Reading *for* Rhetoric

CAROLINE SHRODES
CLIFFORD A. JOSEPHSON
JAMES R. WILSON

San Francisco State University

Reading
for
Rhetoric

Applications to Writing

FOURTH EDITION

Macmillan Publishing Co., Inc.

New York

Macmillan Publishing Co., Inc.
866 Third Avenue, New York, New York 10022

Collier Macmillan Canada, Ltd.

PE1417
S45
1979

Library of Congress Cataloging in Publication Data

Shrodes, Caroline, comp.   (date)
    Reading for rhetoric.

    Bibliography: p.
    1. College readers. 2. English language—Rhetoric.
I. Josephson, Clifford Anthon   II. Wilson,
James R. III. Title.
PE1417.S45 1979   808'.04275   78–5641
ISBN 0–02–410240–7

Printing: 1 2 3 4 5 6 7 8   Year: 9 0 1 2 3 4 5

Acknowledgments

Following are credits for copyright works listed in the order that they appear in the book:

"An 18-Year-Old Looks Back on Life," copyright © 1972 by Joyce Maynard, first appeared in the New York Times. From the book *Looking Back* by Joyce Maynard. Reprinted by permission of Doubleday & Company, Inc.

"My Search for Roots," copyright © 1974 by The Reader's Digest Association, Inc. from *Roots* by Alex Haley. Used by permission of Doubleday & Company, Inc.

"I Become a Student," from *The Autobiography of Lincoln Steffens,* copyright, 1931, by Harcourt Brace Jovanovich, Inc.; renewed, 1959, by Peter Steffens. Reprinted by permission of the publishers.

"A Whole Society of Loners and Dreamers," by William Allen, reprinted by permission from *Saturday Review,* November 11, 1972.

"The Martians" from *The War of the Worlds* by H. G. Wells. Reprinted by permission of A. P. Watt & Son and the Estate of H. G. Wells.

"Memories of a Missouri Farm," pp. 94–115 from *Mark Twain's Autobiography,* Vol. I. Copyright 1924 by Clara Gabrilowitsch; renewed 1952 by Clara Clemens Samossoud. By permission of Harper & Row, Publishers, Inc.

"The Libido for the Ugly," Copyright 1927 by Alfred A. Knopf, Inc. and renewed 1955 by H. L. Mencken. Reprinted from *A Mencken Chrestomathy,* by H. L. Mencken, by permission of Alfred A. Knopf, Inc.

"The Present," from pp. 77–79 in *Pilgrim at Tinker Creek* by Annie Dillard. Copyright © 1974 by Annie Dillard. By permission of Harper & Row, Publishers, Inc.

"The Perfect Crime," from *Mauve Gloves & Madmen, Clutter & Vine* by Tom Wolfe, Copyright © 1973, 1976 by Tom Wolfe. Reprinted with the permission of Farrar, Straus & Giroux, Inc.

"Democracy," from *The Wild Flag* (Houghton-Mifflin); © 1943 E. B. White. Originally in *The New Yorker.*

"Answers to a Questionnaire: The Politics of Women's Liberation," from *The Third World of Women* by Susan Sontag, Copyright © 1973 by Susan Sontag. Reprinted with the permission of Farrar, Straus & Giroux, Inc.

"Lust or Luxuria," *The New Republic,* October 8, 1977, by Henry Fairlie. Reprinted by permission of The New Republic.

"My Wood" from *Abinger Harvest,* copyright 1936, 1964, by E. M. Forster. Reprinted by permission of Harcourt Brace Jovanovich, Inc.

"The Stereotype" from *The Female Eunuch* by Germaine Greer. Copyright © 1970 by Germaine Greer. Used with permission of McGraw-Hill Book Company and MacGibbon & Kee Limited/Granada Publishing Limited.

"Love Is a Fallacy," © 1951 by Max Shulman. Reprinted by permission of the Harold Matson Co., Inc.

"Eastern Cults and Western Culture: Why Young Americans Are Buying Oriental Religions," from *Turning East,* Copyright © 1977 by Harvey Cox. Reprinted by permission of Simon & Schuster, a Division of Gulf & Western Corporation.

"Paranoia," *Harper's,* June 1974, by Hendrik Hertzberg and David C. K. McClelland. Copyright © 1974 by *Harper's Magazine.* All rights reserved. Reprinted from the June 1974 issue by special permission.

Excerpt from *The People Shapers,* Copyright © 1977 by Vance Packard. Reprinted by permission of Little, Brown and Co.

"World of Shadows," from *The Savage and Beautiful Country* by Alan McGlashan. Reprinted by permission of Stonehill Publishing Company (A Division of Stonehill Communications, Inc.), New York. Copyright © 1966, 1967 by Alan McGlashan.

"Diogenes and Alexander," by Gilbert Highet. Copyright © 1963 by American Heritage Publishing Co., Inc. Reprinted by permission from *Horizon* (March 1963).

"Uncaging Skylarks: The Meaning of Transcendent Symbols," from *Where the*

Wasteland Ends by Theodore Roszak, Copyright © 1972 by Theodore Roszak. Reprinted by permission of Doubleday & Company, Inc.

"The Feminine Mind," Copyright 1918, 1922 and renewed 1950 by H. L. Mencken. Reprinted from *A Mencken Chrestomathy*, by H. L. Mencken, by permission of Alfred A. Knopf, Inc.

"When Your Profession Takes You to Hollywood," from *Changing* by Liv Ullman. Copyright © 1976, 1977 by Liv Ullman. Reprinted by permission of Alfred A. Knopf, Inc.

"The Bird and the Machine," Copyright © 1955 by Loren Eiseley. Reprinted from *The Immense Journey*, by Loren Eiseley, by permission of Random House, Inc.

"Semantic Spinach or Mellowing Out in Sunny California," by Cyra McFadden, *The New York Times Magazine*, November 20, 1977, © 1977 by The New York Times Company. Reprinted by permission.

"More Futures Than One," *Playboy*, by Poul Anderson. Reprinted by permission of the author and the author's agents, Scott Meredith Literary Agency, Inc., 845 Third Avenue, New York, New York 10022.

"University Days," Copyright © 1933, 1961 by James Thurber, from *My Life and Hard Times*, published by Harper & Row, Publishers, Inc., originally printed in *The New Yorker*.

"The Bad News About Sharks," *Esquire*, June 1974, by Joy Williams. Reprinted by permission of Esquire Magazine, copyright © 1977 Esquire, Inc.

"Joey: A 'Mechanical Boy,'" *Scientific American*, by Bruno Bettelheim. Reprinted by permission of Scientific American.

"The Generation That Was Never Going to Have to Work," *Esquire*, July 1977, by Mark Jacobson. Reprinted by permission of Esquire Magazine, copyright © 1977 Esquire Magazine Inc.

"The Iks," from *The Lives of a Cell* by Lewis Thomas. Copyright © 1973 by The Massachusetts Medical Society. Reprinted by permission of The Viking Press.

"Friday Night in the Coliseum," *The Atlantic*, March 1972, by William C. Martin. Copyright William C. Martin and Geoff Winningham, 1972.

"Television: More Deeply Than We Suspect, It Has Changed All of Us," *Life*, September 10, 1971, Daniel J. Boorstin for *Life*. Copyright © 1971 by Daniel J. Boorstin. All rights reserved.

"Living Together," *Newsweek*, August 1, 1977. Copyright © 1977 by Newsweek, Inc. All rights reserved. Reprinted by permission.

"How to Say Nothing in Five Hundred Words," from *Understanding English* by Paul Roberts. Copyright © 1958 by Paul Roberts. Used by permission of Harper & Row, Publishers, Inc.

"The Death of Marilyn Monroe," Copyright © 1963 by Diana Trilling. Reprinted from her volume *Claremont Essays* by permission of Harcourt Brace Jovanovich, Inc.

"Words as Weapons" from pp. 214–225 (hardbound edition) in *Black Boy* by Richard Wright. Copyright 1937, 1942, 1944, 1945, by Richard Wright. By permission of Harper & Row, Publishers, Inc.

"What I Have Lived For," by Bertrand Russell from *The Autobiography of Bertrand Russell*.

"The Good Old Medieval Campus," by Arthur Hoppe. Copyright 1968 Chronicle Publishing Company, reprinted by permission of the author.

"Film Negatives: What Can You Do About an Art That Is Simply Too Easy?" by Stanley Kauffmann, reprinted by permission from *Saturday Review*, March 1973.

"The Artist as Housewife," *Ms.*, December 1972, by Erica Jong. Reprinted by permission of Erica Jong, % International Creative Management. Copyright © 1972 by Erica Mann Jong.

"The Devil Speaks" from *Man and Superman* by George Bernard Shaw, reprinted by permission of The Society of Authors on behalf of the Bernard Shaw Estate.

"Where the Kissing Never Stops," reprinted with the permission of Farrar, Straus & Giroux, Inc., from *Slouching Towards Bethlehem* by Joan Didion, Copyright © 1966, 1968 by Joan Didion.

"A Wasp Stings Back," *Newsweek*, September 30, 1974. Copyright © 1974 by Newsweek, Inc. All rights reserved. Reprinted by permission.

"Who Finally Would Do the Dishes?" from *The Prisoner of Sex* by Norman Mailer. Reprinted by permission of the author and the author's agents, Scott Meredith Literary Agency, Inc., 845 Third Avenue, New York, New York 10022.

"The Uses of Ecstasy," excerpted from the book *Education and Ecstasy* by George B. Leonard. Copyright © 1968 by George B. Leonard. Reprinted by permission of Delacorte Press.

"Androgyny," by Andrew Kopkind, from *The Sense of the Seventies* (Dolan and Quinn, eds., Oxford University Press). Reprinted by permission of Andrew Kopkind.

"Angels on a Pin," *Saturday Review*, December 21, 1968, by Alexander Calandra. Reprinted by permission of Alexander Calandra.

"The Last Married Couple Left in Connecticut," by Anatole Broyard, *The New York Times*, October 6, 1977, © 1977 by The New York Times Company. Reprinted by permission.

"Impressions of Japan," first published in *Esquire Magazine*, December 1958, by William Faulkner. Reprinted by permission of Harold Ober Associates Incorporated. Copyright © 1956 by William Faulkner.

"Marrakech," from *Such, Such Were the Joys* by George Orwell, copyright, 1945, 1952, 1953 by Sonia Brownell Orwell; renewed, 1973, by Sonia Pitt-Rivers. Reprinted by permission of Harcourt Brace Jovanovich, Inc.

"Manners of Deceit and the Case for Lying," first published in *Esquire Magazine*, December 1977, by Francine du Plessix Gray. Reprinted by permission of the Author. Copyright © 1977 Francine du Plessix Gray.

"Farewell My Lovely," *The New Yorker*, May 16, 1936. This essay appeared in *The New Yorker* over the pseudonym Lee Strout White. It was suggested by a manuscript submitted to the magazine by Richard Lee Strout and was written by E. B. White. Reprinted by permission. Copr. © 1936, 1964 The New

Yorker Magazine, Inc.; published in book form by G. P. Putnam under the title "Farewell to Model T" in 1936. Reprinted under its original title in "The Second Tree From the Corner" by E. B. White, Harper & Bros., 1954.

"A Noiseless Flash," from *Hiroshima* by John Hersey. Copyright 1946 and renewed 1974 by John Hersey. Originally appeared in *The New Yorker*. Reprinted by permission of Alfred A. Knopf, Inc.

"Notes of a Native Son," from *Notes of a Native Son,* © 1955 by James Baldwin. Reprinted by permission of Beacon Press.

"Sight Into Insight," *Harper's Magazine,* February 1974, by Annie Dillard. Reprinted by permission of the author and her agent Blanche C. Gregory, Inc. Copyright © 1974 by Annie Dillard.

"The Landscape of Our Lives," from *This Is Eric Sevareid,* © 1964 by Eric Sevareid. Reprinted by permission of the Harold Matson Co., Inc.

Foreword

The fourth edition of *Reading for Rhetoric,* like its predecessors, provides a functional approach to rhetoric. We hope that the selections in this book will invite readers to view the human situation with compassion and understanding and move them to respond to the ideas and experiences they have shared. Once involved in reading, they should be willing to scrutinize the means by which the writer has ordered experience. Frequently it is a relief to readers to discover that good writing is not a mysterious abstraction but a rational system of specific techniques that can be learned and applied.

In this fourth edition, forty-seven of the sixty readings are new. We have chosen essays in which the subject matter in some way touches the experience of students. We have included a generous number of short essays similar in length to student compositions. All of the essays can be read with pleasure and insight on more than one level and each demonstrates more than one kind of applied rhetorical principle.

Reading and writing cannot be separated. To improve their writing, students must first learn to be critical readers, especially of their own work. Accordingly, we approach the study of rhetoric inductively to discover the principles applied by skillful writers confronted with the practical problems of writing—of putting ideas into words. Our approach, incremental as well as inductive, departs from that of standard rhetoric texts, which explain rules one at a time in a systematic order. Many editors, faced with the complexity of writing and the simplicity of the rules, place rhetoric and reading at opposite ends of a book and illustrate the principles with fragments: a paragraph of sensory description, logical definition, or graphic illustration; a fragment showing precision of diction or irony of statement. We join reading and rhetoric. Our examples are sufficiently complete in their anatomy to encourage students to note the relationship of the parts to the whole; thus the students become aware of the inseparability of thought and form. The exercises are in no way intended to impose a single method of study or to exhaust the possibilities afforded by the richness of the materials. They are meant instead as a point of departure for original analysis and experiment.

The exercises serve a variety of functions. Each exercise illuminates the purpose, structure, diction, and tone of a selection; each draws attention to the fusion of thought and form at every level— word, sentence, paragraph, and over all organization. Of course, each principle does not receive equal attention in every exercise, for the distinctive quality of the essay or narrative determines the nature of the analysis. It is inevitable, and even desirable, that in ordering and developing complex ideas, a writer should draw upon a number of rhetorical modes and devices. Each analysis, however, focuses upon the primary method of development in order to clarify the means the author uses to achieve a purpose. In each exercise the questions help the reader to determine *how* an individual essay is organized and *why* that organization is appropriate. The exercises also explore the various strategies that distinguish the method and make it the writer's own. The range of rhetorical approach reflected in the exercises encourages students to select with discrimination those methods most appropriate to their own purposes, and each exercise concludes with suggested writing assignments asking students to apply one or more of the rhetorical principles to their own essays.

Reading for Rhetoric is designed to teach students to write with clarity, vigor, and grace, and to secure their commitment to the discipline of writing, not by the prescription of rules but through the testimony of eloquent prose.

C. S.
C. A. J.
J. R. W.

Contents

PART

four Comparison and Contrast

PART

five Illustration   199

PART

six Analysis 251

PART

seven Argument and Persuasion 331

PART

eight Diction and Tone 435

Thematic Grouping of Selections

BEING (AND BECOMING)

Joyce Maynard, *"An 18-Year-Old Looks Back on Life"*
Alex Haley, *"My Search for Roots: A Black American's Story"*
Lincoln Steffens, *"I Become a Student"*
William Allen, *"A Whole Society of Loners and Dreamers"*
Annie Dillard, *"The Present"*
Alan McGlashan, *"World of Shadows"*
Theodore Roszak, *"Uncaging Skylarks: The Meaning of Transcendent Symbols"*
Liv Ullman, *"When Your Profession Takes You to Hollywood"*
Cyra McFadden, *"California Spinach Talk"*
Bruno Bettelheim, *"Joey: A 'Mechanical Boy'"*
Diana Trilling, *"The Death of Marilyn Monroe"*
Erica Jong, *"The Artist as Housewife"*
Joan Didion, *"Joan Baez: Where the Kissing Never Stops"*
George B. Leonard, *"The Uses of Ecstasy"*
Andrew Kopkind, *"Androgyny"*
William Faulkner, *"Impressions of Japan"*
James Baldwin, *"Notes of a Native Son"*
Annie Dillard, *"Sight Into Insight"*

THE SEXES

WOMEN ON WOMEN (AND MEN)
Susan Sontag, *"The Liberated Woman"*

FREEDOM

THE POLITICAL ANIMAL

Reading *for* Rhetoric

one

Identification

Identification seeks to answer the question "Who am I?" or "Who are you?" or "What is that?" Maynard identifies the generation of which she is a member as one of "unfulfilled expectations." Alex Haley relies heavily on detail to give authenticity to his search for his ancestry. Steffens discovers what it means to become an educated person in the context of his experience as a student in the university. William Allen identifies the dreams of a young boy by evoking a mingled sense of hope and fear. Wells gives substance to his imaginary creatures, the Martians, by confronting us with bug-eyed monsters, whose menace is increased by their superiority to us. Twain ties memories to sensory experiences. Mencken identifies the "libido" for the ugly by the objects it creates. Dillard seeks to identify the fleeting moment, the present—catch it if you can.

An 18-Year-Old Looks Back on Life

JOYCE MAYNARD

Every generation thinks it's special—my grandparents because they remember horses and buggies, my parents because of the Depression. The over-30's are special because they knew the Red Scare of Korea, Chuck Berry and beatniks. My older sister is special because she belonged to the first generation of teen-agers (before that, people in their teens were *adolescents*), when being a teen-ager was still fun. And I— I am 18, caught in the middle. Mine is the generation of unfulfilled expectations. "When you're older," my mother promised, "you can wear lipstick." But when the time came, of course, lipstick wasn't being worn. "When we're big, we'll dance like that," my friends and I whispered, watching Chubby Checker twist on "American Bandstand." But we inherited no dance steps, ours was a limp, formless shrug to watered-down music that rarely made the feet tap. "Just wait till we can vote," I said, bursting with 10-year-old fervor, ready to fast, freeze, march and die for peace and freedom as Joan Baez, barefoot, sang "We Shall Overcome." Well, now we can vote, and we're old enough to attend rallies and knock on doors and wave placards, and suddenly it doesn't seem to matter any more. [1]

My generation is special because of what we missed rather than what we got, because in a certain sense we are the first and the last. The first to take technology for granted. (What was a space shot to us, except an hour cut from Social Studies to gather before a TV in the gym as Cape Canaveral counted down?) The first to grow up with TV. My sister was 8 when we got our set, so to her it seemed magic and always somewhat foreign. She had known books already and would never really replace them. But for me, the TV set was, like the kitchen sink and the telephone, a fact of life. [2]

We inherited a previous generation's hand-me-downs and took in the seams, turned up the hems, to make our new fashions. We took drugs from the college kids and made them a high-school commonplace. We got the Beatles, but not those lovable look-alikes in matching suits with barber cuts and songs that made you want to cry. They came to us like a bad joke—aged, bearded, discordant. And we inherited the Vietnam war just after the crest of the wave—too late to burn draft cards and too early not to be drafted. The boys of 1953—my year—will be the last to go. [3]

So where are we now? Generalizing is dangerous. Call us the apathetic generation and we will become that. Say times are changing, nobody cares about prom queens and getting into the college of his choice any more—say that (because it sounds good, it indicates a trend, gives a symmetry to history) and you make a movement and a unit out of a generation unified only in its common fragmentation. If there is a reason why we are where we are, it comes from where we have been. [4]

Like overanxious patients in analysis, we treasure the traumas of our childhood. Ours was more traumatic than most. The Kennedy assassination has become our myth: Talk to us for an evening or two—about movies or summer jobs or Nixon's trip to China or the weather—and the subject will come up ("Where were *you* when you heard?"), as if having lived through Jackie and the red roses, John-John's salute and Oswald's on-camera murder justifies our disenchantment. [5]

We haven't all emerged the same, of course, because our lives were lived in high-school corridors and drive-in hamburger joints as well as in the pages of Time and Life, and the images on the TV screen. National events and personal memory blur so that, for me, Nov. 22, 1963, was a birthday party that had to be called off and Armstrong's moonwalk was my first full can of beer. If you want to know who we are now; if you wonder how we'll vote, or whether we will, or whether, 10 years from now, we'll end up just like all those other generations that thought they were special—with 2.2 kids and a house in Connecticut—if that's what you're wondering, look to the past because, whether we should blame it or not, we do. [6]

I didn't know till years later that they called it the Cuban Missile Crisis. But I remember Castro. (We called him Castor Oil and were awed by his beard—beards were rare in those days.) We might not have worried so much (what would the Communists want with our small New Hampshire town?) except that we lived 10 miles from an air base. Planes buzzed around us like mosquitoes that summer. People talked about fallout shelters in their basements and one family on our street packed their car to go to the mountains. I couldn't understand that. If everybody was going to die, I certainly didn't want to stick around, with my hair falling out and—later—a plague of thalido-mide-type babies. I wanted to go quickly, with my family. [7]

Dying didn't bother me so much—I'd never known anyone who died, and death was unreal, fascinating. (I wanted Doctor Kildare to have more terminal cancer patients and fewer love affairs.) What bothered me was the business of immortality. Sometimes, the grow-ing-up sort of concepts germinate slowly, but the full impact of death hit me like a bomb, in the night. Not only would my body be gone—that I could take—but I would cease to think. That I would no longer be a participant I had realized before; now I saw that I wouldn't even be an observer. What especially alarmed me about The Bomb (always singular like, a few years later, The Pill) was the possibility of total obliteration. All traces of me would be destroyed. There would be no grave and, if there were, no one left to visit it. [8]

Newly philosophical, I pondered the universe. If the earth was in the solar system and the solar system was in the galaxy and the galaxy was in the universe, what was the universe in? And if the sun was just a dot—the head of a pin—what was I? We visited a planetarium that year, in third grade, and saw a dramatization of the sun exploding. Somehow the image of that orange ball zooming toward us merged with my image of The Bomb. The effect was devastating, and for the first time in my life—except for Easter Sundays, when I wished I went to church so I could have a fancy new dress like my Catholic and Protestant friends—I longed for religion. [9]

I was 8 when Joan Baez entered our lives, with long, black, beatnik hair and a dress made out of a burlap bag. When we got her first record (we called her Joan *Baze* then—soon she was simply Joan) we lis-tened all day, to "All My Trials" and "Silver Dagger" and "Wildwood Flower." My sister grew her hair and started wearing sandals, making pilgrimages to Harvard Square. I took up the guitar. We loved her voice and her songs but, even more, we loved the idea of Joan, like the 15th-century Girl of Orleans, burning at society's stake, marching along or singing, solitary, in a prison cell to protest segregation. She was the champion of nonconformity and so—like thousands of others—we joined the masses of her fans. [10]

I knew she must but somehow I could never imagine Jackie Kennedy going to the bathroom. She was too cool and poised and perfect. We had a book about her, filled with color pictures of Jackie painting, in a spotless yellow linen dress, Jackie on the beach with Caroline and

John-John, Jackie riding elephants in India and Jackie, in a long white gown, greeting Khrushchev like Snow White welcoming one of the seven dwarfs. (No, I wasn't betraying Joan in my adoration. Joan was beautiful but human, like us; Jackie was magic.) When, years later, she married Rumpelstiltskin, I felt like a child discovering, in his father's drawer, the Santa Claus suit. And, later still, reading some Ladies' Home Journal exposé ("Jacqueline Onassis's secretary tells all . . .") I felt almost sick. After the first few pages I put the magazine down. I wasn't interested in the fragments, only in the fact that the glass had broken. [11]

If I had spent at the piano the hours I gave to television, on all those afternoons when I came home from school, I would be an accomplished pianist now. Or if I'd danced, or read, or painted. . . . But I turned on the set instead, every day, almost, every year, and sank into an old green easy chair, smothered in quilts, with a bag of Fritos beside me and a glass of milk to wash them down, facing life and death with Dr. Kildare, laughing at Danny Thomas, whispering the answers—out loud sometimes—with "Password" and "To Tell the Truth." Looking back over all those afternoons, I try to convince myself they weren't wasted. I must have learned something; I must, at least, have changed. [12]

What I learned was certainly not what TV tried to teach me. From the reams of trivia collected over years of quiz shows, I remember only the questions, never the answers. I loved "Leave It to Beaver" for the messes Beaver got into, not for the inevitable lecture from Dad at the end of each show. I saw every episode two or three times, witnessed Beaver's aging, his legs getting longer and his voice lower, only to start all over again with young Beaver every fall. (Someone told me recently that the boy who played Beaver Cleaver died in Vietnam. The news was a shock—I kept coming back to it for days until another distressed Beaver fan wrote to tell me that it wasn't true after all.) [13]

I got so I could predict punch lines and endings, not really knowing whether I'd seen the episode before or only watched one like it. There was the bowling-ball routine, for instance: Lucy, Dobie Gillis, Pete and Gladys—they all used it. Somebody would get his finger stuck in a bowling ball (Lucy later updated the gimmick using Liz Taylor's ring) and then they'd have to go to a wedding or give a speech at the P.T.A. or have the boss to dinner, concealing one hand all the while. We weren't supposed to ask questions like "Why don't they just tell the truth?" These shows were built on deviousness, on the longest distance between two points, and on a kind of symmetry which decrees that no loose ends shall be left untied, no lingering doubts allowed. (The Surgeon General is off the track in worrying about TV violence, I think. I grew up in the days before lawmen became peacemakers. What carries over is not the gunfights but the memory that everything always turned out all right.) Optimism shone through all those half hours I spent in the dark shadows of the TV room—out of evil shall come good. [14]

Most of all, the situation comedies steeped me in American culture. I emerged from years of TV viewing indifferent to the museums of France, the architecture of Italy, the literature of England. A perversely homebound American, I pick up paperbacks in bookstores, checking before I buy to see if the characters have foreign names, whether the action takes place in London or New York. Vulgarity and banality fascinate me. More intellectual friends (who watch no TV) can't understand what I see in "My Three Sons." "Nothing happens," they say. "The characters are dull, plastic, faceless. Every show is the same." I guess that's why I watch them—boring repetition is, itself, a rhythm—a steady pulse of flashing Coca-Cola signs, McDonald's Golden Arches and Howard Johnson roofs. [15]

I don't watch TV as an anthropologist, rising loftily above my subject to analyze. Neither do I watch, as some kids now tune in to reruns of "The Lone Ranger" and "Superman" (in the same spirit they enjoy comic books and pop art) for their camp. I watch in earnest. How can I do anything else? Five thousand hours of my life have gone into this box. [16]

There were almost no blacks in our school. They were Negroes then; the word *black* was hard to say at first. *Negro* got hard to say for a while too, so I said nothing at all and was embarrassed. If you had asked me, at 9, to describe Cassius Clay, I would have taken great, liberal pains to be color-blind, mentioning height, build, eye color and shoe size, disregarding skin. I knew black people only from newspapers and the TV screen—picket lines. National Guardsmen at the doors of schools. (There were few black actors on TV then, except for Jack Benny's Rochester.) It was easy, in 1963, to embrace the Negro cause. Later, faced with cold stares from an all-black table in the cafeteria or heckled by a Panther selling newspapers, I first became aware of the fact that maybe the little old lady didn't want to be helped across the street. My visions of black-and-white-together look at me now like

shots from "To Sir With Love." If a black is friendly to me, I wonder as other blacks might, if he's a sellout. [17]

I had no desire to scream or cry or throw jelly beans when I first
saw the Beatles on the Ed Sullivan Show. An eighth-grader would
have been old enough to revert to childhood, but I was too young to
act anything but old. So mostly we laughed at them. We were in fifth
grade, the year of rationality, the calm before the storm. We still
screamed when the boys came near us (which they rarely did) and
said they had cooties. Barbie dolls tempted us. That was the year when
I got my first Barbie. Perhaps they were produced earlier, but they
didn't reach New Hampshire till late that fall, and the stores were always sold out. So at the close of our doll-playing careers there was a
sudden dramatic switch from lumpy, round-bellied Betsy Wetsys and
stiff-legged little-girl dolls to slim, curvy Barbie, just 11 inches tall, with
a huge, expensive wardrobe that included a filmy black negligee and
a mouth that made her look as if she'd just swallowed a lemon. [18]

Barbie wasn't just a toy, but a way of living that moved us suddenly
from tea parties to dates with Ken at the Soda Shoppe. Our short
careers with Barbie, before junior high sent her to the attic, built up
our expectations for teen-age life before we had developed the sophistication to go along with them. Children today are accustomed to having
a tantalizing youth culture all around them. (They play with Barbie
in the nursery school.) For us, it broke like a cloudburst, without
preparation. Caught in the deluge, we were torn—wanted to run for
shelter but tempted, also, to sing in the rain. [19]

Marijuana and the class of '71 moved through high school together.
When we came in, as freshmen, drugs were still strange and new;
marijuana was smoked only by a few marginal figures while those in
the mainstream guzzled beer. It was called pot then—the words grass
and dope came later; hash and acid and pills were almost unheard of.
By my sophomore year, lots of the seniors and even a few younger kids
were trying it. By the time I was a junior—in 1969—grass was no
longer reserved for the hippies; basketball players and cheerleaders and
boys with crew-cuts and boys in black-leather jackets all smoked. And
with senior year—maybe because of the nostalgia craze—there was an
odd liquor revival. In my last month of school, a major bust led to the
suspension of half a dozen boys. They were high on beer. [20]

Now people are saying that the drug era is winding down. (It's those
statisticians with their graphs again, charting social phenomena like

the rise and fall of hemlines.) I doubt if it's real, this abandonment of marijuana. But the frenzy is gone, certainly, the excitement and the fear of getting caught and the worry of where to get good stuff. What's happened to dope is what happens to a new record: you play it constantly, full volume, at first. Then, as you get to know the songs, you play them less often, not because you're tired of them exactly, but just because you know them. They're with you always, but quietly, in your head. [21]

My position was a difficult one, all through those four years when grass took root in Oyster River High. I was on the side of all those things that went along with smoking dope—the clothes, the music, the books, the candidates. More and more of my friends smoked, and many people weren't completely my friends, I think, because I didn't. Drugs took on a disproportionate importance. Why was it I could spend half a dozen evenings with someone without his ever asking me what I thought of Beethoven or Picasso but always, in the first half hour, he'd ask whether I smoked? [22]

It became—like hair length and record collection—a symbol of who you were, and you couldn't be all the other things—progressive and creative and free-thinking—without taking that crumpled roll of dry, brown vegetation and holding it to your lips. You are what you eat—or what you smoke, or what you don't smoke. And when you say "like—you know," you're speaking the code, and suddenly the music of the Grateful Dead and the poetry of Bob Dylan and the general brilliance of Ken Kesey all belong to you as if, in those three fuzzy, mumbled words, you'd created art yourself and uttered the wisdom of the universe. [23]

The freshman women's dorm at Yale has no house mother. We have no check-in hours or drinking rules or punishments for having boys in our rooms past midnight. A guard sits by the door to offer, as they assured us at the beginning of the year, physical—not moral—protection. All of which makes it easy for many girls who feel, after high-school curfews and dating regulations, suddenly liberated. (The first week of school last fall, many girls stayed out all night, every night, displaying next morning the circles under their eyes the way some girls show off engagement rings.) [24]

We all received the "Sex at Yale" book, a thick, black pamphlet filled with charts and diagrams and a lengthy discussion of contraceptive methods. And at the first women's assembly, the discussion moved quickly from course-signing-up procedures to gynecology, where it stayed for much of the evening. Somebody raised her hand to ask where she could fill her pill prescription, someone else wanted to know about abortions. There was no standing in the middle any more—you had to either take out a pen and paper and write down the phone numbers they gave out or stare stonily ahead, implying that those were numbers *you* certainly wouldn't be needing. From then on it seemed the line had been drawn. [25]

But of course the problem is that no lines, no barriers, exist. Where, five years ago a girl's decisions were made for her (she had to be in at 12 and, if she was found—in—with her boyfriend . . .); today the decision rests with her alone. She is surrounded by knowledgeable, sexually experienced girls and if *she* isn't willing to sleep with her boyfriend, somebody else will. It's peer-group pressure, 1972 style—the embarrassment of virginity. [26]

Everyone is raised on nursery rhymes and nonsense stories. But it used to be that when you grew up, the nonsense disappeared. Not for us—it is at the core of our music and literature and art and, in fact, of our lives. Like characters in an Ionesco play, we take absurdity unblinking. In a world where military officials tell us "We had to destroy the village in order to save it," Dylan lyrics make an odd kind of sense. They aren't meant to be understood; they don't jar our sensibilities because we're used to *non sequiturs*. We don't take anything too seriously these days. (Was it a thousand earthquake victims or a million? Does it matter?) The casual butcher's-operation in the film "M*A*S*H" and the comedy in Vonnegut and the album cover showing John and Yoko, bareback, are all part of the new absurdity. The days of the Little Moron joke and the elephant joke and the knock-knock joke are gone. It sounds melodramatic, but the joke these days is life. [27]

You're not supposed to care too much any more. Reactions have been scaled down from screaming and jelly-bean-throwing to nodding your head and maybe—if the music really gets to you (and music's the only thing that does any more)—tapping a finger. We need a passion transfusion, a shot of energy in the veins. It's what I'm most impatient with, in my generation—this languid, I-don't-give-a-s——ism that stems in part, at least, from a culture of put-ons in which any serious expression of emotion is branded sentimental and old-fashioned. The fact that we set such a premium on being cool reveals a lot about my generation; the idea is not to care. You can hear it in the speech of college students today: cultivated monotones, low volume, punctuated with four-letter words that come off sounding only bland. I feel it most of all on Saturday morning, when the sun is shining and the crocuses are about to bloom and, walking through the corridors of my dorm, I see there isn't anyone awake. [28]

I'm basically an optimist. Somehow, no matter what the latest population figures say, I feel everything will work out—just like on TV. I may doubt man's fundamental goodness, but I believe in his power to survive. I say, sometimes, that I wonder if we'll be around in 30 years, but then I forget myself and speak of "when I'm 50. . . ." Death has touched me now—from Vietnam and Biafra and a car accident that makes me buckle my seat belt—but like negative numbers and the sound of a dog whistle (too high-pitched for human ears), it's not a concept I can comprehend. I feel immortal while all the signs around me proclaim that I'm not. [29]

We feel cheated, many of us—the crop of 1953—which is why we complain about inheriting problems we didn't cause. (Childhood notions of justice, reinforced by Perry Mason, linger on. Why should I clean up someone else's mess? Who can I blame?) We're excited also, of course: I can't wait to see how things turn out. But I wish I weren't quite so involved, I wish it weren't my life that's being turned into a suspense thriller. [30]

When my friends and I were little, we had big plans. I would be a famous actress and singer, dancing on the side. I would paint my own sets and compose my own music, writing the script and the lyrics and reviewing the performance for the New York Times. I would marry and have three children (they don't allow us dreams like that any more) and we would live, rich and famous (donating lots to charity, of course, and periodically adopting orphans), in a house we designed ourselves. When I was older I had visions of good works. I saw myself in South American rain forests and African deserts, feeding the hungry and healing the sick with an obsessive selflessness, I see now, as selfish, in the end, as my original plans for stardom. [31]

Now my goal is simpler. I want to be happy. And I want comfort—nice clothes, a nice house, good music and good food, and the feeling that I'm doing some little thing that matters. I'll vote and I'll give to charity, but I won't give myself. I feel a sudden desire to buy land—not a lot, not a business investment, but just a small plot of earth so that whatever they do to the country I'll have a place where I can go—

a kind of fallout shelter, I guess. As some people prepare for their old age, so I prepare for my 20's. A little house, a comfortable chair, peace and quiet—retirement sounds tempting. [32]

PURPOSE AND STRUCTURE

1. How does the author use concrete detail to develop the statement, "Mine is the generation of unfulfilled expectations" (par. 1)?

2. How does Maynard achieve a variety of sentence structure in par. 1?

3. In answering the question "Who am I?" Maynard places herself in her generation to provide a context for her discussion. How does she compare and contrast her generation with that of others?

4. Par. 4 begins by posing a question and ends by expressiong a causal relationship. How do subsequent paragraphs answer the question and develop the causal relationship?

5. How does the author relate personal experience to national events in pars. 6–7?

6. How has the first statement in par. 9 been prepared for in earlier paragraphs? With what details is it developed?

7. How are the comparison and contrast developed between Joan Baez and Jackie Kennedy? How do the details shed light upon both the author and her generation?

8. Maynard's experience with TV dominates pars. 12–16. What is the central thesis and how does she develop it?

9. In par. 17 the author talks about blacks; in pars. 18–19 she discusses the Beatles and Barbie dolls; in pars. 20–23 she writes about drugs. How does each of these subjects cast light on her identity? On her generation?

10. Although Maynard treats a large number of topics and moves from personal experience to the attitudes of her generation, she achieves unity in the essay. What is the unifying principle?

11. In addition to comparison and contrast and to illustration, Maynard employs causal analysis as a method of organization. Cite examples.

12. How does the use of parenthesis, rhetorical questions, and repetition contribute to purpose and tone?

13. How does Maynard relate the use of drugs to the problem of identity?

14. How do the contrasting details in pars. 31–32 give support to Maynard's changed goals?

DICTION AND TONE

1. How does the metaphor that opens par. 3 contribute to purpose and tone?

2. Does the fact that the references are dated make the essay less interesting and effective? What more recent illustrations could be substituted without loss?

3. What is the significance of the allusion to "2.2 kids and a house in Connecticut" (par. 6)? How does it relate to purpose and tone?

4. What are the most graphic details in pars. 10 and 11? How do they contribute to tone?

5. Note the variations in tone from the very personal to the general; from the light touch to the serious; from the optimistic to the cynical. How does the specific subject matter determine the tone? How would you describe the tone of pars. 10–11?

6. How do the allusions to Coca–Cola signs, McDonald's arches, and Howard Johnson roofs in par. 15 contribute to purpose and tone?

7. Maynard says that her generation sets a premium on being "cool." How do her diction and tone give support to that concept?

APPLICATIONS TO WRITING

1. Place yourself in the context of your generation and refer to key personal experiences as well as major events in the country that have influenced your thinking and behavior.

2. Support or refute the proposition that yours is "a generation of unfulfilled expectations" by citing personal and cultural experiences.

3. Trace the evolution of your taste and response to TV by referring to specific programs.

4. Compare and contrast your earlier goals with your current ones. Draw upon specific observations and experiences.

My Search for Roots: A Black American's Story

ALEX HALEY

My earliest memory is of Grandma, Cousin Georgia, Aunt Plus, Aunt Liz and Aunt Till talking on our front porch in Henning, Tenn. At dusk, these wrinkled, graying old ladies would sit in rocking chairs and talk, about slaves and massas and plantations—pieces and patches of family history, passed down across the generations by word of mouth. "Old-timey stuff," Mamma would exclaim. She wanted no part of it. [1]

The furthest-back person Grandma and the others ever mentioned was "the African." They would tell how he was brought here on a ship to a place called "Naplis" and sold as a slave in Virginia. There he mated with another slave, and had a little girl named Kizzy. [2]

When Kizzy became four or five, the old ladies said, her father would point out to her various objects and name them in his native tongue. For example, he would point to a guitar and make a single-syllable sound, *ko*. Pointing to a river that ran near the plantation, he'd say "Kamby Bolongo." And when other slaves addressed him as Toby—the name given him by his massa—the African would strenuously reject it, insisting that his name was "Kin-tay." [3]

Kin-tay often told Kizzy stories about himself. He said that he had been near his village in Africa, chopping wood to make a drum, when he had been set upon by four men, overwhelmed, and kidnapped into slavery. When Kizzy grew up and became a mother, she told her son these stories, and he in turn would tell *his* children. His granddaughter became my grandmother, and she pumped that saga into me as if it were plasma, until I knew by rote the story of the African, and the subsequent generational wending of our family through cotton and tobacco plantations into the Civil War and then freedom. [4]

At 17, during World War II, I enlisted in the Coast Guard, and found myself a messboy on a ship in the Southwest Pacific. To fight boredom, I began to teach myself to become a writer. I stayed on in the service after the war, writing every single night, seven nights a week, for eight years before I sold a story to a magazine. My first story in the Digest was published in June 1954: "The Harlem Nobody Knows." At age 37, I retired from military service, determined to be a full-time writer. Working with the famous Black Muslim spokesman, I did the actual writing for the book *The Autobiography of Malcolm X*. [5]

I remembered still the vivid highlights of my family's story. Could this account possibly be documented for a book? During 1962, between other assignments, I began following the story's trail. In plantation records, wills, census records, I documented bits here, shreds there. By now, Grandma was dead; repeatedly I visited other close sources, most notably our encyclopedic matriarch, "Cousin Georgia" Anderson in Kansas City, Kansas. I went as often as I could to the National Archives in Washington, and the Library of Congress, and the Daughters of the American Revolution Library. [6]

By 1967 I felt I had the seven generations of the U. S. side documented. But the unknown quotient in the riddle of the past continued to be those strange, sharp, angular sounds spoken by the African himself. Since I lived in New York City, I began going to the United Nations lobby, stopping Africans and asking if they recognized the sounds. Every one of them listened to me, then quickly took off. I can well understand: me with a Tennessee accent, trying to imitate African sounds! [7]

Finally, I sought out a linguistics expert who specialized in African languages. To him I repeated the phrases. The sound "Kin-tay," he said, was a Mandinka tribe surname. And "Kamby Bolongo" was probably the Gambia River in Mandinka dialect. Three days later, I was in Africa. [8]

In Banjul, the capital of Gambia, I met with a group of Gambians. They told me how for centuries the history of Africa has been preserved. In the older villages of the back country there are old men, called *griots,* who are in effect living archives. Such men know and, on special occasions, tell the cumulative histories of clans, or families, or villages, as those histories have long been told. Since my forefather had said his name was Kin-tay (properly spelled Kinte), and since the Kinte clan was known in Gambia, they would see what they could do to help me. [9]

I was back in New York when a registered letter came from Gambia. Word had been passed in the back country, and a *griot* of the Kinte clan had, indeed, been found. His name, the letter said, was Kebba Kanga Fofana. I returned to Gambia and organized a safari to locate him. [10]

There is an expression called "the peak experience," a moment which, emotionally, can never again be equaled in your life. I had mine, that first day in the village of Juffure, in the back country in black West Africa. [11]

When our 14-man safari arrived within sight of the village, the people came flocking out of their circular mud huts. From a distance I could see a small, old man with a pillbox hat, an off-white robe and an aura of "somebodiness" about him. The people quickly gathered around me in a kind of horseshoe pattern. The old man looked piercingly into my eyes, and he spoke in Mandinka. Translation came from the interpreters I had brought with me. [12]

"Yes, we have been told by the forefathers that there are many of us from this place who are in exile in that place called America." [13]

Then the old man, who was 73 rains of age—the Gambian way of saying 73 years old, based upon the one rainy season per year—began to tell me the lengthy ancestral history of the Kinte clan. It was clearly a formal occasion for the villagers. They had grown mouse-quiet, and stood rigidly. [14]

Out of the *griot's* head came spilling lineage details incredible to hear. He recited who married whom, two or even three centuries back. I was struck not only by the profusion of details, but also by the Biblical pattern of the way he was speaking. It was something like, "—and so-and-so took as a wife so-and-so, and begat so-and-so. . . ." [15]

The *griot* had talked for some hours, and had got to about 1750 in our calendar. Now he said, through an interpreter, "About the time the king's soldiers came, the eldest of Omoro's four sons, Kunta, went away from this village to chop wood—and he was never seen again. . . ." [16]

Goose pimples came out on me the size of marbles. He just had no way in the world of knowing that what he told me meshed with what I'd heard from the old ladies on the front porch in Henning, Tenn. I got out my notebook, which had in it what Grandma had said about the African. One of the interpreters showed it to the others, and they went to the *griot,* and they all got agitated. Then the *griot* went to the people, and *they* all got agitated. [17]

I don't remember anyone giving an order, but those 70-odd people formed a ring around me, moving counterclockwise, chanting, their bodies close together. I can't begin to describe how I felt. A woman broke from the circle, a scowl on her jet-black face, and came charging toward me. She took her baby and almost roughly thrust it out at me. The gesture meant "Take it!" and I did, clasping the baby to me. Whereupon the woman all but snatched the baby away. Another woman did the same with her baby, then another, and another. [18]

A year later, a famous professor at Harvard would tell me: "You were participating in one of the oldest ceremonies of humankind, called 'the laying on of hands.' In their way, these tribespeople were saying to you, 'Through this flesh, which is us, we are you and you are us.'" [19]

Later, as we drove out over the back-country road, I heard the staccato sound of drums. When we approached the next village, people were packed alongside the dusty road, waving, and the din from them welled louder as we came closer. As I stood up in the Land Rover, I finally realized what it was they were all shouting: "Meester Kinte! Meester Kinte!" In their eyes I was the symbol of all black people in the United States whose forefathers had been torn out of Africa while theirs remained. [20]

Hands before my face, I began crying—crying as I have never cried in my life. Right at that time, crying was all I could do. [21]

I went then to London. I searched and searched, and finally in the British Parliamentary records I found that the "king's soldiers" mentioned by the *griot* referred to a group called "Colonel O'Hare's forces," which had been sent up the Gambia River in 1767 to guard the then British-operated James Fort, a slave fort. [22]

I next went to Lloyds of London, where doors were opened for me to research among all kinds of old maritime records. I pored through the records of slave ships that had sailed from Africa. Volumes upon volumes of these records exist. One afternoon about 2:30, during the seventh week of searching, I was going through my 1023rd set of ship records. I picked up a sheet that had on it the reported movements of 30 slave ships, my eyes stopped at No. 18, and my glance swept across the column entries. This vessel had sailed directly from the Gambia River to America in 1767; her name was the *Lord Ligonier;* and she had arrived at Annapolis (Naplis) the morning of September 29, 1767. [23]

Exactly 200 years later, on September 29, 1967, there was nowhere in the world for me to be except standing on a pier at Annapolis, staring sea-ward across those waters over which my great-great-great-great-grandfather had been brought. And there in Annapolis I inspected the microfilmed records of the *Maryland Gazette*. In the issue of October 1, 1767, on page 3, I found an advertisement informing readers that the *Lord Ligonier* had just arrived from the River Gambia, with "a cargo of choice, healthy SLAVES" to be sold at auction the following Wednesday. [24]

In the years since, I have done extensive research in 50 or so libraries, archives and repositories on three continents. I spent a year combing through countless documents to learn about the culture of Gambia's villages in the 18th and 19th centuries. Desiring to sail over the same waters navigated by the *Lord Ligonier*, I flew to Africa and boarded the freighter *African Star*. I forced myself to spend the ten nights of the crossing in the cold, dark cargo hold, stripped to my underwear, lying on my back on a rough, bare plank. But this was sheer luxury compared to the inhuman ordeal suffered by those millions who, chained and shackled, lay in terror and in their own filth in the stinking darkness through voyages averaging 60 to 70 days. [25]

PURPOSE AND STRUCTURE

1. Identify the grammatical subjects of the sentences in pars. 5, 6, 7, 8.

2. What do these grammatical subjects reveal about the psychological need of the writer? Explain how this psychological need is related to the title. Why is this search so important to Haley when most Americans do not care who their great-great-great-great-grandfathers were?

3. Although Haley's search moves him backward through history, the essay has a chronological development and moves forward in time. List a half-dozen time markers, preferably ones near the beginnings of paragraphs, that move the narrative forward in time.

4. The selection also has a geographical organization. Where does it begin? Where does the middle section occur? Where does it end? Does the location of the end—especially that in par. 24—have anything to do with the subtitle?

5. Par. 5 is a good example of what is sometimes called a coordinate sequence paragraph, one in which the sentences are all on approximately the same level of generalization. Notice that after reading the first sentence you can skip the second sentence and go directly to the third sentence and still make sense of the paragraph. Thus sentence three does not depend on sentence two, or we can say that three is not subordinate to two. Is sentence four coordinate in the same way or does it depend on sentence three? If it depends on sentence three, it is called a subordinate sentence sequence.

6. Is sentence five in par. 5 coordinate or subordinate? Sentence six?

7. In par. 9 explain how each sentence depends on the sentence preceding it, usually on a lower level of generality. This is sometimes called a subordinate sequence paragraph.

8. Is par. 23 a coordinate sequence or subordinate sequence paragraph? Be prepared to defend your answer.

9. Do such details as "One afternoon about 2:30 . . ." and "In the issue of October 1, 1767," help or hinder the article? Explain your answer.

10. What is similar about the sentence structure of the first three sentences of par. 20?

11. Unity in the paragraph requires that all the information in the paragraph relates to the same subject matter. One easy way of achieving unity is to make each sentence have the same subject. The disadvantage of this method is that starting each sentence with the same subject can become monotonous. Explain how in par. 25 Haley achieves unity but avoids monotony.

DICTION AND TONE

1. In par. 4 Haley writes, ". . . she pumped that saga into me as if it were plasma." Explain as fully as you can the richness of the word *plasma* in this context.

2. In par. 6 Haley refers to his Cousin Georgia as "our encyclopedic matriarch." What is a matriarch? Why is this word appropriate at the beginning of his story?

3. At the end of his African experience, Haley writes that he had become the symbol of all those whose "forefathers had been torn out of Africa. . . ." Try substituting some other word for *torn* and see if you can strengthen the force of the sentence.

APPLICATIONS TO WRITING

Write an essay in which you explain how some piece of family history—an anecdote, an exploit of your grandfather, perhaps—first told to you when you were a child, changed meaning for you as you grew older. For example, as a child you may have thought the incident meaningless or just plain normal; as an adolescent, you may have thought it foolish; as a young adult, you may think of it as something to be proud of. Or the attitude may be reversed: you may have been proud of the incident as a child but embarrassed by it as an adult.

You must pay particular attention to your chronological organization, using whatever time markers are appropriate.

I Become a Student

from *The Autobiography of Lincoln Steffens*

LINCOLN STEFFENS

It is possible to get an education at a university. It has been done; not often, but the fact that a proportion, however small, of college students do get a start in interested, methodical study, proves my thesis, and the two personal experiences I have to offer illustrate it and show how to circumvent the faculty, the other students, and the whole college system of mind-fixing. My method might lose a boy his degree, but a degree is not worth so much as the capacity and the drive to learn, and the undergraduate desire for any empty baccalaureate is one of the holds the educational system has on students. Wise students some day will refuse to take degrees, as the best men (in England, for instance) give, but do not themselves accept, titles. [1]

My method was hit on by accident and some instinct. I specialized. With several courses prescribed, I concentrated on the one or two that interested me most, and letting the others go, I worked intensively on my favorites. In my first two years, for example, I worked at English and political economy and read philosophy. At the beginning of my junior year I had several cinches in history. Now I liked history; I had neglected it partly because I rebelled at the way it was taught, as positive knowledge unrelated to politics, art, life, or anything else. The professors gave us chapters out of a few books to read, con, and be quizzed on. Blessed as I was with a "bad memory," I could not commit to it anything that I did not understand and intellectually need. The bare record of the story of man, with names, dates, and irrelative events, bored me. But I had discovered in my readings of literature, philosophy, and political economy that history had light to throw upon unhistorical questions. So I proposed in my junior and senior year to specialize in history, taking all the courses required and those also that I had flunked in. With this in mind I listened attentively to the first introductory talk of Professor William Cary Jones on American constitutional history. He was a dull lecturer, but I noticed that, after telling us what pages of what books we must be prepared in, he mumbled off some other references "for those that may care to dig deeper." [2]

When the rest of the class rushed out into the sunshine, I went up to the professor and, to his surprise, asked for this memorandum. He gave it to me. Up in the library I ran through the required chapters in the two different books, and they differed on several points. Turning to the other authorities, I saw that they disagreed on the same facts and also on others. The librarian, appealed to, helped me search the bookshelves till the library closed, and then I called on Professor Jones for more references. He was astonished, invited me in, and began to approve my industry, which astonished me. I was not trying to be a good boy; I was better than that: I was a curious boy. He lent me a couple of his books, and I went off to my club to read them. They only deepened the mystery, clearing up the historical question, but leaving the answer to be dug for and written. [3]

The historians did not know! History was n   e, but a field for research, a field for me, for any young ma   make discoveries in and write a scientific report a'   As I went on from chapter to chapter, day af sential differences of opinion and of fac do. In this course, American constituti to suspect that the Fathers of the Re stitution of the United States not establish a democratic governmer used as a child to play I was Na' to write a true history of the making of the American Constitution. I did not do it; that chapter has been done or well begun since by two men: Smith of the University of Washington and Beard (then) of Columbia (afterward forced out, perhaps for this very work). I found other events, men, and epochs waiting for students. In all my other courses, in ancient, in European, and in modern history, the disagreeing authorities carried me back to the need of a fresh search for (or of) the original documents or other clinching testimony. Of course I did well in my classes. The history professors soon knew me as a student and seldom put a question to me except when the class had flunked it. Then Professor Jones would say, "Well, Steffens, tell them about it." [4]

Fine. But vanity wasn't my ruling passion then. What I had was a quickening sense that I was learning a method of studying history and that every chapter of it, from the beginning of the world to the end, is crying out to be rewritten. There was something for Youth to do; these superior old men had not done anything, finally. [5]

Years afterward I came out of the graft prosecution office in San Francisco with Rudolph Spreckels, the banker and backer of the investigation. We were to go somewhere, quick, in his car, and we couldn't. The chauffeur was trying to repair something wrong. Mr. Spreckels smiled; he looked closely at the defective part, and to my silent, wondering inquiry he answered: "Always, when I see something badly done or not done at all, I see an opportunity to make a fortune. I never kick at bad work by my class: there's lots of it and we suffer from it. But our failures and neglects are chances for the young fellows coming along and looking for work." [6]

Nothing is done. Everything in the world remains to be done or done over. "The greatest picture is not yet painted, the greatest play isn't written (not even by Shakespeare), the greatest poem is unsung. There isn't in all the world a perfect railroad, nor a good government, nor a sound law." Physics, mathematics, and especially the most advanced and exact of the sciences, are being fundamentally revised. Chemistry is just becoming a science; psychology, economics, and sociology are awaiting a Darwin, whose work in turn is awaiting an Einstein. If the rah-rah boys in our colleges could be told this, they might not all be specialists in football, petting parties, and unearned degrees. They told it, however; they are told to learn what is known. This is ophically speaking. [7]

in my later years at Berkeley, two professors, Moses

and Howison, representing opposite schools of thought, got into a controversy, probably about their classes. They brought together in the house of one of them a few of their picked students, with the evident intention of letting us show in conversation how much or how little we had understood of their respective teachings. I don't remember just what the subject was that they threw into the ring, but we wrestled with it till the professors could stand it no longer. Then they broke in, and while we sat silent and highly entertained, they went at each other hard and fast and long. It was after midnight when, the debate over, we went home. I asked the other fellows what they had got out of it, and their answers showed that they had seen nothing but a fine, fair fight. When I laughed, they asked me what I, the D.S.,[1] had seen that was so much more profound. [8]

I said that I had seen two highly-trained, well-educated Masters of Arts and Doctors of Philosophy disagreeing upon every essential point of thought and knowledge. They had all there was of the sciences; and yet they could not find any knowledge upon which they could base an acceptable conclusion. They had no test of knowledge; they didn't know what is and what is not. And they have no test of right and wrong; they have no basis for even an ethics. [9]

Well, and what of it? They asked me that, and that I did not answer. I was stunned by the discovery that it was philosophically true, in a most literal sense, that nothing is known; that it is precisely the foundation that is lacking for science; that all we call knowledge rested upon assumptions which the scientists did not all accept; and that, likewise, there is no scientfic reason for saying, for example, that stealing is wrong. In brief: there was no scientific basis for an ethics. No wonder men said one thing and did another; no wonder they could settle nothing either in life or in the academies. [10]

I could hardly believe this. Maybe these profes͟ ͟ ͟om I greatly respected, did not know it all. I read the books ͟ ͟ ͟a fresh eye, with a real interest, and I could see that, ͟ ͟ ͟ ͟er branches of knowledge, everything was in the ͟ Rebel though I was, I had got the religion ͟ I was in awe of the authorities in the acad͟ to feel my worship cool and pass. But I ͟ elsewhere, see and hear other professo͟r

[1] Damn Stinker.

sors quoted and looked up to as their high priests. I decided to go as a student to Europe when I was through Berkeley, and I would start with the German universities. [11]

My father listened to my plan, and he was disappointed. He had hoped I would succeed him in his business; it was for that that he was staying in it. When I said that, whatever I might do, I would never go into business, he said rather sadly, that he would sell out his interest and retire. And he did soon after our talk. But he wanted me to stay home and, to keep me, offered to buy an interest in a certain San Francisco daily paper. He had evidently had this in mind for some time. I had always done some writing, verse at the poetical age of puberty, then a novel which my mother alone treasured. Journalism was the business for a boy who liked to write, he thought, and he said I had often spoken of a newspaper as my ambition. No doubt I had in the intervals between my campaigns as Napoleon. But no more. I was now going to be a scientist, a philosopher. He sighed: he thought it over, and with the approval of my mother, who was for every sort of education, he gave his consent. [12]

PURPOSE AND STRUCTURE

1. A number of questions relating to the author's identity, to courses, to professors, to education, and to one's life work are explored, placed in context, and tentatively answered. Formulate each of the questions. How is each answered?

2. What does the physical context (i.e., Berkeley, the classrooms, the library, the professor's home) contribute to the thesis?

3. Select a statement from the essay that sums up the central thesis.

4. In the opening paragraph what does the author tell you about how he will develop and prove his thesis?

5. How does Steffens' view of history and the best method of studying it relate to his central thesis?

6. How do the allusions in par. 4 to Napoleon and a trapper contribute his thesis? How are they similar? How different?

at does par. 7 tell you about Steffens' view of education? How hs that follow (8–11) develop his point of view?

8. In par. 6 there is a time shift. What purpose does it serve?

9. The final paragraph seems to move away from Steffens' experience as a student. How does it relate to the central thesis?

10. How do the direct conversations contribute to the author's purpose?

11. By what means does the reader get a vivid impression of Steffens as a person?

DICTION AND TONE

1. What is the author's attitude toward the university? What words and phrases suggest his negative view?

2. Why does Steffens place "bad memory" in quotation marks?

3. What loaded phrases (par. 7) identify Steffens' view of some of his contemporaries?

4. Try to account for shifts in tone and cite examples.

5. What does use of parallel structure in pars. 7 and 10 contribute to tone?

6. How does the phrase "the religion of scholarship and science" (par. 11), relate to the thesis?

APPLICATIONS TO WRITING

1. Identify yourself as a student by relating a number of personal experiences in the classroom; for example, discuss the way(s) in which a teacher, a subject, a course, a relationship, or an activity affected your thinking and/or your behavior.

2. Answer the question: What does it mean to me to become an educated person?

3. On the basis of the illustrations and self–revelations in the essay describe the character, interests, and deep concerns of Lincoln Steffens.

A Whole Society of Loners and Dreamers

WILLIAM ALLEN

IOWA CITY, Iowa—On Sunday afternoons here, if you're tired of taking walks in the country and fighting off the green-bellied hogflies, your next best choice is thumbing magazines at the downtown drugstore. One Sunday not long ago, when I ran out of anything else to thumb, I started looking through one of those magazines geared toward helping new writers achieve success. I used to pore over them a lot when I was a teen-ager, and the first thing I noticed now was that the ads haven't changed much over the past fifteen years: [1]

"IMAGINE MAKING $5,000 A YEAR WRITING IN YOUR SPARE TIME! Fantastic? Not at all. . . . Hundreds of People Make That Much or More Every Year—and Have Fun Doing It!" [2]

"TO PEOPLE WHO WANT TO WRITE FOR PROFIT BUT CAN'T GET STARTED. Have You Natural Writing Ability? Now a Chance to Test Yourself—FREE!" [3]

"I FIRE WRITERS . . . with enthusiasm for developing God-given talent. You'll 'get fired' too with my 48-lesson home study course. Over-the-shoulder coaching . . . personalized critiques! Amazing sales opportunity the first week. Write for my FREE STARTER KIT." [4]

The ad that struck me the most showed a picture of a handsome and darkly serious young man sitting on a hill, picking his teeth with a weed, and gazing out over the countryside. The caption read: DO YOU HAVE THE "FAULTS" THAT COULD MEAN YOU WERE MEANT TO BE A WRITER? The ad went on to list the outstanding characteristics of writers. They are dreamers, loners, bookworms. They are too impractical, too intense, too idealistic. [5]

When I was fourteen and had just started trying to write, I saw an ad much like this and was overwhelmed by it. That fellow on the hill was just like me, I thought. It was a tremendous feeling to discover that I might not be alone—that there was a whole society of loners and dreamers, that they were called writers, and that by sending off for a free writing IQ test I could find out by return mail if I qualified to climb the hill and chew straw with them. [6]

I took that test and blew the top off it. The writing school said I demonstrated a rare creative potential unlike anything thay had seen in years. They did wonder, though, if I had what it took to stick with them through long months of arduous training to develop my raw talent. If I really did have that kind of fortitude, the next step would be to send in some actual samples of my writing. [7]

Spurred, I sent off everything I had ever written—two stories of about 200 words each. One was about some unidentified creatures who lived in dread of an unidentified monster who came around every week or so to slaughter as many of them as he could. Some of the persecuted creatures had the option of running, hopping, scurrying, or crawling to safety, but the others, for some unexplained reason, couldn't move and had just to stand there and take it. There was a description of the monster's roaring approach. Then the last line hit the reader like a left hook: "The lawn mower ran swiftly over . . ." [8]

The other story I have preserved these many years:

THE RACE

Two gleaming hot rods stand side by side, poised and tensed—eager to scream down the hot asphalt track, each secretly confident that he will be the supreme victor. The time is drawing close now; in just a few minutes the race will be on.

There is a last minute check of both cars . . . everything is ready. A yell rings out for everyone to clear the track. The flagman raises the starting flag above his head, pauses for a second, and with a downward thrust of the flag, he sends the cars leaping forward with frightening speed.

They fly down the track, side by side, neither able to take the lead. They are gaining speed with every second. Faster and faster they go, approaching the half-way mark with incredible momentum. . . .

Wait! Something is wrong—one of the cars is going out of control and skidding toward the other car! The rending sound of ripping metal and sliding tires cuts through the air as the two autos collide and spin crazily off the tracks.

For a moment the tragic panorama is hidden by a self-made curtain of dust, but it isn't a second before the curtain is pulled away by the wind, revealing the horrible sight. There are the two hot rods, one turned over, both broken and smashed. All is quiet. . . .

Two small children, a boy and a girl, get up from the curb where they have been sitting. They eye each other accusingly as they walk slowly across the street where the two broken toy cars lay silent. . . . "Woman driver," grumbles the little boy. [9]

The End

The correspondence school's copy desk quickly replied that the writing samples confirmed my aptitude test results and that they looked forward to working with me to the point of publication and beyond. I couldn't imagine what could be beyond publication but finally figured out they meant to handle my work later as agent-representative. They praised my choice of subject matter, sense of drama, and powerful surprise endings—all of which they said indicated I could sell to the sci-fi market. This made sense, because science fiction was all I had ever read voluntarily except for *Comic Classics* and, as a child, *Uncle Wiggily*. The school was particularly impressed by my style, which they said was practically poetry, in places. They made reference to my use of alliteration ("rending sound of ripping metal") and of metaphor ("self-made curtain of dust . . . pulled away by the wind"). [10]

They were quick to make clear, however, that what I had here were only germs of stories. They need to be expanded to publishable lengths and had to have better character development—particularly the one about the bugs and grass being slaughtered by the lawn mower. They said a good writer could give even an insect an interesting personality. [11]

The next step was to send them $10 for each of the two stories— the standard fee for detailed, over-the-shoulder copy-desk criticism. Then after these stories had been redone and rushed off for publication, I should enroll in their thirty-six-lesson course, in which I would be taught the ins and outs of plotting, characterization, point of vew, theme, tone, and setting. The fee was $10 a lesson, and after my successful completion of the course they would then handle my literary properties, protect my legal rights, etc., for the regular 10 percent. [12]

At this point I began to wonder if I might be going in over my head. I was getting only a dollar a week from my folks and didn't understand half of what the writing school was talking about. In English class I had heard of such terms as "alliteration," "tone," and "point of view" but had no clear idea what they meant. Also I felt like an imposter. I had given my age as twenty-one. Of course, I was strutting because at fourteen I was doing better than anybody they had worked with in years, but I wondered if I could keep it up. "Rending sound of ripping metal" was genius, but could I crank out lines like that on a daily basis? I decided to try. [13]

First I wrote them that I was a little short of cash this month and asked if, just to get started, it would be all right to work on one story for $10 instead of two for $20. They replied that that would be fine— just send in the ten bucks so they could get rolling. [14]

Meanwhile I hadn't been able to get even that much money together. I approached my family and was turned down flat because my father thought there was something unhealthy about people who wanted to write. He was bothered by the school's remark that my writing was like poetry. "If you were a girl, it might be different," he said, and showed me a copy of *Men's Adventure*. "Look here, why don't you get one of these two ninety-eight worm ranches? Or one of these small-game boomerangs?" [15]

After a few days of trying to drum up work around the neighborhood, I realized I wasn't going to be able to pull it off and decided just not to write back. But in a week I got a curt note saying they wanted to help me, were trying to be patient, but I was going to have to be more responsible. They said that writing was 1 percent inspiration and 99 percent perspiration and wondered if in my case the figures might be reversed. [16]

This both goaded and scared me. I wrote back that on account of unexpected medical expenses I could afford to give them only $5 at first. Could they possibly let me have a cut rate? They replied that it was strictly against their policy, but in view of my undeniably vast potential the copy-desk team had voted to go along with me just this once—send the $5. [17]

By mowing lawns and selling bottles, I had by this time scraped together $3, but there my earning potential dropped sharply. Another week went by, and I made only 48 cents more. Then a letter arrived stamped in red, front and back: URGENT! IMPORTANT! DO NOT DISCARD! It said I had violated an agreement based on mutual trust and had exactly twenty-four hours to send in the $5. Without exactly spelling it out, they gave the impression that legal action might be taken. The letter ended: "Frankly, Mr. Allen, we're about at our wits' end with you." [18]

I was hurt as well as shaken. I felt that I just didn't have what it takes. If there ever had been a chance of my climbing that hill and sitting with that elite group of loners and dreamers, it was gone now. I had my mother write them that I had suddenly been struck down with polio and was unable even to write my name, much less take their course. I hung onto the little money I had in case I had to give it to them to avoid a lawsuit, but I didn't hear from them after that. In a few weeks I relaxed and mailed off for the $2.98 worm ranch. [19]

PURPOSE AND STRUCTURE

1. What is the relationship of pars. 2, 3, and 4 to par. 1? The punctuation mark at the end of par. 1 is a clue to the answer. Could pars. 2, 3, and 4 be considered integral parts of par. 1?

2. Par. 6 is a transition paragraph. What does it join?

3. A good general rule is to put first things first. Use this rule to explain why the author begins the first sentence of par. 6 with an adverbial clause.

4. Identify the parallelisms of the last sentence of par. 6 and explain whether they add to or detract from the strength of the paragraph.

5. Verbals are verb forms that are *not* used as predicates. Usually they function as modifiers, as in "the *flying* football." Identify the past participle and present participle verbals in par. 8 and explain how they contribute to the sense of action.

6. In par. 10, show how the sentences work in pairs, with the second sentence of each pair dependent on the first.

7. From evidence in the essay, we can figure out that the writer of the first paragraph is twenty-nine years old. Most of the tale is a flashback to the time when he was only fourteen. Argue for or against an ending that returns the writer to his present age instead of the ending that exists.

DICTION AND TONE

1. Describe the boy's attitude toward his experience. Support your description by supplying details drawn from the young man's language.

2. How can you tell the older man's attitude toward the boy's experience?

3. Analyze the diction of par. 7. Point out as many clichés as you can discover. Comment on the relevance of the language in par. 7 to the quality

of the writing school. Defend the assertion that the diction of par. 7 contributes to the ironic tone of the essay.

4. By your analysis of the diction, prove to your listeners that the story "The Race" was written by a young, untrained writer.

5. Identify an ironical statement near the end of par. 13.

6. Show how the theme of "loners and dreamers" is used as a unifying motif. Do the same for the $2.98 worm ranch.

APPLICATIONS TO WRITING

Write about an experience you had when you were younger, which you took very seriously at the time it happened, but which you now regard as being rather humorous.

The Martians

from *The War of the Worlds*

H. G. WELLS

The fifth cylinder must have fallen right into the midst of the house we had first visited. The building had vanished, completely smashed, pulverised, and dispersed by the blow. The cylinder lay now far beneath the original foundations—deep in a hole, already vastly larger than the pit I had looked into at Woking. The earth all round it had splashed under that tremendous impact—"splashed" is the only word—and lay in heaped piles that hid the masses of the adjacent houses. It had behaved exactly like mud under a violent blow of a hammer. Our house had collapsed backward; the front portion, even on the ground floor, had been destroyed completely; by a chance the kitchen and scullery had escaped, and stood buried now under soil and ruins, closed in by tons of earth on every side save towards the cylinder. Over that aspect we hung now on the very edge of the great circular pit the

Martians were engaged in making. The heavy beating sound was evidently just behind us, and ever and again a bright green vapour drove up like a veil across our peep-hole. [1]

The cylinder was already opened in the centre of the pit, and on the farther edge of the pit, amid the smashed and gravel-heaped shrubbery, one of the great fighting-machines, deserted by its occupant, stood stiff and tall against the evening sky. At first I scarcely noticed the pit and the cylinder although it has been convenient to describe them first, on account of the extraordinary glittering mechanism I saw busy in the excavation, and on account of the strange creatures that were crawling slowly and painfully across the heaped mould near it. [2]

The mechanism it certainly was that held my attention first. It was one of those complicated fabrics that have since been called handling-machines, and the study of which has already given such an enormous impetus to terrestrial invention. As it dawned upon me first it presented a sort of metallic spider with five jointed, agile legs, and with an extraordinary number of jointed levers, bars, and reaching and clutching tentacles about its body. Most of its arms were retracted, but with three long tentacles it was fishing out a number of rods, plates, and bars which lined the covering and apparently strengthened the walls of the cylinder. These, as it extracted them, were lifted out and deposited upon a level surface of earth behind it. [3]

Its motion was so swift, complex, and perfect that at first I did not see it as a machine, in spite of its metallic glitter. The fighting-machines were co-ordinated and animated to an extraordinary pitch, but nothing to compare with this. People who have never seen these structures, and have only the ill-imagined efforts of artists or the imperfect descriptions of such eye-witnesses as myself to go upon, scarcely realise that living quality. [4]

I recall particularly the illustration of one of the first pamphlets to give a consecutive account of the war. The artist had evidently made a hasty study of one of the fighting-machines, and there his knowledge ended. He presented them as tilted, stiff tripods, without either flexibility or subtlety, and with an altogether misleading monotony of effect. The pamphlet containing these renderings had a considerable vogue, and I mention them here simply to warn the reader against the impression they may have created. They were no more like the Martians I saw in action than a Dutch doll is like a human being. To my mind, the pamphlet would have been much better without them. [5]

At first, I say, the handling-machine did not impress me as a machine, but as a crab-like creature with a glittering integument, the controlling Martian whose delicate tentacles actuated its movements seeming to be simply the equivalent of the crab's cerebral portion. But then I perceived the resemblance of its grey-brown, shiny, leathery integument to that of the other sprawling bodies beyond, and the true nature of this dexterous workman dawned upon me. With that realisation my interest shifted to those other creatures, the real Martians. Already I had had a transient impression of these, and the first nausea no longer obscured my observation. Moreover, I was concealed and motionless, and under no urgency of action. [6]

They were, I now saw, the most unearthly creatures it is possible to conceive. They were huge round bodies—or, rather, heads—about four feet in diameter, each body having in front of it a face. This face had no nostrils—indeed, the Martians do not seem to have had any sense of smell, but it had a pair of very large dark-coloured eyes, and just beneath this a kind of fleshy beak. In the back of this head or body—I scarcely know how to speak of it—was the single tight tympanic surface, since known to be anatomically an ear, though it must have been almost useless in our denser air. In a group round the mouth were sixteen slender, almost whip-like tentacles, arranged in two bunches of eight each. These bunches have since been named rather aptly, by that distinguished anatomist, Professor Howes, the *hands*. Even as I saw these Martians for the first time they seemed to be endeavouring to raise themselves on these hands, but of course, with the increased weight of terrestrial conditions, this was impossible. There is reason to suppose that on Mars they may have progressed upon them with some facility. [7]

The internal anatomy, I may remark here, as dissection has since shown, was almost equally simple. The greater part of the structure was the brain, sending enormous nerves to the eyes, ear, and tactile tentacles. Besides this were the bulky lungs, into which the mouth opened, and the heart and its vessels. The pulmonary distress caused by the denser atmosphere and greater gravitational attraction was only too evident in the convulsive movements of the outer skin. [8]

And this was the sum of the Martian organs. Strange as it may seem to a human being, all the complex apparatus of digestion, which makes up the bulk of our bodies, did not exist in the Martians. They were heads—merely heads. Entrails they had none. They did not eat, much less digest. Instead, they took the fresh, living blood of other creatures, and *injected* it into their own veins. I have myself seen this being done, as I shall mention in its place. But, squeamish as I may seem, I cannot bring myself to describe what I could not endure even to continue watching. Let it suffice to say, blood obtained from a still living animal, in most cases from a human being, was run directly by means of a little pipette into the recipient canal. . . . [9]

The bare idea of this is no doubt horribly repulsive to us, but at the same time I think that we should remember how repulsive our carnivorous habits would seem to an intelligent rabbit. [10]

The physiological advantages of the practice of injection are undeniable, if one thinks of the tremendous waste of human time and energy occasioned by eating and the digestive process. Our bodies are half made up of glands and tubes and organs, occupied in turning heterogeneous food into blood. The digestive processes and their reaction upon the nervous system sap our strength and colour our minds. Men go happy or miserable as they have healthy or unhealthy lives, or sound gastric glands. But the Martians were lifted above all these organic fluctuations of mood and emotion. [11]

Their undeniable preference for men as their source of nourishment is partly explained by the nature of the remains of the victims they had brought with them as provisions from Mars. These creatures, to judge from the shrivelled remains that have fallen into human hands, were bipeds with flimsy, silicious skeletons (almost like those of the silicious sponges) and feeble musculature, standing about six feet high and having round, erect heads, and large eyes in flinty sockets. Two or three of these seem to have been brought in each cylinder, and all were killed before earth was reached. It was just as well for them, for the mere attempt to stand upright upon our planet would have broken every bone in their bodies. [12]

And while I am engaged in this description, I may add in this place certain further details which, although they were not all evident to us at the time, will enable the reader who is unacquainted with them to form a clearer picture of these offensive creatures. [13]

In three other points their physiology differed strangely from ours. Their organisms did not sleep, any more than the heart of man sleeps. Since they had no extensive muscular mechanism to recuperate, that periodical extinction was unknown to them. They had little or no sense of fatigue, it would seem. On earth they could never have moved without effort, yet even to the last they kept in action. In twenty-four hours they did twenty-four hours of work, as even on earth is perhaps the case with the ants. [14]

In the next place, wonderful as it seems in a sexual world, the Martians were absolutely without sex, and therefore without any of the tumultuous emotions that arise from that difference among men. A young Martian, there can now be no dispute, was really born upon earth during the war, and it was found attached to its parent, partially *budded* off, just as young lily-bulbs bud off, or like the young animals in the freshwater polyp. [15]

In man, in all the higher terrestrial animals, such a method of increase has disappeared; but even on this earth it was certainly the primitive method. Among the lower animals, up even to those first cousins of the vertebrated animals, the Tunicates, the two processes occur side by side, but finally the sexual method superseded its competitor altogether. On Mars, however, just the reverse has apparently been the case. [16]

It is worthy of remark that a certain speculative writer of quasi-scientific repute, writing long before the Martian invasion, did forecast for man a final structure not unlike the actual Martian condition. His prophecy, I remember, appeared in November or December, 1893, in a long defunct publication, the *Pall Mall Budget,* and I recall a caricature of it in a pre-Martian periodical called *Punch.* He pointed out—writing in a foolish, facetious tone—that the perfection of mechanical appliances must ultimately supersede limbs; the perfection of chemical devices, digestion; that such organs as hair, external nose, teeth, ears, and chin were no longer essential parts of the human being, and that the tendency of natural selection would lie in the direction of their steady diminution through the coming ages. The brain alone remained a cardinal necessity. Only one other part of the body had a strong case for survival, and that was the hand, "teacher and agent of the brain." While the rest of the body dwindled, the hands would grow larger. [17]

There is many a true word written in jest, and here in the Martians we have beyond dispute the actual accomplishment of such a suppression of the animal side of the organism by the intelligence. To me it is quite credible that the Martians may be descended from beings not unlike ourselves, by a gradual development of brain and hands (the latter giving rise to the two bunches of delicate tentacles at last) at the expense of the rest of the body. Without the body the brain would, of course, become a mere selfish intelligence, without any of the emotional substratum of the human being. [18]

The last salient point in which the systems of these creatures differed from ours was in what one might have thought a very trivial particular. Micro-organisms, which cause so much disease and pain on earth, have either never appeared upon Mars or Martian sanitary science eliminated them ages ago. A hundred diseases, all the fevers and contagions of human life, consumption, cancers, tumours and such morbidities never enter the scheme of their life. And speaking of the differences between the life on Mars and terrestrial life, I may allude here to the curious suggestions of the red weed. [19]

Apparently the vegetable kingdom in Mars, instead of having green for a dominant colour, is of a vivid blood-red tint. At any rate, the seeds which the Martians (intentionally or accidentally) brought with them gave rise in all cases to red-coloured growths. Only that known popularly as the red weed, however, gained any footing in competition with terrestrial forms. The red creeper was quite a transitory growth, and few people have seen it growing. For a time, however, the red weed grew with astonishing vigour and luxuriance. It spread up the sides of the pit by the third or fourth day of our imprisonment, and its cactus-like branches formed a carmine fringe to the edges of our triangular window. And afterwards I found it broadcast throughout the country, and especially wherever there was a stream of water. [20]

The Martians had what appears to have been an auditory organ, a single round drum at the back of the head-body, and eyes with a visual range not very different from ours except that, according to Philips, blue and violet were as black to them. It is commonly supposed that they communicated by sounds and tentacular gesticulations; this is asserted, for instance, in the able but hastily compiled pamphlet (written evidently by some one not an eye-witness of Martian actions) to which I have already alluded, and which, so far, has been the chief source of information concerning them. Now no surviving human being saw so much of the Martians in action as I did. I take no credit to myself for an accident, but the fact is so. And I assert that I watched them closely time after time, and that I have seen four, five, and (once) six of them sluggishly performing the most elaborately complicated operations together without either sound or gesture. Their peculiar hooting invariably preceded feeding; it had no modulation, and was, I believe, in no sense a signal, but merely the expiration of air preparatory to the suctional operation. I have a certain claim to at least an elementary knowledge of psychology, and in this matter I am convinced—as firmly as I am convinced of anything—that the Martians interchanged thoughts without any physical intermediation. And I have been convinced of this in spite of strong preconceptions. Before the Martian invasion, as an occasional reader here or there may remember, I had written with some little vehemence against the telepathic theory. [21]

The Martians wore no clothing. Their conceptions of ornament and decorum were necessarily different from ours; and not only were they evidently much less sensible of changes of temperature than we are, but changes of pressure do not seem to have affected their health at all seriously. Yet though they wore no clothing, it was in the other artificial additions to their bodily resources that their great superiority over man lay. We men, with our bicycles and road-skates, our Lilienthal soaring-machines, our guns and sticks and so forth, are just in the beginning of the evolution that the Martians have worked out. They have become practically mere brains, wearing different bodies according to their needs just as men wear suits of clothes and take a bicycle in a hurry or an umbrella in the wet. And of their appliances, perhaps nothing is more wonderful to a man than the curious fact that what is the dominant feature of almost all human devices in mechanism is absent—the *wheel* is absent; among all the things they brought to earth there is no trace or suggestion of their use of wheels. One would have at least expected it in locomotion. And in this connection it is curious to remark that even on this earth Nature has never hit upon the wheel, or has preferred other expedients to its development. And not only did the Martians either not know of (which is incredible), or abstain from, the wheel, but in their apparatus singularly little use is made of the fixed pivot or relatively fixed pivot, with circular motions thereabout confined to one plane. Almost all the joints of the machinery present a complicated system of sliding parts moving over small but beautifully curved friction bearings. And while upon this matter of detail, it is remarkable that the long leverages of their machines are in most cases actuated by a sort of sham musculature of disks in an elastic sheath; these disks become polarised and drawn closely and powerfully together when traversed by a current of electricity. In this way the curious parallelism to animal motions, which was so striking and disturbing to the human beholder, was attained. Such quasi-muscles abounded in the crab-like handling-machine which, on my first peeping out of the slit, I watched unpacking the cylinder. It seemed infinitely more alive than the actual Martians lying beyond it in the sunset light, panting, stirring ineffectual tentacles, and moving feebly after their vast journey across space. [22]

While I was still watching their sluggish motions in the sunlight, and noting each strange detail of their form, the curate reminded me of his presence by pulling violently at my arm. I turned to a scowling face, and silent, eloquent lips. He wanted the slit, which permitted only one of us to peep through; and so I had to forego watching them for a time while he enjoyed that privilege. [23]

When I looked again, the busy handling-machine had already put together several of the pieces of apparatus it had taken out of the cylinder into a shape having an unmistakable likeness to its own; and down on the left a busy little digging mechanism had come into view, emitting jets of green vapour and working its way round the pit, excavating and embanking in a methodical and discriminating manner. This it was which had caused the regular beating noise, and the rhythmic shocks that had kept our ruinous refuge quivering. It piped and whistled as it worked. So far as I could see, the thing was without a directing Martian at all. [24]

PURPOSE AND STRUCTURE

1. In this excerpt from *The War of the Worlds*, H. G. Wells identifies Martians so vividly that we have little difficulty "seeing" them, although they never existed. It is our task to discover the techniques Wells uses to develop this realistic description of creatures that live only in his imagination. What is the function of the setting in which the Martians first appear?

2. What is the *dominant* method of description in par. 7? How does Wells bring the Martians into focus? Does he use significant detail (whole or part)? Or does he use comparison? Or does he describe characteristics or functions?

3. In par. 9, what is the *dominant* method?

4. Ask the same questions about pars. 14, 15, and 16.

5. What methods are used to describe the mechanism in pars. 3 and 6?

6. Now that you have identified the three major techniques Wells uses, analyze the long par. 22 to determine whether or not there are any de-

scriptive techniques in that paragraph that do not fall into one of the three categories named in question 2.

DICTION AND TONE

1. What effect does Wells achieve by referring to illustrations from pamphlets (par. 15) and to writers of quasi-scientific repute (par. 17)?

2. What is the immediate effect of the description of how the Martians nourish themselves (par. 9)?

3. How does Wells counter this effect?

4. How does he establish the tone in pars. 11 and 17?

APPLICATIONS TO WRITING

The three methods or techniques used by Wells—detail, comparison, and characteristics or function—seem simple, but each leads to complexity. Comparison involves the intricacies and subtleties of metaphor and simile. The appropriateness and frequently the freshness of a comparison make it effective. To use detail, the writer must first be observant and then be judicious in selecting those details that contribute to his purpose. Characteristics (or attributes) are usually reported by use of adverbs and adjectives. Occasionally, how a thing functions is a necessary part of description.

1. A UFO has landed in your neighborhood. Identify the creatures that emerge from it, using comparison, significant detail, and characterization.

2. Write a description of an Earthling as a Martian might perceive him.

3. Identify an odd earthly creature you are familiar with. For example, you might describe a sea urchin, a Venus's flytrap, a platypus.

Memories of a Missouri Farm
from *Mark Twain's Autobiography*

MARK TWAIN

My parents removed to Missouri in the early thirties; I do not remember just when, for I was not born then and cared nothing for such things. It was a long journey in those days, and must have been a rough and tiresome one. The home was made in the wee village of Florida, in Monroe County, and I was born there in 1835. The village contained a hundred people and I increased the population by 1 percent. It is more than many of the best men in history could have done for a town. It may not be modest in me to refer to this, but it is true. There is no record of a person doing as much—not even Shakespeare. But I did it for Florida, and it shows that I could have done it for any place—even London, I suppose. [1]

Recently some one in Missouri has sent me a picture of the house I was born in. Heretofore I have always stated that it was a palace, but I shall be more guarded now. [2]

I used to remember my brother Henry walking into a fire outdoors when he was a week old. It was remarkable in me to remember a thing like that, and it was still more remarkable that I should cling to the delusion, for thirty years, that I *did* remember it—for of course it never happened; he would not have been able to walk at that age. If I had stopped to reflect, I should not have burdened my memory with that impossible rubbish so long. It is believed by many people that an impression deposited in a child's memory within the first two years of its life cannot remain there five years, but that is an error. The incident of Benvenuto Cellini and the salamander must be accepted as authentic and trustworthy; and then that remarkable and indisputable instance in the experience of Helen Keller—However, I will speak of that at another time. For many years I believed that I remembered helping my grandfather drink his whisky toddy when I was six weeks old, but I do not tell about that any more, now; I am grown old and my memory is not as active as it used to be. When I was younger I

of Mason and Dixon, nor anywhere in Europe. This is not
experience that is speaking. In Europe it is imagined tha
of serving various kinds of bread blazing hot is "American
too broad a spread; it is custom in the South, but is much
in the North. In the North and in Europe hot br
unhealthy. This is probably another fussy superst
pean superstition that ice-water is unhealthy.
ice-water and does not drink it; and yet,
word for it is better than ours, because i
doesn't. Europe calls it "iced" water. O
from melted ice—a drink which has
have but little acquaintance with.
It seems a pity that the wo
things merely because they
given us any refreshmen
some, except microbes.
selves of each and ev
any way acquired
And health is a
your whole f
The fa
yard w
high

peas, Irish potatoes, sweet potatoes; buttermilk, sw___
watermelons, muskmelons, cantaloupes—all fresh from the garden;
apple pie, peach pie, pumpkin pie, apple dumplings, peach cobbler—I
can't remember the rest. The way that the things were cooked was
perhaps the main splendor—particularly a certain few of the dishes. For
instance, the corn bread, the hot biscuits and wheat bread, and the
fried chicken. These things have never been properly cooked in the
North—in fact, no one there is able to learn the art, so far as my
experience goes. The North thinks it knows how to make corn bread,
but this is mere superstition. Perhaps no bread in the world is quite so
good as Southern corn bread, and perhaps no bread in the world is
quite so bad as the Northern imitation of it. The North seldom tries to
fry chicken, and this is well; the art cannot be learned north of the line

less than that
ead is considered
tion, like the Euro-
Europe does not need
notwithstanding this, its
describes it, whereas ours
ur word describes water made
characterless taste and which we

5]

ld should throw away so many good
are unwholesome. I doubt if God has
which, taken in moderation, is unwhole-
Yet there are people who strictly deprive them-
ry eatable, drinkable, and smokable which has in
a shady reputation. They pay this price for health.
l they get for it. How strange it is! It is like paying out
ortune for a cow that has gone dry. [6]

mhouse stood in the middle of a very large yard, and the
as fenced on three sides with rails and on the rear side with
palings; against these stood the smoke-house; beyond the palings
as the orchard; beyond the orchard were the negro quarters and the
tobacco fields. The front yard was entered over a stile made of sawed-
off logs of graduated heights; I do not remember any gate. In a corner of
the front yard were a dozen lofty hickory trees and a dozen black
walnuts, and in the nutting season riches were to be gathered there. [7]

Down a piece, abreast the house, stood a little log cabin against the
rail fence; and there the woody hill fell sharply away, past the barns,
the corncrib, the stables, and the tobacco-curing house, to a limpid brook
which sang along over its gravelly bed and curved and frisked in and
out and here and there and yonder in the deep shade of overhanging
foliage and vines—a divine place for wading, and it had swimming
pools, too, which were forbidden to us and therefore much frequented
by us. For we were little Christian children and had early been taught
the value of forbidden fruit. [8]

In the little log cabin lived a bedridden white-headed slave woman
whom we visited daily and looked upon with awe, for we believed she

was upward of a thousand years old and had talked with Moses. The younger negroes credited these statistics and had furnished them to us in good faith. We accommodated all the details which came to us about her; and so we believed that she had lost her health in the long desert trip coming out of Egypt, and had never been able to get it back again. She had a round bald place on the crown of her head, and we used to creep around and gaze at it in reverent silence, and reflect that it was caused by fright through seeing Pharaoh drowned. We called her "Aunt" Hannah, Southern fashion. She was superstitious, like the other negroes; also, like them, she was deeply religious. Like them, she had great faith in prayer and employed it in all ordinary exigencies, but not in cases where a dead certainty of result was urgent. Whenever witches were around she tied up the remnant of her wool in little tufts, with white thread, and this promptly made the witches impotent. [9]

All the negroes were friends of ours, and with those of our own age we were in effect comrades. I say in effect, using the phrase as a modification. We were comrades, and yet not comrades; color and condition interposed a subtle line which both parties were conscious of and which rendered complete fusion impossible. We had a faithful and affectionate good friend, ally, and adviser in "Uncle Dan'l," a middle-aged slave whose head was the best one in the negro quarter, whose sympathies were wide and warm, and whose heart was honest and simple and knew no guile. He has served me well these many, many years. I have not seen him for more than half a century, and yet spiritually I have had his welcome company a good part of that time, and have staged him in books under his own name and as "Jim," and carted him all around—to Hannibal, down the Mississippi on a raft, and even across the Desert of Sahara in a balloon—and he has endured it all with the patience and friendliness and loyalty which were his birthright. It was on the farm that I got my strong liking for his race and my appreciation of certain of its fine qualities. This feeling and this estimate have stood the test of sixty years and more, and have suffered no impairment. The black face is as welcome to me now as it was then. [10]

In my schoolboy days I had no aversion to slavery. I was not aware that there was anything wrong about it. No one arraigned it in my hearing; the local papers said nothing against it; the local pulpit taught us that God approved it, that it was a holy thing, and that the doubter need only look in the Bible if he wished to settle his mind—and then the texts were read aloud to us to make the matter sure; if the slaves themselves had an aversion to slavery, they were wise and said nothing. In Hannibal we seldom saw a slave misused; on the farm, never. [11]

There was, however, one small incident of my boyhood days which touched this matter, and it must have meant a good deal to me or it would not have stayed in my memory, clear and sharp, vivid and shadowless, all these slow-drifting years. We had a little slave boy whom we had hired from some one, there in Hannibal. He was from the eastern shore of Maryland, and had been brought away from his family and his friends, halfway across the American continent, and sold. He was a cheery spirit, innocent and gentle, and the noisiest creature that ever was, perhaps. All day long he was singing, whistling, yelling, whooping, laughing—it was maddening, devastating, unendurable. At last, one day, I lost all my temper, and went raging to my mother and said Sandy had been singing for an hour without a single break, and I couldn't stand it, and *wouldn't* she please shut him up. The tears came into her eyes and her lip trembled, and she said something like this: [12]

"Poor thing, when he sings it shows that he is not remembering, and that comforts me; but when he is still I am afraid he is thinking, and I cannot bear it. He will never see his mother again; if he can sing, I must not hinder it, but be thankful for it. If you were older, you would understand me; then that friendless child's noise would make you glad." [13]

It was a simple speech and made up of small words, but it went home, and Sandy's noise was not a trouble to me any more. She never used large words, but she had a natural gift for making small ones do effective work. She lived to reach the neighborhood of ninety years and was capable with her tongue to the last—especially when a meanness or an injustice roused her spirit. She has come handy to me several times in my books, where she figures as Tom Sawyer's Aunt Polly. I fitted her out with a dialect and tried to think up other improvements for her, but did not find any. I used Sandy once, also; it was in *Tom Sawyer.* I tried to get him to whitewash the fence, but it did not work. I do not remember what name I called him by in the book. [14]

I can see the farm yet, with perfect clearness. I can see all its belongings, all its details; the family room of the house, with a "trundle" bed in one corner and a spinning-wheel in another—a wheel whose rising and falling wail, heard from a distance, was the mournfulest of all sounds to me, and made me homesick and low spirited, and filled my atmosphere with the wandering spirits of the dead; the vast fireplace, piled high, on winter nights, with flaming hickory logs from whose ends a sugary sap bubbled out, but did not go to waste, for we scraped it off and ate it; the lazy cat spread out on the rough hearthstones; the drowsy dogs braced against the jambs and blinking; my aunt in one chimney corner, knitting; my uncle in the other, smoking his corn-cob pipe; the slick and carpetless oak floor faintly mirroring the dancing flame tongues and freckled with black indentations where fire coals had popped out and died a leisurely death; half a dozen children romping in the background twilight; "split"-bottomed chairs here and there, some with rockers; a cradle—out of service, but waiting, with confidence; in the early cold mornings a snuggle of children, in shirts and chemises, occupying the hearthstone and procrastinating—they could not bear to leave that comfortable place and go out on the wind-swept floor space between the house and kitchen where the general tin basin stood, and wash. [15]

Along outside of the front fence ran the country road, dusty in the summertime, and a good place for snakes—they liked to lie in it and sun themselves; when they were rattlesnakes or puff adders, we killed them; when they were black snakes, or racers, or belonged to the fabled "hoop" breed, we fled, without shame; when they were "house snakes," or "garters," we carried them home and put them in Aunt Patsy's work basket for a surprise; for she was prejudiced against snakes, and always when she took the basket in her lap and they began to climb out of it it disordered her mind. She never could seem to get used to them; her opportunities went for nothing. And she was always cold toward bats, too, and could not bear them; and yet I think a bat is as friendly a bird as there is. My mother was Aunt Patsy's sister and had the same wild superstitions. A bat is beautifully soft and silky; I do not know any creature that is pleasanter to the touch or is more grateful for caressings, if offered in the right spirit. I know all about these coleoptera, because our great cave, three miles below Hannibal, was multitudinously stocked with them, and often I brought them home to amuse my mother with. It was easy to manage if it was a school day, because then I had ostensibly been to school and hadn't any bats. She was not a suspicious person, but full of trust and confidence; and when I said, "There's something in my coat pocket for you," she would put her hand in. But she always took it out again, herself; I didn't have to tell her. It was remarkable, the way she couldn't learn to like private bats. The more experience she had, the more she could not change her views. [16]

I think she was never in the cave in her life; but everybody else went there. Many excursion parties came from considerable distances up and down the river to visit the cave. It was miles in extent and was a tangled wilderness of narrow and lofty clefts and passages. It was an easy place to get lost in; anybody could do it—including the bats. I got lost in it myself, along with a lady, and our last candle burned down to almost nothing before we glimpsed the search party's lights winding about in the distance. [17]

"Injun Joe," the half-breed, got lost in there once, and would have starved to death if the bats had run short. But there was no chance of that; there were myriads of them. He told me all his story. In the book called *Tom Sawyer* I starved him entirely to death in the cave, but that was in the interest of art; it never happened. "General" Gaines, who was our first town drunkard before Jimmy Finn got the place, was lost in there for the space of a week, and finally pushed his handker-chief out of a hole in a hilltop near Saverton, several miles down the river from the cave's mouth, and somebody saw it and dug him out. There is nothing the matter with his statistics except the handkerchief. I knew him for years and he hadn't any. But it could have been his nose. That would attract attention. [18]

The cave was an uncanny place, for it contained a corpse—the corpse of a young girl of fourteen. It was in a glass cylinder inclosed in a copper one which was suspended from a rail which bridged a narrow passage. The body was preserved in alcohol, and it was said that loafers and rowdies used to drag it up by the hair and look at the dead face. The girl was the daughter of a St. Louis surgeon of extraordinary ability and wide celebrity. He was an eccentric man and did many strange things. He put the poor thing in that forlorn place himself. [19]

Beyond the road where the snakes sunned themselves was a dense young thicket, and through it a dim-lighted path led a quarter of a mile; then out of the dimness one emerged abruptly upon a level great prairie which was covered with wild strawberry plants, vividly starred with prairie pinks, and walled in on all sides by forests. The straw-berries were fragrant and fine, and in the season we were generally there in the crisp freshness of the early morning, while the dew beads still sparkled upon the grass and the woods were ringing with the first songs of the birds. [20]

Down the forest slopes to the left were the swings. They were made of bark stripped from hickory saplings. When they became dry they were dangerous. They usually broke when a child was forty feet in the air, and this was why so many bones had to be mended every year. I had no ill luck myself, but none of my cousins escaped. There were eight of them, and at one time and another they broke fourteen arms among them. But it cost next to nothing, for the doctor worked by the year—twenty-five dollars for the whole family. I remember two of the Florida doctors, Chowning and Meredith. They not only tended an entire family for twenty-five dollars a year, but furnished the medicines themselves. Good measure, too. Only the largest persons could hold a whole dose. Castor oil was the principal beverage. The dose was half a dipperful, with half a dipperful of New Orleans molasses added to help it down and make it taste good, which it never did. The next standby was calomel; the next rhubarb; and the next, jalap. Then they bled the patient, and put mustard plasters on him. It was a dreadful system, and yet the death rate was not heavy. The calomel was nearly sure to salivate the patient and cost him some of his teeth. There were no dentists. When teeth became touched with decay or were otherwise ailing, the doctor knew of but one thing to do—he fetched his tongs and dragged them out. If the jaw remained, it was not his fault. Doctors were not called in cases of ordinary illness; the family grandmother attended to those. Every old woman was a doctor, and gathered her own medicines in the woods, and knew how to compound doses that would stir the vitals of a cast-iron dog. And then there was the "Indian doctor"; a grave savage, remnant of his tribe, deeply read in the mysteries of nature and the secret properties of herbs; and most backwoodsmen had high faith in his powers and could tell of wonderful cures achieved by him. In Mauritius, away off yonder in the solitudes of the Indian Ocean, there is a person who answers to our Indian doctor of the old times. He is a negro, and has had no teaching as a doctor, yet there is one disease which he is master of and can cure and the doctors can't. They send for him when they have a case. It is a child's disease of a strange and deadly sort, and the negro cures it with a herb medicine which he makes, himself, from a prescription which has come down to him from his father and grandfather. He will not let anyone see it. He keeps the secret of its components to himself, and it is feared that he will die without divulging it; then there will be consternation in Mauritius. I was told these things by the people there, in 1896. [21]

We had the "faith doctor," too, in those early days—a woman. Her specialty was toothache. She was a farmer's old wife and lived five miles from Hannibal. She would lay her hand on the patient's jaw and say, "Believe!" and the cure was prompt. Mrs. Utterback. I remember her very well. Twice I rode out there behind my mother, horseback, and saw the cure performed. My mother was the patient. [22]

Doctor Meredith removed to Hannibal, by and by, and was our family physician there, and saved my life several times. Still, he was a good man and meant well. Let it go. [23]

I was always told that I was a sickly and precarious and tiresome and uncertain child, and lived mainly on allopathic medicines during the first seven years of my life. I asked my mother about this, in her old age—she was in her eighty-eighth year—and said: [24]

"I suppose that during all that time you were uneasy about me?" [25]

"Yes, the whole time." [26]

"Afraid I wouldn't live?" [27]

After a reflective pause—ostensibly to think out the facts—"No—afraid you would." [28]

The country schoolhouse was three miles from my uncle's farm. It stood in a clearing in the woods and would hold about twenty-five boys and girls. We attended the school with more or less regularity once or twice a week, in summer, walking to it in the cool of the morning by the forest paths, and back in the gloaming at the end of the day. All the pupils brought their dinners in baskets—corn dodger, buttermilk, and other good things—and sat in the shade of the trees at noon and ate them. It is the part of my education which I look back upon with the most satisfaction. My first visit to the school was when I was seven. A strapping girl of fifteen, in the customary sunbonnet and calico dress, asked me if I "used tobacco"—meaning did I chew it. I said no. It roused her scorn. She reported me to all the crowd, and said: [29]

"Here is a boy seven years old who can't chew tobacco." [30]

By the looks and comments which this produced I realized that I was a degraded object, and was cruelly ashamed of myself. I determined to reform. But I only made myself sick; I was not able to learn to chew tobacco. I learned to smoke fairly well, but that did not conciliate anybody and I remained a poor thing, and characterless. I longed to be respected, but I never was able to rise. Children have but little charity for one another's defects. [31]

As I have said, I spent some part of every year at the farm until I was twelve or thirteen years old. The life which I led there with my cousins was full of charm, and so is the memory of it yet. I can call back the solemn twilight and mystery of the deep woods, the earthy smells, the faint odors of the wild flowers, the sheen of rain-washed foliage, the rattling clatter of drops when the wind shook the trees, the far-off hammering of woodpeckers and the muffled drumming of wood pheasants in the remoteness of the forest, the snapshot glimpses of disturbed wild creatures scurrying through the grass—I can call it all back and make it as real as it ever was, and as blessed. I can call back the prairie, and its loneliness and peace, and a vast hawk hanging motionless in the sky, with his wings spread wide and the blue of the vault showing through the fringe of their end feathers. I can see the woods in their autumn dress, the oaks purple, the hickories washed with gold, the maples and the sumachs luminous with crimson fires, and I can hear the rustle made by the fallen leaves as we plowed through them. I can see the blue clusters of wild grapes hanging among the foliage of the saplings, and I remember the taste of them and the smell. I know how the wild blackberries looked, and how they tasted, and the same with the pawpaws, the hazelnuts, and the persimmons; and I can feel the thumping rain, upon my head, of hickory nuts and walnuts when we were out in the frosty dawn to scramble for them with the pigs, and the gusts of wind loosed them and sent them down. I know the stain of blackberries, and how pretty it is, and I know the stain of walnut hulls, and how little it minds soap and water, also what grudged experience it had of either of them. I know the taste of maple sap, and when to gather it, and how to arrange the troughs and the delivery tubes, and how to boil down the juice, and how to hook the sugar after it is made, also how much better hooked sugar tastes than any that is honestly come by, let bigots say what they will. I know how a prize watermelon looks when it is sunning its fat rotundity among pumpkin vines and "simblins"; I know how to tell when it is ripe without "plugging" it; I know how inviting it looks when it is cooling itself in a tub of water under the bed, waiting; I know how it looks when it lies on the table in the sheltered great floor space between house and kitchen, and the children gathered for the sacrifice and their mouths watering; I know the crackling sound it makes when the carving knife enters its end, and I can see the split fly along in front of the blade as the knife cleaves its way to the other end; I can see its halves fall apart and display the rich red meat and the black seeds, and the heart standing up, a luxury fit for the elect; I know how a boy looks behind a yard-long slice of that melon, and I knew how he feels; for I have been there. I know the taste of the watermelon which has been honestly come by, and I know the taste of the watermelon which has been acquired by art. Both taste good, but the experienced know which tastes best. I know the look of green apples and peaches and pears on the trees, and I know how entertaining they are when they are inside of a person. I know how ripe ones look when they are piled in pyramids under the trees, and how pretty they are and how vivid their colors. I know how a frozen apple looks, in a barrel down cellar in the wintertime, and how hard it is to bite, and how the frost makes the teeth ache, and yet how good it is, notwithstanding. I know the disposition of elderly people to select the specked apples for the children, and I once knew ways to beat the game. I know the look of an apple that is roasting and sizzling on a hearth on a winter's evening, and I know the comfort that comes of eating it hot, along with some sugar and a drench of cream. I know the delicate art and mystery of so cracking hickory nuts and walnuts on a flatiron with a hammer that the kernels will be delivered whole, and I know how the nuts, taken in conjunction with winter apples, cider, and doughnuts, make old people's old tales and old jokes sound fresh and crisp and enchanting, and juggle an evening away before you know what went with the time. I know the look of Uncle Dan'l's kitchen as it was on the privileged nights, when I was a child, and I can see the white and black children grouped on the hearth, with the firelight playing on their faces and the shadows flickering upon the walls, clear back toward the cavernous gloom of the rear, and I can hear Uncle Dan'l telling the immortal tales which Uncle Remus Harris was to gather into his book and charm the world with, by and by; and I can feel again the creepy joy which quivered through me when the time for the ghost story was reached—and the sense of regret, too, which came over me, for it was always the last story of the evening and there was nothing between it and the unwelcome bed. [32]

I can remember the bare wooden stairway in my uncle's house, and the turn to the left above the landing, and the rafters and the slanting roof over my bed, and the squares of moonlight on the floor, and the white cold world of snow outside, seen through the curtainless window. I can remember the howling of the wind and the quaking of the house on stormy nights, and how snug and cozy one felt, under the blankets, listening; and how the powdery snow used to sift in, around the sashes, and lie in little ridges on the floor and make the place look chilly in the morning and curb the wild desire to get up— in case there was any. I can remember how very dark that room was, in the dark of the moon, and how packed it was with ghostly stillness when one woke up by accident away in the night, and forgotten sins came flocking out of the secret chambers of the memory and wanted a hearing; and how ill chosen the time seemed for this kind of business; and how dismal was the hoohooing of the owl and the wailing of the wolf, sent mourning by on the night wind. [33]

I remember the raging of the rain on that roof, summer nights, and how pleasant it was to lie and listen to it, and enjoy the white splendor of the lightning and the majestic booming and crashing of the thunder. It was a very satisfactory room, and there was a lightning rod which was reachable from the window, an adorable and skittish thing to climb up and down, summer nights, when there were duties on hand of a sort to make privacy desirable. [34]

I remember the 'coon and 'possum hunts, nights, with the negroes, and the long marches through the black gloom of the woods, and the excitement which fired everybody when the distant bay of an experienced dog announced that the game was treed; then the wild scramblings and stumblings through briers and bushes and over roots to get to the spot; then the lighting of a fire and the felling of the tree, the joyful frenzy of the dogs and the negroes, and the weird picture it all made in the red glare—I remember it all well, and the delight that everyone got out of it, except the 'coon. [35]

I remember the pigeon seasons, when the birds would come in millions and cover the trees and by their weight break down the branches. They were clubbed to death with sticks; guns were not necessary and were not used. I remember the squirrel hunts, and prairie-chicken hunts, and wild-turkey hunts, and all that; and how we turned out, mornings, while it was still dark, to go on these expeditions, and how chilly and dismal it was, and how often I regretted that I was well enough to go. A toot on a tin horn brought twice as many dogs as were needed, and in their happiness they raced and scampered about, and knocked small people down, and made no end of unnecessary noise. At the word, they vanished away toward the woods, and we drifted silently after them in the melancholy gloom. But presently the gray dawn stole over the world, the birds piped up, then the sun rose and poured light and comfort all around, everything was fresh and dewy and fragrant, and life was a boon again. After three hours of tramping we arrived back wholesomely tired, overladen with game, very hungry, and just in time for breakfast. [36]

PURPOSE AND STRUCTURE

1. At first glance this seems to be a loosely organized piece, with one thought idly leading to another. A large part of the organization is determined by what Twain apparently wants to write about—the farm itself, but more particularly, the *people,* the *activities,* and the *things* that made the farm memorable. How he integrates all of them will be clear if you write out in order the first sentences of the following paragraphs: 5, 7, 16, 20, 21, 29.

2. What subject matter appears between pars. 7 and 16? Between 16 and 20? 21 and 29? 29 and 32?

3. On the basis of your answer to questions 1 and 2, what can you say about the relationship between places and people? Which do you think Twain is more interested in? How can you tell?

4. If you have difficulty completing a 500-word essay, study this selection with care, especially pars. 5, 15, 32. Account for the difference between, "We had a variety of meats, plenty of vegetables, and delicious desserts," and Twain's description of a meal. See Abstraction in the Glossary.

5. In par. 15, although Twain announces that he can "see all its [the farm's] belongings, all its details," he doesn't describe *all* of them. What does he do? Note that rather than merely listing details, Twain makes each detail function in some way. For example, his aunt *knits,* his uncle *smokes.* How do each of the following "work": spinning wheel, hickory logs, sap, dogs, floor, fire coals, cradle?

6. Students frequently try to make their writing vivid by using many adjectives and adverbs to lend color to pallid abstract nouns and verbs instead of relying on specific concrete nouns and verbs that appeal to the

senses. In par. 32, which senses are appealed to in the first half of the paragraph (up to the incident involving the watermelon)?

7. In par. 32 the account of the watermelon is contained in one extraordinarily long sentence. What, if anything, is gained by putting all the independent clauses in one sentence? What does the series of clauses contribute to rhythm and tone? Notice that each clause begins with "I know. . . ." Does this repetition contribute to unity or monotony? Defend your answer.

8. If you are in the habit of thinking of your writing problem as one of language, you have not yet recognized how perception determines what one can write. Remember, it is the experience of small details that makes up a large, general impression. Notice in par. 32 how Twain sees his hawk down to the minutest detail—"with his wings spread wide and the blue of the vault showing through the fringe of their end feathers." Although many may have seen exactly what Twain records, few have the ability to recall it as distinctly and vividly. In the account of the watermelon, what one detail is perfectly familiar to you and yet would have been overlooked if you had been describing a watermelon?

9. How is the topic sentence of par. 32 related to pars. 33, 34, 35, 36?

DICTION AND TONE

1. "It was a simple speech and made up of small words" is Twain's own comment on par. 13. Is any word in par. 12 or 13 not in your active vocabulary or thoroughly familiar to you? On the basis of these two paragraphs what would you say is the relationship between extensive vocabulary and effectiveness? What seems more important than extensive vocabulary?

2. Look at the first sentence in par. 13. It is perfectly balanced. Analyze the sentence so that you can explain what is meant by a balanced sentence.

3. "When I was younger I could remember anything, whether it had happened or not. . . ." What does this remark at the end of par. 3 add to the essay? What does Twain mean by it? Is it in keeping with the rest of the essay?

4. Put in shorter form, "It may not be modest in me" (par. 1). Put "impossible rubbish" in more formal and then in less formal language.

APPLICATIONS TO WRITING

Twain teaches us that generalizations are weak unless supported by relevant details—not any details, but *relevant* ones. Your purpose in writing governs the selection of some details and the rejection of others. For example, the details Twain chooses to report produce an overall effect of coziness in the winter farmhouse. If he had selected such items as drafts, poor lighting, uncomfortable wooden furniture, the general effect would be different.

Write a descriptive essay, using details that will identify the subject clearly in the mind of your reader. In making your presentation of people, places, and things vivid and coherent, you might adopt Twain's method of organization, using a place as a framework. In accounting for the sights, sounds, tastes, smells, and feel of your experience, report the things that originally stimulated them.

Your subject might be "A Street Corner"; "A Friend's Apartment"; "A Ride on Public Transit"; "My Professor's Office." Before writing the essay, compile a list of details that will reveal significant qualities of your subject. For instance, if you describe a room, use details that enable the reader to identify the personality of the room's inhabitant. Don't be satisfied with general observations, but make your details *work*; do not simply catalog or inventory.

The Libido for the Ugly

H. L. MENCKEN

On a Winter day some years ago, coming out of Pittsburgh on one of the expresses of the Pennsylvania Railroad, I rolled eastward for an hour through the coal and steel towns of Westmoreland county. It was familiar ground; boy and man, I had been through it often before. But somehow I had never quite sensed its appalling desolation. Here was the very heart of industrial America, the center of its most lucrative and characteristic activity, the boast and pride of the richest and grandest nation ever seen on earth—and here was a scene so dreadfully hideous, so intolerably bleak and forlorn that it reduced the whole aspiration of man to a macabre and depressing joke. Here was wealth beyond computation, almost beyond imagination—and here were human habitations so abominable that they would have disgraced a race of alley cats. [1]

I am not speaking of mere filth. One expects steel towns to be dirty. What I allude to is the unbroken and agonizing ugliness, the sheer revolting monstrousness, of every house in sight. From East Liberty to Greensburg, a distance of twenty-five miles, there was not one in sight from the train that did not insult and lacerate the eye. Some were so bad, and they were among the most pretentious—churches, stores, warehouses, and the like—that they were downright startling; one blinked before them as one blinks before a man with his face shot away. A few linger in memory, horrible even there: a crazy little church just west of Jeannette, set like a dormer-window on the side of a bare, leprous hill; the headquarters of the Veterans of Foreign Wars at another forlorn town, a steel stadium like a huge rat-trap somewhere further down the line. But most of all I recall the general effect—of hideousness without a break. There was not a single decent house within eyerange from the Pittsburgh suburbs to the Greensburg yards. There was not one that was not misshapen, and there was not one that was not shabby. [2]

The country itself is not uncomely, despite the grime of the endless mills. It is, in form, a narrow river valley, with deep gullies running up into the hills. It is thickly settled, but not noticeably overcrowded. There is still plenty of room for building, even in the larger towns, and there are very few solid blocks. Nearly every house, big and little, has space on all four sides. Obviously, if there were architects of any professional sense or dignity in the region, they would have perfected a chalet to hug the hillsides—a chalet with a high-pitched roof, to throw off the heavy Winter snows, but still essentially a low and clinging building, wider than it was tall. But what have they done? They have taken as their model a brick set on end. This they have converted into a thing of dingy clapboards, with a narrow, low-pitched roof. And the whole they have set upon thin, preposterous brick piers. By the hundreds and thousands these abominable houses cover the bare hillsides, like gravestones in some gigantic and decaying cemetery. On their deep sides they are three, four and even five stories high; on their low sides they bury themselves swinishly in the mud. Not a fifth of them are perpendicular. They lean this way and that, hanging on to their bases precariously. And one and all they are streaked in grime, with dead and eczematous patches of paint peeping through the streaks. [3]

Now and then there is a house of brick. But what brick! When it is new it is the color of a fried egg. When it has taken on the patina of the mills it is the color of an egg long past all hope or caring. Was it necessary to adopt that shocking color? No more than it was necessary to set all of the houses on end. Red brick, even in a steel town, ages with some dignity. Let it become downright black, and it is still sightly, especially if its trimmings are of white stone, with soot in the depths and the high spots washed by the rain. But in Westmoreland they prefer that uremic yellow, and so they have the most loathsome towns and villages ever seen by mortal eye. [4]

I award this championship only after laborious research and incessant prayer. I have seen, I believe, all of the most unlovely towns of the world; they are all to be found in the United States. I have seen the mill towns of decomposing New England and the desert towns of Utah, Arizona and Texas. I am familiar with the back streets of Newark, Brooklyn and Chicago, and have made scientific explorations to Camden, N. J. and Newport News, Va. Safe in a Pullman, I have whirled through the gloomy, God-forsaken villages of Iowa and Kansas, and the malarious tidewater hamlets of Georgia. I have been to Bridgeport, Conn., and to Los Angeles. But nowhere on this earth, at home or abroad, have I seen anything to compare to the villages that huddle along the line of the Pennsylvania from the Pittsburgh yards to Greensburg. They are incomparable in color, and they are incomparable in design. It is as if some titanic and aberrant genius, uncompromisingly inimical to man, had devoted all the ingenuity of Hell to the making of them. They show grotesqueries of ugliness that, in retrospect, become almost diabolical. One cannot imagine mere human beings concocting such dreadful things, and one can scarcely imagine human beings bearing life in them. [5]

Are they so frightful because the valley is full of foreigners—dull, insensate brutes, with no love of beauty in them? Then why didn't these foreigners set up similar abominations in the countries that they came from? You will, in fact, find nothing of the sort in Europe— save perhaps in the more putrid parts of England. There is scarcely an ugly village on the whole Continent. The peasants, however poor, somehow manage to make themselves graceful and charming habitations, even in Spain. But in the American village and small town the pull is always toward ugliness, and in that Westmoreland valley it has been yielded to with an eagerness bordering upon passion. It is incredible that mere ignorance should have achieved such masterpieces of horror. [6]

On certain levels of the American race, indeed, there seems to be a positive libido for the ugly, as on other and less Christian levels there is a libido for the beautiful. It is impossible to put down the wallpaper that defaces the average American home of the lower middle class to mere inadvertence, or to the obscene humor of the manufacturers. Such ghastly designs, it must be obvious, give a genuine delight to a certain type of mind. They meet, in some unfathomable way, its obscure and unintelligible demands. They caress it as "The Palms" caresses it, or the art of the movie, or jazz. The taste for them is as enigmatical and yet as common as the taste for dogmatic theology and the poetry of Edgar A. Guest. [7]

Thus I suspect (though confessedly without knowing) that the vast majority of the honest folk of Westmoreland county, and especially the 100% Americans among them, actually admire the houses they live in, and are proud of them. For the same money they could get vastly better ones, but they prefer what they have got. Certainly there was no pressure upon the Veterans of Foreign Wars to choose the dreadful edifice that bears their banner, for there are plenty of vacant buildings along the track-side, and some of them are appreciably better. They might, indeed, have built a better one of their own. But they chose that clapboarded horror with their eyes open, and having chosen it, they let it mellow into its present shocking depravity. They like it as it is: beside it, the Parthenon would no doubt offend them. In precisely the same way the authors of the rat-trap stadium that I have mentioned made a deliberate choice. After painfully designing and erecting it, they made it perfect in their own sight by putting a completely impossible penthouse, painted a staring yellow, on top of it. The effect is that of a fat woman with a black eye. It is that of a Presbyterian grinning. But they like it. [8]

Here is something that the psychologists have so far neglected: the love of ugliness for its own sake, the lust to make the world intolerable. Its habitat is the United States. Out of the melting pot emerges a race which hates beauty as it hates truth. The etiology of this madness deserves a great deal more study than it has got. There must be causes behind it; it arises and flourishes in obedience to biological laws, and not as a mere act of God. What, precisely, are the terms of those laws? And why do they run stronger in America than elsewhere? Let some honest *Privat Dozent* in pathological sociology apply himself to the problem. [9]

PURPOSE AND STRUCTURE

1. In par. 9 Mencken seems to be identifying a scholarly problem: "Here is something that the psychologists have so far neglected: the love of ugliness for its own sake, the lust to make the world intolerable." Discuss the seriousness of his suggestions for research in psychology and pathological sociology.

2. His essay opens with a description of what he sees from the train as he rolls "eastward for an hour through the coal and steel towns of Westmoreland country" (par. 1). He maintains the unity of the rest of the essay by selecting most of his examples from this same area. What, then, is the purpose of the references to other towns and villages in America (par. 5)? to the villages of Europe (par. 6)? to the Parthenon (par. 8)?

3. The last two sentences of par. 1 repeat a powerful contrast. Notice the use of the dash in each sentence. Why not use a comma or a semicolon instead? Why is this contrast set in the reader's mind early in the essay? What argument could be used against the thesis (par. 7) if Mencken failed to make this point? How does his allusion to "peasants, however poor" (par. 6) and the money of "100% Americans" (par. 8) relate to this point? Why does he exclude "mere filth" (par. 2)?

4. Having developed a thesis—the libido for the ugly—as a result of his examination of Westmoreland, why does Mencken mention wallpaper, "The Palms," motion pictures, jazz, dogmatic theology, and the poetry of Edgar A. Guest (par. 7)?

DICTION AND TONE

1. Mencken's tone is scathing: he speaks of "appalling desolation" (par. 1), of "sheer revolting monstrousness," of a "bare, leprous hill" (par. 2). It is important to understand, however, that the satirical power of his attack is not simply a result of his choice of words, of his diction. His tone is also achieved through structure and image.

Examine par. 4, for instance. It begins by stating that the new brick is the color of a fried egg. What happens to this image in the next sentence? Why does Mencken discuss red brick in the next section of the paragraph? Notice that he returns to yellow in the climax of the paragraph, that "the most loathsome towns and villages ever seen by mortal eye" is tied to "uremic yellow." Is *uremic* an appropriate word at this point in the paragraph?

This careful arrangement of materials is also apparent in par. 3. After describing a possible design, Mencken begins his description of a typical Westmoreland house with a unifying image. What is it? Examine the rest of this paragraph in terms of its structure, its images, its diction. What tone is achieved? How?

Or consider the examples with which Mencken ends his essay (par. 8). Both are planted in par. 2. There is a description of the headquarters of the Veterans of Foreign Wars in par. 2. Why refer to it before par. 8? How is the steel stadium described in par. 2? Would this description be more effective if it were omitted until par. 8? Why is it appropriate to refer to the Parthenon in par. 8? What tone is achieved by comparing the penthouse to "a fat woman with a black eye" (par. 8)? To a "Presbyterian grinning" (par. 8)?

2. Why does Mencken use the uncommon word *libido* in his title?

3. Why does he use the phrase "less Christian levels" (par. 7)?

4. "Macabre and depressing joke" and "race of alley cats" (par. 1) are striking phrases, perhaps too striking. What expectations are set by them? Are the examples of ugliness that follow in the essay anticlimactic? What tone is achieved, for instance, by writing that some buildings were so bad that "one blinked before them as one blinks before a man with his face shot away" (par. 2)?

5. Compare the controlled metaphoric language of Mencken's essay with the literal language in par. 32 of Twain's essay.

APPLICATIONS TO WRITING

1. Mencken compares red and yellow bricks in a simple yet powerful paragraph (par. 5). Write such a paragraph comparing two automobile colors, two paintings, or two TV programs.

2. In par. 3 Mencken compares the typical house of Westmoreland to "a brick set on end." Write a paragraph using such a concrete image to unify a diverse group of particulars.

3. Drive through an unpleasant section of today's suburban sprawl. Write a "Libido for the Ugly" on what you see. Or write a satirical attack on ugliness, describing what you see on a walk downtown. Look at your particular abominations: advertising billboards, public buildings, or new styles in women's (or men's) clothing in store windows. Observe carefully, but pay particular attention to your diction, images, and organization.

4. This essay seems to formulate a scientific hypothesis; actually it satirizes the ugliness of American buildings. Write a satirical identification of a scientific or scholarly problem.

5. Call attention to—that is, identify—a situation by inventing a preposterous hypothesis. For example, that people who commute to work belong to a secret religious cult that has a ritual, epiphany, penance, exorcism, and so on. Or that the experience of registering for college classes is precisely the same as the experience of getting a college education.

The Present

from *Pilgrim at Tinker Creek*

ANNIE DILLARD

Catch it if you can. [1]

It is early March. I am dazed from a long day of interstate driving homeward; I pull in at a gas station in Nowhere, Virginia, north of Lexington. The young boy in charge ("Chick 'at oll?") is offering a free cup of coffee with every gas purchase. We talk in the glass-walled office while my coffee cools enough to drink. He tells me, among other things, that the rival gas station down the road, whose FREE COFFEE sign is visible from the interstate, charges you fifteen cents if you want your coffee in a Styrofoam cup, as opposed, I guess, to your bare hands. [2]

All the time we talk, the boy's new beagle puppy is skidding around the office, sniffing impartially at my shoes and at the wire rack of folded maps. The cheerful human conversation wakes me, recalls me, not to a normal consciousness, but to a kind of energetic readiness. I step outside, followed by the puppy. [3]

I am absolutely alone. There are no other customers. The road is vacant, the interstate is out of sight and earshot. I have hazarded into a new corner of the world, an unknown spot, a Brigadoon. Before me extends a low hill trembling in yellow brome, and behind the hill, filling the sky, rises an enormous mountain ridge, forested, alive and awesome with brilliant blown lights. I have never seen anything so tremulous and live. Overhead, great strips and chunks of cloud dash to the northwest in a gold rush. At my back the sun is setting—how can I not have noticed before that the sun is setting? My mind has been a blank slab of black asphalt for hours, but that doesn't stop the sun's wild wheel. I set my coffee beside me on the curb; I smell loam on the wind; I pat the puppy; I watch the mountain. [4]

My hand works automatically over the puppy's fur, following the line of hair under his ears, down his neck, inside his forelegs, along his hot-skinned belly. [5]

Shadows lope along the mountain's rumpled flanks; they elongate like root tips, like lobes of spilling water, faster and faster. A warm purple pigment pools in each ruck and tuck of the rock; it deepens and spreads, boring crevasses, canyons. As the purple vaults and slides, it tricks out the unleafed forest and rumpled rock in gilt, in shape-shifting patches of glow. These gold lights veer and retract, shatter and glide in a series of dazzling splashes, shrinking, leaking, exploding. The ridge's bosses and hummocks sprout bulging from its side; the whole mountain looms miles closer; the light warms and reddens; the bare forest folds and pleats itself like living protoplasm before my eyes, like a running chart, a wildly scrawling oscillograph on the present moment. The air cools; the puppy's skin is hot. I am more alive than all the world. [6]

This is it, I think, this is it, right now, the present, this empty gas station, here, this western wind, this tang of coffee on the tongue, and I am patting the puppy, I am watching the mountain. And the second I verbalize this awareness in my brain, I cease to see the mountain or feel the puppy. I am opaque, so much black asphalt. But at the same second, the second I know I've lost it, I also realize that the puppy is still squirming on his back under my hand. Nothing has changed for him. He draws his legs down to stretch the skin taut so he feels every fingertip's stroke along his furred and arching side, his flank, his flung-back throat. [7]

I sip my coffee. I look at the mountain, which is still doing its tricks, as you look at a still-beautiful face belonging to a person who was once your lover in another country years ago: with fond nostalgia, and recognition, but no real feeling save a secret astonishment that you are now strangers. Thanks. For the memories. It is ironic that the one thing that all religions recognize as separating us from our creator—our very self-consciousness—is also the one thing that divides us from our fellow creatures. It was a bitter birthday present from evolution, cutting us off at both ends. I get in the car and drive home. [8]

Catch it if you can. The present is an invisible electron; its lightning path traced faintly on a blackened screen is fleet, and fleeing, and gone. [9]

PURPOSE AND STRUCTURE

1. Annie Dillard gives the thesis in the first sentence (par. 1): "Catch it if you can." But she doesn't explain what *it* is until the first sentence of par. 7. What is Dillard's purpose in forcing the reader to wait so long?

2. Dillard ends her essay (par. 9) by fully stating her thesis. Argue for or against using this paragraph as the first paragraph of the essay.

3. Why does explaining (beginning of par. 7) the meaning of "I am more alive than all the world" (end of par. 6) result in Dillard's losing the immediate experience?

4. What separates Dillard from both the beagle puppy (par. 7) and "our creator" (par. 8)? Why is this separation "a bitter birthday present from evolution" (par. 8)?

5. Pars. 2–3 are introductory, pars. 4–6 present the central experience. Why is one sentence so important that it is a separate paragraph (par. 5)? Compare its subject with the preceding and following paragraphs (pars. 4 and 6). Why the contrast in the next to the last sentence (par. 6): "The air cools; the puppy's skin is hot."? The sentence preceding this sentence ends in a climax of emotion (par. 6): "the bare forest folds and pleats itself like living protoplasm before my eyes, like a running chart, a wildly scrawling oscillograph on the present moment." Why end with "the present moment"? Why is the bare forest like living protoplasm?

6. Why is the former lover now a stranger (par. 8)?

7. Dillard seeks to identify the fleeting moment, the present—catch it if you can. Does she succeed? How does she succeed—or fail?

DICTION AND TONE

1. Why does Dillard (par. 7) turn into "so much black asphalt"? Contrast the tone of this image with the tone of pars. 4–6.

2. Why refer to the mountain as "still doing its tricks" (par. 8)?

3. Dillard's tone moves from the light irony of (par. 2), "as opposed, I guess, to your bare hands," to the vividness of (par. 4), "great strips and chunks of cloud dash to the northwest," or "the sun's wild wheel." Why?

4. Why do (par. 6, first sentence) shadows *lope*? Underline the verbs in the rest of the paragraph: notice the vividness of active verbs. Dillard shows perception as action.

APPLICATIONS TO WRITING

1. Catch it if you can: describe a moment of awareness.

2. Dillard captures the present (1) after a long day of interstate driving homeward, (2) after a cheerful human conversation awakens her to a kind of energetic readiness, (3) after stepping outside to find herself absolutely alone. Describe, as she does, how preliminary experiences led to your moment of awareness.

3. Identify, capture a moment when you were "more alive than all the world" (par. 6). Follow Dillard's simple organization: (1) preparation, (2) the moment, (3) loss of awareness.

PART **two**

Definition

Definition—in logic, the placing of the word to be defined in a general class and then demonstrating how it differs from other members of the class; in rhetoric, the meaningful extension (usually enriched by the use of detail, concrete illustrations, anecdote, metaphor) of a logical definition in order to answer fully—though often implicitly—the question, "What is . . . ?" Tom Wolfe defines the perfect crime by identifying the motives and goals of the criminals. E. B. White's evocative definition of democracy is developed by metaphor and analogy. Sontag defines the liberated woman in terms of her activities and responsibilities. Fairlie defines lust by comparing and contrasting it with love. Forster limits his subjects by deliberately excluding peripheral questions and particularizing his general question by personal example. In Greer's extended definition of the female stereotype she excoriates its perpetrators by employing satire, hyperbole, and personification.

The Perfect Crime

from *Mauve Gloves & Madmen, Clutter & Vine*

TOM WOLFE

(This piece was first published in December 1973, two months before the kidnapping of Patty Hearst.)

Remember the old idea of the Perfect Crime? The wife kills her husband by hitting him over the head with a frozen leg of lamb. Then she puts the leg of lamb in the stove and sets the temperature at 450 degrees. When the detective comes by to investigate the murder, she takes the murder weapon out of the oven and garnishes it with parsley and mint sauce and puts it on a Spode platter and serves it to the detective. The detective himself devours and digests the evidence! And eliminates it! The wife—the widow—has only to tote up in her mind the fortune that will be coming her way as soon as her husband's will is probated. How cool! How clever! She scores big! leaves not a trace! is never caught!—the Perfect Crime.[1] [1]

The criminal mind has come a long way since then. Not up, not down; just a long way. Consider the Perfect Crime of the 1970's: [2]

On July 17, 1972, a twenty-two-year-old hair stylist shampooed his own hair and hot-combed it down over his forehead and ears into a John Denver bob, put on a groovy shirt striped with an intricate leaf-repeat pattern and a pair of bell-bottoms with fine chalk-and-pin stripes picking up the tones of the shirt, and walked into a suburban bank near Richmond, Virginia, with a 12-gauge shotgun. He fired two blasts into a wooden door to show he meant business. He took nine women and one man as hostages and herded them into a back room. He spent about five minutes terrifying them and about four hours trying to charm them with jokes and the story of his life. He offered them steak dinners. [3]

---

[1] Tom Wolfe summarizes the plot of a short story, "Lamb to the Slaughter," by Roald Dahl.

"The bank's paying for it!" he said, casting himself in the role of Tyrone Power as Jesse James. [4]

He was disappointed when they asked for pizzas and beer instead, but he got these Low Rent items for them anyway by shouting orders to the bank officials and policemen waiting outside. He also ordered $500,000 in cash and a 1972 white Lincoln Continental to drive away in. He ordered full television and radio coverage of all events, especially the loading of the money into the trunk of the Lincoln. Said conditions having been met, he put down the shotgun, said goodbye to the hostages, and emerged from the bank smiling and waving to the TV cameras and talking a mile a minute into the microphones, right up until the moment when federal officers grabbed him. He put up no struggle at all. They ushered him into the back seat of the white Lincoln Continental, the very one with the half million in the trunk, and drove him off to jail. He was still smiling and waving as the car pulled off. [5]

What on earth, one may ask, could be "perfect" about any such zany, feckless, giddy, goofy attempt at extortion? Nevertheless, it was a casebook example of the Perfect Crime of the 1970's, which is: taking hostages. [6]

Taking hostages is the common core of many different crimes peculiar to the late 1960's and the 1970's: the more than two hundred airplane hijackings since November 1967; most of the prison riots of the same period, such as the Attica uprising; much of the political terrorism, such as the kidnappings at the 1972 Olympics and in Uruguay; and many attempted bank robberies, such as the incident in Stockholm in which two convicts named Olsson and Olofsson kept four hostages in a bank vault for six days. [7]

Most of the Hostage Takers have been people at the ends of their ropes in struggles against what they regard as the enormity of "the system." Moreover, they seem to think that if they can beat the system, they can also deal with more traditional frustrations, i.e., those involving class, love, and money. One of the most sensational of the airplane hijackings was pulled off by an Italian-born U. S. Marine named Raffaele Minichiello. He took his hostages from Los Angeles to Rome in a wild trip that involved many stops and several changes of crew. Minichiello had grown up in the United States but had never learned English properly and felt like a hopelessly awkward Italian country boy (class); felt too gauche to ask American girls out on dates (love); was decorated for bravery while fighting in Vietnam, only to discover

The Perfect Crime 69

that (by his count) he had been euchred out of $200 in the G.I. savings plan (money); drank six beers and broke into a PX, stole an even $200 worth of merchandise; passed out nearby; was cleared by a local civil judge who simply threw the case out; felt elated; rushed to his commanding officer to bring him the good news; was astounded to hear the C.O. start dictating to his secretary orders for a court-martial, felony level, which would ruin his service career ((((((((((((((the unbeatable freaking system!))))))))))))))))). [8]

So what does the modern Master Criminal do? He *takes hostages.* Ostensibly he takes hostages in order to achieve some goal at the end of the line, but in many cases even the internal logic is bananas. Minichiello said his plan was to hijack a plane to Italy, then hide in the countryside and live off the land like a guerrilla. Palestinian and Uruguayan terrorists take hostages ostensibly to call attention to their causes and gain sympathy. The effect, quite predictably, is the opposite, so far as sympathy is concerned, even among true believers. But so what? The master criminal does not really take hostages in order to accomplish such goals. He dreams up such goals in order to Take Hostages. The formula is turned around: the means justify the end. [9]

With one stroke the Hostage Taker creates his own society, his own system: in the bank vault, in the Olympic quarters, in the airplane, in the prison courtyard. On his own small scale the Hostage Taker accomplishes the classic coup d'état as described by Machiavelli:[2] the sudden, short-term use of terror, cold steel, and bloodletting, is necessary, in order to gain respect—then the long charm course . . . to turn respect into love, thereby making it easy to govern. On the face of it, it is astonishing how often hostages come away from their ordeal describing the Hostage Taker as "nice," "considerate," even "likeable," as in the case of both Minichiello and the groovy hair stylist. A female hostage named Kristin Enmark left the Stockholm bank vault on a stretcher waving to one of the Hostage Takers, Clark Olofsson, telling him, "We'll see each other again!" and informing one and all that he had been kind, hadn't harmed her in the slightest, hadn't been as big a threat as the police, in fact. A psychiatrist immediately explained that she was suffering from shell shock, like a line soldier who has been at the front too long, and was repressing her actual feelings as a "de-

[2] Niccolo Machiavelli (1469–1527), Italian political theorist, defended the view that any means may be justifiably employed by a ruler in order to maintain a strong central government.

fense mechanism." Is the same to be said of the twenty-nine American passengers and airline crewmen who were held hostage by Palestinian terrorists in Jordan for almost a month and who, *after being freed*, sent a telegram to Israel's Prime Minister Golda Meir saying: "We wish to affirm that our guards treated us humanely and always did their utmost to protect us against harm and to meet our basic needs"—and urging her to give fresh consideration to the Arab cause in Palestine? Thirteen of the twenty-nine signers were Jews. [10]

Far from being a "defense mechanism," such examples are a grand-scale display of a phenomenon well known to police detectives. One of the techniques of the "third degree" involves the Goon & the Nice Guy. The suspect is put into an interrogation room with two detectives, one of whom plays the role of the violent goon while the other plays the nice guy who seeks to protect him. In a remarkably short time, a few hours, in fact, the victim may form an emotional attachment to the Nice Guy, his "protector," and pour out his soul. In precisely the same manner, the Hostage Taker may soon have the hearts and minds of his subjects as well as their hides. The hostage responds like a dog. He has an urge not only to obey but to be obliging and ingratiating in the bargain. What a delightful and emboldening new world!—especially if one has been for so long as helpless as a Palestinian radical up against the complexities of Cold War politics or a Uruguayan radical up against the endless exfoliations of American power in South America. No possible "ransom" or "prisoner release" could compare with the ecstasy of this moment—when for a change I have these people whimpering like dogs at my feet! [11]

All at once I am not the lowliest subject but the head of state. I demand to negotiate with chiefs of police, mayors, governors, and I get my wish. I even have support on the outside. Nelson Rockefeller was heavily criticized for not coming to Attica and negotiating directly with the Hostage Taker inmates. Many hijackers have demanded to talk to the President of the United States. One hijacked a plane to Dulles International Airport and demanded "a million dollars from Lyndon Johnson." At the very least I finally cut through the red tape. I put an end to the eternal runaround. I make the System spin to my number. At last the top people are listening to *me* . . . and answering . . . quite politely, too, and with quite a little choke in their miserable voices . . . [12]

Above all: as long as I have my hostages, as long as the drama has not been played out, I have the ultimate certification that my new status is real and true—that in the most modern sense my class position is secure: *I am a celebrity!* My existence fills the very atmosphere of the city, the state, the nation. As long as Olsson and Olofsson had their hostages in the Stockholm bank vault, Sweden's national election campaign (one of the more crucial since World War II) came to a halt. Who had time for politics, what with O. & O.'s World on TV around the clock? Nor does my celebrity status end with the event itself. Not necessarily! Minichiello became a hero in Italy and served only a year and a half in jail. He appeared continually on television and in magazines. He was signed up for a book and the leading role in an Italian Western. More impressive, he rated the best tables at all the smart restaurants near the Via del Babuino. His troubles with the chicks were over. Marriage proposals were passed in under his door. Movie actresses thrilled to his courage and good looks in the daily pictorials. *Children want my autograph! Everybody loves me!* [13]

At Attica we Hostage Takers custom-ordered our news coverage. For example, we asked for, and got, Tom Wicker of *The New York Times* and he was obliging. He wrote about us as if we were all Prometheuses[3] in noble deathlock with the forces of repression in a battle for the soul of man. As journalism it was pretty embarrassing stuff—but not half bad as a back rub for the boys in Cellblock D! [14]

The groovy at the suburban bank also custom-ordered his news coverage, asking for certain local broadcasters by name. He was in a jolly mood from the moment he first heard live coverage of his escapade over a transistor radio. When the television crews arrived, he made the hostages stick their heads out the window to be filmed, then acted as if he had done them another service, of the magnitude of the beer & pizzas. When the police brought up the white Lincoln Continental, as he demanded, he broke into a grin and announced to his subjects: "You see what you can get with a gun!" The more intense the radio and television coverage became, the better the Hostage Taker's mood became. The police chief characterized it as the turning point—the pressure that finally flushed him out smiling and unarmed, beaming, waving to pals & gals everywhere, to fans, subjects, devotees from

---

[3] Prometheus, in Greek mythology, was regarded as the founder of civilization and, in later traditions, as the creator of the human race. He stole fire from heaven and bestowed it upon man.

border to border and coast to coast . . . and now, the star of our show
. . . a sunny day, a perfect crime. [15]

PURPOSE AND STRUCTURE

1. In his humorous opening paragraph, Wolfe describes the "old idea" of the Perfect Crime—murder committed for profit. At the end of the paragraph, he lists some additional characteristics. What are they?

2. What does Wolfe consider to be the Perfect Crime of the 1970's (par. 6)?

3. Argue for or against joining pars. 6 and 7.

4. Par. 8 is a nearly perfect example of a traditionally developed paragraph, one in which the opening generalizations are followed by specific details that illustrate the generalizations. Explain this statement by reference to specific parts of the paragraph. Do not overlook the relationship between the first and last sentences.

5. In par. 9, Minichiello and Palestinian and Uruguayan terrorists are cited as examples. What are they examples of?

6. In the first sentence of par. 10, there are a number of allusions. To what do the following refer: "in the bank vault, in the Olympic quarters, in the airplane, in the prison courtyard"? Explain how the words, "creates his own society, his own system," contribute to the unity of the essay.

7. Argue for or against the deletion of par. 11.

8. At the end of par. 11 and throughout pars. 12, 13, and 14, Wolfe shifts from the third person (the Hostage Taker) to the first person (I). Argue that this shift in person is stylistically good or bad, that it can be justified or criticized on psychological grounds.

9. Compare the last words of the first paragraph with the last words of the last paragraph. Now make two short lists, one identifying the main characteristics of the Perfect Crime of the past, the other identifying characteristics of the Perfect Crime of the 1970's.

10. Argue that the word *and* in the next-to-last sentence of par. 3 should be changed to *but*. Explain how this sentence is related to par. 10.

11. Explain how the unity of par. 5 is achieved by controlling the subjects of the sentences.

12. Explain the development of par. 8 in terms of levels of generality.

DICTION AND TONE

1. What difference would it have made if in par. 3 Wolfe had called the criminal a barber instead of a hair stylist?

2. What is Wolfe saying about the criminal by his use of the word *casting* in par. 4?

3. At the beginning of par. 8 Wolfe writes about "the enormity of the system." Is this a correct use of the word *enormity*?

4. What, if anything, does Wolfe gain by using the many parentheses at the end of par. 8? Does he lose anything?

5. What is the effect of Wolfe's use of capital letters for such terms as *Perfect Crime* (par. 1); *Low Rent* (par. 5); *Hostage Takers* (par. 8); *Master Criminal* (par. 9)?

APPLICATIONS TO WRITING

In "The Perfect Crime" Wolfe shows that whereas the perfect crime of yesteryear was committed for profit, the perfect crime of the 1970's was committed for psychological reasons.

Write an essay in which you show that the Perfect Style for doing something has changed over the years because the motive has changed. For example, you may show that a proper style of dress for young people was once designed to win the approval of adults; now the Perfect Style must win the approval of one's peers.

Democracy

E. B. WHITE

July 3, 1943

We received a letter from the Writers' War Board the other day asking for a statement on "The Meaning of Democracy." It presumably is our duty to comply with such a request, and it is certainly our pleasure. [1]

Surely the Board knows what democracy is. It is the line that forms on the right. It is the don't in don't shove. It is the hole in the stuffed shirt through which the sawdust slowly trickles; it is the dent in the high hat. Democracy is the recurrent suspicion that more than half of the people are right more than half of the time. It is the feeling of privacy in the voting booths, the feeling of communion in the libraries, the feeling of vitality everywhere. Democracy is a letter to the editor. Democracy is the score at the beginning of the ninth. It is an idea that hasn't been disproved yet, a song the words of which have not gone bad. It's the mustard on the hot dog and the cream in the rationed coffee. Democracy is a request from a War Board, in the middle of a morning in the middle of a war, wanting to know what democracy is. [2]

PURPOSE AND STRUCTURE

1. How does White use metaphor and analogy to develop his definition of democracy? What does each example have in common? How do the illustrations differ?

2. White begins every sentence or clause in par. 2 with "It is" or "Democracy is." How does the repetition affect purpose and tone? Why isn't the sameness of the structure boring?

DICTION AND TONE

1. Explain how each metaphor contributes to the tone.

2. To what audience would "the hole in the stuffed shirt" and "the dent in the high hat" especially appeal?

3. Although the commentary may be seen as whimsical and as reflecting a light touch, it may also be regarded as very serious. Explain.

4. What images are evoked by the metaphors? To what varied senses does the writer appeal?

APPLICATIONS TO WRITING

1. Assume the request for defining democracy (or freedom, or justice, or compassion) came to you. By the use of metaphor and analogy develop your definition.

2. Compare and contrast a definition of democracy from a text on political theory with White's discussion. Discuss what is gained or lost in a standard definition. Note especially the differences in sentence structure, diction and tone, and use of illustrations.

The Liberated Woman
from *The Third World of Women*

SUSAN SONTAG

I would never describe myself as a liberated woman. Of course, things are never as simple as *that*. But I have always been a feminist. [1]

When I was five years old, I day-dreamed about becoming a bio-chemist and winning the Nobel Prize. (I had just read a biography of Madame Curie.) I stuck with chemistry until the age of ten, when I decided I would become a doctor. At fifteen, I knew I was going to be a writer. That is to say: from the beginning it never even occurred to me that I might be prevented from doing things in "the world" because I was born female. Perhaps because I spent most of my sickly childhood reading and in my chemistry laboratory in the empty garage, growing up in a very provincial part of the United States with a family life so minimal that it could be described as subnuclear, I was curiously innocent of the very existence of a barrier. When, at fifteen, I left home to go to a university, and then took up various careers, the relations that I had with men in my professional life seemed to me, with some exceptions, cordial and untroubled. So I went on not knowing there was a problem. I didn't even know I was a feminist, so unfashionable was that point of view at the time, when I married at the age of seventeen and kept my own name; it seemed to me an equally "personal" act of principle on my part, when I divorced my husband seven years later, to have indignantly rejected my lawyer's automatic bid for alimony, even though I was broke, homeless, and jobless at that moment and I had a six-year-old child to support. [2]

Now and then, people I met would allude to the supposed difficulties of being both independent and a woman; I was always surprised—and sometimes annoyed, because, I thought, they were being obtuse. The problem didn't exist for me—except in the envy and resentment I occasionally felt from other women, the educated, jobless, home stranded wives of the men with whom I worked. I was conscious of being an exception, but it hadn't ever seemed hard to be an exception; and I accepted the advantages I enjoyed as my right. I know better now. [3]

My case is not uncommon. Not so paradoxically, the position of a "liberated" woman in a liberal society where the vast majority of women are *not* liberated can be embarrassingly easy. Granted a good dose of talent and a certain cheerful or merely dogged lack of self-consciousness, one can even escape (as I did) the initial obstacles and derision that are likely to afflict a woman who insists on autonomy. It will not seem so hard for such a woman to lead an independent life; she may even reap some professional advantages from being a woman, such as greater visibility. Her good fortune is like the good fortune of a few blacks in a liberal but still racist society. Every liberal grouping (whether political, professional or artistic) needs its token woman. [4]

What I have learned in the last five years—helped by the women's movement—is to situate my own experience in a certain *political* perspective. My good fortune is really beside the point. What does it prove? Nothing. [5]

Any already "liberated" woman who complacently accepts her privileged situation participates in the oppression of other women. I accuse the overwhelming majority of women with careers in the arts and sciences, in the liberal professions, and in politics of doing just that. [6]

I have often been struck by how misogynistic most successful women are. They are eager to say how silly, boring, superficial, or tiresome they find other women, and how much they prefer the company of men. Like most men, who basically despise and patronize women, most "liberated" women don't like or respect other women. If they don't fear them as sexual rivals, they fear them as professional rivals—wishing to guard their special status as women admitted into largely all-male professional worlds. Most women who pass as being "liberated" are shameless Uncle Toms, eager to flatter their men colleagues, becoming their accomplices in putting down other, less accomplished women, dishonestly minimizing the difficulties they themselves have run into because of being women. The implication of their behavior is that all women can do what they have done, if only they would exert themselves; that the barriers put up by men are flimsy; that it is mainly women themselves who hold themselves back. This simply is not true. [7]

The first responsibility of a "liberated" woman is to lead the fullest, freest, and most imaginative life she can. The second responsibility is her solidarity with other women. She may live and work and make love with men. But she has no right to represent her situation as simpler, or less suspect, or less full of compromises than it really is. Her good relations with men must not be bought at the price of betraying her sisters. [8]

PURPOSE AND STRUCTURE

1. How does Sontag distinguish between "feminist," which she says she has always been, and "liberated woman," which is not how she would describe herself?

2. By what means does she explain her ignorance of the fact she was a feminist?

3. How do the autobiographical details contribute to the definition of a liberated woman?

4. What transition is made between the autobiographical details and the definition of a liberated woman?

5. How does Sontag define women who "pass" as being liberated?

6. Sontag speaks of "a woman who insists on autonomy" (par. 4). What evidences are there that she is such a woman?

7. With what details does she place her own experience in a "political" perspective?

8. How does the last paragraph reflect both a personal and political perspective?

9. How does she account for the changes in her view of women's independence?

10. Sontag defines the liberated woman in terms of her activities and function. What other approaches to definition does she use?

DICTION AND TONE

1. How does Sontag avoid stereotyping (par. 4)?

2. Justify the use of the word *obtuse* in the context in which it is used (par. 3); do the same for *home stranded* (par. 3); *dogged* (par. 4); *misogynistic* (par. 7); *shameless Uncle Toms* (par. 7).

3. Distinguish among the author's use of *"liberated," liberal,* and *liberated* (without quotation marks) in the second sentence of par. 4. Account for the opening phrase of the sentence, "Not so paradoxically."

4. What is a "token woman" (par. 4)?

5. What changes in tone do you note in these few paragraphs?

APPLICATIONS TO WRITING

1. How would you define a liberated woman? Draw on your personal experience, or that of your friends, a public person, or a character in fiction.

2. Trace the evolution of your views of the feminist or the liberated woman and account for any changes in them.

3. Define the liberated man by referring to his attitude toward self, toward women, and toward society.

4. Using Sontag's statement for a thesis, illustrate the three points she makes: "The first responsibility of a 'liberated' woman is to lead the fullest, freest, and most imaginative life she can" (par. 8).

Lust or Luxuria

HENRY FAIRLIE

Lust is not interested in its partners, but only in the gratification of its own craving: not even in the satisfaction of our whole natures, but in the appeasement merely of an appetite which we are unable to subdue. It is therefore a form of self-subjection; in fact of self-emptying. The sign it wears is: "This property is vacant." Anyone may take possession of it for a while. Lustful people may think that they can choose a partner at will for sexual gratification. But they do not really choose; they accept what is available. Lust accepts any partner for a momentary service; anyone may squat in its groin. [1]

Love has meaning only insofar as it includes the idea of its continuance. Even what we rather glibly call a love affair, if it comes to an end, may continue as a memory that is pleasing in our lives, and we can still renew the sense of privilege and reward of having been allowed to know someone with such intimacy and sharing. But Lust dies at the next dawn and, when it returns in the evening, to search where it may, it is with its own past erased. Love wants to enjoy in other ways the human being whom it has enjoyed in bed. But in the morning Lust is always furtive. It dresses as mechanically as it undressed, and heads straight for the door, to return to its own solitude. Like all the sins, it makes us solitary. It is a self-abdication at the very heart of one's own being, of our need and ability to give and receive. [2]

Love is involvement as well as continuance; but Lust will not get involved. This is one of the forms in which we may see it today. If people now engage in indiscriminate and short-lived relationships more than in the past, it is not really for some exquisite sexual pleasure that is thus gained, but because they refuse to become involved and to meet the demands that love makes. They are asking for little more than servicing, such as they might get at a gas station. The fact that it may go to bed with a lot of people is less its offense than the fact that it goes to bed with people for whom it does not care. The characteristic of the "singles" today is not the sexual freedom they supposedly enjoy, but the fact that this freedom is a deception. They are free with only a fraction of their natures. The full array of human emotions is hardly involved. The "singles bar" does not have an obnoxious odor because its clients, before the night is over, may hop into bed with someone whom they have just met, but because they do not even consider that, beyond the morning, either of them may care for the other. As they have made deserts of themselves, so they make deserts of their beds. This is the sin of Lust. Just as it dries up human beings, so it dries up human relationships. The word that comes to mind, when one thinks of it, is that it is parched. Everyone in a "singles bar" seems to have lost moisture, and this is peculiarly the accomplishment of Lust, to make the flesh seem parched, to deprive it of all real dewiness, shrivelling it to no more than a husk. [3]

Lust is not a sin *of* the flesh so much as a sin *against* it. We are present in our flesh to the rest of creation, and particularly we are present in it to each other, revealing and exposing, sensitive to others and even vulnerable to them. When one hears people talk today of the sexual act as if it were rather like emptying one's bladder, one wishes to remind them that people still get hurt. They get hurt in their bodies, not merely from slappings and beatings and whippings, but from more subtle humiliations of which our sexual feelings are registers. Lust is a humiliation of the flesh, of another's and of one's own; and it is a perversity of our time that, in the name of a freedom which is delusive, we not only tolerate this humiliation, but exalt it as a wonder of the modern age. [4]

We have reduced love to sex, sex to the act, and the act to a merely quantitative measurement of it. Sexual love can have infinite expressions, not all of which need to be consummated in the act, and it is this variety of expression that Lust will always diminish. It is not only solitary but uninventive in the slaking of its thirst. Whatever may be said for the sexual investigations that we today pursue and read so avidly, it cannot be denied that they are a little single-minded in their approach to the questions they raise. "People now seem to have sex on their minds," Malcolm Muggeridge once said, "which is a peculiar place to have it." Our obsession with sex is in fact a misplacing and a trivialization of it: a preoccupation with it which has no assocation with the rest of our lives. [5]

More than we care to admit, we all have become voyeurs. "We live in an age in which voyeurism is no longer the side line of the solitary deviate," writes William F. May, "but rather a national pastime, fully institutionalized and naturalized in the mass media." The puritan makes the mistake of thinking that to have sex continually on view is an incitement to it. But it in fact weakens the feelings and passions that sex can and should arouse. Pornographic literature and films do not incite us to strenuous emulation. On the contrary, they are substitutes, evidence not of the strength of our sexual feelings, but of their weakness. We can and usually do indulge in them by ourselves; no one else has to be there; and we have to do nothing with even our own sexuality, except possibly to manipulate ourselves. They are again substitutes for involvement with another person. If they make us Lust at all, it is not for sexual experience with someone else, but merely for the empty cravings and gratifications of Lust itself. We reduce ourselves to the final absurdity: that we will lust after Lust. [6]

What is left to Lust when its cravings at last subside, as subside in the end they will? It is alone. It has died. It has made no bonds, and is in the desert which it has made, with no longer even a craving. It is in its own black hole, where no vice can reach it, and from which its own voice cannot get out. It has collapsed into nothingness. It has burned itself out. Our excessive fear of old age is the fear that must be expected in a society in which Lust has been made a dominating motive. We would not fear it so much, if we did not fear that it will be empty; and we would not fear so much that it will be empty, if we had not emptied our lives already in the pursuit of mere cravings. [7]

To be interested only in pursuit and not in the attainment, to give so much of one's energy only to the seduction, is a prescription for making a desert of one's world and oneself. "Promiscuous love necessitates hypocrisy," Christopher Sykes[1] has said. "To play the part of Don Juan[2] you have to be word-perfect in that of Tartuffe[3] as well." Such hypocrisy is again a form of self-emptying. We become only the words and roles in which we are so practiced, and at last we cannot find who we are behind them. The play of seduction, if it is to be rewarding to the seducer as well as the seduced, requires that their whole personalities be engaged. If love is a journey into another land, then seduction ought to be part of a mutual exploration, to see if the land may be entered and enjoyed together. Lust is incapable of this play, it is not interested in exploring, it does not want to enter any land. But perhaps above all, it has no personality of its own to bring to the encounter, with which to bring into play the personality of the other. [8]

If love is continuance and involvement, perhaps no less it is attention, a constancy of gaze on the object of one's love, so that one may grow to know how to love it as the Other, in all the richness and variety of its aspects. Lust is incapable of this constancy; it has no attention to give. The time span of its interest is determined by the clockwork to which it has reduced its desires. The trouble with sexual infidelity is that it distracts the constancy of our attention to someone else. We remove a part of our gaze, and turn it elsewhere. In fact we remove a part of ourselves, and give it elsewhere. What comes between a couple when one of them is unfaithful is not the other woman, or the other man, *but what now cannot be shared by them.* If a mere sexual act were all that is involved, unfaithfulness would not be such an ever-

[1] Christopher Sykes is a twentieth-century English author, novelist, and literary editor known for his interest in Orientalia.

[2] Don Juan was a fourteenth-century Spanish aristocrat whose name became synonymous with rake or libertine, and who served as the subject of works by Mozart, Molière, Dumas, Byron, and George Bernard Shaw.

[3] Tartuffe is the chief character and title of a Molière comedy (1664); he is a religious hypocrite and imposter who uses religion for self-indulgence.

lasting problem. Even if it is possible to "have sex" (the phrase is revealing) with someone else without loving that person, the fact that no love may have been bestowed elsewhere does not mean that none has been withdrawn. [9]

It is rare for unfaithfulness to do its damage in a single affair. Its danger is that it erodes. Piecemeal it chips away at a relationship, not only at the constancy of our love, but at last at our capacity to love. It empties us of our capacity for loyalty, until we become incapable of forming an enduring relationship with any one individual, whom we have singled out. Our relationships are frayed from the start, like cut-off jeans, because we are no longer capable of discovering the unconditional worth of another human being, or ultimately of oneself. Love requires some effort, but our age encourages us to escape from it. At the first itch of dissatisfaction, the first rankle of difficulty, we can sever the knot, with as little ado as possible, and go to the other side of the fence, where we know that it will be greener. [10]

Perhaps there are few things after which we lust more today than the experiences which we have not so far enjoyed or endured. Since Lust will not take the time or the trouble to explore or develop any relationship to the full, none can satisfy it, and it will whip itself (perhaps an appropriate term in the context) to try anything that will revive its jaded feelings. It is tired of fellatio. Then it will try its hand (hardly the appropriate word in the context) at a little sodomy. Weary of only one partner, it will advance to group sex. Unsure at last of its own sexuality, it will have recourse to bi-sexuality. Bored with the flesh, it will call for chains and leather jackets. Who knows, when, abandoning the last shred of its humanity, it will turn to bestiality? All of this is again often interpreted as a proof that our age is more actively sexual than any before, whereas it is evidence rather than the lustfulness of our age has reduced our sexuality to impotence. [11]

Even the more restrained workouts that are outlined in *The Joy of Sex* amount to instruction for those who live in a time in which the theme and fear of sexual impotence dominate our lives and much of our literature. Our sexuality has been animalized, stripped of the intricacy of feeling with which human beings have endowed it, leaving us to contemplate only the act, and our fear of our impotence in it. It is this animalization from which the sexual manuals cannot escape because they are reflections of it. They might be textbooks for veterinarians, and it is to precisely this kind of dejection that Lust has reduced our sexuality. What ought to be a mutual enchantment, something not on our minds but in our whole beings, is drained of its spontaneous gladness, and the rewards of a long and intricate relationship. [12]

The fascination today with sadism, masochism and fetishism suggests that, just as they reflect a hideous emptiness in the individuals who practice them, they reflect a no less terrible emptiness in our societies. We have said that Lust is a form of self emptying, but there has been emptiness there already. In no other sin does one feel so much of a void, and this void is not only inside, it is also outside in the society. There is a profound failure of our societies to make continuing individual relationships seem part of the much wider social bonds that tie us to them. It is only in and for themselves that they are given any significance, and they are thus emptied of some of their satisfaction. Our fascination with various forms of sexual perversion is a direct result of the fact that our personal relationships now rest only on their own self-justification. It is not surprising that, in such a situation, we say that "anything goes." [13]

There is no more pat shibboleth of our time than the idea that what consenting adults do in private is solely their own business. This is false. What we do in private has repercussions on ourselves, and what we are and believe has repercussions on others. What we do in our own homes will inevitably affect, not only our own behavior outside them, but what we expect and tolerate in the behavior of others. A change in manners or discipline in the family will not leave unchanged the manners and discipline in the wider society. When we recognize how deeply our sexual feelings are registers of our whole beings, it is mere trifling to say that our societies ought not to be constantly alert to the manner in which we employ them. [14]

But if our societies have good reason to be interested in our sexual attitudes and behavior, we have no less reason as individuals to be interested in why our societies have encouraged us to look to sex for such prurient and morbid delectations. The lustful person usually will be found to have only a terrible hollowness at the center of his life, and he is agitated to fill it, not daring to desist lest he should have to confront the desert he has made of himself and his life. He has no spiritual resource to which to turn. But is this not the condition of our societies? They do not know why they are there, except to continue; we hardly know why we are members of them, except to survive. It is all but inevitable in such a condition, with nothing very much outside ourselves to hold our attention for long, that we should agitate the most easily aroused and placable of our physical and emotional urges, if only to reassure ourselves that we are still alive and sentient beings. When our societies reduce most of the rest of life to little more than a series of disconnected episodes, commotions that only distract us, they cannot be surprised that their members reduce their own lives to a series of disconnected encounters, to find distraction in the commotions of their sexual organs. [15]

We do not see how parched our social landscape has become, because it is studded with gawdy and erotogenic allurements to what we conceive to be a pleasure that is within the easy reach of us all. The managers of our society much prefer that we are infatuated with our sexuality, than that we look long and steadily at what they contrive from day to day. They have little to fear as long as we define ourselves by Kinsey, or Masters and Johnson, or Hite, and find our most revolutionary tract in *The Joy of Sex*. They have discovered that, now that religion has been displaced, sex can be made the opiate of the masses. When the entire society is at last tranquilly preoccupied in the morbid practices of onanism, they will know that there is nothing more for them to do but rule forever over the dead. [16]

PURPOSE AND STRUCTURE

1. The author has written his version of the meaning of the seven deadly sins today. How does his definition of lust differ from that in the Bible?

2. By what varied means does the author compare and contrast lust and love? It will be useful to jot down the topic sentences in each paragraph in order to discover the differences.

3. Which contrasts are explicitly made? Which are only implicit? How are the several points brought into unity?

4. In what instances does the author rely on fact; in what cases on opinion?

5. How is the transition made between pars. 2 and 3? How does this transition clarify the author's concept that lust makes the participant "solitary"?

6. What causal relationship is established in par. 3?

7. How does the writer suggest that the supposed freedom of " 'singles' " today is a deception (par. 3)?

8. How do the quotations from Muggeridge and May (pars. 5–6) reflect the author's purpose and tone?

9. In what way is the puritan misguided in his thinking? In what sense does pornographic literature and film reduce us "to the final absurdity" (par. 6)?

10. How does the opening of par. 9 refer back to par. 3?

11. Explain the paradox in par. 11.

12. How does the author suggest that there is a causal relationship with regard to sexual attitudes and practices between the individual and society (pars. 14–16)?

13. In what sense does the final sentence provide a logical conclusion to the thesis advanced?

DICTION AND TONE

1. How does the diction move from formal to informal (par. 1)? Is this shift effective? Explain.

2. Why is *furtive* an appropriate word in par. 2?

3. How does the clause, "servicing, such as they might get at a gas station," contribute to purpose and tone?

4. Account for the use of the pronoun *it* with reference to going to bed (par. 3).

5. How does each of the following words, phrases, and/or metaphors in par. 3 convey the author's tone: "an obnoxious odor"; "deserts of themselves . . . deserts of their beds"; "it is parched . . . lost moisture"; "shrivelling it to no more than a husk"? What does this imagery tell you of the author's attitudes?

6. Identify other recurrent figures of speech used in subsequent paragraphs and examine their contribution to purpose and tone.

7. How does the repetition of *empty* in various forms in pars. 7, 8, 10, and 13 contribute to purpose and tone?

8. How does the language of pars. 12 and 16 suggest the author's contempt for sex manuals?

9. How does the use of parallel structure throughout the essay affect its tone? Cite passages.

10. Although the writer is defining and contrasting abstractions largely in abstract general statements, at the same time he makes his subject matter concrete and graphic. Explain.

APPLICATIONS TO WRITING

1. Using your own words and drawing upon your own experience, write a comparison of love and lust.

2. Compare and contrast any two phenomena by carefully defining each, pointing to causal relationships, and employing language that is concrete and graphic. You might compare and contrast what you assume are male and female attitudes toward love and/or lust; two films that treat the subject differently; pre and postmarital manifestations of love.

My Wood

E. M. FORSTER

A few years ago I wrote a book which dealt in part with the difficulties of the English in India. Feeling that they would have had no difficulties in India themselves, the Americans read the book freely. The more they read it the better it made them feel, and a cheque to the author was the result. I bought a wood with the cheque. It is not a large wood—it contains scarcely any trees, and it is intersected, blast it, by a public footpath. Still, it is the first property that I have owned, so it is right that other people should participate in my shame, and should ask themselves, in accents that will vary in horror, this very important question: What is the effect of property upon the character? Don't let's touch economics; the effect of private ownership upon the community as a whole is another question—a more important question, perhaps, but another one. Let's keep to psychology. If you own things, what's their effect on you? What's the effect on me of my wood? [1]

In the first place, it makes me feel heavy. Property does have this effect. Property produces men of weight, and it was a man of weight who failed to get into the Kingdom of Heaven. He was not wicked, that unfortunate millionaire in the parable, he was only stout; he stuck out in front, not to mention behind, and as he wedged himself this way and that in the crystalline entrance and bruised his well-fed flanks, he saw beneath him a comparatively slim camel passing through the eye of a needle and being woven into the robe of God. The Gospels all through couple stoutness and slowness. They point out what is perfectly obvious, yet seldom realized: that if you have a lot of things you cannot move about a lot, that furniture requires dusting, dusters require servants, servants require insurance stamps, and the whole tangle of them makes you think twice before you accept an invitation to dinner or go for a bathe in the Jordan. Sometimes the Gospels proceed further and say with Tolstoy that property is sinful; they approach the difficult ground of asceticism here, where I cannot follow them. But as to the immediate effects of property on people, they just show straightforward logic. It produces men of weight. Men of weight cannot, by definition, move like the lightning from the East unto the West, and the ascent of a fourteen-stone bishop into a pulpit is thus the exact antithesis of the coming of the Son of Man. My wood makes me feel heavy. [2]

In the second place, it makes me feel it ought to be larger. [3]

The other day I heard a twig snap in it. I was annoyed at first, for I thought that someone was blackberrying, and depreciating the value of the undergrowth. On coming nearer, I saw it was not a man who had trodden on the twig and snapped it, but a bird, and I felt pleased. My bird. The bird was not equally pleased. Ignoring the relation between us, it took fright as soon as it saw the shape of my face, and flew straight over the boundary hedge into a field, the property of Mrs. Henessy, where it sat down with a loud squawk. It had become Mrs. Henessy's bird. Something seemed grossly amiss here, something that would not have occurred had the wood been larger. I could not afford to buy Mrs. Henessy out, I dared not murder her, and limitations of this sort beset me on every side. Ahab did not want that vineyard—he only needed it to round off his property, preparatory to plotting a new curve—and all the land around my wood has become necessary to me in order to round off the wood. A boundary protects. But—poor little thing—the boundary ought in its turn to be protected. Noises on the edge of it.

Children throw stones. A little more, and then a little more, until we reach the sea. Happy Canute! Happier Alexander! And after all, why should even the world be the limit of possession? A rocket containing a Union Jack, will, it is hoped, be shortly fired at the moon. Mars. Sirius. Beyond which . . . But these immensities ended by saddening me. I could not suppose that my wood was the destined nucleus of universal dominion—it is so very small and contains no mineral wealth beyond the blackberries. Nor was I comforted when Mrs. Henessy's bird took alarm for the second time and flew clean away from us all, under the belief that it belonged to itself. [4]

In the third place, property makes its owner feel that he ought to do something to it. Yet he isn't sure what. A restlessness comes over him, a vague sense that he has a personality to express—the same sense which, without any vagueness, leads the artist to an act of creation. Sometimes I think I will cut down such trees as remain in the wood, at other times I want to fill up the gaps between them with new trees. Both impulses are pretentious and empty. They are not honest movements towards money-making or beauty. They spring from a foolish desire to express myself and from an inability to enjoy what I have got. Creation, property, enjoyment form a sinister trinity in the human mind. Creation and enjoyment are both very, very good, yet they are often unattainable without a material basis, and at such moments property pushes itself in as a substitute, saying, "Accept me instead—I'm good enough for all three." It is not enough. It is, as Shakespeare said of lust, "The expense of spirit in a waste of shame"; it is "Before, a joy proposed; behind, a dream." Yet we don't know how to shun it. It is forced on us by our economic system as the alternative to starvation. It is also forced on us by an internal defect in the soul, by the feeling that in property may lie the germs of self-development and of exquisite or heroic deeds. Our life on earth is, and ought to be, material and carnal. But we have not yet learned to manage our materialism and carnality properly; they are still entangled with the desire for ownership, where (in the words of Dante) "Possession is one with loss." [5]

And this brings us to our fourth and final point: the blackberries. [6]

Blackberries are not plentiful in this meagre grove, but they are easily seen from the public footpath which traverses it, and all too easily gathered. Foxgloves, too—people will pull up the foxgloves, and ladies of an educational tendency even grub for toadstools to show them on the Monday in class. Other ladies, less educated, roll down the bracken in the arms of their gentlemen friends. There is paper, there are tins. Pray, does my wood belong to me or doesn't it? And, if it does, should I not own it best by allowing no one else to walk there? There is a wood near Lyme Regis, also cursed by a public footpath, where the owner has not hesitated on this point. He has built high stone walls each side of the path, and has spanned it by bridges, so that the public circulate like termites while he gorges on the blackberries unseen. He really does own his wood, this able chap. Dives in Hell did pretty well, but the gulf dividing him from Lazarus could be traversed by vision, and nothing traverses it here. And perhaps I shall come to this in time. I shall wall in and fence out until I really taste the sweets of property. Enormously stout, endlessly avaricious, pseudocreative, intensely selfish, I shall weave upon my forehead the quadruple crown of possession until those nasty Bolshies come and take it off again and thrust me aside into the outer darkness. [7]

PURPOSE AND STRUCTURE

1. Forster's essay defines an aspect of property. This is a more difficult feat than it seems. For instance, the definition of property in the *Encyclopaedia of Social Sciences* is lengthy, brilliant, and satiric: its point is the near impossibility of defining such a vast entity as property. Forster sees the difficulties clearly and meets them in three ways. First, he presents to the reader a concrete example—"my wood"—which he follows through the essay. Second, he carefully limits the aspect of property that he explores. And third, he is personal in nearly all that he writes about property. Is his final definition purely personal?

2. This little essay is so well organized that it seems to mock organization. The thesis is prepared for and delimited in par. 1. Is it stated twice?

3. The last sentence of the essay begins, "Enormously stout, endlessly avaricious, pseudocreative, intensely selfish. . . ." Find the sections of the essay that develop these points.

DICTION AND TONE

1. Why begin with Americans? Are they involved in the "shame" and "horror" of Forster's question (par. 1)? What tone results from using such words as *shame* and *horror* in a conversational essay?

2. Why does Forster write "blast it" in par. 1?

3. Property "makes you think twice before you accept an invitation to dinner or go for a bathe in the Jordan." Why join these two examples (par. 2)?

4. Forster's bird "flew clean away from us all, under the belief that it belonged to itself" (par. 4). To whom did it belong?

5. In the last half of par. 5 Forster seems to tear through the fabric he has established. The limited definition explodes, the concrete becomes abstract, and the personal becomes entangled with "our life on earth." Has the writer failed in this section of the essay? Explain.

6. The last sentence of the essay contains the phrase "nasty Bolshies." Why not substitute "immoral Bolsheviks"?

APPLICATIONS TO WRITING

1. Forster's essay illustrates one way to approach Definition. Write a definition that is concrete, carefully limited, and personal.

2. A bird flies through par. 4. Its flight makes Forster feel his property should be larger. (Notice the irony of the last sentence.) Write a paragraph in which a concrete movement through space illustrates a general statement. For instance, a ride on the roller coaster may illustrate "Experience is *not* the best teacher." Or the myth of Sisyphus may illustrate "A rolling stone gathers no moss."

The Stereotype
from *The Female Eunuch*

GERMAINE GREER

In that mysterious dimension where the body meets the soul the stereotype is born and has her being. She is more body than soul, more soul than mind. To her belongs all that is beautiful, even the very word beauty itself. All that exists, exists to beautify her. The sun shines only to burnish her skin and gild her hair; the wind blows only to whip up the color in her cheeks; the sea strives to bathe her; flowers die gladly so that her skin may luxuriate in their essence. She is the crown

Taught from infancy that beauty is woman's sceptre, the mind shapes itself to the body, and roaming round its gilt cage, only seeks to adorn its prison.

Mary Woolstonecraft, A Vindication of the Rights of Woman, *1792, p. 90.*

of creation, the masterpiece. The depths of the sea are ransacked for pearl and coral to deck her; the bowels of the earth are laid open that she might wear gold, sapphires, diamonds and rubies. Baby seals are battered with staves, unborn lambs ripped from their mothers' wombs, millions of moles, muskrats, squirrels, minks, ermines, foxes, beavers, chinchillas, ocelots, lynxes, and other small and lovely creatures die untimely deaths that she might have furs. Egrets, ostriches and peacocks, butterflies and beetles yield her their plumage. Men risk their lives hunting leopards for her coats, and crocodiles for her handbags and shoes. Millions of silkworms offer her their yellow labors; even the seamstresses roll seams and whip lace by hand, so that she might be clad in the best that money can buy. [1]

The men of our civilization have stripped themselves of the fineries of the earth so that they might work more freely to plunder the universe for treasures to deck my lady in. New raw materials, new processes, new machines are all brought into her service. My lady must therefore be the chief spender as well as the chief symbol of spending ability and monetary success. While her mate toils in his factory, she totters about the smartest streets and plushiest hotels with his fortune upon her back and bosom, fingers and wrists, continuing that essential expenditure in his house which is her frame and her setting, enjoying that silken idleness which is the necessary condition of maintaining her mate's prestige and her qualification to demonstrate it. Once upon a time only the aristocratic lady could lay claim to the title of crown of creation: only her hands were white enough, her feet tiny enough, her waist narrow enough, her hair long and golden enough; but every well-to-do burgher's wife set herself up to ape my lady and to follow fashion, until my lady was forced to set herself out like a gilded doll overlaid with monstrous rubies and pearls like pigeons' eggs. Nowadays the Queen of England still considers it part of her royal female role to sport as much of the family jewelry as she can manage at any one time on all public occasions, although the male monarchs have escaped such showcase duty, which devolves exclusively upon their wives. [2]

At the same time as woman was becoming the showcase for wealth and caste, while men were slipping into relative anonymity and "handsome is as handsome does," she was emerging as the central emblem of western art. For the Greeks the male and female body had beauty of a human, not necessarily a sexual kind; indeed they may have marginally favored the young male form as the most powerful and perfectly proportioned. Likewise the Romans showed no bias towards the depiction of femininity in their predominantly monumental art. In the Renaissance the female form began to predominate, not only as the mother in the predominate emblem of *madonna col bambino,* but as an aesthetic study in herself. At first naked female forms took their chances in crowd scenes or diptychs of Adam and Eve, but gradually Venus claims ascendancy, Mary Magdalene ceases to be wizened and emaciated, and becomes nubile and ecstatic, portraits of anonymous young women, chosen only for their prettiness, begin to appear, are gradually disrobed, and renamed Flora or Primavera. Painters begin to paint their own wives and mistresses and royal consorts as voluptuous beauties, divesting them of their clothes if desirable, but not of their jewelry. Susanna keeps her bracelets on in the bath, and Hélène Fourment keeps ahold of her fur as well! [3]

What happened to women in painting happened to her in poetry as well. Her beauty was celebrated in terms of the riches which clustered around her: her hair was gold wires, her brow ivory, her lips ruby, her teeth gates of pearl, her breasts alabaster veined with lapis lazuli, her eyes as black as jet. The fragility of her loveliness was emphasized by the inevitable comparisons with the rose, and she was urged to employ her beauty in love-making before it withered on the stem. She was for consumption; other sorts of imagery spoke of her in terms of cherries and cream, lips as sweet as honey and skin white as milk, breasts like cream uncrudded, hard as apples. Some celebrations yearned over her finery as well, her lawn more transparent than morning mist, her lace as delicate as gossamer, the baubles that she toyed with and the favors that she gave. Even now we find the thriller hero describing his classy dames' elegant suits, cheeky hats, well-chosen accessories and footwear; the imagery no longer dwells on jewels and flowers but the consumer emphasis is the same. The mousy secretary blossoms into the feminine stereotype when she reddens her lips, lets down her hair, and puts on something frilly. [4]

Nowadays women are not expected, unless they are Paola di Liegi or Jackie Onassis, and then only on gala occasions, to appear with a king's ransom deployed upon their bodies, but they are required to look expensive, fashionable, well-groomed, and not to be seen in the same dress twice. If the duty of the few may have become less onerous, it has also become the duty of the many. The stereotype marshals an army of servants. She is supplied with cosmetics, underwear, foundation garments, stockings, wigs, postiches and hairdressing as well as her outer garments, her jewels and furs. The effect is to be built up layer by layer, and it is expensive. Splendor has given way to fit, line and cut. The spirit of competition must be kept up, as more and more women struggle towards the top drawer, so that the fashion industry can rely upon an expanding market. Poorer women fake it, ape it, pick up on the fashions a season too late, use crude effects, mistaking the line, the sheen, the gloss of the high-class article for a garish simulacrum. The business is so complex that it must be handled by an expert. The paragons of the stereotype must be dressed, coifed and painted by the experts and the style-setters, although they may be encouraged to give heart to the housewives studying their lives in pulp magazines by claiming a life-long fidelity to their own hair and soap and water. The boast is more usually discouraging than otherwise, unfortunately. [5]

As long as she is young and personable, every woman may cherish the dream that she may leap up the social ladder and dim the sheen of luxury by sheer natural loveliness; the few examples of such a feat are kept before the eye of the public. Fired with hope, optimism and ambition, young women study the latest forms of the stereotype, set out in *Vogue, Nova, Queen* and other glossies, where the mannequins stare from among the advertisements for fabulous real estate, furs and jewels. Nowadays the uniformity of the year's fashions is severely affected by the emergence of the pert female designers who direct their appeal to the working girl, emphasizing variety, comfort, and simple, striking effects. There is no longer a single face of the year: even Twiggy has had to withdraw into marketing and rational personal appearances, while the Shrimp works mostly in New York. Nevertheless the stereotype is still supreme. She has simply allowed herself a little more variation. [6]

The stereotype is the Eternal Feminine. She is the Sexual Object sought by all men, and by all women. She is of neither sex, for she has herself no sex at all. Her value is solely attested by the demand she excites in others. All she must contribute is her existence. She need achieve nothing, for she is the reward of achievement. She need never give positive evidence of her moral character because virtue is assumed from her loveliness, and her passivity. If any man who has no right to her be found with her she will not be punished, for she is morally neuter. The matter is solely one of male rivalry. Innocently she may drive men to madness and war. The more trouble she can cause, the more her stocks go up, for possession of her means more the more demand she excites. Nobody wants a girl whose beauty is imperceptible to all but him; and so men welcome the stereotype because it directs their taste into the most commonly recognized areas of value, although they may protest because some aspects of it do not tally with their fetishes. There is scope in the stereotype's variety for most fetishes. The leg man may follow miniskirts, the tit man can encourage see-through blouses and plunging necklines, although the man who likes fat women may feel constrained to enjoy them in secret. There are stringent limits to

---

The myth of the strong black woman is the other side of the coin of the myth of the beautiful dumb blonde. The white man turned the white woman into a weak-minded, weak-bodied, delicate freak, a sex pot, and placed her on a pedestal; he turned the black woman into a strong self-reliant Amazon and deposited her in his kitchen. . . . The white man turned himself into the Omnipotent Administrator and established himself in the Front Office.

Eldridge Cleaver, "The Allegory of the Black Eunuchs,"
Soul on Ice, *1968, p. 162*

---

the variations on the stereotype, for nothing must interfere with her function as sex object. She may wear leather, so long as she cannot actually handle a motorbike: she may wear rubber, but it ought not to indicate that she is an expert diver or waterskier. If she wears athletic clothes the purpose is to underline her unathleticism. She may sit astride a horse, looking soft and curvy, but she must not crouch over its neck with her rump in the air. [7]

She was created to be the toy of man, his rattle, and it must jingle in his ears whenever, dismissing reason, he chooses to be amused.

Mary Wollstonecraft, A Vindication of the Rights of Woman,
1792, p. 66

Because she is the emblem of spending ability and the chief spender, she is also the most effective seller of this world's goods. Every survey ever held has shown that the image of an attractive woman is the most effective advertising gimmick. She may sit astride the mudguard of a new car, or step into it ablaze with jewels; she may lie at a man's feet stroking his new socks; she may hold the petrol pump in a challenging pose, or dance through woodland glades in slow motion in all the glory of a new shampoo; whatever she does her image sells. The gynolatry of our civilization is written large upon its face, upon hoardings, cinema screens, television, newspapers, magazines, tins, packets, cartons, bottles, all consecrated to the reigning deity, the female fetish. Her dominion must not be thought to entail the rule of women, for she is not a woman. Her glossy lips and mat complexion, her unfocused eyes and flawless fingers, her extraordinary hair all floating and shining, curling and gleaming, reveal the inhuman triumph of cosmetics, lighting, focusing and printing, cropping and composition. She sleeps unruffled, her lips red and juicy and closed, her eyes as crisp and black as if new painted, and her false lashes immaculately curled. Even when she washes her face with a new and creamier toilet soap her expression is as tranquil and vacant and her paint as flawless as ever. If ever she should appear tousled and troubled, her features are miraculously smoothed to their proper veneer by a new washing powder or a bouillon cube. For she is a doll: weeping, pouting or smiling, running or reclining, she is a doll. She is an idol, formed of the concatenation of lines and masses, signifying the lineaments of satisfied impotence. [8]

Her essential quality is castratedness. She absolutely must be young, her body hairless, her flesh buoyant, and *she must not have a sexual organ*. No musculature must distort the smoothness of the lines of her body, although she may be painfully slender or warmly cuddly. Her expression must betray no hint of humor, curiosity or intelligence, although it may signify hauteur to an extent that is actually absurd, or smoldering lust, very feebly signified by drooping eyes and a sullen mouth (for the stereotype's lust equals irrational submission), or, most commonly, vivacity and idiot happiness. Seeing that the world despoils itself for this creature's benefit, she must be happy; the entire structure would topple if she were not. So the image of woman appears plastered on every surface imaginable, smiling interminably. An apple pie evokes a glance of tender beatitude, a washing machine causes hilarity, a cheap box of chocolates brings forth meltingly joyous gratitude, a Coke is the cause of a rictus of unutterable brilliance, even a new stick-on bandage is saluted by a smirk of satisfaction. A real woman licks her lips and opens her mouth and flashes her teeth when photographers appear: *she* must arrive at the premiere of her husband's film in a paroxysm of delight, or his success might be murmured about. The occupational hazard of being a Playboy Bunny is the aching facial muscles brought on by the obligatory smiles. [9]

Discretion is the better part of Valerie
though all of her is nice
lips as warm as strawberries
eyes as cold as ice :
the very best of everything
only will suffice
not for her potatoes
and puddings made of rice
                    Roger McGough, Discretion

So what is the beef? Maybe I couldn't make it. Maybe I don't have a pretty smile, good teeth, nice tits, long legs, a cheeky arse, a sexy voice. Maybe I don't know how to handle men and increase my market value, so that the rewards due to the feminine will accrue to me. Then again, maybe I'm sick of the masquerade. I'm sick of pretending eternal youth. I'm sick of belying my own intelligence, my own will, my own sex. I'm sick of peering at the world through false eyelashes, so everything I see is mixed with a shadow of bought hairs; I'm sick of weighting my head with a dead mane, unable to move my neck freely, terrified of rain, of wind, of dancing too vigorously in case I sweat into my lacquered curls. I'm sick of the Powder Room. I'm sick of pretending that some fatuous male's self-important pronouncements are the objects of my undivided attention, I'm sick of going to films and plays when someone else wants to, and sick of having no opinions of my own about either. I'm sick of being a transvestite. I refuse to be a female impersonator. I am a woman, not a castrate. [10]

April Ashley was born male. All the information supplied by genes, chromosomes, internal and external sexual organs added up to the same thing. April was a man. But he longed to be a woman. He longed for the stereotype, not to embrace, but to be. He wanted soft fabrics, jewels, furs, makeup, the love and protection of men. So he was impotent. He

---

To what end is the laying out of the embroidered Hair, embared Breasts; vermilion Cheeks, alluring looks. Fashion gates, and artful Countenances, effeminate intangling and insnaring Gestures, their Curls and Purls of proclaiming Petulancies, boulstered and laid out with such example and authority in these our days, as with Allowance and beseeming Conveniency?

Doth the world wax barren through decrease of Generations, and become, like the Earth, less fruitful heretofore? Doth the Blood lose his Heat or do the Sunbeams become waterish and less fervent, than formerly they have been, that men should be thus inflamed and persuaded on to lust?

Alex. Niccholes, A Discourse of Marriage and Wiving, *1615,*
pp. 143–52

---

couldn't fancy women at all, although he did not particularly welcome homosexual addresses. He did not think of himself as a pervert, or even as a transvestite, but as a woman cruelly transmogrified into manhood. He tried to die, became a female impersonator, but eventually found a doctor in Casablanca who came up with a more acceptable alternative. He was to be castrated, and his penis used as the lining of a surgically constructed cleft, which would be a vagina. He would be infertile, but that has never affected the attribution of femininity. April returned to England, resplendent. Massive hormone treatment had eradicated his beard, and formed tiny breasts: he had grown his hair and bought feminine clothes during the time he had worked as an impersonator. He became a model, and began to illustrate the feminine stereotype as he was perfectly qualified to do, for he was elegant, voluptuous, beautifully groomed, and in love with his own image. On an ill-fated day he married the heir to a peerage, the Hon. Arthur Corbett, acting out the highest achievement of the feminine dream, and went to live with him in a villa in Marbella. The marriage was never consummated. April's incompetence as a woman is what we must expect from a castrate, but it is not so very different after all from the impotence of feminine women, who submit to sex without desire, with only the infantile pleasure of cuddling and affection, which is their favorite reward. As long as the feminine stereotype remains the definition of the female sex, April Ashley is a woman, regardless of the legal decision ensuing from her divorce. She is as much a casualty of the polarity of the sexes as we all are. Disgraced, unsexed April Ashley is our sister and our symbol. [11]

PURPOSE AND STRUCTURE

1. How does Greer develop and support her extended definition of the stereotype?

2. How do the questions in the body of the text relate to the author's thesis?

3. What does Greer's implicit description of women in pars. 1 and 2 tell you about her attitude toward women? Toward men? Toward society?

4. How do the evolving pictures of women in painting and poetry relate to Greer's concept of the stereotype?

5. How does Greer support her view that woman "was for consumption" (par. 4)? What is the causal relationship between the stereotype and the nature of big business?

6. Account for the seeming paradox in the light of what precedes and follows Greer's statement that the stereotype "is of neither sex, for she has herself no sex at all" (par. 7).

7. How does the introduction of April Ashley in the last paragraph relate to purpose and tone?

DICTION AND TONE

1. Express in your own words the substance of the opening paragraph. What is lost in purpose and tone? How does the use of metaphor, hyperbole, and personification contribute to purpose and tone? Cite examples of each of these figures of speech.

2. In what context does the author employ the first person? How does its use affect purpose and tone?

3. How does the use of parallel structure in pars. 1 and 2 contribute to tone?

4. How do the following words or phrases affect the tone and how can such variations in epithet be reconciled? Relate each to the central definition: "my lady" (par. 2); "she totters" (par. 2); "silken idleness" (par. 2);

"her feet tiny enough" (par. 2); "gilded doll" (par. 2); "the showcase for wealth and caste" (par. 3); "the Eternal Feminine" (par. 7); "Sexual Object" (par. 7); "an idol" (par. 8); "Playboy Bunny" (par. 9); "transvestite" (par. 10); "female impersonator" (par. 10); "a castrate" (par. 10).

5. What tone is reflected in the details of Susanna's keeping her bracelets on in the bath and Hélène holding onto her fur (par. 3)?

6. How does the cliché-ridden diction in par. 4 contribute to tone and advance the author's purpose in defining the feminine stereotype?

7. How does the tone change in par. 10? What purpose does the repetition serve?

8. Check the definitions of *irony* and *satire* in the Glossary and determine how either or both apply to this essay.

APPLICATIONS TO WRITING

1. Write your definition of the male stereotype, drawing your details from your personal experience and observation and from the portrayals of males in advertisements in magazines and on TV.

2. How has the women's movement affected the stereotype? If you have read widely in its literature, define its goals.

3. What is your conception of your appropriate and most fulfilling role as a woman or as a man? Use concrete details in developing your definition.

three

Classification

Classification—an arbitrary, systematic arrangement of categories (classes) so that the larger categories include the smaller. By definition, all members of a class have at least one characteristic in common. While Shulman's purpose is to amuse, his method is classification of logical fallacies. Cox's mode of classification reflects the basic human needs of those who turn East for fulfillment. Hertzberg and McClelland use a wide variety of methods to classify the types of paranoia. Packard arranges people shapers into four categories and then provides an example or illustration of each. McGlashan reviews a number of classic and contemporary theories of dream interpretation before focusing on the dream as a means of penetrating the mystery of the self.

Love Is a Fallacy

MAX SHULMAN

Cool was I and logical. Keen, calculating, perspicacious, acute and astute—I was all of these. My brain was as powerful as a dynamo, as precise as a chemist's scales, as penetrating as a scalpel. And—think of it —I was only eighteen. [1]

It is not often that one so young has such a giant intellect. Take, for example, Petey Burch, my roommate at the University of Minnesota. Same age, same background, but dumb as an ox. A nice enough fellow, you understand, but nothing upstairs. Emotional type. Unstable. Impressionable. Worst of all, a faddist. Fads, I submit, are the very negation of reason. To be swept up in every new craze that comes along, to surrender yourself to idiocy just because everybody else is doing it— this, to me, is the acme of mindlessness. Not, however, to Petey. [2]

One afternoon I found Petey lying on his bed with an expression of such distress on his face that I immediately diagnosed appendicitis. "Don't move," I said. "Don't take a laxative. I'll get a doctor." [3]

"Raccoon," he mumbled thickly. [4]

"Raccoon?" I said, pausing in my flight. [5]

"I want a raccoon coat," he wailed. [6]

I perceived that his trouble was not physical, but mental. "Why do you want a raccoon coat?" [7]

"I should have known it," he cried, pounding his temples. "I should have known they'd come back when the Charleston came back. Like a fool I spent all my money for textbooks, and now I can't get a raccoon coat." [8]

"Can you mean," I said incredulously, "that people are actually wearing raccoon coats again?" [9]

"All the Big Men on Campus are wearing them. Where've you been?" [10]

"In the library," I said, naming a place not frequented by Big Men on Campus. [11]

He leaped from the bed and paced the room. "I've got to have a raccoon coat," he said passionately. "I've got to!" [12]

"Petey, why? Look at it rationally. Raccoon coats are unsanitary. They shed. They smell bad. They weigh too much. They're unsightly. They—" [13]

"You don't understand," he interrupted impatiently. "It's the thing to do. Don't you want to be in the swim?" [14]

"No," I said truthfully. [15]

"Well, I do," he declared. "I'd give anything for a raccoon coat. Anything!" [16]

My brain, that precision instrument, slipped into high gear. "Anything?" I asked, looking at him narrowly. [17]

"Anything," he affirmed in ringing tones. [18]

I stroked my chin thoughtfully. It so happened that I knew where to get my hands on a raccoon coat. My father had had one in his undergraduate days; it lay now in a trunk in the attic back home. It also happened that Petey had something I wanted. He didn't *have* it exactly, but at least he had first rights on it. I refer to his girl, Polly Espy. [19]

I had long coveted Polly Espy. Let me emphasize that my desire for this young woman was not emotional in nature. She was, to be sure, a girl who excited the emotions, but I was not one to let my heart rule my head. I wanted Polly for a shrewdly calculated, entirely cerebral reason. [20]

I was a freshman in law school. In a few years I would be out in practice. I was well aware of the importance of the right kind of wife in furthering a lawyer's career. The successful lawyers I had observed were, almost without exception, married to beautiful, gracious, intelligent women. With one omission, Polly fitted these specifications perfectly. [21]

Beautiful she was. She was not yet of pin-up proportions, but I felt sure that time would supply the lack. She already had the makings. [22]

Gracious she was. By gracious I mean full of graces. She had an erectness of carriage, an ease of bearing, a poise that clearly indicated the best of breeding. At table her manners were exquisite. I had seen her at the Kozy Kampus Korner eating the specialty of the house—a sandwich that contained scraps of pot roast, gravy, chopped nuts, and a dipper of sauerkraut—without even getting her fingers moist. [23]

Intelligent she was not. In fact, she veered in the opposite direction. But I believed that under my guidance she would smarten up. At any rate, it was worth a try. It is, after all, easier to make a beautiful dumb girl smart than to make an ugly smart girl beautiful. [24]

"Petey," I said, "are you in love with Polly Espy?" [25]

"I think she's a keen kid," he replied, "but I don't know if you'd call it love. Why?" [26]

"Do you," I asked, "have any kind of formal arrangement with her? I mean are you going steady or anything like that?" [27]

"No. We see each other quite a bit, but we both have other dates. Why?" [28]

"Is there," I asked, "any other man for whom she has a particular fondness?" [29]

"Not that I know of. Why?" [30]

I nodded with satisfaction. "In other words, if you were out of the picture, the field would be open. Is that right?" [31]

"I guess so. What are you getting at?" [32]

"Nothing, nothing," I said innocently, and took my suitcase out of the closet. [33]

"Where are you going?" asked Petey. [34]

"Home for the weekend." I threw a few things into the bag. [35]

"Listen," he said, clutching my arm eagerly, "while you're home, you couldn't get some money from your old man, could you, and lend it to me so I can buy a raccoon coat?" [36]

"I may do better than that," I said with a mysterious wink and closed my bag and left. [37]

"Look," I said to Petey when I got back Monday morning. I threw open the suitcase and revealed the huge, hairy, gamy object that my father had worn in his Stutz Bearcat in 1925. [38]

"Holy Toledo!" said Petey reverently. He plunged his hands into the raccoon coat and then his face. "Holy Toledo!" he repeated fifteen or twenty times. [39]

"Would you like it?" I asked. [40]

"Oh yes!" he cried, clutching the greasy pelt to him. Then a canny look came into his eyes. "What do you want for it?" [41]

"Your girl," I said, mincing no words. [42]

"Polly?" he said in a horrified whisper. "You want Polly?" [43]

"That's right." [44]

He flung the coat from him. "Never," he said stoutly. [45]

I shrugged. "Okay. If you don't want to be in the swim, I guess it's your business." [46]

I sat down in a chair and pretended to read a book, but out of the corner of my eye I kept watching Petey. He was a torn man. First he looked at the coat with the expression of a waif at a bakery window. Then he turned away and set his jaw resolutely. Then he looked back at the coat, with even more longing in his face. Then he turned away, but with not so much resolution this time. Back and forth his head swiveled, desire waxing, resolution waning. Finally he didn't turn away at all; he just stood and stared with mad lust at the coat. [47]

"It isn't as though I was in love with Polly," he said thickly. "Or going steady or anything like that." [48]

"That's right," I murmured. [49]

"What's Polly to me, or me to Polly?" [50]

"Not a thing," said I. [51]

"It's just been a casual kick—just a few laughs, that's all." [52]

"Try on the coat," said I. [53]

He complied. The coat bunched high over his ears and dropped all the way down to his shoe tops. He looked like a mound of dead raccoons. "Fits fine," he said happily. [54]

I rose from my chair. "Is it a deal?" I asked, extending my hand. [55]

He swallowed. "It's a deal," he said and shook my hand. [56]

I had my first date with Polly the following evening. This was in the nature of a survey; I wanted to find out just how much work I had to do to get her mind up to the standard I required. I took her first to dinner. "Gee, that was a delish dinner," she said as we left the restaurant. Then I took her to a movie. "Gee, that was a marvy movie," she said as we left the theater. And then I took her home. "Gee, I had a sensaysh time," she said as she bade me good night. [57]

I went back to my room with a heavy heart. I had gravely underestimated the size of my task. This girl's lack of information was terrifying. Nor would it be enough merely to supply her with information. First she had to be taught to *think*. This loomed as a project of no small dimensions, and at first I was tempted to give her back to Petey. But then I got to thinking about her abundant physical charms and about the way she entered a room and the way she handled a knife and fork, and I decided to make an effort. [58]

I went about it, as in all things, systematically. I gave her a course in logic. It happened that I, as a law student, was taking a course in logic myself, so I had all the facts at my finger tips. "Polly," I said to her when I picked her up on our next date, "tonight we are going over to the Knoll and talk." [59]

"Oo, terrif," she replied. One thing I will say for this girl: you would go far to find another so agreeable. [60]

We went to the Knoll, the campus trysting place, and we sat down under an old oak, and she looked at me expectantly. "What are we going to talk about?" she asked. [61]

"Logic." [62]

She thought this over for a minute and decided she liked it. "Magnif," she said. [63]

"Logic," I said, clearing my throat, "is the science of thinking. Before we can think correctly, we must first learn to recognize the common fallacies of logic. These we will take up tonight." [64]

"Wow-dow!" she cried, clapping her hands delightedly. [65]

I winced, but went bravely on. "First let us examine the fallacy called Dicto Simpliciter." [66]

"By all means," she urged, batting her lashes eagerly. [67]

"Dicto Simpliciter means an argument based on an unqualified generalization. For example: Exercise is good. Therefore everybody should exercise." [68]

"I agree," said Polly earnestly. "I mean exercise is wonderful. I mean it builds the body and everything." [69]

"Polly," I said gently, "the argument is a fallacy. *Exercise is good* is an unqualified generalization. For instance, if you have heart disease, exercise is bad, not good. Many people are ordered by their doctors *not* to exercise. You must *qualify* the generalization. You must say exercise is *usually* good, or exercise is good *for most people*. Otherwise you have committed a Dicto Simpliciter. Do you see?" [70]

"No," she confessed. "But this is marvy. Do more! Do more!" [71]

"It will be better if you stop tugging at my sleeve," I told her, and when she desisted, I continued. "Next we take up a fallacy called Hasty Generalization. Listen carefully: You can't speak French. I can't speak French. Petey Burch can't speak French. I must therefore conclude that nobody at the University of Minnesota can speak French." [72]

"Really?" said Polly, amazed. *"Nobody?"* [73]

I hid my exasperation. "Polly, it's a fallacy. The generalization is reached too hastily. There are too few instances to support such a conclusion." [74]

"Know any more fallacies?" she asked breathlessly. "This is more fun than dancing even." [75]

I fought off a wave of despair. I was getting nowhere with this girl, absolutely nowhere. Still, I am nothing if not persistent. I continued. "Next comes Post Hoc. Listen to this: Let's not take Bill on our picnic. Every time we take him out with us, it rains." [76]

"I know somebody just like that," she exclaimed. "A girl back home—Eula Becker, her name is. It never fails. Every single time we take her on a picnic—" [77]

"Polly," I said sharply, "it's a fallacy. Eula Becker doesn't *cause* the rain. She has no connection with the rain. You are guilty of Post Hoc if you blame Eula Becker." [78]

"I'll never do it again," she promised contritely. "Are you mad at me?" [79]

I sighed deeply. "No, Polly, I'm not mad." [80]

"Then tell me some more fallacies." [81]

"All right. Let's try Contradictory Premises." [82]

"Yes, let's" she chirped, blinking her eyes happily. [83]

I frowned, but plunged ahead. "Here's an example of Contradictory Premises: If God can do anything, can He make a stone so heavy that He won't be able to lift it?" [84]

"Of course," she replied promptly. [85]

"But if He can do anything, He can lift the stone," I pointed out. [86]

"Yeah," she said thoughtfully. "Well, then I guess He can't make the stone." [87]

"But He can do anything," I reminded her. [88]

She scratched her pretty, empty head. "I'm all confused," she admitted. [89]

"Of course you are. Because when the premises of an argument contradict each other, there can be no argument. If there is an irresistible force, there can be no immovable object. If there is an immovable object, there can be no irresistible force. Get it?" [90]

"Tell me some more of this keen stuff," she said eagerly. [91]

I consulted my watch. "I think we'd better call it a night. I'll take you home now, and you go over all the things you've learned. We'll have another session tomorrow night." [92]

I deposited her at the girls' dormitory, where she assured me that she had had a perfectly terrif evening, and I went glumly home to my room. Petey lay snoring in his bed, the raccoon coat huddled like a great hairy beast at his feet. For a moment I considered waking him and telling him that he could have his girl back. It seemed clear that my project was doomed to failure. The girl simply had a logic-proof head. [93]

But then I reconsidered. I had wasted one evening; I might as well waste another. Who knew? Maybe somewhere in the extinct crater of her mind, a few embers still smoldered. Maybe somehow I could fan them into flame. Admittedly it was not a prospect fraught with hope, but I decided to give it one more try. [94]

Seated under the oak the next evening I said, "Our first fallacy tonight is called Ad Misericordiam." [95]

She quivered with delight. [96]

"Listen closely," I said. "A man applies for a job. When the boss asks him what his qualifications are, he replies that he has a wife and six children at home, the wife is a helpless cripple, the children have nothing to eat, no clothes to wear, no shoes on their feet, there are no beds in the house, no coal in the cellar, and winter is coming." [97]

A tear rolled down each of Polly's pink cheeks. "Oh, this is awful, awful," she sobbed. [98]

"Yes, it's awful," I agreed, "but it's no argument. The man never answered the boss's question about his qualifications. Instead he appealed to the boss's sympathy. He committed the fallacy of Ad Misericordiam. Do you understand?" [99]

"Have you got a handkerchief?" she blubbered. [100]

I handed her a handkerchief and tried to keep from screaming while she wiped her eyes. "Next," I said in a carefully controlled tone, "we will discuss False Analogy. Here is an example: Students should be allowed to look at their textbooks during examinations. After all, surgeons have X-rays to guide them during an operation, lawyers have briefs to guide them during a trial, carpenters have blueprints to guide them when they are building a house. Why, then, shouldn't students be allowed to look at their textbooks during an examination?" [101]

"There now," she said enthusiastically, "is the most marvy idea I've heard in years." [102]

"Polly," I said testily, "the argument is all wrong. Doctors, lawyers, and carpenters aren't taking a test to see how much they have learned, but students are. The situations are altogether different, and you can't make an analogy between them." [103]

"I still think it's a good idea," said Polly. [104]

"Nuts," I muttered. Doggedly I pressed on. "Next we'll try Hypothesis Contrary to Fact." [105]

"Sounds yummy," was Polly's reaction. [106]

"Listen: If Madame Curie had not happened to leave a photographic plate in a drawer with a chunk of pitchblende, the world today would not know about radium." [107]

"True, true," said Polly, nodding her head. "Did you see the movie? Oh, it just knocked me out. That Walter Pidgeon is so dreamy. I mean he fractures me." [108]

"If you can forget Mr. Pidgeon for a moment," I said coldly, "I would like to point out that the statement is a fallacy. Maybe Madame Curie would have discovered radium at some later date. Maybe somebody else would have discovered it. Maybe any number of things would have happened. You can't start with a hypothesis that is not true and then draw any supportable conclusions from it." [109]

"They ought to put Walter Pidgeon in more pictures," said Polly. "I hardly ever see him any more." [110]

One more chance, I decided. But just one more. There is a limit to what flesh and blood can bear. "The next fallacy is called Poisoning the Well." [111]

"How cute!" she gurgled. [112]

"Two men are having a debate. The first one gets up and says, 'My opponent is a notorious liar. You can't believe a word that he is going to say.' . . . Now, Polly, think. Think hard. What's wrong?" [113]

I watched her closely as she knit her creamy brow in concentration. Suddenly a glimmer of intelligence—the first I had seen—came into her eyes. "It's not fair," she said with indignation. "It's not a bit fair. What chance has the second man got if the first man calls him a liar before he even begins talking?" [114]

"Right!" I cried exultantly. "One hundred percent right. It's not fair. The first man has *poisoned the well* before anybody could drink from it. He has hamstrung his opponent before he could even start. . . . Polly, I'm proud of you." [115]

"Pshaw," she murmured, blushing with pleasure. [116]

"You see, my dear, these things aren't so hard. All you have to do is concentrate. Think—examine—evaluate. Come now, let's review everything we have learned." [117]

"Fire away," she said with an airy wave of her hand. [118]

Heartened by the knowledge that Polly was not altogether a cretin, I began a long, patient review of all I had told her. Over and over and over again. I cited instances, pointed out flaws, kept hammering away without let-up. It was like digging a tunnel. At first everything was work, sweat, and darkness. I had no idea when I would reach the light, or even *if* I would. But I persisted. I pounded and clawed and scraped, and finally I was rewarded. I saw a chink of light. And then the chink got bigger and the sun came pouring in and all was bright. [119]

Five grueling nights this took, but it was worth it. I had made a logician out of Polly; I had taught her to think. My job was done. She was worthy of me at last. She was a fit wife for me, a proper hostess for many mansions, a suitable mother for my well-heeled children. [120]

It must not be thought that I was without love for this girl. Quite the contrary. Just as Pygmalion loved the perfect woman he had fashioned, so I loved mine. I determined to acquaint her with my feelings at our very next meeting. The time had come to change our relationship from academic to romantic. [121]

"Polly," I said when next we sat beneath our oak, "tonight we will not discuss fallacies." [122]

"Aw, gee," she said, disappointed. [123]

"My dear," I said, favoring her with a smile, "we have now spent five evenings together. We have gotten along splendidly. It is clear that we are well matched." [124]

"Hasty Generalization," said Polly brightly. [125]

"I beg your pardon," said I. [126]

"Hasty Generalization," she repeated. "How can you say that we are well matched on the basis of only five dates?" [127]

I chuckled with amusement. The dear child had learned her lessons well. "My dear," I said, patting her hand in a tolerant manner, "five dates is plenty. After all, you don't have to eat a whole cake to know that it's good." [128]

"False Analogy," said Polly promptly. "I'm not a cake. I'm a girl." [129]

I chuckled with somewhat less amusement. The dear child had learned her lessons perhaps too well. I decided to change tactics. Obviously the best approach was a simple, strong, direct declaration of love. I paused for a moment while my massive brain chose the proper words. Then I began: [130]

"Polly, I love you. You are the whole world to me, and the moon and the stars and the constellations of outer space. Please, my darling, say that you will go steady with me, for if you will not, life will be meaningless. I will languish. I will refuse my meals. I will wander the face of the earth, a shambling, hollow-eyed hulk." [131]

There, I thought, folding my arms, that ought to do it. [132]

"Ad Misericordiam," said Polly. [133]

I ground my teeth. I was no Pygmalion; I was Frankenstein, and my monster had me by the throat. Frantically I fought back the tide of panic surging through me. At all costs I had to keep cool. [134]

"Well, Polly," I said, forcing a smile, "you certainly have learned your fallacies." [135]

"You're darn right," she said with a vigorous nod. [136]

"And who taught them to you, Polly?" [137]

"You did." [138]

"That's right. So you do owe me something, don't you, my dear? If I hadn't come along you never would have learned about fallacies." [139]

"Hypothesis Contrary to Fact," she said instantly. [140]

I dashed perspiration from my brow. "Polly," I croaked, "you mustn't take all these things so literally. I mean this is just classroom stuff. You know that the things you learn in school don't have anything to do with life." [141]

"Dicto Simpliciter," she said, wagging her finger at me playfully. [142]

That did it. I leaped to my feet, bellowing like a bull. "Will you or will you not go steady with me?" [143]

"I will not," she replied. [144]

"Why not?" I demanded. [145]

"Because this afternoon I promised Petey Burch that I would go steady with him." [146]

I reeled back, overcome with the infamy of it. After he promised, after he made a deal, after he shook my hand! "The rat!" I shrieked, kicking up great chunks of turf. "You can't go with him, Polly. He's a liar. He's a cheat. He's a rat." [147]

"Poisoning the Well," said Polly, "and stop shouting. I think shouting must be a fallacy too." [148]

With an immense effort of will, I modulated my voice. "All right," I said. "You're a logician. Let's look at this thing logically. How could you choose Petey Burch over me? Look at me—a brilliant student, a tremendous intellectual, a man with an assured future. Look at Petey —a knothead, a jitterbug, a guy who'll never know where his next meal is coming from. Can you give me one logical reason why you should go steady with Petey Burch?" [149]

"I certainly can," declared Polly. "He's got a raccoon coat." [150]

PURPOSE AND STRUCTURE

1. While Shulman's purpose is to amuse, his method is classification of logical fallacies. Why begin with "Cool I was and logical" (par. 1)? Why end with "Can you give me one logical reason" (par. 149)? Would you classify Polly's answer (par. 150) as a logical fallacy?

2. Why does the narrator argue that "the things you learn in school don't have anything to do with life" (par. 141)?

3. The narrator decides that Polly is "worthy of me at last" (par. 120). Is she?

4. Does the narrator love Polly (pars. 20, 121)? Discuss. Is love a fallacy?

5. Why is it appropriate that there are rational (par. 13) objections to raccoon coats: "Raccoon coats are unsanitary. They shed. They smell bad. They weigh too much. They're unsightly" (par. 13); they are "huge, hairy, gamy" (par. 38) objects; they look "like a mound of dead raccoons" (par. 54)? Why is it appropriate that Polly should decide to go steady with Petey Burch because of his raccoon coat (par. 150)?

6. Are the narrator's answers to Petey logical (pars. 46, 49, 51, 53)?

7. Much of the humor of Shulman's piece is a result of the unexpected classification—into the various categories of logical fallacies—of the narrator's arguments by Polly. Why is this process of classification amusing to the reader?

DICTION AND TONE

1. At table Polly's manners were exquisite (par. 23). Characterize the tone of the example given.

2. Characterize Polly's diction (for instance, in par. 57).

3. The topic sentence of par. 47 is "He was a torn man." What is the tone of the paragraph?

4. What is the tone of "Maybe somewhere in the extinct crater of her mind, a few embers still smoldered" (par. 94)?

5. What is the tone of the fully developed metaphor in par. 119?

6. Why does the narrator refer to Pygmalion (par. 121)? Why does the narrator refer to Frankenstein (par. 134)?

7. Does the narrator want Polly "for a shrewdly calculated, entirely cerebral reason" (par. 20)?

8. The narrator's brain "was as powerful as a dynamo, as precise as a chemist's scales, as penetrating as a scalpel" (par. 1). What happened when this "massive brain" (par. 130) chose the proper words for a declaration of love?

9. What is the tone of "The dear child had learned her lessons well" (par. 128)?

APPLICATIONS TO WRITING

1. Is love a fallacy? Write a skit or informal narration that classifies some of the logical fallacies caused by love. (Select appropriate fallacies from Shulman.)

2. Polly classifies the narrator's arguments expertly. Apply her method in an argument—write a dialogue—on who shall wash the dishes.

Eastern Cults and Western Culture: Why Young Americans Are Buying Oriental Religions

HARVEY COX

An old Zen story tells of a pilgrim who mounted his horse and crossed formidable mountains and swift rivers seeking a famous roshi, or wise man, in order to ask him how to find true enlightenment. After months of searching, the pilgrim located the teacher in a cave. The roshi listened to the question, and said nothing. The seeker waited. Finally, after hours of silence, the roshi looked at the steed on which the pilgrim had arrived, and asked the pilgrim why he was not looking for a horse instead of enlighten- ment. The pilgrim responded that obviously he already had a horse. The roshi smiled, and retreated to his cave.

In the past decade, this country has seen dozens of Eastern religious cults and movements spring up and flourish, attracting thousands of American youths who are searching for truth, brotherhood, and author- ity. What has provoked this neo-Oriental religious revival? Who are the people caught up in it? Why have they left some more conventional religious life—or none at all—to become seekers or adherents in these new spiritual movements? What does it all mean for American cul- ture? [1]

Large numbers of people are involved in this quest, not just a fringe group. And the extent of their interest has no precedent in American religious history. Although overall estimates vary widely—partly be- cause the movements themselves tend to overstate their membership—I would guess that by now several million Americans have been touched one way or another by some form of neo-Oriental thought or devotional practice. I base this guess not only on the number of actual adherents, but also on those who practice—regularly or sporadically—various forms of meditation, or whose practice of karate or the martial arts goes beyond self-defense to their underlying Buddhist philosophy. [2]

To learn why people join these movements and practice these dis- ciplines, I and some of my students at Harvard Divinity School spent three years informally studying dozens of such groups currently op- erating in Cambridge, Massachusetts. Some of the students were already involved in the movements, while most of them were just curious about what meaning they had to their adherents, why people had joined, and what they were looking for. [3]

To find out, we visited the centers to observe, participate in the meet- ings and the rituals, and talk with the devotees. [4]

Cambridge is known throughout the country primarily as the home of Harvard University. But in recent years it has also become a thriving center of Eastern religious cults and movements, prompting one of my friends to call it "Benares-on-the-Charles." [5]

Within walking distance of Harvard Square, one can find dozens of different neo-Oriental religious movements. A few blocks away stands the Zen center, furnished with black silk cushions, bells, an appropriately wizened and wise-looking resident master, and a visiting Zen swordplay instructor. In the basement of a nearby Episcopal church, the Sufi dancers meet twice a week to twist and turn like the legendary whirling dervishes in a ritual circle, chanting verses from the Koran. Down the street is the Ananda Marga center, specializing in a combination of meditation and community action. [6]

A few blocks south sits the headquarters of the Hare Krishnas, officially known as the International Society for Krishna Consciousness. There, the devotees hold a weekly feast of savory Indian food and a somewhat less piquant introductory lecture on the mysteries of the Krishna devotion. The clean-shaven followers of the chubby young guru, the Maharaj Ji, have a meeting place near Central Square. A group of self-styled Sikhs, immaculately clad in white robes, turbans, and daggers, have opened a vegetarian restaurant called the Golden Temple of Conscious Cookery. Nearby is the International Student Meditation Center, founded several years ago by the Maharishi Mahesh Yoga, the best known of the swamis of the late '60s, where one can learn the art of "transcendental meditation." Recent arrivals include the followers of guru Sri Chinmoy, a former postal clerk living in Queens; the Dharma House, founded by Chogyam Trungpa Rinpoche, the Tibetan Buddhist lama; and dozens of smaller, less stable groups devoted to yoga, Tai Chi, and other exotic pursuits. [7]

I knew that no matter how hard I tried to maintain scholarly objectivity, my inner distrust for all "opiates of the people" might continue to influence me. But I decided to do the study anyway. Although my prejudice against some of the movements was undeniable, I was at least fully aware of it. [8]

During the first several weeks of the study my students and I all had a marvelous time. Together and separately we attended dozens of meditation sessions, feasts, satsangs, introductory lectures, inquirers' meetings, worship services, and study circles. The groups we visited were invariably hospitable. We asked questions, read stacks of tracts and pamphlets, watched, listened, and filled up stacks of tape cartridges. For once we were getting something straight from the source instead of from textbooks. [9]

With all our research, however, I felt something was lacking. As the notebooks piled up, I began to wonder what it would feel like to be on the inside of one of the movements. No one can hope to experience another person's faith as he does. And as a Christian and a professional theologian I realized I was neither a genuine Oriental pilgrim nor an authentic seeker. I was intrigued, curious, fascinated, but not a devotee. Still, I realized I would have to pursue some kind of "inside" knowing and feeling if I were going to understand the disciples I was studying. So I tried to become as much of a participant as I could. I did not merely observe the Sufi dancers; I whirled too. I did not just read about Zen, or visit centers; I "sat." I chanted with the Hare Krishnas. I stood on my head, stretched my torso, and breathed deeply with the yoga practitioners. I spent hours softly intoning a mantra to myself in a favorite form of Hindu devotional practice. [10]

I became a participant not because I thought there was actually something in it for me, but because I wanted to nourish my capacity for empathy. I wanted to find out what I could about the lure of the East on the visceral level. This participant-observer phase of my inquiry took me far away from Benares-on-the-Charles. It led me to spiritual centers in California, Colorado, Texas, and Vermont, and into conversations with Zen abbots, Sufi drummers, and Divine Light devotees. [11]

Only after my search became personal did I finally hit on an approach which seemed both faithful to the movements, and helpful in interpreting them to other people. I had become interested in Eastern spirituality for personal reasons, with a host of internal reservations. My purposes were clearly different from those advanced by the teachers themselves. I was quite sure that mine was a most unusual case. I soon discovered, however, it was not. Once I got to know them, nearly all the people I met turned out to have personal reasons that often had little to do with the official teaching of the movement's leaders. This discovery provided me with the clue I needed. I decided to concentrate not on what the movements and their leaders claim to offer, but on what the individuals who turn to them actually find. [12]

The "East turners" we found in these movements have not moved to India to live in an ashram. They have not left home for the Orient to dwell in a Tibetan temple or a Zen monastery. They still live in Texas or Ohio or New York or somewhere else in the United States. They have not *gone* East, they have *turned* East. There are true seekers and frivolous dilettantes, converts and fellow travelers. Their interest comes in widely varying degrees of seriousness and persistence: some merely sneak a glance at a paperback edition of the *I Ching* or try some yoga postures; others find that one of the Eastern practices becomes im-

portant to them; others leave everything behind and sleep on mats in a
Hare Krishna temple. [13]

One way to find out what kind of people join these movements is to
determine the standard sociological data of their social class, age, race,
sex, education, and ethnic background. Such studies have been done,
but they leave much unsaid. The participants tend to be young, in their
late teens or early 20s. Although some early teen-agers learn how to do
yoga, or read a little Eastern philosophy, few become seriously involved
until late adolescence. The 20s are the prime turning time. [14]

The Eastern religious movements are made up almost exclusively of
white, educated, middle- and upper-middle-class young people. Most
have at least begun college, although some have dropped out after a
year or two. Men and women seem to participate in fairly equal numbers, but men control the leadership groups. There is no predominance
of any particular regional background, although more of the devotees
seem to come from urban than from rural areas, probably because the
movements are generally based in cities. [15]

These young people come from all religious denominations, with
relatively more from liberal Protestant and reform Jewish backgrounds
than the proportion of these groups in the general population would
suggest. This is not surprising, considering the urban, middle-class,
educated milieu in which these groups recruit most of their members.
Few come from strongly atheistic or unusually pious homes. They seem
to have received some religion from their parents, but not enough to
satisfy them. [16]

Despite all these statistics and data and categories, we still don't
know much about the actual human beings who have made this decisive choice. So my students and I asked the people themselves to tell
us in their own words what they found in the groups they belonged to.
Their answers varied, but as we sorted through them, several definite
patterns emerged. [17]

1. Most of the members of these movements seem to be looking for
simple human *friendship*. The reply we heard most often, especially
from those actually living in religious communes or ashrams, told a
story of loneliness, isolation, and the search for a supportive community.
To paraphrase a large number of replies:

They seem to care for me here. I was bummed out, confused, just
wandering around. When I first came here I didn't know what they

*were talking about. They all seemed crazy, and I told them so. But that
didn't seem to bother them. They took me in. They made me feel at
home. Now I feel like I'm a part of it, an important part, too. I belong
here. It's where I was meant to be.* [18]

The newer the convert, the more likely this reply. After a few weeks,
however, the novices begin to learn a more theologically proper answer,
such as, *Krishna called me here,* or *It was my karma.* Many seekers who
drift into such movements looking for intimacy quickly learn to express
their reasons in the group argot. But the need for plain friendship is
clearly their chief motivation. They are looking for warmth, affection,
and close ties of feeling. They don't find it at work, at school, in
churches they attend, or even at home. But they do seem to find it, at
least for a while, in the community of devotees. The groups we visited
provide an island of companionship in what the adherents feel is a
world devoid of fraternity. [19]

2. The East turners are also looking for a way to experience life directly, without the intervention of ideas and concepts. They seek a
kind of *immediacy* they have not been able to find elsewhere. Even
though some young people drift from movement to movement, they do
not seem to be looking for just another kick or "trip" to add to their
collection. [20]

Most are serious, and want a real, personal encounter with God, or
simply with life, nature, and other people:

*All I got at any church I ever went to were sermons or homilies about
God, about "the peace that passes understanding." Words, words, words.
It was all up in the head. I never really felt it. It was all abstract, never
direct, always somebody else's account of it. It was dull and boring. I'd
sit or kneel or stand. I'd listen to or read prayers. But it seemed lifeless.
It was like reading the label instead of eating the contents.* [21]

*But here it really happened to me. I experienced it myself. I don't
have to take someone else's word for it.* [22]

This testimony of direct experience became more understandable
when we noticed that nearly all the neo-Oriental movements include
instruction in some form of spiritual discipline. Initiates learn the
primary techniques of prayer, chanting, contemplation, or meditation.
Teachers rely not only on words, as in most Western religious training,
but also on actual techniques—either quite simple, as in transcendental
meditation, or complex, as in Zen—for inducing the desired forms of

consciousness. At the local Zen center, for example, the teachers sit you down immediately to face a blank wall, and smilingly refuse to answer all but the most elementary questions until you have taken the practical step of trying to meditate. Even after that they keep the ideas to a minimum. Practice and direct exposure are the keys to the kingdom. [23]

3. Some East turners are looking for *authority*. They have turned East to find truth, to lay hold on a message or teaching they can believe and trust. They join these groups as refugees from uncertainty and doubt. They often stress the role of the particular swami or guru whose wisdom or charismatic power has caused such a change in their lives: *I tried everything. I read all the books, went to lectures, listened to different teachers. But all that happened was that I got more confused. I couldn't think straight any more. I couldn't get myself together or make any decisions. Then I met him, and what he said finally made sense. Everything finally clicked. I knew he was for real. I could tell just from the way he spoke that he knew. Now my confusion is over.* [24]

The quest for authority results from a wide range of factors documented by dozens of sociologists: the dissolution of conventional moral codes; the erosion of traditional authorities; the emergence of what Alvin Toffler, the author of *Future Shock,* once called "over-choice." As a result, large numbers of people have begun to suffer a kind of choice-fatigue. They hunger for an authority that will simplify, straighten out, assure; something or somebody that will make their choices fewer and less arduous. For some, the search for authority ends at the swami's feet. [25]

4. A smaller number of people told us in one way or another that they had turned to the East because somehow it seemed more *natural*. These people also seem to have changed their faith-orientation more self-consciously than others, and with deliberate rejection of what they consider the effete, corrupt, or outworn religious tradition of the West. They see in Eastern spirituality a kind of unspoiled purity. In contrast to Western faith, the East seems artless, simple, and fresh. They could often tell us why they had turned *from* some Western religion more clearly than they could say why they had turned *toward* the East. [26]

Western civilization is shot. It is nothing but technology and power and rationalization, corrupted to its core by power and money. It has no contact with nature, feeling, spontaneity. What we need to do now is

learn from the Oriental peoples who have never been ruined by ma-
chines and science, who have kept close to their ancestors' simplicity.
Western religion has invalidated itself. Now only the East is pos-
sible. [27]

The people who talked to us in this vein were often the most widely
read and best educated of the East turners. They could often cite evidence more specifically and phrase their arguments more clearly than
the others. Though they did not put it this way themselves, to me their
decision to turn East often seemed to have some of the quality of a puri-
fication ritual. It was as though they were going through the Western
equivalent of a bath in the Ganges, shedding the tainted and the im-
pure. [28]

These then are the reasons most East turners cite for their choice:
they seek friendship; a direct experience of God and the world; a way
out of intellectual and moral confusion; and a kind of innocence, or a
way of life unmarred by technological overkill. This list of goals shows
that East turners are really not very different from anyone else. They
are looking for what many other people in America are looking for today. They have merely chosen a more visible and dramatic way of looking. The real question, of course, is will they find it? [29]

The ironic aspect of the Turn East is that it is occurring just as many
millions of Asians are involved in an epochal "Turn West" toward
Western science and technology, Western political systems, and Western cultural forms. Just as this great awakening to history has begun to
occur in the real Asia, millions of Americans have fallen in love with
an Asia that is disappearing, or maybe never existed: the "mysterious
Orient" of the old Western myth. In fact, those who yearn for what
they call an "Oriental" approach today are really opting for an archaic
rather than a historical way of life. They may be turning back instead
of turning East. [30]

Two kinds of replies from East turners disturb me because they reveal
a quest that will lead not just to disillusionment but to frustration and
bitterness. One can sympathize with those who hope to regain a lost
innocence—a world free of complications, a world of black and white
choices. But eventually they will find out that no such world will ever
be found. For maturity means learning to live in a complex, shades-of-
gray world. [31]

I feel similar qualms about those who long for an authority so un-questionable and total that they would not have to make hard decisions or chew through choices on their own. [32]

At first, converts to these movements often do seem to find a kind of new innocence. They are "blissed out" with their hassle-free life. The emphasis many of these groups place on the inner life, plus their relega-tion of secular society to an inferior form of reality, means that ad-hering to their teachings will remove the uncomfortable tensions of school, work, or home. Since money, power, and, in some cases, even the capacity to make choices are viewed as illusory or insignificant, the causes of most political tussles disappear. The problem is that the nasty issues of work, politics, and the rest do not really disappear, and even East turners must eventually grapple with them. But as devotees they must do so with a world view that gives them little help, because it re-fuses to recognize that the problems even exist. [33]

I am also troubled by the pursuit of an absolute religious and moral authority that will relieve the discomfort of making decisions. People who hunger for this kind of authority over them suffer from the wounds dealt out by parents, schools, and jobs where they have never been en-couraged to flex their decision-making capabilities. But in order to ma-ture, the last thing they need is one more perfect master to solve their problems for them. [34]

They need friends and families and larger settings in which their confidence in their own capacities will be strengthened. [35]

What the East turners are doing is hardly a prescription for a general cure; rather, it is a symptom of a malaise with which we must all con-tend. Religious remedies to the ills of a culture take two basic forms: one tries to get at the underlying causes of the malady; the other pro-vides a way for people to live in spite of the illness, usually by providing them with an alternative miniworld, sufficiently removed from the one outside so that its perils are kept away from the gate. The East turners have almost all chosen this second form. The only solution they offer to other people is to join them in their miniworld. [36]

But if we all join them, it would soon be a maxiworld with all the problems back again. Part of the answer is that these movements cannot be the answer for everyone. Some East turners have found a haven from the impersonality and vacuousness of the larger society, and, some would say, of its churches. They have rightly located the most severe symptoms of our ailing era. But their solution, though it may work for them individually, at least for a while, is ultimately no solution for the rest of us. [37]

As for the movements themselves, I also worry about their future. For the business of America is business, and that includes the religion business. The greatest irony of the Eastern religious movements is that in their effort to present an alternative to the Western way of life, most have succeeded in adding only one more line of spiritual products to the American religious marketplace. They have become a part of the consumer culture they set out to call in question. [38]

This consumerization of the new religious movements should not surprise us. After all, the genius of any consumer society is its capacity for changing anything, including its critics, into items for distribution and sale. Religious teachings and disciplines—Eastern or Western—can be transformed into commodities, assigned prices, packaged attractively, and made available to prospective buyers. [39]

Conspicuous consumption is no longer a mark of distinction. What we have in its place is something I call the new gluttony, which transforms the entire range of human ideas and emotions into a well-stocked pantry. Today, only the old-fashioned glutton still stuffs his mouth with too many entrees. The new glutton craves experiences: in quantity and variety, more and better, increasingly exotic, and even spiritual. Today's money does not lust after houses, cars, and clothes, but travel, drugs, unusual sights and sounds, exotic tastes, therapies, and new emotional states. If disgrace haunts the affluent, it is not apt to be for failing to *have* something, but rather for failing to have *tried* something. The very thought that out there lurks an experience one has not had now sends the affluent into panic. [40]

No doubt economists as well as theologians could advance explanations for why we are moving from a greed for things to a gluttony of experience. In a system based on encouraging greed, people eventually become sated. It is hard to sell still another television set to the family that already has one in every room. There is a limit somewhere to what most people can stack up. [41]

With experiences, however, there seems to be no such limit, and the experience merchants do not need to plan obsolescence or invent style changes. Their product self-destructs immediately, except for one's memory. Last year's model is unusable not for any reason as trivial as changing hemlines but because it is gone. [42]

Economists can explain the new gluttony in the classical terms of a movement from goods to services. It is the old story of expanding markets, finding new resources and developing novel products. But now the product is an experience that can be sold and delivered to a customer. The resources are virtually infinite for the imaginative entrepreneur, and the market is that growing group of people whose hunger for accumulating mere things has begun to decline. [43]

I think there is an element of spiritual gluttony in the current fascination with Oriental spirituality. We should not blame this on the Oriental traditions themselves, most of which are highly sensitive to the pitfalls of spiritual pride. Nor can we blame the often anguished people who are driven by forces they can neither control nor understand toward searching out more and more exhilarating spiritual experiences. [44]

If there is any fault to be allocated, it lies not with the victims but with the buyer-seller nexus within which the new religious wave is marketed. Despite what may be good intentions all around, the consumer mentality can rot the fragile fruits of Eastern spirituality as soon as they are unpacked. The process is both ironic and pathetic. What begins in Benares as a protest against possessiveness ends up in Boston as still another possession. [45]

No deity, however terrible, no devotion, however deep, no ritual, however splendid, is exempt from the voracious process of trivialization. The smiling Buddha himself and the worldly wise Krishna can be transformed by the new gluttony into collectors' trinkets. It was bad enough for King Midas that everything he touched turned to gold. The acquisition-accumulation pattern of the new gluttony does even more. Reversing the alchemist's course, it transforms rubies and emeralds into plastic, the sacred into the silly, the holy into the hokey. [46]

The gods of the Orient mean one thing there, and something quite different here. This is not to be blamed either on the gods themselves, or on their original devotees, or on their new seekers. It happens because when the gods migrate, or are transported to a civilization where everything is to some extent a commodity, they become commodities too. [47]

The culture barrier that a commodity culture erects against the possibility of genuine interreligious exchange is formidable. It raises the question of whether we in the West can ever hear the voice of the East, can ever learn about the Buddhist or Hindu paths without corrupting them in the process. [48]

Although America today *seems* uncommonly receptive to spiritual ideas and practices from the East, the truth is that we are not really receptive to them at all. True, no stone walls have been erected to keep the pagans out. No orders of Knights Templar have ridden forth to hurl back the infidels. The gates are open, and the citizens seem ready to listen. No wonder many Eastern teachers view America as a fertile ground in which to sow their seeds. [49]

But curiously it is precisely America's receptivity, its eagerness to hear, explore, and experience, that creates the most difficult barrier to our actually learning from Eastern spirituality. The very insatiable hunger for novelty, for intimacy, even for a kind of spirituality that motivates so many Americans to turn toward the East also virtually guarantees that the turn will ultimately fail. [50]

The final paradox is that Easterners have never claimed to be able to save the West. Frequently they deny having any interest in doing so, even if they could. They rarely send missionaries here, and they accept Western novices with reluctance. Although the Western versions of Eastern faiths often claim to bring salvation to the West, at this point they betray the spirit of their sources, and actually worsen the Western dilemma by advertising more than they can deliver. [51]

The spiritual crisis of the West will not be resolved by spiritual importations or individual salvation. It is the crisis of a whole civilization, and one of its major symptoms is the belief that the answer must come from Elsewhere. The crisis can be met only when the West sets aside myths of the Orient, and returns to its own primal roots. [52]

Eventually the spiritual disciplines of the Orient will make a profound contribution to our consciousness and our way of life. Some day, somewhere, we will hear the message the East has for us. But we can only begin to know the real Orient when we are willing to let go of the mythical one. And we can only begin to hear the message of the Oriental religious traditions when we are willing to confront the inner dislocations in our own civilization that caused us to invent the myth of the East in the first place. And when we are willing to do that, we may realize, like the truth seeker in the Zen parable, that what we are seeking so frantically elsewhere may turn out to be the horse we have been riding all along. [53]

PURPOSE AND STRUCTURE

1. How does the Zen story that introduces the essay relate to the author's thesis?

2. The first eleven paragraphs introduce the questions to be explored, the range and possible numbers of Western religious cults, and the author's admitted bias and his efforts to correct for it. As he tried to nourish his capacity for empathy, what discovery provided the clue he needed for an unbiased investigation?

3. What rhetorical devices are used in par. 12 to give emphasis? To what generalization do the particulars lead?

4. Why does the author negate the data supplied in pars. 12–16?

5. The several patterns that emerged after face-to-face interviews were initiated are descriptive of human needs. What are they?

6. How does par. 24 serve as a transitional paragraph? What causal relationship is established?

7. How is comparison and contrast used (pars. 25–27) to clarify one of the reasons for turning East?

8. Par. 28 summarizes the goals of those who have turned East. What other rhetorical and substantive purpose is served by this paragraph?

9. How does Cox's definition of maturity (par. 31) relate to the goals of those who have turned East?

10. With what arguments does Cox offer his view that turning East is a symptom of the ills of the culture?

11. How does Cox support his view that Eastern religious movements have become a part of the consumer culture?

12. How does Cox explain the paradox: "What begins in Benares as a protest against possessiveness ends up in Boston as still another possession" (par. 45)?

13. How do you reconcile the point of view in the final paragraph with the writer's attack on the "East turners"?

14. Justify including this essay under Classification.

DICTION AND TONE

1. Compare the diction and tone of the direct quotes from the "East turners" with those of the writer. How do the italicized comments serve the author's purpose?

2. Examine the figures of speech in par. 27. How do they relate to the direct quotation in par. 26?

3. How does the figurative language in pars. 39–45 acquaint the reader with the difference between what Cox calls "the new gluttony" and "conspicuous consumption"?

4. How do these paragraphs reflect a shift in tone? Identify the tone. What is the paradox in par. 49?

APPLICATIONS TO WRITING

1. Place into categories the ways in which you attempt to satisfy the needs that have led millions of people to respond to one or more Eastern religions.

2. If you have participated in or been sympathetic toward one of the Eastern cults, analyze the reasons for its appeal to you.

3. Classify any group of people you have observed closely in accordance with a clear principle of organization, such as their backgrounds, their personalities, their behavior, or the beliefs they espouse.

Paranoia

HENDRIK HERTZBERG
DAVID C. K. McCLELLAND

Three people, Phil and Sam and Lucy, are at a party. They share enough common experiences, beliefs, and preconceptions to be having a chat. Each contributes, by his talk or by his attentiveness, about as much as the others contribute. Everyone is having a good time. Everyone *seems* to be having a good time. [1]

But suppose Phil is really having a bad time. Perhaps he feels ugly or stupid or out of it; perhaps he is merely depressed. He might excuse himself and go home, but he is afraid of being thought unsociable, so he stays and lets his mind fasten on some premise that seems to explain why he is not enjoying himself. His thoughts begin to congeal around the explanatory premise, which is probably something like, *I'm bad and unhappy and they know it* or *I'm bad and unhappy and they don't know it.* [2]

The conversation goes on:

Lucy: Did you see that new Altman movie—what's it called? [3]
Sam: *Thieves Like Us.* [4]
Phil: Yeah, I saw that. [5]
Sam: Me too. [6]
Lucy: What did you think of it? [7]
Sam: I think it's overrated. [8]

Meanwhile, Phil struggles to establish a connection between the conversation and his premise. He may be thinking, *Why are they talking about movies? They must notice that I'm horrible and miserable, but they know there's no way they can help, so they're trying to take my mind off it.* [9]

Or he may be thinking, *Why are they talking about movies? It must be because they don't notice I'm horrible and miserable. They couldn't care less how I feel.* [10]

Phil fails to notice, among other things, that he, too, is talking about movies. His mind is so full of his own wretchedness that he assumes Sam and Lucy are also preoccupied with it. (The only alternative is that Sam and Lucy are callous and unfeeling.) In fact, Sam and Lucy may simply think they are at a party talking about movies. [11]

Phil, so far, is suffering from little more than a lousy mood. But suppose that Phil's condition is more serious. Suppose that he is paranoid. In that event, the premise dominating his mind will be far from simple, and it will explain far more than why he is unhappy. The premise might be, for example, that an elaborate Mafia conspiracy is trying to control his life. Now Phil will have to work harder to interpret the conversation in a way that "proves" his premise. [12]

Lucy: Did you see that new Altman movie—what's it called? (Phil thinks, *You know damn well what it's called.*) [13]

SAM: *Thieves Like Us.* (Phil thinks, *Thieves indeed. What could be more obvious? You can't fool me.*) [14]

PHIL: Yeah, I saw that. (Phil thinks, *Don't kid yourselves that I don't know what you're really talking about.*) [15]

SAM: Me too. (Phil thinks, *So you know I know—is that what you're saying?*) [16]

LUCY: What did you think of it? (Phil thinks, *You're trying to invade my thoughts.*) [17]

SAM: I think it's overrated. (Phil thinks, *Of course you do—those thieves only steal money, you steal minds.*)
Phil is clearly in a bad way. [18]

A LITTLE SEMANTICS

Paranoia is a word on everyone's lips, but only among mental-health professionals has it acquired a tolerably specific meaning. It refers to a psychosis based on a delusionary premise of self-referred persecution or grandeur (e.g., "The Knights of Columbus control the world and are out to get me," "I am Norman Mailer"), and supported by a complex, rigorously logical system that interprets all or nearly all sense impressions as evidence for that premise. The traditional psychiatric view is that paranoia is an extreme measure for the defense of the integrity of the personality against annihilating guilt. The paranoid (so goes the theory) thrusts his guilt outside himself by denying his hostile or erotic impulses and projecting them onto other people or onto the whole universe. Disintegration is avoided, but at high cost: the paranoid view of reality can make everyday life terrifying and social intercourse problematical. And paranoia is tiring. It requires exhausting mental effort to construct trains of thought demonstrating that random events or details "prove" a wholly unconnected premise. Some paranoids hallucinate, but hallucination is by no means obligatory; paranoia is an interpretive, not a perceptual, dysfunction. [19]

Paranoia is a recent cultural disorder. It follows the adoption of rationalism as the quasiofficial religion of Western man and the collapse of certain communitarian bonds (the extended family, belief in God, the harmony of the spheres) which once made sense of the universe in all its parts. Paranoia substitutes a rigorous (though false) order for chaos, and at the same time dispels the sense of individual insignificance by making the paranoid the focus of all he sees going on around him—a natural response to the confusion of modern life. [20]

Strictly speaking, there was no such thing as paranoia before the mid-nineteenth century, when the word (from the Greek for "beside" and "mind") first surfaced as one of several medical-sounding euphemisms for madness. In an earlier age, the states of mind now explained as paranoia were accounted for differently. The vastness of the difference is suggested if one reflects on the likehood of a president of France placing the command of his country's armed forces in the hands of a teen-age peasant girl who hears voices from God. [21]

Even more recent is the wholesale adoption of the terms "paranoia" and "paranoid" into everyday speech as metaphors for a bewildering variety of experiences. Hippies could no more communicate their thoughts without using "paranoia" and "paranoid" than they could eschew "like," "y'know," and "I mean." In this context the meanings of the terms are blurry but readily comprehensible. "Man, are you ever paranoid." This is not meant as a compliment. The implication is that the accused is imagining a threat where none exists. "I mean, she really makes me paranoid." The speaker feels that "she" is more powerful than he is, making him uncomfortable. "There was a lot of paranoia at that concert." One gathers that the security precautions were excessive. "No thanks, man, I get really paranoid when I smoke dope." Here paranoia is merely a euphemism for fear. "I'm paranoid" is less disturbing, for both speaker and listener, than "I'm frightened." (Psychiatric terminology is central to contemporary etiquette. One says, "I'm having trouble relating to you." One does not say, "I hate your guts.") [22]

In politics, paranoia is a logical consequence of the wrenching loose of power from the rigid social arrangements that once conditioned its exercise, and the resulting preoccupation with questions of "dominate or be dominated." Political and quasipolitical notions, such as the conviction that the telephone company is manipulating reality in order to control one's mind, appear routinely in the delusions of persons suffering from paranoid psychosis. In American public life, as Richard Hofstadter showed in *The Paranoid Style in American Politics*, persecutory themes have cropped up periodically from the beginning. Groups widely believed to have been at the center of the shifting conspiracy against the common weal have at various times included the Masons, the Papists, the Illuminati, Wall Street, the gold hoarders, the outside agitators, the Communists, and—bringing us up to the present—the pointy-headed bureaucrats, the Establishment, the system, the straights, the New Left nihilists, the Mafia, the oil companies, the media, and the CIA.[1] As Lincoln said, you can fool some of the people all of the time. [23]

The Nixon years have been something of a Golden Age of political paranoia. The paranoid strategies of projection, denial, and the use of code language with private meanings ("law and order," "peace with honor," "executive privilege")[2] have been played out on a national scale. The Nixon Administration saw politics as an array of reified conspiracies against it ("the criminal forces as against the peace forces," the Chicago defendants, Ellsberg, the campus bums, the radiclibs, the media) and behaved accordingly. The unprecedented security arrangements at the Washington headquarters of the Committee to Re-Elect the President, designed to counter an imaginary threat of political burglary and wire-tapping, were entrusted to precisely the people who carried out the po-litical burglary and wiretapping of the Democratic National Commit-tee. When the crimes and conspiracies known as Watergate began to come to light, the Administration's two basic responses were denial ("I am not a crook") and projection ("everybody does it"). During the fuss over Pentagon thievery of documents belonging to Henry Kissinger, one "White House source" described his colleagues as "a bunch of paranoids spying on each other." [24]

DOUBLE SPACE

Zero is an extremely bright, self-taught, experimental electronics engi-neer who was the central figure in a small cult in Pontiac, Michigan, one of thousands of local paranoid cults produced by the late counter-culture. Zero and his friends made pilgrimages to hear Pink Floyd, a rock group to whose music and lyrics they attached great importance. They occasionally ingested psychedelic drugs and made midnight visits

[1] The CIA turns up in paranoid delusions perhaps more than any other single organization. Its name is extremely suggestive—"central," "intelligence," and "agency" are all words rich in multiple meanings—and, since the CIA does in fact engage in conspiratorial activities, it can easily be adapted for any scheme involving domination and control by unseen forces. Freud always maintained that every paranoid delusion contains a nugget of truth [Hertzberg and McClel-land's note].

[2] "I don't have to spell it out," the President told a group of milk producers during a tape-recorded meeting [Hertzberg and McClelland's note].

to the main office building of Pontiac Motors, where they intoned mock prayers at the chain-link fence protecting the "temple," a white office monolith lit by floodlights. [25]

Zero lived in a house which would take as long to describe as it would to explicate *Finnegans Wake*.[3] He had used an old chicken coop, later a lampshade factory, as the shell. Inside, he had created an environment from electronic and other debris. The house was too disorienting to be merely a straightforward collection of symbolic junk. No object's use was related to its name. Something that looked and worked like a floor lamp turned out to be a fence post, a telescope, and a plastic cake stand, wired to produce light. Aggregates of machines played the radioactive emissions from one's body back through guitar amplifiers hung from the ceiling. Visual punning marked nearly every object in the house. Overall, it had the impact of a brilliant work of art. But Zero did not consider himself an artist; he regarded his house as a means of self-protection, not of self-expression. [26]

Zero's speech, like his house, was disorienting. In the monologue below, reconstructed by John Farrah, a writer and friend of Zero's, Zero discourses on the great conspiracy he devoted so much energy to protecting himself from. [27]

This isn't something I usually run down. People don't want to hear about it. They figure that if this is true then what's the use. Even if somebody brave like the *National Enquirer* ran it down, which I suppose is impossible, nobody could handle it. [28]

Here's the deal. There's this thing, you know, that would like us all to be very nice polite robots. First, they planned to build androids to replace us. It would either be when you're sleeping or at work or in jail. I used to think that this was unbelievable, but I got busted once, and they really dug on beating me up. I'm sure they get off on offing people, too. You've heard about how every couple of hundred years there's a bunch of people who disappear? Well, they're being offed by GM and getting recycled into new cars. There's a computer under Rochester, Michigan. It completely ran the Vietnam war. That's right, and what's happening now is that the computers of GM have figured out a master scheme to turn us into androids via the food we eat. And McDonald's is the front for the whole thing, and the president of GM is actually Ronald McDonald, who's a front in a scheme to rip off our minds and souls. They're planting

[3] *Finnegans Wake* is James Joyce's last (1939) and most revolutionary experimental novel, notable for its highly complex language and extensive allusions.

electrodes and embalming fluid and synthetic God-knows-what in our food. Did you know that the mostly widely used preservative in white bread is embalming fluid? We're being turned into robots without a hand being laid on us! Maybe those satellites up there are programmed to control us, and it's some kind of worldwide monitoring system. And with all this shit inside us from eating Quarter Pounders that undoubtedly strangle up our minds, who even thinks about all of this? [29]

I worked for Pontiac Motors for a while before I went into the Army, and I used to think that maybe the assembly line was once used to turn our robots. Anyway, there was this food company there that filled all the vending machines and ran the plant cafeterias. It was called Prophet Food. Can you dig that? I mean, it's like saying, "Fuck you, we're going to turn you into androids," you know? Oh, man, I ate one of their hamburgers by mistake once. I got sick and couldn't think straight for a few days. Anyway, every day the workers came in like perfect robots and made the cars that were probably melted down years later and made into bombs or something. Hardly anybody picks up on it—you just had a Big Mac or some other kind of poison and you're driving around trying to relate to the cops. Who's going to be able to think about Pontiac Motors? I mean, you gotta get up tomorrow and be there at 6:28 anyway. So pick up a six-pack and forget about it. It's the whole system. It's its own preservative. And it doesn't matter where you work, man, 'cause it's all GM. Generous Motors. What else is there to say? No one believes it. No one dares even think about it. But it's not their fault. We're all just calcium propionate on this bus. [30]

Like his house, Zero's monologue makes one think of art. The hamburger conspiracy is a striking metaphor for the life Zero sees around him. But Zero is innocent of satiric purpose. He has turned the metaphor on its head. It is not a metaphor to him; it is reality, and he lives inside it. [31]

It is a commonplace of both art and psychology that the line between madness and genius is sometimes difficult to draw. But Zero would seem to fall on one side of it, and a self-aware artist like Thomas Pynchon on the other. In his novel *The Crying of Lot 49,* Pynchon presents a massive conspiracy discovered by a young Southern California housewife, Oedipa Maas. As she begins to find connections between Tupperware, her psychiatrist, a giant corporation called Yoyodyne, perpetual-motion machines, an underground postal system called WASTE, the Mafia, a Jacobean tragedy, the German noble family of Thurn und Taxis, and so on, Oedipa begins to doubt her sanity. [32]

Change your name to Miles, Dean, Serge, and/or Leonard, baby, she advised her reflection in the half-light of that afternoon's vanity mirror. Either way, they'll call it paranoia. They. Either you have stumbled indeed, without the aid of LSD or other indole alkaloids, onto a secret richness and concealed density of dream; onto a network by which X number of Americans are truly communicating whilst reserving their lies, recitations of routine, arid betrayals of spiritual poverty, for the official government delivery system; maybe even onto a real alternative to the existlessness, to the absence of surprise to life, that harrows the head of everybody American you know, and you too, sweetie. Or you are hallucinating it. Or a plot has been mounted against you, so expensive and elaborate, involving items like the forging of stamps and ancient books, constant surveillance of your movements, planting of post horn images all over San Francisco, bribing of librarians, hiring of professional actors and Pierce Inverarity only knows what-all besides, all financed out of the estate in a way either too secret or too involved for your nonlegal mind to know about even though you are co-executor, so labyrinthine that it must have meaning beyond just a practical joke. Or you are fantasying some such plot, in which case you are a nut, Oedipa, out of your skull. [33]

The Crying of Lot 49, like Pynchon's latest book, *Gravity's Rainbow,* is a story whose plot is a plot—a fiction with the structure of a paranoid delusion. Pynchon verbally (like Zero visually) uses puns, metaphors, and layers of symbols so intricately that he ends by making one doubt one's own sanity—which is his purpose. The codes are never explicit, and therein lies the hostility of the arts of paranoia. The reader (or house guest) must work terribly hard to feel even minimally oriented. Neither in art nor in life is paranoia a generous state of mind. [34]

A USEFUL DISORDER

One of Philip K. Dick's most delightful science-fiction novels, *Clans of the Alphane Moon,* is full of paranoids. The story unfolds on an obscure moon that colonists from Earth had used as a mental hospital and then abandoned. Left to their own devices, the former mental patients have organized a workable society, dividing themselves into "clans" according to diagnosis. A psychiatrist from Earth rockets in for a visit, looks around, and speculates on the sociology of the moon. "The paranoids— actually paranoiac schizophrenics—would function as the statesman class," she says. "They'd be in charge of developing political ideology and social programs—they'd have the overall world view." And, she concludes, "Leadership in this society would naturally fall to the paranoids, they'd be superior individuals in terms of initiative, intelligence and just plain innate ability. Of course, they'd have trouble keeping the manics from staging a coup." [35]

No doubt Dick exaggerates. But the fact remains that paranoia (unlike, for example, catatonia) is not necessarily a bar to many kinds of success, including success at leading people. Paranoids, in the course of maintaining and defending their delusionary premises, often develop aptitudes for reasoning, for organization, for argument and persuasion. Paranoids are fond of patterns, and they abhor confusion and uncertainty. For them there are no accidents, and nothing is coincidental. Their dogged tenacity and the supreme confidence with which some of them are able to elucidate their all-embracing theories and nostrums can result in their accession to positions of power. "Though a great many patients with paranoia have to be hospitalized," notes Norman A. Cameron of the Yale School of Medicine, "some do not, and among these an occasional one succeeds in building up a following of persons who believe him to be a genius or inspired." [36]

Paranoids live in a state of perpetual crisis. They are always ready for catastrophe. A psychiatrist has recalled an incident that occurred when he was attached to the staff of a large mental hospital. A gas main had broken, and the poisonous fumes were seeping into the wards. It was vital that the hospital be evacuated, and the staff was undermanned. The expected chaos and panic did not materialize, however, because a group of paranoid schizophrenics, once released from their cells, immediately took charge of the evacuation, organized it, and carried it out quickly and efficiently. These paranoids saw nothing unusual in the fact that the hospital was about to be engulfed by an invisible, deadly, malevolent force. [37]

The average person has many worries, but there is one thing he does not generally worry about. He does not worry that somewhere, without his knowledge, a secret tribunal is about to order him seized, drugged, and imprisoned without the right of appeal. Indeed, anyone who worries overmuch about such a thing, and expresses that worry repeatedly and forcefully enough, would probably be classified as a paranoid schizophrenic. [38]

And, once he is so classified, the probable next step is for a secret tribunal to convene, and, without his knowledge, order him to be seized, drugged, and imprisoned without the right of appeal. Such, at any rate, is the situation in many states of the Union, where commitment laws empower official boards to hospitalize involuntarily a "mentally ill" person whose "illness" renders him unable to appreciate his need for treatment. Whatever else this may prove, it does suggest the power of paranoia to refashion the objective world, as well as the subjective universe, in his own image. [39]

These talents for crisis management and self-fulfilling prophecy are not limited to hospitalized paranoids. Persons who see life as a series of "crises," and who pride themselves on being "the coolest man in the room" when a crisis actually develops, sometimes rise to positions of the highest responsibility. The same is true of people who believe themselves persecuted and harassed by "enemies" who are out to "get" them —and who, as a sort of "protective-reaction strike," persecute and harass these same "enemies." The danger such a person incurs is that with the powers of his high position at his disposal, he may force reality into a conformity with his delusions. He will then find himself besieged by *real* enemies, who will indeed do their best to "get" him. But since such a person has been preparing for precisely this all his life, he will be well equipped to "fight like hell" when his back is against the wall. [40]

MAKING ENEMIES REAL

An individual paranoid may (as one authority puts it) join "some fanatical movement in current vogue, in this way succeeding sometimes in sublimating his excessive zeal and saving himself from further illness." The paranoiac tendencies of social groups sublimate themselves in another fashion. Supermarkets have their security guards; cities have their police forces; states have their state troopers. And nations—which conduct their relations with one another according to rules that are even less binding and explicit than those governing individual behavior—have their armies. [41]

In any large country, it is the solemn duty of the military establishment to be paranoid on behalf of the nation as a whole. Here in the United States, the Department of Defense employs hundreds of superb logicians—"contingency planners"—to imagine the most appalling, most devious, most diabolical horrors that could possibly be perpetrated by other nations against our own. And, so as to be able to deal with any and all such hypothetical nightmares, it employs and equips millions of soldiers, sailors, and airmen at a cost of scores of billions of dollars each year. Although there has not been a large-scale war in nearly thirty years, the Department of Defense maintains at all times what it calls the "capability" of fighting two-and-a-half wars the size of World War II. [42]

The Department of Defense also maintains, at hair-trigger readiness, an arsenal of nuclear weapons, which, if used, would destroy all the major cities of the Soviet Union and China and kill nearly all the people in them. The rationale behind this arsenal is that if we in the United States lacked these weapons, other countries that do possess them would use them against us. Or, to put the rationale more precisely, it is thought to be *more likely* that other countries would attack a disarmed United States than it is thought that the United States and other countries will destroy each other (through inadvertence, miscalculation, or a suicidal-homicidal paroxysm) under the existing "balance of terror" arrangement. [43]

Some people believe that this logic is faulty, that the possibility of an unprovoked nuclear attack on a disarmed United States would be remote—more remote, at least, than the possibility of mutual destruction is now. Some people believe that to maintain an enormously expensive and dangerous "deterrent" against the possibility of such a monstrous, hypothetical crime is to enshrine paranoid delusion as the governing principle of international affairs. The people who believe these things are very few. Most of their fellow citizens regard them as hopelessly naive and unrealistic. [44]

American society at large believes in the usefulness of maintaining an army, but it also recognizes that the military perception of reality is inevitably a distorted one. For this reason, among others, the military has been kept subservient to the civilian authority, even in specifically military matters. The wisdom of this arrangement is apparent when one examines a country like Chile, where the military forces have overthrown the civilian authorities and have begun the task of restructuring society in their own image. When a military government as serious as Chile's goes to work, the result is a terrifying, bloody purge—a kind of political psychotic episode—followed by an attempt to construct a society as rationalized, as well organized, and as free of uncertainty as the most highly articulated paranoid delusion. [45]

POSITIVE PARANOIA

Paranoia is customarily thought of as a distressing experience. It is terrible to be persecuted, even if the perceived mode of persecution happens to be imaginary. Delusions of grandeur, pleasant in themselves, can turn into nightmares when others disbelieve in them. And the shared paranoia of belief in malevolent conspiracies arises from a conviction that something is very wrong with the way things are. [46]

In his book *The Natural Mind*, Andrew Weil describes an anomaly that turned up in psychological testing administered by the Haight-Ashbury Research Project of the Department of Psychiatry of Mount Zion Hospital, in San Francisco. Weil calls this anomaly "positive paranoia." On the Rorschach test, a number of subjects showed a marked "W-tendency." The Rorschach test is a series of ten increasingly fragmented inkblots. Someone who tries to account for every drib and drab of ink is said to have a strong "W-tendency," or "Whole-tendency," which correlates well to paranoia. Yet these particular subjects were unmistakably happy people. The tests said they were paranoid, and in a way they were—each of them thought the universe was a sort of conspiracy organized for his or her own benefit. Such beliefs may be no more realistic than the delusions of "normal" paranoia, but they undoubtedly make for a jollier type of paranoid. [47]

Weil defines paranoia as "the tendency to see external events and things forming patterns that appear to be inimical." (Pattern-seeing, by itself, Weil views as neutral.) Positive paranoia would therefore be the tendency to see events and things forming patterns that appear to be beneficent. By these definitions, however, mere pessimism would qualify as (negative) paranoia, and any religion that posits a benevolent Providence would be a species of positive paranoia. So, for that matter, would any system of social analysis (such as Marxism or classical economics) that finds in the workings of history a progression toward a desirable goal. [48]

Weil's definition seems to us to leave out one element of paranoia. Accordingly, we would amend it to say that paranoia is the tendency to see external events and things forming patterns that appear to be harmful (negative paranoia) or beneficent (positive paranoia), which patterns appear to center upon the person seeing. Now it is not pessimism *per se* that is paranoid, but rather belief in a hostile universe focusing its enmity on oneself. And it is not religion *per se* that is an instance of positive paranoia, but rather a particular kind of religious experience: in Weil's phrase, the perception of the universe as "a radially symmetrical pattern, its center coinciding with the center of focused consciousness." Such experiences are a goal of many kinds of religious and spiritual disciplines. The mandalas of Tibetan Buddhism are, in a sense, maps of precisely this variety of experience. [49]

The concept of positive paranoia is a useful one because it sheds light on the connection between madness and transcendental experience and also because it illuminates what is so seductive about paranoia in general: the comfort of a universe ordered about oneself, a comfort that many people are willing to pay for the currency of anguish. Paranoia is the very opposite of meaninglessness; indeed, paranoia drenches every detail of the world in meaning. [50]

PURPOSE AND STRUCTURE

1. How does the initial dialogue advance the authors' purpose? Write a summary statement of the preliminary incident and compare the effect with the authors' device of leading into their subject.

2. What aspects of thinking and of behavior are reflected in the definition of paranoia subsumed under the heading, "A Little Semantics" (par. 19)?

3. What are the causal relationships established?

4. Examine the different contexts in which *paranoid* is used in everyday speech. How do they relate to the psychiatric definition?

5. How does the use of *paranoia* in everyday speech differ from its use in politics (including the Watergate years)?

6. What are the various means by which the authors classify paranoia?

7. How do the authors justify the statement that paranoia "is not necessarily a bar to many kinds of success" (par. 36)?

8. With what particulars is the section "Making Enemies Real" developed?

9. How does the last section sum up all that has preceded?

10. The essay on paranoia was written for *Harper's Magazine,* a middle-brow publication for lay readers. How well do the authors succeed in clarifying the concept for the lay person? What devices were most helpful?

11. How are positive and negative paranoia compared and contrasted?

DICTION AND TONE

1. Identify the allusion to the teenage peasant girl in par 21.

2. Why are "paranoia" and "paranoid" called "metaphors" (par. 22)?

3. Explain how Zero's monologue and his house make the writers think of art. (pars. 28–34).

4. How does the "self-fulfilling prophecy" operate with paranoids and those not so diagnosed (par. 40)?

5. Show how various aspects of the subject matter determine whether the tone is formal or informal.

APPLICATIONS TO WRITING

Using one or more of the writers' varied methods of classification—the private and public (or political), case histories, the technical and popular, the negative and positive—write an essay classifying some group or phenomena with which you are familiar, such as students, professors, cars, sports, television programs, movies, jobs.

The People Shapers

VANCE PACKARD

There appear to be critical periods in human development when the brain of an infant or child becomes extraordinarily receptive to developing certain aspects of behavior and personality. Benjamin Bloom, an educational psychologist at the University of Chicago, found that each human characteristic has its own growth curve. [1]

The easiest time to make important changes in a child's intelligence, for example, is before the age of 4. By that time intelligence is stabilized to the point at which IQ measurement takes on noteworthy significance, according to Maya Pines in "The Brain Changes." [2]

A number of scientists believe that the brains of young humans accept some imprinting of behavior patterns in those critical periods. By imprinting I mean type of learning that can occur only within a limited period of time early in life and is relatively unmodifiable thereafter. Animals have critical periods for imprinting, for instance. [3]

Jose Delgado, a Spaniard who has been in the forefront of those experimenting with shaping behavior by brain stimulation, talks of what he considers to be imprinting, and suggested a reason why the time element is critical:

"Imprinting decreases at certain ages. Pathways of the brain close at certain ages for every function. You can't become a good musician if you start too late. I did not start to learn English until I was 20, which is why I can't get rid of my Spanish accent. My children have lived in both Spain and America and have no accent." [4]

Child psychologist Eleanore B. Luckey has accepted the concept of imprinting as a development that occurs when the child is extraordinarily impressionable. She has made the interesting proposal that the periods of maximum impressionability be pinpointed for various characteristics, and that a new profession—particularly suited to women—be created: professional imprinter. [5]

The imprinters would go into homes and serve as consultants to natural mothers. If, for example, it is established that personality fixing proceeds most rapidly between the eighth and tenth month, an imprinter specializing in personality might be on hand several hours a week during that period to help optimize the traits particularly desired by the family. [6]

Delgado believes that expert help is needed: "We should try to establish at the earliest possible moment of the baby's life a program of psychogenesis." By that he means the "use of available physiological, psychological and psychiatric knowledge for the formation of the child's personality." [7]

Delgado agrees there is a strong possibility that professional imprinters will emerge. He adds, though: "But to imprint for what? What kind of humans do we want to construct?" [8]

Some scientists, incidentally, believe that personality shaping can be started chemically while the baby is still in the womb. In 1977 *Nature,* a British scientific journal, carried a report on findings by the endocrinologist June Reinisch at Rutgers University. [9]

She was studying the effects of synthetic hormones used to try to prevent miscarriage. (The use of some of the hormones has become controversial.) Mothers treated with progesterones had produced children who on personality tests appeared to be strong on independence and self-confidence. The children whose mothers had been treated with estrogens, in contrast, appeared in tests to be less self-reliant, more inclined to identify with a group. [10]

The already-set personalities of young people can be remodeled or at least profoundly redirected. A number of techniques are being used in this direction. For instance, one, a kind of youthful brainwashing, emerged as a side effect of a federally financed program in Florida. The aim was to rehabilitate adolescents believed to be drug users. [11]

The program, called the Seed, apparently was quite successful in getting the young people off drugs. But the controversy over personality changes accompanying this rehabilitation caused the Department of Health, Education and Welfare to back off. [12]

The youths or "Seedlings" pressed into this program were isolated from family, friends and the outside world. They were stripped of all identification and thrust at a low position into a precise social structure. A Seedling could advance upward in the structure only by rigid right-thinking. [13]

During the U. S. Senate hearings on the program, the statement of a guidance counselor at the North Miami Beach Senior High School who had encountered many returned Seedlings was introduced:

"When they return, they are 'straight,' namely quiet, well dressed, (with) short hair, and not under the influence of drugs compared to their previous appearance of (being) stoned most of the time. However, they seem to be living in a robotlike atmosphere, they won't speak to anyone outside of their own group . . . Seedlings seem to have an informing system on each other and on others that is similar to Nazi Germany. They run in to use the telephone daily, to report against each other to the Seed." [14]

The fact that personality can be transformed by surgery has been known ever since the potentates of the ancient Middle East put eunuchs in charge of their harems. In recent years brain surgeons have become adept at effecting a variety of personality changes by either cutting or burning inside the brain. [15]

Since the brain is the organ of the body fundamental to individual identity, modify it and you will modify identity. The brain can also be modified in its function on a long-term basis by the use of chemicals. For example, the equivalent of castration can apparently now be achieved chemically by treating a person with an anti-androgen drug called cyproterine acetate. [16]

Surgery of the psyche is designed to modify personality, ways of thinking and ways of behaving and feeling. It is also known as mental surgery, lobotomy, sedative neurosurgery and psychosurgery. [17]

In its earliest and still-used form it was the operation called lobotomy. This involves a simple severing of fibers between the frontal lobes and the deeper portions of the brain. Experiments with a chimpanzee had shown that destruction of certain frontal regions of the brain eliminated temper tantrums. [18]

A Portuguese neurologist, Egas Moniz, happened to hear a reference to the chimpanzee experiment at an international meeting and went home and performed lobotomies on 20 long-term psychotics. He claimed improvement in most of the cases and won himself a Nobel Prize. [19]

Today brain structure (and personality) has been changed experimentally by surgical cutting, by burning brain cells with the tip of implanted instruments, by injecting olive oil, by planting radioactive seeds, by ultrasonic beams, by freezing local areas and by proton beams that explode their charge at a specific distance. [20]

Reports of long-term reduction of chronic anxiety in some cases have come from psychosurgeons who use differing techniques and who operate on different areas of the brain. The British have done a considerable amount of work on altering anxiety and depressive states. One team that performed more than 200 operations found that nearly half the patients underwent a change of personality. [21]

If an assertive person is made into a placid person by surgery, it is an irreversible change. He isn't the same person anymore. How much manipulation of personality by intrusion into the brain is justifiable? Should it be restricted to mental hospital patients with certifiable brain damage who want a change, or if they are mentally incompetent, whose closest kin request the operation? [22]

If we get into the business of having surgeons operating on the brains of people judged by them or by governmental authorities to be too aggressive or belligerant for the good of society, psychosurgery can become a convenient tool for social control. [23]

PURPOSE AND STRUCTURE

1. Packard establishes a number of categories of people shapers. These categories are usually diagrammed as follows:

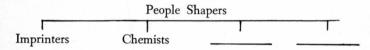

People Shapers

Imprinters   Chemists   _____   _____

Try to complete the chart. Note that each classification has either an example or a subclassification. Add those to the chart.

2. This article appeared in a newspaper as an excerpt from the book *The People Shapers*. Perhaps because it is an excerpt, the classification chart in question 1 is incomplete, for if Packard were to classify all people shapers, he would have to include parents, teachers, psychotherapists, and so on.

Perhaps the fact that this is an excerpt also accounts for the paragraph development. Would you consider par. 3 a very well-developed, a normally developed, or a poorly developed paragraph? Comment on the development of pars. 15, 17 and 20.

3. How are the transitions made between the classifications? What effect does this have on the essay?

4. What is the thesis of this essay? Where is it stated?

5. What do you think constitutes the introduction? The conclusion?

6. Is par. 16, with its discussion of chemical alteration of the brain, out of order? Where do you think would be a better place for it?

DICTION AND TONE

1. What effect is created by the frequent reference to such people as "Benjamin Bloom, an educational psychologist at the University of Chicago"; "Jose Delgado, . . . who has been in the forefront of those experimenting with shaping behavior by brain stimulation"; "child psychologist Eleanor B. Luckey"; "endocrinologist June Reinisch at Rutgers University"?

2. "Seedlings seem to have an informing system on each other and on others that is similar to Nazi Germany" (par. 14). What is wrong with this sentence?

3. "The fact that personality can be transformed by surgery has been known ever since the potentates of the ancient Middle East put eunuchs in charge of their harems. (par. 15). Find a more appropriate and more accurate word than *personality*.

4. "If an assertive person is made into a placid person by surgery, it is an irreversible change." (par. 22). Do we really want to change assertive people into placid ones? Find a more appropriate word than *assertive*.

5. Comment on the general tone of the article. Is it humorous, ironical, serious, persuasive? For example, is the last sentence serious, ironical, or irresponsible?

APPLICATIONS TO WRITING

1. Write an appropriate introduction and conclusion to this essay. Supply transitions wherever you think they are needed.

2. Write an essay like "The People Shapers," but write about people shapers with whom you are familiar: parents, teachers, school counselors, pop culture heroes, peers. Provide an example or illustration of each category.

World of Shadows

from *The Savage and Beautiful Country*

ALAN McGLASHAN

What is "dreaming"? Is it a shadow-play, meaningless and fragmentary? Or a variant of the fortuneteller's crystal? Or a delicate diagnostic convenience for the doctors? Through the centuries dreaming has been looked upon in all three of these ways, now one, now another coming into fashion or falling into disuse. Our own generation has added a fourth, a strictly scientific and physiological approach. And beyond all these, stranger than any of them, lies a fifth possibility, now beginning to emerge for the first time in human history. [1]

There are, and have always been, those who dismiss dreams as a chaos of unrelated details; sturdy, common-sensible folk, holding what could be called the Stuff-and-Nonsense Theory of Dreams. Yet it can hardly be other than unwise to turn away with contempt from any phenomenon big enough and compelling enough to engage the attention of countless generations of human beings. For quite apart from specialists and cranks, ordinary men and women have always been enthralled by dreams and their possible meanings. Dreams are a human preoccupation that is as old as man himself. Naturally so; since they reveal to him glimpses of a whole world of being that might else have remained for ever unknown. [2]

The second attitude to the dreaming mind is to consult it, as one consults a clairvoyant, for hints of what the future holds in store. This would seem silly enough; and often is. But again it ministers to an unassuageable longing of the human heart. Man is an inquisitive creature, and like a ragged urchin outside the Big Top circus, simply cannot resist trying to lift a corner of the tantalizing curtain of Time. He can, of course, make little sense of it; but no matter; to see anything at all is a big thrill. [3]

And by what crazy and fantastic tricks man has tried to gain that forbidden glimpse! Indeed, Oneiromancy, or divination of the future by dreams, begins to appear the height of rationality compared to most of his strategems; compared, for instance, to Ichthyomancy, divination by the entrails of fishes, or Crithomancy, which, believe it or not, is divination by the dough of cakes, or Coscinomancy, by a balanced sieve, or Electryomancy, by a hen picking up grains . . . Admittedly these methods are somewhat outmoded. On the other hand, Necromancy, or divination by communing with the dead, is still with us in the thriving form of Spiritualism; while at this very hour there are young ladies anxiously awaiting the results of Myomancy, or divination by mice. As for the ancient art of Skiomancy, which means divination by shadows, it is perhaps enough to say that the correct name for an X-ray plate is a skiagram. For all our sophistication we are still trying for a small boy's sneak view. [4]

In the light of these highly peculiar activities, dream-divination seems reasonable enough; and, in fact, there is now some impressive support for the scientific use of dreams in relation to future events. Dunne's re-markable books on the subject, for example, have aroused worldwide interest; and the strictly controlled investigations of the Extra-Sensory Perception researchers have provided, among many other things, star-tling evidence of the dreaming mind's capacity to "see ahead." The claims of E.S.P., incidentally, have aroused such solid resistance from orthodox scientists as to raise the possibility that they are of real im-portance. [5]

The third approach to dreams, the therapeutic approach, has had a curiously *regional* history. In the Far East, and among primitive peoples everywhere, the value of dreams for individual and social therapy has been recognized and employed for at least five thousand years, and per-haps far longer. But in the Western world few things are more subject to the whims of fashion than medical opinion; and in these areas the therapeutic status of dreams has sharply fluctuated through the cen-turies. At the moment, owing to its involvement with current psycho-logical theory, it is enjoying something of an intellectual vogue. After many centuries of medical neglect, dreams as valuable curative agents were thrust suddenly upon the Western world's attention by the publi-cation in 1900 of Freud's[1] epoch-making book *The Interpretation of Dreams*. Given some measure of scientific respectability by the impact of this work, the secret perennial human interest in dreams surged into the open. Jung[2] produced his profoundly different approach to the dream-process, and Adler[3] came forward with a third hypothesis. Fol-lowing these three giants a host of minor dream interpreters of varying skill and validity sprang like dragon's teeth from the ground, constitut-ing almost overnight a new and powerful profession. [6]

In one sense there was nothing new in this. More than two thousand years ago Aesculapius, legendary Greek physician and "patron saint" of medicine to this day, used dreams both for diagnosis and treatment. Nearer to our own time, Sir Thomas Browne,[4] wise physician of Nor-wich in the seventeenth century, had a high opinion of the dreaming

[1] Freud was a twentieth-century Viennese physician famous for his develop-ment of psychoanalytic theory and dream interpretation.

[2] Jung was a twentieth-century psychologist noted for his work on myths and archetypes, and for his concept of the collective unconscious.

[3] Adler was a twentieth-century Austrian psychologist noted particularly for stressing power in an individual's relations with others.

[4] Sir Thomas Browne was a seventeenth-century English physician and author famous for his eccentric learning and sonorous prose style.

mind, and declared in his charmingly florid style—"We are somewhat more than ourselves in sleep, and the Slumber of the Body seems to be but the waking of the Soul." Or as the medieval Richard Rolle more briefly and beautifully put it—"I sleep, and my heart wakes." [7]

It seems, therefore, that in one or another of these three modes theories about the meaning and utility of dreams have been a time-honored human concern. But the fourth mode of approach to dreams—the scientific study of their physiological mechanisms—is of very recent origin. In fact, it is only in the last ten years that it has really got under way at all. But now, like the rest of the sciences, it is advancing with vertiginous speed, and fascinating objective facts about the dream-process are emerging almost daily. [8]

Perhaps the most outstanding contemporary researcher in this particular field is Professor Kleitman of Chicago University. Kleitman noticed a short while ago that when a person is asleep there are movements of the eyes under the closed lids at certain regular intervals during the night. It occurred to him that these eye movements might be made because the sleeper is watching, as at a play, the actions of a dream. By waking the sleeper during these periods of eye movements, he found that at such times the sleeper was, in fact, always dreaming, and could invariably remember something of his dream. If the sleeper were waked when his eyes were not moving his sleep appeared to have been dreamless. By these means (checked and confirmed by the demonstration of specific E.E.G. waves which correlated with the eye movements) it has been established that dreams occur to everyone in an unchanging pattern of four to six dreams a night, at regular intervals. [9]

This was interesting enough. But there was more to follow. It was found that if a sleeper were regularly waked at the beginning of each dream-period, in a few nights the dream-deprived person became intensely irritable and forgetful during the day, whereas if he were wakened the same number of times, but during nondreaming periods, this did not occur. It would seem, therefore, that to preserve our psychological health dreams are actually a necessity. Confirming this is the further experimental fact that if a person who has been deprived of dreaming-periods for some nights is then allowed to sleep undisturbed, he dreams about twice as long as usual until he has made up his lost dream-time. Some of Kleitman's findings have been disputed. But for our present purposes, the relevant conclusion arising from these physiological investigations is that for some reason, still unexplained, *we need to dream.* [10]

With so many theories and facts about dreams and the dreaming mind, it might be thought that modern man was reasonably equipped with information on the subject, and that this peculiar nocturnal activity was receiving all, and perhaps more than, the attention it deserved. There are indeed a number of distinguished scientists, including certain psychiatrists, who are at no pains to conceal that this is their opinion. But the odd fact is that the most important question about the dream-process has never yet been asked, far less answered. [11]

This question is concerned with the nature of the dreaming mind itself—not with what it *does,* but what it *is;* a mystery which both the doctors and the clairvoyants, in their haste to extract from dreams something practical and useful, have largely neglected. [12]

The dreaming mind, I suggest, in addition to all its other functions, is an instrument of liberation, capable of breaking up the conventional patterns of human perception, and releasing new forms of awareness. I invite you to regard the dreaming mind as a *file* smuggled into the space-time cell where man lies captive; a cell whose walls and ceiling are our five senses, and whose warders are the inflexible concepts of logic. With the help of this file man might be able—provided always he could evade the vigilance of the Authorities—to saw through the bars of his prison and escape . . . But into what terrifying, what unimaginable world? [13]

Not, certainly, into a world of tranquillity, not into any traditional heaven-haven. The dreaming mind leads—not into Paradise, but into paradox . . . into a world that is fluid and ambiguous and dangerous, a phantasmal world of symbols whose meaning is at once concealed and conveyed by a dazzling and bewildering interplay of opposites . . . And man is afraid of it. The panic reaction of suddenly liberated prisoners swells here to nightmare size. In the last resort man has not dared to use his own escape route. He shudders away from freedom. [14]

Here, then, is one of the unattempted soul-adventures facing modern man. I have no wish to exaggerate its importance. It is only one among many such adventures. But for some minds there could be an incomparable excitement in suddenly recognizing the dreaming mind as an organ of liberation, as an Archimedean point by which man might one day lever his consciousness into a new orbit. This is the fifth possibility of dream interpretation, now at last rising near enough to the conscious level to allow at least two questions about it to be formulated. I will venture to ask them. [15]

Who, or what, is the Dreamer within us? And to whom is the Dreamer talking? [16]

Such questions are admittedly naïve. It will occur at once to many that I am committing the heresy of personification. I am making a graven image of the unimaginable. And in this specific field Jung has declared, "We must not ascribe the functioning of the dream . . . to any 'subject' with a conscious will." This, however, is a statement with which we can all be in agreement. It would indeed be a fallacy to suppose that our dreams are constructed logically and with rational aims in view by any part of the individual conscious mind. Dreams *happen* to us; and what Jung calls "a dark impulse" from far beyond the reach of conscious striving is the final arbiter of the dream pattern. Agreed. And there, for Jung as a declared empiricist, the matter rests. But I suggest that there can be no final prohibition against inquiry into the nature of this "dark impulse." Such an inquiry is nothing less than an attempt to conceptualize something that has not yet arrived at the conscious level; and for this attempt a certain license, a certain *naïveté* of imagery, must be allowed. [17]

Moreover, it is historically justifiable. Many of the forward movements of human consciousness have used some form of personification or analogy as a scaffolding. Pythagoras,[5] for example, held that all numbers had geometrical shapes. Kepler's[6] discoveries in astronomy were motivated by his lifelong belief that there existed a music of the spheres. They may have been mistaken; but they certainly started something. The world would have suffered infinite loss without the advances in consciousness built up by these men within the protection of their faulty imagery. For all their inadequacies we *need* these temporary supports for our new constructions. When the building is completed the scaffolding can be discarded. [18]

[5] Pythagoras was a fifth-century B.C. Greek philosopher and mathematician and founder of the Pythagorean school, which taught that numbers constitute the true nature of things; the school heavily influenced geometry, astronomy, and medicine.

[6] Kepler was a seventeenth-century German scientist known as one of the fathers of modern astronomy and whose name is associated with three laws of planetary motion.

Unrepentantly, therefore, I propose to pursue the personification of this "dark impulse" as an image, the crude image of the Dreamer; in the hope of establishing in men's minds the shadowy outline of a hitherto unrecognized power. [19]

Who, or what, is the Dreamer within us? The question has a numinous feel. We know at once that it is supremely worth asking—and supremely unanswerable. It is unanswerable, perhaps, because the terms employed are ordinary everyday terms that seem to invite an ordinary everyday answer, and on this level no possible answer fits. We lack the categories. We cannot even guess whether the Dreamer is a personality or a force. In some unknown but convincing way we recognize it is both, and neither. In other words, we find ourselves struggling to express something for which the means of communication are lacking, or at least grossly inadequate. [20]

This sounds like the classical difficulty of the mystic. Am I then saying that dreams are mystical experiences? To say "No" to this is to throw away perhaps the nearest analogy there is to the spellbinding power of the dream when taken as a pure experience, not a means to an end. On the other hand, to say "Yes" would be to give an immediate sense of relief to a great many people. "Ah, mysticism," they would say, closing their minds like closing a book, "that's not for me." It is strange that the majority of men are in such haste to dissociate themselves from the "taint" of mysticism that they have never even paused to observe that it has two fundamentally different forms. One is God-mysticism, contemning the world and longing impatiently for union with the Absolute; a form of mysticism that is, in the last resort, in love with death. (This kind is, incidentally, the inspiration of all tragic poetry and drama, and is the reason why such tales, to the bewilderment of simple minds, must always end in death.) The second is Nature-mysticism, which looks at all creation with a delighted wonder, and at all human beings, from mighty saints to monstrous sinners, with a kind of surprised recognition; a mysticism that is, in fact, in love with life. [21]

But in any case, is it not time that we achieved more range and plasticity in our concepts? Must experience be pushed for ever into either a little box labeled "Mysticism" or a little box labeled "Empiricism"? Now, when E.S.P., for instance, is nibbling impudently at the edges of orthodox Science, and Science itself is staring incredulously at its own rationally "impossible" conclusions—now is surely the time to reexamine the modes of human experiencing. [22]

This is why the concept of the Dreamer is among the most fascinating and relevant of the mysteries facing contemporary man. It is nothing less than an invitation to transcend our normal and habitual level of consciousness, to develop a long-latent function, to enter a *terra incognita* of which, paradoxically, we are freeborn citizens. As Dante[7] was led through realms beyond the human range by the ghost of Virgil, so the Dreamer can lead us, through the labyrinthine corridors of sleep, to a realm of being where the human mind blooms phantasmally in new and brilliant and unimagined forms of life. Sleeping could be the archaic *rite d'entrée* to this realm—and the Dreamer could be our ghostly guide. [23]

The identity of the Dreamer . . . who is as close to us as our own unspoken thoughts, who is concerned with our individual destiny while ranging infinitely beyond it, who is a tireless if often terrifying and in-comprehensible Teacher . . . The Dreamer who sees with eyeless eyes, who hears with earless ears, who wakes when the senses sleep . . . Can we draw nearer to this mystery within ourselves? [24]

PURPOSE AND STRUCTURE

1. What are the five categories into which McGlashan classifies his subject of dreams, "the world of shadows"?

2. What rhetorical and substantive purposes are served by the opening questions?

3. With what evidence—subjective or objective—does McGlashan sum up his own view of dreams as predictive of future events (par. 4)?

4. What varied authorities are cited in presenting the therapeutic approach to dreams (pars. 5–6)?

5. How does par. 7 serve as a transition from what precedes and to what follows?

6. How does the author distinguish between a subjective and objective view of dreams?

7. How does the fifth theory differ from the preceding ones? The author utilizes a number of methods of developing it. Identify them.

[7] Dante was a fourteenth-century Italian poet best known for *The Divine Comedy*, an allegory of the progress of the individual soul toward God.

8. How does McGlashan justify what he refers to as "a certain license, a certain *naïveté* of imagery" (pars. 16–17)?

9. How do the comparison and contrast of the two forms of mysticism advance the writer's attempt to explain the fifth theory?

10. Examine the structure of the final paragraph. How do the fragments, parallelisms, and repetitions serve both purpose and tone? What paradoxes are suggested?

DICTION AND TONE

1. How does McGlashan's diction convey to you his own convictions regarding dreams?

2. How does the author establish a tone of tolerance for theories that seem to him irresponsible and even silly? Note particularly the metaphor in par. 3 and the series in par. 4.

3. What purpose do the *italics* serve at the end of par. 10?

4. What are the components of the metaphor in par. 12? How does it contribute to the author's purpose and tone? Ask yourself the same questions of par. 17.

5. How do the diction and tone change as the author develops his fifth theory?

6. What does McGlashan mean by "the heresy of personification" (par. 17)?

7. How does the figure of speech "nibbling impudently at the edges of orthodox Science" contribute to purpose and tone (par. 22)?

APPLICATIONS TO WRITING

1. Use McGlashan's method of classifying a controversial subject into categories and provide illustrative details to illuminate each category. You might wish to explore an area like ESP or UFO's or varieties of science fiction.

2. Examine one or more of your own dreams and attempt to interpret it (or them) in the light of what it might or might not have told you about the "dreaming mind itself."

four

Comparison and Contrast

Comparison and contrast—the presentation of a subject by the indication of similarities between two or more things (comparison) and by the demonstration of differences (contrast). The basic elements in a comparative process, then, are (1) the various entities compared, and (2) the points of likeness or difference between them. To be comparable, they should be members of the same class (see Classification in the Glossary). For example, nature lovers and nature haters, both members of the same class, are comparable. Democracy and communism are not comparable, because the former is a subdivision of a political system and the latter of an economic one. Although nearly all of Highet's essay develops a dramatic contrast between Diogenes and Alexander the Great, the essay ends with a surprising comparison between the two men. The range of effects that may be achieved in comparison and contrast is reflected in Roszak's graphic and moving description of the ways in which the symbols of flight have been debased to the level of a poor counterfeit; in Mencken's preposterous and paradoxical development of the distinctions between men and women; in Huxley's use of the familiar to explain the unfamiliar; in Ullman's mocking portrait of Hollywood's conspicuous consumption, which is contrasted to the spartan life of a barren island in the Baltic; and in Eiseley's counterpointing of bird and machine to express his choice of all that is life supporting.

Diogenes and Alexander

GILBERT HIGHET

Lying on the bare earth, shoeless, bearded, half-naked, he looked like a beggar or a lunatic. He was one, but not the other. He had opened his eyes with the sun at dawn, scratched, done his business like a dog at the roadside, washed at the public fountain, begged a piece of breakfast bread and a few olives, eaten them squatting on the ground, and washed them down with a few handfuls of water scooped from the spring. (Long ago he had owned a rough wooden cup, but he threw it away when he saw a boy drinking out of his hollowed hands.) Having no work to go to and no family to provide for, he was free. As the market place filled up with shoppers and merchants and gossipers and sharpers and slaves and foreigners, he had strolled through it for an hour or two. Everybody knew him, or knew of him. They would throw sharp questions at him and get sharper answers. Sometimes they threw jeers, and got jibes; sometimes bits of food, and got scant thanks; sometimes a mischievous pebble, and got a shower of stones and abuse. They were not quite sure whether he was mad or not. He knew they were mad, all mad, each in a different way; they amused him. Now he was back at his home. [1]

It was not a house, not even a squatter's hut. He thought everybody lived far too elaborately, expensively, anxiously. What good is a house? No one needs privacy: natural acts are not shameful; we all do the same things, and need not hide them. No one needs beds and chairs and such furniture: the animals live healthy lives and sleep on the ground. All we require, since nature did not dress us properly, is one garment to keep us warm, and some shelter from rain and wind. So he had one blanket— to dress him in the daytime and cover him at night—and he slept in a cask. His name was Diogenes. He was the founder of the creed called Cynicism (the word means "doggishness"); he spent much of his life in the rich, lazy, corrupt Greek city of Corinth, mocking and satirizing its people, and occasionally converting one of them. [2]

His home was not a barrel made of wood: too expensive. It was a

157

storage jar made of earthenware, something like a modern fuel tank—no doubt discarded because a break had made it useless. He was not the first to inhabit such a thing: the refugees driven into Athens by the Spartan invasion had been forced to sleep in casks. But he was the first who ever did so by choice, out of principle. [3]

Diogenes was not a degenerate or a maniac. He was a philosopher who wrote plays and poems and essays expounding his doctrine; he talked to those who cared to listen; he had pupils who admired him. But he taught chiefly by example. All should live naturally, he said, for what is natural is normal and cannot possibly be evil or shameful. Live without conventions, which are artificial and false; escape complexities and superfluities and extravagances: only so can you live a free life. The rich man believes he possesses his big house with its many rooms and its elaborate furniture, his pictures and his expensive clothes, his horses and his servants and his bank accounts. He does not. He depends on them, he worries about them, he spends most of his life's energy looking after them; the thought of losing them makes him sick with anxiety. They possess him. He is their slave. In order to procure a quantity of false, perishable goods he has sold the only true, lasting good, his own independence. [4]

There have been many men who grew tired of human society with its complications, and went away to live simply—on a small farm, in a quiet village, in a hermit's cave, or in the darkness of anonymity. Not so Diogenes. He was not a recluse, or a stylite, or a beatnik. He was a missionary. His life's aim was clear to him: it was "to restamp the currency." (He and his father had once been convicted for counterfeiting, long before he turned to philosophy, and this phrase was Diogenes' bold, unembarrassed joke on the subject.) To restamp the currency: to take the clean metal of human life, to erase the old false conventional markings, and to imprint it with its true values. [5]

The other great philosophers of the fourth century before Christ taught mainly their own private pupils. In the shady groves and cool sanctuaries of the Academy, Plato discoursed to a chosen few on the unreality of this contingent existence. Aristotle, among the books and instruments and specimens and archives and research-workers of his Lyceum, pursued investigations and gave lectures that were rightly named *esoteric* "for those within the walls." But for Diogenes, laboratory and specimens and lecture halls and pupils were all to be found in a crowd of ordinary people. Therefore he chose to live in Athens or in the rich city of Corinth, where travelers from all over the Mediterranean world constantly came and went. And, by design, he publicly behaved in such ways as to show people what real life was. He would constantly take up their spiritual coin, ring it on a stone, and laugh at its false superscription. [6]

He thought most people were only half-alive, most men only half-men. At bright noonday he walked through the market place carrying a lighted lamp and inspecting the face of everyone he met. They asked him why. Diogenes answered, "I am trying to find a *man*." [7]

To a gentleman whose servant was putting on his shoes for him, Diogenes said, "You won't be really happy until he wipes your nose for you: that will come after you lose the use of your hands." [8]

Once there was a war scare so serious that it stirred even the lazy, profit-happy Corinthians. They began to drill, clean their weapons, and rebuild their neglected fortifications. Diogenes took his old cask and began to roll it up and down, back and forward. "When you are all so busy," he said, "I felt I ought to do *something!*" [9]

And so he lived—like a dog, some said, because he cared nothing for privacy and other human conventions, and because he showed his teeth and barked at those whom he disliked. Now he was lying in the sunlight, as contented as a dog on the warm ground, happier (he himself used to boast) than the Shah of Persia. Although he knew he was going to have an important visitor, he would not move. [10]

The little square began to fill with people. Page boys elegantly dressed, spearmen speaking a rough foreign dialect, discreet secretaries, hard-browed officers, suave diplomats, they all gradually formed a circle centered on Diogenes. He looked them over, as a sober man looks at a crowd of tottering drunks, and shook his head. He knew who they were. They were the attendants of the conqueror of Greece, the servants of Alexander, the Macedonian king, who was visiting his newly subdued realm. [11]

Only twenty, Alexander was far older and wiser than his years. Like all Macedonians he loved drinking, but he could usually handle it; and toward women he was nobly restrained and chivalrous. Like all Macedonians he loved fighting; he was a magnificent commander, but he was not merely a military automaton. He could think. At thirteen he had become a pupil of the greatest mind in Greece, Aristotle. No exact record of his schooling survives. It is clear, though, that Aristotle took the passionate, half-barbarous boy and gave him the best of Greek culture.

He taught Alexander poetry: the young prince slept with the *Iliad* under his pillow and longed to emulate Achilles, who brought the mighty power of Asia to ruin. He taught him philosophy, in particular the shapes and uses of political power: a few years later Alexander was to create a supranational empire that was not merely a power system but a vehicle for the exchange of Greek and Middle Eastern cultures. [12]

Aristotle taught him the principles of scientific research: during his invasion of the Persian domains Alexander took with him a large corps of scientists, and shipped hundreds of zoological specimens back to Greece for study. Indeed, it was from Aristotle that Alexander learned to seek out everything strange which might be instructive. Jugglers and stunt artists and virtuosos of the absurd he dismissed with a shrug; but on reaching India he was to spend hours discussing the problems of life and death with naked Hindu mystics, and later to see one demonstrate Yoga self-command by burning himself impassively to death. [13]

Now, Alexander was in Corinth to take command of the League of Greek States which, after conquering them, his father Philip had created as a disguise for the New Macedonian Order. He was welcomed and honored and flattered. He was the man of the hour, of the century: he was unanimously appointed commander-in-chief of a new expedition against old, rich, corrupt Asia. Nearly everyone crowded to Corinth in order to congratulate him, to seek employment with him, even simply to see him: soldiers and statesmen, artists and merchants, poets and philosophers. He received their compliments graciously. Only Diogenes, although he lived in Corinth, did not visit the new monarch. With that generosity which Aristotle had taught him was a quality of the truly magnanimous man, Alexander determined to call upon Diogenes. Surely Dio-genes, the God-born, would acknowledge the conqueror's power by some gift of hoarded wisdom. [14]

With his handsome face, his fiery glance, his strong supple body, his purple and gold cloak, and his air of destiny, he moved through the parting crowd, toward the Dog's kennel. When a king approaches, all rise in respect. Diogenes did not rise, he merely sat up on one elbow. When a monarch enters a precinct, all greet him with a bow or an acclamation. Diogenes said nothing. [15]

There was a silence. Some years later Alexander speared his best friend to the wall, for objecting to the exaggerated honors paid to His Majesty; but now he was still young and civil. He spoke first, with a kindly greeting. Looking at the poor broken cask, the single ragged garment, and the rough figure lying on the ground, he said: "Is there anything I can do for you, Diogenes?" [16]

"Yes," said the Dog, "Stand to one side. You're blocking the sunlight." [17]

There was silence, not the ominous silence preceding a burst of fury, but a hush of amazement. Slowly, Alexander turned away. A titter broke out from the elegant Greeks, who were already beginning to make jokes about the Cur that looked at the King. The Macedonian officers, after deciding that Diogenes was not worth the trouble of kicking, were starting to guffaw and nudge one another. Alexander was still silent. To those nearest him he said quietly, "If I were not Alexander, I should be Diogenes." They took it as a paradox, designed to close the awkward little scene with a polite curtain line. But Alexander meant it. He understood Cynicism as the others could not. Later he took one of Diogenes' pupils with him to India as a philosophical interpreter (it was he who spoke to the naked *saddhus*). He was what Diogenes called himself, a *cosmopolitēs*, "citizen of the world." Like Diogenes, he admired the heroic figure of Hercules, the mighty conqueror who labors to help mankind while all others toil and sweat only for themselves. He knew that of all men then alive in the world only Alexander the conqueror and Diogenes the beggar were truly free. [18]

PURPOSE AND STRUCTURE

1. While nearly all of Highet's essay develops a dramatic contrast between Diogenes and Alexander, the essay ends (par. 18) with a surprising comparison between the two men. Is the last sentence of the essay the thesis?

2. Diogenes is not named by Highet until near the end of the second paragraph. Why begin with "he" (par. 1)?

3. The first reference to Alexander occurs at the end of the tenth paragraph. Would it be more effective to begin the contrast between Diogenes and Alexander earlier in the essay—even in the first paragraph?

4. Par. 10 summarizes the first part of the essay (first sentence) and is transitional to the second part (last sentence). What is the purpose of the second sentence? Why begin the sentence with "Now"? Is there any relation between this sentence and the first sentence of the essay?

5. Does Diogenes "acknowledge the conquerer's power by some gift of hoarded wisdom" (par. 14)?

DICTION AND TONE

1. Diogenes' name means the God-born but he was a Cynic—which means doggish. What was the tone of his answer to Alexander (par. 17), god-like or dog-like?

2. What is the tone of Diogenes' joke on " 'to restamp the currency' " (par. 5)?

3. Diogenes taught chiefly by example (par. 4). What is the tone of the examples of his teaching in pars. 7, 8, 9?

4. What is the tone of the phrase the "New Macedonian Order" (par. 14)?

APPLICATIONS TO WRITING

1. Describe a confrontation between two completely different people: two of your friends, two imaginary characters (for example, Chicken Little and Candide), or two public figures (for example, Adolph Hitler and Albert Einstein).

2. Contrast two extremely different individuals—but end your composition with a surprising likeness between the two.

3. Highet has told a famous anecdote (pars. 1, 10, 16, 17)—but he has used the story to develop a powerful contrast between two philosophies of living. What is your philosophy of living? Tell a personal story—possibly describing a confrontation with someone who disagrees with you—which illustrates your way of living.

4. Diogenes taught chiefly by example. Give an example—*not* an abstract statement!—of your beliefs.

Uncaging Skylarks:[1] The Meaning of Transcendent Symbols

from *Where the Wasteland Ends*

THEODORE ROSZAK

> *Ah, no wings of the body could compare*
> *To wings of the spirit!*
> *It is in each of us inborn;*
> *That feeling which arises and ascends*
> *When in the blue heaven overhead*
> *The lark calls out in thrilling song.*
>
> Goethe

THE POPULAR HISTORY OF AVIATION

The musical accompaniment is by Richard Strauss:[2] *Also Sprach Zarathustra.*[3] Over it, a portentous voice announces, "From the beginning of time, man has dreamed of one supreme adventure: to traverse the heavens with the grace of a bird." [1]

And now, a bird appears before us, neatly sailing the wind. From below, a man gazes up, his face filled with fascination and longing. He is shaggy, covered in animal hides . . . a stereotypic caveman. But he has fashioned himself a pair of outsized wings. He ties them on and steps to the edge of a dizzy precipice. And then, as his troglodytic colleagues stand by in awed amazement, as the music rises to a trumpeting crescendo, the original aviator spreads his wings and soars away into the sun . . . only to be transformed in midair into a Boeing 707, the *true* "wings of man." [2]

---

[1] Gerard Manley Hopkins' poem "The Caged Skylark" has a theme similar to the one expressed in this essay.

[2] Richard Strauss was a late nineteenth-century German composer and conductor—the last of the great Romantic composers—known particularly for his tone poems *Don Juan* and *Thus Spake Zarathustra* and his operas *Der Rosenkavalier, Salome,* and *Elektra.*

[3] *Thus Spake Zarathustra* is the theme song of the movie *2001.*

It is a television commercial for a prominent American airline, a slick, pretentious spot announcement that finishes by reminding how all of us can now enjoy the "supreme adventure" for as little as $214 Los Angeles to Atlanta round trip, Mondays through Thursdays, economy fare. [3]

I watch . . . and ponder the wealth of artistic and religious symbolism that lies hidden beneath this popular, potted history of aviation. Classic images of flight and ascendance fill my thoughts . . . the skylark of the Romantic poets . . . Geruda, the divine vulture, the vehicle of the yogis . . . St. Bonaventura's[4] ascent of the mind to God . . . the Taoist[5] holy men who rode the wind in carriages drawn by flying dragons . . . the prophet Elijah[6] in his chariot of fire . . . the Vedic[7] priest scaling his tall pillar, crying from its summit with arms outspread, "We have come to the heaven, to the gods; we have become immortal." I think of the angels pinioned with flame, the furies, genies, and wing-footed gods . . . and behind all these, shining through from the dawn of human consciousness, reflected in a thousand mythical images, the shamanic vision-flight, the ecstasy with wings. [4]

All this passes through my mind, the real but subterranean meaning of flight, buried now beneath a glamorous technology of jet planes and moon rockets, lost, totally lost from the common awareness; and I grow sad to see a noble imagery debased to the level of so poor a counterfeit. [5]

True, there are always the sensitive few, among the artists especially, who can tell the original from the counterfeit; and maybe a few more who have, by way of the drug trip, recaptured something of the primordial meaning of being "high." But for the rest, I think this television commercial—like so many of the clichés on which advertising and the popular arts draw—summarizes the conventional wisdom. It does more

---

[4] Bonaventura (or Bonaventure) was a thirteenth-century Italian theologian, mystic, and philosopher best known for his *The Journey of the Mind,* which sets forth the contemplation of God as the goal of all art and science.

[5] A Taoist is a follower of Taoism, a Chinese religious system based on the teachings of Lao Tzu and Chuang Tzu that opposed Confucianism and emphasized the transcendence of the spirit.

[6] Elijah was an Old Testament Hebrew prophet who lived during the ninth century B.C.

[7] Vedic refers to the four sacred books of the Hindus composed about 2500 B.C.; included in the Vedic writings are the *Upanishads,* a collection of treatises on the nature of man and the universe.

than volumes of scholarship to express the central credo of urban-industrial society: the conviction that only now, under our auspices, do all the best ancestral dreams come true as tangible realities. For us, it goes without question that the aspiration of flight had no significant place in culture until Leonardo da Vinci[8] first looked at a bird and proclaimed it "an instrument working according to mathematical law which it is within the power of man to reproduce." How did Leonardo make flight a realistic proposition? By embedding it in a machine. The machine may not have worked, but it was at least a "practical" step away from mere wishful thinking toward the day when, after generations of experiment with balloons and gliders, industrial technology could finally provide the power and know-how to make heavier-than-air flight a reality. Only then could the "supreme adventure" become available to millions. [6]

THE "REAL THING"

But what has become of that adventure as a matter of living experience? Now that millions are convinced that they possess in fact this ideal that a thousand generations before us could only entertain in dreams, what does it amount to? The question is worth a moment's reflection, because here, I believe, we find an important cause of that chronic despair so characteristic of our culture, that nagging sense of malaise amid world-beating achievement. [7]

All of us who have passed through a major air terminal have been able to see on the thousand tired and anxious faces around us what it means to play the jet-propelled Icarus. The faces of nervous tourists scrambling to locate lost luggage, change money, catch up with the latest rescheduling, clear through customs, find ground transport . . . the faces of jet-fatigued executives routinely shuttling across the globe with heads full of money and worry . . . one struggles among them through congested waiting rooms to find a strong drink or some fresh air . . . never enough places to sit and the air conditioning perpetually overloaded. One waits in traffic queues three miles long to creep into the airport, and, once there, must line up again to check in baggage, obtain information, buy insurance, get a fast snack, load up with duty-free

---

[8] Leonardo da Vinci was a fifteenth-century Italian painter, sculptor, architect, engineer, scientist, poet, and musician.

merchandise. The planes are invariably late departing or arriving; one makes haste only to spend hours waiting among impatient babies and bored adults. [8]

As for the flight itself, is it not universally regarded as so many hours of cramped tedium? Hence the many distractions . . . music by stereophonic earphones, movies, cocktails, magazines, perhaps (for the sagging junior executives on board) stewardesses decked out like harem girls. Rather as if the object were to screen out the entire sensation of flying by turning the plane into a cinema or night club. What is it we say of a successful flight? "Never knew we were in the air." [9]

In the summer of 1971 a man and woman, strangers to one another when they boarded a BOAC jet en route from New York to Australia, are reported to have unsettled a few hundred fellow passengers by having sex in their seat about midway in the trip. An understanding airline spokesman afterwards explained to the press that such antics were not uncommon, because people did after all get bored on these long-distance flights. The obvious remedy, then, is to introduce supersonic transport that will get the tiresome business over with even more quickly. [10]

All this is not meant as a tirade against air transport, but only as an ironic comment on the "supreme adventure" of traversing the heavens as you and I have come to know it. Back in the 1930s, the poet Antoine de Saint-Exupéry could still salvage a bit of high romance from flying the mail routes in a primitive craft open to the elements and equipped with a single risky engine. Today we fly five times faster and ten times higher, but the only romance we may find is that of the BOAC passengers resorting to the oldest amusement of all. Clearly, if air transport is the fulfillment of primeval aspiration, then our ancestors vastly overrated the experience. They expected towering exhilaration; but we know better. After the novelty wears off, it turns out to be a trouble and a bore. *Another* trouble and bore . . . like so many other inconveniencing conveniences of modern life. [11]

Yet how *could* so great and ancient a dream turn out to be so trivial? We are forced to conclude, with a kind of routine disillusionment, that only ignorance of the real thing in all its tedious detail allowed our ancestors to enjoy their dreams. To preserve the dream one must forgo the reality; to possess the reality one must forfeit the dream. Either we resign ourselves to that dismal conclusion, or we must recognize that somewhere along the line we have lost touch with the traditional aspiration. We have made it real—materially, historically real—but at the expense of some other, greater reality . . . something that eludes us for all our power and cunning. [12]

PURPOSE AND STRUCTURE

1. How does the use of the commercial in the opening paragraphs advance the author's purpose and express his tone?

2. With what images does the writer compare and contrast the commercial? How do they advance his purpose and express his tone?

3. How does the author support his view of "a noble imagery debased to the level of so poor a counterfeit" (par. 5)?

4. How does the author reflect his bias in par. 6?

5. How does Roszak answer his own rhetorical questions in par. 7?

6. What details are used in pars. 8–10 to make Roszak's comparison and contrast graphic? What is the subject of his comparison and contrast?

DICTION AND TONE

1. How does the metaphor in the title relate to the subtitle? How is the metaphor developed throughout the passage?

2. How does the language used in the opening paragraphs reveal the author's contempt for the commercial? Specify. How does the diction in pars. 8–10 reflect a similar tone?

3. Account for the adjective *potted* in par. 4.

4. Compare and contrast the tone of par. 4 with that of pars. 1–3.

5. Look up any allusions or words unfamiliar to you in par. 4.

6. Why is *Real Thing* placed in quotation marks in the heading for the second section?

7. Justify the use of the word *trivial* in the last paragraph.

APPLICATIONS TO WRITING

1. Compare and contrast a dream you have cherished with the reality when it has materialized.

2. Can you think of any "inconveniencing conveniences of modern life" (par. 11)? If so, compare and contrast their attributes and deficiencies with those of the commodity they have replaced.

The Feminine Mind

H.   L.   M E N C K E N

A man's women folk, whatever their outward show of respect for his merit and authority, always regard him secretly as an ass, and with something akin to pity. His most gaudy sayings and doings seldom deceive them; they see the actual man within, and know him for a shallow and pathetic fellow. In this fact, perhaps, lies one of the best proofs of feminine intelligence, or, as the common phrase makes it, feminine intuition. The marks of that so-called intuition are simply a sharp and accurate perception of reality, a habitual immunity to emotional enchantment, a relentless capacity for distinguishing clearly between the appearance and the substance. The appearance, in the normal family circle, is a hero, a magnifico, a demigod. The substance is a poor mountebank. [1]

A man's wife, true enough, may envy her husband certain of his more soothing prerogatives and sentimentalities. She may envy him his masculine liberty of movement and occupation, his impenetrable complacency, his peasant-like delight in petty vices, his capacity for hiding the harsh face of reality behind the cloak of romanticism, his general innocence and childishness. But she never envies him his shoddy and preposterous soul. [2]

This shrewd perception of masculine bombast and make-believe, this acute understanding of man as the eternal tragic comedian, is at the bottom of that compassionate irony which passes under the name of the maternal instinct. A woman wishes to mother a man simply because she sees into his helplessness, his need of an amiable environment, his touching self-delusion. That ironical note is not only daily apparent in real life; it sets the whole tone of feminine fiction. The woman novelist, if she be skillful enough to be taken seriously, never takes her heroes so.

From the day of Jane Austen to the day of Selma Lagerlof she has always got into her character study a touch of superior aloofness, of ill-concealed derision. I can't recall a single masculine figure created by a woman who is not, at bottom, a booby. [3]

That it should be necessary, at this late stage in the senility of the human race, to argue that women have a fine and fluent intelligence is surely an eloquent proof of the defective observation, incurable prejudice, and general imbecility of their lords and masters. Women, in fact, are not only intelligent; they have almost a monopoly of certain of the subtler and more utile forms of intelligence. The thing itself, indeed, might be reasonably described as a special feminine character; there is in it, in more than one of its manifestations, a femaleness as palpable as the femaleness of cruelty, masochism or rouge. Men are strong. Men are brave in physical combat. Men are romantic, and love what they conceive to be virtue and beauty. Men incline to faith, hope and charity. Men know how to sweat and endure. Men are amiable and fond. But in so far as they show the true fundamentals of intelligence—in so far as they reveal a capacity for discovering the kernel of eternal verity in the husk of delusion and hallucination and a passion for bringing it forth —to that extent, at least, they are feminine, and still nourished by the milk of their mothers. The essential traits and qualities of the male, the hall-marks of the unpolluted masculine, are at the same time the hall-marks of the numskull. The caveman is all muscles and mush. Without a woman to rule him and think for him, he is a truly lamentable spectacle: a baby with whiskers, a rabbit with the frame of an aurochs, a feeble and preposterous caricature of God. [4]

Here, of course, I do not mean to say that masculinity contributes nothing whatsoever to the complex of chemicophysiological reactions which produces what we call superior ability; all I mean to say is that this complex is impossible without the feminine contribution—that it is a product of the interplay of the two elements. In women of talent we see the opposite picture. They are commonly somewhat mannish, and shave as well as shine. Think of George Sand, Catherine the Great, Elizabeth of England, Rosa Bonheur, Teresa Carreño or Cosima Wagner. Neither sex, without some fertilization of the complementary characters of the other, is capable of the highest reaches of human endeavor. Man, without a saving touch of a woman in him, is too doltish, too naive and romantic, too easily deluded and lulled to sleep by his imagination to be anything above a cavalryman, a theologian or a corporation director. And woman, without some trace of that divine innocence which is masculine, is too harshly the realist for those vast projections of the fancy which lie at the heart of what we call genius. The wholly manly man lacks the wit necessary to give objective form to his soaring and secret dreams, and the wholly womanly woman is apt to be too cynical a creature to dream at all. [5]

What men, in their egotism, constantly mistake for a deficiency of intelligence in woman is merely an incapacity for mastering that mass of small intellectual tricks, that complex of petty knowledges, that collection of cerebral rubberstamps, which constitute the chief mental equipment of the average male. A man thinks that he is more intelligent than his wife because he can add up a column of figures more accurately, or because he is able to distinguish between the ideas of rival politicians, or because he is privy to the minutiae of some sordid and degrading business or profession. But these empty talents, of course, are not really signs of intelligence; they are, in fact, merely a congeries of petty tricks and antics, and their acquirement puts little more strain on the mental powers than a chimpanzee suffers in learning how to catch a penny or scratch a match. [6]

The whole mental baggage of the average business man, or even the average professional man, is inordinately childish. It takes no more actual sagacity to carry on the everyday hawking and haggling of the world, or to ladle out its normal doses of bad medicine and worse law, than it takes to operate a taxicab or fry a pan of fish. No observant person, indeed, can come into close contact with the general run of business and professional men—I confine myself to those who seem to get on in the world, and exclude the admitted failures—without marveling at their intellectual lethargy, their incurable ingenuousness, their appalling lack of ordinary sense. The late Charles Francis Adams, a grandson of one American President and a great-grandson of another, after a long lifetime in intimate association with some of the chief business "geniuses" of the United States, reported in his old age that he had never heard a single one of them say anything worth hearing. These were vigorous and masculine men, and in a man's world they were successful men, but intellectually they were all blank cartridges. [7]

There is, indeed, fair ground for arguing that, if men of that kidney were genuinely intelligent, they would never succeed at their gross and driveling concerns—that their very capacity to master and retain such balderdash as constitutes their stock in trade is proof of their inferior mentality. The notion is certainly supported by the familiar incompetency of admittedly first-rate men for what are called practical concerns. One could not think of Aristotle multiplying 3,472,701 by 99,999 without making a mstake, nor could one think of him remembering the range of this or that railway share for two years, or the number of tenpenny nails in a hundredweight, or the freight on lard from Galveston to Rotterdam. And by the same token one could not imagine him expert at bridge, or at golf, or at any other of the idiotic games at which what are called successful men commonly divert themselves. In his great study of British genius, Havelock Ellis found that an incapacity for such shabby expertness is visible in almost all first-rate men. They are bad at tying cravats. They are puzzled by bookkeeping. They know nothing of party politics. In brief, they are inert and impotent in the very fields of endeavor that see the average men's highest performances, and are easily surpassed by men who, in actual intelligence, are about as far below them as the *Simidoe*. [8]

This lack of skill at manual and mental tricks of a trivial character —which must inevitably appear to a barber as stupidity, and to a successful haberdasher as downright imbecility—is a character that men of the first class share with women of the first, second and even third classes. One seldom hears of women succeeding in the occupations which bring out such expertness most lavishly—for example, tuning pianos, practising law, or writing editorials for newspapers—despite the circumstance that the great majority of such occupations are well within their physical powers, and that few of them offer any very formidable social barriers to female entrance. There is no external reason why they should not prosper at the bar, or as editors of magazines, or as managers of factories, or in the wholesale trade, or as hotel-keepers. The taboos that stand in the way are of very small force; various adventurous women have defied them with impunity, and once the door is entered there remains no special handicap within. But, as everyone knows, the number of women actually practising these trades and professions is very small, and few of them have attained to any distinction in competition with men. [9]

The cause thereof, as I say, is not external, but internal. It lies in the same disconcerting apprehension of the larger realities, the same impatience with the paltry and meretricious, the same disqualification for mechanical routine and empty technic which one finds in the higher varieties of men. Even in the pursuits which, by the custom of Christendom, are especially their own, women seldom show any of that elaborately conventionalized and half automatic proficiency which is the pride and boast of most men. It is a commonplace of observation that a housewife who actually knows how to cook, or who can make her own clothes with enough skill to conceal the fact from the most casual glance, or who is competent to instruct her children in the elements of morals, learning and hygiene—it is a platitude that such a woman is very rare indeed, and that when she is encountered she is not usually esteemed for her general intelligence. [10]

This is particularly true in the United States, where the position of women is higher than in any other civilized or semi-civilized country, and the old assumption of their intellectual inferiority has been most successfully challenged. The American bourgeois dinnertable becomes a monument to the defective technic of the American housewife. The guest who respects his esophagus, invited to feed upon its discordant and ill-prepared victuals, evades the experience as long and as often as he can, and resigns himself to it as he might resign himself to being shaved by a paralytic. Nowhere else in the world have women more leisure and freedom to improve their minds, and nowhere else do they show a higher level of intelligence, but nowhere else is there worse cooking in the home, or a more inept handling of the whole domestic economy, or a larger dependence upon the aid of external substitutes, by men provided, for the skill that is wanting where it theoretically exists. It is surely no mere coincidence that the land of the emancipated and enthroned woman is also the land of canned soup, of canned pork and beans, of whole meals in cans, and of everything else ready made. And nowhere else is there a more striking tendency to throw the whole business of training the minds of children upon professional pedagogues, mostly idiots, and the whole business of developing and caring for their bodies upon pediatricians, playground "experts," sex hygienists and other such professionals, mostly frauds. [11]

In brief, women rebel—often unconsciously, sometimes even submitting all the while—against the dull, mechanical tricks of the trade that the present organization of society compels so many of them to practise for a living, and that rebellion testifies to their intelligence. If they enjoyed and took pride in those tricks, and showed it by diligence and skill, they would be on all fours with such men as are head waiters, accountants, school-masters or carpetbeaters, and proud of it. The inherent tendency of any woman above the most stupid is to evade the whole obligation, and, if she can not actually evade it, to reduce its demands to the minimum. And when some accident purges her, either temporarily or permanently, of the inclination to marriage, and she enters into competition with men in the general business of the world, the sort of career that she commonly carves out offers additional evidence of her mental superiority. In whatever calls for no more than an invariable technic and a feeble chicanery she usually fails; in whatever calls for independent thought and resourcefulness she usually succeeds. Thus she is almost always a failure as a lawyer, for the law requires only an armament of hollow phrases and stereotyped formulae, and a mental habit which puts these phantasms above sense, truth and justice; and she is almost always a failure in business, for business, in the main, is so foul a compound of trivialities and rogueries that her sense of intellectual integrity revolts against it. But she is usually a success as a sick-nurse, for that profession requires ingenuity, quick comprehension, courage in the face of novel and disconcerting situations, and above all, a capacity for penetrating and dominating character; and whenever she comes into competition with men in the arts, particularly on those secondary planes where simple nimbleness of mind is unaided by the master strokes of genius, she holds her own invariably. In the *demi-monde* one will find enough acumen and daring, and enough resilience in the face of special difficulties, to put the equipment of any exclusively male profession to shame. If the work of the average man required half the mental agility and readiness of resource of the work of the average brothelkeeper, the average man would be constantly on the verge of starvation. [12]

Men, as everyone knows, are disposed to question this superior intelligence of women; their egoism demands the denial, and they are seldom reflective enough to dispose of it by logical and evidential analysis. Moreover, there is a certain specious appearance of soundness in their position; they have forced upon women an artificial character which well conceals their real character, and women have found it profitable to encourage the deception. But though every normal man thus cherishes the soothing unction that he is the intellectual superior of all women, and particularly of his wife, he constantly gives the lie to his pretension by consulting and deferring to what he calls her intuition. That is to say, he knows by experience that her judgment in many matters of capital concern is more subtle and searching than his own, and, being disinclined to accredit this great sagacity to a more competent intelligence, he takes refuge behind the doctrine that it is due to some impenetrable and intangible talent for guessing correctly, some half mystical supersense, some vague (and, in essence, infrahuman) instinct. [13]

The true nature of this alleged instinct, however, is revealed by an examination of the situations which inspire a man to call it to his aid. These situations do not arise out of the purely technical problems that are his daily concern, but out of the rarer and more fundamental, and hence enormously more difficult problems which beset him only at long and irregular intervals, and so offer a test, not of his mere capacity for being drilled, but of his capacity for genuine ratiocination. No man, I take it, save one consciously inferior and hen-pecked, would consult his wife about hiring a clerk, or about extending credit to some paltry customer, or about some routine piece of tawdry swindling; but not even the most egoistic man would fail to sound the sentiment of his wife about taking a partner into his business, or about standing for public office, or about marrying off their daughter. Such things are of massive importance; they lie at the foundation of well-being; they call for the best thought that the man confronted by them can muster; the perils hidden in a wrong decision overcome even the clamors of vanity. It is in such situations that the superior mental grasp of women is of obvious utility, and has to be admitted. It is here that they rise above the insignificant sentimentalities, superstitions and formulae of men, and apply to the business their singular talent for separating the appearance from the substance, and so exercise what is called their intuition. [14]

Intuition? Bosh! Women, in fact, are the supreme realists of the race. Apparently illogical, they are the possessors of a rare and subtle superlogic. Apparently whimsical, they hang to the truth with a tenacity which carries them through every phase of its incessant, jelly-like shifting of form. Apparently unobservant and easily deceived, they see with bright and horrible eyes. . . . In men, too, the same merciless perspicacity sometimes shows itself—men recognized to be more aloof and uninflammable than the general—men of special talent for the logical—sardonic men, cynics. Men, too, sometimes have brains. But that is a rare, rare man, I venture, who is as steadily intelligent, as constantly sound in judgment, as little put off by appearances, as the average multipara of forty-eight. [15]

PURPOSE AND STRUCTURE

1. Mencken describes women's failures as evidence of their superiority and men's successes as proof of their inferiority. This unstated paradox is developed by means of comparison and contrast. Locate the paragraphs in which he presents the similarities of men and women, the differences, and both similarities and differences. How does Mencken's definition of the feminine mind (try to sum it up in an inclusive statement) draw upon his comparison of men and women and unify the essay?

2. Before he defines the feminine mind, Mencken brings his subject into focus by the method of *identification*. In par. 1 he identifies the feminine mind through an implied contrast between the inward and outward attitude of woman toward man. Cite other examples of identification.

3. In par. 1 Mencken contrasts woman's outward show of respect toward man and her inward (secret) attitude of contempt and pity. The contrast, explicit or implied, between inward and outward behavior recurs throughout the essay. Where? What purpose does it serve in the development of his definition? What other contrasts are developed in this paragraph? What causal relationship is shown in the first paragraph? What other causal relationships are developed in this essay? How do they contribute to Mencken's argument?
In his description of the three characteristics of the feminine mind, is each element of the series discrete? If not, what is the most general element in the series to which the others are subordinate? Locate other explicit or implied references to this attribute.

4. Analyze the methods of paragraph transition Mencken employs. For example, pars. 1–3 all deal with woman's perception of man: the first, with her inward perception of him; the second, with her perception of him with special relationship to herself (that is, what she does and does not envy); the third, with Mencken's comment upon her perception. How does he provide a bridge between pars. 9 and 10? One way to achieve emphasis is through the cumulative use of illustration. How does the author achieve a cumulative effect without repetition? Underline the topic sentence in each paragraph and note the method of its development before you attempt an answer.

5. Consider the manner in which the author defines "compassionate irony" (par. 3). How has the term been anticipated in par. 1? How does he relate it to maternal instinct? Does he use it as an antithesis? a synonym?

a qualification? Locate previous and subsequent assertions and illustrations which demonstrate both compassion and irony.

6. Is there an inherent contradiction in the point he makes in par. 1 and his use of *aloofness* and *derision* in his literary example in par. 3? Or can they be reconciled? Explain.

7. In par. 1 Mencken describes man and makes assertions about his weakness; he then states that because woman perceives these weaknesses, she is intelligent. In par. 4 there is an interesting use of counterpoint: because he must prove that woman is intelligent, therefore man is defective in his perception. Comment upon the logic or circularity of this kind of reasoning.

8. In the statement in which he recapitulates his definition of intelligence (par. 4) Mencken attributes a feminine quality to men. Far from being a term of disparagement, it is one of high praise. How do you know? To find further evidence, note the topic sentence in par. 5 and the concrete details that support it.

9. How does Mencken establish man's confusion of woman's intelligence with her intuition? How does he establish the speciousness of man's rationalization?

10. By what means does he develop the double antithesis between man's outward scorn and inward respect and woman's outward respect and inward contempt?

11. In par. 4 is a series of perfectly balanced sentences beginning "Men are. . . ." How are they linked with the preceding sentences? In the last paragraph is another masterful example of parallel structure. Analyze its components and note other examples of balance.

DICTION AND TONE

1. Mencken provokes laughter but is serious. What is he serious about? Would his essay be funny if it were not serious? Would he be as effective if he did not make preposterous statements? By specific reference to the text, analyze what these elements contribute to the tone. Could you call it mock seriousness?

2. Which words among the following best describe Mencken's tone: *buffoonery, diatribe, vituperation, invective, flamboyance, relish, bravura, castigation, astringency, stridency, exhibitionism, virtuosity, gusto, imperiousness, dogmatism*? Defend your choice by specific allusions to the text.

3. What tone is established in the first paragraph by the use of *magnifico, demigod, mountebank*? How would you characterize the order and tone of this series? Note the series in par. 4: "cruelty, masochism or rouge." What is the logical relationship among these items? What do they tell you about his tone? In what other series in par. 5 does Mencken use the same technique? He uses the word *femaleness* for the first time in par. 4. What are its connotations? How does its use complicate the purpose and tone of the essay?

4. Mencken uses a series of abstractions such as "virtue," "beauty," "faith," "hope," "charity" (par. 4). In the midst of his idiosyncratic verbs and nouns, what function do they perform? How does the phrase "in the husk of delusion and hallucination" contribute to the tone? Ask the same question of the series: "a baby with whiskers, a rabbit with the frame of an aurochs, a feeble and preposterous caricature of God."

5. How does the allusion to Aristotle (par. 8) exemplify his humor, his tone? He juxtaposes *shabby* with *expertness* (8), *divine* with *innocence* (5), *intellectual* with *tricks* (6) and with *lethargy* (7), *cerebral* with *rubberstamps* (6), *shoddy* and *preposterous* with *soul* (2). What is the effect of these pairings on purpose and tone?

6. From time to time Mencken qualifies his sweeping assertions. Identify statements that are preposterous and phrases or words that are hyperbolic. Note also the times he qualifies opinions that would otherwise tax the reader's credulity. Identify passages in which he modulates an extreme statement.

7. How does the word *infra-human* (par. 13) contribute to his purpose and tone?

8. Show the function of "jelly-like shifting"; "bright and horrible"; "merciless perspicacity"; "uninflammable"; "sardonic"; and "average multipara of forty-eight" in the context of the last paragraph.

9. Mencken asserted in his large work *In Defense of Women*, from which this essay was taken, that it was "pianissimo in tone." How would you sum up its tone?

APPLICATIONS TO WRITING

1. Comment on Mencken's view of men and women in the light of your observation, experience, and reading. Compare the attitudes and the tone in which they are expressed by making specific reference to Mencken, Jong, and Sontag; or compare and contrast any two of these writers.

2. Using the method of comparison and contrast, define the quality of mind of two people close to you.

3. Mencken's attitudes toward women are reflected in a number of essays subsumed under the topic, "Reflections on Human Monogamy" in the fourth series of *Prejudices*. Read especially "The Helpmate," "Woman as Realpolitiker," "Venus at the Domestic Hearth," and "The Rat-Trap," and compare and contrast his views of women with those in "The Feminine Mind." Analyze any differences in method and tone.

The Method of Scientific Investigation
from *Collected Essays,* "Darwiniana"

T. H. HUXLEY

The method of scientific investigation is nothing but the expression of the necessary mode of working of the human mind. It is simply the mode at which all phenomena are reasoned about, rendered precise and exact. There is no more difference, but there is just the same kind of difference, between the mental operations of a man of science and those of an ordinary person, as there is between the operations and methods of a baker or of a butcher weighing out his goods in common scales, and the operations of a chemist in performing a difficult and complex analysis by means of his balance and finely graduated weights. It is not that the action of the scales in the one case, and the balance in the other, differ in the principles of their construction or manner of working; but the beam of one is set on an infinitely finer axis than the other, and of course turns by the addition of a much smaller weight. [1]

You will understand this better, perhaps, if I give you some familiar example. You have all heard it repeated, I dare say, that men of science work by means of induction and deduction, and that by the help of these operations, they, in a sort of sense, wring from Nature certain other things, which are called natural laws, and causes, and that out of these, by some cunning skill of their own, they build up hypotheses and theories. And it is imagined by many, that the operations of the common mind can be by no means compared with these processes, and that they have to be acquired by a sort of special apprenticeship to the craft. To hear all these large words, you would think that the mind of a man of science must be constituted differently from that of his fellow men; but if you will not be frightened by terms, you will discover that you are quite wrong, and that all these terrible apparatus are being used by yourselves every day and every hour of your lives. [2]

There is a well-known incident in one of Molière's plays, where the author makes the hero express unbounded delight on being told that he had been talking prose during the whole of his life. In the same way, I trust that you will take comfort, and be delighted with yourselves, on the discovery that you have been acting on the principles of inductive and deductive philosophy during the same period. Probably there is not one here who has not in the course of the day had occasion to set in motion a complex train of reasoning, of the very same kind, though differing of course in degree, as that which a scientific man goes through in tracing the causes of natural phenomena. [3]

A very trivial circumstance will serve to exemplify this. Suppose you go into a fruiterer's shop, wanting an apple—you take up one, and on biting it, you find it is sour; you look at it, and see that it is hard and green. You take up another one and that too is hard, green, and sour. The shopman offers you a third; but, before biting it, you examine it, and find that it is hard and green, and you immediately say that you will not have it, as it must be sour, like those that you have already tried. [4]

Nothing can be more simple that that, you think; but if you will take the trouble to analyse and trace out into its logical elements what has been done by the mind, you will be greatly surprised. In the first place you have performed the operation of induction. You found that, in two experiences, hardness and greenness in apples went together with sourness. It was so in the first case, and it was confirmed by the second. True, it is a very small basis, but still it is enough to make an induction from; you generalise the facts, and you expect to find sourness in apples where you get hardness and greenness. You found upon that a general law that all hard and green apples are sour; and that, so far as it goes, is a perfect induction. Well, having got your natural law in this way, when you are offered another apple which you find is hard and green, you say, "All hard and green apples are sour; this apple is hard and green, therefore this apple is sour." That train of reasoning is what logicians call a syllogism, and has all its various parts and terms—its major premiss, its minor premiss, and its conclusion. And, by the help of further reasoning, which, if drawn out, would have to be exhibited in two or three other syllogisms, you arrive at your final determination, "I will not have that apple." So that, you see, you have, in the first place, established a law by induction, and upon that you have founded a deduction, and reasoned out the special particular case. Well now, suppose, having got your conclusion of the law, that at some time afterwards, you are discussing the qualities of apples with a friend: you will say to him, "It is a very curious thing, but I find that all hard and green apples are sour!" Your friend says to you, "But how do you know that?" You at once reply, "Oh, because I have tried them over and over again, and have always found them to be so." Well, if we were talking science instead of common sense, we should call that an experimental verification. And, if still opposed, you go further, and say, "I have heard from the people in Somersetshire and Devonshire, where a large number of apples are grown, that they have observed the same thing. It is also found to be the case in Normandy, and in North America. In short, I find it to be the universal experience of mankind wherever attention has been directed to the subject." Whereupon, your friend, unless he is a very unreasonable man, agrees with you, and is convinced that you are quite right in the conclusion you have drawn. He believes, although perhaps he does not know he believes it, that the more extensive verifications are—that the more frequently experiments have been made, and results of the same kind arrived at—that the more varied the conditions under which the same results are attained, the more certain is the ultimate conclusion, and he disputes the question no further. He sees that the experiment has been tried under all sorts of conditions, as to time, place, and people, with the same result; and he says with you, therefore, that the law you have laid down must be a good one, and he must believe it. [5]

In science we do the same thing—the philosopher exercises precisely the same faculties, though in a much more delicate manner. In scientific inquiry it becomes a matter of duty to expose a supposed law to every possible kind of verification, and to take care, moreover, that this is done intentionally, and not left to a mere accident, as in the case of the apples. And in science, as in common life, our confidence in a law is in exact proportion to the absence of variation in the result of our experimental verifications. For instance, if you let go your grasp of an article you may have in your hand, it will immediately fall to the ground. That is a very common verification of one of the best established laws of nature—that of gravitation. The method by which men of science establish the existence of that law is exactly the same as that by which we have established the trivial proposition about the sourness of hard and green apples. But we believe it in such an extensive, thorough, and unhesitating manner because the universal experience of mankind verifies it, and we can verify it ourselves at any time; and that is the strongest possible foundation on which any natural law can rest. [6]

So much, then, by way of proof that the method of establishing laws in science is exactly the same as that pursued in common life. Let us now turn to another matter (though really it is but another phase of the same question), and that is, the method by which, from the relations of certain phenomena, we prove that some stand in the position of causes towards the others. [7]

I want to put the case clearly before you, and I will therefore show you what I mean by another familiar example. I will suppose that one of you, on coming down in the morning to the parlour of your house, finds that a tea-pot and some spoons which had been left in the room on the previous evening are gone—the window is open, and you observe the mark of a dirty hand on the window-frame, and perhaps, in addition to that, you notice the impress of a hob-nailed shoe on the gravel outside. All these phenomena have struck your attention instantly, and before two seconds have passed you say, "Oh, somebody has broken open the window, entered the room, and run off with the spoons and the tea-pot!" That speech is out of your mouth in a moment. And you will probably add, "I know there has; I am quite sure of it!" You mean to say exactly what you know; but in reality you are giving expression to what is, in all essential particulars, an hypothesis. You do not *know* it at all; it is nothing but an hypothesis rapidly framed in your own mind. And it is an hypothesis founded on a long train of inductions and deductions. [8]

What are those inductions and deductions, and how have you got at this hypothesis? You have observed in the first place, that the window is open; but by a train of reasoning involving many inductions and deductions, you have probably arrived long before at the general law—and a very good one it is—that windows do not open of themselves; and you therefore conclude that something has opened the window. A second general law that you have arrived at in the same way is, that tea-pots and spoons do not go out of a window spontaneously, and you are satisfied that, as they are not now where you left them, they have been removed. In the third place, you look at the marks on the window-sill, and the shoe-marks outside, and you say that in all previous experience the former kind of mark has never been produced by anything else but the hand of a human being; and the same experience shows that no other animal but man at present wears shoes with hob-nails in them such as would produce the marks in the gravel. I do not know, even if we could discover any of those "missing links" that are talked about, that they would help us to any other conclusion! At any rate the law which states our present experience is strong enough for my present purpose. You next reach the conclusion that, as these kinds of marks have not been left by any other animal than man, or are liable to be formed in any other way than by a man's hand and shoe, the marks in question have been formed by a man in that way. You have, further, a general law, founded on observation and experience, and that, too, is I am sorry to say, a very universal and unimpeachable one—that some men are thieves; and you assume at once from all these premises—and that is what constitutes your hypothesis—that the man who made the marks outside and on the windowsill, opened the window, got into the room, and stole your tea-pot and spoons. You have now arrived at a *vera causa*—you have assumed a cause which, it is plain, is competent to produce all the phenomena you have observed. You can explain all these phenomena only by the hypothesis of a thief. But that is a hypothetical conclusion, of the justice of which you have no absolute proof at all; it is only rendered highly probable by a series of inductive and deductive reasonings. [9]

I suppose your first action, assuming that you are a man of ordinary common sense, and that you have established this hypothesis to your own satisfaction, will very likely be to go off for the police, and set them on the track of the burglar, with the view to the recovery of your property. But just as you are starting with this object, some person comes in, and on learning what you are about, says, "My good friend, you are going on a great deal too fast. How do you know that the man who really made the marks took the spoons? It might have been a monkey that took them, and the man may have merely looked in afterwards." You would probably reply, "Well, that is all very well, but you see it is contrary to all experience of the way tea-pots and spoons are abstracted; so that, at any rate, your hypothesis is less probable than mine." While you are talking the thing over in this way, another friend arrives, one

of the good kind of people that I was talking of a little while ago. And
he might say, "Oh, my dear sir, you are certainly going on a great deal
too fast. You are most presumptuous. You admit that all these occur-
rences took place when you were fast asleep, at a time when you could
not possibly have known anything about what was taking place. How
do you know that the laws of Nature are not suspended during the
night? It may be that there has been some kind of supernatural interference in this case." In point of fact, he declares that your hypothesis
is one of which you cannot at all demonstrate the truth, and that you
are by no means sure that the laws of Nature are the same when you
are asleep as when you are awake. [10]

Well, now, you cannot at the moment answer that kind of reasoning.
You feel that your worthy friend has you somewhat at a disadvantage.
You will feel perfectly convinced in your own mind, however, that you
are quite right, and you say to him. "My good friend, I can only be
guided by the natural probabilities of the case, and if you will be kind
enough to stand aside and permit me to pass, I will go and fetch the
police." Well, we will suppose that your journey is successful, and that
by good luck you meet with a policeman; that eventually the burglar is
found with your property on his person, and the marks correspond to
his hand and to his boots. Probably any jury would consider those facts
a very good experimental verification of your hypothesis, touching the
cause of the abnormal phenomena observed in your parlour, and would
act accordingly. [11]

Now, in this supposititious case, I have taken phenomena of a very
common kind, in order that you might see what are the different steps
in an ordinary process of reasoning, if you will only take the trouble to
analyse it carefully. All the operations I have described, you will see,
are involved in the mind of any man of sense in leading him to a conclusion as to the course he should take in order to make good a robbery
and punish the offender. I say that you are led, in that case, to your
conclusion by exactly the same train of reasoning as that which a man
of science pursues when he is endeavouring to discover the origin and
laws of the most occult phenomena. The process is, and always must
be, the same; and precisely the same mode of reasoning was employed
by Newton and Laplace in their endeavours to discover and define the
causes of the movements of the heavenly bodies, as you, with your own
common sense, would employ to detect a burglar. The only difference

is, that the nature of the inquiry being more abstruse, every step has to be most carefully watched, so that there may not be a single crack or flaw in your hypothesis. A flaw or crack in many of the hypotheses of daily life may be of little or no moment as affecting the general correctness of the conclusions at which we may arrive; but, in a scientific inquiry, a fallacy, great or small, is always of importance, and is sure to be in the long run constantly productive of mischievous if not fatal results. [12]

Do not allow yourselves to be misled by the common notion that an hypothesis is trustworthy simply because it is an hypothesis. It is often urged, in respect to some scientific conclusion, that, after all, it is only an hypothesis. But what more have we to guide us in nine-tenths of the most important affairs of daily life than hypotheses, and often very ill-based ones? So that in science, where the evidence of an hypothesis is subjected to the most rigid examination, we may rightly pursue the same course. You may have hypotheses, and hypotheses. A man may say, if he likes, that the moon is made of green cheese: that is an hypothesis. But another man, who has devoted a great deal of time and attention to the subject, and availed himself of the most powerful telescopes and the results of the observations of others, declares that in his opinion it is probably composed of materials very similar to those of which our own earth is made up: and that is also only an hypothesis. But I need not tell you that there is an enormous difference in the value of the two hypotheses. That one which is based on sound scientific knowledge is sure to have a corresponding value; and that which is a mere hasty random guess is likely to have but little value. Every great step in our progress in discovering causes has been made in exactly the same way as that which I have detailed to you. A person observing the occurrence of certain facts and phenomena asks, naturally enough, what process, what kind of operation known to occur in Nature, applied to the particular case, will unravel and explain the mystery? Hence you have the scientific hypothesis; and its value will be proportionate to the care and completeness with which its basis had been tested and verified. It is in these matters as in the commonest affairs of practical life; the guess of the fool will be folly, while the guess of the wise man will contain wisdom. In all cases, you see that the value of the result depends on the patience and faithfulness with which the investigator applies to his hypothesis every possible kind of verification. [13]

PURPOSE AND STRUCTURE

1. Huxley provides the general topic or thesis of his essay in one sentence in the first paragraph. Identify the thesis sentence and note its location.

2. An analogy is an extended comparison between two things, one of which is more familiar to the reader than the other. In this way, the unknown is explained in terms of the known, that which is remote and alien in terms of that which is near and familiar. What is the first analogy used?

3. Huxley begins par. 2 with the statement that he is going to give a "familiar example." Of what is it an example?

4. Are there any analogies in the example? If there are, what are the familiar things? The unfamiliar ones?

5. In par. 8, Huxley tells us that he is about to show us "another familiar example." Of what is it an example?

6. The first sentence of par. 5 urges the reader to analyze his thought process. List the steps in the analysis of the process.

7. Outline the steps in the analysis in par. 9.

8. Compare the development of pars. 5 and 6 in terms of levels of generalization. Which paragraph is more particular? Which is more general?

9. Carefully compare the first paragraph of the essay to par. 12. Are they basically the same in content? In what ways do they differ?

DICTION AND TONE

1. What tone is established by the writer's reference to himself as "I" and to the reader as "you"?

2. Explain *induction, deduction,* and *syllogism* (par. 2).

3. There are many words, turns of phrase, and sentences that reveal that this essay was not written for a contemporary audience. For example, no modern American goes to a "fruiterer's shop"; "premise" is spelled "premiss." Cite at least three examples that would convince your listener that the essay is old-fashioned.

APPLICATIONS TO WRITING

Write an essay in which you make use of an analogy. For example, you might show how life often resembles a sports event; how love and marriage resemble a military engagement; how the politics of the country resemble the politics of the family; how the ecology of a garden (a farm, or other small unit) resembles the ecology of the earth.

When Your Profession Takes You to Hollywood
from *Changing*

LIV ULLMAN

I came to Hollywood with a suitcase packed for ten days. I had been invited to the premiere of *The Emigrants*. I remained for many months. [1]

An astounded actress from Trondhjem was showered with offers. People smiled and said welcome, opened their homes, picked fruit from their trees and placed it in my child's hands. [2]

I began working, and Linn and I moved into an enormous house with five bathrooms and a swimming pool and a guest cottage; wrote letters to friends saying that people here must be crazy, but it was fun. My bathroom was the size of an ordinary Oslo apartment. It was so grand that the toilet was built like a throne so that one should never feel confused being a film star when nature called. [3]

"You must cut your hair," said one producer. [4]

"No!" [5]

"I'll make you the biggest star if you'll just dress a little differently." [6]

"I'm used to dressing this way." [7]

"Perhaps you should wear some more make-up. Send the beauty-parlor bill to me." [8]

"Certainly not." [9]

And then they left me alone. After all, I enjoyed the status of a serious actress. I had soul and depth, and was European. I didn't use make-up, and I came from Norway. [10]

I met with generosity, found friends and acquaintances, bathed in heated swimming pools, sat in soft chairs watching films in private screening rooms, walked on long sandy beaches by the sea. [11]

I stood on my lawn in the morning squinting up at the sun, was driven to the studio before most people were awake—at half-past five, when the best of day and night meet. [12]

As I sat in his chair, the make-up artist and I gossiped. He gave me good advice for my new life and was always around, as if he wanted to make sure that I didn't get into difficulties. For many years, even before I was born, he had been bending over world-famous faces, covering them with creams and rouges and powders. The bodies of women who had been the cause of sweet dreams for men all over the world had relaxed here in loose dressing gowns, enjoying a moment of freedom before being taken to the wardrobe and laced in and padded out in the appropriate places. [13]

"Life is so short," said the make-up artist, "and no one can persuade me to give something up today for the possibilities of tomorrow, promises of the future." His neck and hands were covered with chains and amulets, and he jingled gaily as he moved. He wore a little cap to hide his baldness. [14]

"Sparkle," he whispered to me as I went in to the lights and the heat and the cameras. "That's what Shirley Temple's mother always said to her little daughter." [15]

I spent some months in Hollywood and tried to sparkle. When something inside me protested, I reminded myself I would soon be home again. I was looking forward to making a film on the island in Sweden, living with old friends in primitive summer cottages where there was no hot water or electricity. Walk a hundred yards to an outhouse, whatever the weather. [16]

Sit there and see the sea through the cracks in the wall, and feel that it is good to be alive. [17]

When your profession takes you one day to Hollywood and the next to a barren island in the Baltic. [18]

PURPOSE AND STRUCTURE

1. What are the various devices and allusions used to develop Ullman's comparison and contrast? What aspects of the contrast are explicit? What implicit?

2. Relate Ullman's feelings about Hollywood to Greer's comments about the stereotype.

DICTION AND TONE

1. Cite the passages in which Ullman satirizes Hollywood.

2. What tone other than mockery is suggested in this fragment?

3. By what means does the make-up artist come to life?

4. Do the sentence fragments contribute to purpose and tone? Explain your response.

APPLICATIONS TO WRITING

1. Compare and contrast two places in which you have lived and/or visited. Try to use a variety of devices to make the places and the person(s) in your life come alive.

2. If you live in a dormitory or fraternity or cooperative house, compare and contrast your feelings toward your environment with those you had in your own home.

3. Compare and contrast your dream house (or vacation) with the realities of your everyday abode (or working-studying life).

The Bird and the Machine

from *The Immense Journey*

LOREN EISELEY

I suppose their little bones have years ago been lost among the stones and winds of those high glacial pastures. I suppose their feathers blew eventually into the piles of tumbleweed beneath the straggling cattle fences and rotted there in the mountain snows, along with dead steers and all the other things that drift to an end in the corners of the wire. I do not quite know why I should be thinking of birds over the *New York Times* at breakfast, particularly the birds of my youth half a continent away. It is a funny thing what the brain will do with memories and how it will treasure them and finally bring them into odd juxtapositions with other things, as though it wanted to make a design, or get some meaning out of them, whether you want it or not, or even see it. [1]

It used to seem marvelous to me, but I read now that there are machines that can do these things in a small way, machines that can crawl about like animals, and that it may not be long now until they do more things—maybe even make themselves—I saw that piece in the *Times* just now. And then they will, maybe—well, who knows—but you read about it more and more with no one making any protest, and already they can add better than we and reach up and hear things through the dark and finger the guns over the night sky. [2]

This is the new world that I read about at breakfast. This is the world that confronts me in my biological books and journals, until there are times when I sit quietly in my chair and try to hear the little purr of the cogs in my head and the tubes flaring and dying as the messages go through them and the circuits snap shut or open. This is the great age, make no mistake about it; the robot has been born somewhat appropriately along with the atom bomb, and the brain they say now is just another type of more complicated feedback system. The engineers have its basic principles worked out; it's mechanical, you know; nothing to get superstitious about; and man can always improve on nature once he gets the idea. Well, he's got it all right and that's why, I guess, that I sit here in my chair, with the article crunched in my hand, remembering those two birds and that blue mountain sunlight. There is another magazine article on my desk that reads "Machines Are Getting Smarter Every Day." I don't deny it, but I'll still stick with the birds. It's life I believe in, not machines. [3]

Maybe you don't believe there is any difference. A skeleton is all joints and pulleys, I'll admit. And when man was in his simpler stages of machine building in the eighteenth century, he quickly saw the resemblances. "What," wrote Hobbes, "is the heart but a spring, and the nerves but so many strings, and the joints but so many wheels, giving motion to the whole body?" Tinkering about in their shops it was inevitable in the end that men would see the world as a huge machine "subdivided into an infinite number of lesser machines." [4]

The idea took on with a vengeance. Little automatons toured the country—dolls controlled by clockwork. Clocks described as little worlds were taken on tours by their designers. They were made up of moving figures, shifting scenes and other remarkable devices. The life of the cell was unknown. Man, whether he was conceived as possessing a soul or not, moved and jerked about like these tiny puppets. A human being thought of himself in terms of his own tools and implements. He had been fashioned like the puppets he produced and was only a more clever model made by a greater designer. [5]

Then in the nineteenth century, the cell was discovered, and the single machine in its turn was found to be the product of millions of infinitesimal machines—the cells. Now, finally, the cell itself dissolves away into an abstract chemical machine—and that into some intangible, inexpressible flow of energy. The secret seems to lurk all about, the wheels get smaller and smaller, and they turn more rapidly, but when you try to seize it the life is gone—and so, by popular definition, some would say that life was never there in the first place. The wheels and the cogs are the secret and we can make them better in time—machines that will run faster and more accurately than real mice to real cheese. [6]

I have no doubt it can be done, though a mouse harvesting seeds on an autumn thistle is to me a fine sight and more complicated, I think, in his multiform activity, than a machine "mouse" running a maze. Also, I like to think of the possible shape of the future brooding in mice, just as it brooded once in a rather ordinary mousy insectivore who became a man. It leaves a nice fine indeterminate sense of wonder that even an electronic brain hasn't got, because you know perfectly well that if the electronic brain changes, it will be because of something man has done to it. But what man will do to himself he doesn't really know. A certain scale of time and a ghostly intangible thing called change are ticking in him. Powers and potentialities like the oak in the seed, or a red and awful ruin. Either way, it's impressive; and the mouse has it, too. Or those birds, I'll never forget those birds—yet before I measured their significance, I learned the lesson of time first of all. I was young then and left alone in a great desert—part of an expedition that had scattered its men over several hundred miles in order to carry on research more effectively. I learned there that time is a series of planes existing superficially in the same universe. The tempo is a human illusion, a subjective clock ticking in our own kind of protoplasm. [7]

As the long months passed, I began to live on the slower planes and to observe more readily what passed for life there. I sauntered, I passed more and more slowly up and down the canyons in the dry baking heat of midsummer. I slumbered for long hours in the shade of huge brown boulders that had gathered in tilted companies out on the flats. I had forgotten the world of men and the world had forgotten me. Now and then I found a skull in the canyons, and these justified my remaining there. I took a serene cold interest in these discoveries. I had come, like many a naturalist before me, to view life with a wary and subdued attention. I had grown to take pleasure in the divested bone. [8]

I sat once on a high ridge that fell away before me into a waste of sand dunes. I sat through hours of a long afternoon. Finally, as I glanced beside my boot an indistinct configuration caught my eye. It was a coiled rattlesnake, a big one. How long he had sat with me I do not know. I had not frightened him. We were both locked in the sleep-walking tempo of the earlier world, baking in the same high air and sunshine. Perhaps he had been there when I came. He slept on as I left, his coils, so ill discerned by me, dissolving once more among the stones and gravel from which I had barely made him out. [9]

Another time I got on a higher ridge, among some tough little wind-warped pines half covered with sand in a basin-like depression that caught everything carried by the air up to those heights. There were a few thin bones of birds, some cracked shells of indeterminable age, and the knotty fingers of pine roots bulged out of shape from their long and agonizing grasp upon the crevices of the rock. I lay under the pines in the sparse shade and went to sleep once more. [10]

It grew cold finally, for autumn was in the air by then, and the few things that lived thereabouts were sinking down into an even chillier scale of time. In the moments between sleeping and waking I saw the roots about me and slowly, slowly, a foot in what seemed many centuries, I moved my sleep-stiffened hands over the scaling bark and lifted my numbed face after the vanishing sun. I was a great awkward thing of knots and aching limbs, trapped up there in some long, patient endurance that involved the necessity of putting living fingers into rock and by slow, aching expansion bursting those rocks asunder. I suppose, so thin and slow was the time of my pulse by then, that I might have stayed on to drift still deeper into the lower cadences of the frost, or the crystalline life that glistens pebbles, or shines in a snowflake, or dreams in the meteoric iron between the worlds. [11]

It was a dim descent, but time was present in it. Somewhere far down in that scale the notion struck me that one might come the other way. Not many months thereafter I joined some colleagues heading higher into a remote windy tableland where huge bones were reputed to protrude like boulders from the turf. I had drowsed with reptiles and moved with the century-long pulse of trees; now, lethargically, I was climbing back up some invisible ladder of quickening hours. There had been talk of birds in connection with my duties. Birds are intense, fast-living creatures—reptiles, I suppose one might say, that have escaped out of the heavy sleep of time, transformed fairy creatures dancing over sunlit meadows. It is a youthful fancy, no doubt, but because of something that happened up there among the escarpments of that range, it remains with me a lifelong impression. I can never bear to see a bird imprisoned. [12]

We came into that valley through the trailing mists of a spring night. It was a place that looked as though it might never have known the foot of man, but our scouts had been ahead of us and we knew all about the abandoned cabin of stone that lay far up on one hillside. It had been built in the land rush of the last century and then lost to the cattlemen again as the marginal soils failed to take to the plow. [13]

There were spots like this all over that country. Lost graves marked by unlettered stones and old corroding rim-fire cartridge cases lying where somebody had made a stand among the boulders that rimmed the valley. They are all that remain of the range wars; the men are under the stones now. I could see our cavalcade winding in and out through the mist below us: torches, the reflection of the truck lights on our collecting tins and the far-off bumping of a loose dinosaur thigh bone in the bottom of a trailer. I stood on a rock a moment looking down and thinking what it cost in money and equipment to capture the past. [14]

We had, in addition, instructions to lay hands on the present. The word had come through to get them alive—birds, reptiles, anything. A zoo somewhere abroad needed restocking. It was one of those reciprocal matters in which science involves itself. Maybe our museum needed a stray ostrich egg and this was the payoff. Anyhow, my job was to help capture some birds and that was why I was there before the trucks. [15]

The cabin had not been occupied for years. We intended to clean it out and live in it, but there were holes in the roof and the birds had come in and were roosting in the rafters. You could depend on it in a place like this where everything blew away, and even a bird needed some place out of the weather and away from coyotes. A cabin going back to nature in a wild place draws them till they come in, listening at the eaves, I imagine, pecking softly among the shingles till they find a hole and then suddenly the place is theirs and man is forgotten. [16]

Sometimes of late years I find myself thinking the most beautiful sight in the world might be the birds taking over New York after the last man has run away to the hills. I will never live to see it, of course, but I know just how it will sound because I've lived up high and I know the sort of watch birds keep on us. I've listened to sparrows tapping tentatively on the outside of air conditioners when they thought no one was listening, and I know how other birds test the vibrations that come up to them through the television aerials. [17]

"Is he gone?" they ask, and the vibrations come up from below, "Not yet, not yet." [18]

Well, to come back, I got the door open softly and I had the spotlight all ready to turn on and blind whatever birds there were so they couldn't see to get out through the roof. I had a short piece of ladder to put against the far wall where there was a shelf on which I expected to make the biggest haul. I had all the information I needed just like any skilled assassin. I pushed the door open, the hinges squeaking only a little. A bird or two stirred—I could hear them—but nothing flew and there was a faint starlight through the holes in the roof. [19]

I padded across the floor, got the ladder up and the light ready, and slithered up the ladder till my head and arms were over the shelf. Everything was dark as pitch except for the starlight at the little place back of the shelf near the eaves. With the light to blind them, they'd never make it. I had them. I reached my arm carefully over in order to be ready to seize whatever was there and I put the flash on the edge of the shelf where it would stand by itself when I turned it on. That way I'd be able to use both hands. [20]

Everything worked perfectly except for one detail—I didn't know what kind of birds were there. I never thought about it at all, and it wouldn't have mattered if I had. My orders were to get something interesting. I snapped on the flash and sure enough there was a great beating and feathers flying, but instead of my having them, they, or rather he, had me. He had my hand, that is, and for a small hawk not much bigger than my fist he was doing all right. I heard him give one short metallic cry when the light went on and my hand descended on the bird beside him; after that he was busy with his claws and his beak was sunk in my thumb. In the struggle I knocked the lamp over on the shelf, and his mate got her sight back and whisked neatly through the hole in the roof and off among the stars outside. It all happened in fifteen seconds and you might think I would have fallen down the ladder, but no, I had a professional assassin's reputation to keep up, and the bird, of course, made the mistake of thinking the hand was the enemy and not the eyes behind it. He chewed my thumb up pretty effectively and lacerated my hand with his claws, but in the end I got him, having two hands to work with. [21]

He was a sparrow hawk and a fine young male in the prime of life. I was sorry not to catch the pair of them, but as I dripped blood and folded his wings carefully, holding him by the back so that he couldn't strike again, I had to admit the two of them might have been more than I could have handled under the circumstances. The little fellow had saved his mate by diverting me, and that was that. He was born to it, and made no outcry now, resting in my hand hopelessly, but peering toward me in the shadows behind the lamp with a fierce, almost indifferent glance. He neither gave nor expected mercy and something out of the high air passed from him to me, stirring a faint embarrassment. [22]

I quit looking into that eye and managed to get my huge carcass with its fist full of prey back down the ladder. I put the bird in a box too small to allow him to injure himself by struggle and walked out to welcome the arriving trucks. It had been a long day, and camp still to make in the darkness. In the morning that bird would be just another episode. He would go back with the bones in the truck to a small cage in a city where he would spend the rest of his life. And a good thing, too. I sucked my aching thumb and spat out some blood. An assassin has to get used to these things. I had a professional reputation to keep up. [23]

In the morning, with the change that comes on suddenly in that high country, the mist that had hovered below us in the valley was gone. The sky was a deep blue, and one could see for miles over the high outcroppings of stone. I was up early and brought the box in which the little hawk was imprisoned out onto the grass where I was building a cage. A wind as cool as a mountain spring ran over the grass and stirred my hair. It was a fine day to be alive. I looked up and all around and at the hole in the cabin roof out of which the other little hawk had fled. There was no sign of her anywhere that I could see. [24]

"Probably in the next county by now," I thought cynically, but before beginning work I decided I'd have a look at my last night's capture. [25]

Secretively, I looked again all around the camp and up and down and opened the box. I got him right out in my hand with his wings folded properly and I was careful not to startle him. He lay limp in my grasp and I could feel his heart pound under the feathers but he only looked beyond me and up. [26]

I saw him look that last look away beyond me into a sky so full of light I could not follow his gaze. The little breeze flowed over me again, and nearby a mountain aspen shook all its tiny leaves. I suppose I must have had an idea then of what I was going to do, but I never let it come up into consciousness. I just reached over and laid the hawk on the grass. [27]

He lay there a long minute without hope, unmoving, his eyes still fixed on that blue vault above him. It must have been that he was already so far away in heart that he never felt the release from my hand. He never even stood. He just lay with his breast against the grass. [28]

In the next second after that long minute he was gone. Like a flicker of light, he had vanished with my eyes full on him, but without actually seeing even a premonitory wing beat. He was gone straight into that towering emptiness of light and crystal that my eyes could scarcely bear to penetrate. For another long moment there was silence. I could not see him. The light was too intense. Then from far up somewhere a cry came ringing down. [29]

I was young then and had seen little of the world, but when I heard that cry my heart turned over. It was not the cry of the hawk I had captured; for, by shifting my position against the sun, I was now seeing further up. Straight out of the sun's eye, where she must have been soaring restlessly above us for untold hours, hurtled his mate. And from far up, ringing from peak to peak of the summits over us, came a cry of such unutterable and ecstatic joy that it sounds down across the years and tingles among the cups on my quiet breakfast table. [30]

I saw them both now. He was rising fast to meet her. They met in a great soaring gyre that turned to a whirling circle and a dance of wings. Once more, just once, their two voices, joined in a harsh wild medley of question and response, struck and echoed against the pinnacles of the valley. Then they were gone forever somewhere into those upper regions beyond the eyes of men. [31]

I am older now, and sleep less, and have seen most of what there is to see and am not very much impressed any more, I suppose, by anything. "What Next in the Attributes of Machines?" my morning headline runs. "It Might Be the Power to Reproduce Themselves." [32]

I lay the paper down and across my mind a phrase floats insinuatingly: "It does not seem that there is anything in the construction, constituents, or behavior of the human being which it is essentially impossible for science to duplicate and synthesize. On the other hand . . ." [33]

All over the city the cogs in the hard, bright mechanisms have begun to turn. Figures move through computers, names are spelled out, a thoughtful machine selects the fingerprints of a wanted criminal from an array of thousands. In the laboratory an electronic mouse runs swiftly through a maze toward the cheese it can neither taste nor enjoy. On the second run it does better than a living mouse. [34]

"On the other hand . . ." Ah, my mind takes up, on the other hand the machine does not bleed, ache, hang for hours in the empty sky in a torment of hope to learn the fate of another machine, nor does it cry out with joy nor dance in the air with the fierce passion of a bird. Far off, over a distance greater than space, that remote cry from the heart of heaven makes a faint buzzing among my breakfast dishes and passes on and away. [35]

PURPOSE AND STRUCTURE

1. In this essay, Eiseley compares and contrasts "birds" and "machines." In what ways are birds like machines? Make a list of *similarities*. Cite the

paragraph and page number for each of your examples. In what paragraph does the author first mention birds? machines? Describe the contexts or situations in which they are mentioned.

2. What do you think is the main thesis of this essay? How are birds and machines part of the thesis statement? What does each symbolize? Find the sentence (or sentences) that you think state the main topic.

3. What are the *differences* between the bird and the machine? Cite examples of these differences from the beginning (pars. 1–8) and the ending (pars. 32–35) of the essay. Does Eiseley explore the differences between the bird and the machine before or after his thesis statement?

4. What is the topic sentence of par. 4? In what concrete ways does par. 5 expand and illustrate the main topic of par. 4?

5. In par. 7 the concept of "time" is first mentioned. How does the concept of time mark a transition in the subject matter of the essay? Find the sentences in which Eiseley establishes this transition.

6. Examine par. 8. Notice that the *focus* of the pargraph is the subject "I." Make a list of the verbs and verb phrases that follow the subject "I" in this paragraph. Compare the focus of this paragraph with par. 9. Where and how does the focus *shift?*

7. In the lengthy flashback (anecdote) described in pars. 8–23, Eiseley describes time both in terms of "descent" and "ascent." What concrete examples are given to illustrate the author's descent into past time (pars. 8–11)?

8. How does Eiseley contrast birds and reptiles? Cite examples. How do birds symbolize the author's ascent from past to present time in pars. 12 ff.? What do you think is the topic sentence of par. 12? Why?

9. Note the way in which the author makes the transition from the historic past to the historic present in pars. 13–15. List concrete examples of past and present from these paragraphs. What part do light and darkness seem to play in this description, and in the anecdote about the capture of the sparrow hawk in pars. 16–23?

10. How is the concept of "change" illustrated in par. 24? What are the physical changes that indicate a transition from the previous paragraphs? Make a list of the references to "light," "blue sky" and "ascent" in pars. 24–31. How does the use of these images unify the theme of time, and the passage from past to present time which began in par. 12?

11. The last four paragraphs return the reader to the real present, and the comparison and contrast of the "bird" and the "machine." What final *contrast* does the author make to support his thesis statement?

DICTION AND TONE

Note the use of the words and phrases like "cold," "chillier," "vanishing sun" in par. 11. What effect do these words have on the reader? Find other examples in par. 11 that help to establish the tone of this section.

APPLICATIONS TO WRITING

Write an essay in which you compare and contrast two seemingly unlike objects, like Eiseley's "bird" and "machine."

1. Using Eiseley's method, begin by comparing the two things—in what ways are they similar?

2. In your thesis statement show a *preference* for one of these things over the other.

3. In your subsequent paragraphs, support your preference by describing and defining the *differences* between these two things. Give concrete illustrations of the differences; try to use descriptive language in your illustrations that will set a tone for your readers; and use the technique of flashback if you can to illustrate a main point.

4. Write a concluding paragraph that summarizes or restates your thesis.

PART **five**

Illustration

Illustration—at its simplest, a particular member of a class used to explain or dramatize the class. The individual member selected must be a fair representative of the distinctive qualities of the class. At its most complex, an illustration provides the particulars on which a generalization is based; the generalization—a type of person or thing, an idea or abstraction—may or may not be explicitly stated. McFadden illustrates the incidence of mental inertia and debasement of thought that characterizes those who resort to the cliché-ridden psychological patter of the fringe human potential movements. Anderson documents a revolution with illustrations of the changes made in each person's life. Thurber's amusing essay on his "university days" is pure illustration: he states no thesis or generalization. Excerpts from official reports illustrate Williams' sense that sharks are unpredictable. Bettelheim transforms what might have been a mere case history into an illustration of a predicament of contemporary man. The experience of his own life illustrates the irony of Mark Jacobson's thesis.

California Spinach Talk

CYRA McFADDEN

A woman who lives here in the San Francisco Bay Area, where every prospect pleases and only man is vile, is teaching "inner cooking." "I'm out of the closet," a newspaper interview quotes her as saying. "All this time I've been interested in people and feelings, but I've been in the disguise of a cooking teacher." [1]

Joyce Goldstein conducts her classes in "Kitchen Consciousness" in her Berkeley home. Cooking, she believes, is a metaphor for life. It involves "taking risks," "expressing feelings," "releasing body energy" and "sharing space." That her techniques of guided fantasy and gestalt in the kitchen fill yet another need in the collective Bay Area consciousness is apparent in a student testimonial quoted in the same interview: "Joyce's classes have changed my whole outlook in the kitchen. I don't feel all those ought-tos and should-haves anymore. I am a free woman." [2]

I know, I know. It's also a free country. If, as Goldstein suggests, you find cleaning shrimp "a meditative experience," and if you, too, believe that foods have personalities ("the tomato . . . is thin-skinned and bruises easily, but likes to bring things together") that, as we say in the consciousness-raising capital of the Western World, is your own trip. Dig it, relate to it, groove on it, get behind it, even, if you choose. Only spare me your account of the whole transcendent experience. Living here in beautiful Marin county, between the fern bars and the deep blue sea, I hear all the mindless prattle about feelings, human and vegetable, that I can tolerate without "acting out" and drowning the users of the Newspeak of the 70's, like unwanted kittens, in their own hot tubs. [3]

"You've really got a thing about language, haven't you?" said a man who sat next to me at a luncheon recently. "What's your hang-up? I think the whole new language trip is because people are really into being upfront about their feelings these days instead of intellectualizing, so we need a whole new way of describing all that stuff . . . the feelings. I mean, ten years ago we didn't even know they were there. And anyway, you can't say it doesn't communicate. [4]

"Like, right now we're having this discussion, for example, and I say, 'I know where you're coming from.' Are you going to tell me you don't know what I mean by that?" [5]

Arguing with such people, I have learned, is as futile as trying to scrape fresh bubble gum off one's shoe. Still, I insisted that I didn't know what my luncheon partner meant in any concrete sense and that 'I know where you're coming from' was meaningless in the context. Did he mean he knew where I'd grown up, or where I'd been immediately before malevolent fate placed me at the table beside him, or what education and experience had shaped my thinking about the issue between us? [6]

Intellectualizing, said my companion. Nit-picking. I knew very well that he meant that he could relate, that he knew what space I was in. Where my head was coming from. [7]

By this time I wished my head and everything appended to it were elsewhere. "Are you trying to say you understand why I feel the way I do about empty, rubber-stamp language?" I asked, coming down hard on the consonants. [8]

My luncheon partner smiled infuriatingly. "You see?" he said. "I *knew* you knew where I was coming from." [9]

Writer Richard Rosen calls such language psychobabble (his funny and incisive book by the same title has just been published by Atheneum). He defines it as "monotonous patois . . . psychological patter, whose concern is faithfully to catalogue the ego's condition." [10]

I define it as semantic spinach, and I say the hell with it. [11]

Conversations like the above, if one can call such an exchange a conversation, have all but supplanted anything resembling intelligent human discourse here, where the human-potential movement takes the place of other light industry and where the redwood-shingled offices of the healer/masseurs, the gurus and the "life-goals consultants" line the main approach to Mill Valley along with the hamburger stands. They make any real exchange of ideas impossible; block any attempt at true communication; substitute what Orwell called "prefabricated words and phrases" for thought. [12]

Just as surely as the Styrofoam boxes one sees everywhere are evidence of the popularity of McDonald's, such conversations, too, are the fallout from the fast-food-outlet approach to therapy of the 70's. With the self the only subject worth examining, one's purely intuitive "off the wall" response the only reference point, all verbal exchange is soon reduced to a kind of mechanical chatter in the infield. [13]

Speakers of psychobabble, I believe, are not so much concerned with describing feelings "we didn't even know were there" ten years ago as with avoiding any mental exertion whatsoever; any effort at precision of expression, or even thought itself, falls under the pejorative label "intellectualizing." Thus the number of words and phrases in the Bay Area vocabulary that describe mental inertia: "mellowing out," "kicking back," "going with the flow," being "laid back." All suggest that the laid-back, mellowed-out speaker achieves a perfect relation with the universe while in a state of passivity just short of that produced by full anesthetic. [14]

How much easier it is, after all, to "verbalize" in platitudes rather than to think. Trite, cliché-ridden language is always a sign of inattention at best, intellectual laziness at worst. One either speaks or writes the occasional cliché because his mind, for some reason or other, has momentarily switched over to automatic pilot, or he uses prefabricated words and phrases routinely because as far as he's concerned, it's six of one, half a dozen of the other. [15]

Psychobabble is no more difficult to use than drawing the girl on the matchbook cover, and it has another attraction as well: Speakers associate its platitudes with profundity and mouth its Words to Live By in the apparent conviction that having said nothing, they have said it all. [16]

"I can't get behind school right now," said a student in a college composition class of mine, when I warned him that if he continued to show no vital signs, he would fail the course. "But I'm not into F's," he added, "and, anyway, I don't think you ought to lay that authority trip on me. I mean, failing someone . . . wow, that's a value judgment." [17]

"I can't relate to the dude," said another, in a contemporary literature class, pressed for his opinion of a Ray Bradbury short story. [18]

"How about being more specific?" I said. "Do you mean you weren't interested in his ideas, or that you didn't find them sympathetic? Were you bored? Did you have trouble following the action of the story?" [19]

"Actually I didn't exactly read it," said the student. [20]

"For God's sake, how do you know you 'can't relate' then?" I asked, knowing better. [21]

My student turned his serene blue gaze upon me. "I just flashed on it," he explained. [22]

A value judgment. Give me the trench-coat type flasher any time over the one who whips open an empty mind to display his poor excuse for an insight. [23]

What is most alarming about psychobabble, however, is not its appalling smugness but that it spreads like Dutch elm disease. Unlike most cult language—private vocabularies small groups use to distinguish themselves from the larger language community—the fatuous fallout from the human potential movement seems to have jumped all the usual fences. And while elsewhere in the country one hears psychobabble spoken by the members of the "counterculture," here the counterculture has come out from under the counter and become the dominant culture itself, its dialect the language of polite society that one must speak in order to belong. Rock-band roadies, stockbrokers, academics, teeny-boppers, butchers—sometimes it appears that everyone one meets has taken the same course in Deep Feelereze at Berlitz. [24]

"Your arms are crossed. Do you realize that's a very defensive posture?" says the friend I meet in the supermarket. "You're afraid of me. I can tell from your body language." [25]

I'm not afraid, I assure her. My arms are crossed because I couldn't find a cart, and if I adopt a less defensive posture, I will drop a dozen cat-food cans on her foot. [26]

My friend smiles wisely, bemused by my transparent self-deception. Some of the people can fool themselves all of the time, she is thinking. "Look," she says, "it's O.K. *You're* O.K. I just think maybe some time when the vibes are right, we ought to get clear. . . ." [27]

At a dinner party, a new acquaintance tells me about her intimate life. Although she is still "processing" her ex-husband (not, I hope, in the Waring blender her language brings to mind), she just spent a weekend with another man from whom she gets "a lot of ego reinforcement. My therapist keeps telling me to go where the energies are," she says, "so that's what I'm doing, because that's what went wrong last time. I didn't just kick back and go with the energies." [28]

Suddenly I realized why Marin's own George Lucas is getting rich from "Star Wars," a film in which people go where the energies are, at speeds faster than "hyper-space," and deliver themselves of simple-minded philosophy in one-syllable words. [29]

Why has phychobabble saturated Bay Area conversation so? One hears it nearly everywhere else to some extent, it is true, but only in San Francisco, Los Angeles and environs has it all but replaced English. (Los Angeles has its own bizarre variation, incidentally, incorporating film and television industry money talk. Example: "I'm gonna be totally up-front with you, sweetheart. The bottom line is 50 thou and points.") [30]

In part, the appeal is the gravitational pull urban California has always felt toward the new, the Now, the "trendy," no matter how ludicrous its current manifestation. In an area where opening night at the opera featured at least one socialite in an elegant designer gown and a punk-rock safety pin in her hair, one shouldn't be too surprised when a butcher asks, "Could you relate to a pork loin roast?" [31]

Partly responsible, too, is the legacy of the Haight-Ashbury and the Summer of Love. Former flower children whose own vocabulary of peace and love focused on the primacy of feelings, who found concrete reality largely irrelevant, now abound in the hills and canyons of Marin, driving car pools to Montessori school on alternate Thursdays or working as claims adjusters at Fireman's Fund. [32]

Fallen victim to cellulite and revolving credit, wistful for the days of LSD and roses, they naturally embrace a language pattern that declares they have not repudiated their 60's selves. [33]

"Listen," one of them told a friend of mine recently, as they exchanged driver's licenses and phone numbers after a minor traffic accident, "I just want you to know that you've been so beautiful about all this, it's really been a beautiful experience." [34]

My friend said he didn't agree and that most of the traffic accidents he had known couldn't really be described as beautiful, though some were pretty and others compensated for their plainness with lots of charm. [35]

Finally, in these pleasant, prosperous suburbs, enough people have enough money to spend on weekend after weekend at psychological boot camps for civilians like *est* and Silva mind control; consulting holistic healers and doing dream or body work; being Rolfed, getting centered, or—in Marin county—taking their horses to be treated for anxiety by a veterinarian who specializes in equine acupuncture. [36]

What Tom Wolfe calls "the Me decade" can burgeon here under ideal conditions: affluence, leisure and what has been traditionally a high level of tolerance for fads and human foibles. Joyce Goldstein, the Berkeley teacher of inner cooking, might have a little trouble collecting disciples in, say, Missoula, Mont., but she is doing nicely, thank you, in balmy Berkeley. "Joyce is nifty and a half," says another of her students, a woman assistant vice president at Wells Fargo Bank. "I was a cooking cripple until I met her. Now I can't cook, but Joyce has showed me that it's O.K." [37]

One could argue that such preoccupations and diversions are essentially harmless in that they keep people off the streets, or what are called in Los Angeles (to distinguish them from the freeways) the surface roads. In this era of do your own thing, however, my thing, as my luncheon partner some weeks past either understood or didn't, is despair at the effects of 70's egocentrism on the language. [38]

I have read too many essays by and held too many conferences with college students whose written and spoken English had the clarity of Cream of Wheat. [39]

I have listened to too many *est* graduates, living walkie-talkies, tell me, unsolicited, what they were "getting." (Clear, creative divorces, double messages, in touch with themselves, not necessarily in that order.) [40]

I have argued too many times about things that matter to me passionately with people who dismissed both arguments and me with "How come you're so uptight?" or "Your head's really in a funny place, you know?" [41]

Crack-brained California, you say complacently; it's always been Cloud Cuckooland out there. True, but California foolishness has a historic tendency to seep through the water tables and across state lines. What if one day soon it is impossible to carry on a reasonably coherent conversation north of Yucatan and south of the Bering Sea? [42]

Meanwhile I stand on the roof of my Mill Valley house, watching the flood of psychobabble rising, ever rising, and wishing I knew how to turn the situation around. It won't be easy. The psychobabblers not only outnumber the rest of us, but, what is worse, they have The Force on their side. [43]

PURPOSE AND STRUCTURE

1. State the author's thesis in your own words. What is the advantage of beginning with a series of illustrations and delaying, until the third paragraph, any direct and general statement of the author's views?

2. How would you describe the shift in structure in pars. 10–16?

3. How do the particulars in pars. 12–13 illustrate the writer's thesis? What ironical contrast is drawn?

4. How does the incident in pars. 17–23 give credence to the author's thesis?

5. How does the allusion to *Star Wars* relate to the generalization and its illustrations in pars. 24–29?

6. What causal relationships are illustrated in pars. 30–37?

7. With what generalization and illustrations does McFadden express her despair in pars. 38–43?

DICTION AND TONE

1. What clue does the spinach metaphor in the title give you regarding the author's attitude toward her subject? What clues in the first three paragraphs reveal that the writer is being satirical? Distinguish between the language that directly and indirectly conveys her indignation.

2. What does the image of the tomato contribute to tone and purpose (par. 3)?

3. How does the writer distinguish "true communication" from " 'prefabricated words and phrases' " (par. 12)? How does she relate "mental inertia" to "psychobabble" (par. 14)?

4. How do the following details or figures of speech relate to purpose and contribute to tone: "the styrofoam boxes . . . of McDonalds" (par. 13); "the fast-food-outlet approach to therapy of the 70's" (par. 13); "a state of passivity just short of that produced by full anesthetic" (par. 14); "his mind . . . has momentarily switched over to automatic pilot" (par. 15); "it's six of one, half a dozen of the other" (par. 15); "the girl on the matchbook cover" (par. 16)?

5. How does the comparison and contrast in par. 23 function in relation to purpose and tone? Why is the use of the verb *whips* effective?

6. Why is the allusion to "The Force" in the final sentence an effective way to sum up the author's thesis and to reflect its dominant tone?

APPLICATIONS TO WRITING

1. With notebook or tape recorder constantly available, record a number of conversations in your dormitory or home, at lunch or dinner, at work, in the halls, before or after class, wherever you and your contemporaries congregate. Using the conversations as illustrations, draw some generalizations about your own language habits and those of your contemporaries.

2. If you have had experience in one or more of the human potential movements, support or refute the author's point of view toward them by formulating a general statement and illustrating it by using concrete detail.

3. Write a satirical sketch of one of the subcultures with which you are familiar, illustrating its language, its activities and its outlook on life.

More Futures Than One

POUL ANDERSON

He was born in 1970, to an upper-middle-class white American family that thought of itself as beleaguered. [1]

Not that his parents were unenlightened or fanatical. On the contrary, both were college graduates, enjoyed foreign travel, left good impressions wherever they went and had friends in more than one circle. Political independents, they split their ballots as often as not. He, a rising young corporation lawyer, was a bit more conservative than she, who had flirted with radicalism in her student days. But their arguments only added liveliness to a loving relationship. At root they wanted the same things for themselves, their children and the world. [2]

They were both afraid. [3]

Their nightmares were shared, but certain ones came most sharply to each. He saw crime and hatred tearing his country apart and, waiting behind them, insurrection. He feared these things less in themselves than he feared the reaction they could provoke—the end of Jefferson's dreams in tyranny and genocide. Abroad, he saw spreading chaos, implacable enmity and weapons that could lay waste the earth. She saw barrenness: of the soil, the flesh and the spirit. Wasn't the start of the great famines predicted for about 1980? North America and Europe might survive a while longer; but at what cost? Faceless mobs packed elbow to elbow in rotting cities and junk-yard countryside, the almighty state equipped with snooper systems and data banks to control every action, on a planet so gutted and poisoned that the very possibility of life seemed to be going down the same drain that was about to swallow the last vestiges of beauty and serenity. Was that any future to offer your children? [4]

They had two, John and Jane. They said those names were a declaration of independence from the neonyms—Jax and Jeri and Lord knew what else—that had become the real mark of conformity. Maybe they meant it, though they said it with a laugh. In spite of their fears, they laughed quite a bit—though the children's first two decades were, in fact, hard. History would look back on them and shudder. But John and Jane remembered that time in much the way their grandparents remembered the Great Depression, their parents the Korean War or anyone who is not too cruelly unfortunate remembers growing up. In the background was trouble; sometimes it struck close, as when a cousin came home dead from Burma, or the streets of their suburb resounded to the boots of the National Guard, or inflation wrecked their father's business. But mostly they were busy exploring their existence. [5]

And somehow existence continued. Somehow the ultimate catastrophes never quite came. Enough people never quit working for reform and public compassion on the one hand, for order and public decency on the other. No matter the scale on which madness ran loose, no matter the face it wore, they resisted it. Disagreeing among themselves, often profoundly, they nonetheless made common cause against the real enemy and worked together to achieve the traditional, sane equality of dissatisfaction. [6]

It turned out that lawlessness could be curbed without extreme measures. When investments in education and opportunity began to pay off, the younger generation simply grew bored by talk of revolt. A high-level industrial economy proved to have remarkable powers of recuperation even from funny money. The first tactical nuclear weapon fired in anger did not automatically trigger the detonation of everything. A peace of exhaustion was not a hopelessly bad foundation on which to start building enforceable international agreements. Population patterns generally followed that of Japan as soon as the means were commonly available. The environment could be cleaned up and rehabilitated. Pollution-free machines were feasible to make and sell. A massive American reaction set in against bureaucratic interference in private affairs. None of this was perfect, none was clear-cut nor had any definite beginning or cause. But once more—as after the fall of Rome or the wars of religion—man was groping his way back toward the light. [7]

And the most savage of those years witnessed some of the most superb achievements the race had yet reached. They were in science and technology—the arts would not regain any important creativity for a while —but they were not on that account any less Bach fugues of theory, Parthenons of mechanism. John had been begotten on the joyful night man first spent on the moon. He was still in grade school when permanent bases were established there; and by then, visits to Earth-orbital stations were routine. Between lunar resources and free-space assembly, the construction of interplanetary craft had become almost cheap. This was good, because the demand for them waxed as knowledge led to spatial industries. John was in high school at the time of the Mars and Venus landings. Radiation screens and thermal conversion were then about to open up innermost Mercury and really efficient nuclear engines were being developed for expeditions to the remote outer worlds. Speculation about reaching the stars became official. [8]

On Earth, the changes were more obviously fundamental, and many of them were disturbing. Few denied that the controlled thermonuclear reaction—clean power, its source literally inexhaustible—was a good thing. Nor was there any serious argument against progress in fuel cells, energy storage units and other devices that, together, would push the combustion engine into well-deserved extinction. True, while alarmists predicted that such techniques as desalinization and food synthesis would merely fill the planet with more starvelings, those landmarks of engineering forestalled worldwide famine until such other techniques as the one-year contraceptive pill could show results. [9]

But controversy went on over the effects of biology, medicine, psychology. The cracking of the genetic code made prostheses and organ transplants obsolete after the organs would be regrown. More importantly, DNA modification brought an end to diseases such as diabetes and, indirectly, to cancer. But would man now start tinkering with his own evolution? What ghastliness might his unwisdom bring on? The dangers in the growing variety of psycho-drugs and brain stimulators were not reduced by becoming a trite topic at cocktail parties. New methods of education helped ram enough poor people into the twentieth century that the threatened uprisings faded away. But since these methods involved conditioning, right down to the neural level, did they not invite any dictator to produce a nation of willing slaves? Man-computer linkages (temporary ones using electro-magnetic induction, not wires into anybody's skull) had vastly extended the range of human control, experience and thinking capability. But were they not potentially dehumanizing? And what of the machines themselves, the robots, the enormous automatic systems, the ubiquitous and ever more eerily gifted computers? What would they do to us? [10]

Thus, as mankind staggered toward a degree of tranquillity and common sense, John and Jane's father wondered how relevant politics had been in the first place. It seemed to him that the future belonged to those blind, impersonal, unpredictable and uncontrollable forces associated with pure and applied science. He was an intelligent man and a concerned one. He was right about an ongoing revolution that was to alter the world. But he was looking in the wrong direction. The real cataclysm was happening elsewhere. His mistake was scarcely his fault. The revolutionaries didn't know either. [11]

They were running secondhand-book stores that tended to specialize, and head shops of a thousand different kinds, and artists' cooperatives, and schools teaching assorted Japanese athletics, and home workshops, and small-circulation magazines, and their own movie companies, and subsistence farms with up-to-date equipment that took advantage of cheap power, and tiny laboratories that drew on public data-retrieval and computer systems, and consultation services that did likewise, and on and on. By these means they became independent. [12]

They weren't beat, hippie, conservative, utopian; they weren't activists nor disciples. They weren't artsy-craftsy. They weren't do-it-yourselfers. They weren't the rich kids who followed sun and surf around the planet nor those who opted out to groove on rock and pot. They weren't the middle-class middle-aged men who, in real or fancied desperation, carried for a while those anesthetic guns that became the compromise between lethal weapons and none. They weren't those young men who, understanding the transfigured technology as their elders never would, used it to make themselves millionaries before the age of 30 and then used the money for their pet causes. They weren't the American blacks, *chicanos*, Indians, Orientals who decided—usually in a quiet fashion—that the culture of their liberal white friends wasn't for them after all. They weren't the medievalists who, a few years before John was born, brought back the tournaments, costumes, food and manners of a bygone era, raised banners and pavilions and generally spent a large part of their time playing an elaborate game. They weren't the many who discovered that, in a world of machines, personal service—anything human, from gardening to carpentry to counseling—is in such demand that those who render it can work when and where they choose. The revolutionaries were none of these, because they were all of them and more. They fitted into no category whatsoever. [13]

Has the point been made? In an ultraproductive, largely automated economy, which has rationalized its distribution system so that everyone can have the necessities of life, labor becomes voluntary. Some kinds of it are rewarded with a high material standard of living; but if you prefer different activities, you can trade that standard off to whatever extent you wish. The way out of the rat-race is to renounce cheese and go after flowers, which are free. Enough will always want cheese to keep the wheel turning. [14]

Many of the revolutionaries had at various times described themselves as radical, hippie, Afro or what have you. Many still did when John reached his maturity. Others had invented new labels, were prophesying new salvations and trying out new life styles. But none of that was important. The revolution had already taken place. Every way of living that was not a direct threat to someone else's had become possible. [15]

PURPOSE AND STRUCTURE

1. Par. 4 has a number of levels of generality. The topic sentence is the most general. Which sentence is it? The nightmares "he" sees are at a lower level of generality. Demonstrate how the author could have made the nightmares even more particular.

2. In the same paragraph she sees barrenness "of the soil, the flesh and the spirit." How does the author attempt to illustrate each of these? Is he equally successful with all three?

3. How does the author achieve a transition between pars. 4 and 5?

4. Argue that in par. 6 the high level of generality makes the paragraph difficult to understand. Be very specific and particular in your remarks.

5. Par. 7 appears to be a string of unrelated sentences. Is there any coherence in the paragraph? If there is, how is it achieved?

6. Find as many similarities as you can between pars. 13 and 7.

7. Pars. 9 and 10 list advantages and disadvantages that accrue to mankind. In light of these paragraphs, argue that the first sentence of par. 11 is illogical.

8. In par. 14 the author asks, "Has the point been made"? Has it? What is the point?

DICTION AND TONE

1. In par. 4, explain the allusion to "Jefferson's dreams."

2. Explain what the author means in par. 8 by "Bach fugues of theory, Parthenons of mechanism."

3. What effect is created by naming the children John and Jane instead of Jax and Jeri?

4. What effect is created by the list of activities in par. 12? By the list of people in par. 13?

APPLICATIONS TO WRITING

Write an essay in which you regard the future first pessimistically, then optimistically. You should consider social, technological, and scientific developments, but you must present these developments in as concrete, specific terms as possible.

University Days

I passed all the other courses that I took at the University, but I could never pass botany. This was because all botany students had to spend several hours a week in a laboratory looking through a microscope. I never once saw a cell through a microscope. This used to enrage my instructor. He would wander around the laboratory pleased with the progress all the students were making in drawing the involved and, so I am told, interesting structure of flower cells, until he came to me. I would just be standing there. "I can't see anything," I would say. He would begin patiently enough, explaining how anybody can see through a microscope, but he would always end up in a fury, claiming that I could *too* see through a microscope but just pretended that I couldn't. "It takes away from the beauty of flowers anyway," I used to tell him. "We are not concerned with beauty in this course," he would say. "We are concerned solely with what I may call the *mechanics* of flars." "Well," I'd say, "I can't see anything." "Try it just once again," he'd say, and I would put my eye to the microscope and see nothing at all, except now and again a nebulous milky substance— a phenomenon of maladjustment. You were supposed to see a vivid, restless clockwork of sharply defined plant cells. "I see what looks like a lot of milk," I would tell him. This, he claimed, was the result of my not having adjusted the microscope properly, so he would readjust it for me, or rather, for himself. And I would look again and see milk. [1]

I finally took a deferred pass, as they called it, and waited a year and tried again. (You had to pass one of the biological sciences or you couldn't graduate.) The professor had come back from vacation brown as a berry, bright-eyed, and eager to explain cell-structure again to his classes. "Well," he said to me, cheerily, when we met in the first laboratory hour of the semester, "we're going to see cells this time, aren't we?" "Yes, sir," I said. Students to right of me and to left of me and in front of me were seeing cells; what's more, they were quietly drawing pictures of them in their notebooks. Of course, I didn't see anything. [2]

"We'll try it," the professor said to me, grimly, "with every adjustment of the microscope known to man. As God is my witness, I'll arrange this glass so that you see cells through it or I'll give up teaching. In twenty-two years of botany, I—" He cut off abruptly for he was beginning to quiver all over, like Lionel Barrymore, and he genuinely wished to hold onto his temper; his scenes with me had taken a great deal out of him. [3]

So we tried it with every adjustment of the microscope known to man. With only one of them did I see anything but blackness or the familiar lacteal opacity, and that time I saw, to my pleasure and amazement, a variegated constellation of flecks, specks, and dots. These I hastily drew. The instructor, noting my activity, came back from an adjoining desk, a smile on his lips and his eyebrows high in hope. He looked at my cell drawing. "What's that?" he demanded, with a hint of a squeal in his voice. "That's what I saw," I said. "You didn't, you didn't, you *did*n't!" he screamed, losing control of his temper instantly, and he bent over and squinted into the microscope. His head snapped up. "That's your eye!" he shouted. "You've fixed the lens so that it reflects! You've drawn your eye!" [4]

Another course that I didn't like, but somehow managed to pass, was economics. I went to that class straight from the botany class, which didn't help me any in understanding either subject. I used to get them mixed up. But not as mixed up as another student in my economics class who came there direct from a physics laboratory. He was a tackle on the football team, named Bolenciecwcz. At that time Ohio State University had one of the best football teams in the country, and Bolenciecwcz was one of its outstanding stars. In order to be eligible to play it was necessary for him to keep up in his studies, a very difficult matter, for while he was not dumber than an ox he was not any smarter. Most of his professors were lenient and helped him along. None gave him more hints, in answering questions, or asked him simpler ones than the economics professor, a thin, timid man named Bassum. One day when we were on the subject of transportation and distribution, it came Bolenciecwcz's turn to answer a question. "Name one means of transportation," the professor said to him. No light came into the big tackle's eyes. "Just any means of transportation," said the professor. Bolenciecwcz sat staring at him. "That is," pursued the professor, "any medium, agency, or method of going from one place to another." Bolenciecwcz had the look of a man who is being led into a trap.

You may choose among steam, horse-drawn, or electrically propelled vehicles," said the instructor. "I might suggest the one which we commonly take in making long journeys across land." There was a profound silence in which everybody stirred uneasily, including Bolenciecwcz and Mr. Bassum. Mr. Bassum abruptly broke this silence in an amazing manner. "Choo-choo-choo," he said, in a low voice, and turned instantly scarlet. He glanced appealingly around the room. All of us, of course, shared Mr. Bassum's desire that Bolenciecwcz should stay abreast of the class in economics, for the Illinois game, one of the hardest and most important of the season, was only a week off. "Toot, toot, too-tooooooot!" some student with a deep voice moaned, and we all looked encouragingly at Bolenciecwcz. Somebody else gave a fine imitation of a locomotive letting off steam. Mr. Bassum himself rounded off the little show. "Ding, dong, ding, dong," he said, hopefully. Bolenciecwcz was staring at the floor now, trying to think, his great brow furrowed, his huge hands rubbing together, his face red. [5]

"How did you come to college this year, Mr. Bolenciecwcz?" asked the professor. "*Chuf*fa, chuffa, *chuf*fa, chuffa." [6]

"M'father sent me," said the football player. [7]

"What on?" asked Bassum. [8]

"I git an 'lowance," said the tackle, in a low, husky voice, obviously embarrassed. [9]

"No, no," said Bassum. "Name a means of transportation. What did you *ride* here on?" [10]

"Train," said Bolenciecwcz. [11]

"Quite right," said the professor. "Now, Mr. Nugent, will you tell us—" [12]

If I went through anguish in botany and economics—for different reasons—gymnasium work was even worse. I don't even like to think about it. They wouldn't let you play games or join in the exercises with your glasses on and I couldn't see with mine off. I bumped into professors, horizontal bars, agricultural students, and swinging iron rings. Not being able to see, I could take it but I couldn't dish it out. Also, in order to pass gymnasium (and you had to pass it to graduate) you had to learn to swim if you didn't know how. I didn't like the swimming pool, I didn't like swimming, and I didn't like the swimming instructor, and after all these years I still don't. I never swam but I passed my gym work anyway, by having another student give my gymnasium number (978) and swim across the pool in my place. He was a quiet, amiable blonde youth, number 473, and he would have seen through a microscope for me if we could have got away with it, but we couldn't get away with it. Another thing I didn't like about gymnasium work was that they made you strip the day you registered. It is impossible for me to be happy when I am stripped and being asked a lot of questions. Still, I did better than a lanky agricultural student who was cross-examined just before I was. They asked each student what college he was in—that is, whether Arts, Engineering, Commerce, or Agriculture. "What college are you in?" the instructor snapped at the youth in front of me. "Ohio State University," he said promptly. [13]

It wasn't that agricultural student but it was another a whole lot like him who decided to take up journalism, possibly on the ground that when farming went to hell he could fall back on newspaper work. He didn't realize, of course, that that would be very much like falling back full-length on a kit of carpenter's tools. Haskins didn't seem cut out for journalism, being too embarrassed to talk to anybody and unable to use a typewriter, but the editor of the college paper assigned him to the cow barns, the sheep house, the horse pavilion, and the animal husbandry department generally. This was a genuinely big "beat," for it took up five times as much ground and got ten times as great a legislative appropriation as the College of Liberal Arts. The agricultural student knew animals, but nevertheless his stories were dull and colorlessly written. He took all afternoon on each of them, on account of having to hunt for each letter on the typewriter. Once in a while he had to ask somebody to help him hunt. "C" and "L," in particular, were hard letters for him to find. His editor finally got pretty much annoyed at the farmer-journalist because his pieces were so uninteresting. "See here, Haskins," he snapped at him one day. "Why is it we never have anything hot from you on the horse pavillion? Here we have two hundred head of horses on this campus—more than any other university in the Western Conference except Purdue—and yet you never get any real low down on them. Now shoot over to the horse barns and dig up something lively." Haskins shambled out and came back in about an hour; he said he had something. "Well, start it off snappily," said the editor. "Something people will read." Haskins set to work and in a couple of hours brought a sheet of typewritten paper to the desk; it was a two-hundred-word story about some disease that had broken out among the horses. Its opening sentence was simple but arresting. It read: "Who has noticed the sores on the tops of the horses in the animal husbandry building?" [14]

Ohio State was a land grant university and therefore two years of military drill was compulsory. We drilled with old Springfield rifles and studied the tactics of the Civil War even though the World War was going on at the time. At 11 o'clock each morning thousands of freshmen and sophomores used to deploy over the campus, moodily creeping up on the old chemistry building. It was good training for the kind of warfare that was waged at Shiloh but it had no connection with what was going on in Europe. Some people used to think there was German money behind it, but they didn't dare say so or they would have been thrown in jail as German spies. It was a period of muddy thought and marked, I believe, the decline of higher education in the Middle West. [15]

As a soldier I was never any good at all. Most of the cadets were glumly indifferent soldiers, but I was no good at all. Once General Littlefield, who was commandant of the cadet corps, popped up in front of me during regimental drill and snapped, "You are the main trouble with the university!" I think he meant that my type was the main trouble with the university but he may have meant me individually. I was mediocre at drill, certainly—that is, until my senior year. By that time I had drilled longer than anybody else in the Western Conference, having failed at military at the end of each preceding year so that I had to do it all over again. I was the only senior still in uniform. The uniform which, when new, had made me look like an interurban railway conductor, now that it had become faded and too tight made me look like Bert Williams in his bellboy act. This had a definitely bad effect on my morale. Even so, I had become by sheer practice little short of wonderful at squad maneuvers. [16]

One day General Littlefield picked our company out of the whole regiment and tried to get it mixed up by putting it through one movement after another as fast as we could execute them: squads right, squads left, squads on right into line, squads right about, squads left front into line, etc. In about three minutes one hundred and nine men were marching in one direction and I was marching away from them at an angle of forty degrees, all alone. "Company, halt!" shouted General Littlefield. "That man is the only man who has it right!" I was made a corporal for my achievement. [17]

The next day General Littlefield summoned me to his office. He was swatting flies when I went in. I was silent and he was silent too, for a long time. I don't think he remembered me or why he had sent for me, but he didn't want to admit it. He swatted some more flies, keeping his eyes on them narrowly before he let go with the swatter. "Button up your coat!" he snapped. Looking back on it now I can see that he meant me although he was looking at a fly, but I just stood there. Another fly came to rest on a paper in front of the general and began rubbing its hind legs together. The general lifted the swatter cautiously. I moved restlessly and the fly flew away. "You startled him!" barked General Littlefield, looking at me severely. I said I was sorry. "That won't help the situation!" snapped the general, with cold military logic. I didn't see what I could do except offer to chase some more flies toward his desk, but I didn't say anything. He stared out the window at the faraway figures of co-eds crossing the campus toward the library. Finally, he told me I could go. So I went. He either didn't know which cadet I was or else he forgot what he wanted to see me about. It may have been that he wished to apologize for having called me the main trouble with the university; or maybe he had decided to compliment me on my brilliant drilling of the day before and then at the last minute decided not to. I don't know. I don't think about it much any more. [18]

PURPOSE AND STRUCTURE

1. Does Thurber's essay have an introduction (par. 1)? Does Thurber's essay have a thesis? Does Thurber's essay have a conclusion? Discuss.

2. Thurber's transitions are minimal: see the beginning of pars. 4, 13, 14. (The last section of his essay—pars. 15–18—is not explicitly related to the rest of the essay.) Should Thurber tighten up and elaborate his transitions? Discuss.

3. What is the point that Thurber is making about his "University Days"? Does he state his point explicitly?

4. Typically, illustrations are tied to generalizations, abstractions, or theses. There are five illustrations in Thurber's essay. Are they integrated with a series of general points or a thesis? Should they be?

DICTION AND TONE

1. Thurber's diction is simple and natural. What is the tone of his essay?

2. Usually Thurber saw milk when he looked through the microscope, but one time he saw, to his pleasure and amazement, "a variegated constellation of flecks, specks, and dots" (par. 4). What was he looking at?

3. Bolenciecwcz (par. 5) was not "dumber than an ox." How bright was he?

4. Would you omit the gymnasium numbers (978 and 473) in par. 13? Discuss.

5. Does the news story start off snappily (par. 14, last sentence)?

6. Thurber sees a reflection of his own eye in the microscope—and once, in military drill, one hundred men are marching in one direction and Thurber is marching away from them at an angle of forty degrees, all alone. What is funny about these episodes? What do these stories say about the relationship between Thurber and the University? What is the tone of the final paragraph (par. 18)?

APPLICATIONS TO WRITING

1. Without explicitly generalizing, tell a story about your college days. (If they began yesterday, tell about yesterday.)

2. Sum up—in three illustrations—your real experience of college.

3. State a generalization and illustrate it.

The Bad News About Sharks

JOY WILLIAMS

There's something out there waiting for us and that's the truth. Wasps and abandoned refrigerators. Ski-mobiles and barbed wire. Dehydration, myxedema[1] and the three-hundred-year-old elm on the

---

[1] Myxedema is a disease producing a cretinoid appearance of the face, slow speech, and dullness of intellect.

curve. Explosions and wrecks and electrocutions. Funny-tasting pies. There are cycles and moments. There are fatal hours. The chop waits in the night and the bright sunshine, and each piece of earth is good enough and greedy for our ending. Dying is the message all right, but the messengers are bums. Petty. Common. Hasty. We're shot or burned. Our bones start breaking. Cars make waffles of us. We keel over. Or it begins with trouble in the voiding parts. Not many of us die from love or terror these days, and there are few thoughts left which touch us with true horror. But there are some, certainly. There's one. Earth's nightmare is the sea. [1]

Q. What did you hear? A. I heard an awful splash that sounded like an explosion. Q. What did you see? A. I saw a swimmer trying to get away from a shark, swimming with his arms. (*Extract of evidence re the death of Brian Derry, Safety Bay, Tasmania, 1959.*) [2]

The dark angel must be forgiven, although he has no regard for human dignity. [3]

The known food of the West Coast white shark includes pieces of basking sharks (*Cetorhinus maximus*), grey smoothhound sharks (*Mustelus californicus*), Pacific mackerel (*Scomber japonicus*), cabezone (*Scorpaenichthys marmoratus*), halibut (*Paralichthys californicus*), sea otter (*Enhydra lutris*), and man. [4]

When men catch sharks, they do not simply kill them, they mutilate them as though in the grip of an ancient rite. They hatchet fins, chop out jaws, slit open bellies and grind up claspers[2] or ovaries beneath the heels of their boots. Scientists and fishermen alike seem to be always stomping and skidding around in the blood and viscera of a ruined shark. Men hate sharks. They hate them a *lot*. But what does it matter? The reality of the creature's existence cannot truly be confronted. The shark is deft and original and very ancient. Dead or alive, it inhabits impossible depths and will inhabit them forever. [5]

Swedenborg said that Devils are things which after Death choose Hell. Who among us knows the extent of the sea's true abyss? [6]

On May 5, 1959, at about five-forty-five P.M., the deceased and a friend, Shirley O'Neill, were swimming at Bakers Beach, off the

---

[2] Claspers are copulatory organs of male sharks and skates.

Golden Gate, and were about 30 yards from shore, swimming parallel to each other and talking back and forth, when suddenly Miss O'Neill saw the deceased disappear under the water and the tail of a large fish shoot out of the water nearby. Deceased then rose to the surface. Miss O'Neill started for shore and then, seeing that the deceased was in obvious distress, returned to assist deceased back to shore. When they arrived ashore, it was noted that deceased was suffering from partial amputation of the left shoulder and arm, multiple lacerations of left chest and multiple deep lacerations of right shoulder, arm and chest. Authorities were notified. (*History taken from Coroner's Register re the death of Albert Kogler in California.*) [7]

The shark as cruising destroyer, acting, for some, as bizarre *machina,* attacks approximately twenty-five people a year. That's not many. Nevertheless, the thought of a big fish lunching on a fated bather is known to create concern out of all proportion to the amount of injury or loss of life incurred statistically. Somewhere or other, there's a Bronze Whaler or a Grey Nurse or a White Death out to do the purely unspeakable. Rolling and trimming, balancing and pivoting, flying with baseball eyes through the sea, without malice or immoral intent, a percentage of sharks bite a percentage of people. The chosen can be a silver-suited diver or a black pearler or a little boy in a hemmed T-shirt or a woman bathing with her gentleman friend after lunch or a kid on a fluorescent surfboard with a singing keg. [8]

At the time of the incident, all the spear fishermen (Wilson, Hitt, Kirkman, Churchill and Skinner) were similarly equipped and Graeme Hitt was wearing a ¼-inch wet suit (parka-hooded jacket, trousers and boots) with a yellow 8-inch diameter Southern Sea Divers emblem on the back, blue fins, black face mask, blue snorkel with white top and brown leather glove on left hand. He was carrying a green spear gun loaded with gum rubbers. About 30 minutes before the attack, Skinner speared a blue moki which broke free and about 20 minutes later this was respeared by Kirkman after it had been found swimming on its side about 10 feet below the water in a distressed fashion. This fish and about eight others were contained in three floats at the time of the attack. All had their necks broken to kill them, a practice which is considered to be preferable to and safer than towing dying, struggling fish around on the surface. Two of these floats were recovered near the end of the mole by rod fishermen with surf-casting gear. None of the fish had been touched. There is no tangible reason why Graeme Hitt was attacked in preference to the other men other than that he was the person swimming on the surface nearest to where the shark appeared. (*Fatal. Aramoana, Otago Harbour, New Zealand, 1968.*) [9]

A shark can attack anybody. Yes, they just don't seem to care. It's man who persists in believing there are common factors associated with the elected. Bathing-suit color or frame of mind or torn hangnail or mucky water or whatever. Avoid the common factor, man thinks, and you'll live to leave the sea. [10]

The pressure exerted by the jaws of a typical 8-foot shark is three metric tons a square centimeter. [11]

The shark is not in the Tarot; it is not in the Signs of Heaven. Its strict reality remains beneath the waters of the world. [12]

Many people choose to believe that the shark is dumb, cowardly and unexceptional. These people take comfort in their thoughts. [13]

The attack took place in very heavy surf on a dull cloudy afternoon following a cyclone. The victim was catching body shoots with his friends. They were in the surf about 120 yards from shore and all caught a wave and were shooting toward the beach. Victim was attacked by a shark which made the first pass at his buttocks, removing the greater portion of them. As the shark made a second pass the victim attempted to fend it off with his hands and consequently lost his left hand. The shark then discontinued the attack. (*Non-fatal attack on Leo Ryan, Burleigh Heads, Queensland, Australia, 1950.*) [14]

Sharks are not deterred consistently by anything. It is quite useless to proffer advice although, of course, there are those who have. Most suggestions are too preliminary to be helpful (don't swim alone or at night or in bloody water or in water where sharks have been sighted) or too much after the fact (all efforts should be made to control hemorrhage as quickly as possible). There are dozens of actions one *might* take. Remain calm; bop the fish smartly on the snout; leave the water as unobtrusively as possible. Most skin divers sincerely believe that any aggressive motion, even shouting underwater, will frighten off a shark, although this is only sometimes true. Most swimmers believe, bless them, that splashing or clapping is a deterrent, although evidence shows that splashing or thrashing or even the tremors caused by relatively smooth swimming is what attracts the shark to the area in the first place. [15]

Nothing works constantly, that's all. There is no universally correct action to take. There is nothing really to *do* in case of shark attack. Possess the foolishness of God. Know that this is so. [16]

The International Shark Attack File, begun in 1958, is presently contained in eleven large filing drawers in a trailer at the Mote Marine Laboratory, Siesta Key, Florida. There are 1700 cases on record which represent only a fraction of the attacks which have actually occurred. [17]

The files are in folders which hang in the drawers from metal Pendaflex frames. Red raised plastic inserts on the far right of a folder indicate fatal encounters; clear ones on the far left denote non-fatal ones. Staggered in between are markers which are green (provoked or doubtful attacks), yellow (air-sea disasters), and blue (boats). It all has an obsessive, commanding neatness about it, and people always seem impressed when they open a drawer and see what appears to be a vast amount of highly organized information. [18]

All of this "evidence" was gathered together in a project created by and contracted between the U.S. Navy and the Smithsonian Institution, which believed that we have enough troubles in this life without having to worry about being eaten by a fish. Information was accumulated in order to become data which would then be fed into a "retrieval system." There were facts and now there were going to be questions. How can one keep from being in the right place at the right time? There were questions and now there were going to be answers. What were these sharks thinking of? Conclusions would be reached. [19]

More than $100,000 has been spent in establishing and maintaining the Shark Attack File over the years, and there is so much of everything—medical and scientific reports, newspaper clippings, morgue photographs, military letter reports, first-person accounts, slides, tapes—that one cannot be blamed for being confident that conclusions would be reached. [20]

A shark attacking a human being probably never strikes from mere hunger, but rather because, under varying circumstances, the victim assumes a suggestion of food which the shark, out of pure aggressive-ness, is unable to resist, hungry or not. [21]

Cases number 683 and 1333. In these two Australian attacks the victims were swimming to retrieve tennis balls thrown into the water. [22]

Case No. 1017: The shark attacked Mr. Hoogvorst at 9 A.M. when the tide was ebbing. The victim was a strong swimmer and accustomed to swimming far out to sea under the influence of alcohol and dagga. Mr. Hoogvorst had an open wound caused by a blister on the heel of his right foot. Mr. Hoogvorst was unemployed. Mr. Hoogvorst was wearing a royal-blue bathing costume. [23]

Case No. 637: Two fishermen battled with a 8-foot shark which jumped into their 14-foot boat. Richard Crew, 52, said the shark leaped straight at him. "The shark must have been attracted or in-furiated by my green yachting jacket," Crew said. [24]

Case No. 317: The wound was full of sand and about the size of a dinner plate. . . . [25]

Once a camera crew shooting still another film on sharks came to the Mote Marine Lab. They climbed up to the observation decks above the pens and filmed the starved sharks used in the buoyancy studies and the dead sharks used in the attempted training of Simo the porpoise to be an aggressive maim-machine himself. Then they came into the trailer and jumbled up all the files in the International Shark Attack File, placing all the fatal cases with their bright red indicators into four drawers. Then a hand slowly dragged out these drawers one after another as the camera moved lugubriously back-ward. Then they called it on the sound track The Roll of the Dead. [26]

Case No. 994: When the shark attacked, Steffans was holding the girl, Hobbs, in his arms and ducking her playfully in the water. They were in approximately 3 feet of water some 15 feet from shore. The 10-foot shark made three rolling attacks on the couple. During the attack both Hobbs and Steffans were screaming and shouting but this had no effect on the shark, as it remained in the area and was seen cruising in the vicinity for at least one hour after the attack. The victim Hobbs had lost so much blood that there was no evidence of bleeding after she was removed from the water. A number of sharks were caught at the beach the next day. However, there is no evidence avail-able which would suggest that the shark responsible had been caught.

Three of the sharks caught had had their bodies eaten by other sharks. It is thought that one of these latter sharks may have been responsible. (*Fatal. Lambert's Beach, Queensland, Australia, 12/28/61.*) [27]

Case No. 714: Shark attacked coming in straight, making a quarter twist clockwise to bite. Shark subsequently attacked five times with same attacking procedure except that the shark made a full-circle turn in front (ocean side) of victim. Shark continued to swim around area of attack until a small boat was launched. The shark attacked the boat. Shark was gaffed, caught and beached. Shark was killed, photographed and buried after being identified as a 9-foot female. (*Non-fatal. Coral Beach, Bermuda, May, 1960.*) [28]

Case No. 376: The shark was three-quarters upside down on a sand patch, jerking its head and lashing its tail. The victim was held between the shark's jaws at about his waist; his legs were not visible. . . . The victim had been carrying a yellow-handled abalone iron and had been pushing an inflated black inner tube to which a burlap sack was attached. (*Fatal. La Jolla Cove, California, 6/14/59.*) [29]

Case No. 405: Billy Weaver, 15, had been surfing with several companions when the incident occurred. The body was recovered by skin-diving. The shark, variously estimated at 15 to 25 feet in length, was still cruising nearby, its dorsal fin about a foot and a half out of the water. The shark bite had stripped away the flesh six inches above the knee and completely removed the right leg from the knee joint. The victim died from loss of blood, drowning, shock or a combination of all three. (*Lanikai, Oahu, Hawaii, 12/13/58.*) [30]

Thirty-eight percent of all people attacked die. That's a statistic and a discovery of sorts, but its relevance is illusive. There are things which are not being said. It is simply too dreadful. The more detailed the account, the more one becomes aware that there is nothing to be grasped. Despite our painful bondage to fact, we realize that both the form and formality of documentation bring us nothing but emptiness. [31]

The murky water and distance from the boat precluded adequate witnessing of the terminal event. If the victim were in the process of having his upper extremity avulsed[3] by a large fish, he would have

---

[3] Avulse means to pluck or pull off.

little opportunity to release his leaded belt or to render an intelligent vocal appraisal of his dealings at that moment. (*Office of the Medical Examiner, Dade County, Florida.*) [32]

I am sorry to inform you that because of limited refrigeration facilities, we have been forced to dispose of the shark. However, the shark has been identified as a *Caracharhinus springeri*. It was 10 feet long, medium-grey color with a white belly and definitely did have a mid-dorsal ridge. The human parts recovered were 18 inches from the anus 24 hours after the attack. The human part (hand) showed little effect from the body processes. (*U.S. Navy letter report re fatal attack on John Gibson, Magens Bay, Virgin Islands.*) [33]

The sensory systems of sharks, although beautifully interrelated, nevertheless result in a decidedly limited behavioral repertoire. Once they have initiated a specific pattern of behavior, they are not readily distracted or inhibited. Often they continue to attack their prey despite a variety of normally distracting and noxious stimuli, even including severe bodily crippling. [34]

Such an object! Both primitive and futuristic with its simple core of mystery, with its actions, exact, obsessed and inexplicable. . . . [35]

Case No. 236: . . . The movements of the shark were at all times deliberate and leisurely. Neither during the initial strike nor while making subsequent strikes nor while convoying the swimmers toward shore did its speed impress any observer. It made no abrupt lunges and never seemed to be exerting itself. . . . Wilson was struck four times by the shark, at least twice while he was being rescued and closely surrounded by five swimmers. (*Fatal. Imperial Beach, California, 1950.*) [36]

Case No. 807: The light was poor. The victim was standing on submerged rocks next to the edge of a channel when he felt something touch his right foot. He attempted to touch the severed foot with his right hand and was severely bitten across that hand. . . . A shark of esitimated length 7 feet followed the lifesavers as they carried him out. (*Non-fatal. Winkelspruit, South Africa, 1/6/61.*) [37]

Case No. 1406: The victim endeavored to fight the shark off and bit it on its snout to make it release its grip on his right leg but without effect. A surf-club member first reached the victim, who said, "Help me, please, the shark's still there." The rescuer could not see the shark and did not believe the victim until he tried to drag him ashore. Five other lifesavers then arrived and half pulled and half carried the shark and victim to knee-deep water. The shark was struck with a surfboard but would not release its grip until dragged ashore and its jaws pried open. (*Non-fatal attack. Coledale Beach, Australia, 2/26/66.*) [38]

Such a deep imperviousness to life! Such silence. Such . . . invisibility. As though created instantly, when needed, out of the sea itself. Day and night, without cessation, death approaches. What can be learned from the shark but negation? The facts presented by computer readout of the files' contents are reasonable, negative, and ultimately of no help to anyone. [39]

The shark likes blood and fish, but it often attacks man when neither of these excitants[4] is present. It strikes in the rain and the bright sunshine, off crowded beaches and in rivers seventy miles from the sea. Neither month nor time of day nor condition of sea or sky nor depth of water nor distance from shore are applicable to the probability of attack. Neither shade of skin nor the presence of sweat or urine is applicable. Nothing is applicable. [40]

Review of data in the Shark Attack File, particularly wound characteristics [many wounds seemingly produced by open-jaw slashing with the upper teeth], led to the conclusion that a significant fraction of shark attacks on humans appear to be motivated by factors other than hunger. (*Office of Naval Research, excerpt of final report, Project NR 104-025 PO 1-0017.*) [41]

What more is there to know? Sharks move boneless from the sea light into the darkness of our worst imaginings. And as the impossible terminus, as the inconceivable hazard, they slip from our dreams into the sea. [42]

Case No. 1559: FELT AWFUL THUD SAYS BITTEN BATHER. [43]

---

[4] Excitants are stimulants.

PURPOSE AND STRUCTURE

1. Analyze par. 1 carefully in terms of levels of generalizations and the use of detail. Be sure to explain the full significance of each item in the series of sentence fragments that ends with "Funny-tasting pies." Are there any other generalizations? What are they? Explain fully as many details or images as you can.

2. Is there coherence in par. 1? If there is, how is it achieved?

3. There is no transition between pars. 1 and 2. Or between pars. 2 and 3. Or between pars. 3 and 4. Argue for or against the position that juxtapositions of this kind make for incoherence and lack of organization.

4. The conventional essay announces its thesis early, and the body develops the thesis. In this essay, a central idea is restated over a half-dozen times in different places. What is the main idea of the essay?

5. Pars. 3, 4, 11, 12 and 13 are short and undeveloped. Some of them are almost cryptic. Are they effective in this essay? Can you account for their effectiveness or lack of it? How effective would they be in a traditional essay?

6. Argue that the author's use of parallelisms in par. 36 contributes to making the paragraph "deliberate and leisurely."

7. Argue that in par. 8 verbals, rather than the predicates, give a dynamic sense to the paragraph.

DICTION AND TONE

1. Explain how the odd mixture of abstract and concrete language in par. 7 contributes to the tone.

2. Explain par. 12, especially the references to the "Tarot" and to the "Signs of Heaven."

3. How does the style of the excerpts from "The International Shark Attack File" differ from that of the author's paragraphs?

APPLICATIONS TO WRITING

Write an essay with the title, "The Bad News About X," where X may be anything you are familiar with: radial tires, seat-belts, blood transfusions, microwave ovens, drugs (LSD, heroin), abortions, muggings, city life, motorcycles.

Like Joy Williams, intersperse your expository paragraphs with ones that are written in an "official" style. Make your illustrations carry the burden of your meaning.

Joey: A "Mechanical Boy"

BRUNO BETTELHEIM

Joey, when we began our work with him, was a mechanical boy. He functioned as if by remote control, run by machines of his own powerfully creative fantasy. Not only did he himself believe that he was a machine but, more remarkably, he created this impression in others. Even while he performed actions that are intrinsically human, they never appeared to be other than machine-started and executed. On the other hand, when the machine was not working he had to concentrate on recollecting his presence, for he seemed not to exist. A human body that functions as if it were a machine and a machine that duplicates human functions are equally fascinating and frightening. Perhaps they are so uncanny because they remind us that the human body can operate without a human spirit, that body can exist without soul. And Joey was a child who had been robbed of his humanity. [1]

Not every child who possesses a fantasy world is possessed by it. Normal children may retreat into realms of imaginary glory or magic powers, but they are easily recalled from these excursions. Disturbed children are not always able to make the return trip; they remain withdrawn, prisoners of the inner world of delusion and fantasy. In many ways Joey presented a classic example of this state of infantile autism. In any age, when the individual has escaped into a delusional world, he has usually fashioned it from bits and pieces of the world at hand. Joey, in his time and world, chose the machine and froze himself in its image. His story has a general relevance to the understanding of emotional development in a machine age. [2]

Joey's delusion is not uncommon among schizophrenic children today. He wanted to be rid of his unbearable humanity, to become completely automatic. He so nearly succeeded in attaining this goal that he could almost convince others, as well as himself, of his mechanical character. The descriptions of autistic children in the literature take for their point of departure and comparison the normal or abnormal human being. To do justice to Joey I would have to compare him simultaneously to a most inept infant and a highly complex piece of machinery. Often we had to force ourselves by a conscious act of will to realize that Joey was a child. Again and again his acting-out of his delusions froze our own ability to respond as human beings. [3]

During Joey's first weeks with us we would watch absorbedly as this at once fragile-looking and imperious nine-year-old went about his mechanical existence. Entering the dining room, for example, he would string an imaginary wire from his "energy source"—an imaginary electric outlet—to the table. There he "insulated" himself with paper napkins and finally plugged himself in. Only then could Joey eat, for he firmly believed that the "current" ran his ingestive apparatus. So skillful was the pantomime that one had to look twice to be sure there was neither wire nor outlet nor plug. Children and members of our staff spontaneously avoided stepping on the "wires" for fear of interrupting what seemed the source of his very life. [4]

For long periods of time, when his "machinery" was idle, he would sit so quietly that he would disappear from the focus of the most conscientious observation. Yet in the next moment he might be "working" and the center of our captivated attention. Many times a day he would turn himself on and shift noisily through a sequence of higher and higher gears until he "exploded," screaming "crash, crash!" and hurling items from his ever present apparatus—radio tubes, light bulbs, even motors or, lacking these, any handy breakable object. (Joey had an astonishing knack for snatching bulbs and tubes unobserved.) As soon as the object thrown had shattered, he would cease his screaming and wild jumping and retire to mute, motionless nonexistence. [5]

Our maids, inured to difficult children, were exceptionally attentive to Joey; they were apparently moved by his extreme infantile fragility, so strangely coupled with megalomaniacal superiority. Occasionally some of the apparatus he fixed to his bed to "live him" during his sleep would fall down in disarray. This machinery he contrived from masking tape, cardboard, wire and other paraphernalia. Usually the maids would pick up such things and leave them on a table for the children to find, or disregard them entirely. But Joey's machine they carefully restored: "Joey must have the carburetor so he can breathe." Similarly they were on the alert to pick up and preserve the motors that ran him during the day and the exhaust pipes through which he exhaled. [6]

How had Joey become a human machine? From intensive interviews with his parents we learned that the process had begun even before birth. Schizophrenia often results from parental rejection, sometimes combined ambivalently with love. Joey, on the other hand, had been completely ignored. [7]

"I never knew I was pregnant," his mother said, meaning that she had already excluded Joey from her consciousness. His birth, she said, "did not make any difference." Joey's father, a rootless draftee in the wartime civilian army, was equally unready for parenthood. So, of course, are many young couples. Fortunately most such parents lose their indifference upon the baby's birth. But not Joey's parents. "I did not want to see or nurse him," his mother declared. "I had no feeling of actual dislike—I simply didn't want to take care of him." For the first three months of his life Joey "cried most of the time." A colicky baby, he was kept on a rigid four-hour feeding schedule, was not touched unless necessary and was never cuddled or played with. The mother, preoccupied with herself, usually left Joey alone in the crib or playpen during the day. The father discharged his frustrations by punishing Joey when the child cried at night. [8]

Soon the father left for overseas duty, and the mother took Joey, now a year and a half old, to live with her at her parents' home. On his arrival the grandparents noticed that ominous changes had occurred in the child. Strong and healthy at birth, he had become frail and irritable; a responsive baby, he had become remote and inaccessible. When he began to master speech, he talked only to himself. At an early date he became preoccupied with machinery, including an old electric fan which he could take apart and put together again with surprising deftness. [9]

Joey's mother impressed us with a fey quality that expressed her insecurity, her detachment from the world and her low physical vitality. We were struck especially by her total indifference as she talked about Joey. This seemed much more remarkable than the actual mistakes she made in handling him. Certainly he was left to cry for hours when hungry, because she fed him on a rigid schedule; he was toilet-trained with great rigidity so that he would give no trouble. These things happen to many children. But Joey's existence never registered with his mother. In her recollections he was fused at one moment with one event or person; at another, with something or somebody else. When she told us about his birth and infancy, it was as if she were talking about some vague acquaintance, and soon her thoughts would wander off to another person or to herself. [10]

When Joey was not yet four, his nursery school suggested that he enter a special school for disturbed children. At the new school his autism was immediately recognized. During his three years there he experienced a slow improvement. Unfortunately a subsequent two years in a parochial school destroyed this progress. He began to develop compulsive defenses, which he called his "preventions." He could not drink, for example, except through elaborate piping systems built of straws. Liquids had to be "pumped" into him, in his fantasy, or he could not suck. Eventually his behavior became so upsetting that he could not be kept in the parochial school. At home things did not improve. Three months before entering the Orthogenic School he made a serious attempt at suicide. [11]

To us Joey's pathological behavior seemed the external expression of an overwhelming effort to remain almost nonexistent as a person. For weeks Joey's only reply when addressed was "Bam." Unless he thus neutralized whatever we said, there would be an explosion, for Joey plainly wished to close off every form of contact not mediated by machinery. Even when he was bathed he rocked back and forth with mute, engine-like regularity, flooding the bathroom. If he stopped rocking, he did this like a machine too; suddenly he went completely rigid. Only once, after months of being lifted from his bath and carried to bed, did a small expression of puzzled pleasure appear on his face as he said very softly: "They even carry you to your bed here." [12]

For a long time after he began to talk he would never refer to anyone by name, but only as "that person" or "the little person" or "the big person." He was unable to designate by its true name anything to which he attached feelings. Nor could he name his anxieties except through neologisms or word contaminations. For a long time he spoke about "master paintings" and "a master painting room" (*i.e.*, masturbating and masturbating room). One of his machines, the "criticizer," prevented him from "saying words which have unpleasant feelings." Yet he gave personal names to the tubes and motors in his collection of machinery. Moreover, these dead things had feelings; the tubes bled when hurt and sometimes got sick. He consistently maintained this reversal between animate and inanimate objects. [13]

In Joey's machine world everything, on pain of instant destruction, obeyed inhibitory laws much more stringent than those of physics. When we came to know him better, it was plain that in his moments of silent withdrawal, with his machine switched off, Joey was absorbed in pondering the compulsive laws of his private universe. His pre-occupation with machinery made it difficult to establish even practical contacts with him. If he wanted to do something with a counselor, such as play with a toy that had caught his vague attention, he could not do so: "I'd like this very much, but first I have to turn off the machine." But by the time he had fulfilled all the requirements of his preventions, he had lost interest. When a toy was offered to him, he could not touch it because his motors and his tubes did not leave him a hand free. Even certain colors were dangerous and had to be strictly avoided in toys and clothing, because "some colors turn off the current, and I can't touch them because I can't live without the current." [14]

Joey was convinced that machines were better than people. Once when he bumped into one of the pipes on our jungle gym he kicked it so violently that his teacher had to restrain him to keep him from injuring himself. When she explained that the pipe was much harder than his foot, Joey replied: "That proves it. Machines are better than the body. They don't break; they're much harder and stronger." If he lost or forgot something, it merely proved that his brain ought to be thrown away and replaced by machinery. If he spilled something his arm should be broken and twisted off because it did not work properly. When his head or arm failed to work as it should, he tried to punish it by hitting it. Even Joey's feelings were mechanical. Much later in his therapy, when he had formed a timid attachment to another child and had been rebuffed, Joey cried: "He broke my feelings." [15]

Gradually we began to understand what had seemed to be contra-dictory in Joey's behavior—why he held on to the motors and tubes, then suddenly destroyed them in a fury, then set out immediately and urgently to equip himself with new and larger tubes. Joey had created these machines to run his body and mind because it was too painful to be human. But again and again he became dissatisfied with their failure to meet his need and rebellious at the way they frustrated his will. In a recurrent frenzy he "exploded" his light bulbs and tubes, and for a moment became a human being—for one crowning instant he came alive. But as soon as he had asserted his dominance through the self-created explosion, he felt his life ebbing away. To keep on existing he had immediately to restore his machines and replenish the electricity that supplied his life energy. [16]

What deep-seated fears and needs underlay Joey's delusional system? We were long in finding out, for Joey's preventions effectively concealed the secret of his autistic behavior. In the meantime we dealt with his peripheral problems one by one. [17]

During his first year with us Joey's most trying problem was toilet behavior. This surprised us, for Joey's personality was not "anal" in the Freudian sense; his original personality damage had antedated the period of his toilet-training. Rigid and early toilet-training, however, had certainly contributed to his anxieties. It was our effort to help Joey with this problem that led to his first recognition of us as human beings. [18]

Going to the toilet, like everything else in Joey's life, was surrounded by elaborate preventions. We had to accompany him; he had to take off all his clothes; he could only squat, not sit, on the toilet seat; he had to touch the wall with one hand, in which he also clutched frantically the vacuum tubes that powered his elimination. He was terrified lest his whole body be sucked down. [19]

To counteract this fear we gave him a metal wastebasket in lieu of a toilet. Eventually, when eliminating into the wastebasket, he no longer needed to take off all his clothes, nor to hold on to the wall. He still needed the tubes and motors which, he believed, moved his bowels for him. But here again the all-important machinery was itself a source of new terrors. In Joey's world the gadgets had to move their bowels, too. He was terribly concerned that they should, but since they were so much more powerful than men, he was also terrified that if his tubes moved their bowels, their feces would fill all of space and leave him no room to live. He was thus always caught in some fearful contradiction. [20]

Our readiness to accept his toilet habits, which obviously entailed some hardship for his counselors, gave Joey the confidence to express his obsessions in drawings. Drawing these fantasies was the first step toward letting us in, however distantly, to what concerned him most deeply. It was the first step in a year-long process of externalizing his anal preoccupations. As a result he began seeing feces everywhere; the whole world became to him a mire of excrement. At the same time he began to eliminate freely wherever he happened to be. But with this release from his infantile imprisonment in compulsive rules, the toilet and the whole process of elimination became less dangerous. Thus far it had been beyond Joey's comprehension that anybody could possibly move his bowels without mechanical aid. Now Joey took a further step forward; defecation became the first physiological process he could perform without the help of vacuum tubes. It must not be thought that he was proud of this ability. Taking pride in an achievement presupposes that one accomplishes it of one's own free will. He still did not feel himself an autonomous person who could do things on his own. To Joey defecation still seemed enslaved to some incomprehensible but utterly binding cosmic law, perhaps the law his parents had imposed on him when he was being toilet-trained. [21]

It was not simply that his parents had subjected him to rigid, early training. Many children are so trained. But in most cases the parents have a deep emotional investment in the child's performance. The child's response in turn makes training an occasion for interaction between them and for the building of genuine relationships. Joey's parents had no emotional investment in him. His obedience gave them no satisfaction and won him no affection or approval. As a toilet-trained child he saved his mother labor, just as household machines saved her labor. As a machine he was not loved for his performance, nor could he love himself. [22]

So it had been with all other aspects of Joey's existence with his parents. Their reactions to his eating or noneating, sleeping or wakening, urinating or defecating, being dressed or undressed, washed or bathed did not flow from any unitary interest in him, deeply embedded in their personalities. By treating him mechanically his parents made him a machine. The various functions of life—even the parts of his body—bore no integrating relationship to one another or to any sense of self that was acknowledged and confirmed by others. Though he had acquired mastery over some functions, such as toilet-training and speech, he had acquired them separately and kept them isolated from each other. Toilet-training had thus not gained him a pleasant feeling of body mastery; speech had not led to communication of thought or feeling. On the contrary, each achievement only steered him away from self-mastery and integration. Toilet-training had enslaved him. Speech left him talking in neologisms that obstructed his and our ability to relate to each other. In Joey's development the normal process of growth had been made to run backward. Whatever he had learned put him not at the end of his infantile development toward integration but, on the contrary, farther behind than he was at its very beginning. Had we understood this sooner, his first years with us would have been less baffling. [23]

It is unlikely that Joey's calamity could befall a child in any time and culture but our own. He suffered no physical deprivation; he starved for human contact. Just to be taken care of is not enough for relating. It is a necessary but not a sufficient condition. At the extreme where utter scarcity reigns, the forming of relationships is certainly hampered. But our society of mechanized plenty often makes for equal difficulties in a child's learning to relate. Where parents can provide the simple creature-comforts for their children only at the cost of significant effort, it is likely that they will feel pleasure in being able to provide for them; it is this, the parents' pleasure, that gives children a sense of personal worth and sets the process of relation in motion. But if comfort is so readily available that the parents feel no particular pleasure in winning it for their children, then the children cannot develop the feeling of being worthwhile around the satisfaction of their basic needs. Of course parents and children can and do develop relationships around other situations. But matters are then no longer so simple and direct. The child must be on the receiving end of care and concern given with pleasure and without the exaction of return if he is to feel loved and worthy of respect and consideration. This feeling gives him the ability to trust; he can entrust his well-being to persons to whom he is so important. Out of such trust the child learns to form close and stable relationships. [24]

For Joey relationship with his parents was empty of pleasure in comfort-giving as in all other situations. His was an extreme instance of a plight that sends many schizophrenic children to our clinics and hospitals. Many months passed before he could relate to us; his despair that anybody could like him made contact impossible. [25]

When Joey could finally trust us enough to let himself become more infantile, he began to play at being a papoose. There was a corresponding change in his fantasies. He drew endless pictures of himself as an electrical papoose. Totally enclosed, suspended in empty space, he is run by unknown, unseen powers through wireless electricity. [26]

As we eventually came to understand, the heart of Joey's delusional system was the artificial, mechanical womb he had created and into which he had locked himself. In his papoose fantasies lay the wish to be entirely reborn in a womb. His new experiences in the school suggested that life, after all, might be worth living. Now he was searching for a way to be reborn in a better way. Since machines were better than men, what was more natural than to try rebirth through them? This was the deeper meaning of his electrical papoose. [27]

As Joey made progress, his pictures of himself became more dominant in his drawings. Though still machine-operated, he has grown in self-importance. Another great step forward is represented in a picture in which he has acquired hands that do something, and he has had the courage to make a picture of the machine that runs him. Later still the papoose became a person, rather than a robot encased in glass. [28]

Eventually Joey began to create an imaginary family at the school: the "Carr" family. Why the Carr family? In the car he was enclosed as he had been in his papoose, but at least the car was not stationary; it could move. More important, in a car one was not only driven but also could drive. The Carr family was Joey's way of exploring the possibility of leaving the school, of living with a good family in a safe, protecting car. [29]

Joey at last broke through his prison. In this brief account it has not been possible to trace the painfully slow process of his first true relations with other human beings. Suffice it to say that he ceased to be a mechanical boy and became a human child. This newborn child was, however, nearly 12 years old. To recover the lost time is a tremendous task. That work has occupied Joey and us ever since. Sometimes he sets to it with a will; at other times the difficulty of real life makes him regret that he ever came out of his shell. But he has never wanted to return to his mechanical life. [30]

One last detail and this fragment of Joey's story has been told. When Joey was 12, he made a float for our Memorial Day parade. It carried the slogan: "Feelings are more important than anything under the sun." Feelings, Joey had learned, are what makes for humanity; their absence, for a mechanical existence. With this knowledge Joey entered the human condition. [31]

PURPOSE AND STRUCTURE

In this essay Bettelheim clarifies the general concept of emotional development in a machine age by drawing upon the experiences of a single individual, Joey, as an illustration. The illustration in turn is developed by means of analogy. By taking an extreme and atypical example of a boy who "froze himself" (par. 2) in the image of the machine the author dramatizes his general concept.

1. What is meant by "mechanical boy"? Underline the details that explain the title.

2. How does the author account for Joey's behavior?

3. With what details in par. 1 does the author develop his analogy?

4. How do the two meanings of the word *possess* underlie the contrast made in par. 2? What causal relationships are established in the last three sentences of the paragraph?

5. What dual comparison is made in par. 3? What two concepts in this paragraph are repetitions of those previously mentioned? What new causal relationship is advanced?

6. What illustrations in par. 4 develop the image of Joey's mechanical existence? How do the last two sentences of the paragraph derive from them?

7. What is the relationship of par. 6 to pars. 4 and 5?

8. What illustrations develop the causal relationships advanced in pars. 7–10?

9. What further particulars in par. 12 support the opening generalization?

10. What comparison and contrast is developed in par. 13? What is its relationship to par. 12?

11. What causal relationship is developed in par. 14?

12. Note how par. 16 serves a transitional purpose in summing up what has been previously stated. How does par. 17 serve a transitional purpose?

13. How do pars. 18–23 illustrate the generalization that "in Joey's development the normal process of growth had been made to run backward"?

In par. 23 what kind of relationship is implied by the words "had been made"?

14. How does the analogy of labor-saving devices in par. 22 contribute to your understanding of Joey's problem? How does the succeeding paragraph further illuminate the analogy?

15. How does the author develop the opening topic sentence in par. 24?

16. What is the relationship of pars. 26–29 to par. 30?

17. What is the relationship of Joey's Memorial Day slogan to the concluding sentence; to the author's central purpose?

18. With what concrete illustrations does the author make clear each of the following dualities: human-mechanical; fragile-imperious; internalize-externalize; explosions-preventions?

19. Formulate your own definition of childhood schizophrenia by referring to specific details in the text.

DICTION AND TONE

1. The word *froze,* or a synonym, is used throughout the essay. Comment on its relevance to structural purpose and tone.

2. How does the diction, appropriate to the vocabulary of a machine, contribute to the tone? provide emphasis? Refer both to the author's descriptions and to Joey's own choice of words.

3. Identify the irony in par. 13.

4. Discuss the appropriateness of the word *work* in par. 30.

5. What is Bettelheim's attitude toward Joey? toward his mother? How do you know?

6. From what point of view does the author narrate the story of Joey? Is he speaking solely as a psychiatrist? Is he also passing judgment upon society? Discuss.

APPLICATIONS TO WRITING

1. Describe a sensitive or rebellious child or adolescent by providing concrete illustrations of his behavior and by showing your subject interacting with family, friends, or teachers.

2. Clarify a general concept by drawing upon the experiences of a single individual. Beginning with an observation about the family, the university, an occupation, a leisure activity, attempt to clarify and illustrate your concept by narrating the experiences of a single individual.

3. Analyze the means by which the author transforms what might have been a medical case history into a moving portrait of Joey. Examine a number of case histories in psychiatric texts. What are the differences in intention, tone, perspective, and diction in the two modes of writing?

The Generation That Was Never Going to Have to Work

MARK JACOBSON

I could see this good-bye was going to be hard to take. It wasn't going to be quite as memorable as the time I got on a plane in the Manila airport and saw a Filipino soldier push my wife, Andrea, away from the observation-deck rail with his submachine-gun butt. This was just going to be one of those standard midnight-Greyhounds-out-of-the-Port-Authority-Bus-Terminal good-byes. But as the Forty-second Street night vermin eyeballed us blowing kisses to each other through the exhaust fumes, I could see this good-bye was going to be hard to take. [1]

It was raining, cold, and there were plenty of muggers around with nothing to do. That made it a perfect night to walk all the way downtown and drive myself crazy thinking about it again. Andrea was off to dissect another horse gut or dog belly or whatever else she chops up at veterinary school in Ithaca. That's what she had been doing in the Philippines the year before. The stateside schools, picky bastards, wouldn't take her the first time around. The Filipinos would. That was fun. The martial-law government over there turned off her phone so we couldn't even give Bell Telephone $6.75 the first three minutes to tell each other how much we hated being apart. When Cornell let Andrea in we were happy; at least we would be in the same hemisphere. But 249 miles is the same as 8000 when you turn over at night. She's got another three years to go. Then she'll be a respectable professional. It's a great job; you can make a mint if you don't mind looking down the throats of Park Avenue poodles. But knowing her, she'd rather work in a clinic or a zoo. [2]

Still, the next three years is going to be a long time for Port Authority good-byes. I could, of course, make it easier for us. I could go up to Ithaca to live. Personally I can't stand the place: it's terminal white bread. But I suppose I could sneer and bear it. Except that I can't. I have a job running after dope pushers and baseball players for *The Village Voice*. The money's not great, but they let me write almost anything I want, as long as there's blood in it. [3]

It's what some people would call a career. Shirley MacLaine and Dean Martin might call it a *Career*. That's just what I'll call it too. In fact, that's what Andrea and I are today: two career mongers. We got ambition. The stuff Marlon Brando once said (in *On the Waterfront*) he figured he could live longer without. [4]

And walking home in the rain I figured I agreed with Brando— ambition was definitely something that could put a killer bee up your ass. Misused, ambition had twisted whole generations into making war and non-biodegradable products. Both Andrea and I once swore to expunge the rot from our systems. So in the end the joke turned out to be on us, the two sweethearts being kept apart by work. How the hell did we get in this fix? We used to be such well-adjusted hippies. [5]

Go back, if you will, to the days of hippiedom, the pre-Manson era. I cringe at some of the things I did, like taking the bizarro grey acid from the bearded man wearing the dress in the red pickup on the road to San Luis Potosí. But everyone has stories like that. It was our special time, the time from which we remember the stoned faces the same way your old man remembers the faces of the guys in the fox-hole at the Battle of the Bulge. That was when we had a common goal. A mission. When we felt a moral duty to hold out on capitalism's call to oblivion. [6]

Work was the bottom line of the bad guy's world: nine to five was the basic gear in the Rockefellers' nefarious machinery. Something to be avoided at all costs. We were different from the beatniks, those poetry-spouting, sneaker-footed sots. Their TV spokesman, Maynard G. Krebs, said, *"Work?"* and got faint when Dobie Gillis suggested he get a job. Maynard got laughs from middle America because he was an isolated lazy bum. We weren't isolated lazy bums, hell no, we were a holy army trying to save the human race. And that scared them. [7]

We would shut down the process by refusing to refuel it. Even if it was necessary to work—for good reasons like unemployment insurance or the presence of a particularly good Mexican dope crop—we would withhold our brains. One time in the Sixties, my uncle, at the urging of my beside-herself mother, offered me a job buying for his garment-center business. He knew I'd been to college (Wisconsin, N.Y.U., Berkeley twice, San Francisco Art Institute—no degree), so he said, "Start with the trimmings, soon you can buy maybe the fabrics, then who knows . . . someday you might own the business." Sly stuff, but I wasn't about to be bought off. I demanded the only other open job, truck helper. Bamboozled, my uncle, who'd worked his way up from an underwear hawker in Mays' basement, gave me the job. A perfect position: no chance for advancement and you get to hang out with the blacks. Once inside, I began to sabotage. Tony the Driver, an ex-mob torpedo, could shift gears perfectly with three bottles of Chianti in his expanded gut. But when I laid a little bit of the evil weed on him, he lost control. Gears started grinding. He stopped the truck and told me to get out. I had the rest of the day off, he said. The next night I received a panicked call from my uncle, demanding, "What did you do to my driver?" Seems Big Tony went to take a piss somewhere in Greenpoint and misplaced the truck—with its six thousand garments. My uncle broke my mother's heart by firing me, which sweetened an already great victory for the people. [8]

Getting married did not slow our crusade against the workaday world. The parents thought we were weakening, but marriage was just a ploy. We used the gelt[1] we got to buy my garment-center uncle's Ford van: it came cheap after I convinced him the transmission was shot. Our parents thought we'd consummate the marriage at The Holiday Inn; instead, we slept in the truck and took off for California the next morning (commonly called "splitting for the Coast"). Out there, we reckoned, you never had to work. Sure, there were occasional gigs. Like the time the local rabbi hired us to transport a bunch of signed Ben Shahn[2] lithographs to San Diego. The paintings got ripped off around Santa Maria. I'm not sure if they were ever recovered but we

[1] Gelt is the Yiddish (Middle High German) word for money.
[2] Ben Shahn (1898–1969) was an American artist and painter.

didn't care; we were living in The New Land. There was honor in standing in the food-stamp line and in following a welfare-food-choices cookbook. Instead of calling for "one tablespoon sugar," the cookbook said, "one tablespoon carbohydrates." After all those years of pretending manners over the pot roast, it was *so* prole[3] to say, "Pass the fat." [9]

Aggressive irresponsibility was our bag and we were good at it. The only thing Andrea and I really wanted was to be together. Fifteen minutes was a long time to be apart. Work was ridiculous; singing the Silhouettes' old forty-five *Get a Job,* "Yip, yip, yip, mum, mum, mum, get a job, sha, na, na, na," was as close as we wanted to get to it. There were so many other more interesting things to do. But as the Berkeley years rolled by, we began to realize we'd done it all: drugs, getting arrested (during People's Park while telling salesgirls at Hink's Department Store to give up their burdens and join "the revolution") and going back to the land. Winds of change were rumbling. [10]

I remember that evil day as if it were yesterday. I was lying in a hammock on the porch of our house, dreaming about the opening shot in *Touch of Evil.* I was, by this time, a class A film freak, specializing in the American Cinema 1940–1960. It wasn't bad, because I parlayed the passion into running the film series at college. I paid myself $50 a week to put up three or four posters around campus. It was written off as "advertising"; they never suspected a thing. Anyway I was four minutes into the shot (it is seven minutes long) when I spied Andrea pedaling up the road. She was riding the green ten speed we bought with money we made the year before selling Shaklee's Basic-H organic all-purpose cleaner door to door. [11]

She was mad. And I knew why. Just the other day our most recent dog, Concho, had keeled over with terminal distemper. We had terrible luck with animals. It started with Billie, the wedding gift that got flattened by a semi in Colorado. Then there was Richie, Rocco, Snooky and Do-lang: all stolen, lost or runaway. This last one was the final straw as far as Andrea was concerned. We took Concho to the vet, but the guy wouldn't even look at him. We hadn't paid our bill. The dog died in the truck on the way home. [12]

Who was to know this death in the family would lead to Port Au-

---

[3] Prole is slang for proletariat.

thority Bus Terminal good-byes? But one thing was certain: the hippie jig was up. It ended the moment Andrea dragged the bicycle up the steps, looked at me in the hammock and said, "Self-actualization." [13]

Aggh. That miserable phrase, the despicable concept that seared through a generation of comfortable sloth. Self-actualization was far more devastating than simplistic hippie credos like "Get your head together." Clones[4] from Texas with endless blue eyes and crooked grins "got their heads together" after they were busted for having fifty tabs of acid taped to the battery caps of their VW buses. It usually meant getting serious about your pottery. But self-actualization—that smacked of making something of yourself, of personal ambition. No longer could our "nation" find solace in collective abstinence from "de system"; self-actualization was the hippie version of the work ethic. [14]

The dead dogs self-actualized Andrea. She got a job with the vet to pay off our bills. But she wasn't the only one plunging back into the work morass. Honey George, who never left the Caffé Mediterraneum except to do wheelies down the avenue on his motorcycle, disappeared. We figured he'd been kidnapped because, although he had the smelliest armpits in Berkeley, we knew he was from Jewish royalty in Shaker Heights. Later we got a letter from him telling us his relatives set him up running a rubber factory in New Jersey. He also added, in a postscript, that he'd shot himself in the foot, "to show my contempt for my position as a captain of industry." [15]

Smooth Paulie, once the only white Ivy Leaguer in the Harlem street gangs, pulled an El Topo by becoming a Zen monk. The religious life didn't satisfy the pimp side of his nature, so he became the business manager of an American Zen center. One of his plans was to operate franchised Tassajara bread outlets. [16]

Ollie, who pulled the highest grades ever in Maryland on the medical boards and then immediately moved to California to make stained glass, went back home to practice medicine. Time was when dope dealing was the only refuge for the closet capitalists among us. Now plant stores and natural-food restaurants were everywhere. No one seemed fun anymore. [17]

Any of us who actually listened during those interminable Eldridge Cleaver speeches at Sproul Hall Plaza knew what was happening. It

---

[4] Clones are more than one offspring propagated from one original seed. All have an identical genetic inheritance.

was, like, all economics, man. The slightest breath of the Nixonian recession (undoubtedly a Cointelpro plot to bring the country's wayward children back into the fold) had exposed the holy army as a bunch of middle-class kids. [18]

Besides, the welfare department was wise to us. I was trying desperately to self-actualize. I was into movies. I wrote a screenplay treatment from a kids' book called *Never Cry Wolf*, which took me two months. Spent eight dollars to have a Hare Krishna type it and hitchhiked to L. A. to show it around. When I got there I found out Warners had bought the book years ago and wasn't planning to do anything with it. My protests went unheeded by an indifferent story editor. No matter, there were other opportunities. [19]

A one-shot dope deal brought a Bolex Rex-5 camera into my life. It was to be the basis of a big-time production company. But the only work anyone offered came from a fifty-year-old ex-husband of Pauline Kael, who owned one of the local cinemas. He had recently tape-recorded a hundred hours of his revelations. I had seen the movie, and better, before, but I consented to put the visual accompaniment to his narration. No doubt it would have been as great as *Steppenwolf*, but a slimy Brazilian who'd been crashing at our place stole the camera and put me out of business. [20]

My mother, always sharp to any unsteadiness on my part, was back in action. If I was ready to make my peace with capitalism, she had the perfect compromise. There were more uncles. This batch was in Local 306 of the moving picture projectionists' union. Visual sense, it seemed, ran in the family. These uncles would use their influence to get me enrolled in a projectionists' school in Queens. [21]

Karma-wise, it didn't seem a bad nine-to-five. Seven dollars an hour and getting to handle film. Andrea and I agreed to return to New York. For six months I learned to "strike the arc," "frame the show" and do other arcane motor skills. The goddamn class met three times a week, but I never missed a lesson. I felt beaten and this, just like Honey George's gunshot wound, was my penance. I passed the written test for the license even though I was so stoned I couldn't see the page. After all that college, I could pass a test in a coma. The guys with eight kids and mortgages studied for weeks and failed. [22]

Everything was mellow until my first on-the-job training session. The local told us we could pick any theater in the city and the union projectionist there was contract-bound to help us learn to "operate." I scanned the *New York Post* movie section and picked the Thalia, then an "art house." It was playing a double of *Rebel Without A Cause* and Rossellini's film *Open City.* I didn't understand the thematic reasoning behind the bill, but it was the best in town that day. [23]

I went up to the projection booth and found that the old guy running the show wasn't exactly a cinéaste. He barely looked up from his *Daily News* when I came in; but he did get a load of my shoulder-length hair. Then he started complaining. First about me, but mostly about working "in an old, dumpy booth where they show these old goddamn movies that got all these goddamn splices in them." Just about that time the print of *Rebel* broke in the projector. This was supposed to be the pinnacle of an operator's cool: making a splice in the film without the audience's missing much. This guy's technique was to rip whole sections of the movie out of the machine and throw them on the floor. [24]

"Stupid fucking old movie," he said as the film curled around wounded on the linoleum. [25]

I was aghast; this man was censoring art. He tore more. Finally I picked up a mangled section of James Dean arguing with his parents and fled. [26]

I had seen the inside of the nine-to-five beast and was repelled. I put my projectionist's license on my wall. I would use it for inspiration, to remind myself of what that Berkeley nonsense was really all about. But I suppose it was the specter of my old man that saved me from unconditional surrender to day laboring. He's an all-star woodworker/craftsman; you should see some of the stuff he can make. But he grew up during the Depression and was taught to know the buck. What did it get him? A job as a ceramics teacher in a junior high school, where he watched the same snot-nosed kids make the same ashtrays for thirty-two years. No way I was getting railroaded like that. [27]

I stumbled around the city, determined to hold out. I drove a cab to pay the rent. Hacking was an out-and-out horror, but it had its reassuring aspects. I wasn't alone. The garage was filled with other unreconstituted hippies. They were all there: the actors, trumpet players, philosophers, film freaks and defrocked priests, still withholding their brains. The garage was like a bunker for battered warriors. We sat around waiting for cabs and talked about it for hours: how did it go wrong, weren't we the generation that wasn't going to have to waste time working? [28]

Meanwhile, the heat was on. Andrea was self-actualizing like mad, working at the Animal Medical Center as a nurse. She had already decided she was going to be a doctor. Her sense of purpose was frightening. I accused her of selling out to the fascist notions of the women's movement. I felt like a leper. Around me exponents of the "new maturity," a stance several budding capitalists from our old crowd were affecting, said, "Grow up, fool. You see Abbie and Jerry and the rest of them acting silly. Get with it." I asked, what were these washed-up radicals to me or me to them, but the message hit home. [29]

More compromises. . . . While driving, I noticed I was picking up a lot of gay guys who wanted to go to deserted factory buildings in the middle of the night. A little investigation revealed they were frequenting discos. This was back in early 1974, before hustle records started advertising on the late-night TV movies. No one knew much about these discos. A friend of mine told me it might make a good magazine article. I didn't know much about magazine writing, but I put together some notes, complete with ample sociological insight, and went to *The SoHo Weekly News,* a bohemian paper on the lower East Side of Manhattan. It was a sleazy sheet, but I figured that because it was small, it must be feisty and honest. They paid ten dollars, an insane but seemingly honorable price. Michael Goldstein, an unpleasant sort who published the rag, read my pieces quickly. Then he held his tummy and told me they were crap, I was crap and should get out of his office and back into the cab. [30]

It was depressing. If this turkey wouldn't give me ten bucks, what was I supposed to do, get back in the cab? Anyway, to cut it short, I showed the stuff to a guy who liked it. He recommended I take it to *New York* magazine, then an uptown glitz book. They liked it too and gave me $1,000, of which I should have sent Michael Goldstein at least ten dollars. [31]

After that I was hooked. As a hippie cabdriver, I was a thirty-five-cent tip; as a hippie cabdriver/writer I was a hot property. I even got a chance to write about all my old buddies down at the garage. Mary Tyler Moore's people picked up the article for a TV sit-com. "It's the story of your generation," the M.T.M. lawyer said. "It's very salable." Imagine that. Who would have guessed being a failed hippie was commercial? [32]

Mind you now, I'm not complaining. After Andrea becomes a vet and I a famous writer, we'll be rolling in the dough. We're two young people on the way up. Maybe they'll feature us in the Couples section of

People magazine. We certainly deserve to be included in any rubbish story about working couples, even if we're not "bi-coastal" anymore. In fact, just the other day I conceived my first-ever passion for a specific automobile, one of those Mercedes sports models. The choice shocked me because it had little to do with funk, wit or taste. It just looks rich. [33]

I do find it ironic that we live apart, while most of the couples who made up the generation that supposedly didn't know how to love would suffer all kinds of abuse to stay together. But when you've got a job to do, you've got to do it. We're committed. It's our choice. [34]

There will be plenty of time to talk it over soon. The semester's almost over. Andrea will be home for the summer. She's going to work with a vet at the racetrack, which will be nice because I want to write a story about nags. She'll be able to give me *info*. We do, however, plan a vacation, probably stopping in Key West, one of our favorite places. We like it because it's a rock out in the middle of the sea and there's only one road in and out. It's the last stop for most of its inhabitants. There are a lot of people down there who never quite self-actualized; maybe they couldn't take the strain. But we know people who have lived in Key West since the Human Be-In and haven't worked yet. The only thing they do is go out on the pier and clap as the sun goes beneath the horizon. Last time we watched them do it we felt embarrassed for them and envious at the same time. [35]

PURPOSE AND STRUCTURE

1. At first glance this appears to be a personal narrative about two people whose careers keep them separate. Prove to the satisfaction of your class that this is an essay. Be sure to discuss the relationship between the title and the text and to discover internal evidence to support your position.

2. If this is an essay, what is the thesis? Is the thesis expressed in a sentence? a paragraph? more than one paragraph? Or is it implicit?

3. In par. 8, Jacobson tells the story of being hired by his uncle to help on a truck. What is the point of the story?

4. What are some of Jacobson's illustrations of "aggressive irresponsibility" (par. 10)?

5. What examples does Jacobson give of getting "your head together"

(par. 14)? How does getting "your head together" differ from self-actualization?

6. Pars. 15, 16, 17, and 18 contain accounts of Honey George, Smooth Paulie, Ollie, and other unnamed hippies. What do these stories illustrate?

7. When Jacobson reports to the projection booth for his first on-the-job training session, what is the title of the film being shown? What is the relevance of this title to the essay? He picks up a mangled section of the film. Does this torn section of film have any relevance to the essay?

DICTION AND TONE

1. Jacobson mixes many levels of usage: formal, informal, colloquial, slang. Argue that this mixture makes the tone confusing. Or argue that the level of usage is appropriate to the context. In either case, support your argument with examples from the text.

2. At the end of par. 18 Jacobson refers to a "holy army." What holy army is this? Is it referred to at any other point in the essay?

3. Explain: "aggressive irresponsibility" (par. 10); "evil day" (par. 11); "generation of comfortable sloth" (par. 14).

APPLICATIONS TO WRITING

Write an essay about a personal experience that changed your values, taste, or attitude, or that altered your life style. Make your personal experience illustrate the experience of an entire class of people. For example, your change in musical taste (from rock to country-western or from rock to classical) may illustrate the change in taste of many of your contemporaries. Or your change in attitude toward school (or work, or athletics) may illustrate a change experienced by many others. The important thing is that your personal experience should be made to illustrate the experience of a class or category of people.

PART six

Analysis

Analysis—a method of exposition by logical division, applicable to anything that can be divided into component parts. For example, in "The Iks" Thomas has a double analysis: in the first half of the essay he analyzes the causes of the behavior of the Iks; in the second half, the causes of the behavior of communities of men. Martin analyzes a huge, inchoate list of types of professional wrestlers: "Crushers, Killers, Bruisers, and Butchers, Commies, Nazis, Japs, and A-rabs . . . " and eighteen more. But Boorstin simply divides his subject into four parts and then develops each part equally. In "Living Together," the editors of *Newsweek* attempt to establish some of the causes for the increase in cohabitation and for the decline of marriage. Like Boorstin, Roberts arbitrarily divides his subject into a number of reasonable parts and then richly illustrates each. In her discussion of Marilyn Monroe's personality, Trilling distinguishes among the possible causes of her suicide, and concludes that she is a victim of her own remarkable gifts. In the excerpt from his autobiography, Wright interweaves in his deceptively simple narrative a number of experiences and themes that are unified by their causal relationships: his omnivorous reading led to his discovery that words are indeed weapons; his increasing awareness of the vast distance between himself and the world in which he lived strengthened his fearsome determination to leave the South. Russell simplifies his long and complex career by dividing the forces governing his life into three overwhelming passions.

The Iks

from *The Lives of a Cell*

LEWIS THOMAS

The small tribe of Iks, formerly nomadic hunters and gatherers in the mountain valleys of northern Uganda, have become celebrities, literary symbols for the ultimate fate of disheartened, heartless mankind at large. Two disastrously conclusive things happened to them: the government decided to have a national park, so they were compelled by law to give up hunting in the valleys and become farmers on poor hillside soil, and then they were visited for two years by an anthropologist who detested them and wrote a book about them.[1] [1]

The message of the book is that the Iks have transformed themselves into an irreversibly disagreeable collection of unattached, brutish creatures, totally selfish and loveless, in response to the dismantling of their traditional culture. Moreover, this is what the rest of us are like in our inner selves, and we will all turn into Iks when the structure of our society comes all unhinged. [2]

The argument rests, of course, on certain assumptions about the core of human beings, and is necessarily speculative. You have to agree in advance that man is fundamentally a bad lot, out for himself alone, displaying such graces as affection and compassion only as learned habits. If you take this view, the story of the Iks can be used to confirm it. These people seem to be living together, clustered in small, dense villages, but they are really solitary, unrelated individuals with no evident use for each other. They talk, but only to make ill-tempered demands and cold refusals. They share nothing. They never sing. They turn the children out to forage as soon as they can walk, and desert the elders to starve whenever they can, and the foraging children snatch food from the mouths of the helpless elders. It is a mean society. [3]

They breed without love or even casual regard. They defecate on each

---

[1] Turnbull, C. M., *The Mountain People* (New York: Simon and Schuster, 1972).

other's doorsteps. They watch their neighbors for signs of misfortune, and only then do they laugh. In the book they do a lot of laughing, having so much bad luck. Several times they even laughed at the anthropologist, who found this especially repellent (one senses, between the lines, that the scholar is not himself the world's luckiest man). Worse, they took him into the family, snatched his food, defecated on his doorstep, and hooted dislike at him. They gave him two bad years. [4]

It is a depressing book. If, as he suggests, there is only Ikness at the center of each of us, our sole hope for hanging on to the name of humanity will be in endlessly mending the structure of our society, and it is changing so quickly and completely that we may never find the threads in time. Meanwhile, left to ourselves alone, solitary, we will become the same joyless, zestless, untouching lone animals. [5]

But this may be too narrow a view. For one thing, the Iks are extraordinary. They are absolutely astonishing, in fact. The anthropologist has never seen people like them anywhere, nor have I. You'd think, if they were simply examples of the common essence of mankind, they'd seem more recognizable. Instead, they are bizarre, anomalous. I have known my share of peculiar, difficult, nervous, grabby people, but I've never encountered any genuinely, consistently detestable human beings in all my life. The Iks sound more like abnormalities, maladies. [6]

I cannot accept it. I do not believe that the Iks are representative of isolated, revealed man, unobscured by social habits. I believe their behavior is something extra, something laid on. This unremitting, compulsive repellence is a kind of complicated ritual. They must have learned to act this way; they copied it, somehow. [7]

I have a theory, then. The Iks have gone crazy. [8]

The solitary Ik, isolated in the ruins of an exploded culture, has built a new defense for himself. If you live in an unworkable society you can make up one of your own, and this is what the Iks have done. Each Ik has become a group, a one-man tribe on its own, a constituency. [9]

Now everything falls into place. This is why they do seem, after all, vaguely familiar to all of us. We've seen them before. This is precisely the way groups of one size or another, ranging from committees to nations, behave. It is, of course, this aspect of humanity that has lagged behind the rest of evolution, and this is why the Ik seems so primitive. In his absolute selfishness, his incapacity to give anything away, no matter what, he is a successful committee. When he stands at the door of his hut, shouting insults at his neighbors in a loud harangue, he is city addressing another city. [10]

Cities have all the Ik characteristics. They defecate on doorsteps, in rivers and lakes, their own or anyone else's. They leave rubbish. They detest all neighboring cities, give nothing away. They even build institutions for deserting elders out of sight. [11]

Nations are the most Iklike of all. No wonder the Iks seem familiar. For total greed, rapacity, heartlessness, and irresponsibility there is nothing to match a nation. Nations, by law, are solitary, self-centered, withdrawn into themselves. There is no such thing as affection between nations, and certainly no nation ever loved another. They bawl insults from their doorsteps, defecate into whole oceans, snatch all the food, survive by detestation, take joy in the bad luck of others, celebrate the death of others, live for the death of others. [12]

That's it, and I shall stop worrying about the book. It does not signify that man is a sparse, inhuman thing at his center. He's all right. It only says what we've always known and never had enough time to worry about, that we haven't yet learned how to stay human when assembled in masses. The Ik, in his despair, is acting out this failure, and perhaps we should pay closer attention. Nations have themselves become too frightening to think about, but we might learn some things by watching these people. [13]

PURPOSE AND STRUCTURE

1. In the first sentence, the author claims that the Iks have become "literary symbols." Is this claim supported consistently or does the author lose his focus? Cite evidence.

2. Support the assertion that the first half of par. 3 is a subordinate sequence paragraph and the second half a coordinate sequence paragraph, one in which the sentences are at approximately the same level of generality and therefore give the effect of lists.

3. Explain why the method of development of pars. 3 and 4 is appropriate to the author's *analysis* of the Iks.

4. Argue for or against joining par. 4 to par. 3.

5. Argue that par. 10 has all these characteristics: subordinate sequence paragraph; development by comparison; development by illustration.

6. Identify the transition between par. 10 and par. 11.

7. Show how some of the effects of par. 3 are achieved by the use of co-ordinating conjunctions.

8. Does the author assign any cause to the behavior of the Iks? In which paragraphs does he make this assignment most clearly? Does he assign any cause to the behavior of groups of men? Are these causes in any way comparable?

9. In par. 4, what elementary device does the author use in order to maintain focus in the paragraph?

DICTION AND TONE

1. What does the title contribute to your feeling about the piece?

2. What effect is created by juxtaposing as two disasters the government's banning of hunting and the visit of the anthropologist?

3. Explain the apparent paradox in par. 4, ". . . they do a lot of laughing, having so much bad luck."

4. In par. 6 the Iks are called "examples of the common essence of mankind," and also "anomalous." Can they be both?

5. Par. 12 begins "Nations are the most Iklike of all." Is it an allowable language procedure to take a noun like *Ik* and convert it into another part of speech?

APPLICATIONS TO WRITING

Analyze the main characteristics of a cultural subgroup (high school students, fraternity members, 4-H members, members of a motorcycle club) and then compare these characteristics with those of another, more numerous group such as blue-collar workers, retired people, farm workers, CB operators.

Friday Night in the Coliseum

WILLIAM C. MARTIN

"When I die, I want to be cremated, and I want my ashes scattered in the Coliseum on Friday night. It's in my will." Thus spoke a little old lady who hasn't missed a Friday night wrestling match for—well, she's not exactly sure, but "it's been a long time, son, a long time." On Friday night, fifty times a year, more than 6500 fans stream into the Coliseum in downtown Houston for promoter Paul Boesch's weekly offering of Crushers, Killers, Bruisers, and Butchers, Commies, Nazis, Japs, and A-rabs, Dukes, Lords, and Barons, Professors and Doctors, Cowboys and Indians, Spoilers and Sissies, Farmers and Lumberjacks, Bulls and Mad Dogs, Masked Men and Midgets, Nice Girls and Bitches, and at least one Clean-cut, Finely Muscled Young Man who never fights dirty until provoked beyond reason and who represents the Last, Best, Black, Brown, Red, or White Hope for Truth, Justice, and the American Way. [1]

Though scoffed at by much of the public as a kind of gladiatorial theater in which showmanship counts for more than genuine athletic skill, professional wrestling enjoys steadily increasing success not only in Houston but in hundreds of tank towns and major cities all over America. This is not, of course, the first time around. Pro wrestling has been part of the American scene for more than a century and has enjoyed several periods of wide popularity. For most fans over thirty, however, it began sometime around 1949, with the arrival of television. Lou Thesz was world champion in those days, but the man who symbolized professional wrestling to most people was Gorgeous George, a consummate exhibitionist whose long golden curls, brocade and satin robes, and outrageously effeminate manner drew huge crowds wherever he went, all hoping to see a local he-man give him the beating he so obviously deserved. [2]

The Gorgeous One's success at the box office ushered in a new era of wrestler-showmen, each trying to appear more outrageous than the others. For many, villainy has provided the surest route to fame and fortune. The overwhelming majority of professional wrestling matches pit the Good, the Pure, and the True against the Bad, the Mean, and the Ugly, and a man with a flair for provoking anger and hatred has an assured future in the sport. Since shortly after World War II, the most dependable source of high displeasure has been the Foreign Menace, usually an unreconstructed Nazi or a wily Japanese who insults the memory of our boys in uniform with actions so contemptuous one cannot fail to be proud that our side won the war. [3]

Houston's most recent Nazi was Baron von Raschke, a snarling Hun with an Iron Cross on his cape and red swastikas on his shoes, who acknowledged his prefight introductions with a sharply executed goose step. Raschke, however, managed to make one think of George Lincoln Rockwell more often than Hitler or Goebbels, and so never really achieved first-class menacehood. It must be disappointing to be a Nazi and not have people take you seriously. [4]

Now, Japs [sic], especially Big Japs, are a different story. For one thing, they all know karate and can break railroad ties with their bare hands. For another, they are sneaky. So when Toru Tanaka climbs into the ring in that red silk outfit with the dragon on the back, and bows to the crowd and smiles that unspeakably wicked smile, and then caps it off by throwing salt all over everything in a ceremony designed to win the favor of god knows how many of those pagan deities Japanese people worship, you just know that nice young man up there in the ring with him is in serious trouble. [5]

Another major Foreign Menace is, of course, the Russian. Russian wrestlers are named Ivan, Boris, or Nikita, and although they have defected from Russia in quest of a few capitalist dollars, they still retain a lot of typically Communist characteristics, like boasting that Russians invented certain well-known wrestling techniques and predicting flatly that the World Champion's belt will one day hang from the Kremlin wall. Furthermore, they value nothing unless it serves their own selfish aims. After a twenty-year partnership with Lord Charles Montague, Boris Malenko states flatly, "I owe his lordship nothing. Remember one thing about us Russians. When we have no more use for anybody or anything, we let them go. Friendship means nothing to a Russian. When we get through with the Arabs and Castro, you will see what I mean. When we want something we don't care who we step on." [6]

Wrestling fans are generally an egalitarian lot, at least among themselves, and they do not appreciate those who put on airs. So they are easily angered by another strain of crowd displeaser one might call Titled Snobs and Pointy-Headed Intellectuals. These villains, who love to call themselves "Professor" or "Doctor" or "Lord" Somebody-or-other, use the standard bag of tricks—pulling a man down by his hair, rubbing his eyes with objects secreted in trunks or shoes, stomping his face while he lies wounded and helpless—but their real specialty is treating the fans like ignorant yahoos. They walk and speak with disdain for common folk, and never miss a chance to belittle the crowd in sesquipedalian put-downs or to declare that their raucous and uncouth behavior calls for nothing less than a letter to the *Times,* to inform proper Englishmen of the deplorable state of manners in the Colonies. [7]

A third prominent villain is the Big Mean Sonofabitch. Dick the Bruiser, Cowboy Bill Watts, Butcher Vachone, Killer Kowalski—these men do not need swastikas and monocles and big words to make you hate them. They have the bile of human meanness by the quart in every vein. If a guileless child hands a Sonofabitch a program to autograph, he will often brush it aside or tear it into pieces and throw it on the floor. It isn't that he has forgotten what it was like to be a child. As a child, he kicked crutches from under crippled newsboys and cheated on tests and smoked in the rest room. Now, at 260 pounds, he goes into the ring not just to win, but to injure and maim. Even before the match begins, he attacks his trusting opponent from behind, pounding his head into the turnbuckle, kicking him in the kidneys, stomping him in the groin, and generally seeking to put him at a disadvantage. These are bad people. None of us is really safe as long as they go unpunished. [8]

Fortunately, these hellish legions do not hold sway unchallenged by the forces of Right. For every villain there is a hero who seeks to hold his own against what seem to be incredible odds. Heroes also fall into identifiable categories. Most of them are trim and handsome young men in their twenties or early thirties, the sort that little boys want to grow up to be, and men want to have as friends, and women want to have, also. Personable Bobby Shane wins hearts when he wrestles in his red, white, and blue muscle suit with the "USA" monogram; and when Tim Woods, dressed all in white, is introduced as a graduate of Michigan State University, older folk nod approvingly. They want their sons and grandsons to go to college, even though they didn't have a chance to go themselves, and it is reassuring to see living proof that not everybody who goes to college is out burning draft cards and blowing up banks. [9]

Though quick to capitalize on the jingoist appeal of matches involving Menacing Foreigners, few promoters will risk a match that might divide the house along racial lines. So black and brown wrestlers usually appear in the role of Hero, behind whom virtually the entire crowd can unite. Browns—Mexicans, Mexican-Americans, and Puerto Ricans—are almost invariably handsome, lithe, and acrobatic. They fight "scientifically" and seldom resort to roughhouse tactics until they have endured so much that the legendary Latin temper can no longer be contained. If a black chooses to play the villain, he will soften the racial element; when Buster Lloyd, the Harlem Hangman, came into town, he belittled the skills of his opponents not because they were white, but because they were Texans and therefore little challenge for a man who learned to fight at the corner of Lenox Avenue and 125th Street. Several white grapplers might have been able to handle Buster, but the hero selected to take his measure and send him packing back to Harlem was Tiger Conway, a black Texan. [10]

The purest of pure Americans, of course, and a people well acquainted with villainy, are Red Indians. Most wrestling circuits feature a Red Indian from time to time; in Houston, ex-Jets linebacker Chief Wahoo McDaniel is the top attraction and has wrestled in the Coliseum more than a hundred times in the last three years. Like Chief White Owl, Chief Suni War Cloud, and Chief Billy Two Rivers, Wahoo enters the ring in moccasin-style boots, warbonnet, and other Indian authentica. He can endure great pain and injustice without flinching or retaliating in kind, but when enraged, or sometimes just to get the old adrenalin going, he will rip into a furious war dance and level his opponent with a series of karate-like Tomahawk Chops to the chest or scalp, then force him into submission with the dreaded Choctaw Death Lock. [11]

Although no Nazi fights clean and few Red Indians fight dirty, not all wrestlers can be characterized so unambiguously. The Masked Man, for example, is sinister-looking, and usually evil, with a name indicative of his intentions: The Destroyer, The Assassin, The Hangman, and Spoilers One, Two, and Three. But some masked men, like Mr. Wrestling and Mil Mascaras (who stars in Mexican movies as a masked crime-fighting wrestler), are great favorites, and Clawman has tried to dignify mask-wearing by having Mrs. Clawman and the Clawchildren sit at ringside in matching masks. [12]

The majority of Houston's wrestling fans appear to be working-class folk. The white and Mexican-American men still wear crew cuts and well-oiled pompadours, and many black men and boys cut their hair close to the scalp. Family men, often with several children in tow, wear Perma-Prest slacks and plaid sport shirts with the T-shirt showing at the neck. Others, who stand around before the matches drinking Lone Star Beer and looking for friendly ladies, favor cowboy boots, fancy Levis, and Western shirts with the top two or three pearl buttons already unsnapped. Occasionally, a black dude in a purple jump suit and gold ruffled shirt shows up, but the brothers in nondescript trousers and short-sleeve knits far outnumber him. The women cling stubbornly to bouffant hairstyles, frequently in shades blonder or redder or blacker than hair usually gets, and at least 80 percent wear pants of some sort. [13]

One basic reason these people come to the Coliseum is reflected in the motto displayed in Boesch's office: "Professional Wrestling: the sport that gives you your money's worth." Approximately half the Houston cards feature at least one championship bout or a battle for the right to meet the men's, women's, midgets', tag-team, or Brass Knucks champion of Texas, the United States, or the World. If fans grow jaded with championships, Boesch adds extra wrestlers to produce two-, three-, and four-man team matches, heavyweight-midget teams, man-woman teams, and Battles Royale, in which ten men try to throw each other over the top rope, the grand prize going to the last man left in the ring. . . . [14]

For many regulars, Friday night at the Coliseum is the major social event of the week. All over the arena blacks, browns, and whites visit easily across ethnic lines, in perverse defiance of stereotypes about blue-collar prejudices. A lot of people in the ringside section know each other, by sight if not by name. Mrs. Elizabeth Chappell, better known simply as "Mama," has been coming to the matches for more than twenty-five years. Between bouts, she walks around the ring, visiting with old friends and making new ones. When she beats on a fallen villain with a huge mallet she carries in a shopping bag, folks shout, "Attaway, Mama! Git him!" and agree that "things don't really start to pick up till Mama gets here." When a dapper young insurance salesman flies into a rage at a referee's decision, the fans nudge one another and grin about how "old Freddy really gets worked up, don't he?" [15]

Professional wrestling offers fans an almost unparalleled opportunity to indulge aggressive and violent impulses. A few appreciate the finer points of a take-down or a switch or a Fireman's Carry, but most would walk out on the NCAA wrestling finals or a collegiate match between Lehigh and Oklahoma. They want hitting and kicking and stomping and bleeding. Especially bleeding. [16]

Virtually all bouts incite a high level of crowd noise, but the sight of fresh blood streaming from a wrestler's forehead immediately raises the decibel level well into the danger zone. This is what they came to see. If both men bleed, what follows is nothing less than orgiastic frenzy. Mere main events and world championships and tag-team matches eventually run together to form murky puddles in the back regions of the mind, but no one forgets the night he saw real blood. One woman recalled such a peak experience in tones that seemed almost religious: "One night, about six or seven years ago, Cowboy Ellis was hit against the post and got three gashes in his head. I grabbed him when he rolled out of the ring and got blood on my dress all the way from the neckline to the hem. I thought he would bleed to death in my arms. I never washed that dress. I've still got it at the house. I keep it in a drawer all by itself." [17]

The lust for blood is not simply ghoulish, but a desire to witness the stigmata, the apparently irrefutable proof that what is seen is genuine. Wrestling fans freely acknowledge that much of the action is faked, that many punches are pulled, that the moisture that flies through the air after a blow is not sweat but spit, and that men blunt the full effect of stomping opponents by allowing the heel to hit the canvas before the ball of the foot slaps the conveniently outstretched arm. They not only acknowledge the illusion; they jeer when it is badly performed: "Aw my goodness! He can't even make it look good!" Still, they constantly try to convince themselves and each other that at least part of what they are seeing on a given night is real. When Thunderbolt Patterson throws Bobby Shane through the ropes onto the concrete, a woman shouts defiantly. "Was that real? Tell me that wasn't real!" And when Johnny Valentine and Ernie Ladd are both disqualified after a three-fall slugfest, a young man tells his buddy, "I think that was real. You know, sometimes they do get mad. One time Killer Kowalski got so mad he tore old Yukon Eric's ear plumb off." But when blood flows, no one seeks or needs confirmation. [18]

The effects on fans of viewing such violence are disputed. Some experiments with children and college students offer evidence that observing violent behavior either produces no change or raises the level of aggressive tendencies in the spectator. Other research, however, indicates that wrestling fans do experience a decrease in aggressive tendencies after viewing wrestling matches. Still, manipulating hatred and aggressive tendencies is not without its risks. Every wrestler has seen or heard about the time when some fan went berserk and clubbed or burned or cut or shot a villain who played his role too convincingly, and Tim Woods, it is said, has had only nine fingers since the night a challenger from the audience grabbed his hand, bit down extra hard, and spat the tenth out onto the mat. Then, too, the possibility always exists that in the highly charged atmosphere of the arena, a wrestler may lose control of himself and cause real damage to his opponent. If he were alive today, old Yukon Eric could tell you something about that. [19]

The Portrayal of Life that unfolds in the ring is no naïve melodrama in which virtue always triumphs and cheaters never win. Whatever else these folk know, they know that life is tough and filled with conflict, hostility, and frustration. For every man who presses toward the prize with pure heart and clean hands, a dozen Foreigners and so-called Intellectuals and Sonsofbitches seek to bring him down with treachery and brute force and outright meanness. And even if he overcomes these, there are other, basically decent men who seek to defeat him in open competition. . . . [20]

PURPOSE AND STRUCTURE

1. Martin's analysis of the varieties of wrestlers begins with a huge, inchoate list: "Crushers, Killers, Bruisers, and Butchers, Commies, Nazis, Japs, and A-rabs, Dukes, Lords and Barons, Professors and Doctors, Cowboys and Indians, Spoilers and Sissies, Farmers and Lumberjacks, Bulls and Mad Dogs, Masked Men and Midgets, Nice Girls and Bitches, and at least one Clean-cut, Finely Muscled Young Man who never fights dirty until provoked beyond reason and who represents the Last, Best, Black, Brown,

Red or White Hope for Truth, Justice, and the American Way" (par. 1). Why begin with this list? What is the result of capitalizing even adjectives: "Last, Best, Black, Brown, Red or White"? Why is this slightly puzzling list an effective introduction to an analysis? (Notice that Martin takes care—through unobtrusive groupings signaled by the use of "and"—that the reader does not completely lose his way.)

2. In the preceding list who are "the Good, the Pure, and the True" (par. 3)? Who are "the Bad, the Mean, and the Ugly" (par. 3)? (Most of the remainder of Martin's article consists of an analysis of this list (par. 1) of wrestler–showmen.

3. Why has the Foreign Menace (par. 3) been most successful at the box office? According to Martin's analysis, what are the three kinds of Foreign Menace (pars. 3–6)?

4. Why are "Japs [sic], especially Big Japs," (par. 5) a more serious Foreign Menace than Nazis?

5. "The Big Mean Sonofabitch[es] . . . . do not need swastikas and monocles and big words to make you hate them" (par. 8). Why not?

6. Why is the following transition appropriate: "Fortunately, these hellish legions do not hold sway unchallenged by the forces of Right" (par. 9)?

7. Analyze the categories that Heroes fall into: "For every villain there is a hero who seeks to hold his own against what seem to be incredible odds. Heroes also fall into identifiable categories" (par. 9).

8. Why conclude the analysis of the types of wrestlers with the ambiguous Masked Man (par. 12)?

9. Is the "Portrayal of Life" (par. 20) in the ring a naive melodrama?

DICTION AND TONE

1. Why introduce an article on wrestling with this quotation from a little old lady: " 'When I die, I want to be cremated, and I want my ashes scattered in the Coliseum on Friday night. It's in my will.' "? Does the rest of the article explain her puzzling fervor? Is the tone of this quotation appropriate?

2. The Coliseum referred to in the title is in downtown Houston. What happened at the original Coliseum in ancient Rome?

3. What is the tone of the phrase "high displeasure" (par. 3)? Is it an appropriate description of the audience referred to in Martin's article?

4. What are "actions so contemptuous" (par. 3)? Are they contemptible actions? Discuss.

5. What is the tone of: " 'When we want something we don't care who we step on.' " (par. 6)? Why is this statement from a Foreign Menace appropriate?

6. Why does Toru Tanaka smile "that unspeakably wicked smile" (par. 5)? Why does he cap "it off by throwing salt all over everything" (par. 5)?

7. Why do Titled Snobs and Pointy-Headed Intellectuals "never miss a chance to belittle the crowd in sesquipedalian putdowns" (par. 7)?

8. Should *Sonofabitch* (par. 8) be Son of a Bitch? Discuss the names of these Big Mean Sonofabitches: "Dick the Bruiser, Cowboy Bill Watts, Butcher Vachone, Killer Kowalski" (par. 8).

9. What is the tone of "They have the bile of human meanness by the quart in every vein" (par. 8)?

10. What is the tone of "These are bad people. None of us is really safe as long as they go unpunished" (par. 8)?

APPLICATIONS TO WRITING

1. In Pro wrestling the complicated world we live in is reflected in simple dramatic stereotypes. Analyze another reflection of the real world: situation comedies on TV, elections for student body officers, or college professors' personalities and teaching methods.

2. Write an analysis of a Pro wrestling match. (Make use of Martin's categories or develop your own.)

3. Martin makes a short and informal analysis of violence and audience reaction (pars. 15–19). Develop your own analysis of this subject.

Television: More Deeply Than We Suspect, It Has Changed All of Us

DANIEL J. BOORSTIN

Just as the printing press democratized learning, so the television set has democratized experience. But while our experience now is more equal than ever before, it is also more separate. And no Supreme Court ruling can correct this segregation, no federal commission can police it. It is built into our TV sets. [1]

SEGREGATION FROM ONE ANOTHER

When a colonial housewife went to the village to draw water for her family, she saw friends, gathered gossip, shared the laughs and laments of her neighbors. When her great-great-granddaughter was blessed with running water, and no longer had to go to the well, this made life easier, but also less interesting. Running electricity, mail delivery and the telephone removed more reasons for leaving the house. And now the climax of it all is Television. [2]

For television gives the American housewife in her kitchen her own private theater, her window on the world. Every room with a set becomes a private room with a view—a TV booth. Television brings in a supply of information, knowledge, news, romance, and advertisements —without her having to set foot outside her door. The range and variety and vividness of these experiences of course excel anything she gets outside, even while she spends hours driving around in her automobile. At home she now has her own private faucet of hot and cold running images. [3]

But always before, to see a performance was to share an experience with a visible audience. At a concert, or a ball game, or a political rally, the audience was half the fun. What and whom you saw in the audience was at least as interesting, and often humanly more important, than what you saw on the stage. While watching TV, the lonely American is thrust back on herself. She can, of course, exclaim or applaud or hiss, but nobody hears except the family in the living room. The other people at the performance take the invisible forms of "canned" laughter and applause. [4]

And while myriad island audiences gather nightly around their sets, much as cave-dwelling ancestors gathered around the fire, for warmth and safety and a feeling of togetherness, now, with more and more two-TV families, a member of the family can actually withdraw and watch in complete privacy. [5]

SEGREGATION FROM THE SOURCE

In the 1920s, in the early days of radio, "broadcast" entered the language with a new meaning. Before then it meant "to sow seeds over the whole surface, instead of in drills or rows," but now it meant to diffuse messages or images to unidentified people at unknown destinations. The mystery of the anonymous audience was what made sensible businessmen doubt whether radio would ever pay. They had seen the telegraph and the telephone prosper by delivering a message, composed by the sender, to a particular recipient. They thought the commercial future of radio might depend on devising ways to keep the radio message private so that it could be sent to only one specific person. [6]

The essential novelty of wireless communication—that those who received "broadcast" messages were no longer addressees, but a vast mysterious audience—was destined, in the long run, to create unforeseen new opportunities and new problems for Americans in the age of television, to create a new sense of isolation and confinement and frustration for those who saw the images. For television was a one-way window. Just as Americans were segregated from the millions of other Americans who were watching the same program, so each of them was segregated in a fantastic new way from those who put on the program and who, presumably, aimed to please. The viewer could see whatever they offered, but nobody (except the family in the living room) could know for sure how he reacted to what he saw. [7]

While the American felt isolated from those who filled the TV screen, he also felt a new isolation from his government, from those who collected his taxes, who provided his public services, and who made the crucial decisions of peace or war. Of course, periodically he still had the traditional opportunity to express his preference on the ballot. But now there was a disturbing and frustrating new disproportion between how often and how vividly his government and his political leaders could get their message to him and how often and how vividly he could get his to them. Even if elected representatives were no more inaccessible to him than they had ever been before, in a strange new way he surely felt more isolated from them. They could talk his ear off on TV and if he wanted to respond, all he could do was write them a letter. Except indirectly through the pollsters, Americans were offered no new modern avenue comparable to television by which to get their message back. They were left to rely on a venerable, almost obsolete 19th-century institution, the post office. [8]

SEGREGATION FROM THE PAST

Of all the forces which have tempted us to lose our sense of history, none has been more potent than television. While, of course, television levels distance—puts us closer and more vividly present in Washington than we are in our state capital and takes us all instantly to the moon —it has had a less noticeable but equally potent effect on our sense of time. Because television enables us to be there, anywhere, instantly, precisely because it fills the instant present moment with experience so engrossing and overwhelming, it dulls our sense of the past. If it had not been possible for us all to accompany Scott and Irwin on their voyage of exploration on the moon, we would have had to wait to be engrossed in retrospect by the vivid chronicle of some Francis Parkman or Samuel Eliot Morison, and there would then have been no possible doubt that the moon journey was part of the stream of our history. But with television we saw that historic event—as we now see more and more of whatever goes on in our country—as only another vivid item in the present. [9]

Almost everything about television tempts the medium to a time-myopia—to focus our interest on the here-and-now, the exciting, disturbing, inspiring, or catastrophic instantaneous now. Meanwhile, the high cost of network time and the need to offer something for everybody produce a discontinuity of programming, a constant shifting from one thing to another, an emphasis on the staccato and motley character of experience—at the cost of our sense of unity with the past. [10]

But history is a flowing stream. We are held together by its continuities, by people willing to sit there and do their jobs, by the unspoken faiths of people who still believe much of what their fathers believed. That makes a dull program. So the American begins to think of the outside world as if there too the program changed every half hour. [11]

SEGREGATION FROM REALITY

Of all the miracles of television none is more remarkable than its power to give to so many hours of our experience a new vagueness. Americans have become increasingly accustomed to see somethingor-other, happening somewhere-or-other, at sometime-or-other. The common-sense hallmarks of authentic first-hand experience (the ordinary facts which a jury expects a witness to supply to prove he actually experienced what he says) now begin to be absent, or to be only ambiguously present, in our television-experience. For our TV-experience we don't need to go out to see anything in particular. We just turn the knob. Then we wonder while we watch. Is this program "live" or is it "taped"? Is it merely an animation or a "simulation"? Is this a rerun? Where does it originate? When (if ever) did it really occur? Is this happening to actors or to real people? Is this a commercial? A spoof of a commercial? A documentary? Or pure fiction? [12]

Almost never do we see a TV event from what used to be the individual human point of view. For TV is many-eyed, and alert to avoid the monotony of one person's limited vision. And each camera gives us a close-up that somehow dominates the screen. Dick Cavett or Zsa Zsa Gabor fills the screen just like Dave Scott or President Nixon. Everything becomes theater, any actor—or even a spectator—holds center stage. Our TV perspective makes us understandably reluctant to go back to the seats on the side and in the rear which are ours in real life. [13]

The experience flowing through our television channels is a miscellaneous mix of entertainment, instruction, news, uplift, exhortation, and guess what. Old compartments of experience which separated going to church, or to a lecture, from going to a play or a movie or to a ball game, from going to a political rally or stopping to hear a patent-medicine salesman's pitch—on television, such compartments are dissolved. Here at last is a supermarket of surrogate experience. Successful programming offers entertainment (under the guise of instruction), instruction (under the guise of entertainment), political persuasion (with the appeal of advertising) and advertising (with the appeal of drama). [14]

A new miasma—which no machine before could emit—enshrouds the world of TV. We begin to be so accustomed to this foggy world, so at home and solaced and comforted within and by its blurry edges, that reality itself becomes slightly irritating. [15]

Here is a great, rich, literate, equalitarian nation suddenly fragmented into mysterious anonymous island-audiences, newly separated from one another, newly isolated from their entertainers and their educators and their political representatives, suddenly enshrouded in a fog of new ambiguities. Unlike other comparable changes in human experience, the new segregation came with rocket speed. Television conquered America in less than a generation. No wonder its powers are bewildering and hard to define. It took 500 years for the printing press to democratize learning. Then the people, who at last could know as much as their "betters," demanded the power to govern themselves. As late as 1671, the governor of colonial Virginia, Sir William Berkeley, thanked God that the printing press (breeder of heresy and disobedience) had not yet arrived in his colony, and prayed that printing would never come to Virginia. By the early 19th century, aristocrats and men of letters would record (with Thomas Carlyle) that movable type had disbanded hired armies and cashiered kings, and somehow created "a whole new democratic world." [16]

With dizzying speed television has democratized experience. Like the printing press, it threatens—and promises—a transformation. Is it any wonder that, like the printing press before it, television has met a cool reception from intellectuals and academics and the other custodians of traditional avenues of experience? [17]

Can TV-democratized experience carry us to a new society, beyond the traditional democracy of learning and politics? The great test is whether somehow we can find ways in and through television itself to break down the walls of the new segregation—the walls which separate us from one another, from the sources of knowledge and power, from the past, from the real world outside. We see clues to our frustrations in the rise of endless dreary talk-shows, as much as in the sudden increase in mass demonstrations. We must find ways outside TV to restore the sense of personal presence, the sense of neighborhood, of visible fellowship, of publicly shared enthusiasm and dismay. We must find ways within TV to allow the anonymous audience to express its views, not merely through sampling and statistical averages, but person-to-person. We must find ways to decentralize and define and separate TV audiences into smaller, more specific interest-groups, who have the competence to judge what they see, and then to give the audiences an opportunity to react and communicate their reactions. We must try every institutional and technological device—from more specialized stations to pay TV, to cable TV, and other devices still unimagined. [18]

Over a century ago, Thoreau warned that men were becoming "the tools of their tools." While this new-world nation has thrived on change and on novelty, our prosperity and our survival have depended on our ability to adapt strange new tools to wise old purposes. We cannot allow ourselves to drift in the channels of television. Many admirable features of American life today—the new poignance of our conscience, the wondrous universalizing of our experiences, the sharing of the exotic, the remote, the unexpected—come from television. But they will come to little unless we find ways to overcome the new provincialism, the new isolation, the new frustrations and the new confusion which come from our new segregation. [19]

PURPOSE AND STRUCTURE

1. Compare pars. 1 and 2 in terms of levels of generality.

2. Is there a thesis in these two paragraphs? Where is it stated?

3. Explain the last line of par. 3.

4. In par. 7 Boorstin writes, "Just as Americans were segregated from the millions of other Americans who were watching the same program, so each of them was segregated in a fantastic new way from those who put on the program and who, presumably, aimed to please." Where is the first half of this sentence developed? Where the second half?

5. Argue that pars. 9, 10, and 11, constitute a mini-essay, with a thesis, development of the thesis, and a conclusion.

6. Do the same for pars. 12, 13, 14, and 15.

7. By detailed reference to the text of the essay, demonstrate that the first sentence of par. 16 is a summary sentence. Relate the sentence to the title of the essay.

8. The second sentence of par. 18 is also a summary sentence. Show that it identifies the four parts of Boorstin's analysis.

9. Analyze the levels of generality of the sentences in par. 14. For example, sentence 2 is at a lower level than sentence 1. Is sentence 3 lower or higher than sentence 2? Is sentence 4 higher or lower than 3? At what point would the paragraph have been improved by the addition of example or illustration?

DICTION AND TONE

1. In the first paragraph Boorstin writes that television has "democratized experience," that our experiences are now "equal" but "separate," and that no "Supreme Court ruling can correct this segregation." This is terminology from our recent political past. Argue for the appropriateness or inappropriateness of this language.

2. Hyperbole is an exaggeration for effect. For example, par. 3 begins, "For television gives the American housewife in her kitchen her own private theater. . . ." Find three other examples of hyperbole.

3. In par. 10, Boorstin refers to "time-myopia." What is "time-myopia"?

4. Later in the same paragraph, he refers to "the stacatto . . . character of experience." In what field of specialization is "stacatto" generally used? Can it be used the way Boorstin uses it?

APPLICATIONS TO WRITING

1. Write an essay in which you analyze the effects of a particular program—or set of programs—on the audience. You may want to take the elements Boorstin identified—isolation of members of the audience from each other, isolation from the source of the program, isolation from the past, and isolation from reality—and show how they do or do not apply to your subject.

2. Write an essay in which you analyze the reasons for the decline of interest in serious literature.

3. Write an essay in which you analyze the reasons for the decline of college enrollments in the liberal arts.

Living Together

NEWSWEEK

"The whole concept of having a family scares me right now," says Stephen Fenichell, 21. *"I wouldn't even want to have a dog. All the possessions I have in the world fit in the back of a station wagon."* Still, for the past four years, Steve has been living with Mary Jane Reilly, 22, in dormitories at Harvard College. *"Sometimes I would like a symbolic statement that says this is my legitimate boyfriend,"* says Mary. *"It might turn out to be more convenient later on to be married. At least if I went to visit my relatives with Steve, they wouldn't make us sleep in separate rooms."*

"Sometimes I look at Maureen and feel like I've only known her for two weeks," says Ed Myers, 27. *"Being married would destroy that feeling. It's very irresponsible in a way, but I like that."* Last spring, after living together for five years, Ed and Maureen O'Leary, 27, put a down-payment on a modest house in Atlanta and moved in. Maureen's Irish Catholic family press constantly for a wedding, Ed says, and *"I'm not sure Maureen can hold out. It'll make me retch, but I'll do it just to make them happy."*

"It's cool with our friends, it's cool with our neighbors—our biggest inconvenience is that we don't know what to call each other." For fully ten years, Ron Nagle, 39, has been living with Cindy Ehrlich, 31, his 13-year-old son, Thatcher, and their two dogs. Ron and Cindy own a house together in San Francisco and celebrate anniversaries the same way married couples do. *"We used to talk about marriage a lot more than we do now,"* says Cindy, *"though we might consider it if we decided to have a child—or if we get inspired by a Cary Grant movie where he ran off and got married."*

It used to be called "living in sin"—and Jimmy Carter and millions of other Americans still think of it that way. Last winter, the President even asked a group of government workers to cut it out and get married. And it used to be done mostly by the very rich, who could afford to flout society's rules, and the very poor, who had nothing to lose by ignoring them. But now it's a way of life that takes in college students, divorcees, pensioners and thousands of young adults in transition from swingledom to suburbia. [1]

Since 1970, Census Bureau figures show, the number of unmarried people of the opposite sex sharing a household has doubled, from 654,000 to 1.3 million—and that almost surely understates the total. "Of all the revolutions that began in the 1960s, this is the only one that took hold among young people," says theologian and social critic Martin Marty. "It is not a momentary phenomenon, but a symbolic shift in attitudes that has great social significance." [2]

And as social shifts go, this one went with blinding speed. It was only nine years ago that a Barnard College sophomore named Linda LeClair created an instant scandal by admitting that she had been living, unmarried, with a man. The news made the front page of The New York Times and LeClair was nearly booted out of college. To-day, few major colleges retain parietal rules and many have coed dormitories. If Doris Day and Rock Hudson were models of uptight virtue in the movies of their day, modern film protagonists, such as Sylvester Stallone and Talia Shire in "Rocky" and Woody Allen and Diane Keaton in "Annie Hall," casually shack up. And if celebrities themselves see nothing new in having live-in lovers, they haven't always flaunted them so openly. People magazine makes a staple of happily unmarried couples, and one recent cover subject, 18-year-old actress Linda Blair, burbled about the 19-year-old musician she lives with—in her parents' house in Westport, Conn. "Mom says nothing stands in the way of love," Linda explains. [3]

Linda Blair's parents are still the exception, however. Most surveys show that the great majority of parents think that cohabitation is immoral, emotionally unhealthy and unwise. And for the millions of Americans who retain strong and formal religious ties, what used to be called "living in sin" remains just that. "It is unmitigated adultery, which is clearly forbidden in the Bible, seriously injurious to the well-being of families and a sin against God," says Foy Valentine, executive secretary of the Christian Life Commission of the Southern Baptist Convention. [4]

Social scientists believe the trend toward living together indicates an alarming loss of faith in institutions. "The real issue is not cohabitation but the meaning of marriage," says sociologist Richard Sennett. "Something about making a lifetime commitment of marriage doesn't work any more—that's what cohabiting shows. The idea of a permanent commitment to another human being has lost its meaning." Psychologist Urie Bronfenbrenner believes that cohabitation is seriously weakening the family and undermining the sense of obligation in all love and work relationships. "Society needs some kind of custom or institution in which people are committed to each other, no matter what," he says. "In sleeping together you don't develop those commitments." [5]

People choose to live together for many reasons—but wariness about the troubled prospects of modern marriage may be the key one. One out of three marriages of couples between 25 and 35 years old will end in divorce and it is partly because of such bleak statistics that, for better or for worse, many people are moving so cautiously toward making lifelong commitments. The women's movement has encouraged its followers to demand the same rights and privileges as men, and many women argue that cohabitation offers the best of both worlds—intimate relationships on the one hand, and freedom from the traditional roles they might adopt in marriage, including economic dependence, on the other. At the same time, with premarital sex widely tolerated and contraception and abortion readily available, couples can openly enjoy intimate relationships without getting married. [6]

Some people cohabit because they are philosophically opposed to marriage, and others see cohabitation as a practical short-term option when the lease is up or a roommate moves out. But for most couples, living together is a positive trial period or prelude to marriage. "I discovered a lot I never could in a marriage," says 20-year-old student Pamela Brown, who has been living with her boyfriend for the past year in Portland, Maine. "When we lived apart we ate every meal together. Now we don't eat together all the time. If I had been married I would have felt the pressure of filling the wife-and-cook role. I believe in marriage but I'm not ready for it yet. I want a career first." Most couples who live together do marry sooner or later, especially when they want to have children. [7]

Cohabitation may be delaying marriage. Since 1960, the incidence of never-married women 20–24 years old has jumped from 28 percent to 40 percent; among men aged 23, the never-marrieds jumped from 42 percent to 52 percent just since 1970. But conclusive views on its effects are difficult to come by, partly because research in the area is so spotty. While cohabitation has rapidly become a favorite dissertation subject for Ph.D. students and a Cohabitation Newsletter is published for those in the field, the research has focused almost exclusively on college students, the sampling techniques have been notably unscientific and studies aimed at long-term comparisons of couples are almost nonexistent. Most important, the research is frustratingly inconclusive both as to whether cohabitation is generally more or less satisfying than marriage, and whether it helps set the groundwork for better and more enduring relationships. [8]

This uncertainty is reflected—sometimes ludicrously—in the difficulty couples have trying to find labels for each other and their arrangements. "That is no accident," says San Francisco psychotherapist Lillian Rubin. "Language and custom tend to interact." The absence of such a terminology here, she says, implies that "there is not yet agreement that this is really a legitimate form of coupling." Elizabeth L. Post, author of "The New Emily Post's Etiquette," suggests "covivant" as the most appropriate way to refer to one's roommate. Others have suggested such exotica as attaché, compañera, unlywed, paramour, apartmate, checkmate and swain. Some try coy double entendres such as 'spose ("'spose they'll get married?") and sin-law. Parents, suggests Washington, D. C., writer Jane Otten, may finally have to settle for "my daughter's er and my son's um." Most people talk about their "friends," with or without special stress, or just use unadorned first names. [9]

Cohabitation creates considerable problems of protocol, especially in Washington, some of which journalist Sally Quinn wryly described in a recent Washington Post article. According to Quinn—who shares a house with her executive editor, Ben Bradlee—social secretaries are "having nervous breakdowns" over addressing invitations, making introductions and seating guests according to the rank of their roommates. For invitations, both names can be listed on the envelope, alphabetically and on separate lines. When it comes to inviting one partner and not the other, there are no easy answers. The same is true of introductions, although Elizabeth Post suggests an interesting compromise—use "friend" for elders and "the person I live with" for peers. As for seating arrangements, says Quinn, "for now, the protocol demands that the spouse assume the rank of the spouse and an unranked roommate is simply not counted." [10]

At the White House, where the President's views on living together are well known, protocol problems have been obviated by a rash of marriages since January. Although staffers insist that Carter does not interfere with their personal lives, the fact is that a number of his aides have belatedly tied the knot—including Jack Watson, Greg Schneiders, Tim Kraft and Rex Granum, Federal Trade Commission head Mike Pertschuk and State Department official Richard Holbrooke. "It does seem to defy the laws of probability," admits one White House insider. [11]

At most other houses, the stickiest protocol problems arise when children show up for visits with their mates. Many parents remain adamantly opposed to letting them sleep together. "I'd never let any of my children shack up in my house on a weekend," says a Westchester, N. Y., mother of four. "I insist on my standards being respected." Columnist Ann Landers, who unstintingly opposes cohabitation, agrees that parents have the right to set the rules in their own household, but cautions them not to be "judgmental" about their children's arrangements. [12]

More and more parents, however, are trying to adapt to the new morality—no matter how difficult it may prove. Peggy Scott, a New York City mother of four, first confronted the situation six years ago. "We arrived for a weekend at our Vermont house, only to find that my 19-year-old son had been living there with his girlfriend for about ten days. My husband and I felt very shaken up and incredulous and there was this terrible moment where we didn't know what to do. They were not trying to conceal it, though, so we welcomed the girl and just hoped everything would come out all right." It has, at least to parental eyes: they eventually got married. Today, when the Scotts' other sons come home for weekends, they are permitted to stay in the same room with their mates. "It was a very hard decision," says Mrs. Scott, "but I knew they were living together during the week, so what difference did the weekend make?" [13]

But if societal sanctions against cohabitation are easing, there are still certain legal barriers that remain. Cohabitation, where two unmarried people share a residence and have sexual relations, is against the law in twenty states, with penalties for conviction ranging as high as a three-year jail sentence in Massachusetts and Arizona. Fornication—

sexual intercourse between a man and a woman who are unmarried—is a crime in sixteen states. But such laws are rarely enforced. [14]

For the most part, childless couples living together face only minor hassles—mostly economic. While cohabitors usually get the same rates as married people for life insurance and face no greater problems in obtaining mortgages than do married couples, disadvantages often include higher auto- and home-insurance rates, exclusion from family medical plans, scattered difficulty in renting apartments and traveling in foreign countries, and perhaps most important, a lack of legal standing for their children. Income-tax rates give the best break to the married couple in which only one member works. For moderate-income couples in which both partners work, the tax bite is worse in many cases for those who are married, since they are entitled to a single standard deduction compared with two for singles living together. For example, a married couple earning a joint income of $20,000 may pay nearly $400 more in taxes than a comparable cohabiting couple. [15]

Old people complain that, for them, the social-security system invites living in sin. Louis Marathon, 80, and Madeline Clarke, 81, met in a Miami nursing home last year and lived together for several months, between his hospital stays. A former schoolteacher, Madeline received $285 a month from her husband's social-security benefits. Lou gets a World War I veteran's pension of $425 a month (he received no social security since he had been self-employed). Last June, they got married and Madeline may now lose her benefits. "If they cut her off, I'll go to the VA and get an increase as a married man," says Louis, a double amputee. Even if their money is reduced, however, the Marathons are glad they married. "There's more respect," says Madeline, who is almost blind. "If we live together, it's just common-law, and with that anyone could get disgusted and walk out." [16]

Is living together any different from marriage? Research indicates that people who live together are less likely than others to be involved with formal religions, and that they see themselves as more liberated from traditional sex roles but just as monogamous as their married counterparts. But beyond that it is almost impossible to generalize. On the one hand, cohabitation can be a sensible way to explore a loving relationship. On the other, it tends to rule out experiments outside one rigid structure. The one conclusion from all the evidence is that the degree of commitment among people living together is considerably less than that of married couples. [17]

For Rich, 31, and Ilene, 25, both recently graduated from Boston College, living together was anything but a romantic adventure in young love. "It is much cheaper," says Rich. "We share the costs on rent and food." Both anticipate marriage eventually, though not necessarily to each other, and they don't even agree on how and where they'd like to live. Rich wants to look for work in a rural setting; Ilene would prefer an urban one. "We're trying to work on it but I'm not sure a compromise can be reached," says Ilene. Whatever happens, both Rich and Ilene say that their experience has been a good one. [18]

According to author Gail Sheehy, whose book "Passages" explores the stages of adult life, Rich and Ilene's attitude may be appropriate for them. "Establishing what you want to do and who you are is necessary before you can truly believe that commitment to another person does not threaten your own individuality," she says. "The whole stage in which one is trying to gain a footing in the adult world requires that one put hope and effort into trials. Like early friendship, they may dissolve, but how are you going to learn without trying?" [19]

What troubles some social critics about the notion of trial intimacy is that it undermines the concept of enduring loyalty that is integral to marriage. "Intimate bonding should be based on deep concepts of fidelity," says Martin Marty. "A lot that is convenient and exploratory undercuts that. There is no society when everything is based on ad hoc, and if we can't trust each other, we have no lives." Notre Dame campus chaplain William Toohey sees living together as part of the problem of making open-end promises. "I think it is a weakness in society that we have a feverish desire not to be hurt," he says. "Dammit, life is vulnerability. You've got to give of yourself and it does make you vulnerable." [20]

Couples who have married after living together confirm the fact that the institution deepens their sense of commitment. Lenny, 29, and Inger, 33, married last May after living together for four years in Washington, D. C. "One thing it has done is make me realize I am going to drop dead someday," says Lenny, an attorney. "The job has become more serious. I need to get the career going and I'm feeling more responsible." "Until you get married you aren't aware of being part of something that's bigger than yourself," says Inger. [21]

For Katie Charles, who is getting married in August after five years of cohabitation, the very things she once feared might encroach on her independence now are welcome. "It's a real step, standing up before your friends and saying I'm going to make my life with this person," says the 30-year-old Chicago mental-health counselor. "Before it was somewhat temporary. Now I'm turned on to the idea of being a family. I'm becoming more traditional than I thought I was. It's a return to the values I learned as I was growing up." [22]

But the values many young people bring to marriage these days are changing, too. Married couples are just as likely to pursue separate careers and intermingle roles as those who live together. And the problems of married couples and those living together are remarkably similar. "Most of the problems unmarried couples have—sex, money, power, the need for space—are the same ones married couples mention," says Dr. Frederick G. Humphrey, president of the American Association of Marriage and Family Counselors. "Unmarried couples may want the pseudointellectual belief that they are free to leave, but when they split up, the emotional pain and trauma is often virtually identical to married couples getting a divorce." In fact, so many unmarried couples are seeking counseling these days that the AAMFC is seriously considering retitling its members "relationship counselors." [23]

Unlike cohabitation, however, marriage is reinforced by its traditions and religious associations. "Marriage is a form of intimate coercion," says Sennett. "That's why it is ritualized so strongly. It's a legal way of saying you can trust someone to be there." Los Angeles actress Elizabeth Allensworth, for instance, believes that the relationship she had with her former boyfriend might have survived had they been married. As her career got under way, problems developed over independence and money. "All the hostilities, I think, would have been dealt with in a different way if we'd been married," she says. "That's a much more long-range ball game, not just a here-and-now situation. For a couple that's living together, it's so easy to say the hell with you, I'm leaving." [24]

Some believe, however, that the very fragility of living together makes cohabitors less likely than married folk to take each other for granted. "Married people are more apt to put up with a problem rather than divorce, but couples living together are more likely to try and work out the differences between them," says New York psychiatrist Avodah

Offit. "There is the fear of losing each other." But there is also, for many couples, the unspoken issue of "if you really loved me, you would marry me." During almost a year of living together, Jenny and Mark Bluestein had spats over staying out late and small jealousies. "It was the tensions and feelings of wanting to possess without being possessed," says Mark, 25, who works for a beauty shop in St. Louis. "We were both suffering through different insecurities about each other so we both said, 'OK, I'll show you I do too love you.' We got married to solidify the commitment, to reassure each other." [25]

Many people—especially mothers—believe that the insecurities of living together harm women more than men. "I'm bitterly opposed to living together," says Mrs. Dorothy Grossman, a Nashville mother of four grown daughters, some of whom have tried cohabiting. "A woman is more subservient to a man if she enters this type of arrangement. The woman goes and sets up house, gives more than 50 percent of the effort, and when it breaks up she always gets the bad deal. It's almost always the man who walks out." [26]

Some research indicates that the level of commitment among women who live together with men is indeed consistently higher than that of their partners. Ohio State sociologist Nancy Moore Clatworthy interviewed 100 young couples in Columbus, Ohio, and concluded that most of the women consented to living with men only because they felt their partners wanted to. "The women had feelings of guilt," she says. "Living-together couples often haven't proved what they wanted to prove—that marriage is the same as cohabitation." [27]

But in one way, that may be changing. Last December, the California Supreme Court ruled that singer Michelle Triola had the right to pursue her claim for both support payments and property rights from actor Lee Marvin, the man she had lived with for seven years. The ruling said that in the absence of a legal marriage contract—or even a verbal agreement—the court can infer a contract from the conduct of the parties. As a result, Triola—and others in her situation—may have the right at least to communal property if not support after a relationship breaks up. [28]

Since he represented Triola, Los Angeles lawyer Marvin M. Mitchelson has already taken on four more celebrity cases. "A problem with the Marvin-Triola decision," says Mitchelson, "is that it states that the court can examine the relationship of the parties to determine who contributed what. So you get back to a fault system"—just what the no-fault divorce law was designed to eliminate. It also means the courts may have to decide the value of services and the equity of imposing the economic obligations of lawful spouses on people who have rejected matrimony to avoid such obligations. Mitchelson foresees that the California finding may encourage couples to sign what he calls "non-nuptial agreements" spelling out what obligations they are and are not taking on. [29]

Although non-nuptial contracts have been advocated over the years, perhaps no one has taken the concept quite as far as Edmund Van Deusen, a 53-year-old California writer. Himself the product of a failed marriage, Van Deusen advertised in a newspaper for a partner. He offered to pay her $500 a month to live with him, provide companionship but not necessarily sex or love, and perform light household duties. That was five years ago. Since then he has been sharing his Laguna Beach home with the woman he chose—under a contract that includes a 30-day cancellation clause on either side. Neither one has exercised it. "A marriage contract is 24 hours a day," Van Deusen says. "We only commit a bargained amount of our time. It allows people who live together to follow familiar rules that also guarantee independence." [30]

At the moment, the overwhelming majority of Americans still strongly disapprove of living together "without benefit of clergy," and even the people involved in those relationships find them not wholly comfortable. If the divorce rate continues to climb, widespread cohabitation may one day peacefully coexist with marriage, either as an interim option or as a practical alternative. But if it is to be the trend of the future, couples will discover that it is no magic solution: the problems of living together take as much time and effort to work out as the problems of modern marriage. [31]

PURPOSE AND STRUCTURE

1. What is the thesis sentence of par. 7? Demonstrate that the unity of the paragraph is maintained by controlling the subject of the sentences.

2. In par. 16, what proportion of the paragraph is thesis, what proportion illustration? Again, demonstrate that sentence subjects contribute significantly to paragraph unity.

3. In par. 14 the second sentence and the next-to-last sentence contain appositives. From your examination of the sentences, explain what an appositive is and what it can contribute to a sentence.

4. A noun clause, like any clause, has a subject and a verb. It is a *noun* clause because it functions in a sentence just as a noun would function. The second sentence of par. 17 contains two parallel noun clauses. Identify the clauses and explain the parallelism. Identify the noun clause in the last sentence of the paragraph. What are some of the characteristics of sentences that contain noun clauses?

5. " 'The job has become more serious. I need to get the career going and I'm feeling more responsible.' " (par. 21) Compare the quotation with the following: "Because I'm feeling more responsible, the job has become more serious and therefore I need to get the career going." Which makes its point more clearly and more forcefully? Why?

6. What is the topic sentence of par. 15? How many examples support this topic sentence?

7. Should par. 6 be made into two paragraphs? If so, where should the paragraph break? Should par. 5 be made a part of the development of par. 6?

8. How is the transition made between pars. 10 and 11? Between 11 and 12?

DICTION AND TONE

1. In pars. 1 and 4 the term " 'living in sin' " is placed in quotation marks, but in par. 16 it isn't. What difference in meaning and effect is created by this difference in technique?

2. The term "from swingledom to suburbia" appears at the end of par. 1. What effect does the term *swingledom* have on you? Do you think it is an imaginative joining of two words? Do you think it is too cute for the essay? Do you think the alliteration with *suburbia* is good-humored, memorable, or what?

3. The term "parietal rules" is used in par. 3. Not all that many readers know what the word *parietal* means. First, guess at its meaning from the context. Then look it up in an unabridged dictionary.
    What is your opinion of using a word like *parietal* in the essay? Does it add to the tone? Does it interfere with communication? Is it all right be-

cause you understand the general meaning of the sentence even though you do not understand this word?

4. Par. 9 contains a list of terms used to refer to one's living partner. Evaluate the advantages and disadvantages of each of these terms. How should people who are living together refer to each other?

5. The term "shack up" is used in par. 3 and in par. 13. Does it have a different tone in the different contexts? Is it more appropriate in one context than in another?

APPLICATIONS TO WRITING

Because it touches on cultural, social, economic, and psychological problems, an essay like "Living Together" is difficult to write unless the writer does research. You may have to do some research to accomplish this assignment.

Write an essay in which you analyze a problem of cultural change. For example, fifty years ago anyone who could afford to do so moved to the city. Today those who can afford to do so move out of the city. This change has its social, economic, and psychological dimensions. There are many other such changes underway: changes in the role of education; changes in work and employment patterns; changes in technological developments; changes in attitudes toward science and religion.

How to Say Nothing in Five Hundred Words

PAUL ROBERTS

It's Friday afternoon, and you have almost survived another week of classes. You are just looking forward dreamily to the weekend when the English instructor says: "For Monday you will turn in a five-hundred-word composition on college football." [1]

Well, that puts a good hole in the weekend. You don't have any strong views on college football one way or the other. You get rather excited during the season and go to all the home games and find it rather more fun than not. On the other hand, the class has been reading

Robert Hutchins in the anthology and perhaps Shaw's "Eighty-Yard Run," and from the class discussion you have got the idea that the instructor thinks college football is for the birds. You are no fool. You can figure out what side to take. [2]

After dinner you get out the portable typewriter that you got for high school graduation. You might as well get it over with and enjoy Saturday and Sunday. Five hundred words is about two double-spaced pages with normal margins. You put in a sheet of paper, think up a title, and you're off:

WHY COLLEGE FOOTBALL SHOULD BE ABOLISHED
College football should be abolished because it's bad for the school and also bad for the players. The players are so busy practicing that they don't have any time for their studies.

This, you feel, is a mighty good start. The only trouble is that it's only thirty-two words. You still have four hundred and sixty-eight to go, and you've pretty well exhausted the subject. It comes to you that you do your best thinking in the morning, so you put away the typewriter and go to the movies. But the next morning you have to do your washing and some math problems, and in the afternoon you go to the game. The English instructor turns up too, and you wonder if you've taken the right side after all. Saturday night you have a date, and Sunday morning you have to go to church. (You can't let English assignments interfere with your religion.) What with one thing and another, it's ten o'clock Sunday night before you get out the typewriter again. You make a pot of coffee and start to fill out your views on college football. Put a little meat on the bones. [3]

WHY COLLEGE FOOTBALL SHOULD BE ABOLISHED
In my opinion, it seems to me that college football should be abolished. The reason why I think this to be true is because I feel that football is bad for the colleges in nearly every respect. As Robert Hutchins says in his article in our anthology in which he discusses college football, it would be better if the colleges had race horses and had races with one another, because then the horses would not have to attend classes. I firmly agree with Mr. Hutchins on this point, and I am sure that many other students would agree to. [4]

One reason why it seems to me that college football is bad is that it has become too commercial. In the olden times when people played football just for the fun of it, maybe college football was all right, but they do not play football just for the fun of it now as they used to in the old days. Nowadays college football is what you might call a big business. Maybe this is not true at all schools, and I don't think it is especially true here at State, but certainly this is the case at most colleges and universities in America nowadays, as Mr. Hutchins points out in his very interesting article. Actually the coaches and alumni go around to the high schools and offer the high school stars large salaries to come to their colleges and play football for them. There was one case where a high school star was offered a convertible if he would play football for a certain college. [5]

Another reason for abolishing college football is that it is bad for the players. They do not have time to get a college education, because they are so busy playing football. A football player has to practice every afternoon from three to six and then he is so tired that he can't concentrate on his studies. He just feels like dropping off to sleep after dinner, and then the next day he goes to his classes without having studied and maybe he fails the test. [6]

(Good ripe stuff so far, but you're still a hundred and fifty-one words from home. One more push.) [7]

Also I think college football is bad for the colleges and the universities because not very many students get to participate in it. Out of a college of ten thousand students only seventy-five or a hundred play football, if that many. Football is what you might call a spectator sport. That means that most people go to watch it but do not play it themselves. [8]

(Four hundred and fifteen. Well, you still have the conclusion, and when you retype it, you can make the margins a little wider.) [9]

These are the reasons why I agree with Mr. Hutchins that college football should be abolished in American colleges and universities. [10]

On Monday you turn it in, moderately hopeful, and on Friday it comes back marked "weak in content" and sporting a big "D." [11]

This essay is exaggerated a little, not much. The English instructor will recognize it as reasonably typical of what an assignment on college football will bring in. He knows that nearly half of the class will contrive in five hundred words to say that college football is too commercial and bad for the players. Most of the other half will inform him that college football builds character and prepares one for life and brings prestige to the school. As he reads paper after paper all saying the same thing in almost the same words, all bloodless, five hundred words dripping out of nothing, he wonders how he allowed himself to get trapped into teaching English when he might have had a happy and interesting life as an electrician or a confidence man. [12]

Well, you may ask, what can you do about it? The subject is one on which you have few convictions and little information. Can you be expected to make a dull subject interesting? As a matter of fact, this is precisely what you are expected to do. This is the writer's essential task. All subjects, except sex, are dull until somebody makes them interesting. The writer's job is to find the argument, the approach, the angle, the wording that will take the reader with him. This is seldom easy, and it is particularly hard in subjects that have been much discussed: College Football, Fraternities, Popular Music, Is Chivalry Dead?, and the like. You will feel that there is nothing you can do with such subjects except repeat the old bromides. But there are some things you can do which will make your papers, if not throbbingly alive, at least less insufferably tedious than they might otherwise be. [13]

AVOID THE OBVIOUS CONTENT

Say the assignment is college football. Say that you've decided to be against it. Begin by putting down the arguments that come to your mind: it is too commercial, it takes the students' minds off their studies, it is hard on the players, it makes the university a kind of circus instead of an intellectual center, for most schools it is financially ruinous. Can you think of any more arguments, just off hand? All right. Now when you write your paper, *make sure that you don't use any of the material on this list.* If these are the points that leap to your mind, they will leap to everyone else's too, and whether you get a "C" or a "D" may depend on whether the instructor reads your paper early when he is fresh and tolerant or late, when the sentence "In my opinion, college football has become too commercial," inexorably repeated, has brought him to the brink of lunacy. [14]

Be against college football for some reason or reasons of your own. If they are keen and perceptive ones, that's splendid. But even if they are trivial or foolish or indefensible, you are still ahead so long as they are not everybody else's reasons too. Be against it because the colleges don't spend enough money on it to make it worthwhile, because it is bad for the characters of the spectators, because the players are forced to attend classes, because the football stars hog all the beautiful women, because it competes with baseball and is therefore un-American and possibly Communist-inspired. There are lots of more or less unused reasons for being against college football. [15]

Sometimes it is a good idea to sum up and dispose of the trite and conventional points before going on to your own. This has the advantage of indicating to the reader that you are going to be neither trite nor conventional. Something like this:

We are often told that college football should be abolished because it has become too commercial or because it is bad for the players. These arguments are no doubt very cogent, but they don't really go to the heart of the matter. [16]

Then you go to the heart of the matter. [17]

TAKE THE LESS USUAL SIDE

One rather simple way of getting into your paper is to take the side of the argument that most of the citizens will want to avoid. If the assignment is an essay on dogs, you can, if you choose, explain that dogs are faithful and lovable companions, intelligent, useful as guardians of the house and protectors of children, indispensable in police work—in short, when all is said and done, man's best friends. Or you can suggest that those big brown eyes conceal, more often than not, a vacuity of mind and an inconstancy of purpose; that the dogs you have known most intimately have been mangy, ill-tempered brutes, incapable of instruction; and that only your nobility of mind and fear of arrest prevent you from kicking the flea-ridden animals when you pass them on the street [18]

Naturally personal convictions will sometimes dictate your approach. If the assigned subject is "Is Methodism Rewarding to the Individual?" and you are a pious Methodist, you have really no choice. But few assigned subjects, if any, will fall in this category. Most of them will lie in broad areas of discussion with much to be said on both sides.

They are intellectual exercises, and it is legitimate to argue now one way and now another, as debaters do in similar circumstances. Always take the side that looks to you hardest, least defensible. It will almost always turn out to be easier to write interestingly on that side. [19]

This general advice applies where you have a choice of subjects. If you are to choose among "The Value of Fraternities" and "My Favorite High School Teacher" and "What I Think About Beetles," by all means plump for the beetles. By the time the instructor gets to your paper, he will be up to his ears in tedious tales about the French teacher at Bloombury High and assertions about how fraternities build character and prepare one for life. Your views on beetles, whatever they are, are bound to be a refreshing change. [20]

Don't worry too much about figuring out what the instructor thinks about the subject so that you can cuddle up with him. Chances are his views are no stronger than yours. If he does have convictions and you oppose him, his problem is to keep from grading you higher than you deserve in order to show he is not biased. This doesn't mean that you should always cantankerously dissent from what the instructor says; that gets tiresome too. And if the subject assigned is "My Pet Peeve," do not begin, "My pet peeve is the English instructor who assigns papers on 'my pet peeve.'" This was still funny during the War of 1812, but it has sort of lost its edge since then. It is in general good manners to avoid personalities. [21]

SLIP OUT OF ABSTRACTION

If you will study the essay on college football [near the beginning of this essay], you will perceive that one reason for its appalling dullness is that it never gets down to particulars. It is just a series of not very glittering generalities: "football is bad for the colleges," "it has become too commercial," "football is a big business," "it is bad for the players," and so on. Such round phrases thudding against the reader's brain are unlikely to convince him, though they may well render him unconscious. [22]

If you want the reader to believe that college football is bad for the players, you have to do more than say so. You have to display the evil. Take your roommate, Alfred Simkins, the second-string center. Picture poor old Alfy coming home from football practice every evening, bruised and aching, agonizingly tired, scarcely able to shovel the mashed potatoes into his mouth. Let us see him staggering up to the room, getting out his econ textbook, peering desperately at it with his good eye, falling asleep and failing the test in the morning. Let us share his unbearable tension as Saturday draws near. Will he fail, be demoted, lose his monthly allowance, be forced to return to the coal mines? And if he succeeds, what will be his reward? Perhaps a slight ripple of applause when the third-string center replaces him, a moment of elation in the locker room if the team wins, of despair if it loses. What will he look back on when he graduates from college? Toil and torn ligaments. And what will be his future? He is not good enough for pro football, and he is too obscure and weak in econ to succeed in stocks and bonds. College football is tearing the heart from Alfy Simkins and, when it finishes with him, will callously toss aside the shattered hulk. [23]

This is no doubt a weak enough argument for the abolition of college football, but it is a sight better than saying, in three or four variations, that college football (in your opinion) is bad for the players. [24]

Look at the work of any professional writer and notice how constantly he is moving from the generality, the abstract statement, to the concrete example, the facts and figures, the illustrations. If he is writing on juvenile delinquency, he does not just tell you that juveniles are (it seems to him) delinquent and that (in his opinion) something should be done about it. He shows you juveniles being delinquent, tearing up movie theatres in Buffalo, stabbing high school principals in Dallas, smoking marijuana in Palo Alto. And more than likely he is moving toward some specific remedy, not just a general wringing of the hands. [25]

It is no doubt possible to be *too* concrete, too illustrative or anecdotal, but few inexperienced writers err this way. For most the soundest advice is to be seeking always for the picture, to be always turning general remarks into seeable examples. Don't say, "Sororities teach girls the social graces." Say, "Sorority life teaches a girl how to carry on a conversation while pouring tea, without sloshing the tea into the saucer." Don't say, "I like certain kinds of popular music very much." Say, "Whenever I hear Gerber Sprinklittle play 'Mississippi Man' on the trombone, my socks creep up my ankles." [26]

GET RID OF OBVIOUS PADDING

The student toiling away at his weekly English theme is too often tormented by a figure: five hundred words. How, he asks himself, is he to achieve this staggering total? Obviously by never using one word when he can somehow work in ten. [27]

He is therefore seldom content with a plain statement like "Fast driving is dangerous." This has only four words in it. He takes thought, and the sentence becomes:

In my opinion, fast driving is dangerous. [28]

Better, but he can do better still:

In my opinion, fast driving would seem to be rather dangerous. [29]

If he is really adept, it may come out:

In my humble opinion, though I do not claim to be an expert on this complicated subject, fast driving, in most circumstances, would seem to be rather dangerous in many respects, or at least so it would seem to me. [30]

Thus four words have been turned into forty, and not an iota of content has been added. [31]

Now this is a way to go about reaching five hundred words, and if you are content with a "D" grade, it is as good a way as any. But if you aim higher, you must work differently. Instead of stuffing your sentences with straw, you must try steadily to get rid of the padding, to make your sentences lean and tough. If you are really working at it, your first draft will greatly exceed the required total, and then you will work it down, thus:

It is thought in some quarters that fraternities do not contribute as much as might be expected to campus life. [32]
Some people think that fraternities contribute little to campus life. [33]
The average doctor who practices in small towns or in the country must toil night and day to heal the sick. [34]
Most country doctors work long hours. [35]

When I was a little girl, I suffered from shyness and embarrassment in the presence of others. [36]

I was a shy little girl. [37]

It is absolutely necessary for the person employed as a marine fireman to give the matter of steam pressure his undivided attention at all times. [38]

The fireman has to keep his eye on the steam gauge. [39]

You may ask how you can arrive at five hundred words at this rate. Simple. You dig up more real content. Instead of taking a couple of obvious points off the surface of the topic and then circling warily around them for six paragraphs, you work in and explore, figure out the details. You illustrate. You say that fast driving is dangerous, and then you prove it. How long does it take to stop a car at forty and at eighty? How far can you see at night? What happens when a tire blows? What happens in a head-on collision at fifty miles an hour? Pretty soon your paper will be full of broken glass and blood and headless torsos, and reaching five hundred words will not really be a problem. [40]

CALL A FOOL A FOOL

Some of the padding in freshman themes is to be blamed not on anxiety about the word minimum but on excessive timidity. The student writes, "In my opinion, the principal of my high school acted in ways that I believe every unbiased person would have to call foolish." This isn't exactly what he means. What he means is, "My high school principal was a fool." If he was a fool, call him a fool. Hedging the thing about with "in-my-opinion's" and "it-seems-to-me's" and "as-I-see-it's" and "at-least-from-my-point-of-view's" gains you nothing. Delete these phrases whenever they creep into your paper. [41]

The student's tendency to hedge stems from a modesty that in other circumstances would be commendable. He is, he realizes, young and inexperienced, and he half suspects that he is dopey and fuzzy-minded beyond the average. Probably only too true. But it doesn't help to announce your incompetence six times in every paragraph. Decide what you want to say and say it as vigorously as possible, without apology and in plain words. [42]

Linguistic diffidence can take various forms. One is what we call *euphemism.* This is the tendency to call a spade "a certain garden implement" or women's underwear "unmentionables." It is stronger in some eras than others and in some people than others but it always operates more or less in subjects that are touchy or taboo: death, sex, madness, and so on. Thus we shrink from saying "He died last night" but say instead "passed away," "left us," "joined his Maker," "went to his reward." Or we try to take off the tension with a lighter cliché: "kicked the bucket," "cashed in his chips," "handed in his dinner pail." We have found all sorts of ways to avoid saying *mad:* "mentally ill," "touched," "not quite right upstairs," "feeble-minded," "innocent," "simple," "off his trolley," "not in his right mind." Even such a now plain word as *insane* began as a euphemism with the meaning "not healthy." [43]

Modern science, particularly psychology, contributes many polysyllables in which we can wrap our thoughts and blunt their force. To many writers there is no such thing as a bad schoolboy. Schoolboys are maladjusted or unoriented or misunderstood or in the need of guidance or lacking in continued success toward satisfactory integration of the personality as a social unit, but they are never bad. Psychology no doubt makes us better men and women, more sympathetic and tolerant, but it doesn't make writing any easier. Had Shakespeare been confronted with psychology, "To be or not to be" might have come out, "To continue as a social unit or not to do so. That is the personality problem. Whether 'tis a better sign of integration at the conscious level to display a psychic tolerance toward the maladjustments and repressions induced by one's lack of orientation in one's environment or—" But Hamlet would never have finished the soliloquy. [44]

Writing in the modern world, you cannot altogether avoid modern jargon. Nor, in an effort to get away from euphemism, should you salt your paper with four-letter words. But you can do much if you will mount guard against those roundabout phrases, those echoing polysyllables that tend to slip into your writing to rob it of its crispness and force. [45]

BEWARE OF PAT EXPRESSIONS

Other things being equal, avoid phrases like "other things being equal." Those sentences that come to you whole, or in two or three doughy lumps, are sure to be bad sentences. They are no creation of yours but pieces of common thought floating in the community soup. [46]

Pat expressions are hard, often impossible, to avoid, because they come too easily to be noticed and seem too necessary to be dispensed with. No writer avoids them altogether, but good writers avoid them more often than poor writers. [47]

By "pat expressions" we mean such tags as "to all practical intents and purposes," "the pure and simple truth," "from where I sit," "the time of his life," "to the ends of the earth," "in the twinkling of an eye," "as sure as you're born," "over my dead body," "under cover of darkness," "took the easy way out," "when all is said and done," "told him time and time again," "parted the best of friends," "stand up and be counted," "gave him the best years of her life," "worked her fingers to the bone." Like other clichés, these expressions were once forceful. Now we should use them only when we can't possibly think of anything else. [48]

Some pat expressions stand like a wall between the writer and thought. Such a one is "the American way of life." Many student writers feel that when they have said that something accords with the American way of life or does not they have exhausted the subject. Actually, they have stopped at the highest level of abstraction. The American way of life is the complicated set of bonds between a hundred and eighty million ways. All of us know this when we think about it, but the tag phrase too often keeps us from thinking about it. [49]

So with many another phrase dear to the politician: "this great land of ours," "the man in the street," "our national heritage." These may prove our patriotism or give a clue to our political beliefs, but otherwise they add nothing to the paper except words. [50]

COLORFUL WORDS

The writer builds with words, and no builder uses a raw material more slippery and elusive and treacherous. A writer's work is a constant struggle to get the right word in the right place, to find that particular word that will convey his meaning exactly, that will persuade the reader or soothe him or startle or amuse him. He never succeeds altogether—

sometimes he feels that he scarcely succeeds at all—but such successes as he has are what make the thing worth doing. [51]

There is no book of rules for this game. One progresses through everlasting experiment on the basis of ever-widening experience. There are few useful generalizations that one can make about words as words, but there are perhaps a few. [52]

Some words are what we call "colorful." By this we mean that they are calculated to produce a picture or induce an emotion. They are dressy instead of plain, specific instead of general, loud instead of soft. Thus, in place of "Her heart beat," we may write, "Her heart *pounded, throbbed, fluttered, danced.*" Instead of "He sat in his chair," we may say, "He *lounged, sprawled, coiled.*" Instead of "It was hot," we may say, "It was *blistering, sultry, muggy, suffocating, steamy, wilting.*" [53]

However, it should not be supposed that the fancy word is always better. Often it is as well to write "Her heart beat" or "It was hot" if that is all it did or all it was. Ages differ in how they like their prose. The nineteenth century liked it rich and smoky. The twentieth has usually preferred it lean and cool. The twentieth century writer, like all writers, is forever seeking the exact word, but he is wary of sounding feverish. He tends to pitch it low, to understate it, to throw it away. He knows that if he gets too colorful, the audience is likely to giggle. [54]

See how this strikes you: "As the rich, golden glow of the sunset died away along the eternal western hills, Angela's limpid blue eyes looked softly and trustingly into Montague's flashing brown ones, and her heart pounded like a drum in time with the joyous song surging in her soul." Some people like that sort of thing, but most modern readers would say, "Good grief," and turn on the television. [55]

COLORED WORDS

Some words we would call not so much colorful as colored—that is, loaded with associations, good or bad. All words—except perhaps structure words—have associations of some sort. We have said that the meaning of a word is the sum of the contexts in which it occurs. When we hear a word, we hear with it an echo of all the situations in which we have heard it before. [56]

In some words, these echoes are obvious and discussable. The word *mother*, for example, has, for most people, agreeable associations. When you hear *mother* you probably think of home, safety, love, food, and various other pleasant things. If one writes, "She was like a mother to me," he gets an effect which he would not get in "She was like an aunt to me." The advertiser makes use of the associations of *mother* by working it in when he talks about his product. The politician works it in when he talks about himself. [57]

So also with such words as *home, liberty, fireside, contentment, patriot, tenderness, sacrifice, childlike, manly, bluff, limpid*. All of these words are loaded with associations that would be rather hard to indicate in a straightforward definition. There is more than a literal difference between "They sat around the fireside" and "They sat around the stove." They might have been equally warm and happy around the stove, but *fireside* suggests leisure, grace, quiet tradition, congenial company, and *stove* does not. [58]

Conversely, some words have bad associations. *Mother* suggests pleasant things, but *mother-in-law* does not. Many mothers-in-law are heroically lovable and some mothers drink gin all day and beat their children insensible, but these facts of life are beside the point. The point is that *mother* sounds good and *mother-in-law* does not. [59]

Or consider the word *intellectual*. This would seem to be a complimentary term, but in point of fact it is not, for it has picked up associations of impracticality and ineffectuality and general dopiness. So also such words as *liberal, reactionary, Communist, socialist, capitalist, radical, schoolteacher, truck driver, undertaker, operator, salesman, huckster, speculator*. These convey meaning on the literal level, but beyond that—sometimes, in some places—they convey contempt on the part of the speaker. [60]

The question of whether to use loaded words or not depends on what is being written. The scientist, the scholar, try to avoid them; for the poet, the advertising writer, the public speaker, they are standard equipment. But every writer should take care that they do not substitute for thought. If you write, "Anyone who thinks that is nothing but a Socialist (or Communist or capitalist)" you have said nothing except that you don't like people who think that and such remarks are effective only with the most naive readers. It is always a bad mistake to think your readers more naive than they really are. [61]

COLORLESS WORDS

But probably most student writers come to grief not with words that are colorful or those that are colored but with those that have no color at all. A pet example is *nice,* a word we would find it hard to dispense with in casual conversation but which is no longer capable of adding much to a description. Colorless words are those of such general meaning that in a particular sentence they mean nothing. Slang adjectives like *cool* ("That's real cool") tend to explode all over the language. They are applied to everything, lose their original force, and quickly die. [62]

Beware also of nouns of very general meaning, like *circumstances, cases, instances, aspects, factors, relationships, attitudes, eventualities,* etc. In most circumstances you will find that those cases of writing which contain too many instances of words like these will in this and other aspects have factors leading to unsatisfactory relationships with the reader resulting in unfavorable attitudes on his part and perhaps other eventualities, like a grade of "D." Notice also what "etc." means. It means "I'd like to make this list longer, but I can't think of any more examples." [63]

PURPOSE AND STRUCTURE

1. Unlike most essays, this one has subheadings at the beginning of new sections. This gives the reader the impression that each section is equally important. Is it? Is the section "Call a Fool a Fool" as important as the section that precedes it, "Get Rid of Obvious Padding," or is one a subsection of the other?

2. Are there any other sections closely related to each other? Which ones?

3. Could some of the sections be placed in a different order without changing the meaning of the essay?

4. Approximately what percentage of par. 23 is illustration? 10 percent? 50 percent? 90 percent? What is the point of the illustration? Relate the development of par. 23 to the title of the section in which it appears.

5. How many examples are cited in par. 22? What are they examples of?

6. Apply the information in the section "Colored Words" to the Mencken essay, "A Libido for the Ugly." List at least five strongly colored words that Mencken uses.

7. If you were to lengthen this essay by adding three sections, what sections would you add? Be prepared to defend your answer.

DICTION AND TONE

Starting with the section entitled, "Avoid the Obvious Comment," add one illustration to each section. Try to make your illustration so much like the author's that the casual reader would have difficulty telling them apart.

APPLICATIONS TO WRITING

Apply the information in each section to an analysis of H. L. Mencken's essay, "A Libido for the Ugly."

The Death of Marilyn Monroe

DIANA TRILLING

On a Sunday morning in August 1962, Marilyn Monroe, aged thirty-six, was found dead in the bedroom of her home in Los Angeles, her hand on the telephone as if she had just received or, far more likely, been about to make a call. On the night table next to her bed stood a formidable array of medicines, among them a bottle that had held twenty-five Nembutal pills, now empty. Two weeks later a team of psychiatrists, appointed by the state in conformity with California law, brought in its report on the background and circumstances of her death, declaring it a suicide. There had of course never been any suggestion of foul play. The death was clearly self-inflicted, a climax of extended mental suffering. In fact, it was soon revealed that on Saturday evening Marilyn Monroe had made an emergency call to the psychoanalyst who had been treating her for her acute sleeplessness, her anxieties and depression, and that he had paid her a visit. But the formal psychiatric verdict had to do with the highly technical question of whether the overdose of barbiturates was purposeful or accidental: had Marilyn Monroe *intended* to kill herself when she took the twenty-five sleeping pills? The jury of experts now ruled it was purposeful: she had wanted to die. [1]

It is an opinion, or at least a formulation, that can bear, I believe, a certain amount of modification. Obviously, I'm not proposing that Marilyn Monroe's death was accidental in the sense that she took so large a dose of pills with no knowledge of their lethal properties. But I think it would be more precise to call this kind of death incidental rather than purposeful—incidental to the desire to escape the pain of living. I am not a psychiatrist and I never knew Marilyn Monroe, but it seems to me that a person can want to be released from consciousness without seeking actual death; that someone can want to stop living without wishing to die. And this is my feeling about Marilyn Monroe, that even when she had spoken of "wanting to die" she really meant that she wanted to end her suffering, not her life. She wanted to destroy consciousness rather than herself. Then, having taken the pills, she realized she might never return from the sleep she craved so passionately and reached for the phone for help. [2]

But this is of course only speculation, and more appropriately engaged in by the medical profession than by the layman. For the rest of us, the motives surrounding Marilyn Monroe's suicide fade in importance before the all-encompassing reality of the act itself: Marilyn Monroe terminated her life. While the medical experts pondered the delicate difference between accident and suicide, the public recognized that the inevitable had at last occurred: Marilyn Monroe had killed herself. Shocked and grieved as everyone was, no one was at all surprised that she had died by her own hand, because for some years now the world had been prepared for just some such tragic outcome to one of the extraordinary careers of our time. [3]

The potentiality of suicide or, at any rate, the threat of extreme mental breakdown had been, after all, conveyed to us by virtually every news story about Marilyn Monroe of recent years. I don't mean that it had been spelled out that she would one day take her life or otherwise go off the deep psychic end. But no one seemed able to write about her without reassuring us that despite her instability and the graveness of her emotional problems, she was still vital and eager, still, however precariously, a going concern. Marilyn Monroe was an earnest, ambitious actress, determined to improve her skill; Marilyn Monroe had failed in several marriages but she was still in pursuit of fulfillment in love; Marilyn Monroe had several times miscarried but she still looked forward to having children; Marilyn Monroe was seriously engaged in psychoanalysis; Marilyn Monroe's figure was better than ever; she was learning to be prompter; she was coping, or was struggling to cope, with whatever it was that had intervened in the making of her last picture—so, on the well-worn track, ran all the news stories. Even what may have been her last interview to appear in print (by the time it came out, she was already dead) sounded the same dominant chord of hopefulness, telling us of a Marilyn Monroe full of confidence that she would improve her acting and find her roles, and that between the two therapies, hard work and psychoanalysis, she would achieve the peace of mind that had for so long eluded her. [4]

Where there is this much need for optimism, surely there is great peril, and the public got the message. But what is striking is the fact that throughout this period of her mounting difficulties, with which we were made so familiar, the popular image remained intact. Whatever we were told of her weak hold on life, we retained our image of Marilyn Monroe as the very embodiment of life energy. I think my response to her death was the common one: it came to me with the impact of a personal deprivation but I also felt it as I might a catastrophe in history or in nature; there was less in life, there was less of life, because she had ceased to exist. In her loss life itself had been injured. [5]

In my own instance, it happens that she was already an established star before I knew her as anything except the latest pin-up girl. There is always this shield of irony some of us raise between ourselves and any object of popular adulation, and I had made my dull point of snubbing her pictures. Then one evening I chanced on a television trailer for *Bus Stop,* and there she was. I'm not even sure I knew whom I was seeing on the screen, but a light had gone on in the room. Where everything had been gray there was all at once an illumination, a glow of something beyond the ordinarily human. It was a remarkable moment, of a kind I don't recall having had with any other actress, and it has its place with certain rare, cherished experiences of art such as my youthful remembrance of Pavlova,[1] the most perfect of performing artists, whose control of her body was like a radiance, or even the quite recent experience of seeing some photographs of Nijinsky[2] in motion. Marilyn Monroe was in motion, too, which is important, since no still picture could quite catch her electric quality; in posed pictures the redundancy of flesh was what first imposed itself, dimming one's perception of its peculiar aliveness, of the translucence that infused body with spirit. In a moment's flash of light, the ironies with which I had resisted this sex idol, this object of an undifferentiating public taste, dropped from me never to be restored. [6]

But mine was a minority problem; the world had long since recognized Marilyn Monroe's unique gift of physical being and responded to it as any such gift of life demands. From the start of her public career it had acknowledged the genius of biology or chemistry or whatever it was that set this young woman apart from the general kind. And once it had admitted her magic, nothing it was to learn of her "morbidity" could weigh against the conviction that she was alive in a way not granted the rest of us, or, more accurately, that she communicated such a charge of vitality as altered our imagination of life, which is of course the whole job and wonder of art. [7]

Since her death it has occurred to me that perhaps the reason we were able to keep these two aspects in which we knew Marilyn Monroe—her life affirmation and her impulse to death—in such discreet balance was that they never presented themselves to us as mutually exclusive but, on the contrary, as two intimately related, even expectable, facets of her extraordinary endowment. It is as if the world that loved Marilyn Monroe understood that her superabundant biology had necessarily to provoke its own restraint, that this is the cruel law by which nature, or at least nature within civilization, punishes those of us who ask too much of life or bring too much to life. We are told that when one of the senses is defective, nature frequently provides a compensation in another of the senses; the blind often hear better than the seeing, or have a sharper sense of touch. What we are not told but perhaps understand nonetheless is the working of nature's system of

[1] Pavlova was an early twentieth-century Russian ballerina of immense popularity, particularly well known for her performance of *The Dying Swan*.
[2] Nijinsky was a twentieth-century Russian ballet dancer and choreographer considered by many critics to be the greatest male dancer of the century.

negative compensation—the price we pay for gift, the revenge that life seems so regularly to take upon distinction. Certainly our awareness of the more, the plus, in Marilyn Monroe prepared us for some sort of minus. The fact that this young woman whose biological gift was so out of the ordinary was in mental pain seemed to balance the ledger. And one can speculate that had we not known of her emotional suffering, we would have been prepared for some other awful fate for her—an airplane disaster, maybe, or a deforming illness. So superstition may be thought of as an accurate reading of the harder rules of life. [8]

And yet it is difficult to suppose the gods could be all that jealous. Had Marilyn Monroe not been enough punished in childhood to ensure her against further misfortune? Once this poor forlorn girl had been so magically brought into her own, the most superstitious of us had the right to ask happiness for her ever after. It was impossible to think of Marilyn Monroe except as Cinderella. The strange power of her physical being seemed best explained and justified by the extreme circumstances of her early life—the illegitimate birth, the mad mother, the orphanage and near-mad foster homes, the rape by one of her early guardians. If there was no good fairy in Marilyn Monroe's life and no Prince Charming, unless Hollywood, this didn't rob her story of its fairy-book miraculousness; it merely assimilated to the old tale our newer legend of the self-made hero or heroine. Grace Kelly had had her good Philadelphia family to pave her path and validate her right to a crown. But Marilyn Monroe reigned only by virtue of her beauty and her determination to be raised out of the squalor and darkness, and to shine in the full, the fullest, light. It is scarcely a surprise that the brighter her radiance, the more we listened for the stroke of midnight that would put a limit on such transcendence. [9]

But it was not only the distance Marilyn Monroe had traveled from her unhappy beginnings that represented for us a challenge of reality, to be punished by reality. If her gift is to be regarded not as that of the stage or screen, which I think it primarily was not, but as the gift of biology, she was among those who are greatly touched with power; she was of the true company of artists. And her talent was so out of the range of the usual that we were bound to feel of it that it was not to be contained in society as we know it; therefore it proposed its own dissolution. Like any great artistic gift, Marilyn Monroe's power of biology was explosive, a primitive and savage force. It had, therefore and inevitably, to be a danger both to herself and to the world in which it did its work. All art is fierce in the measure that it matters, finally, and in its savagery it chooses either to push against society, against the restrictions that hedge it in, or against the artist himself. And no doubt it is the incapacity of most human beings to sustain this inordinate pressure that accounts for the fact that the artist is an exception in any civilized population. To mediate between the assault upon oneself and upon society, to keep alive in the battle and come out more or less intact, is a giant undertaking in which the native endowment of what we call talent is probably but a small element. [10]

Among the very few weapons available to the artist in this monstrous struggle, naïveté can be the most useful. But it is not at all my impression that Marilyn Monroe was a naïve person. I think she was innocent, which is very different. To be naïve is to be simple or stupid on the basis of experience, and Marilyn Monroe was far from stupid; no one who was stupid could have been so quick to turn her wit against herself, or to manage the ruefulness with which she habitually replied to awkward questioning. To be innocent is to suffer one's experience without being able to learn self-protection from it; as if willessly, innocence is at the mercy of experience, unable to mobilize counterforces to fortune. [11]

Of Ernest Hemingway, for example, I feel much as I do of Marilyn Monroe, that he was unable to marshal any adequate defense against the painful events of his childhood, and this despite his famous toughness and the courage he could call upon in war, in hunting, in all the dangerous enterprises that seduced him. He was an innocent man, not a naïve man, though not always intelligent. Marilyn Monroe offers us a similar paradox. Even while she symbolized an extreme of experience, of sexual knowingness, she took each new circumstance of life, as it came to her or as she sought it, like a newborn babe. And yet this was what made her luminous—her innocence. The glow was not rubbed off her by her experience of the ugliness of life because finally, in some vital depth, she had been untouched by it. [12]

From the psychiatrist's point of view, too much innocence, a radical disproportion between what has happened to a person and what he has absorbed from his experience, is a symptom, and alarming. It can indicate a rude break in his connection with himself, and if he is in treatment, it suggests a difficult cure, since, in emotional logic, he will probably be as impervious to the therapy as to the events through which he has passed, and yet without any mitigation of suffering. In the creative spheres, an excess of innocence unquestionably exercises an enormous fascination on us; it produces the purity of expression which leads us to say of an artistic creation or performance that it is "out of this world." But the psychiatric judgment has to pick its way on tiptoe between the gift and the pathology. What constitutes a person's art may eventually spell his emotional undoing. [13]

I can suppose of Marilyn Monroe that she was peculiarly elusive to the psychiatrists or analysts who tried to help her, that emotionally speaking she presented herself to them as a kind of blank page on which nothing had been written, failing to make the connection between herself and them even as she pleaded for it. And yet disconnection was at the heart of her gift, it defined her charm for the world, much as Hemingway's dissociation from his own experience was determinative of his gift. [14]

For several decades, scores of writers have tried to imitate Hemingway's style: the flexibility and purity of his prose, the bright, cogent distance he was able to put between himself and the object under examination. But none has succeeded. And I believe this is because his prose was, among many other things, a direct report of the unbridgeable distance between external reality and his emotions. Just so, Marilyn Monroe was inimitable. Hollywood, Broadway, the night clubs: they all regularly produce their quota of sex queens, but the public takes them and leaves them, or doesn't really take them; the world is not enslaved as it was by Marilyn Monroe because none but Marilyn Monroe could suggest such a purity of sexual delight. The boldness with which she could parade herself and yet never be gross, her sexual flamboyance and bravado which yet breathed an air of mystery and even reticence, her voice which carried such ripe overtones of erotic excitement and yet was the voice of a shy child—these complications were integral to her gift. And they described a young woman trapped in some never-never land of unawareness. [15]

What I imply here, of course, is a considerable factitiousness in Marilyn Monroe as a sexual figure. Certainly the two or three men I've known who met her in "real life" were agreed on her lack of direct sexual impact; she was sweet and beautiful and lovely, yes, but somehow not all the arousing woman they had expected. The nature of true sexuality is most difficult to define, so much of what we find sexually compelling has its source in phantasies that have little to do with the primary sexual instinct. Especially in the case of a movie star we enter a realm where dream and biology make their easiest merger. The art of acting is the art of *performing as if,* and the success of this feat of suggestion depends upon the degree to which it speaks to some phantasy of the onlookers. [16]

Marilyn Monroe spoke to our dreams as much as to our animal nature, but in a most unusual way. For what she appealed to was our determination to be rid of phantasy and to get down to the rock-bottom actuality. She gratified our wish to confront our erotic desires without romance, without diversion. And working within a civilization like ours, in which sexuality is so surrounded with restraints and fears and prohibitions, she perhaps came as close as possible to giving us the real thing. But she didn't give us the real thing; she merely acted as if she were giving it to us. She glamorized sexuality to the point at which it lost its terror for us; and maybe it was this veil that she raised to sexual reality that permitted women, no less than men, to respond to her so generously. Instinctively, I think, women understood that this seemingly most sexual of female creatures was no threat to them. [17]

The myth of Marilyn Monroe was thus even more of a myth than we realized, for this girl who was supposed to release us from our dreams into sexual actuality was in all probability not actual even to herself. Least of all could she have been sexually actual to herself and at the same time such a marvelous public performer of sex, such a conscious artist of sex. And we can conjecture that it was this deep alienation from her own feelings, including her sexual feeling, that enabled her to sustain the disorder of her early years even as long and as well as she did, and to speak of her awful childhood so simply and publicly. For most of us, the smallest "shame" in our past must be kept locked from others. We prefer that the least menacing of skeletons remain in the closet lest our current image of ourselves be violated by its emergence into the open. But Marilyn Monroe had no need for such reserves. She told the public the most gruesome facts of her personal history, for all the world as if we on the outside were worthy of such confidences—except that in some odd, generous response to her innocence, we exceeded ourselves in her instance and didn't take the advantage of her that we might have. Judged from the point of view of what we require of the artist, that he have the will and fearlessness to rise above the conventions which bind those of us with less gift,

Marilyn Monroe's candor about her early life was something to be celebrated. But from another point of view her frankness was a warning that the normal barriers of self-protection were down or non-existent, leaving her grievously exposed to the winds of circumstance. [18]

And indeed the very word "exposed" is a key word in the pattern of her life. She was an actress and she exposed her person and her personality to the public gaze. She was an exposed human being who told the truth about herself too readily, too publicly. And more than most actresses, she exposed her body, with but inadequate understanding of what this involved. We recall, for instance, the awkward little scandal about her having once posed naked for a calendar and the bewildered poise, the really untoward innocence and failure of comprehension, with which she met the dismay of her studio, as if to say, "But that was me yesterday when I needed money. That isn't me today; today I have money." Just as today and yesterday were discontinuous with each other, she was discontinuous with herself, held together, one feels, only and all too temporarily by her success. [19]

And this success was perhaps more intimately connected with her awareness of her physical appeal than we always understood. It may well have been the fact that she was so much and so admiringly in the public eye that gave Marilyn Monroe the largest part of her sense of a personal identity. Not long before her death, we now discover, she had herself photographed in the nude, carefully editing the many pictures as if to be certain she left the best possible record for posterity. The photographs leave, however, a record only of wasted beauty at least of the famous body—while Marilyn Monroe's face is lovely as ever, apparently unscarred by her intense suffering, her body looked ravaged and ill, already drained of life. Recently the pictures have been published in an expensive magazine devoted to erotica. If their high price, prohibitive to the general buyer, could be interpreted as a precaution against their being too easily available to a sensation-seeking audience, the restraint was not really necessary. At the last, the nude Marilyn Monroe could excite no decent viewer to anything but the gentlest pity, and much fear. [20]

But even before this ultimate moment the public success had been threatened. The great career was already failing. There had not been a Marilyn Monroe movie for a long time, and the last film she had worked on had had to be halted because she was unable to appear. And there was no private life to fall back upon, not even the formal structure of one: no marriage, no family, apparently not even friends. One had come, indeed, to think of her as the loneliest of people, so that it was not without bitterness that, on her death, one discovered that it was not only oneself who had wished to help her but many other strangers, especially women to whose protectiveness her extreme vulnerability spoke so directly. But we were the friends of whom she knew nothing, and among the people she knew it would seem that real relationships were out of reach across the desert emptiness that barricades whoever is out of touch with his feelings. One thinks of her that last evening of her life, alone and distraught, groping for human comfort and finding nothing but those endless bottles of medicine, and one confronts a pathos worse than tragedy. [21]

Certainly it strains justice as well as imagination that the world's most glamorous woman should have been alone, with no date, on a Saturday night—for it was, in fact, a Saturday night when she killed herself. On other nights but Saturday, we are allowed our own company. Saturday night is when all American boys and girls must prove themselves sexually. This is when we must be "out," out in the world where we can be seen among the sexually chosen. Yet the American girl who symbolized sexual success for all of us spent her last Saturday night alone in despair. Every man in the country would have wanted to date Marilyn Monroe, or so he would say, but no man who knew her did. [22]

Or, contemplating her loneliness, we think of her funeral, which, contrived to give her the peace and privacy that had so strenuously eluded her throughout her life, yet by its very restraint and limited attendance reminded us of the limitations of her actual connection with the world. Joe DiMaggio,[3] who had been her husband for a few brief months earlier in her career, was the chief mourner. It was DiMaggio to whom, she had told us, it was impossible to be married because he had no conversation; at meals, instead of talking to her, he read the papers or looked at television. The more recent husband, *with* conversation, was not present, no doubt for his own inviolable reasons, but it was saddening. I do not know what, if anything, was read at the service, but I'd like to think it was of an elevated and literary kind,

---

[3] Joe DiMaggio is a twentieth-century American baseball player and member of the Baseball Hall of Fame who played almost his entire career with the New York Yankees.

such as might be read at the funeral of a person of the first intellectual rank. [23]

For of the cruelties directed at this young woman even by the public that loved her, it seems to me that the most biting, and unworthy of the supposedly enlightened people who were particularly guilty of it, was the mockery of her wish to be educated, or thought educated. Granting our right to be a bit confused when our sex idol protests a taste for Dostoevsky,[4] surely the source of our discomfort must yet be located in our suspicions of Dostoevsky's worth for us and in our own sexual unease rather than in Marilyn Monroe. For what our mockery signifies is our disbelief that anyone who has enough sexuality needs to read Dostoevsky. The notion that someone with Marilyn Monroe's sexual advantages could have wanted anything except to make love robbed us of a prize illusion, that enough sexual possibility is enough everything. [24]

I doubt that sex was enough anything for Marilyn Monroe, except the means for advancing herself in the world. One of the touching revelations of her early life was her description of how she discovered that somehow she was sexually different from other girls her age: the boys all whistled at her and crowded to her like bears to honey, so she came to realize that she must have something special about her, which she could use to rise above her poor circumstances. Her sexual awareness, that is, came to her from outside herself. It would be my guess that it remained outside her always, leaving a great emptiness, where a true sexuality would have supplied her with a sense of herself as a person with connection and content. [25]

This void she tried to fill in every way available, with worldly goods, with fame and public attention and marriage, and also in ways that turned out to be unavailable, like children and domesticity— nothing could be more moving than the eagerness with which she seized upon a Jewish mother-in-law, even upon Jewish ceremonials and cooking, as if in the home life of her last husband's people she would find the secret of emotional plenitude. She also tried to fill her emptiness with books and learning. How mean-spirited can we be, to have denied her whatever might have added to her confidence that she was really a solid person and not just an uninhabited body? [26]

[4] Dostoevsky was a nineteenth-century Russian novelist recognized as one of the most influential writers of modern literature; with Tolstoy, he ranks as the master of the realistic novel.

And that she had the intellectual capacity for education there can be no question, had it but been matched with emotional capacity. No one without a sharp native intelligence could have spoofed herself as gracefully as she did or parried reporters with such finesse. If we are to judge by her interviews, she was as singularly lacking in the endemic off-stage dullness of actors and actresses, the trained courtesy and charm that is only another boring statement of their self-love, as she was deficient in the established defenses of her profession: one recalls no instance of even implied jealousy of her colleagues or of censure of others—directors, script-writers, husbands—for her own failures. Her generosity of spirit, indeed, was part of the shine that was on her. But unfortunately it spared everyone but herself; she had never studied self-justification. To herself she was not kind. She made fun of herself and of all that she had to go on in life: her biology. Certainly this added to her lovableness but it cut from under her the little ground that she could call her own. When she exhibited her sexual abundance with that wonderful, gay exaggeration of hers, or looked wide-eyed upon the havoc she wrought, it was her way of saying, "Don't be afraid. I don't take myself seriously so you don't have to take me seriously either." Her talent for comedy, in other words, was a public beneficence but a personal depredation, for, far more than most people, she precisely needed the assurance that she weighed in the scheme of human life, that she had substance and reality, that she had all the qualifications that make for a person we take seriously. Herself a supplicant, she gave us comfort. Herself a beggar, she distributed alms. [27]

At her death, several writers of good will who undertook to deal with the tragedy of her suicide blamed it on Hollywood. In the industry that had made millions from her and in the methods by which Hollywood had exploited her, they found the explanation of her failed life; they wrote about her as the sacrificial lamb on the altar of American vulgarity and greed. I share their disgust with Hollywood and I honor their need to isolate Marilyn Monroe from the nastiness that fed on her, but I find it impossible to believe that this girl would have been an iota better off were Hollywood to have been other than what we all know it to be, a madness in our culture. [28]

The self-destructiveness that Marilyn Monroe carried within her had not been put there by the "system," however overbearing in its ugliness. Just as her sweetness was her own, and immune to the influences of Hollywood, her terrors were also her own. They were not implanted in her, though undoubtedly they were increased, by the grandiosity of being a star. Neither for better nor worse, I feel, was she essentially falsified or distorted by her public role, though she must often have suffered cruelly from the inescapability of the public glare. In fact, it would be my conjecture that had she never gone into the movies and become rich and world-famous, her troubled spirit would long since have had its way with her. She would have been equally undone, and sooner, and with none of the many alleviations and compensations that she must have known in these years of success. [29]

This doesn't mean that I don't think she was a "victim." But she was not primarily a victim of Hollywood commercialism, or exploitation, or of the inhumanity of the press. She was not even primarily a victim of the narcissistic inflation that so regularly attends the grim business of being a great screen personality. Primarily she was a victim of her gift, a biological victim, a victim of life itself. It is one of the excesses of contemporary thought that we like to blame our very faulty culture for tragedies that are inherent in human existence—at least, inherent in human existence in civilization. I think Marilyn Monroe was a tragedy of civilization, but this is something quite else again from, and even more poignant than, being a specifically American tragedy. [30]

PURPOSE AND STRUCTURE

1. Trilling considers a large number of facts and opinions—her own and others—to arrive at a hypothesis. What is it? How does she marshal the evidence for her "speculation"?

2. What causal relationships are established in her efforts to account for the suicide? How does Trilling's verdict compare with that of the jury of experts?

3. How does the first sentence in par. 2 provide a transition from the first paragraph?

4. How do the comparisons and contrasts in par. 4 advance her speculation and affect tone? Specify. What characteristics are placed in opposition?

5. How does the opening sentence of par. 5 serve as a transition from the preceding paragraph, and as an introduction to what follows?

6. With what details have you been prepared for the generalization concluding par. 5: "In her loss life itself had been injured"?

7. Pars. 7–8 express alternative aspects of the author's speculation. How is each supported? Which is more convincing and why?

8. Trilling extends her analysis of Marilyn Monroe to the nature and function of art and artist. What are her views of the latter? How do they relate to her explanation of Monroe's suicide?

9. How does the author support her statement that "in the case of a movie star we enter a realm where dream and biology make their easiest merger" (par. 16)?

10. How did Marilyn Monroe's liking for Dostoevsky rob us of a prized illusion?

DICTION AND TONE

1. Examine the use of the words *incidental, accidental,* and *purposeful.* How is each used in context?

2. Explain the seeming paradox—"someone can want to stop living without wishing to die"—in relation to Marilyn Monroe. How is repetition used to support this assertion?

3. How does the phrase, "shield of irony," pertain to Trilling's attitude toward Marilyn Monroe?

4. To what is the phrase "redundancy of flesh" contrasted (par. 6)?

5. In what contexts are the phrases "life affirmation" and "impulse to death" used throughout the essay?

6. How is the phrase "negative compensation" used in context (par. 8)? How does it advance Trilling's thesis (par. 7)?

7. How do the details, the metaphors, the allusions, and especially the diction throughout the essay support Trilling's view that Marilyn Monroe's gift was primarily one not of stage or screen but of biology? Cite examples of verbs, adjectives and nouns that reinforce this concept.

8. How does Trilling draw upon her view of Marilyn Monroe to distinguish between "naive" and "innocent"? What does she regard as the paradox that is shared in Hemingway's and Monroe's lives?

9. Explain the use of the phrase "on tiptoe" in the psychiatric judgment regarding the gift and the pathology (par. 13).

10. What are the several contexts in which the key word *exposed* is used in relation to Marilyn Monroe's life?

11. How does the adjective *discontinuous* relate to the author's thesis (par. 19)?

12. When she talks of Hollywood, what is the author's tone?

13. Identify the tone of Trilling's analysis of Marilyn Monroe. Cite examples of diction that make evident her warm feelings toward Monroe.

14. In the final paragraph Trilling says she believes Marilyn Monroe was a "victim." In your own words explain how she *was* and *was not* a victim. Distinguish among the kinds of victims noted and between a "tragedy of civilization" and a "specifically American tragedy."

15. How does the author define sexuality? What distinctions does she make when she uses the words *sexual* and *erotic*?

APPLICATIONS TO WRITING

1. Throughout the essay Trilling presents a variety of facts and opinions—hers and those of others—concerning Marilyn Monroe. After weighing them reflectively she arrives at a hypothesis based largely upon causal relationships: Given these causes, these effects follow. Write about someone you know well—weigh the seemingly contradictory aspects of that person's character and attempt an analysis based upon a causal relationship.

2. Write an analysis of the way in which phantasies and dreams are or are not gratified by film or television. Be specific in your references and suggest what cause leads to what effects.

Words as Weapons

from *Black Boy*

RICHARD WRIGHT

One morning I arrived early at work and went into the bank lobby where the Negro porter was mopping. I stood at a counter and picked up the Memphis *Commercial Appeal* and began my free reading of the press. I came finally to the editorial page and saw an article dealing with one H. L. Mencken. I knew by hearsay that he was the editor of the *American Mercury,* but aside from that I knew nothing about him. The article was a furious denunciation of Mencken, concluding with one, hot, short sentence: Mencken is a fool. [1]

I wondered what on earth this Mencken had done to call down upon him the scorn of the South. The only people I had ever heard denounced in the South were Negroes, and this man was not a Negro. Then what ideas did Mencken hold that made a newspaper like the *Commercial Appeal* castigate him publicly? Undoubtedly he must be advocating ideas that the South did not like. Were there, then, people other than Negroes who criticized the South? I knew that during the Civil War the South had hated northern whites, but I had not encountered such hate during my life. Knowing no more of Mencken than I did at that moment, I felt a vague sympathy for him. Had not the South, which had assigned me the role of a non-man, cast at him its hardest words? [2]

Now, how could I find out about this Mencken? There was a huge library near the riverfront, but I knew that Negroes were not allowed to patronize its shelves any more than they were the parks and playgrounds of the city. I had gone into the library several times to get books for the white men on the job. Which of them would now help me to get books? And how could I read them without causing concern to the white men with whom I worked? I had so far been successful in hiding my thoughts and feelings from them, but I knew that I would create hostility if I went about this business of reading in a clumsy way. [3]

I weighed the personalities of the men on the job. There was Don, a Jew; but I distrusted him. His position was not much better than mine and I knew that he was uneasy and insecure; he had always treated me in an offhand, bantering way that barely concealed his contempt. I was afraid to ask him to help me to get books; his frantic desire to demonstrate a racial solidarity with the whites against Negroes might make him betray me. [4]

Then how about the boss? No, he was a Baptist and I had the suspicion that he would not be quite able to comprehend why a black boy would want to read Mencken. There were other white men on the job whose attitudes showed clearly that they were Kluxers or sympathizers, and they were out of the question. [5]

There remained only one man whose attitude did not fit into an anti-Negro category, for I had heard the white men refer to him as a "Pope lover." He was an Irish Catholic and was hated by the white Southerners. I knew that he read books, because I had got him volumes from the library several times. Since he, too, was an object of hatred, I felt that he might refuse me but would hardly betray me. I hesitated, weighing and balancing the imponderable realities. [6]

One morning I paused before the Catholic fellow's desk. [7]

"I want to ask you a favor," I whispered to him. [8]

"What is it?" [9]

"I want to read. I can't get books from the library. I wonder if you'd let me use your card?" [10]

He looked at me suspiciously. [11]

"My card is full most of the time," he said. [12]

"I see," I said and waited, posing my question silently. [13]

"You're not trying to get me into trouble, are you boy?" he asked, staring at me. [14]

"Oh, no sir." [15]

"What book do you want?" [16]

"A book by H. L. Mencken." [17]

"Which one?" [18]

"I don't know. Has he written more than one?" [19]

"He has written several." [20]

"I didn't know that." [21]

"What makes you want to read Mencken?" [22]

"Oh, I just saw his name in the newspaper," I said. [23]

"It's good of you to want to read," he said. "But you ought to read the right things." [24]

I said nothing. Would he want to supervise my reading? [25]

"Let me think," he said. "I'll figure out something." [26]

I turned from him and he called me back. He stared at me quizzically. [27]

"Richard, don't mention this to the other white men," he said. [28]

"I understand," I said. "I won't say a word." [29]

A few days later he called me to him. [30]

"I've got a card in my wife's name," he said. "Here's mine." [31]

"Thank you, sir." [32]

"Do you think you can manage it?" [33]

"I'll manage fine," I said. [34]

"If they suspect you, you'll get in trouble," he said. [35]

That afternoon I addressed myself to forging a note. Now, what were the names of books written by H. L. Mencken? I did not know any of them. I finally wrote what I thought would be a foolproof note: *Dear Madam: Will you please let this nigger boy*—I used the word "nigger" to make the librarian feel that I could not possibly be the author of the note—*have some books by H. L. Mencken?* I forged the white man's name. [36]

I entered the library as I had always done when on errands for whites, but I felt that I would somehow slip up and betray myself. I doffed my hat, stood a respectful distance from the desk, looked as unbookish as possible, and waited for the white patrons to be taken care of. When the desk was clear of people, I still waited. The white librarian looked at me. [37]

"What do you want, boy?" [38]

As though I did not possess the power of speech, I stepped forward and simply handed her the forged note, not parting my lips. [39]

"What books by Mencken does he want?" she asked. [40]

"I don't know, ma'am," I said, avoiding her eyes. [41]

"Who gave you this card?" [42]

"Mr. Falk," I said. [43]

"Where is he?" [44]

"He's at work, at the M———— Optical Company," I said. "I've been in here for him before." [45]

"I remember," the woman said. "But he never wrote notes like this." [46]

Oh, God, she's suspicious. Perhaps she would not let me have the books? If she had turned her back at that moment, I would have ducked out the door and never gone back. Then I thought of a bold idea. [47]

"You can call him up, ma'am," I said, my heart pounding. [48]

"You're not using these books, are you?" she asked pointedly. [49]

"Oh, no, ma'am. I can't read." [50]

"I don't know what he wants by Mencken," she said under her breath. [51]

I knew now that I had won; she was thinking of other things and the race question had gone out of her mind. She went to the shelves. Once or twice she looked over her shoulder at me, as though she was still doubtful. Finally she came forward with two books in her hand. [52]

"I'm sending him two books," she said. "But tell Mr. Falk to come in next time, or send me the names of the books he wants. I don't know what he wants to read." [53]

I said nothing. She stamped the card and handed me the books. Not daring to glance at them, I went out of the library, fearing that the woman would call me back for further questioning. A block away from the library I opened one of the books and read a title: *A Book of Prefaces*. I was nearing my nineteenth birthday and I did not know how to pronounce the word "preface." I thumbed the pages and saw strange words and strange names. I shook my head, disappointed. I looked at the other book; it was called *Prejudices*. I knew what that word meant; I had heard it all my life. And right off I was on guard against Mencken's books. Why would a man want to call a book *Prejudices*? The word was so stained with all my memories of racial hate that I could not conceive of anybody using it for a title. Perhaps I had made a mistake about Mencken? A man who had prejudices must be wrong. [54]

When I showed the books to Mr. Falk, he looked at me and frowned. [55]

"That librarian might telephone you," I warned him. [56]

"That's all right," he said. "But when you're through reading those books, I want you to tell me what you get out of them." [57]

That night in my rented room, while letting the hot water run over my can of pork and beans in the sink, I opened *A Book of Prefaces* and began to read. I was jarred and shocked by the style, the clear, clean, sweeping sentences. Why did he write like that? And how did one write like that? I pictured the man as a raging demon, slashing with his pen, consumed with hate, denouncing everything American, extolling everything European or German, laughing at the weaknesses of people, mocking God, authority. What was this? I stood up, trying to realize what reality lay behind the meaning of the words. . . . Yes, this man was fighting, fighting with words. He was using words as a weapon, using them as one would use a club. Could words be weapons? No. It frightened me. I read on and what amazed me was not what he said, but how on earth anybody had the courage to say it. [58]

Occasionally I glanced up to reassure myself that I was alone in the room. Who were these men about whom Mencken was talking so passionately? Who was Anatole France? Joseph Conrad? Sinclair Lewis, Sherwood Anderson, Dostoevski, George Moore, Gustave Flaubert, Maupassant, Tolstoy, Frank Harris, Mark Twain, Thomas Hardy, Arnold Bennett, Stephen Crane, Zola, Norris, Gorky, Bergson, Ibsen, Balzac, Bernard Shaw, Dumas, Poe, Thomas Mann, O. Henry, Dreiser, H. G. Wells, Gogol, T. S. Eliot, Gide, Baudelaire, Edgar Lee Masters, Stendhal, Turgenev, Huneker, Nietzsche, and scores of others? Were these men real? Did they exist or had they existed? And how did one pronounce their names? [59]

I ran across many words whose meanings I did not know, and I either looked them up in a dictionary or, before I had a chance to do that, encountered the word in a context that made its meaning clear. But what strange world was this? I concluded the book with the conviction that I had somehow overlooked something terribly important in life. I had once tried to write, had once reveled in feeling, had let my crude imagination roam, but the impulse to dream had been slowly beaten out of me by experience. Now it surged up again and I hungered for books, new ways of looking and seeing. It was not a matter of believing or disbelieving what I read, but of feeling something new, of being affected by something that made the book of the world different. [60]

As dawn broke I ate my pork and beans, feeling dopey, sleepy. I went to work, but the mood of the book would not die; it lingered, coloring everything I saw, heard, did. I now felt that I knew what the white men were feeling. Merely because I had read a book that had spoken of how they lived and thought, I identified myself with that book. I felt vaguely guilty. Would I, filled with bookish notions, act in a manner that would make the whites dislike me? [61]

I forged more notes and my trips to the library became frequent. Reading grew into a passion. My first serious novel was Sinclair Lewis's *Main Street*. It made me see my boss, Mr. Gerald, and identify him as an American type. I would smile when I saw him lugging his golf bags into the office. I had always felt a vast distance separating me from the boss, and now I felt closer to him, though still distant. I felt now that I knew him, that I could feel the very limits of his narrow life. And this had happened because I had read a novel about a mythical man called George F. Babbitt. [62]

The plots and stories in the novels did not interest me so much as the point of view revealed. I gave myself over to each novel without reserve, without trying to criticize it; it was enough for me to see and feel something different. And for me, everything was something different. Reading was like a drug, a dope. The novels created moods in which I lived for days. But I could not conquer my sense of guilt, my feeling that the white men around me knew that I was changing, that I had begun to regard them differently. [63]

Whenever I brought a book to the job, I wrapped it in newspaper— a habit that was to persist for years in other cities and under other circumstances. But some of the white men pried into my packages when I was absent and they questioned me. [64]

"Boy, what are you reading those books for?" [65]

"Oh, I don't know, sir." [66]

"That's deep stuff you're reading, boy." [67]

"I'm just killing time, sir." [68]

"You'll addle your brains if you don't watch out." [69]

I read Dreiser's *Jennie Gerhardt* and *Sister Carrie* and they revived in me a vivid sense of my mother's suffering; I was overwhelmed. I grew silent, wondering about the life around me. It would have been impossible for me to have told anyone what I derived from these novels, for it was nothing less than a sense of life itself. All my life had shaped me for the realism, the naturalism of the modern novel, and I could not read enough of them. [70]

Steeped in new moods and ideas, I bought a ream of paper and tried to write; but nothing would come, or what did come was flat beyond telling. I discovered that more than desire and feeling were necessary to write and I dropped the idea. Yet I still wondered how it was possible to know people sufficiently to write about them? Could I ever learn about life and people? To me, with my vast ignorance, my Jim Crow station in life, it seemed a task impossible of achievement. I now knew what being a Negro meant. I could endure the hunger. I had learned to live with hate. But to feel that there were feelings denied me, that the very breath of life itself was beyond my reach, that more than anything else hurt, wounded me. I had a new hunger. [71]

In buoying me up, reading also cast me down, made me see what was possible, what I had missed. My tension returned, new, terrible, bitter, surging, almost too great to be contained. I no longer *felt* that the world about me was hostile, killing; I *knew* it. A million times I asked myself what I could do to save myself, and there were no answers. I seemed forever condemned, ringed by walls. [72]

I did not discuss my reading with Mr. Falk, who had lent me his library card; it would have meant talking about myself and that would have been too painful. I smiled each day, fighting desperately to maintain my old behavior, to keep my disposition seemingly sunny. But some of the white men discerned that I had begun to brood. [73]

"Wake up there, boy!" Mr. Olin said one day. [74]

"Sir!" I answered for the lack of a better word. [75]

"You act like you've stolen something," he said. [76]

I laughed in the way I knew he expected me to laugh, but I resolved to be more conscious of myself, to watch my every act, to guard and hide the new knowledge that was dawning within me. [77]

If I went north, would it be possible for me to build a new life then? But how could a man build a life upon vague, unformed yearnings? I wanted to write and I did not even know the English language. I bought English grammars and found them dull. I felt that I was getting a better sense of the language from novels than from grammars. I read hard, discarding a writer as soon as I felt that I had grasped his point of view. At night the printed page stood before my eyes in sleep. [78]

Mrs. Moss, my landlady, asked me one Sunday morning:

"Son, what is this you keep on reading?" [79]

"Oh, nothing. Just novels." [80]

"What you get out of 'em?" [81]

"I'm just killing time," I said. [82]

"I hope you know your own mind," she said in a tone which implied that she doubted if I had a mind. [83]

I knew of no Negroes who read the books I liked and wondered if Negroes ever thought of them. I knew that there were Negro doctors, lawyers, newspapermen, but I never saw any of them. When I read a Negro newspaper I never caught the faintest echo of my preoccupation in its pages. I felt trapped and occasionally, for a few days, I would stop reading. But a vague hunger would come over me for books, books that opened up new avenues of feeling and seeing, and again I would forge another note to the white librarian. Again I would read and wonder as only the naïve and unlettered can read and wonder, feeling that I carried a secret, criminal burden about with me each day. [84]

That winter my mother and brother came and we set up house-keeping, buying furniture on the installment plan, being cheated and yet knowing no way to avoid it. I began to eat warm food and to my surprise found that regular meals enabled me to read faster. I may have lived through many illnesses and survived them, never suspecting that I was ill. My brother obtained a job and we began to save toward the trip north, plotting our time, setting tentative dates for departure. I told none of the white men on the job that I did not like the life I was living, and because my life was completely conditioned by what they said or did, it would have been tantamount to challenging them. [85]

I could calculate my chances for life in the South as a Negro fairly clearly now. [86]

I could fight the southern whites by organizing with other Negroes, as my grandfather had done. But I knew that I could never win that way; there were many whites and there were but few blacks. They were strong and we were weak. Outright black rebellion could never win. If I fought openly I would die and I did not want to die. News of lynchings were frequent. [87]

I could submit and live the life of a genial slave, but that was impossible. All of my life had shaped me to live by my own feelings and thoughts. I could make up to Bess and marry her and inherit the house. But that, too, would be the life of a slave; if I did that, I would crush to death something within me, and I would hate myself as much as I knew the whites already hated those who had submitted. Neither could I ever willingly present myself to be kicked, as Shorty had done. I would rather have died than do that. [88]

I could drain off my restlessness by fighting with Shorty and Harrison. I had seen many Negroes solve the problem of being black by transferring their hatred of themselves to others with a black skin and fighting them. I would have to be cold to do that, and I was not cold and I could never be. [89]

I could, of course, forget what I had read, thrust the whites out of my mind, forget them; and find release from anxiety and longing in sex and alcohol. But the memory of how my father had conducted himself made that course repugnant. If I did not want others to violate my life, how could I voluntarily violate it myself? [90]

I had no hope whatever of being a professional man. Not only had I been so conditioned that I did not desire it, but the fulfillment of such an ambition was beyond my capabilities. Well-to-do Negroes lived in a world that was almost as alien to me as the world inhabited by whites. [91]

What, then, was there? I held my life in my mind, in my consciousness each day, feeling at times that I would stumble and drop it, spill it forever. My reading had created a vast sense of distance between me and the world in which I lived and tried to make a living, and that sense of distance was increasing each day. My days and nights were one long, quiet, continuously contained dream of terror, tension, and anxiety. I wondered how long I could bear it. [92]

The accidental visit of Aunt Maggie to Memphis formed a practical basis for my planning to go north. Aunt Maggie's husband, the "uncle" who had fled from Arkansas in the dead of night, had deserted her; and now she was casting about for a living. My mother, Aunt Maggie, my brother, and I held long conferences, speculating on the prospects of jobs and the costs of apartments in Chicago. And every time we conferred, we defeated ourselves. It was impossible for all four of us to go at once; we did not have enough money. [93]

Finally sheer wish and hope prevailed over common sense and facts. We discovered that if we waited until we were prepared to go, we would never leave, we would never amass enough money to see us through. We would have to gamble. We finally decided that Aunt Maggie and I would go first, even though it was winter, and prepare a place for my mother and brother. Why wait until next week or next month? If we were going, why not go at once? [94]

Next loomed the problem of leaving my job cleanly, smoothly, without arguments or scenes. How could I present the fact of leaving to my boss? Yes, I would pose as an innocent boy; I would tell him that my aunt was taking me and my paralyzed mother to Chicago. That would create in his mind the impression that I was not asserting my will; it would block any expression of dislike on his part for my act. I knew that southern whites hated the idea of Negroes leaving to live in places where the racial atmosphere was different. [95]

It worked as I had planned. When I broke the news of my leaving two days before I left—I was afraid to tell it sooner for fear that I would create hostility on the part of the whites with whom I worked—the boss leaned back in his swivel chair and gave me the longest and most considerate look he had ever given me. [96]

"Chicago?" he repeated softly. [97]

"Yes, sir." [98]

"Boy, you won't like it up there," he said. [99]

"Well, I have to go where my family is, sir," I said. [100]

The other white office workers paused in their tasks and listened. I grew self-conscious, tense. [101]

"It's cold up there," he said. [102]

"Yes, sir. They say it is," I said, keeping my voice in a neutral tone. [103]

He became conscious that I was watching him and he looked away, laughing uneasily to cover his concern and dislike. [104]

"Now, boy," he said banteringly, "don't you go up there and fall into that lake." [105]

"Oh, no sir," I said, smiling as though there existed the possibility of my falling accidentally into Lake Michigan. [106]

He was serious again, staring at me. I looked at the floor. [107]

"You think you'll do any better up there?" he asked. [108]

"I don't know, sir." [109]

"You seem to've been getting along all right down here," he said. [110]

"Oh, yes, sir. If it wasn't for my mother's going, I'd stay right here and work," I lied as earnestly as possible. [111]

"Well, why not stay? You can send her money," he suggested. [112]

He had trapped me. I knew that staying now would never do. I could not have controlled my relations with the whites if I had remained after having told them that I wanted to go north. [113]

"Well, I want to be with my mother," I said. [114]

"You want to be with your mother," he repeated idly. "Well, Richard, we enjoyed having you with us." [115]

"And I enjoyed working here," I lied. [116]

There was silence; I stood awkwardly, then moved to the door. There was still silence; white faces were looking strangely at me. I went upstairs, feeling like a criminal. The word soon spread through the factory and the white men looked at me with new eyes. They came to me. [117]

"So you're going north, hunh?" [118]

"Yes, sir. My family's taking me with 'em." [119]

"The North's no good for your people, boy." [120]

"I'll try to get along, sir." [121]

"Don't believe all the stories you hear about the North." [122]

"No, sir. I don't." [123]

"You'll come back here where your friends are." [124]

"Well, sir. I don't know." [125]

"How're you going to act up there?" [126]

"Just like I act down here, sir." [127]

"Would you speak to a white girl up there?" [128]

"Oh, no, sir. I'll act there just like I act here." [129]

"Aw, no, you won't. You'll change. Niggers change when they go north." [130]

I wanted to tell him that I was going north precisely to change, but I did not. [131]

"I'll be the same," I said, trying to indicate that I had no imagination whatever. [132]

As I talked I felt that I was acting out a dream. I did not want to lie, yet I had to lie to conceal what I felt. A white censor was standing over me and, like dreams forming a curtain for the safety of sleep, so did my lies form a screen of safety for my living moments. [133]

"Boy, I bet you've been reading too many of them damn books." [134]

"Oh, no, sir." [135]

I made my last errand to the post office, put my bag away, washed my hands, and pulled on my cap. I shot a quick glance about the factory; most of the men were working late. One or two looked up. Mr. Falk, to whom I had returned my library card, gave me a quick, secret smile. I walked to the elevator and rode down with Shorty. [136]

"You lucky bastard," he said bitterly. [137]

"Why do you say that?" [138]

"You saved your goddamn money and now you're gone." [139]

"My problems are just starting," I said. [140]

"You'll never have any problems as hard as the ones you had here," he said. [141]

"I hope not," I said. "But life is tricky." [142]

"Sometimes I get so goddamn mad I want to kill everybody," he spat in a rage. [143]

"You can leave," I said. [144]

"I'll never leave this goddamn South," he railed. "I'm always saying I am, but I won't . . . I'm lazy. I like to sleep too goddamn much. I'll die here. Or maybe they'll kill me." [145]

I stepped from the elevator into the street, half expecting someone to call me back and tell me that it was all a dream, that I was not leaving. [146]

This was the culture from which I sprang. This was the terror from which I fled. [147]

PURPOSE AND STRUCTURE

1. This excerpt from Richard Wright's autobiography narrates in a deceptively simple fashion a number of his experiences in the South that culminated in his decision to move to the North. What characteristics of style, substance, and organization create a sense of simplicity?

2. Although deceptively simple, *Black Boy* treats a very complex subject that is logically divisible into a number of interrelated themes. What are they? How are they interwoven into a unified whole?

3. A narrative such as Wright's does not proceed with the logical ordering of ideas that characterizes formal analysis in an essay; however, there is a logical progression in the movement of *Black Boy* in the form of cause and effect relationships that are dramatized for the reader. What are they?

4. How does the series of rhetorical questions contribute to purpose and tone (pars. 2–3)? Do they all serve the same purpose? Examine the question: "Were there, then, people other than Negroes who criticized the South?" Is the author being disingenuous, or has a new idea just occurred to him?

5. With what concrete details are you prepared for the narrator's choice of a fellow conspirator in the withdrawal of books (pars. 4–6)?

6. What does the dialogue tell you about his collaborator's character (pars. 8–35)?

7. With what details are you made aware of Wright's role playing and the desperate need for it?

8. What sometimes conflicting concerns and feelings followed Wright's steeping himself in Mencken and his subsequent reading? How does he account for the fact that "in buoying me up, reading also cast me down" (pars. 58–72)?

9. With what details does Wright communicate the effects of the identifications he makes in his reading? Refer especially to his response to Mencken, Lewis, and Dreiser. Compare your response to Mencken with that of Wright.

10. How are you prepared for the statement that "I no longer *felt* that the world about me was hostile, killing; I *knew* it"? To what cause does he assign this bitterness (pars. 60–72)?

11. What are the causal relationships that Wright analyzes in his consideration of remaining in the South (pars. 86–92)?

12. Why did Wright want to create in his boss's mind the impression that he was not asserting his will (par. 95)? With what replies to the boss's questions does he act out this role (pars. 98–116)?

13. How does the author use dialogue to advance the narrative? What other purposes does it serve?

DICTION AND TONE

1. How do the following words or phrases in context convey the author's purpose and tone: "stained" (par. 54); "raging demon . . . slashing . . . consumed" (par. 58); "felt trapped" (par. 84); "vague hunger" (par. 84); "secret, criminal burden" (par. 84); "genial slave" (par. 88); "crush to death something within me" (par. 88); "feeling like a criminal" (par. 117); "a white censor" (par. 133)?

2. Account for the images in the sentence: "I held my life in my mind . . . spill it forever" (par. 92).

3. Discuss the ironic effect of the juxtaposition of the last two sentences.

APPLICATIONS TO WRITING

1. Using the approach to analysis in "Words as Weapons" narrate a series of experiences that have had an influence upon your thinking and your activities. Clarify the connection between these events by reminding yourself of the causal relationship: given this situation or experience in which your sense of self has been sharpened, this or that event or change logically followed.

2. In a formal or informal essay, analyze the impact that a book, a film, a play, a sermon, a lecture, a class discussion had upon your thinking and/or behavior. What new ways of looking and seeing did it provide?

3. On the basis of your experience discuss Wright's belief that he was getting a better sense of the language from novels than from grammars.

4. Have you observed any hostility among your contemporaries or others vented against those who read for pleasure? If so, write a causal analysis of the contempt often expressed toward the omniverous reader (whether black or white) in your attempt to account for it.

5. Write an analysis in which you develop or challenge Wright's statement in relation to your own reading experiences: "The plots and stories in the novels did not interest me as much as the point of view revealed" (par. 63), or "Reading was like a drug, a dope" (par. 63).

6. Place yourself in a situation in which role playing has been or might be necessary. Dramatize the difference between your real feelings and those you express by means of alternating dialogue and introspection.

7. Analyze the reasons for an identification you have made with a character in a book.

A Life Worth Living

from *The Autobiography of Bertrand Russell*

BERTRAND RUSSELL

Three passions, simple but overwhelmingly strong, have governed my life: the longing for love, the search for knowledge, and unbearable pity for the suffering of mankind. These passions, like great winds, have blown me hither and thither, in a wayward course, over a deep ocean of anguish, reaching to the very verge of despair. [1]

I have sought love, first, because it brings ecstasy—ecstasy so great that I would often have sacrificed all the rest of life for a few hours of this joy. I have sought it, next, because it relieves loneliness—that terrible loneliness in which one shivering consciousness looks over the rim of the world into the cold unfathomable lifeless abyss. I have sought it, finally, because in the union of love I have seen, in a mystic miniature, the prefiguring vision of the heaven that saints and poets have imagined. This is what I sought, and though it might seem too good for human life, this is what—at last—I have found. [2]

With equal passion I have sought knowledge. I have wished to understand the hearts of men. I have wished to know why the stars shine. And I have tried to apprehend the Pythagorean power by which number holds sway above the flux.[1] A little of this, but not much, I have achieved. [3]

Love and knowledge, so far as they were possible, led upward toward the heavens. But always pity brought me back to earth. Echoes of cries of pain reverberate in my heart. Children in famine, victims tortured by oppressors, helpless old people a hated burden to their sons, and the whole world of loneliness, poverty, and pain make a mockery of what human life should be. I long to alleviate the evil, but I cannot, and I too suffer. [4]

[1] Pythagoras was a fifth-century B.C. Greek philosopher and mathematician and founder of the Pythagorean school, which taught that numbers constitute the true nature of things; the school heavily influenced geometry, astronomy, and medicine.

This has been my life. I have found it worth living, and would gladly live it again if the chance were offered me. [5]

PURPOSE AND STRUCTURE

1. "A Life Worth Living" is an example of the five-paragraph essay. From your examination of this article, describe the main features of the five-paragraph essay.

2. Which of pars. 2, 3, or 4 contains the most details? Which the least? Which is easier to understand?

3. Which sentences in par. 2 are parallel? Which elements of those sentences are parallel?

4. Are there any elements in par. 3 which are parallel? If so, what are they? How do they differ from the parallel elements in par. 2?

5. In par. 2, if we omit words like *first, next,* and *finally* does the order or sequence make much difference? Is par. 2 therefore a coordinate sequence or a subordinate sequence paragraph?

6. The last sentence of par. 4 is as follows: "I long to alleviate the evil, but I cannot, and I too suffer." The sentence, "Because I failed to alleviate the evil, I too suffer," is just as acceptable grammatically. Show why, in the context of this essay, the original is the preferable sentence.

DICTION AND TONE

1. What effect does the parallelism of pars. 2 and 3 have on such a short essay? Does it make the selection repetitious or monotonous? Or lyrical and poetical? Defend your answer.

2. In par. 3 Russell writes, "I wished to understand the hearts of men." Did he make a mistake here? Did he intend the "minds" instead of the "hearts" of men? What is the difference?

3. Also in par. 3 he writes, "I have wished to know why the stars shine." But we know why the stars shine; they shine because they burn gases, the same as our sun. Obviously Russell intended more than the literal meaning of this question. What does he intend to ask?

4. Also in par. 3 he writes, "And I have tried to apprehend the Pythagorean power by which number holds sway above the flux." Argue for the

need of a statement at some lower level of generality—an illustration, perhaps—to make this sentence more immediately comprehensible. Why do
you think Russell didn't provide the illustration?

APPLICATIONS TO WRITING

Write a five paragraph essay, taking special care in the first paragraph to
announce the three main points that you will develop in the body of your
essay. Like Russell, you may want to write about your own feelings or
beliefs, or—if you know them—the feelings or beliefs of your family.

seven

Argument and Persuasion

Argument and persuasion are reciprocally related. Formal argument often consists of the following parts: the *proposition,* an assertion that leads to the *issue;* the *issue,* the aspect of the proposition that the writer is attempting to prove and the question on which the whole argument rests; the *evidence,* the facts and opinions that the author offers as testimony. He may order the evidence deductively by proceeding from certain premises to a *conclusion* or inductively by generalizing from a number of instances and drawing a *conclusion.* Informal arguments frequently make greater use of the methods of exposition than they do of formal logic. Argument is a mode of discourse; *the* argument, a line of reasoning. (See Deduction, Induction, Logic, and Analogy in the Glossary.)

The purpose of argument is to persuade. The attempt to distinguish between argument and persuasion is sometimes made by reference to means (argument makes appeals to reason; persuasion, to emotions); sometimes to ends (argument causes someone to change his mind; persuasion moves him to action). These distinctions, however, are more academic than functional, for in practice argument and persuasion are not discrete entities. Yet the proof in argument rests largely upon the objectivity of evidence; the proof in persuasion, upon a subtle and controlled use of language. The diction employed, as well as such literary devices as irony, satire, paradox, metaphor, and allusion, will establish the tone, which in turn may affect the reader's judgment of the objectivity of the evidence and the degree to which he is persuaded by it. Hoppe argues that today's university (Skarewe U) is a diploma mill. If we go back to the Good Old Medieval Campus (no credits, no grades, no requirements, no diplomas) we will end with well-educated students. Kauffman argues that film is too easy a medium. The filmgoer sits in the dark in a near fetal position and falls into a "brothel lethargy." In "The Artist as Housewife" the formal components of Jong's argument are less arresting than the amusing digressions, the myriad, wry rhetorical questions, and the acerbic cumulative detail, all of which reflect the intensity of her effort to persuade. Mark Twain attacks the literary art of James Fenimore Cooper by presenting arguments that are so palpably exaggerated and so unfair that they are amusing—and, because they are so funny, they are persuasive. In the excerpt from *Man and Superman* the Devil supports his argument that man is "the most destructive of all destroyers" by alluding to a succession of his bestial acts. Although the argument in "Joan Baez: Where the Kissing Never Stops" can be divided into proposition, issue, evidence, and conclusion, Didion's power to persuade is largely dependent upon the tone of her discourse, which both disarms and delights the reader in its reliance upon irony, paradox, and subtle humor. Claiborne makes one argument for the Wasps: for three hundred years no Wasp nation has endured an absolute monarchy or dictatorship. The persuasive power of "A Modest Proposal" lies in its sustained irony: Swift simulates an amorality that is cumulatively revealed in an exaggerated rationality and a view of man that reduces him to an object to be used. Mailer's argument moves from the question of who finally would do the dishes to the ultimate responsibility of women to choose the fathers of their children. Leonard argues that "the natural condition of the human organism is joy" and that significant learning can take place only when accompanied by delight. Kopkind draws upon a variety of sources—from pop culture to psychology—to support his view that the acceptance of androgyny is crucial for the successful functioning of the next stages of social evolution. In his effort to persuade the reader of the limitations of conventional answers, Calandra employs a parable in which the student engages in an academic lark.

The Good Old Medieval Campus

A R T H U R   H O P P E

Once upon a time in the country called Wonderfuland there was a 500-year-old institution named Skarewe University. It issued Diplomas. [1]

Just about everybody went to Skarewe University. They spent exactly four years studying exactly 16 required courses in thisology and thatology. They did this to get a Diploma. [2]

Diplomas were very valuable. If you showed one to a prospective employer he gave you more money. No one knew why. [3]

But the country fell on uneasy times. Even the students at Skarewe University caused trouble. They demanded this and they demanded that. And they got everything they demanded. Until, finally, they couldn't think of anything else to demand. [4]

"I know," said one student one day, "let's demand that they abolish Diplomas!" [5]

And, not having anything else to do, the students went on a Diploma Strike. [6]

The President of Skarewe University was stunned. "If we don't issue Diplomas," he said, "we will lose our standing in the academic community." [7]

The business community was shocked. "Without diplomas," employers said, "how can we tell a college graduate from an uneducated man?" [8]

Editorial writers viewed with alarm. "These radicals would destroy the very purpose of dear old Skarewe U.," they wrote. "They should be forced to accept their Diplomas whether they like it or not." [9]

The trustees were furious. "Abolishing Diplomas will set our university back 500 years," they thundered. "It will become a medieval institution!" [10]

And it did. [11]

From the very day that Diplomas were abolished, 64.3 percent of the students quit to go engage in more financially-rewarding pursuits. And those who were left found parking spaces for their cars—for the first time since the Middle Ages. [12]

Just as in the Middle Ages, students now attended Skarewe University solely to gain knowledge and wisdom. [13]

And as there were no required courses, teachers who imparted knowledge and wisdom gave well-attended lectures. And those who didn't, didn't. Just as in medieval times. [14]

Just as in medieval times, students pursued only the studies that interested them and read only the books that stimulated them. And all, being constantly interested and stimulated, were dedicated scholars. [15]

Thus it was that Skarewe University became what it had been 500 years before—a vast smorgasbord of knowledge and wisdom from which the student could select that which delighted and enriched him. [16]

So everybody was happy. The President was happy to head such a distinguished community of scholars. The trustees were happy there were no more riots. And the taxpayers were happy they no longer had to purchase educations for those who didn't want them. [17]

Even prospective employers were happy. For, oddly enough, even without a Diploma, you could still pick out the applicant who had gone through college—because for the first time in 500 years, he was a well-educated man. [18]

PURPOSE AND STRUCTURE

1. The structure of Hoppe's persuasive satire is clear if the reader examines the paragraphs that contain a reference to 500 years: pars. 1, 10, 16, and 18. How do these paragraphs function in Hoppe's argument?

2. Hoppe's newspaper piece is an amusing parable rather than a serious argument. But if examined carefully, the argument is discovered to be carefully structured: the *proposition* is stated in par. 10, the *issue* in par. 16. In which paragraphs is the *evidence* presented?

3. How does par. 3 prepare the reader for the proposition?

DICTION AND TONE

1. " 'Skarewe U.' " (par. 9) is a curious name for a university. How is it pronounced?

2. "Required courses in thisology and thatology" (par. 2) sound rather boring. Why? They are required for a "Diploma." What does this tell you about the value of a "Diploma"?

3. Is par. 8 making the point that the college graduates are uneducated men?

APPLICATIONS TO WRITING

1. Do you go to Skarewe U? Accept Hoppe's argument (for your own insidious, subversive purposes) and describe the *real* "Good Old Medieval Campus." (Make up your own examples of the most popular courses or use these: Ed. 68, Breathing in Deep Sleep; Ornithology 72, Bird Walking with Beach Birds; Psychology 70, Sex Contacts with UFO's; P.E. 899 [Graduate Course] Levitation; English 71, Literature for the Non-Reader.)

2. Turn Hoppe's argument around: argue that today's university is failing precisely because it offers a vast smorgasbord of intellectual hors d'oeuvres instead of an integrated education.

3. Satirize another institution as Hoppe does: present-day banks, the Army, the modern American family, automobiles.

Film Negatives: What Can You Do About an Art That Is Simply Too Easy?

STANLEY KAUFFMANN

I'm tired—and hope you are, too—of that recurrent article in which the writer, usually a professional literary person, takes a look at the film scene and finds it wanting. He says in effect that he has been hearing a great deal about film as the New Art, so he has finally consented to go to five or ten current successful films and has found them pretentious or distorted or cheap. Imagine the sort of article that would result if a nonliterary person, after hearing a lot about the art of the novel, then did nothing more than read any ten current best sellers. [1]

But I do want to play devil's advocate against film for a bit: partly because I dislike the sort of article described above, which finds what it sets out to find; partly because I'm one of those who have hailed the power and importance of film. I'm still hailing, but I have some worries. [2]

Certainly no one needs to prove the high degree of interest in film. Although the audience is smaller than it was twenty-five or thirty years ago, there are plentiful reasons to believe that qualitatively it is stratospheres beyond the pre–World War II audience that went to film theaters once or twice a week like automobiles to filling stations. Today's audience has much more knowledge about its enthusiasm. [3]

Just because of this distilled and intensified film furor, proved further by the flood of film books in recent years, I thought this might be a good time for one film enthusiast to take a cool look at that furor—*because* of his enthusiasm. Here are notes on some aspects of film that have been bothering me for a while. [4]

FILMGOING IS TOO EASY

I'm not talking about admission prices or the widespread availability of film. I mean the frame of mind. [5]

I mean that it is easier to see a film than to read a book—easier even than to listen to some music. I don't suggest that, if something is easy, it is automatically bad, but this particular ease is frequently taken as proof in itself that film is more apposite to our times than other arts, is richer and more rewarding. There are reasons why film *is* especially apposite for us, but this ease isn't one of them. In one of his novels Edward Hyams writes that the real objection to brothels is that they make us emotionally lazy. There is something of a whorehouse feeling about this film ease, a whiff of lazy gratification in the darkness. [6]

I'm not inveighing against pleasure in filmgoing—not after all the pleasures I've had from it in five decades—nor against the enjoyment of all kinds of films, even some bad ones. I'm concerned about the assumption that there is an absolute equivalence between plunking one's behind into a film-theater seat and a serious cultural act, that the first always and invariably equals the second; more, that the act of attending a film subsumes all other possible cultural and intellectual acts; even more, that it certifies one's contemporaneity. [7]

Only cultural blockheads try to turn clocks backward, and if (as is said) college students now see twenty films for every book they read, then that preference is the product of current pressures and hungers and must be recognized as a cultural condition. Progress can be made *from* that condition, not against it. But culture is a word with both a sociological and an esthetic meaning. The "twenty-to-one" fact, if it is a fact, can be recognized sociologically without being exalted esthetically. Seeing a Humphrey Bogart series at a film society is an experience that no one should either miss or condescend to, but it's esthetic sloth to believe that seeing the Bogart series is a priestly act on the slopes of Parnassus simply because one has done it in the Film Age. [8]

From the same seat we see both junk films and good films, but in a way good films reprove us for indiscriminate rump-plumping. Good films ask us to do something in that seat, make demands on us, help dispel that brothel lethargy (without destroying pleasure). Good films, from *Swing Time* with Fred Astaire to Kurosawa's *Ikiru,* show us that there is more to film culture than film slavishness, that we are cultural trespassers if we have no values, and that values are formed (a) within the art and (b) by comparison with other arts. As for the first, it is Fred Astaire who teaches us that the most we can get from Busby Berkeley are the slumming pleasures of camp—which means a very easily earned sense of superiority. As for the second: if you don't know Mozart, you don't know Renoir's *Rules of the Game.* If you don't know Strindberg, you don't know Bergman. If you don't know Frederic Remington, you don't know John Ford. [9]

Film slavishness today is a worse narcotic that the shopgirl-shoeclerk escapism of Joan Crawford's heyday because now it has a pietistic rationale. Today the person who submerges himself in B movies of the 1930s tells us that he isn't like the first audiences for those pictures, he is investigating American culture. This would be equally true if he burrowed through Faith Baldwin novels of the period. Not that such things as Baldwin research are unheard of, but they are much less appealing because they—even they—are more difficult than just watching films and lack the inherent power of the lowest film. Film has a wide range of magics, and one of them is that it *can* transmute junk—to a degree—into something better than it could be in any other art. But that alchemy is limited. Not to see where it ends and how it can be abused is film blindness. Orson Welles elevated Booth Tarkington's *The Magnificent Ambersons* into a film that is artistic stratospheres above the original novel, but all his huffing and puffing on *Touch of Evil* only emphasized the vacuous melodrama of Whit Masterson's book. [10]

I suggest that any person, particularly a young person, who thinks that a slump in a film-theater seat with his feet up will bring his mind all it needs for growth and his spirit all it needs for challenge is more interested in the position itself—a near fetal one—than in what he is getting through it. [11]

How to share all the miracles and possibilities of film without making a joke of the medium or a fool of yourself—that is becoming a cultural question of some importance. [12]

FILMMAKING IS TOO EASY

By which, obviously, I don't mean the raising of capital or the production of a good film. I mean that the basic act of motion-picture photography is relatively easy—and is deluding. [13]

It's easier to take a good photograph of a tree than to make a good drawing of a tree or write a good sentence about one. It's easier to assemble a film, particularly a short one, that has some superficial resemblance to art than it is to paint a picture or write a story that produces equivalent effects. Color photography has now made the matter worse; any fool can now ladle lush beauty over anything. (See such vacuous professional productions as *Greaser's Palace* and *Images.*) [14]

All this makes an esthetic problem that is disturbing intelligent film teachers in colleges, even in high schools. The easiness described above leads to quick self-satisfaction, and a teacher sometimes finds it hard to convince a student that there is more to a film than making it look good, that all of the physical world is aching to "act," that physicality is actually quite hammy, that the film camera provides easy outlets for that hamminess, and that the person who merely presses a camera button can take relatively little credit. [15]

Films have to *begin further on,* esthetically, than other arts because they take the first steps so easily. This is certainly not to say that, after those first steps, the film travels further than other arts; it rarely travels as far. But film starts with enormous representational power, enormous symbolic power, just by virtue of its innate properties. All film stuns us, at least for a second or two, just by being flashed in front of us; and the fact that any film student or mere film wallower can use that stunning effect to some degree proves little about him. For four years I looked at about 150 student films a year, from all over the country. I saw much that was technically competent and much more that was briefly eye-catching, but I saw few films that moved past competence, past initial effects. Most of them seemed content just to *be* films! Filmmaking is susceptible of being the greatest con game in the history of the arts, uniquely dangerous in that it often deceives the maker more than the audience. [16]

A grossly simple analogy: The crossbar in pole vaulting is much higher than in high jumping. This doesn't mean that the pole vaulter is the better athlete, only that he has an initial advantage. The critical question for film is: What does the filmmaker do after his initial advantage? [17]

THE ODDS ARE HEAVY TODAY AGAINST A NEW ART

By the beginning of the twentieth century, when film started, was it too late in the history of Western culture to begin a new art? To anticipate, my answer is no; but the question is central and well worth examining. [18]

The older arts all entered this century with huge bodies of work behind them, including supreme masterpieces. Cultural changes in six decades have smitten them hard, have made many artists believe that the dominant modes in their arts are finished: the mimetic novel, the designed painting, the literary drama, music made by traditional instruments, and so on. Buttressed by their ancient histories, these arts have nonetheless been shaken. [19]

Right in the middle of this cultural tempest, a new art, an infant without a history of its own, was born. [20]

Its newness is, in one way, an advantage. If film lacks the confidence that a past can provide, it is spared the burden on its back that a past can also be. But in addition to its infancy, in addition to the batterings of twentieth-century change, the film has a unique problem. The money needs of filmmaking, and therefore the pressures on filmmakers from outsiders, have always been horrendous, and promise to continue so. Money pressures exist throughout the world of film, even in countries with systems of film subsidy, even in communist countries where the film industry belongs to the state. In the United States the problems caused by money pressures have varied: from the formulas imposed by the factory assembly lines in the humming Hollywood days to—paradoxically—the *lack* of factory routine today, which leaves producers baffled and money men floundering. The causes change, but the money harassments are constant—greater than in any other art. [21]

One might have thought that the Film Generation, first discernible in the late 1950s, would make a difference to the course and development of American film art, even in the midst of all these difficulties. One might have hoped for this particularly within a decade or so because of the tremendous growth in film education. Between 1964 and 1969 the number of college film courses in the United States increased by 84 per cent. The latest American Film Institute (AFI) survey (1971–1972) reports that there are 2,460 teachers of film and allied subjects like television at 613 schools, that there are 22,466 students at the 194 schools that offer extensive programs, and that of those schools 51 offer degrees in film. This would have sounded like fantasy in 1960. [22]

And what, so far, has been the effect of all this education in filmmaking? Production is the most important aspect of study in all these programs. How has it helped the new art in this century of crisis? Not very much. Most of the films now being made reflect a technical sophistication that is miles ahead of 1960, but the quality of theatrical feature films, which are the heart of the matter, has not in any serious, sustained sense benefited from the astronomical rise in film education. The range of subject matter has widened healthily, and there have been occasional good films from new people. But, ironically, the most interesting of the newcomers have not come from film schools—such directors of widely differing ages and temperaments as Barbara Loden (*Wanda*), Peter Fonda (*The Hired Hand*), and Frank Gilroy (*Desperate Characters*). There have been successful film school graduates; in fact, the most successful picture in history, *The Godfather,* was directed by former UCLA student Francis Ford Coppola. Still, for all its slickness, what is *The Godfather* but a film that made many people mistake length for size and that reveled in previously established artistic limits? And what can be expected from Coppola but more, perhaps bigger, successes? [23]

Film education so far seems to reflect, to underscore, the strengths and defects of American life: the ability to master technology and the belief that this mastery is the reason for the existence of the technology. Just as many music school graduates know more about orchestration than Brahms ever dreamed of, so the film school graduate knows more of film technique than Jean Vigo did. But the questions do not often arise about why he has bothered to learn it, who the person *is* that has learned the technique, what relation there can be between the art medium and the transformation of his own experience. Compare this situation with the records of some new foreign directors of the past decade, men whose acquisition of technique seems to have been accompanied by other enrichments, all of which have been married to artistic purpose: such men as Jan Troell (*The Emigrants*), Dusan Makaveyev (*Love Affair*), Marco Bellocchio (*China Is Near*), and Alain Tanner (*La Salamandre*). [24]

There are no AFI statistics about the employment of film school graduates, but given economic conditions, it seems logical to assume that many have gone into TV, and into TV's busiest area, the commercial. Take a careful look at the next commercial you see that comes from a big national sponsor. (Stanley Kubrick reportedly said that he couldn't afford to spend proportionately on a feature what is spent on such a commercial—often more than $100,000 a minute.) Count the cuts and dissolves. That's step one, and will itself probably amaze you. The next time you see it—and you'll see it again—note the zoom shots, the crane and dolly shots, the helicopter shots, the opticals, the split screens, the special effects, and, most of all, the subtlety of the lighting. In sum, you are watching a highly compressed encyclopedia of film language: of film techniques and film "vision" evolved by good men and by great men in pursuit of good storytelling or pursuit of an art, all now being cleverly utilized by an army of well-trained vicarious salesmen. And that army must, logic tells us, include many film school graduates. In itself, this is merely predictable on a statistical basis, just as a lot of art school graduates end up in ad agencies; but there are other art school graduates who are doing a great deal for American painting, and that's where the analogy with film breaks down. [25]

Inarguably, it's harder to get started as a film director than as a painter. That condition has to be changed, for all our sakes. I'm not going to try to slough off this enormously complex dilemma in one glib paragraph. But there are ideas in the wind at least to help the situation —for instance, ideas about subsidy and new techniques of distribution. And what I'm particularly talking about is not the situation but the willingness of so many film school graduates (on the basis of what I see and am told) to *accept* it. Who's going to change the situation if they don't? [26]

Still, without any willed affirmation, my prognosis has to be cheery. The long-range reply to the gloomy statement that opened the last section is no, it is not too late to start a new art—not because I say so but on the evidence. That evidence simply is that there are many, many fine films. They exist. It can be done because it has been done. [27]

No film that I know has reached the greatest heights of art, if greatness means something more than its use in the lingo of film journals, if it means Shakespeare and Michelangelo and Mozart. But when you remember that film is so young, so beleaguered by the century into which it popped, so harassed by commercial pressures everywhere, and *still* has produced so many fine works in seventy years, you must feel optimistic. You must feel that it was important to civilization that film be invented and that anything still possible to art is possible to film. [28]

Some of those fine works came from America; most of the world's film images and mythology and impetus came from America. Nothing can be done by film that—in any final arbitrary sense—cannot be done by American film. The trouble so far is not so much that high expectations have been disappointed as that low expectations have been fulfilled. [29]

PURPOSE AND STRUCTURE

1. Kauffmann is "tired" (par. 1) of that recurrent article that criticizes the film scene. Why begin with this statement? What is the relationship between par. 1 and the statement of the thesis in pars. 2 and 4?

2. Why argue that filmgoing is too easy (par. 6)? Why argue that there "is something of a whorehouse feeling about this film ease, a whiff of lazy gratification in the darkness" (par. 6)?

3. Kauffmann's argument is presented in three parts. Are the subtitles necessary?

4. Kauffmann argues that filmmaking "is susceptible of being the greatest con game in the history of the arts" (par. 16). Why?

5. Is the filmmaker a pole vaulter or a high jumper (par. 17)? Why use this analogy to sum up the second part of the argument?

6. Kauffmann negates his own argument at the beginning of the third section (par. 18). Would it be more effective to withhold this information until the end of the section?

7. Kauffmann's prognosis is "cheery" (par. 27). Why, then, follow this statement with "No film I know has reached the greatest heights of art" (par. 28)?

8. Kauffmann plays the devil's advocate (par. 2); that is to say, he presents unpopular arguments. But his argument is unpolemical, even tentative. Would his essay be more effective if he took a stronger position: Should "Film Negatives" be more negative?

DICTION AND TONE

1. What is the tone of "the slumming pleasures of camp" (par. 9)?

2. How does the diction of these phrases function in Kauffmann's argument that filmgoing is too easy: "plunking one's behind into a film-theatre seat" (par. 7), "brothel lethargy" (par. 9), "the position itself—a near fetal one" (par. 11)?

3. What is the tone of "any fool can now ladle lush beauty over anything" (par. 14)? Of "physicality is . . . quite hammy" (par. 15)?

4. Is Kauffmann arguing against some filmmakers or some members of the audience in the phrase "mere film wallower" (par. 16)?

5. What is the tone of "without any willed affirmation" (par. 27)?

6. What is the tone of "low expectations have been fulfilled" (par. 29)? Why is that a "trouble" (par. 29)?

APPLICATIONS TO WRITING

1. Answer Kauffmann. Write an argument entitled "Film Positives."

2. Argue that great art can be best perceived in a "near fetal" (par. 11)

position in the dark: that great art should "stun" with its enormous power (par. 16).

3. Argue an unpopular position as tentatively as Kauffmann does.

The Artist as Housewife

E R I C A J O N G

God knows it's hard enough to be an artist at all, so why make a fetish about sex? The future's a mouth. Death's got no sex. The artist propelled by her horror of death and some frantic energy which feels half like hunger, half like hot pants, races forward (she hopes) in a futile effort to outrun time, knowing all the while that the race is rigged, doomed, and ridiculous. The odds are with the house. [1]

Being an artist of any sex is such a difficult business that it seems almost ungenerous and naïve to speak of the special problems of the woman artist. The problems of becoming an artist are the problems of selfhood. The reason a woman has greater problems becoming an artist is because she has greater problems becoming a self. She can't believe in her existence past 30. She can't believe her own voice. She can't see herself as a grown-up. She can't leave the room without a big wooden *pass.* [2]

This is crucial in life but even more crucial in art. A woman can go on thinking of herself as a dependent little girl and still get by, if she sticks to the stereotyped roles a woman is supposed to play in our society. Frau Doktor. Frau Architect. Mrs. George Blank. Mrs. Harry Blank. Harold's mother. Mother of charge plates, bank checks, bankbooks; insurance beneficiary, fund raiser, den mother, graduate student, researcher, secretary. . . . As long as she goes on taking orders, as long as she doesn't have to tell herself what to do, and be accountable to herself for finishing things. . . . But an artist takes orders only from her inner voice and is accountable only to herself for finishing things. Well, what if you have no inner voice, or none you can distinguish? Or what if you have three inner voices and all three of them are saying conflicting things? Or what if the only inner voice which you can conjure up is male because you can't really conceive of authority as soprano? [3]

Just about the most common complaint of talented women, artists manqué, women who aspire to be artists, is that they *can't finish things*. Partly because finishing implies being judged—but also because finishing things means being grown up. More important, it means possibly succeeding at something. And success, for women, is always partly failure. [4]

Don't get a doctorate or you'll never find a husband. [5]

Don't be too successful or men will be scared of you. [6]

The implication is always that if you're a success with your brain (or talent or whatever), you'll be a failure with your cunt (or womb or whatever). Success at one end brings failure at the other (Edna St. Vincent Millay's candle notwithstanding). No wonder women are ambivalent about success. Most of them are so ambivalent, in fact, that when success seems imminent they go through the most complex machinations to ward it off. Very often they succeed, too. [7]

The main problem of a poet is to raise a voice. We can suffer all kinds of kinks and flaws in a poet's work except lack of authenticity. Authenticity is a difficult thing to define, but roughly it has to do with our sense of the poet as a *mensch,* a human being, an *author* (with the accent on authority). Poets arrive at authenticity in very different ways. Each poet finds her own road by walking it—sometimes backward, sometimes at a trot. To achieve authenticity you have to know who you are and approximately why. You have to know yourself not only as defined by the roles you play but also as a creature with an inner life, a creature built around an inner darkness. Because women are always encouraged to see themselves as role players and helpers ("helpmate" as a synonym for "wife" is illuminating here,) rather than as separate beings, they find it hard to grasp this authentic sense of self. They have too many easy cop-outs. [8]

Probably men are just as lazy and would cop out if they could. Surely men have similar and very crushing problems of selfhood and identity. The only difference is that men haven't got the built-in escape from identity that women have. They can't take refuge in being Arnold's father or Mr. Betty Jones. Women not only can, but are encouraged to, are often forbidden not to, are browbeaten into believing that independence is "castrating," "phallic," or "dikey." [9]

It's not that women lack the inner darkness—one might almost argue that women are ideally suited to be artists because of their built-in darkness, and the mysteries they are privy to—but women don't explore that darkness as men do. And in art, the exploration is all. Everyone has talent. What is rare is the courage to follow the talent to the dark place where it leads. [10]

Of course, it's also a question of trust. Katherine Anne Porter said that becoming a writer was all a question of learning to trust yourself, to trust your own voice. And that's just what most women can't do. That's why they are always seeking someone to dictate to them, someone to be their perennial graduate student adviser, someone to give them gold stars for being good girls. [11]

Naming is the crucial activity of the poet; and naming is a form of self-creation. In theory, there's nothing wrong with a woman's changing names for each new husband, except that often she will come to feel that she has no name at all. (All men are mirrors. Which one will she look into today?) So her first name, her little girl name is the only one which winds up sounding real to her. [12]

Erica. [13]

Erica X. [14]

My father (death) has come to get me. [15]

May I please leave the room? [16]

I have a sleep-over date. [17]

If women artists often elect to use their maiden (or even maternal) names, it's in a sort of last-ditch attempt to assert an unchanging, identity in the face of the constant shifts of identity which are thought in our society to constitute femininity. Changing names all the time is only symbolic of this. It's only disturbing because it mirrors the inner uncertainty. [18]

To have ten identities (wife, mother, mistress, cook, maid, chauffeur, tutor, governess, banker, poet?) is really to have none—or at least none you can believe in. You always feel like a dilettante. You always feel fragmented. You always feel like a little girl. Characteristically, women think of themselves as first names (children): men think of themselves as last names (grown-ups). [19]

And what about "writing like a man" and the word "poetess" (which has come to be used like the word "nigrah")? I know of no woman writer who hasn't confessed the occasional temptation to send her work out under a masculine nom de plume, or under initials, or under the "protection" of some male friend or lover. I know women who can never finish a novel because they insist on making their narrators men, and women poets who are hung up on "androgynous poems" in an attempt to fool the first readers (often self-hating women like themselves). [20]

But sex—it seems so obvious one shouldn't even have to say it—is a part of identity, and if a writer's problem is to find her human identity, only more so, then how can she manage this while concealing her sex? [21]

She can't. [22]

I knew I wanted to be a writer from the time I was 10 or 11 and, starting then, I attempted to write stories. The most notable thing about these otherwise not very memorable stories was that the main character was always male. I never tried to write about women and I never thought anyone would be interested in a woman's point of view. I assumed that what people wanted to hear was how men thought women were, not what women themselves thought they were. None of this was quite conscious, though. I wrote about boys in the same way a black child draws blond hair (like mine) on the faces in her sketchbook. [23]

Yet I did not think of myself as self-hating, and it was only years later (when I was in my late twenties) that I realized how my self-hatred had always paralyzed me as a writer. In high school, I thought I loved myself and I was full of dreams of glory. At 14, I declared myself a feminist, read bits and pieces of *The Second Sex,* and ostentatiously carried the book around. I talked about never wanting to marry —or at the very least not until I was 30 (which then must have seemed like old age to me). But for all my bravado, whenever I sat down to write, I wrote about men. Why? I never asked myself why. [24]

It may also be relevant to point out that until I was 20 or so, all the characters I invented had WASP names—names like Mitch Mitchell, Robert Robertson, Elizabeth Anderson, Bob Briggs, Duane Blaine. Names like the ones you saw in school readers. Names like the ones you heard on radio soap operas. None of the kids I grew up with had such names. They were all Weinbergers and Hamburgers and Blotniks and Briskins and Friskins. There were even some Singhs and Tsangs and Wongs and Fongs. There were even some McGraths and Kennedys and McCabes. The Mitchells in my high school class could be counted on the digits of one severely frostbitten foot, or one leprous hand. But they were in all my stories. [25]

This only proves that one's own experience is less convincing than the cultural norm. In fact, one has to be strong indeed to *trust* one's own experience. Children characteristically lack this strength. And most women, in our culture, are encouraged to remain children. I know two little girls whose mother is a full-time practicing physician who works a very long day and works at home. The children see the patients come and go. They know their mother is a doctor, and yet one of them returned from nursery school with the news that men were doctors and women had to be nurses. All her mother's reasoning and all the child's own experience could not dissuade her. [26]

So, too, with my feelings about writers. I spent my whole bookish life identifying with writers and nearly all the writers who mattered were men. Even though there were women writers, and even though I read them and loved them, they did not seem to *matter*. If they were good, they were good *in spite of* being women. If they were bad, it was *because* they were women. I had, in short, internalized all the dominant cultural stereotypes. And the result was that I could scarcely even imagine a woman as an author. Even when I read Boswell, it was with him that I identified and not with the women he knew. Their lives seemed so constricted and dull compared with his dashing around London. I, too, loved wordplay and clever conversation. I, too, was a clown. I, too, was clever and a bit ridiculous. I was Boswell. The differences in our sexes honestly never occurred to me. [27]

So, naturally, when I sat down to write, I chose a male narrator. Not because I was deluded that I was a man—but because I was very much a woman, and being a woman means, unfortunately, believing a lot of male definitions (even when they cause you to give up significant parts of your own identity). [28]

Of course there were women writers, too, but that didn't seem to change anything. There was Dorothy Parker, whose stories I had by heart and whose bittersweet verses I'd recite whenever I could find a baffled adolescent boy who'd listen. There was Edna St. Vincent Millay, whose sonnets I had memorized from my mother's old, leather-bound, gold-tooled, tear-stained editions (with the crushed violets between the pages). There was Simone de Beauvoir, who seemed so remotely intellectual and French. There was Colette, who wrote of a baffling theatrical world of lesbian love whose significance eluded me then. And there was Virginia Woolf, whose style, at that point in my life, was too rich for my blood. [29]

Except for Parker and Millay (whom I mythicized as much as read), it was to the male writers that I had to go. I even learned about women from them—trusting what they said, even when it implied my own inferiority. [30]

I had learned what an orgasm was from D. H. Lawrence, disguised as Lady Chatterley. I learned from him that all women worship "the Phallos"—as he so quaintly spelled it. (For years I measured my orgasms against Lady Chatterley's and wondered what was *wrong* with me. It honestly never occurred to me that Lady Chatterley's creator was a man, and perhaps not the best judge of female orgasms. It honestly never occurred to me to trust myself or other women.) I learned from Shaw that women can be artists. I learned from Dostoevski that they have no religious feeling. I learned from Swift and Pope that they have too much religious feeling (and therefore can never be quite rational). I learned from Faulkner that they are earth-mothers and at one with the moon and the tide and the crops. I learned from Freud that they have deficient superegos and are ever "incomplete" because they lack the one thing in this world worth having: a penis. [31]

I didn't really become an avid reader of poetry until college. The modern poets I loved best then were Yeats and Eliot, Auden and Dylan Thomas. Diverse as they were, they had in common the assumption of a male viewpoint and a masculine voice, and when I imitated them, I tried to sound either male or neuter. Despite Emily Dickinson, poetry, for me, was a masculine noun. It came as a revelation to discover contemporary women poets like Anne Sexton, Sylvia Plath, Muriel Rukeyser, Carolyn Kizer, Adrienne Rich, and Denise Levertov, and to realize that strong poetry could be written out of the self that I had systematically (though perhaps unconsciously) repressed. And it was not until I allowed the femaleness of my personality to surface in my work that I began to write anything halfway honest. [32]

I remember the year when I began to write seriously, when I threw out all my college poems and began again. What I noticed most persistently about my earliest poems was the fact that they did not engage my individuality very deeply. I had written clever poems about Italian ruins and villas, nightingales and the graves of poets—but I had tried always to avoid revealing myself in any way. I had assumed a stock poetic voice and a public manner. It was as though I disdained myself, felt I had no *right* to have a self. Obviously an impossible situation for a poet. [33]

How did this change? It's hard to chronicle in detail because the change was gradual and I can't retrace each step. I was living in Europe

in a kind of cultural and intellectual isolation. I was part of no consciousness-raising group. I was part of no writing seminar. Yet gradually
I managed to raise my own consciousness as a poet. The main steps
were these: first I owned up to being Jewish, urban, and American;
then I owned up to my femaleness. [34]

It was in Germany that I first set myself the task of writing as if my
life depended on it (and of writing every day). For an atheistic New
York Jew who had been raised to feel as indifferent to religion as possible, Germany was an overwhelming experience. Suddenly I felt as
paranoid as a Jew in hiding during the Nazi period. For the first time
I began to confess to my primal terror, to my sense of being a victim.
I began to delve into my own fears and fantasies, and finally I began
to write about these things. Little by little, I was able to strip away the
disguises. I was able to stop disdaining myself. I was able to stop feeling
that what I was (and therefore what I had to write about) must, of
necessity, be unimportant. [35]

From persecuted Jew to persecuted woman is not a very long step.
When you begin to open up your own sense of vulnerability and make
poetry of it, you are on your way to understanding your femaleness as
well. That was the progression for me. First I confessed to being a
victim. Then I identified with victims. Finally, I was able to cast off
the mask of the WASP male oppressor which I (and my writing) had
worn for so long. [36]

From then on, it was just a question of burrowing deeper and deeper.
I no longer had anything to hide. Once I confessed to my vulnerability,
I was able to explore it, and from that everything followed. I stopped
writing about ruins and nightingales. I was able to make poetry out of
the everyday activities of my life: peeling onions, a trip to the gyne-
cologist, a student demonstration, my own midnight terrors and dreams
—all the things I would have previously dismissed as trivial. [37]

Because of my own history, I think women poets have to insist on
their right to write like women. Where their experience of the world
is different, women writers ought to reflect that difference. They ought
to feel a complete freedom about subject matter. But most important,
our definition of femininity has to change. As long as femininity is
associated with ruffles and flourishes and a lack of directness and
honesty, women artists will feel a deep sense of ambivalence about
their own femaleness. In a culture where *woman* is a synonym for

second-rate, there's no mystery about why women want to "write like men." [38]

In cultural life, as elsewhere, women are damned if they do and damned if they don't. They are often paralyzed and afraid to write because they feel their experience is trivial, yet if they write outside of their experience, they are condemned as inauthentic. No matter how great their achievement, they are always called *women* artists rather than artists. No wonder they are so afraid to write, and having written are so afraid to submit their work for display or judgment. Even their greatest successes are tinged with failure. They are never praised without being patronized. Their jacket photographs are reviewed instead of their books. [39]

When I was in college, I remember listening (and growing increasingly depressed) as a visiting writer went on and on about how women couldn't possibly be authors. Their experience was too limited, he said. They didn't know blood and guts and fucking whores and puking in the streets, he growled. At the time this silly cliché made me miserable. How could a girl hope to be a writer unless she had a history more lurid than that of Moll Flanders? (It never occurred to me then that this let out most men, too.) It was the old Hemingway-Miller-Mailer routine. The writer as tough guy. The writer as Tarzan crossed with King Kong. Naturally, if you believed that *machismo* garbage, you had to believe that (most) women couldn't be authors. And certainly men who had empathy with women (or indeed with anyone) were excluded, too. [40]

A few years later, when I got to know Neruda's elemental odes about lemons and artichokes, and Ponge's prose poems about soap and seashells and oysters, and William Carlos Williams's red wheelbarrow, and Gary Snyder's essay about the poet as tender of the earth household, I was able to reconsider the relation between the poet and the housewife and find it far more congenial than any growling male writer of the Tarzan-King Kong school would want to believe. The trouble with the phallic-warmongering-whoring image of the damned, doomed artist was not only that it so often backfired (literally in Hemingway's case, figuratively in the case of others), but that it was essentially so destructive and so false. It came out of a sensibility which can only be called imperialist: man against nature and man against woman. What was needed was a different concept of potency (and *poetency*) and a different concept of the artist. Perhaps all artists were, in a sense, house-wives: tenders of the earth household. Perhaps a nurturing sensibility had never been more needed. Besides, it was the inner experience, not the outer one, which was crucial. One of the things which makes a poet a poet is the ability to see the world in a grain of sand or eternity in a wild flower (or in an onion). As Valéry says, "It is with our own sub-stance that we imagine and create a stone, a plant, a movement, an *object:* any object is perhaps only the beginning of ourselves." [41]

Like blacks, women will have to learn first to love their own bodies; and women poets will have to learn to write about their bodies. Their breasts: those two blind animals with painted eyes. Their cunts: those furry deaf-mutes speaking a red tongue. The astounding royal purple of their blood. It will not do to continue to confuse the pen with the penis. Despite all the cultural stereotypes which equate femininity with second-rateness, women artists will have to learn to explore their own femininity and to define its true nature. Just as male artists will have to confront their envy of women (which often takes the form of assert-ing that women can't be artists), women artists will have to confront their own bodies and the symbolic implications of their bodies. It seems to me not accidental that two of the most prolific and courageous contemporary women poets (Anne Sexton and Denise Levertov) long ago attempted to write about their bodies and never attempted to con-ceal that they were women. [42]

Nor does it seem accidental that one of the few female artists to fully explore her own anger at being a woman (Sylvia Plath) could never return from that exploration. Plath's extraordinary burst of creativity after childbirth bears witness to the kind of power hidden in women if only it could be tapped. We can no longer doubt its existence. Our problem is how to tap it without going mad. [43]

The pseudocompliment ("you write like a man"), and the contempt in which the term "poetess" is held both attest to the fact that all of us (even feminists) continue to regard masculinity as a standard of ex-cellence. We still use the word "feminine" as if it were synonymous with foolish, frivolous, and silly. In his sniggeringly sexist introduction to *Ariel,* Robert Lowell "compliments" Sylvia Plath (who is too dead to hear) by saying that she is "hardly a person at all, or a woman, certainly not another 'poetess'. . . ." No wonder Lady Lazarus rises out of the ash with her red hair—"And I eat men like air." [44]

Note also the Kirkus-Service blurb on the back of Marge Piercy's second book of poems: 'Angry, alive, loving, real poetry: not feminine, but powerfully female." As if "feminine" and "real poetry" were opposites. [45]

Since authenticity is the key to everything, it seems particularly fatal for a woman artist to become a surrogate male. Nearly all the women poets of our time who have succeeded in becoming individual voices know this. They explore the fact of being female and go beyond it, but they never deny it. Of course, they pay dearly for this in condescending reviews (which seldom fail to disparage their sex in some way or other), and their reputations are somehow never taken as seriously as those of male poets of the same (or lesser) quality. But at least they go on writing and publishing; they go on working. Yet they are so pitifully few in number! For the handful of Levertovs, Plaths, Richs, Piercys, Swensons, Wakoskis, Sextons—there must be thousands of talented women, sitting on unfinished books, wondering how to make themselves sound unfeminine. [46]

I think that as we become more aware of the deep relationship between poetry and ecology, we will begin to revalue the female sensibility in poetry (and in all the arts). We will begin to value the exploration of femaleness (as many ancient civilizations did) rather than to reject it. [47]

But if there's too much male chauvinism in literature and in the literary world, the answer to it is not female chauvinism. Beyond the initial freedom women writers need (of allowing themselves to write like women), there's the greater goal of the mature artist: to become artistically bisexual. [48]

Virginia Woolf points out that the process of developing as an artist means at some point transcending gender. It means having empathy for both sexes, partaking of both halves of humanity and reconciling them in one's work. [49]

At just about this point I anticipate a howl of outrage about my use of the words "male" and "female" and my assumption that there is such a thing as "female sensibility" in poetry or elsewhere. Unfortunately, the terms male and female have become so loaded and politicized, so laden with old prejudices, that they are almost useless for purposes of communication. We don't know what masculine really means, nor what feminine really means. We assume them to be opposites and we may not even be right about that. Yet we are stuck with these words. They are deeply embedded in language and in our minds (which language in part helped to shape). What shall we do with masculine and feminine? Does it do anyone any good just to pretend that they don't exist? [50]

Gradually, we will redefine them. Gradually, society will change its false notions of male and female, and perhaps they will cease to be antitheses. Gradually, male experience and female experience will cease to be so disparate, and then maybe we will not have to worry about women understanding their own self-hatred as a prerequisite to authentic creative work. But what are we to do in the meantime? In our society, men and women still *do* have different life patterns and different experiences. Shouldn't each sex be permitted an authentic expression of its own experience? [51]

Luckily, the artist has an answer. The artist is not finally male or female, but both at once. It is as though the artist were one of those African votive figurines which have breasts, a pregnant belly, and a penis. I think of Leopold Bloom giving birth, or Orlando changing sexes with the centuries. I think of the artist as a mental hermaphrodite, or as a shaman who exploits sexuality in order to get beyond sexuality. The artist starts by exploring her/his particular sexual identity, but this is only the beginning. It is only a necessary way inward. Once women writers are able to write freely about being women, they will be able to write freely about being human. They will be able to explore the world with the confidence that it really belongs to them—just as male writers have done. [52]

Women artists cannot escape exploring their own sexuality because the connection between sex and inspiration is intimate. They are both forms of intense energy. They connect and correspond. The relationship between the artist and the Muse is a sexual relationship in which it is impossible to tell who is fucking and who is being fucked. If sex and creativity are often seen by dictators as subversive activities, it's because they lead to the knowledge that you own your own body (and with it your own voice), and that's the most revolutionary insight of all. [53]

PURPOSE AND STRUCTURE

1. State the thesis of the first and second paragraphs in your own words. How do the key concepts advance the writer's purpose? What causal relationships are established?

2. What is the purpose and effect of the series of parallel sentences concluding par. 2?

3. What is the referent for *this* in par. 3? What details in pars. 3–7 give support to the thesis expressed in par. 2?

4. How has the transition been made to par. 8?

5. With what kinds of detail does Jong develop her definition of authenticity (pars. 8–22)? How are comparison and contrast and illustration used to define it?

6. In what literal and metaphorical sense is "naming" a crucial activity of the poet (pars. 12–22)?

7. What previous statements provide the transition for the rhetorical questions and answers (pars. 21–22)?

8. Account for the shift in person and purpose in par. 23. In what specific ways does the commentary (pars. 23–33) illustrate the general statements that have been made previously?

9. What purpose is served by the italicized words in par. 27?

10. With what supporting details does Jong specify what she learned from male writers? What generalization would you make about the nature of what she learned (pars. 31–32)?

11. What cause-effect relationships are established in pars. 32–38? How do they relate to the problems of achieving both selfhood and artistic integrity?

12. How does the Valéry statement provide a transition from the paragraphs that have preceded and to those immediately following (par. 41)?

13. Jong alludes to the deep relationship between poetry and ecology (par. 47). What does she mean? In what particulars has the essay prepared the reader for this generalization?

14. How has the substance of Jong's argument prepared you for her agreement with Virginia Woolf that artistic development requires "transcending gender" (par. 49)? How does par. 52 directly support this admonition? In what sense is *human* the key word in par. 52? Demonstrate how the final paragraph logically follows the point of view expressed in par. 52 and in the entire essay.

15. How do the substance and tone of the essay lend support to both title and subtitle?

16. Although Jong's approach to her subject is informal, the essay includes a formal proposition, an issue, evidence, and a conclusion. Identify them. To what extent does her evidence rest upon objectively marshaled detail? To what extent does she try to persuade by means of other literary devices? What are they? If you were moved or persuaded, identify the means used. If you were alienated, what were the devices that turned you off?

DICTION AND TONE

1. Define the tone of the first paragraph. Note particularly the effect of the diction, sentence structure, and figurative language. Compare the tone and purpose in pars. 1 and 2.

2. Study the following metaphors in context. How do they affect the tone and purpose: "The future's a mouth" (par. 1); "The odds are with the house" (par. 1); "She can't leave the room without a big wooden *pass*" (par. 2); "you can't really conceive of authority as a soprano" (par. 3); "by walking it—sometimes backward, sometimes at a trot" (par. 8); "All men are mirrors" (par. 12); "that *machismo* garbage" (par. 40)?

3. How do the listing of occupations, activities, and names and the series of rhetorical questions affect tone and purpose (par. 3)?

4. Justify the many single-sentence (or word or phrase) paragraphs. How do they affect purpose and tone?

5. Describe the tone of the section beginning with par. 5 and continuing through par. 22. How does the tone change beginning with par. 23?

6. Can you justify in the context in which it appears Jong's use of the word *imperialist* (par. 41)?

7. In your opinion, are the variations in tone consciously controlled to persuade the reader? Do the author's bitterness, wit, and acerbity help to persuade you or do they weaken her argument? Refer directly to the text in your response.

APPLICATIONS TO WRITING

1. Develop an argument in the Aristotelian sense of discovered judgment on one of the following topics taken from Jong's essay: "The Odds Are with the House"; "The Problems of Becoming an Artist Are the Prob-

lems of Selfhood"; "The Stereotyped Roles a Woman Is Supposed to Play in Our Society"; "Self-accountability"; "An Artist Takes Orders Only from an Inner Voice"; "Success for Women Is Always Partly Failure"; "Don't Be Too Successful or Men Will Be Scared of You"; "Women Are Ambivalent About Success"; "To Achieve Authenticity You Have to Know Who You Are and Approximately Why"; "Men Have Very Similar and Very Crushing Problems of Selfhood and Identity"; "You Have to Know Yourself Not Only as Defined by the Roles You Play but Also as a Creature with an Inner Life"; "In Art, the Exploration Is All"; "Naming Is a Form of Self-creation"; "All Men Are Mirrors"; "I Always Feel like a Dilettante"; "Sex Is a Part of Identity"; "I Was Full of Dreams of Glory"; "One's Own Experience Is Less Convincing than the Cultural Norm"; "I Was Able to Strip Away the Disguises"; "I Identified with Victims"; "Our Definition of Femininity Has to Change"; "The Writer as Tough Guy"; "The Relation-ship Between Poetry and Ecology"; "We Don't Know What Masculine (or Feminine) Really Means."

2. Discuss the evolution of your views about femininity and masculinity.

3. Discuss the explicit or implicit attitudes toward women reflected in the work of a poet or novelist of your choice; or in the essays of Mencken, Sontag, or Greer.

Fenimore Cooper's Literary Offences

MARK TWAIN

The Pathfinder and *The Deerslayer* stand at the head of Cooper's novels as artistic creations. There are others of his works which contain parts as perfect as are to be found in these, and scenes even more thrilling. Not one can be compared with either of them as a finished whole.

The defects in both of these tales are comparatively slight. They were pure works of art.

—*Prof. Lounsbury*

The five tales reveal an extraordinary fullness of invention.

. . . One of the very greatest characters in fiction, "Natty Bumppo.". . .

The craft of the woodsman, the tricks of the trapper, all the delicate art of the forest, were familiar to Cooper from his youth up.

—*Prof. Brander Matthews*

> Cooper is the greatest artist in the domain of romantic fiction yet pro-
> duced by America.
>
> —*Wilkie Collins*

It seems to me that it was far from right for the Professor of English
Literature in Yale, the Professor of English Literature in Columbia,
and Wilkie Collins, to deliver opinions on Cooper's literature without
having read some of it. It would have been much more decorous to
keep silent and let persons talk who have read Cooper. [1]

Cooper's art has some defects. In one place in *Deerslayer,* and in
the restricted space of two-thirds of a page, Cooper has scored 114 offences against literary art out of a possible 115. It breaks the record. [2]

There are nineteen rules governing literary art in the domain of
romantic fiction—some say twenty-two. In *Deerslayer* Cooper violated
eighteen of them. These eighteen require:

1. That a tale shall accomplish something and arrive somewhere. But
   the *Deerslayer* tale accomplishes nothing and arrives in the air. [3]
2. They require that the episodes of a tale shall be necessary parts of
   the tale, and shall help to develop it. But as the *Deerslayer* tale is
   not a tale, and accomplishes nothing and arrives nowhere, the episodes have no rightful place in the work, since there was nothing
   for them to develop. [4]
3. They require that the personages in a tale shall be alive, except in
   the case of corpses, and that always the reader shall be able to tell
   the corpses from the others. But this detail has often been overlooked in the *Deerslayer* tale. [5]
4. They require that the personages in a tale, both dead and alive,
   shall exhibit a sufficient excuse for being there. But this detail also
   has been overlooked in the *Deerslayer* tale. [6]
5. They require that when the personages of a tale deal in conversation, the talk shall sound like human talk, and be talk such as
   human beings would be likely to talk in the given circumstances,
   and have a discoverable meaning, also a discoverable purpose, and
   a show of relevancy, and remain in the neighborhood of the subject
   in hand, and be interesting to the reader, and help out the tale, and
   stop when the people cannot think of anything more to say. But
   this requirement has been ignored from the beginning of the *Deerslayer* tale to the end of it. [7]

6. They require that when the author describes the character of a personage in his tale, the conduct and conversation of that personage shall justify said description. But this law gets little or no attention in the *Deerslayer* tale, as "Natty Bumppo's" case will amply prove. [8]

7. They require that when a personage talks like an illustrated, gilt-edged, tree-calf, hand-tooled, seven-dollar Friendship's Offering in the beginning of a paragraph, he shall not talk like a negro minstrel in the end of it. But this rule is flung down and danced upon in the *Deerslayer* tale. [9]

8. They require that crass stupidities shall not be played upon the reader as "the craft of the woodsman, the delicate art of the forest," by either the author or the people in the tale. But this rule is persistently violated in the *Deerslayer* tale. [10]

9. They require that the personages of a tale shall confine themselves to possibilities and let miracles alone; or, if they venture a miracle, the author must so plausibly set it forth as to make it look possible and reasonable. But these rules are not respected in the *Deerslayer* tale. [11]

10. They require that the author shall make the reader feel a deep interest in the personages of his tale and in their fate; and that he shall make the reader love the good people in the tale and hate the bad ones. But the reader of the *Deerslayer* tale dislikes the good people in it, is indifferent to the others, and wishes they would all get drowned together. [12]

11. They require that the characters in a tale shall be so clearly defined that the reader can tell beforehand what each will do in a given emergency. But in the *Deerslayer* tale this rule is vacated. [13]

In addition to these large rules there are some little ones. These require that the author shall

12. *Say* what he is proposing to say, not merely come near it. [14]
13. Use the right word, not its second cousin. [15]
14. Eschew surplusage. [16]
15. Not omit necessary details. [17]
16. Avoid slovenliness of form. [18]
17. Use good grammar. [19]
18. Employ a simple and straightforward style. [20]

Even these seven are coldly and persistently violated in the *Deer-slayer* tale. [21]

Cooper's gift in the way of invention was not a rich endowment: but such as it was he liked to work it, he was pleased with the effects, and indeed he did some quite sweet things with it. In his little box of stage properties he kept six or eight cunning devices, tricks, artifices for his savages and woodsmen to deceive and circumvent each other with, and he was never so happy as when he was working these innocent things and seeing them go. A favorite one was to make a moccasined person tread in the tracks of the moccasined enemy, and thus hide his own trail. Cooper wore out barrels and barrels of moccasins in working that trick. Another stage-property that he pulled out of his box pretty frequently was his broken twig. He prized his broken twig above all the rest of his effects, and worked it the hardest. It is a restful chapter in any book of his when somebody doesn't step on a dry twig and alarm all the reds and whites for two hundred yards around. Every time a Cooper person is in peril, and absolute silence is worth four dollars a minute, he is sure to step on a dry twig. There may be a hundred handier things to step on, but that wouldn't satisfy Cooper. Cooper requires him to turn out and find a dry twig; and if he can't do it, go and borrow one. In fact the Leather Stocking Series ought to have been called the Broken Twig Series. [22]

I am sorry there is not room to put in a few dozen instances of the delicate art of the forest, as practiced by Natty Bumppo and some of the other Cooperian experts. Perhaps we may venture two or three samples. Cooper was a sailor—a naval officer; yet he gravely tells us how a vessel, driving toward a lee shore in a gale, is steered for a particular spot by her skipper because he knows of an *undertow* there which will hold her back against the gale and save her. For just pure woodcraft, or sailorcraft, or whatever it is, isn't that neat? For several years Cooper was daily in the society of artillery, and he ought to have noticed that when a cannon ball strikes the ground it either buries itself or skips a hundred feet or so; skips again a hundred feet or so—and so on, till it finally gets tired and rolls. Now in one place he loses some "females"—as he always calls women—in the edge of a wood near a plain at night in a fog, on purpose to give Bumppo a chance to show off the delicate art of the forest before the reader. These mislaid people are hunting for a fort. They hear a cannon-blast, and a cannon-ball presently comes rolling into the wood and stops at their feet. To the females this suggests nothing. The case is very different with the admirable Bumppo. I wish I may never know peace again if he doesn't strike out promptly and *follow the track* of that cannon-ball across the plain through the dense fog and find the fort. Isn't it a daisy? If Cooper had any real knowledge of Nature's ways of doing things, he had a most delicate art in concealing the fact. For instances: one of his acute Indian experts, Chingachgook (pronounced Chicago, I think), has lost the trail of a person he is tracking through the forest. Apparently that trail is hopelessly lost. Neither you nor I could ever have guessed out the way to find it. It was very different with Chicago. Chicago was not stumped for long. He turned a running stream out of its course, and there, in the slush in its old bed, were that person's moccasin-tracks. The current did not wash them away, as it would have done in all other like cases—no, even the eternal laws of Nature have to vacate when Cooper wants to put up a delicate job of wood-craft on the reader. [23]

We must be a little wary when Brander Matthews tells us that Cooper's books "reveal an extraordinary fullness of invention." As a rule, I am quite willing to accept Brander Matthews's literary judgments and applaud his lucid and graceful phrasing of them; but that particular statement needs to be taken with a few tons of salt. Bless your heart, Cooper hadn't any more invention than a horse; and I don't mean a high class horse, either; I mean a clothes horse. It would be very difficult to find a really clever "situation" in Cooper's books; and still more difficult to find one of any kind which he has failed to render absurd by his handling of it. Look at the episodes of "the caves" and at the celebrated scuffle between Maqua and those others on the table-land a few days later; and at Hurry Harry's queer water-transit from the castle to the ark; and at Deerslayer's half hour with his first corpse; and at the quarrel between Hurry Harry and Deerslayer later; and at —but choose for yourself; you can't go amiss. [24]

If Cooper had been an observer, his inventive faculty would have worked better, not more interestingly, but more rationally, more plausibly. Cooper's proudest creations in the way of "situations" suffer noticeably from the absence of the observer's protecting gift. Cooper's eye was splendidly inaccurate. Cooper seldom saw anything correctly. He saw nearly all things as through a glass eye, darkly. Of course a man who cannot see the commonest little everyday matters accurately is working at a disadvantage when he is constructing a "situation." In the *Deerslayer* tale Cooper has a stream which is fifty feet wide, where it flows out of a lake; it presently narrows to twenty as it meanders along for no given reason, and yet, when a stream acts like that it ought to be required to explain itself. Fourteen pages later the width of the brook's outlet from the lake has suddenly shrunk thirty feet and become the "narrowest part of the stream." This shrinkage is not accounted for. The stream has bends in it, a sure indication that it has alluvial banks, and cuts them; yet these bends are only thirty and fifty feet long. If Cooper had been a nice and punctilious observer he would have noticed that the bends were oftener nine hundred feet long than short of it. [25]

Cooper made the exit of that stream fifty feet wide in the first place, for no particular reason; in the second place, he narrowed it to less than twenty to accommodate some Indians. He bends a "sapling" to the form of an arch over this narrow passage, and conceals six Indians in its foliage. They are "laying" for a settler's scow or ark which is coming up the stream on its way to the lake; it is being hauled against the stiff current by a rope whose stationary end is anchored in the lake; its rate of progress cannot be more than a mile an hour. Cooper describes the ark, but pretty obscurely. In the matter of dimensions "it was little more than a modern canal boat." Let us guess, then, that it was about 140 feet long. It was of "greater breadth than common." Let us guess, then, that it was about sixteen feet wide. This leviathan had been prowling down bends which were but a third as long as itself, and scraping between banks where it had only two feet of space to spare on each side. We cannot too much admire this miracle. A low-roofed log dwelling occupies "two-third's of the ark's length"—a dwelling ninety feet long and sixteen feet wide, let us say—a kind of vestibule train. The dwelling has two rooms—each forty-five feet long and sixteen feet wide, let us guess. One of them is the bed-room of the Hutter girls, Judith and Hetty; the other is the parlor, in the daytime, at night it is papa's bed chamber. The ark is arriving at the stream's exit, now, whose width has been reduced to less than twenty feet to accommodate the Indians—say to eighteen. There is a foot to spare on each side of the boat. Did the Indians notice that there was going to be a tight squeeze there? Did they notice that they could make money by climbing down out of that arched sapling and just stepping aboard when the ark scraped by? No; other Indians would have noticed these things, but Cooper's Indians never notice anything. Cooper thinks they are marvellous creatures for noticing, but he was almost always in error about his Indians. There was seldom a sane one among them. [26]

The ark is 140 feet long; the dwelling is 90 feet long. The idea of the Indians is to drop softly and secretly from the arched sapling to the dwelling as the ark creeps along under it at the rate of a mile an hour, and butcher the family. It will take the ark a minute and half to pass under. It will take the 90-foot dwelling a minute to pass under. Now, then, what did the six Indians do? It would take you thirty years to guess, and even then you would have to give it up, I believe. Therefore, I will tell you what the Indians did. Their chief, a person of quite extraordinary intellect for a Cooper Indian, warily watched the canal boat as it squeezed along under him, and when he had got his calculations fined down to exactly the right shade, as he judged, he let go and dropped. And *missed the house!* That is actually what he did. He missed the house, and landed in the stern of the scow. It was not much of a fall, yet it knocked him silly. He lay there unconscious. If the house had been 97 feet long, he would have made the trip. The fault was Cooper's, not his. The error lay in the construction of the house. Cooper was no architect. [27]

There still remained in the roost five Indians. The boat has passed under and is now out of their reach. Let me explain what the five did —you would not be able to reason it out for yourself. No. 1 jumped for the boat, but fell in the water astern of it. Then No. 2 jumped for the boat, but fell in the water still further astern of it. Then No. 3 jumped for the boat, and fell a good way astern of it. Then No. 4 jumped for the boat, and fell in the water *away* astern. Then even No. 5 made a jump for the boat—for he was a Cooper Indian. In the matter of intellect, the difference between a Cooper Indian and the Indian that stands in front of the cigar shop is not spacious. The scow episode is really a sublime burst of invention; but it does not thrill, because the inaccuracy of the details throws a sort of air of fictitiousness and general improbability over it. This comes of Cooper's inadequacy as an observer. [28]

The reader will find some examples of Cooper's high talent for inaccurate observation in the account of the shooting match in *The Path-*

finder. "A common wrought nail was driven lightly into the target, its head having been first touched with paint." The color of the paint is not stated—an important omission, but Cooper deals freely in important omissions. No, after all, it was not an important omission; for this nail head is *a hundred yards* from the marksman and could not be seen by them at that distance no matter what its color might be. How far can the best eyes see a common house fly? A hundred yards? It is quite impossible. Very well, eyes that cannot see a house fly that is a hundred yards away cannot see an ordinary nail head at that distance, for the size of the two objects is the same. It takes a keen eye to see a fly or a nail head at fifty yards—one hundred and fifty feet. Can the reader do it? [29]

The nail was lightly driven, its head painted, and game called. Then the Cooper miracles began. The bullet of the first marksman chipped an edge of the nail head; the next man's bullet drove the nail a little way into the target—and removed all the paint. Haven't the miracles gone far enough now? Not to suit Cooper; for the purpose of this whole scheme is to show off his prodigy, Deerslayer-Hawkeye-Long-Rifle-Leather-Stocking-Pathfinder-Bumppo before the ladies. [30]

"Be all ready to clench it, boys!" cried out Pathfinder, stepping into his friend's tracks the instant they were vacant. "Never mind a new nail; I can see that, though the paint is gone, and what I can see, I can hit at a hundred yards, though it were only a mosquitos's eye. Be ready to clench!" [31]

The rifle cracked, the bullet sped its way and the head of the nail was buried in the wood, covered by the piece of flattened lead. [32]

There, you see, is a man who could hunt flies with a rifle, and command a ducal salary in a Wild West show to-day, if we had him back with us. [33]

The recorded feat is certainly surprising, just as it stands; but it is not surprising enough for Cooper. Cooper adds a touch. He has made Pathfinder do this miracle with another man's rifle, and not only that, but Pathfinder did not have even the advantage of loading it himself. He had everything against him, and yet he made that impossible shot, and not only made it, but did it with absolute confidence, saying, "Be ready to clench." Now a person like that would have undertaken that same feat with a brickbat, and with Cooper to help he would have achieved it, too. [34]

Pathfinder showed off handsomely that day before the ladies. His very first feat was a thing which no Wild West show can touch. He was standing with the group of marksmen, observing—a hundred yards from the target, mind: one Jasper raised his rifle and drove the centre of the bull's-eye. Then the quartermaster fired. The target exhibited no result this time. There was a laugh. "It's a dead miss," said Major Lundie. Pathfinder waited an impressive moment or two, then said in that calm, indifferent, know-it-all way of his, "No, Major—he has covered Jasper's bullet, as will be seen if anyone will take the trouble to examine the target." [35]

Wasn't it remarkable! How *could* he see that little pellet fly through the air and enter that distant bullet-hole? Yet that is what he did; for nothing is impossible to a Cooper person. Did any of those people have any deep-seated doubts about this thing? No; for that would imply sanity, and these were all Cooper people. [36]

The respect for Pathfinder's skill and for his *quickness and accuracy of sight* (the italics are mine) was so profound and general, that the instant he made this declaration the spectators began to distrust their own opinions, and a dozen rushed to the target in order to ascertain the fact. There, sure enough, it was found that the quartermaster's bullet had gone through the hole made by Jasper's, and that, too, so accurately as to require a minute examination to be certain of the circumstance, which, however, was soon clearly established by discovering one bullet over the other in the stump against which the target was placed. [37]

They made a "minute" examination; but never mind, how could they know that there were two bullets in that hole without digging the latest one out, for neither probe nor eyesight could prove the presence of any more than one bullet. Did they dig? No; as we shall see. It is the Pathfinder's turn now; he steps out before the ladies, takes aim, and fires. [38]

But alas! here is a disappointment; an incredible, an unimaginable disappointment—for the target's aspect is unchanged; there is nothing there but that same old bullet hole! [39]

"If one dared to hint at such a thing," cried Major Duncan, "I should say that the Pathfinder has also missed the target." [40]

As nobody had missed it yet, the "also" was not necessary; but never mind about that, for the Pathfinder is going to speak. [41]

"No; no, Major," said he, confidently, "that *would* be a risky declaration. I didn't load the piece, and can't say what was in it, but if it was lead, you will find the bullet driving down those of the Quartermaster and Jasper, else is not my name Pathfinder." [42]

A shout from the target announced the truth of this assertion. [43]

Is the miracle sufficient as it stands? Not for Cooper. The Pathfinder speaks again, as he "now slowly advances towards the stage occupied by the females":

"That's not all, boys, that's not all; if you find the target touched at all, I'll own to a miss. The Quartermaster cut the wood, but you'll find no wood cut by that last messenger." [44]

The miracle is at last complete. He knew—doubtless *saw*—at the distance of a hundred yards—that his bullet had passed into the hole *without fraying the edges*. There were now three bullets in that one hole—three bullets imbedded processionally in the body of the stump back of the target. Everybody knew this—somehow or other—and yet nobody had dug any of them out to make sure. Cooper is not a close observer, but he is interesting. He is certainly always that, no matter what happens. And he is more interesting when he is not noticing what he is about than when he is. This is a considerable merit. [45]

The conversations in the Cooper books have a curious sound in our modern ears. To believe that such talk really ever came out of people's mouths would be to believe that there was a time when time was of no value to a person who thought he had something to say; when it was the custom to spread a two-minute remark out to ten; when a man's mouth was a rolling-mill, and busied itself all day long in turning four-foot pigs of thought into thirty-foot bars of conversational railroad iron by attenuation; when subjects were seldom faithfully stuck to, but the talk wandered all around and arrived nowhere; when conversations consisted mainly of irrelevances, with here and there a relevancy, a relevancy with an embarrassed look, as not being able to explain how it got there. [46]

Cooper was certainly not a master in the construction of dialogue. Inaccurate observation defeated him here as it defeated him in so many other enterprises of his. He even failed to notice that the man who talks corrupt English six days in the week must and will talk it on the seventh, and can't help himself. In the *Deerslayer* story he lets

Deerslayer talk the showiest kind of book talk sometimes, and at other times the basest of base dialects. For instance, when some one asks him if he has a sweetheart, and if so, where she abides, this is the majestic answer:

"She's in the forest—hanging from the boughs of the trees, in a soft rain—in the dew on the open grass—the clouds that float about in the blue heavens—the birds that sing in the woods—the sweet springs where I slake my thirst—and in all the other glorious gifts that come from God's Providence!" [47]

And he preceded that, a little before, with this:

"It consarns me as all things that touches a fri'nd consarns a fri'nd." [48]

And this is another of his remarks:

"If I was Injin born, now, I might tell of this, or carry in the scalp and boast of the expl'ite afore the whole tribe; or if my inimy had only been a bear"—and so on. [49]

We cannot imagine such a thing as a veteran Scotch Commander-in-Chief comporting himself in the field like a windy melodramatic actor, but Cooper could. On one occasion Alice and Cora were being chased by the French through a fog in the neighborhood of their father's fort:

"Point de quartier aux coquins!" cried an eager pursuer, who seemed to direct the operations of the enemy. [50]
"Stand firm and be ready, my gallant 60ths!" suddenly exclaimed a voice above them; "wait to see the enemy; fire low, and sweep the glacis." [51]
"Father! father!" exclaimed a piercing cry from out the mist; "it is I! Alice! thy own Elsie! spare, O! save your daughters!" [52]
"Hold!" shouted the former speaker, in the awful tones of parental agony, the sound reaching even to the woods, and rolling back in solemn echo. " 'Tis she! God has restored me my children! Throw open the sally-port; to the field, 60ths, to the field; pull not a trigger, lest ye kill my lambs! Drive off these dogs of France with your steel." [53]

Cooper's word-sense was singularly dull. When a person has a poor ear for music he will flat and sharp right along without knowing it. He keeps near the tune, but it is *not* the tune. When a person has a poor ear for words, the result is a literary flatting and sharping; you perceive what he is intending to say, but you also perceive that he doesn't *say* it. This is Cooper. He was not a word-musician. His ear was satisfied with the *approximate* word. I will furnish some circumstantial evidence in support of this charge. My instances are gathered from half a dozen pages of the tale called *Deerslayer*. He uses "verbal," for "oral"; "precision," for "facility"; "phenomena," for "marvels"; "necessary," for "predetermined"; "unsophisticated," for "primitive"; "preparation," for "expectancy"; "rebuked," for "subdued"; "dependant on," for "resulting from"; "fact," for "condition"; "fact," for "conjecture"; "precaution," for "caution"; "explain," for "determine"; "mortified," for "disappointed"; "meretricious," for "factitious"; "materially," for "considerably"; "decreasing," for "deepening"; "increasing," for "disappearing"; "embedded," for "enclosed"; "treacherous," for "hostile"; "stood," for "stooped"; "softened," for "replaced"; "rejoined," for "remarked"; "situation," for "condition"; "different," for "differing"; "insensible," for "unsentient"; "brevity," for "celerity"; "distrusted," for "suspicious"; "mental imbecility," for "imbecility"; "eyes," for "sight"; "counteracting," for "opposing"; "funeral obsequies," for "obsequies." [54]

There have been daring people in the world who claimed that Cooper could write English, but they are all dead now—all dead but Lounsbury. I don't remember that Lounsbury makes the claim in so many words, still he makes it, for he says that *Deerslayer* is a "pure work of art." Pure, in that connection, means faultless—faultless in all details—and language is a detail. If Mr. Lounsbury had only compared Cooper's English with the English which he writes himself—but it is plain that he didn't; and so it is likely that he imagines until this day that Cooper's is as clean and compact as his own. Now I feel sure, deep down in my heart, that Cooper wrote about the poorest English that exists in our language, and that the English of *Deerslayer* is the very worst than even Cooper ever wrote. [55]

I may be mistaken, but it does seem to me that *Deerslayer* is not a work of art in any sense; it does seem to me that it is destitute of every detail that goes to the making of a work of art; in truth, it seems to me that *Deerslayer* is just simply a literary *delirium tremens*. [56]

A work of art? It has no invention; it has no order, system, sequence, or result; it has no lifelikeness, no thrill, no stir, no seeming of reality; its characters are confusedly drawn, and by their acts and words they prove that they are not the sort of people the author claims that they are; its humor is pathetic; its pathos is funny; its conversations are—oh! indescribable; its love-scenes odious; its English a crime against the language. [57]

Counting these out, what is left is Art. I think we must all admit that. [58]

PURPOSE AND STRUCTURE

1. Twain begins by quoting three authorities on Cooper's art. Why does Twain suggest that it would have been more decorous for these critics to have kept silent (par. 1)? Is his suggestion fair-minded?

2. Twain points out that "Cooper's art has some defects" (par. 2). This seems a fairly restrained criticism of Cooper. How many defects are "some"?

3. Twain does not give his source for the nineteen—or "some say twenty-two" (par. 3)—rules governing literary art in the domain of romantic fiction. Discuss where Twain got these rules.

4. Twain covers eighteen rules rather rapidly. Do you feel he should have developed each one more fully? Discuss.

5. The topic sentence of paragraph 54 is "Cooper's word-sense is singularly dull." Does Twain cite specific examples? Discuss the examples.

DICTION AND TONE

1. Why call the "Leatherstocking Series" the "Broken Twig Series"? (par. 22).

2. How did Cooper wear out "barrels and barrels of moccasins" (par. 22)?

3. Cooper "did some quite sweet things with" (par. 22) invention. What are they? Is Twain praising Cooper?

4. Is the third rule (par. 5) too demanding? Discuss.

5. According to Twain, how is "Chingachgook" pronounced (par. 23)? Why?

6. Cooper, according to Twain, "hadn't anymore invention than a horse" (par. 24). What kind of a horse?

7. What does Twain mean when he states that Cooper "saw nearly all things as through a glass eye" (par. 25)? Why add the word *darkly*?

8. Twain is amusing but is he persuasive? Discuss. Why state that Cooper, in the restricted space of two thirds of a page, has scored 114 offenses against literary art out of a possible 115 (par. 2)? Does Twain expect the reader to believe that? Usually, transparent exaggeration will work against the argument. Does it here? Has Twain made you laugh? Is paragraph 54 convincing? Has Twain influenced your attitude toward Cooper?

APPLICATIONS TO WRITING

1. Choose a book you dislike and write an attack like Twain's. (Modest understatement and wild burlesque should be combined.)

2. Write a humorous attack on a famous politician or TV personality using the mock-serious tone of Twain.

The Devil Speaks
from *Man and Superman*

GEORGE BERNARD SHAW

The Devil. And is Man any the less destroying himself for all this boasted brain of his? Have you walked up and down upon the earth lately? I have; and I have examined Man's wonderful inventions. And I tell you that in the arts of life man invents nothing; but in the arts of death he outdoes Nature herself, and produces by chemistry and machinery all the slaughter of plague, pestilence, and famine. The peasant I tempt today eats and drinks what was eaten and drunk by the peasants of ten thousand years ago; and the house he lives in has not altered as much in a thousand centuries as the fashion of a lady's bonnet in a score of weeks. But when he goes out to slay, he carries a marvel of mechanism that lets loose at the touch of his finger all the hidden molecular energies, and leaves the javelin, the arrow, the blowpipe of his fathers far behind. In the arts of peace Man is a bungler. I have seen his cotton factories and the like, with machinery that a greedy dog could have invented if it had wanted money instead of food. I know his clumsy typewriters and bungling locomotives and tedious bicycles: they are toys compared to the Maxim gun, the submarine torpedo boat. There is nothing in Man's industrial machinery but his greed and sloth: his heart is in his weapons. This marvellous force of Life of which you boast is a force of Death: Man measures his strength by his destructiveness. What is his religion? An excuse for hating me. What is his law? An excuse for hanging you. What is his morality? Gentility! an excuse for consuming without producing. What is his art? An excuse for gloating over pictures of slaughter. What are his politics? Either the worship of a despot because a despot can kill, or parliamentary cockfighting. I spent an evening lately in a certain celebrated legislature, and heard the pot lecturing the kettle for its blackness, and ministers answering questions. When I left I chalked up on the door the old nursery saying "Ask no questions and you will be told no lies." I bought a sixpenny family magazine, and found it full of pictures of young men shooting and stabbing one another. I saw a man die: he was a London bricklayer's laborer with seven children. He left seventeen pounds club money; and his wife spent it all on his funeral and went into the workhouse with the children next day. She would not have spent sevenpence on her children's schooling: the law had to force her to let them be taught gratuitously; but on death she spent all she had. Their imagination glows, their energies rise up at the idea of death, these people: they love it; and the more horrible it is the more they enjoy it. Hell is a place far above their comprehension: they derive their notion of it from two of the greatest fools that ever lived, an Italian and an Englishman. The Italian described it as a place of mud, frost, filth, fire, and venomous serpents: all torture. This ass, when he was not lying about me, was maundering about some woman whom he saw once in the street. The Englishman described me as being expelled from Heaven by cannons and gunpowder; and to this day every Briton believes that the whole of his silly story is in the Bible. What else he says I do not know; for it is all in a long poem which neither I nor anyone else ever succeeded in wading through. It is the same in everything. The highest form of literature is the tragedy, a play in which everybody is murdered at the end. In the old chronicles you read of earthquakes and pestilences, and are told that these shewed the power and majesty of God and the littleness of Man. Nowadays the chronicles describe battles. In a battle two bodies of men shoot at one another with bullets and explosive shells until one body runs away, when the others chase the fugitives on horseback and cut them to pieces as they fly. And this, the chronicle concludes, shews the greatness and majesty of empires, and the littleness of the vanquished. Over such battles the people run about the streets yelling with delight, and egg their Governments on to spend hundreds of millions of money in the slaughter, whilst the strongest Ministers dare not spend an extra penny in the pound against the poverty and pestilence through which they themselves daily walk. I could give you a thousand instances; but they all come to the same thing: the power that governs the earth is not the power of Life but of Death; and the inner need that has nerved Life to the effort of organizing itself into the human being is not the need for higher life but for a more efficient engine of destruction. The plague, the famine, the earthquake, the tempest were too spasmodic in their action; the tiger and crocodile were too easily satiated and not cruel enough: something more constantly, more ruthlessly, more ingeniously destructive was needed; and that something was Man, the inventor of the rack, the stake, the gallows, the electric chair; of sword and gun and poison gas: above all, of justice, duty, patriotism, and all the other isms by which even those who are clever enough to be humanely disposed are persuaded to become the most destructive of all the destroyers. [1]

PURPOSE AND DICTION

1. The Devil's argument is powerful and passionate. He has stated (just before our excerpt) that "all Man's reason has done for him is to make him beastlier than any beast." What evidence for this conviction can you find in his argument?

2. Study the structure of the sentences and account for their effectiveness. Note the repetition, parallel structure, rhythmic quality, and other rhetorical devices. Summarize the argument. What is lost in the summary?

3. Note the repeated use of the first person (to be expected in a dialogue): "I have," "I tell you," "I tempt," "as I have seen," "I know." What would be lost in purpose and tone were each of the sentences to be phrased without the personal pronoun?

4. What is the *issue*, the question upon which the Devil's argument rests? What concrete evidence does the Devil marshal to support his argument?

5. What is the function of the series of rhetorical questions?

6. Who are the Italian and the Englishman whom the Devil refers to as fools? Why does he so regard them?

7. What does the Devil think of "the majesty of empires"?

8. Analyze the structure of the concluding sentence. Break it up into two or more sentences. What has been gained or lost?

9. How are comparison and contrast used in developing the argument?

DICTION AND TONE

1. Identify the tone of the Devil's speech by making reference to specific words, phrases, and constructions.

2. Account for the use of the verb *nerved* in the next to the last sentence. Would any other word be as appropriate in the context?

3. Is the phrase "a more efficient engine of destruction" used literally or metaphorically or both? Explain.

4. How are paradox, irony, metaphor, and allusion used? Cite examples of each.

5. To what degree does the Devil's argument rest upon objectivity of evidence? upon the subtle and controlled use of language? Cite examples.

APPLICATIONS TO WRITING

1. Reply to the Devil employing a similar sentence structure, a similar method of asking and answering rhetorical questions, and similar persuasive techniques.

2. Attempt to persuade a friend who is convinced that the destructive forces in man are dominant that the life force can assert itself if only man will change his ways.

Joan Baez: Where the Kissing Never Stops
from *Slouching Towards Bethlehem*

JOAN DIDION

Outside the Monterey County Courthouse in Salinas, California, the Downtown Merchants' Christmas decorations glittered in the thin sunlight that makes the winter lettuce grow. Inside, the crowd blinked uneasily in the blinding television lights. The occasion was a meeting of the Monterey County Board of Supervisors, and the issue, on this warm afternoon before Christmas 1965, was whether or not a small school in the Carmel Valley, the Institute for the Study of Nonviolence, owned by Miss Joan Baez, was in violation of Section 32-C of the Monterey County Zoning Code, which prohibits land use "detrimental to the peace, morals, or general welfare of Monterey County." Mrs. Gerald Petkuss, who lived across the road from the school, had put the problem another way. "We wonder what kind of people would go to a school like this," she asked quite early in the controversy. "Why they aren't out working and making money." [1]

Mrs. Petkuss was a plump young matron with an air of bewildered determination, and she came to the rostrum in a strawberry-pink knit dress to say that she had been plagued "by people associated with Miss Baez's school coming up to ask where it was although they knew perfectly *well* where it was—one gentleman I remember had a beard." [2]

"Well I don't *care*," Mrs. Petkuss cried when someone in the front row giggled. "I have three small children, that's a big responsibility, and I don't like to have to worry about . . ." Mrs. Petkuss paused delicately. "About who's around." [3]

The hearing lasted from two until 7:15 P.M., five hours and fifteen minutes of participatory democracy during which it was suggested, on the one hand, that the Monterey County Board of Supervisors was turning our country into Nazi Germany, and, on the other, that the presence of Miss Baez and her fifteen students in the Carmel Valley would lead to "Berkeley-type" demonstrations, demoralize trainees at Fort Ord, paralyze Army convoys using the Carmel Valley road, and send property values plummeting throughout the county. "Frankly, I can't conceive of anyone buying property near such an operation," declared Mrs. Petkuss's husband, who is a veterinarian. Both Dr. and Mrs. Petkuss, the latter near tears, said that they were particularly offended by Miss Baez's presence on her property during weekends. It seemed that she did not always stay inside. She sat out under trees, and walked around the property. [4]

"We don't start until one," someone from the school objected. "Even if we did make noise, which we don't, the Petkuss could sleep until one, I don't see what the problem is." [5]

The Petkusses' lawyer jumped up. "The *prob*lem is that the Petkusses happen to have a very beautiful swimming pool, they'd like to have guests out on weekends, like to use the pool." [6]

"They'd have to stand up on a table to see the school." [7]

"They will, too," shouted a young woman who had already indicated her approval of Miss Baez by reading aloud to the supervisors a passage from John Stuart Mill's *On Liberty*. "They'll be out with spyglasses." [8]

"That is *not* true," Mrs. Petkuss keened. "We see the school out of three bedroom windows, out of one living-room window, it's the only direction we can *look*." [9]

Miss Baez sat very still in the front row. She was wearing a long-sleeved navy-blue dress with an Irish lace collar and cuffs, and she kept her hands folded in her lap. She is extraordinary looking, far more so that her photographs suggest, since the camera seems to emphasize an Indian cast to her features and fails to record either the startling fineness and clarity of her bones and eyes or, her most striking characteristic, her absolute directness, her absence of guile. She has a great natural style, and she is what used to be called a lady. "Scum," hissed an old man with a snap-on bow tie who had identified himself as "a veteran of two wars" and who is a regular at such meetings. "*Spaniel*." He seemed to be referring to the length of Miss Baez's hair, and was trying to get her attention by tapping with his walking stick, but her eyes did not flicker from the rostrum. After a while she got up, and stood until the room was completely quiet. Her opponents sat tensed, ready to spring up and counter whatever defense she was planning to make of her politics, of her school, of beards, of "Berkeley-type" demonstrations and disorder in general. [10]

"Everybody's talking about their forty- and fifty-thousand-dollar houses and their property values going down," she drawled finally, keeping her clear voice low and gazing levelly at the supervisors. "I'd just like to say one thing. I have more than one *hundred* thousand dollars invested in the Carmel Valley, and I'm interested in protecting my property too." The property owner smiled disingenuously at Dr. and Mrs. Petkuss then, and took her seat amid complete silence. [11]

She is an interesting girl, a girl who might have interested Henry James, at about the time he did Verena Tarrant, in *The Bostonians*. Joan Baez grew up in the more evangelistic thickets of the middle class, the daughter of a Quaker physics teacher, the granddaughter of two Protestant ministers, an English-Scottish Episcopalian on her mother's side, a Mexican Methodist on her father's. She was born on Staten Island, but raised on the edges of the academic community all over the country; until she found Carmel, she did not really come from anywhere. When it was time to go to high school, her father was teaching at Stanford, and so she went to Palo Alto High School, where she taught herself "House of the Rising Sun" on a Sears, Roebuck guitar, tried to achieve a vibrato by tapping her throat with her finger, and made headlines by refusing to leave the school during a bomb drill. When it was time to go to college, her father was at M.I.T. and Harvard, and so she went a month to Boston University, dropped out, and for a long while sang in coffee bars around Harvard Square. She did not much like the Harvard Square life ("They just lie in their pads, smoke pot, and do stupid things like that," said the ministers' granddaughter of her acquaintances there), but she did not yet know another. [12]

In the summer of 1959, a friend took her to the first Newport Folk Festival. She arrived in Newport in a Cadillac hearse with "JOAN BAEZ" painted on the side, sang a few songs to 13,000 people, and there it was, the new life. Her first album sold more copies than the work of any other female folksinger in record history. By the end of 1961 Vanguard had released her second album, and her total sales were behind those of only Harry Belafonte, the Kingston Trio, and the

Weavers. She had finished her first long tour, had given a concert at Carnegie Hall which was sold out two months in advance, and had turned down $100,000 worth of concert dates because she would work only a few months a year. [13]

She was the right girl at the right time. She had only a small repertory of Child ballads ("What's Joanie still doing with this Mary Hamilton?" Bob Dylan would fret later), never trained her pure soprano and annoyed some purists because she was indifferent to the origins of her material and sang everything "sad." But she rode in with the folk wave just as it was cresting. She could reach an audience in a way that neither the purists nor the more commercial folksingers seemed to be able to do. If her interest was never in the money, neither was it really in the music: she was interested instead in something that went on between her and the audience. "The easiest kind of relationship for me is with ten thousand people," she said. "The hardest is with one." [14]

She did not want, then or ever, to entertain; she wanted to move people, to establish with them some communion of emotion. By the end of 1963 she had found, in the protest movement, something upon which she could focus the emotion. She went into the South. She sang at Negro colleges, and she was always there where the barricade was, Selma, Montgomery, Birmingham. She sang at the Lincoln Memorial after the March on Washington. She told the Internal Revenue Service that she did not intend to pay the sixty percent of her income tax that she calculated went to the defense establishment. She became the voice that meant protest, although she would always maintain a curious distance from the movement's more ambiguous moments. ("I got pretty sick of those Southern marches after a while," she could say later. "All these big entertainers renting little planes and flying down, always about 35,000 people in town.") She had recorded only a handful of albums, but she had seen her face on the cover of *Time*. She was just twenty-two. [15]

Joan Baez was a personality before she was entirely a person, and, like anyone to whom that happens, she is in a sense the hapless victim of what others have seen in her, written about her, wanted her to be and not to be. The roles assigned to her are various, but variations on a single theme. She is the Madonna of the disaffected. She is the pawn of the protest movement. She is the unhappy analysand. She is the singer who would not train her voice, the rebel who drives the Jaguar too fast, the Rima who hides with the birds and the deer. Above all, she is the girl who "feels" things, who has hung on to the freshness and pain of adolescence, the girl ever wounded, ever young. Now, at an age when the wounds begin to heal whether one wants them to or not, Joan Baez rarely leaves the Carmel Valley. [16]

Although all Baez activities tend to take on certain ominous overtones in the collective consciousness of Monterey County, what actually goes on at Miss Baez's Institute for the Study of Nonviolence, which was allowed to continue operating in the Carmel Valley by a three-two vote of the supervisors, is so apparently ingenuous as to disarm even veterans of two wars who wear snap-on bow ties. Four days a week, Miss Baez and her fifteen students meet at the school for lunch: potato salad, Kool-Aid, and hot dogs broiled on a portable barbecue. After lunch they do ballet exercises to Beatles records, and after that they sit around on the bare floor beneath a photomural of Cypress Point and discuss their reading: *Gandhi on Nonviolence,* Louis Fischer's *Life of Mahatma Gandhi,* Jerome Frank's *Breaking the Thought Barrier,* Thoreau's *On Civil Disobedience,* Krishnamurti's *The First and Last Freedom* and *Think on These Things,* C. Wright Mills's *The Power Elite,* Huxley's *Ends and Means,* and Marshall McLuhan's *Understanding Media.* On the fifth day, they meet as usual but spend the afternoon in total silence, which involves not only not talking but also not reading, not writing, and not smoking. Even on discussion days, this silence is invoked for regular twenty-minute or hour intervals, a regimen described by one student as "invaluable for clearing your mind of personal hangups" and by Miss Baez as "just about the most important thing about the school." [17]

There are no admission requirements, other than that applicants must be at least eighteen years old; admission to each session is granted to the first fifteen who write and ask to come. They come from all over, and they are on the average very young, very earnest, and not very much in touch with the larger scene, less refugees from it than children who do not quite apprehend it. They worry a great deal about "responding to one another with beauty and tenderness," and their response to one another is in fact so tender that an afternoon at the school tends to drift perilously into the never-never. They debate whether or not it was a wise tactic for the Vietnam Day Committee at Berkeley to try to reason with Hell's Angels "on the hip level." [18]

"O.K." someone argues. "So the Angels just shrug and say 'our thing's violence.' How can the V.D.C. guy answer that?" [19]

They discuss a proposal from Berkeley for an International Non-violent Army: "The idea is, we go to Vietnam and we go into these villages, and then if they burn them, we burn too." [20]

"It has a beautiful simplicity," someone says. [21]

Most of them are too young to have been around for the memorable events of protest, and the few who have been active tell stories to those who have not, stories which begin "One night at the Scranton Y . . ." or "Recently when we were sitting in at the A.E.C. . . ." and "We had this eleven-year-old on the Canada-to-Cuba march who was at the time corresponding with a Gandhian, and he. . . ." They talk about Allen Ginsberg, "the only one, the only beautiful voice, the only one talking." Ginsberg had suggested that the V.D.C. send women carrying babies and flowers to the Oakland Army Terminal. [22]

"Babies and flowers," a pretty little girl breathes. "But that's so *beautiful*, that's the whole *point*." [23]

"Ginsberg was down here one weekend," recalls a dreamy boy with curly golden hair. "He brought a copy of the *Fuck Songbag*, but we burned it." He giggles. He is holding a clear violet marble up to the window, turning it in the sunlight. "Joan gave it to me," he says. "One night at her house, when we all had a party and gave each other presents. It was like Christmas but it wasn't." [24]

The school itself is an old whitewashed adobe house quite far out among the yellow hills and dusty scrub oaks of the Upper Carmel valley. Oleanders support a torn wire fence around the school, and there is no sign, no identification at all. The adobe was a one-room county school until 1950; after that it was occupied in turn by the So Help Me Hannah Poison Oak Remedy Laboratory and by a small shotgun-shell manufacturing business, two enterprises which apparently did not present the threat to property values that Miss Baez does. She bought her place in the fall of 1965, after the County Planning Commission told her that zoning prohibited her from running the school in her house, which is on a ten-acre piece a few miles away. Miss Baez is the vice president of the Institute, and its sponsor; the $120 fee paid by each student for each six-week session includes lodging, at an apartment house in Pacific Grove, and does not meet the school's expenses. Miss Baez not only has a $40,000 investment in the school property but is responsible as well for the salary of Ira Sandperl, who is the president of the Institute, the leader of the discussions, and in fact the *eminence gris* of the entire project. "You might think we're starting in a very small way," Ira Sandperl says. "Sometimes the smallest things can change the course of history. Look at the Benedictine order." [25]

In a way it is impossible to talk about Joan Baez without talking about Ira Sandperl. "One of the men on the Planning Commission said I was being led down the primrose path by the lunatic fringe," Miss Baez giggles. "Ira said maybe he's the lunatic and his beard's the fringe." Ira Sandperl is a forty-two-year-old native of St. Louis who has, besides the beard, a shaved head, a large nuclear-disarmament emblem on his corduroy jacket, glittering and slightly messianic eyes, a high cracked laugh and the general look of a man who has, all his life, followed some imperceptibly but fatally askew rainbow. He has spent a good deal of time in pacifist movements around San Francisco, Berkeley, and Palo Alto, and was, at the time he and Miss Baez hit upon the idea of the Institute, working in a Palo Alto bookstore. [26]

Ira Sandperl first met Joan Baez when she was sixteen and was brought by her father to a Quaker meeting in Palo Alto. "There was something magic, something different about her even then," he recalls. "I remember once she was singing at a meeting where I was speaking. The audience was so responsive that night that I said 'Honey, when you grow up we'll have to be an evangelical team.'" He smiles, and spreads his hands. [27]

The two became close, according to Ira Sandperl, after Miss Baez's father went to live in Paris as a UNESCO advisor. "I was the oldest friend around, so naturally she turned to me." He was with her at the time of the Berkeley demonstrations in the fall of 1964. "We were actually the outside agitators you heard so much about," he says. "Basically we wanted to turn an *un*violent movement into a *non*violent one. Joan was *enor*mously instrumental in pulling the movement out of its slump, although the boys may not admit it now." [28]

A month or so after her appearance at Berkeley, Joan Baez talked to Ira Sandperl about the possibility of tutoring her for a year. "She found herself among politically knowledgeable people," he says, "and while she had strong *feel*ings, she didn't know any of the socio-economic-political-historical terms of nonviolence." [29]

"It was all vague," she interrupts, nervously brushing her hair back. "I want it to be less vague." [30]

They decided to make it not a year's private tutorial but a school to go on indefinitely, and enrolled the first students late in the summer of 1965. The Institute aligns itself with no movements ("Some of the kids are just leading us into another long, big, violent mess," Miss Baez says), and there is in fact a marked distrust of most activist organizations. Ira Sandperl, for example, had little use for the V.D.C., because the V.D.C. believed in nonviolence only as a limited tactic, accepted conventional power blocs, and even ran one of its leaders for Congress, which is anathema to Sandperl. "Darling, let me put it this way. In civil rights, now, the President signs a bill, who does he call to witness it? Adam Powell? No. He calls Rustin, Farmer, King, *none* of them in the conventional power structure." He pauses, as if envisioning a day when he and Miss Baez will be called upon to witness the signing of a bill outlawing violence. "I'm not optimistic, darling, but I'm hopeful. There's a difference. I'm hopeful." [31]

The gas heater sputters on and off and Miss Baez watches it, her duffel coat drawn up around her shoulders. "Everybody says I'm politically naïve, and I am," she says after a while. It is something she says frequently to people she does not know. "So are the people running politics, or we wouldn't be in wars, would we." [32]

The door opens and a short middle-aged man wearing handmade sandals walks in. He is Manuel Greenhill, Miss Baez's manager, and although he has been her manager for five years, he has never before visited the Institute, and he has never before met Ira Sandperl. [33]

"At last!" Ira Sandperl cries, jumping up. "The disembodied voice on the telephone is here at last! There *is* a Manny Greenhill! There is an Ira Sandperl! Here I am! Here's the villain!" [34]

It is difficult to arrange to see Joan Baez, at least for anyone not tuned to the underground circuits of the protest movement. The New York company for which she records, Vanguard, will give only Manny Greenhill's number, in Boston. "Try Area Code 415, prefix DA 4, number 4321," Manny Greenhill will rasp. Area Code 415, DA 4-4321 will connect the caller with Keppler's Bookstore in Palo Alto, which is where Ira Sandperl used to work. Someone at the bookstore will take a number, and, after checking with Carmel to see if anyone there cares to hear from the caller, will call back, disclosing a Carmel number. The Carmel number is not, as one might think by now, for Miss Baez, but for an answering service. The service will take a number, and, after some days or weeks, a call may or may not be received from Judy Flynn, Miss Baez's secretary. Miss Flynn says that she will "try to contact" Miss Baez. "I don't see people," says the heart of this curiously improvised web of wrong numbers, disconnected telephones, and unreturned calls. "I lock the gate and hope nobody comes, but they come anyway. Somebody's been telling them where I live." [35]

She lives quietly. She reads, and she talks to the people who have been told where she lives, and occasionally she and Ira Sandperl go to San Francisco, to see friends, to talk about the peace movement. She sees her two sisters and she sees Ira Sandperl. She believes that her days at the Institute talking and listening to Ira Sandperl are bringing her closer to contentment than anything she has done so far. "Certainly than the singing. I used to stand up there and think I'm getting so many thousand dollars, and for what?" She is defensive about her income ("Oh, I have some money from somewhere"), vague about her plans. "There are some things I want to do. I want to try some rock 'n' roll and some classical music. But I'm not going to start worrying about the charts and the sales because then where are you?" [36]

Exactly where it is she wants to be seems an open question, bewildering to her and even more so to her manager. If he is asked what his most celebrated client is doing now and plans to do in the future, Manny Greenhill talks about "lots of plans," "other areas," and "her own choice." Finally he hits upon something: "Listen, she just did a documentary for Canadian television, *Variety* gave it a great review, let me read you." [37]

Manny Greenhill reads. "Let's see. Here *Variety* says *'planned only a twenty-minute interview but when CBC officials in Toronto saw the film they decided to go with a special—'*" He interrupts himself. "That's pretty newsworthy right there. Let's see now. Here they quote her ideas on peace . . . you know those . . . here she says *'every time I go to Hollywood I want to throw up'* . . . let's not get into that . . . here now, *'her impersonations of Ringo Starr and George Harrison were dead-on,'* get that, that's good." [38]

Manny Greenhill is hoping to get Miss Baez to write a book, to be in a movie, and to get around to recording the rock 'n' roll songs. He will not discuss her income, although he will say, at once jaunty and bleak, "but it won't be much *this* year." Miss Baez let him schedule only one concert for 1966 (down from an average of thirty a year), has accepted only one regular club booking in her entire career, and is virtually never on television. "What's she going to do on Andy Williams?" Manny Greenhill shrugs. "One time she sang one of Pat Boone's songs with him," he adds, "which proves she can get along, but still. We don't want her up there with some dance routine behind her." Greenhill keeps an eye on her political appearances, and tries to prevent the use of her name. "We say, if they use her name it's a concert. The point is, if they haven't used her name, then if she doesn't like the looks of it she can get out." He is resigned to the school's cutting into her schedule. "Listen," he says. "I've always encouraged her to be political. I may not be active, but let's say I'm concerned." He squints into the sun. "Let's say maybe I'm just too old." [39]

To encourage Joan Baez to be "political" is really only to encourage Joan Baez to continue "feeling" things, for her politics are still, as she herself said, "all vague." Her approach is instinctive, pragmatic, not too far from that of any League of Women Voters member. "Frankly, I'm down on Communism," is her latest word on that subject. On recent events in the pacifist movement, she has this to say: "Burning draft cards doesn't make sense, and burning themselves makes even less." When she was at Palo Alto High School and refused to leave the building during a bomb drill, she was not motivated by theory; she did it because "it was the practical thing to do, I mean it seemed to me this drill was impractical, all these people thinking they could get into some kind of little shelter and be saved with canned water." She has made appearances for Democratic administrations, and is frequently quoted as saying: "There's never been a good Republican folksinger"; it is scarcely the diction of the new radicalism. Her concert program includes some of her thoughts about "waiting on the eve of destruction," and her thoughts are these:

My life is a crystal teardrop. There are snowflakes falling in the teardrop and little figures trudging around in slow motion. If I were to look into the teardrop for the next million years, I might never find out who the people are, and what they are doing. [40]

Sometimes I get lonesome for a storm. A full-blown storm where everything changes. The sky goes through four days in an hour, the trees wail, little animals skitter in the mud and everything gets dark and goes completely wild. But it's really God—playing music in his favorite cathedral in heaven —shattering stained glass—playing a gigantic organ—thundering on the keys—perfect harmony—perfect joy. [41]

Although Miss Baez does not actually talk this way when she is kept from the typewriter, she does try, perhaps unconsciously, to hang on to the innocence and turbulence and capacity for wonder, however ersatz or shallow, of her own or of anyone's adolescence. This openness, this vulnerability, is of course precisely the reason why she is so able to "come through" to all the young and lonely and inarticulate, to all those who suspect that no one else in the world understands about beauty and hurt and love and brotherhood. Perhaps because she is older now, Miss Baez is sometimes troubled that she means, to a great many of her admirers, everything that is beautiful and true. [42]

"I'm not very happy with my thinking about it," she says. "Sometimes I tell myself, 'Come on, Baez, you're just like everybody else,' but then I'm not happy with that either." [43]

"Not everybody else has the voice," Ira Sandperl interrupts dotingly. [44]

"Oh, it's all right to have the *voice,* the *voice* is all right . . ." [45]

She breaks off and concentrates for a long while on the buckle of her shoe. [46]

So now the girl whose life is a crystal teardrop has her own place, a place where the sun shines and the ambiguities can be set aside a little while longer, a place where everyone can be warm and loving and share confidences. "One day we went around the room and told a little about ourselves," she confides, "and I discovered that *boy,* I'd had it pretty easy." The late afternoon sun streaks the clean wooden floor and the birds sing in the scrub oaks and the beautiful children sit in their coats on the floor and listen to Ira Sandperl. [47]

"Are you a vegetarian, Ira?" someone asks idly.[48]

"Yes. Yes, I am." [49]

"Tell them, Ira," Joan Baez says. "It's nice." [50]

He leans back and looks toward the ceiling. "I was in the Sierra once." He pauses, and Joan Baez smiles approvingly. "I saw this magnificent tree *growing* out of bare rock, *thrusting* itself . . . and I thought *all right, tree,* if you want to live that much, *all right! All right!* O.K.! I won't chop you! I won't eat you! The one thing we all have in common is that we all want to *live!"* [51]

"But what about vegetables," a girl murmurs. [52]

"Well, I realized, of course, that as long as I was in *this flesh* and *this blood* I couldn't be *perfectly* nonviolent." [53]

It is getting late. Fifty cents apiece is collected for the next day's lunch, and someone reads a request from the Monterey County Board of Supervisors that citizens fly American flags to show that "Kooks, Commies, and Cowards do not represent our County," and someone else brings up the Vietnam Day Committee, and a dissident member who had visited Carmel. [54]

"Marv's an honest-to-God nonviolenter," Ira Sandperl declares. "A man of honesty and love." [55]

"He said he's an anarchist," someone interjects doubtfully. [56]

"Right," Ira Sandperl agrees. "Absolutely." [57]

"Would the V.D.C. call Gandhi bourgeois?" [58]

"Oh, they must know better, but they lead such bourgeois lives themselves . . ." [59]

"That's so true," says the dreamy blond boy with the violet marble. "You walk into their office, they're so unfriendly, so unfriendly and cold . . ." [60]

Everyone smiles lovingly at him. By now the sky outside is the color of his marble, but they are all reluctant about gathering up their books and magazines and records, about finding their car keys and ending the day, and by the time they are ready to leave Joan Baez is eating potato salad with her fingers from a bowl in the refrigerator, and everyone stays to share it, just a little while longer where it is warm. [61]

PURPOSE AND STRUCTURE

1. Why does Didion introduce her portrait with the proceedings of the board of supervisors? What would be gained or lost if the essay began with the description of Joan Baez in par. 10 or with the review of her background in par. 12?

2. What is the issue upon which the argument rests? What is the nature of the evidence presented as testimony by Dr. and Mrs. Petkuss, by their lawyer, by Joan Baez?

3. How do the details of Joan Baez's background (par. 12) prepare you for what follows?

4. " 'The easiest kind of relationship for me is with ten thousand people. . . . The hardest is with one.' " How does this statement (par. 14) illuminate her personality, her singing, her activities?

5. What is the nature of the evidence implicit in the account of the students and the activities of the Institute (pars. 17–24)?

6. Determine the focus in each of the several sections. What is the principle of organization? What demarcates one section from another? Could any section be eliminated without a substantive loss? How does the structure of the essay affect the argument?

7. " 'Everybody says I'm politically naïve, and I am. . . . So are the people running politics, or we wouldn't be in wars, would we' " (par. 32). How do these remarks of Joan Baez enhance our understanding of her? of the issue? of the evidence?

8. Why does Ira Sandperl say he is the villain (par. 34)?

DICTION AND TONE

1. What do the remarks of Mrs. Gerald Petkuss (pars. 1–3) contribute to purpose and tone?

2. What does Joan Baez's presence on her property during weekends have to do with the Petkusses' objection to the Institute (pars. 4–9)? What does it tell you about the Petkusses? about Didion's attitude toward them?

3. How does Didion employ satire, irony, and direct ridicule to persuade the reader? Cite specific passages. Is any of the satire directed at Joan Baez's associates and followers? Document your answer.

4. How does the phrase "her absence of guile" illuminate the character of Joan Baez (par. 10)? How does it illuminate the issue?

5. Why does Joan Baez smile "disingenuously" at the Petkusses (par. 11)?

6. Examine the descriptive phrases in par. 16. To what degree are they critical of Joan Baez? sympathetic? contradictory? congruent?

7. Identify the author's tone in pars. 17–24.

8. The phrase "threat to property values" recurs a number of times. How does it contribute to tone? How does it illuminate the issue?

9. The last two sections of the essay (pars. 35–46 and pars. 47–61) include a wide range of particulars about Joan Baez's associates, activities, thoughts, and feelings. How does the tone contribute to our understanding

of Joan Baez? of the issue? of the evidence? Of what does Didion wish to persuade the reader? Of what are you persuaded?

10. How does the phrase used to describe Joan Baez's life, "a crystal teardrop" (par. 47), relate to what has preceded? Is it an apt metaphor? Explain.

11. ". . . and the ambiguities can be set aside a little while longer . . ." (par. 47). Elaborate on the meaning of this remark of Didion's by referring to specific passages in the essay.

12. Interpret the subtitle of the portrait—"Where the Kissing Never Stops"—by alluding to both the substance and tone of the essay. In the light of your documented explanation, how would you sum up Didion's attitude toward her subject?

APPLICATIONS TO WRITING

1. Attend a meeting of your board of supervisors or of a committee in which there is a controversial issue to be resolved. Present the issue and the evidence and characterize the participants by means of narrative and dialogue.

2. Select one of your classes in which a large part of the hour is devoted to discussion. Characterize one of your contemporaries or your instructor by using the discussion as a point of departure.

3. Place a public figure of your choice in a variety of settings and situations that indirectly illuminate the person's character.

4. Satirize an individual or group by drawing upon a variety of approaches: brief character sketches, dialogue, introspection, description of setting, delineation of behavior, or whatever means enable you to give the reader a sense of immediacy and drama.

5. Justify the placement of the Didion essay under the rhetorical category of "Argument and Persuasion." Analyze the issue(s), the nature of the evidence, the subtle and controlled use of language, the literary devices that establish the tone, and finally the degree to which, and of what, you are persuaded.

A Wasp Stings Back

ROBERT CLAIBORNE

Over the past few years, American pop culture has acquired a new folk antihero: the Wasp. One slick magazine tells us that the White Anglo-Saxon Protestants rule New York City, while other media gurus credit (or discredit) them with ruling the country—and, by inference, ruining it. A Polish-American declares in a leading newspaper that Wasps have "no sense of honor." *Newsweek* patronizingly describes Chautauqua as a citadel of "Wasp values," while other folklorists characterize these values more explicitly as a compulsive commitment to the work ethic, emotional uptightness and sexual inhibition. The Wasps, in fact, are rapidly becoming the one minority that every other ethnic group—blacks, Italians, chicanos, Jews, Poles and all the rest—feels absolutely free to dump on. I have not yet had a friend greet me with "Did you hear the one about the two Wasps who . . . ?"—but any day now! [1]

I come of a long line of Wasps; if you disregard my French great-great-grandmother and a couple of putatively Irish ancestors of the same vintage, a rather pure line. My mother has long been one of the Colonial Dames, an organization some of whose members consider the Daughters of the American Revolution rather parvenu. My umpty-umpth Wasp great-grandfather, William Claiborne, founded the first European settlement in what is now Maryland (his farm and trading post were later ripped off by the Catholic Lord Baltimore, Maryland politics being much the same then as now). [2]

As a Wasp, the mildest thing I can say about the stereotype emerging from the current wave of anti-Wasp chic is that I don't recognize myself. As regards emotional uptightness and sexual inhibition, modesty forbids comment—though I dare say various friends and lovers of mine could testify on these points if they cared to. I will admit to enjoying work—because I am lucky enough to be able to work at what I enjoy—but not, I think, to the point of compulsiveness. And so far as ruling America, or even New York, is concerned, I can say flatly that (a) it's a damn lie because (b) if I *did* rule them, both would be in better shape than they are. Indeed I and all my Wasp relatives, taken in a lump, have far less clout with the powers that run this country than any one of the Buckleys or Kennedys (Irish Catholic), the Sulzbergers or Guggenheims (Jewish), or the late A. P. Giannini (Italian) of the Bank of America. [3]

Admittedly, both corporate and (to a lesser extent) political America are dominated by Wasps—just as (let us say) the garment industry is dominated by Jews, and organized crime by Italians. But to conclude from this that The Wasps are the American elite is as silly as to say that The Jews are cloak-and-suiters or The Italians are gangsters. Wasps, like other ethnics, come in all varieties, including criminals—political, corporate and otherwise. [4]

More seriously, I would like to say a word for the maligned "Wasp values," one of them in particular. As a matter of historical fact, it was we Wasps—by which I mean here the English-speaking peoples—who invented the idea of *limited governments*: that there are some things that no king, President or other official is allowed to do. It began more than seven centuries ago, with Magna Carta, and continued (to cite only the high spots) through the wrangles between Parliament and the Stuart kings, the Puritan Revolution of 1640, the English Bill of Rights of 1688, the American Revolution and our own Bill of Rights and Constitution. [5]

The Wasp principle of limited government emerged through protracted struggle with the much older principle of unlimited government. This latter was never more cogently expressed than at the trial of Charles I, when the hapless monarch informed his judges that, as an anointed king, he was not accountable to any court in the land. A not dissimilar position was taken more recently by another Wasp head of state—and with no more success; executive privilege went over no better in 1974 than divine right did in 1649. The notion that a king, a President or any other official can do as he damn well pleases has never played in Peoria—or Liverpool or Glasgow, Melbourne or Toronto. For more than 300 years, no Wasp nation has endured an absolute monarchy, dictatorship or any other form of unlimited government—which is something no Frenchman, Italian, German, Pole, Russian or Hispanic can say. [6]

It is perfectly true, of course, that we Wasps have on occasion imposed unlimited governments on other (usually darker) peoples. We have, that is, acted in much the same way as have most other nations that possessed the requisite power and opportunity—including many Third World nations whose leaders delight in lecturing us on political morality (for recent information on this point, consult the files on Biafra, Bangladesh and Brazil, Indian tribes of). Yet even here, Wasp values have played an honorable part. When you start with the idea that Englishmen are entitled to self-government, you end by conceding the same right to Africans and Indians. If you begin by declaring that all (white) men are created equal, you must sooner or later face up to the fact that blacks are also men—and conform your conduct, however reluctantly, to your values. [7]

Keeping the Wasp faith hasn't always been easy. We Wasps, like other people, don't always live up to our own principles, and those of us who don't, if occupying positions of power, can pose formidable problems to the rest of us. Time after time, in the name of anti-Communism, peace with honor or some other slippery shibboleth, we have been conned or bullied into tolerating government interference with our liberties and privacy in all sorts of covert—and sometimes overt—ways; time after time we have had to relearn the lesson that eternal vigilance is the price of liberty. [8]

It was a Wasp who uttered that last thought. And it was a congress of Wasps who, about the same time, denounced the executive privilege of George III and committed to the cause of liberty their lives, their fortune and—*pace* my Polish-American compatriot—their sacred honor. [9]

PURPOSE AND STRUCTURE

1. Claiborne's informal diction and casual tone disguise the care with which he presents his argument. Pars. 1–4 introduce the arguments against Wasps; par. 5 states the proposition—that Wasps invented the idea of limited governments; par. 6 presents the issue—"For more than 300 years no Wasp nation has endured an absolute monarchy, dictatorship or any other form of unlimited government—which is something no Frenchman, Italian, German, Pole, Russian, or Hispanic can say." What is the purpose of pars. 7–9?

2. What is the purpose of par. 3?

3. Are The Jews "cloak-and-suiters" (par. 4)? Are The Italians "gangsters" (par. 4)? Are The Wasps the "American elite" (par. 4)? Why does Claiborne ask the questions about Jews and Italians?

4. What is the function of the first sentence of par. 5?

5. In what nations are the following cities: Peoria, Liverpool, Glasgow, Melbourne, Toronto (par. 6)? Why are none of these the capitals of their nations?

6. Why is par. 9 a powerful conclusion to Claiborne's argument?

DICTION AND TONE

1. Claiborne's diction is informal: "feels absolutely free to dump on" (par. 1). Would his argument be more persuasive if he were more formal? Rewrite par. 1 omitting ironic diction ("media gurus," "folklorists") and slang. Compare the effectiveness of the two versions.

2. Would par. 3 be more effective if the tone were less mild?

3. Why is the informal diction ("My umpty-umpth Wasp great-grandfather" and "ripped off") of the last sentence of par. 2 especially persuasive?

APPLICATIONS TO WRITING

1. If you are not a Wasp, present your argument for your ethnic group. If you are a Wasp, sting the Wasps.

2. Defend another antihero of American pop culture. Choose your own or one of these: the McDonald's hamburger, readers of modern Gothic novels, *Playboy* magazine and its male readers, *Cosmopolitan* magazine and its female readers, Archy Bunker.

3. What is your most deeply-held belief? Argue for it as gracefully and informally as Claiborne argues.

A Modest Proposal

for Preventing the Children of Ireland from Being a Burden to Their Parents or Country

JONATHAN SWIFT

It is a melancholy object to those who walk through this great town or travel in the country, when they see the streets, the roads, and cabin-doors crowded with beggars of the female sex, followed by three, four, or six children, all in rags, and importuning every passenger for an alms. These mothers instead of being able to work for their honest livelihood, are forced to employ all their time in strolling to beg sustenance for their helpless infants, who, as they grow up, either turn thieves for want of work, or leave their dear native country, to fight for the Pretender in Spain, or sell themselves to the Barbadoes. [1]

I think it is agreed by all parties, that this prodigious number of children in the arms, or on the backs, or at the heels of their mothers, and frequently of their fathers, is in the present deplorable state of the kingdom a very great additional grievance; and therefore whoever could find out a fair, cheap, and easy method of making these children sound and useful members of the common-wealth, would deserve so well of the public as to have his statue set up for a preserver of the nation. [2]

But my intention is very far from being confined to provide only for the children of professed beggars; it is of a much greater extent, and shall take in the whole number of infants at a certain age, who are born of parents in effect as little able to support them, as those who demand our charity in the streets. [3]

As to my own part, having turned my thoughts, for many years, upon this important subject, and maturely weighed the several schemes of other projectors, I have always found them grossly mistaken in their computation. It is true, a child just dropt from its dam, may be supported by her milk for a solar year with little other nourishment, at most not above the value of two shillings, which the mother may certainly get, or the value in scraps, by her lawful occupation of begging; and it is exactly at one year old that I propose to provide for them in such a manner, as, instead of being a charge upon their parents, or the parish, or wanting food and raiment for the rest of their lives, they shall, on the contrary, contribute to the feeding and partly to the clothing of many thousands. [4]

There is likewise another great advantage in my scheme, that it will prevent those voluntary abortions, and that horrid practice of women murdering their bastard children, alas! too frequent among us—sacrificing the poor innocent babes, I doubt, more to avoid the expense than the shame—which would move tears and pity in the most savage and inhuman breast. [5]

The number of souls in this kingdom being usually reckoned one million and a half, of these I calculate there may be about two hundred thousand couple whose wives are breeders; from which number I subtract thirty thousand couples, who are able to maintain their own children, although I apprehend there cannot be so many, under the present distresses of the kingdom; but this being granted, there will remain an hundred and seventy thousand breeders. I again subtract fifty thousand, for those women who miscarry, or whose children die by accident or disease within the year. There only remain an hundred and twenty thousand children of poor parents annually born: The question therefore is, How this number shall be reared, and provided for? which, as I have already said, under the present situation of affairs, is utterly impossible by all the methods hitherto proposed; for we can neither employ them in handicraft or agriculture; we neither build houses, (I mean in the country) nor cultivate land: They can very seldom pick up a livelihood by stealing till they arrive at six years old, except where they are of towardly parts, although, I confess, they learn the rudiments much earlier; during which time they can however be properly looked upon only as probationers; as I have been informed by a principal gentleman in the county of Cavan, who protested to me, that he never knew above one or two instances under the age of six, even in a part of the kingdom so renowned for the quickest proficiency in that art. [6]

I am assured by our merchants, that a boy or a girl before twelve years old, is no salable commodity, and even when they come to this age, they will not yield above three pounds, or three pounds and half a crown at most, on the exchange; which cannot turn to account either to the parents or kingdom, the charge of nutriment and rags having been at least four times that value. [7]

I shall now therefore humbly propose my own thoughts, which I hope will not be liable to the least objection. [8]

I have been assured by a very knowing American of my acquaintance in London, that a young healthy child well nursed is at a year old a most delicious, nourishing, and wholesome food, whether stewed, roasted, baked, or boiled; and I make no doubt that it will equally serve in a fricassee, or a ragout. [9]

I do therefore humbly offer it to publick consideration, that of the hundred and twenty thousand children, already computed, twenty thousand may be reserved for breed, whereof only one fourth part to be males; which is more than we allow to sheep, black cattle, or swine; and my reason is that these children are seldom fruits of marriage, a circumstance not much regarded by our savages; therefore one male will be sufficient to serve four females. That the remaining hundred thousand may, at a year old, be offered in the sale to the persons of quality and fortune through the kingdom; always advising the mother to let them suck plentifully in the last month, so as to render them plump and fat for a good table. A child will make two dishes at an entertainment for friends; and when the family dines alone, the fore or hind quarter will make a reasonable dish, and seasoned with a little pepper or salt will be very good boiled on the fourth day, especially in winter. [10]

I have reckoned upon a medium that a child just born will weigh 12 pounds, and in a solar year, if tolerably nursed, increaseth to 28 pounds. [11]

I grant this food will be somewhat dear, and therefore very proper for landlords, who, as they have already devoured most of the parents, seem to have the best title to the children. [12]

Infants' flesh will be in season throughout the year, but more plentiful in March, and a little before and after; for we are told by a grave author, an eminent French physician, that fish being a prolific diet, there are more children born in Roman Catholic countries about nine months after Lent than at any other season; therefore, reckoning a year after Lent, the markets will be more glutted than usual, because the number of popish infants is at least three to one in this kingdom: and therefore it will have one other collateral advantage, by lessening the number of papists among us. [13]

I have already computed the charge of nursing a beggar's child (in which list I reckon all cottagers, laborers, and four-fifths of the farmers) to be about two shillings per annum, rags included; and I believe no gentleman would repine to give ten shillings for the carcass of a good fat child, which, as I have said, will make four dishes of excellent nutritive meat, when he hath only some particular friend or his own family to dine with him. Thus the squire will learn to be a good landlord, and grow popular among his tenants; the mother will have eight shillings net profit, and be fit for work till she produces another child. [14]

Those who are more thrifty (as I must confess the times require) may flay the carcass, the skin of which artificially dressed will make admirable gloves for ladies, and summer boots for the fine gentlemen. [15]

As to our city of Dublin, shambles may be appointed for this purpose in the most convenient parts of it, and butchers we may be assured will not be wanting; although I rather recommend buying the children alive and dressing them hot from the knife, as we do roasting pigs. [16]

A very worthy person, a true lover of his country, and whose virtues I highly esteem, was lately pleased in discoursing on this matter to offer a refinement upon my scheme. He said that many gentlemen of this kingdom, having of late destroyed their deer, he conceived that the want of venison might be well supplied by the bodies of young lads and maidens, not exceeding fourteen years of age nor under twelve; so great a number of both sexes in every country being now ready to starve for want of work and service; and these to be disposed of by their parents if alive, or otherwise by their nearest relations. But with due deference to so excellent a friend, and so deserving a patriot, I cannot be altogether in his sentiments; for as to the males, my American acquaintance assured me from frequent experience, that their flesh was generally tough and lean, like that of our schoolboys, by continual exercise, and their taste disagreeable, and to fatten them would not answer the charge. Then as to the females, it would, I think with humble submission, be a loss to the publick, because they soon would become breeders themselves: And besides it is not improbable that some scrupulous people might be apt to censure such a practice (although indeed very unjustly) as a little bordering upon cruelty, which, I confess, hath always been with me the strongest objection against any project, how well soever intended. [17]

But in order to justify my friend, he confessed that this expedient was put into his head by the famous Psalmanazar, a native of the island Formosa, who came from thence to London, above twenty years ago, and in conversation told my friend, that in his country when any young person happened to be put to death, the executioner sold the carcass to persons of quality, as a prime dainty, and that, in his time, the body of a plump girl of fifteen, who was crucified for an attempt to poison the Emperor, was sold to his Imperial Majesty's prime minister of state, and other great mandarins of the court, in joints from the gibbet, at four hundred crowns. Neither indeed can I deny, that if the same use were made of several plump young girls in this town, who, without one single groat to their fortunes, cannot stir abroad without a chair, and appear at a play-house and assemblies in foreign fineries which they never will pay for, the kingdom would not be the worse. [18]

Some persons of a desponding spirit are in great concern about that vast number of poor people, who are aged, diseased, or maimed, and I have been desired to employ my thoughts what course may be taken, to ease the nation of so grievous an encumbrance. But I am not in the least pain upon that matter, because it is very well known, that they are every day dying, and rotting, by cold, and famine, and filth, and vermin, as fast as can be reasonably expected. And as to the younger labourers, they are now in almost as hopeful a condition. They cannot get work, and consequently pine away for want of nourishment, to a degree, that if at any time they are accidentally hired to common labour, they have not strength to perform it, and thus the country and themselves are happily delivered from the evils to come. [19]

I have too long digressed, and therefore shall return to my subject. I think the advantages by the proposal which I have made are obvious and many, as well as of the highest importance. [20]

For *first*, as I have already observed, it would greatly lessen the number of papists, with whom we are yearly over-run, being the principal breeders of the nation, as well as our most dangerous enemies, and who stay at home on purpose with a design to deliver the kingdom to the Pretender, hoping to take their advantage by the absence of so many good Protestants, who have chosen rather to leave their country, than stay at home, and pay tithes against their conscience to an Episcopal curate. [21]

Secondly, the poorer tenants will have something valuable of their own, which by law may be made liable to distress and help to pay their landlord's rent, their corn and cattle being already seized, and money a thing unknown. [22]

Thirdly, whereas the maintenance of an hundred thousand children, from two years old and upward, cannot be computed at less than ten shillings apiece per annum, the nation's stock will be thereby increased fifty thousand pounds per annum, besides the profit of a new dish introduced to the tables of all gentlemen of fortune in the kingdom who have any refinement in taste. And the money will circulate among ourselves, the goods being entirely of our own growth and manufacture. [23]

Fourthly, the constant breeders, beside the gain of eight shillings sterling per annum by the sale of their children, will be rid of the charge of maintaining them after the first year. [24]

Fifthly, this food would likewise bring great custom to taverns, where the vintners will certainly be so prudent as to procure the best receipts for dressing it to perfection, and consequently have their houses frequented by all the fine gentlemen who justly value themselves upon their knowledge in good eating; and a skillful cook, who understands how to oblige his guests, will contrive to make it as expensive as they please. [25]

Sixthly, this would be a great inducement to marriage, which all wise nations have either encouraged by rewards or enforced by laws and penalties. It would increase the care and the tenderness of mothers toward their children, when they were sure of a settlement for life to the poor babes, provided in some sort by the public, to their annual profit instead of expense. We should soon see an honest emulation among the married women, which of them could bring the fattest child to the market. Men would become as fond of their wives during the time of their pregnancy as they are now of their mares in foal, their cows in calf, their sows when they are ready to farrow; nor offer to beat or kick them (as is too frequent a practice) for fear of a miscarriage. [26]

Many other advantages might be enumerated. For instance, the addition of some thousand carcasses in our exportation of barreled beef, the propagation of swine's flesh, and improvement in the art of making good bacon, so much wanted among us by the great destruction of pigs, too frequent at our tables; which are no way comparable in taste or magnificence to a well-grown, fat, yearling child, which roasted whole will make a considerable figure at a lord mayor's feast or any other public entertainment. But this and many others I omit, being studious of brevity. [27]

Supposing that one thousand families in this city would be constant customers for infants' flesh, besides others who might have it at merry meetings, particularly at weddings and christenings, I compute that Dublin would take off annually about twenty thousand carcasses; and the rest of the kingdom (where probably they will be sold somewhat cheaper) the remaining eighty thousand. [28]

I can think of no one objection that will possibly be raised against this proposal, unless it should be urged that the number of people will be thereby much lessened in the kingdom. This I freely own, and 'twas indeed one principal design in offering it to the world. I desire the reader will observe that I calculate my remedy for this one individual kingdom of Ireland, and for no other that ever was, is, or, I think, ever can be upon earth. Therefore let no man talk to me of other expedients: of taxing our absentees at five shillings a pound: of using neither clothes, nor household furniture, except what is of our own growth and manufacture: of utterly rejecting the materials and instruments that promote foreign luxury: of curing the expensiveness of pride, vanity, idleness, and gaming in our women: of introducing a vein of parsimony, prudence and temperance: of learning to love our country, wherein we differ even from Laplanders, and the inhabitants of Topinamboo: of quitting our animosities, and factions, nor act any longer like the Jews, who were murdering one another at the very moment their city was taken: of being a little cautious not to sell our country and consciences for nothing: of teaching landlords to have at least one degree of mercy towards their tenants. Lastly, of putting a spirit of honesty, industry, and skill into our shopkeepers, who, if a resolution could now be taken to buy only our native goods, would immediately unite to cheat and exact upon us in the price, the measure, and the goodness, nor could ever yet be brought to make one fair proposal of just dealing, though often and earnestly invited to it. [29]

Therefore I repeat, let no man talk to me of these and the like expedients, till he hath at least some glimpse of hope, that there will ever be some hearty and sincere attempt to put them in practice. [30]

But as to my self, having been wearied out for many years with offering vain, idle, visionary thoughts, and at length utterly despairing of success, I fortunately fell upon this proposal, which as it is wholly new, so it hath something solid and real, of no expense and little trouble, full in our own power, and whereby we can incur no danger in disobliging England. For this kind of commodity will not bear exportation, the flesh being of too tender a consistence, to admit a long continuance in salt, although perhaps I could name a country, which would be glad to eat up our whole nation without it. [31]

After all, I am not so violently bent upon my own opinion, as to reject any offer, proposed by wise men, which shall be found equally innocent, cheap, easy, and effectual. But before something of that kind shall be advanced in contradiction to my scheme, and offering a better, I desire the author or authors, will be pleased maturely to consider two points. *First*, as things now stand, how they will be able to find food and raiment for a hundred thousand useless mouths and backs. And *Secondly*, there being a round million of creatures in human figure throughout this kingdom, whose whole subsistence put into a common stock would leave them in debt two millions of pounds sterling, adding those who are beggars by profession, to the bulk of farmers, cottagers and labourers, with their wives and children, who are beggars in effect; I desire those politicians, who dislike my overture, and may perhaps be so bold to attempt an answer, that they will first ask the parents of these mortals, whether they would not at this day think it a great happiness to have been sold for food at a year old, in the manner I prescribe, and thereby have avoided such a perpetual scene of misfortunes as they have since gone through, by the oppression of landlords, the impossibility of paying rent without money or trade, the want of common sustenance, with neither house nor clothes to cover them from the inclemencies of the weather, and the most inevitable prospect of entailing the like or greater miseries upon their breed for ever. [32]

I profess, in the sincerity of my heart, that I have not the least personal interest in endeavoring to promote this necessary work, having no other motive than the public good of my country, by advancing our trade, providing for infants, relieving the poor, and giving some pleasure to the rich. I have no children by which I can propose to get a single penny; the youngest being nine years old, and my wife past child-bearing. [33]

PURPOSE AND STRUCTURE

1. In discussing "A Modest Proposal" it is important to distinguish between the character of Swift and the character he *assumes* for the purpose of writing the essay. This assumed character, frequently referred to as a mask through which Swift writes, will hereafter be called the *narrator*. This distinction is important, for the effectiveness of the essay depends in part upon the narrator's inability to comprehend fully all the implications of what he is suggesting. He is morally blind. As you will see, Swift reveals this blindness by degrees; at the same time he develops a complex but narrow narrator whose two dominant characteristics are his extreme rationality and his conception of humanity solely in terms of economics—utility and value. (See Irony, Perspective, Tone in Glossary.)

2. The first seven paragraphs—up to "I shall now therefore humbly propose my own thoughts"—constitute an introduction. Identify at least two purposes of this lengthy introduction.

3. What is your impression of the narrator of the first three paragraphs? Consider such language as "this great town," "dear native country," "sound and useful members of the common-wealth." Whom or what does he sound like?

4. The moral nature of the narrator begins to emerge in par. 4. What one word dehumanizes his fellow countrymen?

5. Par. 6 continues this dehumanization. What one word in the first sentence reveals the narrator's attitudes toward people? Notice how the choice of words maintains his tone.

6. In par. 6 the narrator assumes a highly objective attitude. What does he gain? What do the mathematical tabulations say about the narrator? about the proposal itself?

7. Some of the horror of "A Modest Proposal" grows out of the narrator's inability to consider human misery in any terms other than economic ones. Swift handles this inability in an increasingly subtle fashion. For example, the narrator lists six advantages to his proposal. In the sixth advantage, what does he assume to be the source of decent human behavior? How is this consistent with his character?

8. The last two sentences of the essay are especially revealing as a commentary on human nature. In them the narrator anticipates an objection to his proposal and answers it. What is the objection he anticipates? If his anticipation is correct, what does this say about his audience?

DICTION AND TONE

1. In par. 2 notice how "present deplorable state of the kingdom" makes the presence of starving children regrettable not for the children's sakes, but for the nation's. What words in the rest of the paragraph sustain this attitude?

2. In the last sentence of par. 6, what is the effect of *livelihood, towardly, probationers, renowned?*

3. In par. 7, what is the effect of *commodity?*

4. Par. 9 is straightforward—almost blunt—and yet rather elegantly written. Discrepancy between elegance of statement and blunt meaning is usually discouraged. What is gained here?

5. Compare the first and last sentences of par. 10. Which evokes the most horror? Defend your answer using some of the principles discussed under Abstraction in the Glossary.

6. Par. 12 is a brilliant sentence. What is the significance of *therefore?* Of *proper?* Is *devoured* meant literally? Why is "best title" particularly appropriate?

7. In par. 14 is *gentleman* appropriate? Why *"fine* gentlemen" in par. 15?

8. In par. 19, explain the effect of "as fast as can be reasonably expected."

APPLICATIONS TO WRITING

1. Write your own modest proposal. You may suggest solutions to problems in such areas as unemployment, food distribution, education, race relations, foreign policy. If you prefer, focus attention on some problem in your school or community. A few words of caution: Swift makes only *one* outlandish assumption—that children be consumed as food—and the remainder of his argument follows quite logically. The more outlandish assumptions you make, the weaker your essay will be. Notice also that your essay must be logical. Consistency of tone, highly important, will depend on your ability to maintain a good "mask" and on your sense of appropriate diction.

2. "A Modest Proposal" is frequently called the greatest piece of sustained irony in English literature. Write an extended definition of irony

based on your understanding of this essay. Support your generalizations with evidence from the essay.

Who Finally Would Do the Dishes?
from *The Prisoner of Sex*

NORMAN MAILER

Still he had not answered the question with which he began. Who finally would do the dishes? And passed in his reading through an Agreement drawn between husband and wife where every piece of housework was divided, and duty-shifts to baby-sit were divided, and weekends where the man worked to compensate the wife for chores of weekday transportation. Shopping was balanced, cooking was split, so was the transportation of children. It was a crystal of a contract bound to serve as model for many another, and began on this high and fundamental premise:

We reject the notion that the work which brings in more money is more valuable. The ability to earn more money is already a privilege which must not be compounded by enabling the larger earner to buy out his/her duties and put the burden on the one who earns less, or on someone hired from outside. [1]

We believe that each member of the family has an equal right to his/her own time, work, value, choices. As long as all duties are performed, each person may use his/her extra time any way he/she chooses. If he/she wants to use it making money, fine. If he/she wants to spend it with spouse, fine. If not, fine. [2]

As parents we believe we must share all responsibility for taking care of our children and home—not only the work, but the responsibility. At least during the first year of this agreement, *sharing responsibility* shall mean:

1. Dividing the *jobs* (see "Job Breakdown" below); and
2. Dividing the *time* (see "Schedule" below) for which each parent is responsible. [3]

There were details which stung:

10. Cleaning: Husband does all the house-cleaning, in exchange for wife's extra childcare (3:00 to 6:30 daily) and sick care. [4]
11. Laundry: Wife does most home laundry. Husband does all dry cleaning delivery and pick up. Wife strips beds, husband remakes them. [5]

No, he would not be married to such a woman. If he were obliged to have a roommate, he would pick a man. The question had been answered. He could love a woman and she might even sprain her back before a hundred sinks of dishes in a month, but he would not be happy to help her if his work should suffer, no, not unless her work was as valuable as his own. But he was complacent with the importance of respecting his work—what an agony for a man if work were meaningless: then all such rights were lost before a woman. So it was another corollary of Liberation that as technique reduced labor to activities which were often absurd, like punching the buttons on an automatic machine, so did the housework of women take on magnitude, for their work was directed at least to a basic end. And thinking of that Marriage Agreement which was nearly the equal of a legal code, he was reminded of his old campaign for mayor when Breslin[1] and himself had called for New York City to become the fifty-first state and had preached Power to the Neighborhoods and offered the idea that a modern man would do well to live in a small society of his own choosing, in a legally constituted village within the city, or a corporate zone, in a traditional religious park or a revolutionary commune—the value would be to discover which of one's social ideas were able to work. For nothing was more difficult to learn in the modern world. Of course, it had been a scheme with all the profound naïveté of assuming that people voted as an expression of their desire when he had yet to learn the electorate obtained satisfaction by venting their hate. Still he wondered if it was not likely that the politics of government and property would yet begin to alter into the politics of sex. Perhaps he had been living with the subject too closely, but he saw no major reason why one could not await a world—assuming there would be a world—where people would found their politics on the fundamental demands they

[1] Jimmy Breslin is a New York newspaperman, syndicated columnist, and unsuccessful candidate for New York City Council President.

would make of sex. So might there yet be towns within the city which were homosexual, and whole blocks legally organized for married couples who thought the orgy was ground for the progessive action of the day. And there would be mournful areas of the city deserted on Sunday, all suitable for the mood of masturbators who liked the open air and the street, perhaps even pseudo-Victorian quarters where brothels could again be found. There could be city turfs steaming with the nuances of bisexuals living on top of bisexuals, and funky tracts for old-fashioned lovers where the man was the rock of the home; there would always be horizons blocked by housing projects vast as the legislation which had gone into the division of household duties between women and men. There would be every kind of world in the city, but their laws would be founded on sex. It was, he supposed, the rationalized end of that violence which had once existed between men and women as the crossed potential of their love, violence which was part perhaps of the force to achieve and the force to scourge, it had been that violence which entered into all the irrationality of love, "the rooting out of the old bodily shame" of which Lawrence[2] had spoke, and the rooting out of the fear in women that they were more violent than their men, and would betray them, or destroy them in the transcendence of sex; yes, the play of violence had been the drama of love between a man and a woman, for too little, and they were friends never to be gripped by any attraction which could send them far; too much, and they were ruined, or love was ruined, or they must degenerate to bully and victim, become no better than a transmission belt to bring in the violence and injustice of the world outside, bring it in to poison the cowardice of their home. But the violence of lovers was on its way to disappear in all the other deaths of the primitive which one could anticipate as the human became the human unit—human violence would go to some place outside (like the smog) where it could return to kill them by slow degree—and equally. But he had made his determination on beginning his piece that he would not write of sex and violence too long, for that would oblige him to end in the unnatural position of explaining what he had attempted in other work. So he would step aside by remarking that a look at sex and violence was the proper ground of a novel and he would rather try it there. And content himself now with one last look at

[2] D. H. Lawrence was a twentieth-century English novelist, poet, short story writer, and essayist who rebelled against Anglo-Saxon puritanism and social conventions.

his remark that "the prime responsibility of a woman probably is to be on earth long enough to find the best mate for herself, and conceive children who will improve the species." Was it too late now to suggest that in the search for the best mate was concealed the bravery of a woman, and to find the best mate, whatever ugly or brutal or tyrannical or unbalanced or heart-searing son of misery he might appear, his values nonetheless, mysterious fellow of values, would inevitably present themselves in those twenty-three chromosomes able to cut through fashion, tradition, and class. [6]

There is a famous study of neurotics which shows that patients who received psychoanalysis had an improvement rate of 44 percent; psychotherapy was more effective—a rate of 64 percent; and 72 percent was the unhappiest improvement, for that was the rate of cure of patients who had never been treated at all. The Eysenck study it is called, and later studies confirm its results. It was, the prisoner decided, a way of telling us that the taste in the mouth of explaining too much is the seating of the next disease. One cannot improve the human condition through comfort and security, or through generalized sympathy and support—it is possible the untreated patients got better because the violence of their neurosis was not drained. The cure of the human was in his leap. [7]

But now he could comprehend why woman bridled at the thought she must "find the best mate for herself and . . . improve the species." How full of death was the idea if one looked at any scheme which brought people who were fundamentally unattracted to each other down marriage aisles, their qualifications superb, their qualities neuter. So he was grateful to a writer who wrote a book. *The Lady,* published in 1910, Emily James Putnam, first dean of Barnard. She was a writer with a whip of the loveliest wit. He would give the last quotation to her for she had given the hint of a way. [8]

Apart from the crude economic question, the things that most women mean when they speak of "happiness," that is, love and children and the little republic of the home, depend upon the favour of men, and the qualities that win this favour are not in general those that are most useful for other purposes. A girl should not be too intelligent or too good or too highly differentiated in any direction. Like a ready-made garment she should be designed to fit the average man. She should have "just about as much religion as my William likes." The age-long operation of this rule, by which the least strongly individualised women are the most likely to have a chance to transmit their qualities, has given it the air of a natural law. [9]

It was finally obvious. Women must have their rights to a life which would allow them to look for a mate. And there would be no free search until they were liberated. So let woman be what she would, and what she could. Let her cohabit on elephants if she had to, and fuck with Borzoi hounds, let her bed with eight pricks and a whistle, yes, give her freedom and let her burn it, or blow it, or build it to triumph or collapse. Let her conceive her children, and kill them in the womb if she thought they did not have it, let her travel to the moon, write the great American novel, and allow her husband to send her off to work with her lunch pail and a cigar; she could kiss the cooze of forty-one Rockettes in Macy's store window; she could legislate, incarcerate, and wear a uniform; she could die of every male disease, and years of burden was the first, for she might learn that women worked at onerous duties and men worked for egos which were worse than onerous and often insane. So women could have the right to die of men's diseases, yes, and might try to live with men's egos in their own skull case and he would cheer them on their way—would he? Yes, he thought that perhaps they may as well do what they desired if the anger of the centuries was having its say. Finally, he would agree with everything they asked but to quit the womb, for finally a day had to come when women shattered the pearl of their love for pristine and feminine will and found the man, yes that man in the million who could become the point of the seed which would give an egg back to nature, and let the woman return with a babe who came from the root of God's desire to go all the way, wherever was that way. And who was there to know that God was not the greatest lover of them all? The idiocy was to assume the oyster and the clam knew more than the trees and the grass. (Unless dear God was black and half-Jewish and a woman, and small and mean as motherwit. We will never know until we take the trip. And so saying realized he had been able to end a portentous piece in the soft sweet flesh of parentheses.) [10]

PURPOSE AND STRUCTURE

1. Is Mailer's initial question one that *leads to* the issue or is it the central issue itself? Examine the facts and opinions in the subsequent paragraphs to determine your answer. If it is not the issue, what is?

2. Does Mailer proceed deductively by moving from certain premises to a conclusion or inductively by generalizing from a number of instances and drawing a conclusion? Cite evidence for your decision.

3. How does Mailer develop his idea that the politics of government and property might yet become the politics of sex?

4. Par. 6 treats a number of interrelated topics. Jot them down so that you can determine how they relate to each other and how they may be subsumed under a topic sentence. Formulate the topic sentence.

5. How does the Eysenck study relate to Mailer's argument?

6. Is there a contradiction between his statement in par. 6 concerning " 'the prime responsibility of a woman' " and that in par. 10?

7. Note the parallel structure within parallel structure in the final paragraph. How does it contribute to purpose and tone?

8. With what statements does Mailer make concessions, if any?

9. Examine the details in par. 10. What do they tell you about Mailer's attitude toward men and women? toward himself?

DICTION AND TONE

1. How does the tone change after the citations from the marriage contract?

2. How is the tone affected by Mailer's use of the third person? By referring back to his attitudes, account for Mailer's alluding to himself as "the prisoner" (par. 7).

3. Interpret the statement, "the cure of the human was in his leap" (par. 7). How does the metaphor relate to what has preceded?

4. How do you interpret "their qualifications superb, their qualities neuter" (par. 8)?

5. Why does Mailer call these paragraphs "portentous" (10)?

6. What does the final parenthesis contribute to tone?

7. In the quotation from *The Lady* (par. 9) it is suggested that " 'like a ready-made garment she (a girl) should be designed to fit the average man.' " To what degree does Mailer's argument support or refute this view?

8. Is Mailer trying to persuade the reader? Of what? What evidence is there that he is trying to persuade himself? Of what?

9. Is the diction in the final paragraph demeaning to women? to men? to Mailer?

APPLICATIONS TO WRITING

1. Write an argument refuting any or all of Mailer's statements. Clarify your issue and provide concrete evidence on which to rest your argument.

2. Write a marriage contract with which you could happily live and introduce it with the premises on which it is based.

3. Discuss your views of the prime responsibility of women or of men.

The Uses of Ecstasy
from *Education and Ecstasy*

GEORGE B. LEONARD

Unlimited amounts of power are coming into human hands, perhaps surpassing what even Huxley[1] could have imagined a few short years ago. For example, the "breeder" reactors now under development promise to produce more nuclear fuel than they can use. Human control of the death rate already has set into motion a possibly catastrophic population rise, though the means for controlling the birth rate also are available. Both time and distance in the old sense have been annihilated. The whole globe is intimately intertwined with the means of achieving understanding or destruction. [1]

This situation, despite attempts at drawing historical parallels, cannot be viewed simply as more of the same. It is something entirely new,

[1] Aldous Huxley was a twentieth-century English novelist, satirist, and essayist, whose later novels—such as *Brave New World*—are concerned with the dangers of so-called scientific progress.

calling for entirely new responses. What is more important, it seems to demand a new kind of human being—one who is not driven by narrow competition, eager acquisition and aggression, but who spends his life in the joyful pursuit of learning. Such a human being, I feel, will result not so much through changed ideologies or economic systems as through changes in the process I have called "education." The idea of education as the most effective human change agent is by no means new. But I have tried to broaden and simplify education's definition, to expand its domain, to link it with the new technology and to alter the relationship between educator and learner. As a chief ingredient in all this, as well as an alternative to the old reinforcers, I have named "ecstasy"—joy, *ananda*,[2] the ultimate delight. [2]

Our society knows little about this ingredient. In fact, every civilization in our direct lineage has tended to fear and shun it as a threat to reason and order. In a sense, they have been right. It is hard to imagine a more revolutionary statement for us than "The natural condition of the human organism is joy." For, if this is true, we are being daily cheated, and perhaps the social system that so ruthlessly steals our birthright *should* be overthrown. [3]

How many of us can live through three or four utterly joyful days without feeling, shortly afterwards, that our plane will crash or that we shall be struck with lightning? It is deeply embedded, this societal teaching. And when a highly visible segment of our young people, sometimes through shortsighted means, devotes all its days and nights to the pursuit of joy, how many of us do not feel deeply threatened? Joy *does* threaten things-as-they-are. Ecstasy, like nuclear energy, *is* dangerous. The only thing that may turn out to be more dangerous is shunning it and clinging to the old ways that clearly are dragging us toward destruction. [4]

Perhaps it is time for scholars and pundits to engage in the serious study of delight. What are its dangers? What are its uses? I would suggest three primarily negative considerations as a beginning:

1. *Ecstasy is not necessarily opposed to reason.* On the other hand, it may help light the way toward relationships, societies and educational systems in which reason and emotion are no longer at odds; in which, in fact, the two are so in tune that the terms themselves, as opposites, will atrophy. [5]

[2] Bliss—one of the three characteristics of Brahma.

2. *Ecstasy is not necessarily opposed to order.* On the other hand, it may help us redefine order. In the new definition, a balanced natural ecology in which all creatures grow and act freely represents order. Our free-learning and joyful Kennedy School represents a far higher, more elegant form of order than does a school in which "order" is forced and artificial. Life is an ordering force. Man is an ordering animal. Order will continue to evolve. Ecstasy is implicated in changing not the quantity, but the quality of order. [6]

3. *Ecstasy is neither immoral nor moral in itself.* At times, forms of ecstasy have powered some of mankind's most destructive movements. The Third Reich, for example, exhibited a certain ecstatic mania. But Hitler's "joy" was used to bolster the old reinforcement system—competition, acquisition and aggression—carried to the most destructive extremes. It was not brought into play as an *alternative* reinforcement system designed to replace the old. [7]

In dealing with ecstasy, as with all powerful forces, context is crucial. The context I have suggested is neither the wantonly Dionysian[3] nor the purely contemplative, but the educational. Ecstasy is education's most powerful ally. It is reinforcer for and substance of the moment of learning. [8]

Knowing this, the master teacher pursues delight. Even those best known as great lecturers have turned their lecture halls into theaters, shameless in their use of spells and enchantments. Great men, as every schoolboy knows, have greeted their moments of learning with crazy joy. We learn how Archimedes[4] leaped crying, "Eureka!," from his bathtub; how Handel,[5] on finishing the "Hallelujah Chorus," told his servant, "I did think I did see all Heaven before me, and the great God himself"; how Nietzsche[6] wrote *Thus Spake Zarathustra:*

---

[3] *Dionysian* pertains to the Greek god of fertility and wine; the term is associated with celebration, sensuality, and passion, and is used in opposition to *Apollonian,* the rational and cerebral.

[4] Archimedes was a Syracusan mathematician, astronomer, and inventor (200 B.C.) whose treatises on the sphere and cylinder are still used.

[5] Handel was an eighteenth-century German composer and one of the greatest figures of the late Baroque period in music.

[6] Nietzsche was a nineteenth-century German philosopher, scholar, and poet who opposed the systematic philosophy of Hegel and rejected Western bourgeois civilization.

There is an ecstasy such that the immense strain of it is sometimes re-laxed by a flood of tears, along with which one's steps either rush or in-voluntarily lag, alternately. There is the feeling that one is completely out of hand, with the very distinct consciousness of an endless number of fine thrills and quiverings to the very toes. [9]

What we fail to acknowledge is that every child starts out as an Archimedes, a Handel, a Nietzsche. The eight-month-old who succeeds in balancing one block on another has made a connection no less mo-mentous for him than Nietzsche's. He cannot verbalize it so eloquently and probably would not bother to if he could; such moments are not so rare for him as for Nietzsche. Much of his life at that age, in fact, is learning. The possibility of an endless series of ecstatic moments stretches before him. We quell the ecstasy and the learning, but this is hard work and rarely is it entirely successful. Explaining why he was unable to think about scientific problems for a year after his final exams, Albert Einstein said:

It is in fact nothing short of a miracle that the modern methods of in-struction have not yet entirely strangled the holy curiosity of inquiry. . . . It is a very grave mistake to think that the enjoyment of seeing and search-ing can be promoted by means of coercion and a sense of duty. [10]

And yet, life and joy cannot be subdued. The blade of grass shatters the concrete. The spring flowers bloom in Hiroshima. An Einstein emerges from the European academies. Those who would reduce, con-trol, quell must lose in the end. The ecstatic forces of life, growth and change are too numerous, too various, too tumultuous. [11]

In the eighteenth century, the Swedish botanist Carolus Linnaeus thought he had catalogued all the species of animals and plants in the world, a total of 4,345. He was wrong. Biologists today estimate they have classified nearly two million different kinds of animals; botanists have identified more than 300,000 kinds of plants. And that is only a beginning. Entomologists believe that, if all forms of insects alone could be counted, they would total from two to ten million. Faced with this profusion, scientists have run out of suitable Latin and Greek names, and now grope for impressive-sounding words that mean nothing what-ever in any language. And all this life, the affirmation of development and change, has taken place in the surface film of an average-size planet of an average-size star in one of hundreds of millions of galaxies. If this planet were the size of an orange, the habitat of all living things would be no thicker than a piece of paper. [12]

Life has one ultimate message, "Yes!" repeated in infinite number and variety. Human life, channeled for millennia by Civilization, is only just beginning to express the diversity and range of which it is easily capable. To deny is to swim against the current of existence. To affirm, to follow ecstasy in learning—in spite of injustice, suffering, confusion and disappointment—is to move more easily toward an education, a society that would free the enormous potential of man. [13]

July the Fourth. A lake in the Georgia woods. The soft, still air of afternoon vibrates with a thousand lives: the mad, monotonous trance music of the cicadas rising and falling above the chatter of crickets, the drone of bees; cries of a Cooper's hawk on a dead tree across the lake; birdsong all around, a different blend for every change of sky or air. The acoustics are incredible. Sound floats across the lake, touches me, immediate and eternal. All is one and I am that one. [14]

I walk slowly toward the lake's edge. A blacksnake whistles away through high grasses. A pair of white herons that have been working their way around the borders of the lake rise with undulating, confident strokes. Disdainful, taking their own time, they fly on to a spot appropriately distant from me. *Perfect.* Over the water, a flycatcher shoots straight upward with wings fluttering fast, then spreading motionless at the apogee—a moment frozen in thin air. A buzzard, an inverted shadow, cruises overhead. And there on a slim pine branch (pine needles spread like star points) a tiny warbler is silhouetted, upside down. [15]

A turtle rests on the bank. I pick it up. Dark brown shell; long, translucent bear claws clawing air. A yellow spotted head lengthens, cranes around. Impersonal eyes see nothing, see everything. I return the turtle to its bank. Squatting down, I watch a dragonfly less than an inch long with wings like amber cellophane quivering on a weed in the burnt gold of late afternoon. [16]

What now? A green grasshopper, disturbed by my movements, has jumped into the lake. He kicks as in a spasm, then lies in the water. Two ripples move out, concentric circles signaling his plight. He kicks again, moving toward the tangled bank. Will he make it? Two more spasmodic kicks and he's in shallow water. The bottom is visible. Almost safe. And the fish is there, a light shadow appearing, fully in position, without movement. Though only as long as a hand, the fish is somehow terribly sinister. *Snakkk!* A sharp report, a mouth sound. Empty water. [17]

Later, just before the sun goes down, blue shadows settle into the spaces beneath the trees across the lake. The sky is a confusion of shifting clouds and colors. With twilight's advance, the colors richen, the sky comes to rest. After sundown, I take a rowboat out onto the water. The air is cooling, the trees are utterly still. White morning glories on the bank are closed for the night. Turtles peep out of the still water, curious rather than predatory. A wood thrush sings, its trill swelling suddenly to fill all the evening like a distended balloon. A wren sings, a cardinal, a warbler—all sweet singers. [18]

Darkness approaches. The songs end. Something is swimming, making steady progress along the shore toward my boat. The swimmer goes into the bank for a moment, curves out again, its ripples making a precise triangle behind it. It sees me, dives. And now I know the night hunters have awakened. Two frogs croak tentatively. A night hawk sweeps across the lake. I can barely make out a possum moving deliberately along the opposite bank. I head the boat back toward the bank. The lake is a faint gleam, the trees black silhouettes. [19]

This world is elegantly interconnected and all-involving. It cannot be compartmentalized. It does not cease. [20]

William Golding's[7] novel of some years back, *Lord of the Flies,* generally has been interpreted as a bitter commentary on man's nature. In it, a group of children, marooned on a deserted island, turn from Ralph, the voice of Civilized reason, and Piggy, his myopic egghead sidekick, to join Jack, who has been interpreted as the villain, the savage, the dark spirit in man that invariably emerges when the Civilized restraints are removed. [21]

But Golding stacked the deck in a way that comments more on Civilization than on "human nature." Ralph is "good," but dull, unimaginative and indecisive. Piggy has "mind," but not much else. He is physically and sensorially inept. Jack, on the other hand, is physically and mentally alert, resourceful, imaginative and creative. He encour-

[7] William Golding is a twentieth-century novelist best known for *Lord of the Flies.* He calls his books fables that express his worldview that men are basically evil.

ages his followers in games and chants, colorful costumes and face paint, ceremonies and a sense of community. He organizes successful pig hunts and provides his meat-hungry children with torchlit feasts. Meanwhile, Ralph and his dispirited followers sicken on their unvarying diet of fruit. What child would not follow Jack? When Golding makes Jack's group evil, he reveals the usual inability in our time to equate the ecstatic with the good. When he makes Civilized Ralph dull and inept, he reveals what he really feels about Civilization as he knows it. [22]

When men must serve as predictable, prefabricated components of a rigid social machine, the ecstatic is not particularly useful and may, in fact, erode the compartments so necessary for the machine's functioning. But when a society moves away from the mechanistic, when an individual may function as a free-roving seeker, when what we now term "leisure" occupies most of an individual's hours, ecstasy may usefully accompany almost every act. Technology is preparing a world in which we may be learners all life long. In this world, delight will not be a luxury but a necessity. [23]

I can recall little of what happened in school the winter I was fifteen. Perhaps that was the year everyone in my English class had to do a chapter-by-chapter synopsis of *Treasure Island*. But the afternoons and nights of that period still are vivid. I was infected with the ham-radio bug. My next-door neighbor, a boy two years older, had got me started, and I lived for months in a state of delicious excitement. I would rush home from school, knowing the day would not be long enough. I would work steadily, practicing code, devouring ham manuals and magazines, poring over catalogues of radio parts, building simple shortwave receivers. I loved everything about it. When later I read Gerard Manley Hopkins'[8] "Pied Beauty," the phrase, "all trades, their gear and tackle and trim," immediately summoned up the coils and condensers, the softly glowing vacuum tubes, the sizzle and smell of hot solder, the shining curls of metal drilled out of a chassis. [24]

One night, my radio experience came to a moment of climax. For weeks I had been working on my first major effort, a four-tube regenerative shortwave receiver. The design was "my own," derived

---

[8] Gerard Manley Hopkins was a late nineteenth-century English poet and Jesuit priest known for his innovations in poetic technique.

from circuits in the manuals and approved by my knowledgeable friend. Every part was of the highest quality, all housed in a professional-looking black metal cabinet. Every knob and dial was carefully positioned for efficiency and esthetics, and there was an oversized, freewheeling band-spread tuning knob. That particular night I had been working ever since running most of the way home from school. I had skipped dinner, fiercely overriding my parents' protests. And now, at about eleven o'clock, I soldered the last connection. [25]

With trembling hands, I connected the ground and the antenna, plugged in the socket and switched on the set. There was a low, reassuring hum and, after a suspenseful wait, the four tubes lit up. I increased the volume. Dead silence. Nothing. I checked all the switches and dials. No problem there. Perhaps it was the speaker. I plugged in the earphones. Still nothing. [26]

I couldn't imagine what was the matter. For the next hour or so, I went over every connection, traced the circuit until I was dizzy. Since I had splurged on all-new parts, I didn't even consider that one of them might be defective. The mystery, so powerful and unfathomable, could obviously have been cleared up in a few minutes by any well-equipped radio repairman. But, for me, its unraveling was momentous. [27]

The radio's circuit consisted of two stages. The first stage converted radio frequency waves to electrical impulses of an audible frequency; the second stage served as an amplifier for the electrical impulses coming from the first stage. I hit upon the idea of tapping the earphones in at the end of the first stage. Success! Static, code, voices. This seemed to indicate to me that the trouble lay somewhere in the second stage. On an impulse, however, I tied in a microphone at the very beginning of the second stage. Success again. The second stage worked. I could hear my voice coming from the speaker. [28]

At that very instant, the answer was clear: Both stages worked separately. The trouble had to lie in the coupling between them. My eyes went to a little green and silver coil (*the broken connection between subconscious and conscious, the hidden flaw between individual and community*). It *had* to be that impedance coil. With this certainty, I was quite overcome. I would gladly have broken into a radio store to get another one, but my friend, I found, had a spare. I tied it in, not bothering for the moment to solder it. And a universe poured into my room from the star-filled night. I spun the dial: a ham in Louisiana, in California; short wave broadcasts from England, Germany, Mexico,

Brazil. There was no end to it. I had put out new sensors. Where there had been nothing, there was *all of this.* [29]

Ecstasy is one of the trickier conditions to write about. But if there is such a thing as being transported, I was transported that night. And I was, as with every true learning experience, forever afterwards changed. [30]

Every child, every person can delight in learning. A new education is already here, thrusting up in spite of every barrier we have been able to build. Why not help it happen? [31]

PURPOSE AND STRUCTURE

1. What is the issue upon which the argument rests?

2. How does the writer's belief that "both time and distance in the old sense have been annihilated" relate to his argument?

3. What oppositions are set up in par. 2?

4. On what basis does the author assert that " 'the natural condition of the human organism is joy' " (par. 3)? Why is it a revolutionary statement?

5. On what three considerations does Leonard build his argument? Is the evidence offered in support of each point subjective or objective? Explain.

6. What is the point of the allusion to the Swedish botanist Carolus Linnaeus (par. 12)? How does it advance the argument?

7. How does Leonard draw upon the past to persuade the reader? What devices does he use to make it come alive?

8. How does the ultimate message, " 'Yes!,' " advance the argument and affect the tone (par. 13)?

9. How does personal reminiscence in pars. 13–18 relate to his argument?

10. To what senses does Leonard appeal in pars. 13–18?

11. How does par. 20 sum up the preceding paragraphs? How does its assertion relate to the uses of ecstasy?

12. In what sense does the author suggest that ecstasy may be dangerous?

DICTION AND TONE

1. What are the characteristics of human response that Leonard would replace with joy (par. 2)?

2. What does Leonard mean when he says "context is crucial" (par. 8)?

3. To what audience do you think this essay is directed? Justify your answer.

4. Compare and contrast the tone in pars. 1–12 with that in the ensuing paragraphs. Which is more persuasive? In spite of the difference in tone, how does the writer achieve unity?

5. Why does Leonard capitalize *Civilized* and *Civilization* (pars. 21–22)?

6. How does Leonard use the novel *Lord of the Flies* to distinguish between "Civilization" and " 'human nature' " (pars. 21–22)? How does the description of Jack make it obvious that the children would follow him?

7. How does Leonard's use of language convey his disdain for aspects of our culture?

8. How does the metaphor of the social machine affect the argument and the tone (par. 23)?

9. Identify and comment upon the varieties of tone employed in this essay.

APPLICATIONS TO WRITING

1. Develop an argument in which you take a position pro or con on the benefits and learning derived from sources other than those involved in your formal education. Move, as Leonard does, from the formal statement to the personal reminiscence.

2. "I was, as with every true learning experience, forever afterwards changed" (par. 30). Using Leonard's assertion as a thesis, write an argument developing it.

Androgyny

ANDREW KOPKIND

You see them in shopping malls and Manhattan boutiques, in locker rooms and ladies' lounges, in school rooms, factories, kitchens, bedrooms, on television and in the movies. They wear pants suits and leisure suits, jeans and caftans, blow-dry haircuts, herbal perfumes; they are rock singers who twirl their hips, coeds who dig the Alaskan pipeline, a football tackle who crochets, a Brownie in the Little League, a President-elect who broadcasts love and compassion and weeps at the news of his election. They practice the many ways of androgyny, but they rarely recognize its profound novelty. They are—we are—skirting the edge of a revolution in sexual consciousness so radical that it could make the disruptions of the last decade seem like tantrums in a sandbox. [1]

Androgyny—literally, man-woman—is as old as prehistoric myth and as new as next fall's fashions. It is as banal as unisex hairdos and as basic as human equality, as pop as David Bowie and as cultivated as Virginia Woolf. It stretches from Bloomsbury to Bloomingdale's. Its expressions are the many mixtures of manners, styles and values assigned by custom—or law—to only one or the other sex: dominance, breadwinning, decisiveness to males; dependence, child rearing, tenderness to females. Convention calls it a sin, or a joke, to reassign those roles; both comedy and religion contain plenty of cautionary tales on the subject. But androgyny implies not a mere exchange or reversal of the roles, but liberation from them, the removal of the stereotypes of sex, an escape from the jailhouse of gender. [2]

"Behavior should have no gender," Stanford psychologist Sandra Bem insists. What people do for a living, what they wear, how they express themselves or how they confront the everyday world has nothing to do with their sex types. That, at least, is the androgynous ideal. If true androgynes evolve from this heavily stereotyped society, they will be tender and dominant, dependent and decisive, ambitious and nurturing according to their human temperament, not their gender. [3]

But for most people, the reality of manners and morals in our sex-polarized civilization is so far from that ideal plane that it is hard to see how it will be reached, what is pushing us there—and why it should be an ideal in the first place. [4]

Simply to sense the androgynous current that runs beneath the surface of ordinary events is difficult enough. The heads that bob up seem only tenuously connected: Mick Jagger, Patti Smith, Twyla Tharp, Lauren Hutton, Cary Grant; tuxedoed women in *Vogue*; families that share a hair dryer in TV commercials; middle-aged couples in matching acrylic leisure/pants suits; father minding the kids while mothers go to the office. They all partake of an androgynous sensibility that was almost unknown a generation ago. Some people *look* androgynous: they incorporate masculine and feminine body characteristics and mannerisms in a hybrid whole. Others *behave* androgynously: they work, play or act in ways not completely "appropriate" to their gender. And still others *feel* androgynous: their emotions do not correspond to the list of acceptable passions assigned to their sex. [5]

There is no uniform scale yet in use that measures the development of an androgynous personality (although Sandra Bem is working on the problem: she believes healthy sexual adjustment should be plotted against androgynous perfection, not masculine/feminine polarity). Nor is there a way to chart the movement toward androgyny in the society at large. But almost everyone has impressions that something peculiar is happening to sex roles. By and large, role changing is still a joke or a sin. But one morning, not too far in the future, the critical mass of Americans may wake up and realize that androgyny is on its way—and all hell will break loose. [6]

The trend began decades ago, but between the death of Victoria and the dawn of Aquarius androgyny was confined to hothouse environments of intellectuals, actors, musicians and other freaks. It hardly moved out of Bloomsbury,[1] Greenwich Village or the Hollywood Hills. [7]

Then the marshaled forces of the sexual revolution in the late 1960s propelled androgyny out of its bohemian closets and into Middle American family rooms. The bottom line of feminism and gay liberation has been the obliteration of socially defined roles. Women no longer have to look, act or feel the way men's fantasies dictate. Homo-

---

[1] See paragraph 31.

sexuals can be free of the emotional straitjackets tailored by hetero-sexual demands. In back of those battlelines, others removed from the struggles have the opportunity—and the impetus—to summon up those parts of themselves that were always restrained by propriety. [8]

In the beginning the muse of androgyny created denim, unstyled and impersonal, then washed, crushed, crimped and flared—but preemi-nently the unisex texture. Soon men and women were sharing work boots, hiking boots, Frye boots, clogs, Adidas sneakers, Earth Shoes; jogging suits, snowmobile suits, jumpsuits, silk shirts, beads and bracelets, pendants and necklaces, turquoise rings, perfumes. [9]

"Men's scents used to be a joke," Annette Green of New York's Fragrance Foundation reports. "Hai Karate advertised with grunts. And then Aramis came along and it took the male perfume market seriously." And no wonder. American men last year spent $208 million on cologne, an increase of 18 percent over the previous year. According to *Beauty Fashion* magazine, "the sound barrier of masculinity has been smashed and the blue-collar worker does not consider it 'faggish' to use the heavier colognes." [10]

The androgynous sensibility invaded high fashion: Gernreich and Courreges added a dimension of spacey, sexy masculinity to feminine frills. Cardin began tailoring men's clothes to emphasize sleek figures and forms. Men and women could now wear their new suits with the same style of turtleneck sweater—and a piece of jewelry if they chose. The Marlboro dude became the Winston androgyne, showing off his gold good-luck charm hanging deep in his cleavage, his blow-dry hair immobile in strong wind or calm. [11]

The imported flotsam and jetsam of the Third World made its way from hippie head shops and college-town bazaars to fashionable unisex boutiques. Most of it was well-suited for androgynous wear: who knew whether maharajas or maharanis wore a particular style of shirt or piece of jewelry; who cared whether a camel driver or his wife fancied sheep-skin jackets. At home any sex could play the import game. [12]

Better than the Third World as a spring of unisex styles was Outer Space. If sex-typed fashions could be altered on the road from Morocco, they were ready-to-wear from Krypton. Androgyny is a prevailing theme in futurist and other-worldly literature: men and women in sci-fi movies set centuries ahead in time are often identically clothed, ornamented—and conveniently bald, whether because of evolution or advanced barbering. Space is the great sex leveler. Technology and convenience, at least, demand that Soviet male and female cosmonauts wear unisex clothing, perform the same tasks and treat each other as equals. It might somehow be awkward for a cosmonaut man to hold the space hatch open for a cosmonaut woman on their way down the stairs to a new planet. [13]

Space and science fiction allow a different kind of escape from mundane sex roles. Two of the most androgynous rock stars—David Bowie and Elton John—have futurist personae: Bowie has been, on different occasions, Ziggy Stardust (a man from Mars) and the Man Who Fell to Earth. John plays as Captain Fantastic and sings in "Rocket Man," one of his early hits, "I'm not the man they think I am at home/Oh! no, no, no/I'm a rocket man." And the most twisted androgynous fantasy of all is Alice Cooper, who transcends sex roles altogether with the force of corruption and mockery. [14]

The politics of pure androgyny has always had significant historical support, while under social attack. Philosophers and psychologists have maintained that each human has "masculine" and "feminine" characteristics, but society channels individuals into that category in which behavior matches sexual appearance. The other half—the unused complement of traits—is then lost, forgotten or repressed, often with dire results for the person's psyche or soul. [15]

Aristophanes, Plato's character in *The Symposium,* formulated the famous allegory of three original sexes—male, female and hermaphrodite—split into halves by Zeus; each half has spent the succeeding aeons searching for its mate to regain completion (as homosexual man, lesbian female and heterosexual). Hinduism, Buddhism and Zoroastrianism all contain visions of Creation that postulate androgynous beings cleaved into single, incomplete sexes. Freud and Jung saw evidence of continuing conflict between masculine and feminine instincts, or unconscious memories in the individual. Contemporary psychotherapists often encourage patients to awaken their submerged "other" selves to achieve healthy wholeness. In therapy, if not in life, men are supposed to cry and solicit affection, women are helped to express anger and assert their independence. D. H. Lawrence—by turns an egregious male chauvinist and prophet of androgyny—saw in "The Rainbow" the evolution of a feminine principle that would renew the world spoiled by men. Proust, Artaud, Cocteau, Apollinaire—there is a hidden literary history of androgyny that only now can be understood in a social context. [16]

But the doctors—of the church, of philosophy, of medicine and literature—have not always been helpful. They customarily confuse androgynous behavior with sexual preference or with gender identity. Their confusion has become common fallacy, so that many people mistake androgyny for bisexuality or homosexuality or neuter sexuality—or with hermaphroditism or transsexuality. It is none of the above. Androgyny is the principle that *unties* gender and sexual orientation from human activity. Androgynous people can be male or female, heterosexual or homosexual. They can be as sexually hot as Jagger or Dietrich or as cool as Bowie or Audrey Hepburn. They move toward an existence in which those aspects of sexuality do not confine their behavior. [17]

As for sexual preference, Sandra Bem argues that it is utterly irrelevant "to anything other than the individual's own love or pleasure," and should be ignored as a social fact, no more or less interesting than the color of one's eyes or the length of fingernails. Roles of emotion or behavior based on sex, she continues, are not only absurd but destructive of human health and happiness; to be poured into a masculine or feminine mold makes both men and women unable to cope with the complexities of life. [18]

In a series of devilishly clever experiments, in which subjects chose simple tasks or performed certain actions, Bem saw that the most highly "polarized" men and women neither enjoyed themselves nor performed effectively. In one test, in which subjects were supposed to interact with a tiny kitten, the "super-feminine" women could not deal with the nurturing task, while the more androgynous women handled the situation best. Bem and her colleagues have a long way to go to flesh out their pioneering studies. But they seem to have discovered that traditional sex roles constrict both men and women and impair their power to fulfill themselves in work and play. [19]

But if orientation and roles are irrelevant and absurd, gender clearly is not. "Even if people were all to become psychologically androgynous, the world would continue to consist of two sexes, male and female would continue to be one of the first and most basic dichotomies that young children would learn and no one would grow up ignorant of or even indifferent to his or her gender," Bem writes. The point is that even gender has limited relevance: it does not demand inevitable roles. Women can be comfortable with their female bodies, but they do not have to bear or raise children—unless they want to. Men can be secure in their masculine physiques, but they do not have to chase girls, play basketball, father families or join the career rat race—unless it pleases them to do so. Such decisions can be left to individual personality and inclination. [20]

Finally, it does not really matter whether traits of temperament are inherited or acquired, or even if they are in some ways attached to gender. Perhaps there are evolved "feminine" or "masculine" qualities— or perhaps they are arbitrarily assigned, like "masculine" and "feminine" rhymes, or "male" and "female" plugs and sockets. Not to worry: one follows or ignores the logic of one's instincts or wishes—not what social convention determines them to require. "Androgyny," Columbia Professor Carolyn Heilbrun writes, "seeks to liberate the individual from the confines of the appropriate." [21]

Definitions are necessary and distinctions are required precisely because androgyny is so ill-considered in our culture. We cannot describe it in our "dead language," as Adrienne Rich says scornfully, because our concepts and the words that signify them are tied to sex-role stereotypes. An aboriginal Eskimo who never left the North Pole could describe a world without snow only in terms of snow. We sexual aborigines can describe a world without sex roles only in terms of sex roles. [22]

Alexandra Kaplan and Joan Bean, whose compilation of recent research papers on androgyny (*Beyond Sex-Role Stereotypes*) marks the beginning of a new approach to sexual psychology, contend that androgynous people have always existed, but until now they have been "invisible" to social scientists—and almost everyone else except the odd poet or the chroniclers of the bizarre. So there is no readily available vocabulary to describe the "hybrid" androgynous qualities that are being born: the trait between dominance and dependence, synthesizing tender and competitive, or combining assertive and nurturing. [23]

If a man steps out of his assigned roles he is denigrated as a "sissy." If a woman oversteps hers, she is chastised as "mannish." More than most men, who have the power to set the language as well as the rules of social games, women and homosexuals have always known the perils of exceeding propriety. Even after a decade of women's liberation, females who dress, behave or work in previously "masculine" territory are conspicuous, isolated and subtly or blatantly condemned (often with patronizing praise). In the same way, gay men who inhabit the "feminine" category of man-loving are pushed into grotesque expressions of all the other qualities in that sex role: they are called "queens" and they act out that assigned part with mincing manners, campy styles and drag. If society says that a woman in a "man's job" is mannish, she will act that way; if it says gays are "sissies," they will ultimately act out their own parodies. [24]

Not only homosexuals are deformed by such typecasting. Men of whatever sexual orientation who exhibit tenderness or shyness, or who easily express their feelings, are usually treated with contempt or condescension. One of the saddest examples of the genre was Adlai Stevenson, whose sensitive, slightly vulnerable wit was widely deprecated in Washington as evidence of his lack of guts, vigor, clout—in short, "balls." Lyndon Johnson despised him for it: "Why, he has to sit down to pee," Johnson once said of Stevenson. So much for the popularity of androgynous qualities. [25]

Senator Muskie's well-known outburst of emotion in New Hampshire during his 1972 presidential primary campaign probably cost him the Democratic nomination. And this year, Jimmy Carter's lack of "decisiveness," his rhetoric of "compassion" and his soft-spoken manners surely diminished his popularity in those constituencies least responsive to those slightly androgynous qualities. Not for nothing did Carter slip in the polls as his personality became more familiar. Americans expect their presidents to be high up on the index of masculinity (self-reliant, defends own beliefs, independent, assertive, strong personality, competitive, individualistic, etc.) and nowhere near the items on the femininity list (yielding, shy, gullible, soft-spoken, compassionate, childlike, eager to soothe hurt feelings, etc.). [26]

Early in the primaries a particularly astute though unliberated aunt of a friend of mine saw Carter on television and decided some "presidential" dimension of masculinity was missing. *"Faigele!"* she pronounced in her Bronx Yiddish idiom—"Fairy!"—and walked away from the TV. Her idiom had no other word for what she saw. [27]

Carter is hardly a sexual ideologue's vision of an androgyne, nor did Muskie or Stevenson come close to that idea. Beneath their thinnish skins beat macho hearts. But it's obvious that, more than many political leaders, they moved slightly centerward from the polar masculine stereotype. Kennedy spoke of vigor and strength, Carter conveyed compassion and love. No matter how real or disingenuous either candidate's rhetoric may have been, the identity they projected was strikingly different. One writer on sexual topics recently mused that Carter's victory was an important sign of a changing national consciousness, and that perhaps an androgyne could someday be president of the United States. [28]

The President-elect is presumably no *faigele,* despite Aunt Frieda's suspicions, nor are most of the men who are beginning to acquire androgynous manners. But a sex-stereotyped society can imagine no other category for androgynous men except a sexual one. Similarly, most of the women who wear "man's style" clothes, sport unisex tastes and invade masculine precincts of work or study are not lesbians. Yet custom gives androgynous women pejorative labels and locks them in a sexual role. Even an acquisition of high fashion does not always help: the classiest models are called "Vogue dykes," an epithet that manages to combine the joke and the sin of androgyny. The most glaring irony of all is that in a more androgynous world it would not be necessary, or even intelligent, to make any distinctions or disclaimers of sexual orientation in relation to behavior. [29]

But in the sex-typed world there is clearly a connection between homosexual and feminist *culture* and androgynous *styles.* Gays in large measure make up the androgynous vanguard; feminists are both theoreticians and practitioners of androgyny. Sexual outcasts (it makes no difference whether self or society does the casting) are able to invent new roles because they are not allowed to maintain the old ones. Self-reliant, assertive women have to develop their own feminist culture: the dominant society will not let them back into the world of wallflowers and housewives on their own terms. Gay men who have been consigned to the "sissy" world of emotional self-consciousness cannot travel back to the land of passionless masculinity and cold rationality. But their new makeshift culture contains the available models for later androgynous styles. [30]

The preeminent example of an androgynous community in the early years of the century, way before the recent liberation movements were born, was the Bloomsbury set, the informal but internally cohesive group of English writers, critics, artists and floating intellectuals who hung on in a slightly unfashionable section of London during and after the First World War. At its center was Virginia Woolf, her husband Leonard, sister Vanessa Bell and brother-in-law Clive Bell, the biographer Lytton Strachey, the economist John Maynard Keynes and the critic Roger Fry. On the periphery, but very much revered, was the novelist E. M. Forster. [31]

The artistic and intellectual output of Bloomsbury was prodigious. But, most of all, it was a unique model of a civilized community based on equality. The members recognized the basis of their civilization: "The equality of the sexes, the outer manifestation of the equality of the masculine and feminine impulses, are essential to civilization," Carolyn Heilbrun writes of Bloomsbury in her trenchant study *Toward a Recognition of Androgyny*. Virginia Woolf was convinced that she and her world were approaching androgyny, although she feared that the ideal would explode as it neared reality; perfection and completion could not exist in imperfect, fragmented surroundings. She saw a signal of androgyny in a single, silent falling leaf, "pointing to a force in things which one has overlooked." [32]

Many of the Bloomsbury setters were homosexual or bisexual, and the byways of "inappropriate" sexuality were always very much in their hearts and minds. There were famous romantic triangles and quad-rangles, scandalous ruptures of ceremony, hilarious practical jokes. Lytton Strachey appeared before the tribunal trying him for conscientious objection to military service wearing earrings, shoulder-length hair, an outlandish robe, and carrying an air pillow, which he blew up before the judges. He said it was necessary for his hemorrhoids. When asked what action he would take if a German soldier attempted to rape his sister, he replied impishly, "I should try to interpose my body." The Bloomsbury biographer, David Gadd, calls Strachey's response "a memorable reply whose monstrous ambiguity was fully appreciated by Lytton's three sisters," who were in the courtroom. But despite the famous japes, a premium was placed on the conquest of the vices of the old social order: jealousy, competitiveness, vindictiveness. Because of the sexual orientation of many in the group, its self-proclaimed androgyny has always been confused with the preferences of the members. But the truth of the situation was the other way around: the members' extraordinary sexual orientation gave them both perspective and motivation to explore innovative, androgynous relationships. [33]

Bloomsbury gives historic context and some intellectual nuances to the new androgyny, but not much more. When you look for androgyny today you are apt to find it in much less transcendental places. Former Los Angeles Ram Rosey Greer crochets his own pretty things and sings a pop song, "It's All Right to Cry," but he owes little of his sensibility to Lytton Strachey. It is seen in fleeting glimpses: Minnesota Viking Fran Tarkenton sending a touchdown pass to teammate Sammy White, and the two of them celebrating the event by holding hands as they walk back down the field—not in the old back-slapping jock gesture but in a manner that two schoolgirls would have used. [34]

On the screen it is the androgynous Fred Astaire in *That's Entertainment, II,* soft-shoeing alongside the heavily masculine Gene Kelly— still charming and still macho after all these years. Or Garbo, Dietrich or Katherine Hepburn, in almost any of their old roles—but especially opposite leading men with an androgynous bent: Grant, for example, not Gable. [35]

In fact, there's so much androgynous manhood around that some new Hollywood stars are making a buck on the backlash. Sylvester Stallone, writer and hero of *Rocky,* told *The New York Times'* Judy Klemesrud, "I don't think that even Women's Lib wants all men to become limp-wristed librarians. I don't know what's happening to men these days. There's a trend toward a sleek, subdued sophistication and a lack of participation in sports. In discos, men and women look almost alike, and if you were a little bleary-eyed, you'd get them mixed up. I think it's wrong. . . . There doesn't seem to be enough real men to go around." [36]

Bloomsbury had indicated that in its origins androgyny would flower in the upper registers of social class and intellect, and that it would be carried along on a politically progressive, countercultural movement. Those connections still hold. Androgyny in the seventies has been limited to the educated middle class and the radical counterculture. You look for androgynous styles in *Vogue* and Bloomingdale's, not *McCall's* and Penny's. Economic status and social registry somehow give people the security to discard the anchors of sex roles. [37]

Androgyny in the twentieth century may have begun in England, but it is hardly surprising that it is blooming in America. There are both particular and general forces contributing to its forward motion. The economic necessity for women to work—and its social acceptance —has made the old roles of housewifery, and the emotions that go with them, absurd and often dysfunctional. Simply to break through conventional feminine roles is to move towards an androgynous synthesis. [38]

But beyond that, the constellation of brand-new needs, demands and desires in "postindustrial" America has brought across-the-board changes in consciousness. For instance, the transformation of the nature of work from farm and factory to "services" has propelled many young men out of traditional "masculine" work roles and the emotional haberdashery suited to those jobs. Their new roles often let them share family roles formerly consigned to women. The men do not automatically become androgynous, but they are not so securely tied to the masculine pole any more. [39]

Along the leading edge of change, the vectors point toward equality —in the political economy as well as the political culture. If the coming issue in government is redistribution of wealth, the issue in human relationships is the redistribution of power. It is equality not for its own sake, not because it is self-evident or endowed by the Creator, but because the next stages of social evolution cannot function well without it. The sage political economist Robert Heilbroner wrote recently that the gross inequalities of American capitalism will destroy it. In the same way, gross inequalities in communities and families will destroy them. Alexandra Kaplan and Joan Bean see androgyny growing as the structure of the acquisitive society weakens. "A society that supports androgyny would probably not be based on capitalistic consumerism, which is a direct outgrowth of the competitive, achievement-oriented values of the male model. Flexibility in sex-role norms seems to be more related to a social-welfare economy," they say. [40]

Gloria Steinem noted recently that hard and fast distinctions between the sexes always accompany stages of imperial expansion in a society—those times when men think it necessary to keep women semislaves, in order to bear and rear offspring for the expanding nation. As we near a no-growth, resource-short, shrinking political economy in America, she continues, the polarized patriarchy will begin to break up. [41]

In time, evolutionary changes may follow the economic ones. If women are less necessary as sexual objects and men as sexual subjects, their physical characteristics could be transformed. Gone would be the classic Rubenesque female, two-thirds breasts and hips; gone too the stallionoid male, the walking phallic symbol. There need be no dimunition of sexual activity or pleasure. In fact, psychologists find that sexual fulfillment is increased as partners move toward an androgynous center. One writer told me, "Men and women who keep to the myth of their sex type stay separated even when they're together. They are afraid of each other, always aware of the differences. They may extol those differences, but the important ones aren't in their sex attributes but in their humanity. Androgyny doesn't mean a race of sexless androids, but a wider variety of sexual possibilities than exists now." [42]

The convulsions that will accompany the collapse of the old sexual culture will make most recent political events seem puny by comparison. In fact, they may have already begun. A great deal of nonsense will be loosed upon the world, as freed men and women scramble for new standards of behavior and anchors of being. People will mistake transient excesses for final accountings, bemoan the leveling of differences, extol the former virtues. Those with vested interests in polarized roles will predict the direst consequences of androgyny. They will not only be men. Or women. Renee Richards, the transsexual, sees only calamity arising as the familiar signposts fall. [43]

"If someone can be sex-tied," she sighs, "there's so much less anxiety. I mean, I'd rather have pink rooms for girls and blue for boys. How can you tell who's who in a yellow room?" [44]

PURPOSE AND STRUCTURE

1. What is the issue the writer is attempting to prove? What evidence does he offer to support his argument?

2. Why is the topic sentence placed at the end of par. 1 instead of at the beginning? What is gained or lost?

3. The dominant method of organization used to develop the argument in pars. 2 and 3 is comparison and contrast. Cite examples. What other modes of development are used?

4. How is a transition made between pars. 2 and 3?

5. How does the writer classify the androgynous personality in par. 5?

6. How is each of the following fields drawn upon to provide evidence: popular culture, fashion, the third world, space and science fiction, history, politics, philosophy, psychology, psychotherapy, and literature?

7. How do Bem's experiments and theories advance the argument?

8. How does the discussion of the Bloomsbury group advance the argument (pars. 31–34)?

9. What causal relationships are expressed in pars. 38–39?

10. What does the final paragraph contribute to purpose and tone?

DICTION AND TONE

1. What do the phrases "jail house of gender" (par. 2) and "emotional straitjackets" (par. 8) tell you about the writer's purpose and tone?

2. Explain the use of the descriptive adjective *hothouse* in par. 7.

3. Cite a number of the shifts from formal to informal diction and try to account for them.

4. What does Heilbrun mean by liberating " 'the individual from the confines of the appropriate' " (par. 21)?

5. What does Kopkind mean when he observes that the sex roles to which individuals are assigned by society will ultimately be acted out by them in the form of parodies (par. 24)?

6. What is the author's attitude toward the typecasting he illustrates (pars. 25–30)? How do you know?

7. How does Kopkind's statement that "some new Hollywood stars are making a buck on the backlash" relate to his purpose and express his tone (par. 36)?

APPLICATIONS TO WRITING

1. In developing his argument, the author draws upon a large number of sources to which you do not have immediate access. Support or refute any of his statements by drawing upon your personal experience, observations, or reading. Be sure you clearly delineate the issue on which your argument is based.

2. Compare and contrast the attitudes of Sontag, Greer, Jong, Mailer, and Kopkind or any two of them. What do the issues they discuss have in common? What are their differences in perspective?

Angels on a Pin

A Modern Parable

ALEXANDER CALANDRA

Some time ago I received a call from a colleague who asked if I would be the referee on the grading of an examination question. He was about to give a student a zero for his answer to a physics question, while the student claimed he should receive a perfect score and would if the system were not set up against the student. The instructor and the student agreed to submit this to an impartial arbiter, and I was selected. [1]

I went to my colleague's office and read the examination question: "Show how it is possible to determine the height of a tall building with the aid of a barometer." [2]

The student had answered: "Take a barometer to the top of the building, attach a long rope to it, lower the barometer to the street, and then bring it up, measuring the length of the rope. The length of the rope is the height of the building." [3]

I pointed out that the student really had a strong case for full credit, since he had answered the question completely and correctly. On the other hand, if full credit was given, it could well contribute to a high grade for the student in his physics course. A high grade is supposed to certify competence in physics, but the answer did not confirm this. I suggested that the student have another try at answering the question. I was not surprised that my colleague agreed, but I was surprised that the student did. [4]

I gave the student six minutes to answer the question with the warning that the answer should show some knowledge of physics. At the end of five minutes, he had not written anything. I asked if he wished to give up, but he said no. He had many answers to this problem; he was just thinking of the best one. I excused myself for interrupting him and asked him to please go on. In the next minute he dashed off his answer which read: [5]

"Take the barometer to the top of the building and lean over the edge of the roof. Drop that barometer, timing its fall with a stop-watch. Then using the formula $S = \frac{1}{2} at^2$, calculate the height of the building." [6]

At this point I asked my colleague if *he* would give up. He conceded, and I gave the student almost full credit. [7]

In leaving my colleague's office, I recalled that the student had said he had many other answers to the problem, so I asked him what they were. "Oh yes," said the student. "There are a great many ways of getting the height of a tall building with a barometer. For example, you could take the barometer out on a sunny day and measure the height of the barometer and the length of its shadow, and the length of the shadow of the building, and by the use of a simple proportion, determine the height of the building." [8]

"Fine," I asked. "And the others?" [9]

"Yes," said the student. "There is a very basic measurement method that you will like. In this method you take the barometer and begin to walk up the stairs. As you climb the stairs, you mark off the length of the barometer along the wall. You then count the number of marks, and this will give you the height of the building in barometer units. A very direct method." [10]

"Of course, if you want a more sophisticated method, you can tie the barometer to the end of a string, swing it as a pendulum, and determine the value of 'g' at the street level and at the top of the building. From the difference of the two values of 'g' the height of the building can be calculated." [11]

Finally, he concluded, there are many other ways of solving the problem. "Probably the best," he said, "is to take the barometer to the basement and knock on the superintendent's door. When the superintendent answers, you speak to him as follows: 'Mr. Superintendent, here I have a fine barometer. If you tell me the height of this building, I will give you this barometer.'" [12]

At this point I asked the student if he really did know the conventional answer to this question. He admitted that he did, said that he was fed up with high school and college instructors trying to teach him how to think, using the "scientific method," and to explore the deep inner logic of the subject in a pedantic way, as is often done in the new mathematics, rather than teaching him the structure of the subject. With this in mind, he decided to revive scholasticism as an academic lark to challenge the Sputnik-panicked classrooms of America. [13]

PURPOSE AND STRUCTURE

1. The subtitle of this piece is "A Modern Parable." In what sense modern? In what sense a parable?

2. Formulate the issue that is argued. How does the writer marshal his evidence?

3. What is the relationship of Calandra's argument to Lincoln Steffens' experience as a student?

4. How does the title relate to the argument?

5. What was the student rebelling against?

6. In a simple statement, sum up the author's purpose.

DICTION AND TONE

1. How does the author reflect his attitude toward students? Toward colleagues?

2. In what sense were the student's answers an "academic lark"?

3. How does the sequence of "correct" answers establish the tone?

4. How does the author's approach to the issue serve to persuade? Whom is the author attempting to persuade? Who will be persuaded?

APPLICATIONS TO WRITING

1. Select an issue growing out of your high school or college experience, your family life, or your observations at work. Using the form of a parable, attempt to persuade a predesignated person or group.

2. By drawing on your personal experience and observation, write an argument in which the central issue is the nature and effects of grading. Be as specific as possible. If you are advocating the elimination of grades to the administration, your language and tone will differ from that which you would employ if you were defending grades to your peers.

eight

Diction and Tone

Diction—style as determined by choice of words. Good diction is characterized by precision and appropriateness to subject matter, weak diction by the use of inappropriate, vague, or trite words. The relationship between the kinds of words a writer selects and his subject matter in large part determines tone. Broyard describes the sad plight of the last married couple in Connecticut, all of whose friends have divorced. Faulkner's impressions of Japan are paradoxical ("the overcast sinks slowly upward") and almost nonverbal ("the splashed symbols of the characters"), whereas Orwell's impressions of Marrakech have a cinematic immediacy. Du Plessix Gray believes that deceit and lying—used with compassion and civility—are necessary in the love relationship. Lee Strout White (E. B. White) bids farewell to the Model T Ford as an aging male kisses an old flame good-bye. Hersey's diction does not reflect his subject matter; his language is deliberately flat and reportorial. Baldwin's diction is a striking combination of formal public language and informal private language. Dillard shows that sight and insight are one: that it is "the noise of useless interior babble" that keeps us from seeing. Sevareid tells us that the modern city is becoming like a medieval town with its garbage in the streets and its footpads: "the juggernaut of time" is going backwards.

The Last Married Couple Left

ANATOLE BROYARD

It's been raining in Connecticut and all our friends are divorcing. We're worried, my wife and I. We don't want to be sticks in the mud, the only married persons in the neighborhood. It's a troubling situation from many angles. Ecologically, for example, all these divorces could spell disaster. With everyone pulling up roots, the whole area may wash away. [1]

The husbands will leave, of course, and the wives stay behind. With mixed feelings, I imagine a matriarchal society, myself the only man. Will I be popular or a pariah, the target of their bitterness? What will this do to our dinner parties? I see an immensely long table lined with women, stretching into the distance like a de Chirico vista.[1] [2]

How will they react to being alone, all these divorced women? Will they roam the fields and roads in packs, or hide, like Gothic heroines, behind locked doors and drawn shades? Perhaps they'll become androgynous, independent, a new breed we won't know what to do with. [3]

And the husbands who are fleeing to New York City, how will they manage? Will they frequent massage parlors, lurk in Central Park? I see them joining athletic clubs, sitting in the men's bar after 57 games of squash, staring into their drinks with lost eyes. [4]

Maybe, my wife says, we're being too pessimistic. She paints a more sanguine picture: the women learning belly dancing, studying semiotics at the New School, holding self-help clinics, enjoying their sisterhood. [5]

The men will write novels, quit their suffocating careers, take karate lessons. They'll wrestle nude in their Greenwich Village studios, like Gerald and Birkin in *Women In Love*,[2] reaffirm their atavistic ties, their bonding instincts. They'll play volley ball in Washington Square to the beat of conga drums. [6]

---

[1] Giorgio de Chirico (1881–   ) is an Italian surrealist painter.
[2] *Women in Love* is a novel by D. H. Lawrence (1885–1930), English author.

But the children, what about the children? At night, on the wind, we will hear the sound of their crying. I will be a big brother or foster father to 50 boys—do I have enough masculinity to go around? Not necessary, my wife says. Children are so plastic. They can adapt to anything. In a world where we are all alienated, what's one parent more or less? [7]

Feeling that there is no longer any reason to be polite, that in fact it's gone out of style, we confront our friends who are divorcing. "What seems to be the matter?" Accusations burst out like abscesses, we are spattered with the symptomatology of marriage in the 70's. [8]

"She refuses to develop a backhand." "He only likes to make love in the swimming pool." "She sneers at my driving." "He begins all his sentences with 'hopefully.'" "She won't quit shaving her armpits." "His hips are too wide." "She flirts with the dog." "He hates foreign films." [9]

Their problems do not seem insurmountable, we suggest, but they disagree. They're divorcing. "Our evenings lack promise," a husband says, quoting a Donald Barthelme[3] story. "We doubled our loneliness by marrying" his wife says, quoting Jean Cocteau.[4] "The heaviest object in the world is the body of the woman one has ceased to love," the husband says, quoting Vauvenargues.[5] "Every man is an island entire in himself," his wife says, paraphrasing John Donne. [10]

They moved to Connecticut, these couples, to get away from the noise and dirt of the city and now they have discovered the noise and dirt of the self, so they are divorcing. They want to unlearn all the lessons, to be new again to someone. [11]

"Will you still love us?" they ask. "Of course," we answer. "We will always love you, together or apart, now and forever." [12]

At night, in bed, we talk about it, my wife and I. Can we really salvage one. We go over the couples, one by one. Marcus is so manic. Without Kate's silences to soak him up and soften his edges, he'll be like a dentist's drill. And if he isn't there, what will we say to her? Alison is as dependent as a newborn baby: Unless Saul is at her side, she'll want to sit in our laps. And if he isn't fathering her, he'll start

---

[3] Donald Barthelme (1931–   ) is an American writer.
[4] Jean Cocteau (1889–1963) was a French writer, artist, and filmmaker.
[5] Marquis de Vauvenargues (1715–1747) was a French moralist.

on us. Hilary has all the money: When she divorces Jules, she'll be too rich for us and he'll be too poor. Andrew and Liza are both so sexy: Once they separate, nobody will be safe with either of them. In every case, the answer is the same: United they stand, divided they fall into the impossible category. [13]

We look at each other, the last married couple in Connecticut, with wild surmise. The thing we have always dreaded and desired has finally come about. We are alone together. [14]

PURPOSE AND STRUCTURE

1. Broyard's newspaper piece is as short as a student theme. His purpose and tone are established with great economy in the title and the first paragraph. The first sentence joins "raining" and "divorcing." The third sentence compares "sticks in the mud" and "married persons." Par. 1 ends with a possible ecological disaster. Is the reader meant to take it seriously?

2. The third sentence (par. 1) mentions the thesis very casually. Should Broyard state the thesis more formally? How does the fourth sentence (par. 1) prepare the reader for the organization of the piece?

3. Par. 14 concludes the essay by restating the thesis. Is the reader left with the feeling that the last married couple in Connecticut can be called (see par. 1) "sticks in the mud"?

4. Pars. 2 to 7—on the results of divorce—contain a dialogue between husband and wife. The husband imagines dinner parties in a matriarchal society (par. 2), divorced women roaming the fields and roads in packs (par. 3), husbands in New York massage parlors (par. 4). Contrast the wife's views in pars. 5–6. Par. 7 concludes the dialogue. Do the husband and wife remain in character?

5. Pars. 8 to 11—on the causes of divorce—are summed up (par. 11): "They want to unlearn all the lessons, to be new again to someone." Does the writer imply that it is possible to "unlearn all the lessons"?

6. The question in par. 12 is answered twice, once in par. 12 and again in par. 13. Which answer is the correct one? Why give two different answers?

7. This fanciful essay—which seems to wander wherever Broyard's pleasure beckons—is actually very tightly organized. Par. 1 introduces; pars. 2–7 discuss the results of divorce, pars. 8–11 the causes, pars. 12–14 conclude the essay. Why is par. 13 the climax of the essay?

8. The last sentence of par. 13 says something serious about marriage. In what way is this sentence a summary of par. 13? Of *all* the effects of divorcing mentioned in Broyard's essay?

DICTION AND TONE

1. Is the reader expected to believe (par. 9) that divorces are caused by flirting "with the dog" or beginning sentences with "hopefully"?

2. Par. 9 consists entirely of quoted reasons for divorcing. What is the tone of the paragraph? Why use direct quotations?

3. Par. 10 gives a series of literary quotations. What is the cumulative tone of the paragraph?

4. What is the tone of "I see an immensely long table lined with women, stretching into the distance like a de Chirico vista" (par. 2)? Of "Perhaps they'll become androgynous, independent, a new breed we won't know what to do with" (par. 3)?

5. Most of the diction in Broyard's piece is simple and stripped ("divorcing" instead of getting a divorce). Why then does he heighten his diction in par. 14: "with wild surmise" and "dreaded and desired"?

6. Broyard's journalistic paragraphs are short and rapid. Should pars. 8 and 9 be joined? The last three paragraphs—the climax of the piece—vary most in length: shortest (par. 12), longest (par. 13), next to shortest (par. 14). Is this variation in length a reflection of the internal structure of the paragraphs or is it external and arbitrary?

7. The tone of Broyard's piece is conveyed and controlled by Broyard's superb journalistic style, his diction, and his sentence structure. Underline the main clauses—that is, the independent clauses—in par. 1. Note their simplicity. Notice the variety, richness, and precision added by appositives and modifiers before and after the main clauses. Examine other paragraphs in the same way.

APPLICATIONS TO WRITING

1. Is that old gang of yours breaking up? Tell how. Achieve your tone as Broyard does, with specific and economical illustrations that are (1) subtly exaggerated: "the women learning belly dancing, studying semiotics

at the New School, holding self-help clinics, enjoying their sisterhood" (par. 5); or (2) farcically exaggerated: "Will they roam the fields and the roads in packs, or hide, like Gothic heroines, behind locked doors and drawn shades? Perhaps they'll become androgynous, independent, a new breed we won't know what to do with" (par. 3).

2. Are you the last single? Are all your friends coupling or tripling; are all the pleasing singles turning into impossible combinations? Describe your plight, with special attention to par. 13 as the mirror image of your own problem.

3. Have you been pulling up roots lately? Is your social life in danger of becoming an ecological disaster (par. 1)? Contrast two periods in your life: rootedness vs. rootlessness.

Impressions of Japan

WILLIAM FAULKNER

The engines are long since throttled back; the overcast sinks slowly upward with no semblance whatever of speed until suddenly you see the aircraft's shadow scudding the cottony hillocks; and now speed has returned again, aircraft and shadow now rushing toward one another as toward one mutual headlong destruction. [1]

To break through the overcast and fling that shadow once more down, upon an island. It looks like land, like any other air-found landfall, yet you know it is an island, almost as if you saw both seabound flanks of it at the same instant, like a transparent slide; an island more miraculously found in the waste of water than Wake or Guam even, since here is a civilization, an ordered and ancient homogeny of the human race. [2]

It is visible and audible, spoken and written too: a communication between man and man because human speaks it; you hear and see them. But to this one western ear and eye it means nothing because it resembles nothing which that western eye remembers; there is nothing to measure it against, nothing for memory and habit to say,

"Why, this looks like the word for house or home or happiness"; not even just cryptic but acrostic too, as though the splashed symbols of the characters held not mere communication but something urgent and important beyond just information, promising toward some ultimate wisdom or knowledge containing the secret of man's salvation. But then no more, because there is nothing for western memory to measure it against; so not the mind to listen but only the ear to hear that chirrup and skitter of syllables like the cries of birds in the mouths of children, like music in the mouths of women and young girls. [3]

The faces: Van Gogh and Manet would have loved them: that of the pilgrim with staff and pack and dusty with walking, mounting the stairs toward the Temple in the early sunlight; the Temple lay brother or perhaps servant, his gown tucked about his thighs, squatting in the gate of the compound before beginning, or perhaps having already set it into motion, the day; that of the old woman vending peanuts beneath the gate for tourists to feed the pigeons with: a face worn with living and remembering, as though not one life had been long enough but rather every separate breath had been needed to etch into it all those fine and myriad lines; a face durable and now even a comfort to her, as if it had by now blotted up whatever had ever ached or sorrowed behind it, leaving it free now of anguishes and the griefs and the enduring: here is one anyway who never read Faulkner and neither knows nor cares why he came to Japan nor gives one single damn what he thinks of Ernest Hemingway. [4]

He is much too busy to have time to bother about whether he is happy or not, quite dirty, perhaps five years old, past-less and apparently immune even from parents, playing in the gutter with the stub of a cigarette. [5]

The bowl of mountains containing the lake is as full of hard rapid air as the mouth of a wind tunnel; for some time now we have been thinking that maybe it is already too late to take a reef in the mainsail: yet there it is. It is only a skiff yet to the western eye it is as invincibly and irrevocably alien as a Chinese junk, driven by a battered U.S.-made outboard engine and containing a woman in a kimono beneath an open paper parasol such as would have excited no comment in a sunny reach of the English Thames, as fragile and invulnerable in the center of that hard blue bowl of wind as a butterfly in the eye of a typhoon. [6]

The geisha's mass of blue-black lacquered hair encloses the painted face like a helmet, surmounts, crowns the slender body's ordered and ritual posturing like a grenadier's bearskin busby, too heavy in appearance for that slender throat to bear, the painted fixed expressionless face immobile and immune also above the studied posturing: yet behind that painted and lifeless mask is something quick and alive and elfin: or more than elfin: puckish: or more than puckish even: sardonic and quizzical, a gift for comedy, and more: for burlesque and caricature: for a sly and vicious revenge on the race of men. [7]

Kimono. It covers her from throat to ankles; with a gesture as feminine as the placing of a flower or as female as the cradling of a child, the hands can be concealed into the sleeves until there remains one unbroken chalice-shape of modesty proclaiming femininity where nudity would merely parade mammalian femaleness. A modesty which flaunts its own immodestness like the crimson rose tossed by no more than one white flick of hand, from the balcony window—modesty, than which there is nothing more immodest and which therefore is a woman's dearest possession; she should defend it with her life. [8]

Loyalty. In her western clothes, blouse and skirt, she is merely one dumpy and nondescript young woman, though in kimono at the deft balanced rapid tripping glide she too comes into her own share of that national heritage of feminine magic. Though she has more than that; she partakes of her share of that other quality which women have in this land which was not given them by what they have on: loyalty, constancy, fidelity, not for, but at least one hopes not without, reward. She does not speak my language nor I hers, yet in two days she knows my countryman's habit of waking soon after first light so that each morning when I open my eyes a coffee tray is already on the balcony table; she knows I like a fresh room to breakfast in when I return from walking, and it is so: the room done for the day and the table set and the morning paper ready; she asks without words why I have no clothes to be laundered today, and without word asks permission to sew the buttons and darn the socks; she calls me wise man and teacher, who am neither, when speaking of me to others; she is proud to have me for her client and, I hope, pleased that I try to deserve that pride and match with courtesy that loyalty. There is a lot of loose loyalty in this land. Even a little of it is too valuable to be ignored. I would wish that all of it were deserved or at least appreciated as I have tried to do. [9]

This is the same rice paddy which I know back home in Arkansas and Mississippi and Louisiana, where it replaces now and then the cotton. This one is merely a little smaller and a little more fiercely cultivated, right up to the single row of beans which line the very edge of the irrigation canals, the work here done by hand where in my country machines do it since we have more machines than we have people; nature is the same: only the economy is different. [10]

And the names are the same names too: Jonathan and Winesap and Delicious; the heavy August foliage is blue-grey with the same spray which we use. But there the resemblance ceases: every single apple enclosed in this twist of paper until that whole tree to this western eye becomes significant and festive and ceremonial like the symbolical tree of the western rite of Christmas. Only it is more significant here: where in the West there is one small often artificial tree to a family, wrested from the living dirt to be decked in ritual tinsel and then to die as though the tree were not the protagonist of a rite but the victim of a sacrifice, here not one tree to a family but every tree of all is dressed and decked to proclaim and salute older gods than Christ: Demeter and Ceres. [11]

Briefer and faster now, toward the journey's nearing end: goldenrod, as evocative of dust and autumn and hay fever as ever in Mississippi, against a tall bamboo fence. [12]

The scenery is beautiful but the faces are better still. The swift supple narrow grace with which the young girl bows and in that same one glowing motion recovers, tougher through very tenderness than the rigid culture which bent her is as the willow bough itself to the hard gust which can never do more than sway it. [13]

The tools they use evoke the ones Noah must have built his ark with, yet the framework of the house seems to rise and stand without nails in the fitted joints or even the need for nails, as if here were a magic, an art in the simple building of man's habitations which our western ancestors seemed to have lost somewhere when they moved. [14]

And always the water, the sound, the plash and drip of it, as if here were a people making constant oblation to water as some peoples do to what they call their luck. [15]

So kind the people that with three words the guest can go anywhere and live: Gohan; Sake; Arrigato. [16]

And one more word: [17]

Tomorrow now the aircraft lightens, a moment more and the wheels will wrench free of the ground, already dragging its shadow back toward the overcast before the wheels are even tucked up, into the overcast and then through it, the land, the island gone now which memory will always know though eye no longer remembers. [18]

Sayonara. [19]

PURPOSE AND STRUCTURE

1. Faulkner's impressions of Japan begin (par. 1) in paradox ("the overcast sinks slowly upward") and in destruction ("aircraft and shadow now rushing toward one another as toward one mutual headlong destruction"). How does this paragraph prepare the reader for the rest of the essay?

2. Par. 3 is about communication. What do the "splashed symbols of the characters" say to Faulkner? Do they communicate information? If the mind cannot listen, can the ear hear? How does what the ear hears (end of par. 3) prepare the reader for what the eye sees (beginning of par. 4 and the rest of the essay)?

3. Par. 4 is about faces: the face of the old woman selling peanuts is elaborately described. Should the faces of the pilgrim and the Temple lay brother also be described?

4. The reader is lost for a moment at the beginning of par. 5. Who is "he"? Why does Faulkner treat the reader as if the reader were a slightly puzzled traveler?

5. Faulkner begins his visit to Japan by hearing and seeing: "But to this one western ear and eye it means nothing because it resembles nothing which the western eye remembers" (par. 3). But Faulkner almost immediately begins to recognize the humanity in the faces (pars. 4 and 7). Why, then, make this point? Later in the essay (par. 9) Faulkner perceives loyalty in his servant and even recognizes "the same rice paddy which I know back home in Arkansas and Mississippi and Louisiana" (par. 10). What has happened to Faulkner?

6. Par. 18 returns to the paradoxes of par. 1: "Tomorrow now" with the aircraft "already dragging its shadow back toward the overcast" but there is no feeling of "mutual headlong destruction" (par. 1). Why not?

DICTION AND TONE

1. The "splashed symbols of the characters" (par. 3) do not give information but promise some ultimate wisdom Faulkner is trying to reach

through the "chirrup and skitter of syllables like the cries of birds." Why refer to "the cries of birds"?

2. The diction of the description of the geisha's face (par. 7) is formal and complex, almost ritualistic: "encloses the painted face like a helmet, surmounts, crowns the slender body's ordered and ritual posturing like a grenadier's bearskin busby." What is behind that mask? What is the tone of the powerful contrast in par. 7?

3. What is the tone of Faulkner's paradoxical description of the modesty of the kimono (par. 8)?

4. The Japanese language is, for Faulkner, "like music in the mouths of women and young girls" (par. 3), significant but meaningless. Why, then, does Faulkner end his essay with three Japanese words (par. 16) and, finally, a single Japanese word (par. 19)? Have these words become meaningful for Faulkner? What is the tone of his statement: "So kind the people that with three words the guest can go anywhere and live" (par. 16)?

APPLICATIONS TO WRITING

1. What did you do last summer? Describe your vacation.

2. Faulkner writes about foreignness and human separation; he tells how they were overcome. If you have had a similar experience, describe it.

3. Faulkner makes his reader experience the foreignness of the Japanese and his separation from them by confronting his reader with some of the same incoherence and fragmentation which Faulkner experienced in Japan. But, just as Faulkner's experience of Japan was finally a coherent one, so is his essay. Attempt a similar essay.

Marrakech

GEORGE ORWELL

As the corpse went past the flies left the restaurant table in a cloud and rushed after it, but they came back a few minutes later. [1]

The little crowd of mourners—all men and boys, no women—threaded their way across the market place between the piles of pomegranates and the taxis and the camels, wailing a short chant over and over again. What really appeals to the flies is that the corpses here are never put into coffins, they are merely wrapped in a piece of rag and carried on a rough wooden bier on the shoulders of four friends. When the friends get to the burying-ground they hack an oblong hole a foot or two deep, dump the body in it and fling over it a little of the dried-up, lumpy earth, which is like broken brick. No gravestone, no name, no identifying mark of any kind. The burying-ground is merely a huge waste of hummocky earth, like a derelict building-lot. After a month or two no one can even be certain where his own relatives are buried. [2]

When you walk through a town like this—two hundred thousand inhabitants, of whom at least twenty thousand own literally nothing except the rags they stand up in—when you see how the people live, and still more how easily they die, it is always difficult to believe that you are walking among human beings. All colonial empires are in reality founded upon that fact. The people have brown faces—besides, there are so many of them! Are they really the same flesh as yourself? Do they even have names? Or are they merely a kind of undifferentiated brown stuff, about as individual as bees or coral insects? They rise out of the earth, they sweat and starve for a few years, and then they sink back into the nameless mounds of the graveyard and nobody notices that they are gone. And even the graves themselves soon fade back into the soil. Sometimes, out for a walk, as you break your way through the prickly pear, you notice that it is rather bumpy underfoot, and only a certain regularity in the bumps tells you that you are walking over skeletons. [3]

I was feeding one of the gazelles in the public gardens. [4]

Gazelles are almost the only animals that look good to eat when they are still alive, in fact, one can hardly look at their hindquarters without thinking of a mint sauce. The gazelle I was feeding seemed to know that this thought was in my mind, for though it took the piece of bread I was holding out it obviously did not like me. It nibbled rapidly at the bread, then lowered its head and tried to butt me, then took another nibble and then butted again. Probably its idea was that if it could drive me away the bread would somehow remain hanging in mid-air. [5]

An Arab navvy working on the path nearby lowered his heavy hoe and sidled slowly towards us. He looked from the gazelle to the bread and from the bread to the gazelle, with a sort of quiet amazement, as though he had never seen anything quite like this before. Finally he said shyly in French:

"I could eat some of that bread." [6]

I tore off a piece and he stowed it gratefully in some secret place under his rags. This man is an employee of the Municipality. [7]

When you go through the Jewish quarters you gather some idea of what the medieval ghettoes were probably like. Under their Moorish rulers the Jews were only allowed to own land in certain restricted areas, and after centuries of this kind of treatment they have ceased to bother about overcrowding. Many of the streets are a good deal less than six feet wide, the houses are completely windowless, and sore-eyed children cluster everywhere in unbelievable numbers, like clouds of flies. Down the centre of the street there is generally running a little river of urine. [8]

In the bazaar huge families of Jews, all dressed in the long black robe and little black skull-cap, are working in dark fly-infested booths that look like caves. A carpenter sits crosslegged at a prehistoric lathe, turning chair-legs at lightning speed. He works the lathe with a bow in his right hand and guides the chisel with his left foot, and thanks to a lifetime of sitting in this position his left leg is warped out of shape. At his side his grandson, aged six, is already starting on the simpler parts of the job. [9]

I was just passing the coppersmiths' booths when somebody noticed that I was lighting a cigarette. Instantly, from the dark holes all round, there was a frenzied rush of Jews, many of them old grandfathers with flowing grey beards, all clamouring for a cigarette. Even a blind man somewhere at the back of one of the booths heard a rumour of cigarettes and came crawling out, groping in the air with his hand. In about a minute I had used up the whole packet. None of these people, I suppose, works less than twelve hours a day, and every one of them looks on a cigarette as a more or less impossible luxury. [10]

As the Jews live in self-contained communities they follow the same trades as the Arabs, except for agriculture. Fruit-sellers, potters, silversmiths, blacksmiths, butchers, leatherworkers, tailors, water-carriers, beggars, porters—whichever way you look you see nothing but Jews. As a matter of fact there are thirteen thousand of them, all living in the space of a few acres. A good job Hitler wasn't here. Perhaps he was on his way, however. You hear the usual dark rumours about the Jews, not only from the Arabs but from the poorer Europeans. [11]

"Yes *mon vieux,* they took my job away from me and gave it to a Jew. The Jews! They're the real rulers of this country, you know. They've got all the money. They control the banks, finance—everything." [12]

"But," I said, "isn't it a fact that the average Jew is a labourer working for about a penny an hour?" [13]

"Ah, that's only for show! They're all money lenders really. They're cunning, the Jews." [14]

In just the same way, a couple of hundred years ago, poor old women used to be burned for witchcraft when they could not even work enough magic to get themselves a square meal. [15]

All people who work with their hands are partly invisible, and the more important the work they do, the less visible they are. Still, a white skin is always fairly conspicuous. In northern Europe, when you see a labourer ploughing a field, you probably give him a second glance. In a hot country, anywhere south of Gibraltar or east of Suez, the chances are that you don't even see him. I have noticed this again and again. In a tropical landscape one's eye takes in everything except the human beings. It takes in the dried-up soil, the prickly pear, the palm tree and the distant mountain, but it always misses the peasant hoeing at his patch. He is the same colour as the earth, and a great deal less interesting to look at. [16]

It is only because of this that the starved countries of Asia and Africa are accepted as tourist resorts. No one would think of running cheap trips to the Distressed Areas. But where the human beings have brown skins their poverty is simply not noticed. What does Morocco mean to a Frenchman? An orange grove or a job in Government service. Or to an Englishman? Camels, castles, palm trees, Foreign Legionnaires, brass trays, and bandits. One could probably live there for years without noticing that for nine-tenths of the people the reality of life is an endless, back-breaking struggle to wring a little food out of an eroded soil. [17]

Most of Morocco is so desolate that no wild animal bigger than a hare can live on it. Huge areas which were once covered with forest have turned into a treeless waste where the soil is exactly like broken-up brick. Nevertheless a good deal of it is cultivated, with frightful labour. Everything is done by hand. Long lines of women, bent double like inverted capital L's, work their way slowly across the fields, tearing up the prickly weeds with their hands, and the peasant gathering lucerne for fodder pulls it up stalk by stalk instead of reaping it, thus saving an inch or two on each stalk. The plough is a wretched wooden thing, so frail that one can easily carry it on one's shoulder, and fitted underneath with a rough iron spike which stirs the soil to a depth of about four inches. This is as much as the strength of the animals is equal to. It is usual to plough with a cow and a donkey yoked together. Two donkeys would not be quite strong enough, but on the other hand two cows would cost a little more to feed. The peasants possess no harrows, they merely plough the soil several times over in different directions, finally leaving it in rough furrows, after which the whole field has to be shaped with hoes into small oblong patches to conserve water. Except for a day or two after the rare rainstorms there is never enough water. Along the edges of the fields channels are hacked out to a depth of thirty or forty feet to get at the tiny trickles which run through the subsoil. [18]

Every afternoon a file of very old women passes down the road outside my house, each carrying a load of firewood. All of them are mummified with age and the sun, and all of them are tiny. It seems to be generally the case in primitive communities that the women, when they get beyond a certain age, shrink to the size of children. One day a poor old creature who could not have been more than four feet tall crept past me under a vast load of wood. I stopped her and put a five-sou piece (a little more than a farthing) into her hand. She answered with a shrill wail, almost a scream, which was partly gratitude but mainly surprise. I suppose that from her point of view, by taking any notice of her, I seemed almost to be violating a law of nature. She accepted her status as an old woman, that is to say as a beast of burden. When a family is travelling it is quite usual to see a father and a grown-up son riding ahead on donkeys, and an old woman following on foot, carrying the baggage. [19]

But what is strange about these people is their invisibility. For several weeks, always at about the same time of day, the file of old women had hobbled past the house with their firewood, and though they had registered themselves on my eyeballs I cannot truly say that I had seen them. Firewood was passing—that was how I saw it. It was only that one day I happened to be walking behind them, and the curious up-and-down motion of a load of wood drew my attention to the human being beneath it. Then for the first time I noticed the poor old earth-coloured bodies, bodies reduced to bones and leathery skin, bent double under the crushing weight. Yet I suppose I had not been five minutes on Moroccan soil before I noticed the overloading of the donkeys and was infuriated by it. There is no question that the donkeys are damnably treated. The Moroccan donkey is hardly bigger than a St. Bernard dog, it carries a load which in the British Army would be considered too much for a fifteen-hands mule, and very often its packsaddle is not taken off its back for weeks together. But what is peculiarly pitiful is that it is the most willing creature on earth, it follows its master like a dog and does not need either bridle or halter. After a dozen years of devoted work it suddenly drops dead, whereupon its master tips it into the ditch and the village dogs have torn its guts out before it is cold. [20]

This kind of thing makes one's blood boil, whereas—on the whole— the plight of the human beings does not. I am not commenting, merely pointing to a fact. People with brown skins are next door to invisible. Anyone can be sorry for the donkey with its galled back, but it is generally owing to some kind of accident if one even notices the old woman under her load of sticks. [21]

As the storks flew northward the Negroes were marching southward —a long, dusty column, infantry, screw-gun batteries, and then more infantry, four or five thousand men in all, winding up the road with a clumping of boots and a clatter of iron wheels. [22]

They were Senegalese, the blackest Negroes in Africa, so black that sometimes it is difficult to see whereabouts on their necks the hair begins. Their splendid bodies were hidden in reach-me-down khaki uniforms, their feet squashed into boots that looked like blocks of wood, and every tin hat seemed to be a couple of sizes too small. It was very hot and the men had marched a long way. They slumped under the weight of their packs and the curiously sensitive black faces were glistening with sweat. [23]

As they went past, a tall, very young Negro turned and caught my eye. But the look he gave me was not in the least the kind of look you might expect. Not hostile, not contemptuous, not sullen, not even inquisitive. It was the shy, wide-eyed Negro look, which actually is a look of profound respect. I saw how it was. This wretched boy, who is a French citizen and has therefore been dragged from the forest to scrub floors and catch syphilis in garrison towns, actually has feelings of reverence before a white skin. He has been taught that the white race are his masters, and he still believes it. [24]

But there is one thought which every white man (and in this connection it doesn't matter twopence if he calls himself a socialist) thinks when he sees a black army marching past. "How much longer can we go on kidding these people? How long before they turn their guns in the other direction?" [25]

It was curious, really. Every white man there had this thought stowed somewhere or other in his mind. I had it, so had the other onlookers, so had the officers on their sweating chargers and the white N.C.O.'s marching in the ranks. It was a kind of secret which we all knew and were too clever to tell; only the Negroes didn't know it. And really it was like watching a flock of cattle to see the long column, a mile or two miles of armed men, flowing peacefully up the road, while the great white birds drifted over them in the opposite direction, glittering like scraps of paper. [26]

PURPOSE AND STRUCTURE

1. Instead of *telling* the reader that the natives are poor, Orwell *shows* poverty in at least five ways. Identify them. Explain the difference between telling and showing.

2. By showing instead of telling, Orwell maintains the point of view of an objective reporter. How then can you tell that he is outraged at the spectacle of misery?

3. State clearly in one sentence the significance of the incident involving the cigarettes. Compare your statement with Orwell's report. What specific details and particulars make his account more vivid than your summary? What is the topic sentence of par. 10?

4. Could pars. 4–7 just as well come after 8–15 as before? Could other groups of paragraphs be rearranged? What does this indicate about the organization? What gives the essay coherence?

5. Notice the lack of transition between parts of the essay. What is gained by avoiding logical transitions and abruptly juxtaposing the elements?

DICTION AND TONE

1. List all the words revealing Orwell's lack of objectivity in reporting on the Moroccan donkeys. Why does he reveal his feelings about the donkeys but conceal his feelings about the people?

2. Orwell frequently uses a more particular verb than the general one to *walk*. For example, "The little crowd of mourners . . . *threaded their way*" (par. 2). What verbs does he use in place of *to walk* in par. 19?

3. In par. 2, circle the verbs relating to the burial. What feelings are evoked?

4. In par. 3 Orwell addresses the reader by writing, "When *you* walk through a town like this. . . ." What would be the difference in tone if he had written, "When *one* walks . . ."? How does this tone contribute to his purpose?

5. In how many ways are the storks and the Negro soldiers different? What is the effect of placing these contrasting elements together?

APPLICATIONS TO WRITING

Write an essay in which you describe objectively a highly moving scene or situation. Select a scene of poverty, one evoking pity, terror, or revulsion. Although you must make an effort to maintain an objective tone, your real but unstated feelings should be evident to the reader.

Manners of Deceit and the Case for Lying

FRANCINE DU PLESSIX GRAY

The Countess of O. was an American whose adroitness was much admired in Paris society. One particularly spectacular conquest had typified her skills: Although she was neither wealthy, famous nor very beautiful, she had married, long past forty, one of Europe's most desirable industrialists. She knew how to exaggerate, which is the beginning of both flattery and deceit. Upon first meeting the Count of O., she had greeted him with the words "Ah, you are the *poet.*" The count was very sensitive about the existence of his only work, a slender collection of Victorian verse that he had long ago translated into French. He proposed to her the following week. [1]

I met her in an immense country house where the arts of fibbery played a relatively minor role. For both the owner's wife and his mistress, though they kept a distance of some twelve rooms between them, had chosen to torture each other for years by summering there simultaneously. The host alone was serene. No need, on his part, for tall tales of yachting races or grouse shooting in Scotland. His household was thus conducive to the following table talk between two weekend guests, the worldly countess and the young American to whom I had been married for barely a year. [2]

"What would you expect most of a wife?" she asked over the Brie, in the tartly playful Gallic tone intended to trigger an exchange of gallantries. Alas, my husband was so candid, so impulsive, so American, that the earnestness of his reply descended upon his dinner partner like an invasion of paratroopers. [3]

"I expect her," he said, "to always tell me the truth." [4]

"*Quelle horreur!*" she screamed, amid a clatter of dessertspoons. She composed herself and stared at him with maternal severity, adding: "When my husband proposed to me I said the following. I said, 'Yes, I'll marry you, but only on one condition: that you never, *never* tell me the truth.'" [5]

I appreciated her genius instantly. For some years before, I had had a lover who tortured me with his passion for the unadulterated truth. Some lovers tyrannize us by lying, which is the fabrication of fact; others by deceit, which is the withholding of information. But this fetishist of the authentic—who insisted on discussing every daily detail of his often deviant life—was a pervert who used candor as his only whip. And I have never been so miserable before or since. Whether he had shared a bacchanal with a triad of famous beauties, picked up a manicurist at a bar or dined at the home of the prepubescent heiress whom he had chosen as his eventual bride, he described his encounters with the sordid and loving detail, the naturalistic precision, of a botanist's journal. These accountings (I must stress that they were strictly unsolicited) began by being wounding and soon became tedious. I pleaded with him to remain silent. I begged him to lie, since he seemed incapable of deceit. I threatened to leave him. I insulted him. I announced that he had turned senile at the age of thirty-two. I paraphrased Montaigne—"I scarcely inquire of a footman whether he is chaste; I inquire whether he is diligent"—stressing that I did not ask of a lover that he be faithful but that he remain interesting. But being French, and mean, he continued talking. [6]

For a year I lived a folie à deux with this voluptuary of the sincere, experiencing the sadism of absolute truthfulness. If I stayed on as long as I did, it was in great part due to my fascination for the following paradox: No one I have known lied more to himself than this man who refused to deceive. He thought of himself not only as a gifted lover and novelist but also—supreme proof of his self-delusion—as an utterly debased renegade, a mini-Sade. Nonsense! He was, in fact, a weak, spoiled, often tender, comfort-loving mamma's boy. He could not bear to lie to his mother any more than he could bear to deceive me, and always left my flat at three A.M. so that he could be in bed when she brought him his breakfast tray. And the end of the affair left me, aged twenty-three, with the following conviction: that to deceive with caution and compassion, to withhold judiciously, for instance, the daily data of our temptations, is one of the foundations of a happy love and can only be practiced by those relatively free of *self*-deceit. [7]

Yet what if he had invented all those encounters and orgies as a way to write, in his life, the novel he could never put to paper . . . what if he had actually been lying all the time to torture me? [8]

He would have been equally perverse. The extremes of truth telling can be as tainted with the banality of evil as the most contrived duplicity. [9]

In America today, we lie to one another as much as if not more than ever, while having lost many deceits indispensable to three crucial aspects of civilized life: manners, privacy and the art of conversation. For the fibs that go under the name of diplomacy, tact and etiquette are not merely sociobiological means of avoiding strife and psychic pain; they're also masks, plumages, camouflages, for our true identity, which is the last thing we should wish to disclose casually in public. The art of good table talk, for instance, thrives on an intricate network of hypocrisy and masquerade. And that perennial yardstick of manners, the dinner party, has long been ruled by codes far more stringent than the tabooed voicing of "What a ghastly dress, darling" and "This stew is inedible," or such obligatory lies as "I adore your house." Until a generation ago, it had been a dictum never to discuss money or sex at the table, issues without which the texture of human personality cannot possibly be plumbed. It remains a code in France never to ask of a stranger at a party what he or she "does" in life. And well-mannered Britishers can be equally duplicitous about their political convictions. ("What do you think of Mrs. Thatcher?" I asked one of my hosts in England just last year. "Lovely skin," he retorted, plunging into his blancmange.) [10]

The recent withering of these many masks, the decline of these restraints, frequently turn our American dinner parties into group-therapeutic horror shows. Vainly attempting to discuss Kafka, the Bible, the breeding of Siamese cats or the inundation of Venice, I am too often subjected to the tediously intimate details of some dinner partner's sexual, digestive, financial and psychoanalytic habits. Instead of being buoyed by the objectivity and serious playfulness that is the essence of good talk, our dinner fare has become glutted with that confessionalism, voyeurism and public subjectivity that presently rule our mores under the banners of openness and authenticity. And this reversion to a frontier ethic is not to be disassociated from the general demise of manners that has led to a generation of eighteen-year-olds who do not shake hands, rise for elders, care for grammar or use forks anymore. We are presented, here as elsewhere, with the illusions of false freedom. Only that most deceitful of literary forms, the epigram, can sum up the situation with proper pungency: Nothing so much prevents our being authentic as our efforts to seem so. [11]

Some observations on technology: The snoopy voyeurism of the contemporary media nosing in on such delicate negotiations as the Middle East peace talks may create a greater need than ever for "secret," hence duplicitous, diplomacy. [12]

Before the advent of planes, telephones and doctors' beepers invaded our privacy, it was considerably harder to discover a lover's or spouse's infidelities. Thus, within the confines of traditional marriages, in which they must plead squash practice or the dentist for each fornication, men might lie more today than ever before. [13]

Women may also be led to lie more than ever, being biologically endowed with that gift for sexual hypocrisy that is their most precious weapon. Tyrannized as they are by the myth of sexual performance, fearful of losing their mate if they don't come to orgasm every time, they are tempted to answer each "Was it good for *you*, sweetie?" with the frequent fibbery of "Just marvelous." [14]

Let us imagine a broad-based pyramid whose apex points to the sky. The prevalence of untruth seems to be most massive at the bottom level, seems to thrive in the measure to which we are earthbound, locked in struggles for material power. Machiavelli was the first artist to stress the need for prevarication at the pyramid's base, on the immense ground floor of government and international relations. And the best ambassadors have been honest men sent abroad to lie for their country. [15]

I see the domain of love as located somewhere in the middle of the pyramid. For it is both the grandeur and the tragedy of love that it feeds on infinitely deeper drives for possessiveness and power than the emotion of friendship. One of the most interesting lessons we have learned from our so-called sexual liberation is that the relaxation of mores has done little to decrease the pain of abrogated trust, the agony of jealousy. And I believe that both the discipline of fidelity and a measured use of the untruth offer more alternatives for the future than the brutal sincerity of the open marriage. [16]

At the ethereal summit of the pyramid, the domain of friendship offers much repose to those of us who treasure candor. For this human bond least tainted by physical pleasure or material profit, most powerfully anchored in free will, most liberated from any oath of constancy, is by its very nature freer of deceit than any other relation we can know. Friendship, in this sense, is the human condition most resemblant to what may be humanity's most beautiful and necessary lie—the promise of an afterlife. It is only in this projected celestial sphere, where there are no childbirth pains, no lust for "fame, wealth and the love of women," that one could speak the truth of our inner thoughts in total freedom and abundance. Whereas to abolish the civility of compassionate deceit in any still-human sphere, to invade the privacy of one another's temptations and illusions, would be to create a veritable hell on earth. [17]

PURPOSE AND STRUCTURE

1. In the last three paragraphs "love" (par. 16) is located between diplomacy and friendship. Why?

2. What is the function of each of the five parts of du Plessix Gray's essay: pars. 1–5, 6–9, 10–11, 12–14, and 15–17?

3. What was the result in the marriage where "the arts of fibbery played a relatively minor role" (par. 2)?

4. What are the three ways lovers "tyrannize" (par. 6)? Why is the example of the truthful lover important in the argument of the essay? What is the tone of "No one I have known lied more to himself than this man who refused to deceive" (par. 7)?

5. The last sentence of par. 16 is a kind of thesis statement. What, then, is the purpose of the last sentence of the essay (par. 17)?

DICTION AND TONE

1. In the last paragraph (par. 17) "friendship" is compared to "the promise of an afterlife." Why is the comparison ironic?

2. Why have the best ambassadors been "honest men" (par. 15)?

3. Why does du Plessix Gray refer to untruth as "the civility of compassionate deceit" (par. 17)?

4. Why does du Plessix Gray refer to our "so-called" (par. 16) sexual liberation?

5. Why refer to the "brutal sincerity" (par. 16) of open marriage?

6. What is the tone of the reference to the "most precious weapon" (par. 14) of women?

7. Why is the lover in par. 6 called a "fetishist," a "pervert"?

8. Why has our "dinner fare become glutted with confessionalism, voyeurism, and public subjectivity" (par. 11)?

APPLICATIONS TO WRITING

1. Answer du Plessix Gray, using her own weapons—irony, sophisticated anecdote, and subtle exaggeration: Deceit and lying have created "a ver-

itable hell on earth" (par. 17). What we need is the civility of compassionate truth.

2. Compare and contrast two love relationships: one truthful, one deceitful.

3. Compare and contrast friendship and love.

4. Write on the following epigram: "Nothing so much prevents our being authentic as our efforts to seem so" (par. 11).

Farewell, My Lovely

An aging male kisses an old flame good-bye, circa 1936.

LEE STROUT WHITE (E. B. WHITE)

I see by the new Sears Roebuck catalogue that it is still possible to buy an axle for a 1909 Model T Ford, but I am not deceived. The great days have faded, the end is in sight. Only one page in the current catalogue is devoted to parts and accessories for the Model T; yet everyone remembers springtimes when the Ford gadget section was larger than men's clothing, almost as large as household furnishings. The last Model T was built in 1927, and the car is fading from what scholars call the American scene—which is an understatement, because to a few million people who grew up with it, the old Ford practically *was* the American scene. [1]

It was the miracle God had wrought. And it was patently the sort of thing that could only happen once. Mechanically uncanny, it was like nothing that had ever come to the world before. Flourishing industries rose and fell with it. As a vehicle, it was hardworking, commonplace, heroic; and it often seemed to transmit those qualities to the persons who rode in it. My own generation identifies it with youth, with its gaudy, irretrievable excitements; before it fades into the mist, I would like to pay it the tribute of the sigh that is not a sob, and set down random entries in a shape somewhat less cumbersome than a Sears Roebuck catalogue. [2]

The Model T was distinguished from all other makes of cars by the fact that its transmission was of a type known as planetary—which was half metaphysics, half sheer friction. Engineers accepted the word "planetary" in its epicyclic sense, but I was always conscious that it also meant "wandering," "erratic." Because of the peculiar nature of this planetary element, there was always, in Model T, a certain dull rapport between engine and wheels, and even when the car was in a state known as neutral, it trembled with a deep imperative and tended to inch forward. There was never a moment when the bands were not faintly egging the machine on. In this respect it was like a horse, rolling the bit on its tongue, and country people brought to it the same technique they used with draft animals. [3]

Its most remarkable quality was its rate of acceleration. In its palmy days the Model T could take off faster than anything on the road. The reason was simple. To get under way, you simply hooked the third finger of the right hand around a lever on the steering column, pulled down hard, and shoved your left foot forcibly against the low-speed pedal. These were simple, positive motions; the car responded by lunging forward with a roar. After a few seconds of this turmoil, you took your toe off the pedal, eased up a mite on the throttle, and the car, possessed of only two forward speeds, catapulted directly into high with a series of ugly jerks and was off on its glorious errand. The abruptness of this departure was never equaled in other cars of the period. The human leg was (and still is) incapable of letting in a clutch with anything like the forthright abandon that used to send Model T on its way. Letting in a clutch is a negative, hesitant motion, depending on delicate nervous control; pushing down the Ford pedal was a simple, country motion—an expansive act, which came as natural as kicking an old door to make it budge. [4]

The driver of the old Model T was a man enthroned. The car, with top up, stood seven feet high. The driver sat on top of the gas tank, brooding it with his own body. When he wanted gasoline, he alighted, along with everything else in the front seat; the seat was pulled off, the metal cap unscrewed, and a wooden stick thrust down to sound the liquid in the well. There were always a couple of these sounding sticks kicking around in the ratty subcushion regions of a flivver. Refueling was more of a social function then, because the driver had to unbend, whether he wanted to or not. Directly in front of the driver was the windshield—high, uncompromisingly erect. Nobody talked about air resistance, and the four cylinders pushed the car through the atmosphere with a simple disregard of physical law. [5]

There was this about a Model T: the purchaser never regarded his purchase as a complete, finished product. When you bought a Ford, you figured you had a start—a vibrant, spirited framework to which could be screwed an almost limitless assortment of decorative and functional hardware. Driving away from the agency, hugging the new wheel between your knees, you were already full of creative worry. A Ford was born naked as a baby, and a flourishing industry grew up out of correcting its rare deficiencies and combating its fascinating diseases. Those were the great days of lily-painting. I have been looking at some old Sears Roebuck catalogues, and they bring everything back so clear. [6]

First you bought a Ruby Safety Reflector for the rear, so that your posterior would glow in another's car's brilliance. Then you invested thirty-nine cents in some radiator Moto Wings, a popular ornament which gave the Pegasus touch to the machine and did something god-like to the owner. For nine cents you bought a fanbelt guide to keep the belt from slipping off the pulley. [7]

You bought a radiator compound to stop leaks. This was as much a part of everybody's equipment as aspirin tablets are of a medicine cabinet. You bought special oil to prevent chattering, a clamp-on dash light, a patching outfit, a tool box which you bolted to the running board, a sun visor, a steering-column brace to keep the column rigid, and a set of emergency containers for gas, oil, and water—three thin, disclike cans which reposed in a case on the running board during long, important journeys—red for gas, gray for water, green for oil. It was only a beginning. After the car was about a year old, steps were taken to check the alarming disintegration. (Model T was full of tumors, but they were benign.) A set of antirattlers (ninety-eight cents) was a popular panacea. You hooked them on to the gas and spark rods, to the brake pull rod, and to the steering-rod connections. Hood silencers, of black rubber, were applied to the fluttering hood. Shock-absorbers and snubbers gave "complete relaxation." Some people bought rubber pedal pads, to fit over the standard metal pedals. (I didn't like these, I remember.) Persons of a suspicious or pugnacious turn of mind bought a rear-view mirror; but most Model T owners weren't worried by what was coming from behind because they would soon enough see it out in front. They rode in a state of cheerful catalepsy. Quite a large mutinous clique among Ford owners went over to a foot accelerator (you could buy one and screw it to the floor board), but there was a certain madness in these people, because the Model T, just as she stood, had a choice of three foot pedals to push, and there were plenty of moments when both feet were occupied in the routine performance of duty and when the only way to speed up the engine was with the hand throttle. [8]

Gadget bred gadget. Owners not only bought ready-made gadgets, they invented gadgets to meet special needs. I myself drove my car directly from the agency to the blacksmith's and had the smith affix two enormous iron brackets to the port running board to support an army trunk. [9]

People who owned closed models builded along different lines: they bought ball grip handles for opening doors, window antirattlers, and de-luxe flower vases of the cut-glass antisplash type. People with delicate sensibilities garnished their car with a device called the Donna Lee Automobile Disseminator—a porous vase guaranteed, according to Sears, to fill the car with a "faint clean odor of lavender." The gap between open cars and closed cars was not as great then as it is now: for $11.95, Sears Roebuck converted your touring car into a sedan and you went forth renewed. One agreeable quality of the old Fords was that they had no bumpers, and their fenders softened and wilted with the years and permitted the driver to squeeze in and out of tight places. [10]

Tires were 30 × 3½, cost about twelve dollars, and punctured readily. Everybody carried a jiffy patching set, with a nutmeg grater to roughen the tube before the goo was spread on. Everybody was capable of putting on a patch, expected to have to, and did have to. [11]

During my association with Model T's, self-starters were not a prevalent accessory. They were expensive and under suspicion. Your car came equipped with a serviceable crank, and the first thing you learned was how to Get Results. It was a special trick, and until you learned it (usually from another Ford owner, but sometimes by a period of appalling experimentation) you might as well have been winding up an awning. The trick was to leave the ignition switch off, proceed to the animal's head, pull the choke (which was a little wire protruding through the radiator) and give the crank two or three nonchalant upward lifts. Then, whistling as though thinking about something else, you would saunter back to the driver's cabin, turn the ignition on, return to the crank, and this time, catching it on the down stroke, give it a quick spin with plenty of That. If this procedure was followed, the engine almost always responded—first with a few scattered explosions, then with a tumultuous gunfire, which you checked by racing around to the driver's seat and retarding the throttle. Often, if the emergency brake hadn't been pulled all the way back, the car advanced on you the instant the first explosion occurred and you would hold it back by leaning your weight against it. I can still feel my old Ford nuzzling me at the curb, as though looking for an apple in my pocket. [12]

In zero weather, ordinary cranking became an impossibility, except for giants. The oil thickened, and it became necessary to jack up the rear wheels, which, for some planetary reason, eased the throw. [13]

The lore and legend that governed the Ford were boundless. Owners had their own theories about everything; they discussed mutual problems in that wise, infinitely resourceful way old women discuss rheumatism. Exact knowledge was pretty scarce, and often proved less effective than superstition. Dropping a camphor ball into the gas tank was a popular expedient; it seemed to have a tonic effect on both man and machine. There wasn't much to base exact knowledge on. The Ford driver flew blind. He didn't know the temperature of his engine, the speed of his car, the amount of his fuel, or the pressure of his oil (the old Ford lubricated itself by what was amiably described as the "splash system"). A speedometer cost money and was an extra, like a windshield-wiper. The dashboard of the early models was bare save for an ignition key; later models, grown effete, boasted an ammeter which pulsated alarmingly with the throbbing of the car. Under the dash was a box of coils, with vibrators, which you adjusted or thought you adjusted. Whatever the driver learned of his motor, he learned not through instruments but through sudden developments. I remember that the timer was one of the vital organs about which there was ample doctrine. When everything else had been checked, you "had a look" at the timer. It was an extravagantly odd little device, simple in construction, mysterious in function. It contained a roller, held by a spring, and there were four contact points on the inside of the case against which, many people believed, the roller rolled. I have had a timer apart on a sick Ford many times. But I never really knew what I was up to—I was just showing off before God. There were almost as many schools of thought as there were timers. Some people, when things went wrong, just clenched their teeth and gave the timer a smart crack with a wrench. Other people opened it up and blew on it. There was a school that held that the timer needed large amounts of oil; they fixed it by frequent baptism. And there was a school that was positive it was meant to run dry as a bone; these people were continually taking it off and wiping it. I remember once spitting into a timer; not in anger, but in a spirit of research. You see, the Model T driver moved in the realm of metaphysics. He believed his car could be hexed. [14]

One reason the Ford anatomy was never reduced to an exact science was that, having "fixed" it, the owner couldn't honestly claim that the treatment had brought about the cure. There were too many authenticated cases of Fords fixing themselves—restored naturally to health after a short rest. Farmers soon discovered this, and it fitted nicely with their draft-horse philosophy: "Let 'er cool off and she'll snap into it again." [15]

A Ford owner had Number One Bearing constantly in mind. This bearing, being at the front end of the motor, was the one that always burned out, because the oil didn't reach it when the car was climbing hills. (That's what I was always told, anyway.) The oil used to recede and leave Number One dry as a clam flat; you had to watch that bearing like a hawk. It was like a weak heart—you could hear it start knocking, and that was when you stopped to let her cool off. Try as you would to keep the oil supply right, in the end Number One always went out. "Number One Bearing burned out on me and I had to have her replaced," you would say, wisely; and your companions always had a lot to tell about how to protect and pamper Number One to keep her alive. [16]

Sprinkled not too liberally among the millions of amateur witch doctors who drove Fords and applied their own abominable cures were the heaven-sent mechanics who could really make the car talk. These professionals turned up in undreamed-of spots. One time, on the banks of the Columbia River in Washington, I heard the rear end go out of my Model T when I was trying to whip it up a steep incline onto the deck of a ferry. Something snapped; the car slid backward into the mud. It seemed to me like the end of the trail. But the captain of the ferry, observing the withered remnant, spoke up. [17]

"What's got her?" he asked. [18]

"I guess it's the rear end," I replied, listlessly. The captain leaned over the rail and stared. Then I saw that there was a hunger in his eyes that set him off from other men. [19]

"Tell you what," he said, carelessly, trying to cover up his eagerness, "let's pull the son of a bitch up onto the boat, and I'll help you fix her while we're going back and forth on the river." [20]

We did just this. All that day I plied between the towns of Pasco and Kennewick, while the skipper (who had once worked in a Ford garage) directed the amazing work of resetting the bones of my car. [21]

Springtime in the heyday of the Model T was a delirious season. Owning a car was still a major excitement, roads were still wonderful and bad. The Fords were obviously conceived in madness: any car which was capable of going from forward into reverse without any perceptible mechanical hiatus was bound to be a mighty challenging thing to the human imagination. Boys used to veer them off the highway into a level pasture and run wild with them, as though they were cutting up with a girl. Most everybody used the reverse pedal quite as much as the regular foot brake—it distributed the wear over the bands and wore them all down evenly. That was the big trick, to wear all the bands down evenly, so that the final chattering would be total and the whole unit scream for renewal. [22]

The days were golden, the nights were dim and strange. I still recall with trembling those loud, nocturnal crises when you drew up to a signpost and raced the engine so the lights would be bright enough to read destinations by. I have never been really planetary since. I suppose it's time to say goodbye. Farewell, my lovely! [23]

PURPOSE AND STRUCTURE

1. Should White's thesis be more sharply delimited: "random entries in a shape somewhat less cumbersome than a Sears Roebuck catalogue" (par. 2)? Why is it appropriate to refer to a "Sears Roebuck catalogue"?

2. White introduces his thesis (first sentence, par. 2) by describing the Model T as "the miracle God had wrought" and as "Mechanically uncanny" (par. 2). How does this description prepare for the discussion of the Model T's "planetary" transmission (par. 3)?

3. Par. 4 is on acceleration. How does the last half of par. 3 prepare the reader for this subject?

4. Is the list of accessories too long (pars. 6–beginning of 12)? It is an extremely specific list, for instance, "the Donna Lee Automobile Disseminator—a porous vase guaranteed, according to Sears, to fill the car with a 'faint clean odor of lavender'" (par. 10). Should such specific references be omitted? Discuss.

5. White's list of accessories ends with self-starters. Why?

6. The Model T transmission was "planetary—which was half metaphysics" (par. 3). In what way was the timer also "in the realm of metaphysics" (par. 14)?

DICTION AND TONE

1. The title and the subtitle ("An aging male kisses an old flame goodbye, circa 1936") do not prepare the reader for the subject of the essay: the passing of the Model T Ford. Yet both are appropriate. Why?

2. Why is it an *understatement* (par. 1) to say that the Model T is fading from the American scene?

3. Why compare the Model T to a horse, "rolling the bit on its tongue" (par. 3)? "Nuzzling me at the curb" (par. 12)? "'Let 'er cool off'" (par. 15)?

4. What is the tone of "the car, possessed of only two forward speeds, catapulted directly into high with a series of ugly jerks and was off on its glorious errand" (par. 4)?

5. What is the tone of "brooding it with his own body" (par. 5)?

6. Why use the phrase "withered remnant" (par. 17)? "Resetting the bones of my car" (par. 21)?

7. What is the tone of "roads were still wonderful and bad" (par. 22)?

8. What does White mean by: "I have never been really planetary since" (par. 23)?

APPLICATIONS TO WRITING

1. Bid farewell to a favorite gadget, toy, fad, or style that was once popular.

2. What made your own springtimes "delirious" (par. 22), "a major excitement"?

A Noiseless Flash

from *Hiroshima*

JOHN HERSEY

At exactly fifteen minutes past eight in the morning, on August 6, 1945, Japanese time, at the moment when the atomic bomb flashed above Hiroshima, Miss Toshiko Sasaki, a clerk in the personnel department of the East Asia Tin Works, had just sat down at her place in the plant office and was turning her head to speak to the girl at the next desk. At that same moment, Dr. Masakazu Fujii was settling down cross-legged to read the Osaka *Asahi* on the porch of his private hospital, overhanging one of the seven deltaic rivers which divide Hiroshima; Mrs. Hatsuyo Nakamura, a tailor's widow, stood by the window of her kitchen, watching a neighbor tearing down his house because it lay in the path of an air-raid-defense fire lane; Father Wilhelm Kleinsorge, a German priest of the Society of Jesus, reclined in his underwear on a cot on the top floor of his order's three-story mission house, reading a Jesuit magazine, *Stimmen der Zeit*; Dr. Terufumi Sasaki, a young member of the surgical staff of the city's large modern Red Cross Hospital, walked along one of the hospital corridors with a blood specimen for a Wassermann test in his hand; and the Reverend Mr. Kiyoshi Tanimoto, pastor of the Hiroshima Methodist Church, paused at the door of a rich man's house in Koi, the city's western suburb, and prepared to unload a handcart full of things he had evacuated from town in fear of the massive B-29 raid which everyone expected Hiroshima to suffer. A hundred thousand people were killed by the atomic bomb, and these six were among the survivors. They still wonder why they lived when so many others died. Each of them counts many small items of chance or volition—a step taken in time, a decision to go indoors, catching one streetcar instead of the next—that spared him. And now each knows that in the act of survival he lived a dozen lives and saw more death than he ever thought he would see. At the time, none of them knew anything. [1]

The Reverend Mr. Tanimoto got up at five o'clock that morning. He was alone in the parsonage, because for some time his wife had been commuting with their year-old baby to spend nights with a friend in Ushida, a suburb to the north. Of all the important cities of Japan, only two, Kyoto and Hiroshima, had not been visited in strength by B-*san*, or Mr. B, as the Japanese, with a mixture of respect and un-happy familiarity, called the B-29; and Mr. Tanimoto, like all his neighbors and friends, was almost sick with anxiety. He had heard uncomfortably detailed accounts of mass raids on Kure, Iwakuni, Tokuyama, and other nearby towns; he was sure Hiroshima's turn would come soon. He had slept badly the night before, because there had been several air-raid warnings. Hiroshima had been getting such warnings almost every night for weeks, for at that time the B-29s were using Lake Biwa, northeast of Hiroshima, as a rendezvous point, and no matter what city the Americans planned to hit, the Superfortresses streamed in over the coast near Hiroshima. The frequency of the warnings and the continued abstinence of Mr. B with respect to Hiroshima had made its citizens jittery; a rumor was going around that the Americans were saving something special for the city. [2]

Mr. Tanimoto is a small man, quick to talk, laugh, and cry. He wears his black hair parted in the middle and rather long; the promi-nence of the frontal bones just above his eyebrows and the smallness of his mustache, mouth, and chin give him a strange, old-young look, boyish and yet wise, weak and yet fiery. He moves nervously and fast, but with a restraint which suggests that he is a cautious, thoughtful man. He showed, indeed, just those qualities in the uneasy days before the bomb fell. Besides having his wife spend the nights in Ushida, Mr. Tanimoto had been carrying all the portable things from his church, in the close-packed residential district called Nagaragawa, to a house that belonged to a rayon manufacturer in Koi, two miles from the center of town. The rayon man, a Mr. Matsui, had opened his then unoccupied estate to a large number of his friends and ac-quaintances, so that they might evacuate whatever they wished to a safe distance from the probable target area. Mr. Tanimoto had had no difficulty in moving chairs, hymnals, Bibles, altar gear, and church records by pushcart himself, but the organ console and an upright piano required some aid. A friend of his named Matsuo had, the day before, helped him get the piano out to Koi; in return, he had promised this day to assist Mr. Matsuo in hauling out a daughter's belongings. That is why he had risen so early. [3]

Mr. Tanimoto cooked his own breakfast. He felt awfully tired. The effort of moving the piano the day before, a sleepless night, weeks of worry and unbalanced diet, the cares of his parish—all combined to make him feel hardly adequate to the new day's work. There was another thing, too; Mr. Tanimoto had studied theology at Emory College, in Atlanta, Georgia; he had graduated in 1940; he spoke excellent English; he dressed in American clothes; he had corresponded with many American friends right up to the time the war began; and among a people obsessed with a fear of being spied upon—perhaps almost obsessed himself—he found himself growing increasingly uneasy. The police had questioned him several times, and just a few days before, he had heard that an influential acquaintance, a Mr. Tanaka, a retired officer of the Toyo Kisen Kaisha steamship line, an anti-Christian, a man famous in Hiroshima for his showy philanthropies and notorious for his personal tyrannies, had been telling people that Tanimoto should not be trusted. In compensation, to show himself publicly a good Japanese, Mr. Tanimoto had taken on the chairmanship of his local *tonarigumi*, or Neighborhood Association, and to his other duties and concerns this position had added the business of organizing air-raid defense for about twenty families. [4]

Before six o'clock that morning, Mr. Tanimoto started for Mr. Matsuo's house. There he found that their burden was to be a *tansu*, a large Japanese cabinet, full of clothing and household goods. The two men set out. The morning was perfectly clear and so warm that the day promised to be uncomfortable. A few minutes after they started, the air-raid siren went off—a minute-long blast that warned of approaching planes but indicated to the people of Hiroshima only a slight degree of danger, since it sounded every morning at this time, when an American weather plane came over. The two men pulled and pushed the handcart through the city streets. Hiroshima was a fan-shaped city, lying mostly on the six islands formed by the seven estuarial rivers that branch out from the Ota River; its main commercial and residential districts, covering about four square miles in the center of the city, contained three-quarters of its population, which had been reduced by several evacuation programs from a wartime peak of 380,000 to about 245,000. Factories and other residential districts, or suburbs, lay compactly around the edges of the city. To the south were the docks, an airport, and the island-studded Inland Sea. A rim of mountains runs around the other three sides of the delta. Mr. Tanimoto and Mr. Matsuo took their way through the shopping center, already full of people, and across two of the rivers to the sloping streets of Koi, and up them to the outskirts and foothills. As they started up a valley away from the tight-ranked houses, the all-clear sounded. (The Japanese radar operators, detecting only three planes, supposed that they comprised a reconnaissance.) Pushing the handcart up to the rayon man's house was tiring, and the men, after they had maneuvered their load into the driveway and to the front steps, paused to rest awhile. They stood with a wing of the house between them and the city. Like most homes in this part of Japan, the house consisted of a wooden frame and wooden walls supporting a heavy tile roof. Its front hall, packed with rolls of bedding and clothing, looked like a cool cave full of fat cushions. Opposite the house, to the right of the front door, there was a large, finicky rock garden. There was no sound of planes. The morning was still; the place was cool and pleasant. [5]

Then a tremendous flash of light cut across the sky. Mr. Tanimoto has a distinct recollection that it travelled from east to west, from the city toward the hills. It seemed a sheet of sun. Both he and Mr. Matsuo reacted in terror—and both had time to react (for they were 3,500 yards, or two miles, from the center of the explosion). Mr. Matsuo dashed up the front steps into the house and dived among the bedrolls and buried himself there. Mr. Tanimoto took four or five steps and threw himself between two big rocks in the garden. He bellied up very hard against one of them. As his face was against the stone, he did not see what happened. He felt a sudden pressure, and then splinters and pieces of board and fragments of tile fell on him. He heard no roar. (Almost no one in Hiroshima recalls hearing any noise of the bomb. But a fisherman in his sampan on the Inland Sea near Tsuzu, the man with whom Mr. Tanimoto's mother-in-law and sister-in-law were living, saw the flash and heard a tremendous explosion; he was nearly twenty miles from Hiroshima, but the thunder was greater than when the B-29s hit Iwakuni, only five miles away.) [6]

When he dared, Mr. Tanimoto raised his head and saw that the rayon man's house had collapsed. He thought a bomb had fallen directly on it. Such clouds of dust had risen that there was a sort of twilight around. In panic, not thinking for the moment of Mr. Matsuo under the ruins, he dashed out into the street. He noticed as he ran that the concrete wall of the estate had fallen over—toward the house rather than away from it. In the street, the first thing he saw was a squad of soldiers who had been burrowing into the hillside opposite, making one of the thousands of dugouts in which the Japanese apparently intended to resist invasion, hill by hill, life for life; the soldiers were coming out of the hole, where they should have been safe, and blood was running from their heads, chests, and backs. They were silent and dazed. [7]

Under what seemed to be a local dust cloud, the day grew darker and darker. [8]

At nearly midnight, the night before the bomb was dropped, an announcer on the city's radio station said that about two hundred B-29s were approaching southern Honshu and advised the population of Hiroshima to evacuate to their designated "safe areas." Mrs. Hatsuyo Nakamura, the tailor's widow, who lived in the section called Nobori-cho and who had long had a habit of doing as she was told, got her three children—a ten-year-old boy, Toshio, an eight-year-old girl, Yaeko, and a five-year-old girl, Myeko—out of bed and dressed them and walked with them to the military area known as the East Parade Ground, on the northeast edge of the city. There she unrolled some mats and the children lay down on them. They slept until about two, when they were awakened by the roar of the planes going over Hiroshima. [9]

As soon as the planes had passed, Mrs. Nakamura started back with her children. They reached home a little after two-thirty and she immediately turned on the radio, which, to her distress, was just then broadcasting a fresh warning. When she looked at the children and saw how tired they were, and when she thought of the number of trips they had made in past weeks, all to no purpose, to the East Parade Ground, she decided that in spite of the instructions on the radio, she simply could not face starting out all over again. She put the children in their bedrolls on the floor, lay down herself at three o'clock, and fell asleep at once, so soundly that when planes passed over later, she did not waken to their sound. [10]

The siren jarred her awake at about seven. She arose, dressed quickly,

and hurried to the house of Mr. Nakamoto, the head of her Neighborhood Association, and asked him what she should do. He said that she
should remain at home unless an urgent warning—a series of inter-
mittent blasts of the sirens—was sounded. She returned home, lit the
stove in the kitchen, set some rice to cook, and sat down to read that
morning's Hiroshima *Chugoku*. To her relief, the all-clear sounded at
eight o'clock. She heard the children stirring, so she went and gave
each of them a handful of peanuts and told them to stay on their
bedrolls, because they were tired from the night's walk. She had hoped
that they would go back to sleep, but the man in the house directly to
the south began to make a terrible hullabaloo of hammering, wedging,
ripping, and splitting. The prefectural government, convinced, as
everyone in Hiroshima was, that the city would be attacked soon, had
begun to press with threats and warnings for the completion of wide
fire lanes, which, it was hoped, might act in conjunction with the
rivers to localize any fires started by an incendiary raid; and the
neighbor was reluctantly sacrificing his home to the city's safety. Just
the day before, the prefecture had ordered all able-bodied girls from the
secondary schools to spend a few days helping to clear these lanes, and
they started work soon after the all-clear sounded. [11]

Mrs. Nakamura went back to the kitchen, looked at the rice, and
began watching the man next door. At first, she was annoyed with him
for making so much noise, but then she was moved almost to tears by
pity. Her emotion was specifically directed toward her neighbor, tearing
down his home, board by board, at a time when there was so much
unavoidable destruction, but undoubtedly she also felt a generalized,
community pity, to say nothing of self-pity. She had not had an easy
time. Her husband, Isawa, had gone into the Army just after Myeko
was born, and she had heard nothing from or of him for a long time,
until, on March 5, 1942, she received a seven-word telegram: "Isawa
died an honorable death at Singapore." She learned later that he had
died on February 15th, the day Singapore fell, and that he had been a
corporal. Isawa had been a not particularly prosperous tailor, and his
only capital was a Sankoku sewing machine. After his death, when his
allotments stopped coming, Mrs. Nakamura got out the machine and
began to take in piece-work herself, and since then had supported the
children, but poorly, by sewing. [12]

As Mrs. Nakamura stood watching her neighbor, everything flashed
whiter than any white she had ever seen. She did not notice what hap-

pened to the man next door; the reflex of a mother set her in motion toward her children. She had taken a single step (the house was 1,350 yards, or three-quarters of a mile, from the center of the explosion) when something picked her up and she seemed to fly into the next room over the raised sleeping platform, pursued by parts of her house. [13]

Timbers fell around her as she landed, and a shower of tiles pommelled her; everything became dark, for she was buried. The debris did not cover her deeply. She rose up and freed herself. She heard a child cry, "Mother, help me!," and saw her youngest—Myeko, the five-year-old—buried up to her breast and unable to move. As Mrs. Nakamura started frantically to claw her way toward the baby, she could see or hear nothing of her other children. [14]

In the days right before the bombing, Dr. Masakazu Fujii, being prosperous, hedonistic, and at the time not too busy, had been allowing himself the luxury of sleeping until nine or nine-thirty, but fortunately he had to get up early the morning the bomb was dropped to see a house guest off on a train. He rose at six, and half an hour later walked with his friend to the station, not far away, across two of the rivers. He was back home by seven, just as the siren sounded its sustained warning. He ate breakfast and then, because the morning was already hot, undressed down to his underwear and went out on the porch to read the paper. This porch—in fact, the whole building—was curiously constructed. Dr. Fujii was the proprietor of a peculiarly Japanese institution: a private, single-doctor hospital. This building, perched beside and over the water of the Kyo River, and next to the bridge of the same name, contained thirty rooms for thirty patients and their kinfolk—for, according to Japanese custom, when a person falls sick and goes to a hospital, one or more members of his family go and live there with him, to cook for him, bathe, massage, and read to him, and to offer incessant familial sympathy, without which a Japanese patient would be miserable indeed. Dr. Fujii had no beds—only straw mats—for his patients. He did, however, have all sorts of modern equipment; an X-ray machine, diathermy apparatus, and a fine tiled laboratory. The structure rested two-thirds on the land, one-third on piles over the tidal waters of the Kyo. This overhang, the part of the building where Dr. Fujii lived, was queer-looking, but it was cool in summer and from the porch, which faced away from the center of the city, the prospect of the river, with pleasure boats drifting up and down it, was always refreshing. Dr. Fujii had occasionally had anxious moments when the Ota and its mouth branches rose to flood, but the piling was apparently firm enough and the house had always held. [15]

Dr. Fujii had been relatively idle for about a month because in July, as the number of untouched cities in Japan dwindled and as Hiroshima seemed more and more inevitably a target, he began turning patients away, on the ground that in case of a fire raid he would not be able to evacuate them. Now he had only two patients left—a woman from Yano, injured in the shoulder, and a young man of twenty-five recovering from burns he had suffered when the steel factory near Hiroshima in which he worked had been hit. Dr. Fujii had six nurses to tend his patients. His wife and children were safe; his wife and one son were living outside Osaka, and another son and two daughters were in the country on Kyushu. A niece was living with him, and a maid and a manservant. He had little to do and did not mind, for he had saved some money. At fifty, he was healthy, convivial, and calm, and he was pleased to pass the evenings drinking whiskey with friends, always sensibly and for the sake of conversation. Before the war, he had affected brands imported from Scotland and America; now he was perfectly satisfied with the best Japanese brand, Suntory. [16]

Dr. Fujii sat down cross-legged in his underwear on the spotless matting of the porch, put on his glasses, and started reading the Osaka *Asahi.* He liked to read the Osaka news because his wife was there. He saw the flash. To him—faced away from the center and looking at his paper—it seemed a brillant yellow. Startled, he began to rise to his feet. In that moment (he was 1,550 yards from the center), the hospital leaned behind his rising and, with a terrible ripping noise, toppled into the river. The Doctor, still in the act of getting to his feet, was thrown forward and around and over; he was buffeted and gripped; he lost track of everything, because things were so speeded up; he felt the water. [17]

Dr. Fujii hardly had time to think that he was dying before he realized that he was alive, squeezed tightly by two long timbers in a V across his chest, like a morsel suspended between two huge chopsticks—held upright, so that he could not move, with his head miraculously above water and his torso and legs in it. The remains of his hospital were all around him in a mad assortment of splintered lumber and materials for the relief of pain. His left shoulder hurt terribly. His glasses were gone. [18]

Father Wilhelm Kleinsorge, of the Society of Jesus, was, on the morning of the explosion, in rather frail condition. The Japanese wartime diet had not sustained him, and he felt the strain of being a foreigner in an increasingly xenophobic Japan; even a German, since the defeat of the Fatherland, was unpopular. Father Kleinsorge had, at thirty-eight, the look of a boy growing too fast—thin in the face, with a prominent Adam's apple, a hollow chest, dangling hands, big feet. He walked clumsily, leaning forward a little. He was tired all the time. To make matters worse, he had suffered for two days, along with Father Cieslik, a fellow-priest, from a rather painful and urgent diarrhea, which they blamed on the beans and black ration bread they were obliged to eat. Two other priests then living in the mission compound, which was in the Nobori-cho section—Father Superior LaSalle and Father Schiffer—had happily escaped this affliction. [19]

Father Kleinsorge woke up about six the morning the bomb was dropped, and half an hour later—he was a bit tardy because of his sickness—he began to read Mass in the mission chapel, a small Japanese-style wooden building which was without pews, since its worshippers knelt on the usual Japanese matted floor, facing an altar graced with splendid silks, brass, silver, and heavy embroideries. This morning, a Monday, the only worshippers were Mr. Takemoto, a theological student living in the mission house; Mr. Fukai, the secretary of the diocese; Mrs. Murata, the mission's devoutly Christian housekeeper; and his fellow-priests. After Mass, while Father Kleinsorge was reading the Prayers of Thanksgiving, the siren sounded. He stopped the service and the missionaries retired across the compound to the bigger building. There, in his room on the ground floor, to the right of the front door, Father Kleinsorge changed into a military uniform which he had acquired when he was teaching at the Rokko Middle School in Kobe and which he wore during air-raid alerts. [20]

After an alarm, Father Kleinsorge always went out and scanned the sky, and in this instance, when he stepped outside, he was glad to see only the single weather plane that flew over Hiroshima each day about this time. Satisfied that nothing would happen, he went in and breakfasted with the other Fathers on substitute coffee and ration bread, which, under the circumstances, was especially repugnant to him. The Fathers sat and talked awhile, until, at eight, they heard the all-clear. They went then to various parts of the building. Father Schiffer retired to his room to do some writing. Father Cieslik sat in his room in a straight chair with a pillow over his stomach to ease his pain, and read. Father Superior LaSalle stood at the window of his room, thinking. Father Kleinsorge went up to a room on the third floor, took off all his clothes except his underwear, and stretched out on his right side on a cot and began reading his *Stimmen der Zeit*. [21]

After the terrible flash—which, Father Kleinsorge later realized, reminded him of something he had read as a boy about a large meteor colliding with the earth—he had time (since he was 1,400 yards from the center) for one thought: A bomb has fallen directly on us. Then, for a few seconds or minutes, he went out of his mind. [22]

Father Kleinsorge never knew how he got out of the house. The next things he was conscious of were that he was wandering around in the mission's vegetable garden in his underwear, bleeding slightly from small cuts along his left flank; that all the buildings round about had fallen down except the Jesuits' mission house, which had long before been braced and double-braced by a priest named Gropper, who was terrified of earthquakes; that the day had turned dark; and that Murata-*san*, the housekeeper, was nearby, crying over and over, "*Shu Jesusu, awaremi tamai!* Our Lord Jesus, have pity on us!" [23]

On the train on the way into Hiroshima from the country, where he lived with his mother, Dr. Terufumi Sasaki, the Red Cross Hospital surgeon, thought over an unpleasant nightmare he had had the night before. His mother's home was in Mukaihara, thirty miles from the city, and it took him two hours by train and tram to reach the hospital. He had slept uneasily all night and had awakened an hour earlier than usual, and, feeling sluggish and slightly feverish, had debated whether to go to the hospital at all; his sense of duty finally forced him to go, and he had started out on an earlier train than he took most mornings. The dream had particularly frightened him because it was so closely associated, on the surface at least, with a disturbing actuality. He was only twenty-five years old and had just completed his training at the Eastern Medical University, in Tsingtao, China. He was something of an idealist and was much distressed by the inadequacy of medical facilities in the country town where his mother lived. Quite on his own, and without a permit, he had begun visiting a few sick people out there in the evenings, after his eight hours at the hospital and four hours' commuting. He had recently learned that the penalty for practicing without a permit was severe; a fellow-doctor whom he had asked about it had given him a serious scolding. Nevertheless, he had continued to practice. In his dream, he had been at the bedside of a country patient when the police and the doctor he had consulted burst into the room, seized him, dragged him outside, and beat him up cruelly. On the train, he just about decided to give up the work in Mukaihara, since he felt it would be impossible to get a permit, because the authorities would hold that it would conflict with his duties at the Red Cross Hospital. [24]

At the terminus, he caught a streetcar at once. (He later calculated that if he had taken his customary train that morning, and if he had had to wait a few minutes for the streetcar, as often happened, he would have been close to the center at the time of the explosion and would surely have perished.) He arrived at the hospital at seven-forty and reported to the chief surgeon. A few minutes later, he went to a room on the first floor and drew blood from the arm of a man in order to perform a Wassermann test. The laboratory containing the incubators for the test was on the third floor. With the blood specimen in his left hand, walking in a kind of distraction he had felt all morning, probably because of the dream and his restless night, he started along the main corridor on his way toward the stairs. He was one step beyond an open window when the light of the bomb was reflected, like a gigantic photographic flash, in the corridor. He ducked down on one knee and said to himself, as only a Japanese would, "Sasaki, *gambare!* Be brave!" Just then (the building was 1,650 yards from the center), the blast ripped through the hospital. The glasses he was wearing flew off his face; the bottle of blood crashed against one wall; his Japanese slippers zipped out from under his feet—but otherwise, thanks to where he stood, he was untouched. [25]

Dr. Sasaki shouted the name of the chief surgeon and rushed around to the man's office and found him terribly cut by glass. The hospital was in horrible confusion: heavy partitions and ceilings had fallen on patients, beds had overturned, windows had blown in and cut people, blood was spattered on the walls and floors, instruments were everywhere, many of the patients were running about screaming, many more lay dead. (A colleague working in the laboratory to which Dr.

Sasaki had been walking was dead; Dr. Sasaki's patient, whom he had just left and who a few moments before had been dreadfully afraid of syphilis, was also dead.) Dr. Sasaki found himself the only doctor in the hospital who was unhurt. [26]

Dr. Sasaki, who believed that the enemy had hit only the building he was in, got bandages and began to bind the wounds of those inside the hospital; while outside, all over Hiroshima, maimed and dying citizens turned their unsteady steps toward the Red Cross Hospital to begin an invasion that was to make Dr. Sasaki forget his private nightmare for a long, long time. [27]

Miss Toshiko Sasaki, the East Asia Tin Works clerk, who is not related to Dr. Sasaki, got up at three o'clock in the morning on the day the bomb fell. There was extra housework to do. Here eleven-month-old brother, Akio, had come down the day before with a serious stomach upset; her mother had taken him to the Tamura Pediatric Hospital and was staying there with him. Miss Sasaki, who was about twenty, had to cook breakfast for her father, a brother, a sister, and herself, and— since the hospital, because of the war, was unable to provide food—to prepare a whole day's meals for her mother and the baby, in time for her father, who worked in a factory making rubber earplugs for artillery crews, to take the food by on his way to the plant. When she had finished and had cleaned and put away the cooking things, it was nearly seven. The family lived in Koi, and she had a forty-five minute trip to the tin works, in the section of town called Kannonmachi. She was in charge of the personnel records in the factory. She left Koi at seven, and as soon as she reached the plant, she went with some of the other girls from the personnel department to the factory auditorium. A prominent local Navy man, a former employee, had committed suicide the day before by throwing himself under a train—a death considered honorable enough to warrant a memorial service, which was to be held at the tin works at ten o'clock that morning. In the large hall, Miss Sasaki and the others made suitable preparations for the meeting. This work took about twenty minutes. [28]

Miss Sasaki went back to her office and sat down at her desk. She was quite far from the windows, which were off to her left, and behind her were a couple of tall bookcases containing all the books of the factory library, which the personnel department had organized. She settled herself at her desk, put some things in a drawer, and shifted papers. She thought that before she began to make entries in her lists of new employees, discharges, and departures for the Army, she would chat for a moment with the girl at her right. Just as she turned her head away from the windows, the room was filled with a blinding light. She was paralyzed by fear, fixed still in her chair for a long moment (the plant was 1,600 yards from the center). [29]

Everything fell, and Miss Sasaki lost consciousness. The ceiling dropped suddenly and the wooden floor above collapsed in splinters and the people up there came down and the roof above them gave way; but principally and first of all, the bookcases right behind her swooped forward and the contents threw her down, with the left leg horribly twisted and breaking underneath her. There, in the tin factory, in the first moment of the atomic age, a human being was crushed by books. [30]

PURPOSE AND STRUCTURE

1. The first two words of Hersey's report are *At exactly*. Why begin with these words?

2. Miss Toshiko Sasaki is introduced in the first sentence, the other five survivors in the second sentence (par. 1). Would it be more effective to introduce all six in the second sentence, rewriting the first sentence to end with the word *Hiroshima?* Would it be more effective to present each of the survivors in a separate sentence? Rewrite, or argue for Hersey's two sentences.

3. Hersey introduces the six survivors in one order (par. 1) and describes their experiences in another order (pars. 2–30). Why? Would it be more effective for the sections of the report to follow the sequence of the introduction?

4. Is the last sentence of the introduction (par. 1) too general? Formulate it more precisely or argue for its present form.

5. The introduction describes precisely what each of the six survivors was doing at the moment of the flash. Thus the reader begins with the climax of each episode. Does this knowledge reduce the interest of the detailed episodes? Would it be preferable to save this information for the end of each episode? Discuss.

6. The first sentence of par. 2 identifies Mr. Tanimoto and gives the time ("five o'clock that morning"). The second sentence gives further informa-

tion about him. Then the rest of the paragraph is an exposition of his situation. How much of it is peculiar to Mr. Tanimoto? Could this information have been attached to any of the other five victims? Is it most relevant to Mr. Tanimoto? Why place this information at this point in the essay?

7. The last sentence of par. 3 ("That is why he had risen so early") refers back to the first sentence of par. 2. What portions of these paragraphs tell why he rose so early?

8. The first sentence of par. 4 is the next point in time after Mr. Tanimoto got up. Is the second sentence ("He felt awfully tired") the topic sentence of par. 4? Discuss.

9. In par. 5 there is a geographical description of the city ("Hiroshima was a fan-shaped city, lying mostly on the six islands formed by the seven estuarial rivers . . ."). The sentence preceding this description ("The two men pulled and pushed the handcart through the city streets") and the words following it ("Mr. Tanimoto and Mr. Matsuo took their way through the shopping center . . .") seem to have little to do with the description. Why describe the city here? Would this description be preferable at the beginning of the essay? Where is the best place in the essay for such information?

10. Why end the episode with this detail (par. 8)? Why is the same detail introduced in par. 7?

11. The fourth sentence in par. 6 consists of three simple independent clauses joined by conjunctions. The usual punctuation would be to separate the clauses with commas. Why, then, does Hersey use a dash and parentheses?

12. The distance of each of the victims from the center of the explosion is given in pars. 6, 13, 17, 22, 25, and 29. Is this information most relevant at the particular points chosen by Hersey? Rewrite this section of each of these paragraphs, attempting a more effective arrangement of the material without using parentheses.

13. Choose five other examples of parenthetical statements. Compare and contrast their rhetorical functions with five parenthetical examples from the magazine *Consumer Reports* (published by Consumers Union). Note: Parentheses are sometimes used in technical writing (carrying a heavy load of statistical or comparative data) to locate complicated modifiers freely.

14. Par. 30, the conclusion of "A Noiseless Flash," is not ordered chronologically, though the events are located in time. Why end with what happened "first of all"?

15. Is it accurate to say "Everything fell" (par. 30)?

16. Why refer to "tin factory" in the last sentence of par. 30?

17. Why does Hersey call it "the first moment of the atomic age" (par. 30)? Discuss whether these words can be considered part of the thesis of the essay. Can it be argued that other "moments" are just as relevant to the meaning of Hersey's essay? (One example might be 1905, the year Albert Einstein created the special theory of relativity—one of whose propositions was that mass and energy are equivalent.)

18. Can the last words of the essay ("a human being was crushed by books") be considered part of the thesis? Discuss.

DICTION AND TONE

1. The diction of "A Noiseless Flash" is reportorial—careful, flat, and conventional. But the manner in which the writer communicates his attitude toward his subject—his tone—is complex.

Consider Hersey's first two sentences. They are densely factual ("overhanging one of the seven deltaic rivers which divide Hiroshima") and almost obsessively exact ("reclined in his underwear on a cot on the top floor of the order's three-story mission house, reading a Jesuit magazine, *Stimmen der Zeit*"). The sentences are overladen with detail. How do they prepare the reader for the rest of the essay?

2. Write a short introductory paragraph to "A Noiseless Flash," setting it in historical perspective and commenting on the moral, military, and political implications. Discuss whether Hersey should have used such an introduction.

3. Search the essay for comments or generalizations made by Hersey. Has Hersey failed to take advantage of his material, to develop relevant generalizations from his data? Formulate a generalization and develop a paragraph using the factual material of "A Noiseless Flash" as evidence. Compare the tone of your paragraph with the tone of "A Noiseless Flash," with its relative paucity of overt moralizing or intellectual analysis. Has Hersey failed to communicate his attitude toward his materials—failed, in other words, to establish his tone? Discuss. If you believe he has communicated his tone, attempt a statement of it. Point to details, organizing principles, or diction as evidence for your statement.

4. Why use the word *estuarial* (par. 5)? Would a more common word or phrase be better?

5. Why "finicky rock garden" (par. 5)? Would you omit this detail?

APPLICATIONS TO WRITING

The factual density and precision of Hersey's "A Noiseless Flash" almost convince the reader that here is a transcription of reality, that everything is included from moment to moment. In part the reader's impression is a result of (1) diction that does not call attention to itself ("flat"), (2) careful selection of details ("facts"), (3) effective arrangement of the details, and (4) control of tone (primarily through the last two elements). Try to employ these four methods in the following applications to writing.

1. Describe fifteen minutes of your day in chronological sequence, including necessary exposition as Hersey does. (See pars. 2, 3, 4, 5.)

2. Describe an automobile accident, beginning with the moment of impact, then cutting back to an earlier time and returning to the impact.

3. Begin with a moment from basketball—say, the last score of the game. Freeze the instant the ball leaves the hand of the scorer, describing the position of each player. Then describe how each player reached this point, beginning sixty seconds before this time.

Notes of a Native Son

JAMES BALDWIN

On the 29th of July, in 1943, my father died. On the same day, a few hours later, his last child was born. Over a month before this, while all our energies were concentrated in waiting for these events, there had been, in Detroit, one of the bloodiest race riots of the century. A few hours after my father's funeral, while he lay in state in the undertaker's chapel, a race riot broke out in Harlem. On the morning of the 3rd of August, we drove my father to the graveyard through a wilderness of smashed plate glass. [1]

The day of my father's funeral had also been my nineteenth birthday. As we drove him to the graveyard, the spoils of injustice, anarchy, discontent, and hatred were all around us. It seemed to me that God himself had devised, to mark my father's end, the most sustained and brutally dissonant of codas. And it seemed to me, too, that the violence which rose all about us as my father left the world had been devised as a corrective for the pride of his eldest son. I had declined to believe in that apocalypse which had been central to my father's vision; very well, life seemed to be saying, here is something that will certainly pass for an apocalypse until the real thing comes along. I had inclined to be contemptuous of my father for the conditions of his life, for the conditions of our lives. When his life had ended I began to wonder about that life and also, in a new way, to be apprehensive about my own. [2]

I had not known my father very well. We had got on badly, partly because we shared, in our different fashions, the vice of stubborn pride. When he was dead I realized that I had hardly ever spoken to him. When he had been dead a long time I began to wish I had. It seems to be typical of life in America, where opportunities, real and fancied, are thicker than anywhere else on the globe, that the second generation has no time to talk to the first. No one, including my father, seems to have known exactly how old he was, but his mother had been born during slavery. He was of the first generation of free men. He, along with thousands of other Negroes, came North after 1919 and I was part of that generation which had never seen the landscape of what Negroes sometimes call the Old Country. [3]

He had been born in New Orleans and had been a quite young man there during the time that Louis Armstrong, a boy, was running errands for the dives and honky-tonks of what was always presented to me as one of the most wicked of cities—to this day, whenever I think of New Orleans, I also helplessly think of Sodom and Gomorrah. My father never mentioned Louis Armstrong, except to forbid us to play his records; but there was a picture of him on our wall for a long time. One of my father's strong-willed female relatives had placed it there and forbade my father to take it down. He never did, but he eventually maneuvered her out of the house and when, some years later, she was in trouble and near death, he refused to do anything to help her. [4]

He was, I think, very handsome. I gather this from photographs and from my own memories of him, dressed in his Sunday best and on his way to preach a sermon somewhere, when I was little. Handsome, proud, and ingrown, "like a toe-nail," somebody said. But he looked to

me, as I grew older, like pictures I had seen of African tribal chieftains:
he really should have been naked, with war-paint on and barbaric
mementos, standing among spears. He could be chilling in the pulpit
and indescribably cruel in his personal life and he was certainly the
most bitter man I have ever met; yet it must be said that there was
something else in him, buried in him, which lent him his tremendous
power and, even, a rather crushing charm. It had something to do with
his blackness, I think—he was very black—with his blackness and his
beauty, and with the fact that he knew that he was black but did not
know that he was beautiful. He claimed to be proud of his blackness
but it had also been the cause of much humiliation and it had fixed
bleak boundaries to his life. He was not a young man when we
were growing up and he had already suffered many kinds of ruin; in
his outrageously demanding and protective way he loved his children,
who were black like him and menaced, like him; and all these things
sometimes showed in his face when he tried, never to my knowledge
with any success, to establish contact with any of us. When he took
one of his children on his knee to play, the child always became fretful
and began to cry; when he tried to help one of us with our homework
the absolutely unabating tension which emanated from him caused our
minds and our tongues to become paralyzed, so that he, scarcely knowing why, flew into a rage and the child, not knowing why, was punished. If it ever entered his head to bring a surprise home for his
children, it was, almost unfailingly, the wrong surprise and even the big
watermelons he often brought home on his back in the summertime led
to the most appalling scenes. I do not remember, in all those years, that
one of his children was ever glad to see him come home. From what I
was able to gather of his early life, it seemed that this inability to
establish contact with other people had always marked him and had
been one of the things which had driven him out of New Orleans.
There was something in him, therefore, groping and tentative, which
was never expressed and which was buried with him. One saw it most
clearly when he was facing new people and hoping to impress them.
But he never did, not for long. We went from church to smaller and
more improbable church, he found himself in less and less demand as
a minister, and by the time he died none of his friends had come to
see him for a long time. He had lived and died in an intolerable
bitterness of spirit and it frightened me, as we drove him to the graveyard through those unquiet, ruined streets, to see how powerful and

overflowing this bitterness could be and to realize that this bitterness now was mine. [5]

When he died I had been away from home for a little over a year. In that year I had had time to become aware of the meaning of all my father's bitter warnings, had discovered the secret of his proudly pursed lips and rigid carriage: I had discovered the weight of white people in the world. I saw that this had been for my ancestors and now would be for me an awful thing to live with and that the bitterness which had helped to kill my father could also kill me. [6]

He had been ill a long time—in the mind, as we now realized, re-living instances of his fantastic intransigence in the new light of his affliction and endeavoring to feel a sorrow for him which never, quite, came true. We had not known that he was being eaten up by para-noia, and the discovery that his cruelty, to our bodies and our minds, had been one of the symptoms of his illness was not, then, enough to enable us to forgive him. The younger children felt, quite simply, relief that he would not be coming home anymore. My mother's observa-tion that it was he, after all, who had kept them alive all these years meant nothing because the problems of keeping children alive are not real for children. The older children felt, with my father gone, that they could invite their friends to the house without fear that their friends would be insulted or, as had sometimes happened with me, being told that their friends were in league with the devil and intended to rob our family of everything we owned. (I didn't fail to wonder, and it made me hate him, what on earth we owned that anybody else would want.) [7]

His illness was beyond all hope of healing before anyone realized that he was ill. He had always been so strange and had lived, like a prophet, in such unimaginably close communion with the Lord that his long silences which were punctuated by moans and hallelujahs and snatches of old songs while he sat at the living-room window never seemed odd to us. It was not until he refused to eat because, he said, his family was trying to poison him that my mother was forced to accept as a fact what had, until then, been only an unwilling suspicion. When he was committed, it was discovered that he had tuberculosis and, as it turned out, the disease of his mind allowed the disease of his body to destroy him. For the doctors could not force him to eat, either, and, though he was fed intravenously, it was clear from the beginning that there was no hope for him. [8]

In my mind's eye I could see him, sitting at the window, locked up in his terrors; hating and fearing every living soul including his children who had betrayed him, too, by reaching towards the world which had despised him. There were nine of us. I began to wonder what it could have felt like for such a man to have had nine children whom he could barely feed. He used to make little jokes about our poverty, which never, of course, seemed very funny to us; they could not have seemed very funny to him, either, or else our all too feeble response to them would never have caused such rages. He spent great energy and achieved, to our chagrin, no small amount of success in keeping us away from the people who surrounded us, people who had all-night rent parties to which we listened when we should have been sleeping, people who cursed and drank and flashed razor blades on Lenox Avenue. He could not understand why, if they had so much energy to spare, they could not use it to make their lives better. He treated almost everybody on our block with a most uncharitable asperity and neither they, nor, of course, their children were slow to reciprocate. [9]

The only white people who came to our house were welfare workers and bill collectors. It was almost always my mother who dealt with them, for my father's temper, which was at the mercy of his pride, was never to be trusted. It was clear that he felt their very presence in his home to be a violation: this was conveyed by his carriage, almost ludicrously stiff, and by his voice, harsh and vindictively polite. When I was around nine or ten I wrote a play which was directed by a young, white schoolteacher, a woman, who then took an interest in me, and gave me books to read and, in order to corroborate my theatrical bent, decided to take me to see what she somewhat tactlessly referred to as "real" plays. Theater-going was forbidden in our house, but, with the really cruel intuitiveness of a child, I suspected that the color of this woman's skin would carry the day for me. When, at school, she suggested taking me to the theater, I did not, as I might have done if she had been a Negro, find a way of discouraging her, but agreed that she should pick me up at my house one evening. I then, very cleverly, left all the rest to my mother, who suggested to my father, as I knew she would, that it would not be very nice to let such a kind woman make the trip for nothing. Also, since it was a schoolteacher, I imagine that my mother countered the idea of sin with the idea of "education," which word, even with my father, carried a kind of bitter weight. [10]

Before the teacher came my father took me aside to ask *why* she was coming, what *interest* she could possibly have in our house, in a boy like me. I said I didn't know but I, too, suggested that it had something to do with education. And I understood that my father was waiting for me to say something—I didn't quite know what; perhaps that I wanted his protection against this teacher and her "education." I said none of these things and the teacher came and we went out. It was clear, during the brief interview in our living room, that my father was agreeing very much against his will and that he would have refused permission if he had dared. The fact that he did not dare caused me to despise him: I had no way of knowing that he was facing in that living room a wholly unprecedented and frightening situation. [11]

Later, when my father had been laid off from his job, this woman became very important to us. She was really a very sweet and generous woman and went to a great deal of trouble to be of help to us, particularly during one awful winter. My mother called her by the highest name she knew: She said she was a "christian." My father could scarcely disagree but during the four or five years of our relatively close association he never trusted her and was always trying to surprise in her open, Midwestern face the genuine, cunningly hidden, and hideous motivation. In later years, particularly when it began to be clear that this "education" of mine was going to lead me to perdition, he became more explicit and warned me that my white friends in high school were not really my friends and that I would see, when I was older, how white people would do anything to keep a Negro down. Some of them could be nice, he admitted, but none of them were to be trusted and most of them were not even nice. The best thing was to have as little to do with them as possible. I did not feel this way and I was certain, in my innocence, that I never would. [12]

But the year which preceded my father's death had made a great change in my life. I had been living in New Jersey, working in defense plants, working and living among southerners, white and black. I knew about the south, of course, and about how southerners treated Negroes and how they expected them to behave, but it had never entered my mind that anyone would look at me and expect *me* to behave that way. I learned in New Jersey that to be a Negro meant, precisely, that one was never looked at but was simply at the mercy of the reflexes the color of one's skin caused in other people. I acted in New Jersey as I had always acted, that is as though I thought a great deal of myself—I had to *act* that way—with results that were, simply, unbelievable. I had scarcely arrived before I had earned the enmity, which was extraordinarily ingenious, of all my superiors and nearly all my co-workers. In the beginning, to make matters worse, I simply did not know what was happening. I did not know what I had done, and I shortly began to wonder what *anyone* could possibly do, to bring about such unanimous, active, and unbearably vocal hostility. I knew about jim-crow but I had never experienced it. I went to the same self-service restaurant three times and stood with all the Princeton boys before the counter, waiting for a hamburger and coffee; it was always an extraordinarily long time before anything was set before me; but it was not until the fourth visit that I learned that, in fact, nothing had ever been set before me: I had simply picked something up. Negroes were not served there, I was told, and they had been waiting for me to realize that I was always the only Negro present. Once I was told this, I determined to go there all the time. But now they were ready for me and, though some dreadful scenes were subsequently enacted in that restaurant, I never ate there again. [13]

It was the same story all over New Jersey, in bars, bowling alleys, diners, places to live. I was always being forced to leave, silently, or with mutual imprecations. I very shortly became notorious and children giggled behind me when I passed and their elders whispered or shouted—they really believed that I was mad. And it did begin to work on my mind, of course; I began to be afraid to go anywhere and to compensate for this I went places to which I really should not have gone and where, God knows, I had no desire to be. My reputation in town naturally enhanced my reputation at work and my working day became one long series of acrobatics designed to keep me out of trouble. I cannot say that these acrobatics succeeded. It began to seem that the machinery of the organization I worked for was turning over, day and night, with but one aim: to eject me. I was fired once, and contrived, with the aid of a friend from New York, to get back on the payroll; was fired again, and bounced back again. It took a while to fire me for the third time, but the third time took. There were no loopholes anywhere. There was not even any way of getting back inside the gates. [14]

That year in New Jersey lives in my mind as though it were the year during which, having an unsuspected predilection for it, I first contracted some dread, chronic disease, the unfailing symptom of which is a kind of blind fever, a pounding in the skull and fire in the bowels.

Once this disease is contracted, one can never be really carefree again, for the fever, without an instant's warning, can recur at any moment. It can wreck more important things than race relations. There is not a Negro alive who does not have this rage in his blood—one has the choice, merely, of living with it consciously or surrendering to it. As for me, this fever has recurred in me, and does, and will until the day I die. [15]

My last night in New Jersey, a white friend from New York took me to the nearest big town, Trenton, to go to the movies and have a few drinks. As it turned out, he also saved me from, at the very least, a violent whipping. Almost every detail of that night stands out very clearly in my memory. I even remember the name of the movie we saw because its title impressed me as being so patly ironical. It was a movie about the German occupation of France, starring Maureen O'Hara and Charles Laughton and called *This Land Is Mine*. I remember the name of the diner we walked into when the movie ended: it was the "American Diner." When we walked in the counterman asked what we wanted and I remember answering with the casual sharpness which had become my habit: "We want a hamburger and a cup of coffee, what do you think we want?" I do not know why, after a year of such rebuffs, I so completely failed to anticipate his answer, which was, of course, "We don't serve Negroes here." This reply failed to discompose me, at least for the moment. I made some sardonic comment about the name of the diner and we walked out into the streets. [16]

This was the time of what was called the "brown-out," when the lights in all American cities were very dim. When we re-entered the streets something happened to me which had the force of an optical illusion, or a nightmare. The streets were very crowded and I was facing north. People were moving in every direction but it seemed to me, in that instant, that all of the people I could see, and many more than that, were moving toward me, against me, and that everyone was white. I remember how their faces gleamed. And I felt, like a physical sensation, a *click* at the nape of my neck as though some interior string connecting my head to my body had been cut. I began to walk. I heard my friend call after me, but I ignored him. Heaven only knows what was going on in his mind, but he had the good sense not to touch me— I don't know what would have happened if he had—and to keep me in sight. I don't know what was going on in my mind, either; I certainly had no conscious plan. I wanted to do something to crush these white faces, which were crushing me. I walked for perhaps a block or two until I came to an enormous, glittering, and fashionable restaurant in which I knew not even the intercession of the Virgin would cause me to be served. I pushed through the doors and took the first vacant seat I saw, at a table for two, and waited. [17]

I do not know how long I waited and I rather wonder, until today, what I could possibly have looked like. Whatever I looked like, I frightened the waitress who shortly appeared, and the moment she appeared all of my fury flowed towards her. I hated her for her white face, and for her great, astounded, frightened eyes. I felt that if she found a black man so frightening I would make her fright worthwhile. [18]

She did not ask me what I wanted, but repeated, as though she had learned it somewhere, "We don't serve Negroes here." She did not say it with the blunt, derisive hostility to which I had grown so accustomed, but, rather, with a note of apology in her voice, and fear. This made me colder and more murderous than ever. I felt I had to do something with my hands. I wanted her to come close enough for me to get her neck between my hands. [19]

So I pretended not to have understood her, hoping to draw her closer. And she did step a very short step closer, with her pencil poised incongruously over her pad, and repeated the formula: ". . . don't serve Negroes here." [20]

Somehow, with the repetition of that phrase, which was already ringing in my head like a thousand bells of a nightmare, I realized that she would never come any closer and that I would have to strike from a distance. There was nothing on the table but an ordinary watermug half full of water, and I picked this up and hurled it with all my strength at her. She ducked and it missed her and shattered against the mirror behind the bar. And, with that sound, my frozen blood abruptly thawed, I returned from wherever I had been, I *saw*, for the first time, the restaurant, the people with their mouths open, already, as it seemed to me, rising as one man, and I realized what I had done, and where I was, and I was frightened. I rose and began running for the door. A round, potbellied man grabbed me by the nape of the neck just as I reached the doors and began to beat me about the face. I kicked him and got loose and ran into the streets. My friend whispered, *"Run!"* and I ran. [21]

My friend stayed outside the restaurant long enough to misdirect my pursuers and police, who arrived, he told me, at once. I do not know what I said to him when he came to my room that night. I could not have said much. I felt, in the oddest, most awful way, that I had somehow betrayed him. I lived it over and over and over again, the way one relives an automobile accident after it has happened and one finds oneself alone and safe. I could not get over two facts, both equally difficult for the imagination to grasp, and one was that I could have been murdered. But the other was that I had been ready to commit murder. I saw nothing very clearly but I did see this: that my life, my *real* life, was in danger, and not from anything other people might do but from the hatred I carried in my own heart. [22]

II

I had returned home around the second week in June—in great haste because it seemed that my father's death and my mother's confinement were both but a matter of hours. In the case of my mother, it soon became clear that she had simply made a miscalculation. This had always been her tendency and I don't believe that a single one of us arrived in the world, or has since arrived anywhere else, on time. But none of us dawdled so intolerably about the business of being born as did my baby sister. We sometimes amused ourselves, during those endless, stifling weeks, by picturing the baby sitting within in the safe, warm, dark, bitterly regretting the necessity of becoming a part of our chaos and stubbornly putting it off as long as possible. I understood her perfectly and congratulated her on showing such good sense so soon. Death, however, sat as purposefully at my father's bedside as life stirred within my mother's womb and it was harder to understand why he so lingered in that long shadow. It seemed that he had bent, and for a long time, too, all of his energies towards dying. Now death was ready for him but my father held back. [23]

All of Harlem, indeed, seemed to be infected by waiting. I had never before known it to be so violently still. Racial tensions throughout this country were exacerbated during the early years of the war, partly because the labor market brought together hundreds of thousands of ill-prepared people and partly because Negro soldiers, regardless of where they were born, received their military training in the south. What happened in defense plants and army camps had repercussions, naturally,

in every Negro ghetto. The situation in Harlem had grown bad enough
for clergymen, policemen, educators, politicians, and social workers to
assert in one breath that there was no "crime wave" and to offer, in the
very next breath, suggestions as to how to combat it. These suggestions
always seemed to involve playgrounds, despite the fact that racial
skirmishes were occurring in the playgrounds, too. Playground or not,
crime wave or not, the Harlem police force had been augmented in
March, and the unrest grew—perhaps, in fact, partly as a result of
the ghetto's instinctive hatred of policemen. Perhaps the most revealing
news item, out of the steady parade of reports of muggings, stabbings,
shootings, assaults, gang wars, and accusations of police brutality, is the
item concerning six Negro girls who set upon a white girl in the subway because, as they all too accurately put it, she was stepping on their
toes. Indeed she was, all over the nation. [24]

I had never before been so aware of policemen, on foot, on horseback,
on corners, everywhere, always two by two. Nor had I ever been so
aware of small knots of people. They were on stoops and on corners and
in doorways, and what was striking about them, I think, was that they
did not seem to be talking. Never, when I passed these groups, did the
usual sound of a curse or a laugh ring out and neither did there seem
to be any hum of gossip. There was certainly, on the other hand,
occurring between them communication extraordinarily intense. Another thing that was striking was the unexpected diversity of the people
who made up these groups. Usually, for example, one would see a
group of sharpies standing on the street corner, jiving the passing
chicks; or a group of older men, usually, for some reason, in the vicinity
of a barber shop, discussing baseball scores, or the numbers, or making
rather chilling observations about women they had known. Women, in
a general way, tended to be seen less often together—unless they were
church women, or very young girls, or prostitutes met together for an
unprofessional instant. But that summer I saw the strangest combinations: large, respectable, churchly matrons standing on the stoops or the
corners with their hair tied up, together with a girl in sleazy satin whose
face bore the marks of gin and the razor, or heavy-set, abrupt, no-
nonsense older men, in company with the most disreputable and
fanatical "race" men, or these same "race" men with the sharpies, or
these sharpies with the churchly women. Seventh Day Adventists and
Methodists and Spiritualists seemed to be hobnobbing with Holyrollers
and they were all, alike, entangled with the most flagrant disbelievers;

something heavy in their stance seemed to indicate that they had all, incredibly, seen a common vision, and on each face there seemed to be the same strange, bitter shadow. [25]

The churchly women and the matter-of-fact, no-nonsense men had children in the Army. The sleazy girls they talked to had lovers there, the sharpies and the "race" men had friends and brothers there. It would have demanded an unquestioning patriotism, happily as uncommon in this country as it is undesirable, for these people not to have been disturbed by the bitter letters they received, by the newspaper stories they read, not to have been enraged by the posters, then to be found all over New York, which described the Japanese as "yellow-bellied Japs." It was only the "race" men, to be sure, who spoke ceaselessly of being revenged—how this vengeance was to be exacted was not clear—for the indignities and dangers suffered by Negro boys in uniform; but everybody felt a directionless, hopeless bitterness, as well as that panic which can scarcely be suppressed when one knows that a human being one loves is beyond one's reach, and in danger. This helplessness and this gnawing uneasiness does something, at length, to even the toughest mind. Perhaps the best way to sum all this up is to say that the people I knew felt, mainly, a peculiar kind of relief when they knew that their boys were being shipped out of the south, to do battle overseas. It was, perhaps, like feeling that the most dangerous part of a dangerous journey had been passed and that now, even if death should come, it would come with honor and without the complicity of their countrymen. Such a death would be, in short, a fact with which one could hope to live. [26]

It was on the 28th of July, which I believe was a Wednesday, that I visited my father for the first time during his illness and for the last time in his life. The moment I saw him I knew why I had put off this visit so long. I had told my mother that I did not want to see him because I hated him. But this was not true. It was only that I *had* hated him and I wanted to hold on to this hatred. I did not want to look on him as a ruin: it was not a ruin I had hated. I imagine that one of the reasons people cling to their hates so stubbornly is because they sense, once hate is gone, that they will be forced to deal with pain. [27]

We traveled out to him, his older sister and myself, to what seemed to be the very end of a very Long Island. It was hot and dusty and we wrangled, my aunt and I, all the way out, over the fact that I had recently begun to smoke and, as she said, to give myself airs. But I knew that she wrangled with me because she could not bear to face the fact of her brother's dying. Neither could I endure the reality of her despair, her unstated bafflement as to what had happened to her brother's life, and her own. So we wrangled and I smoked and from time to time she fell into a heavy reverie. Covertly, I watched her face, which was the face of an old woman; it had fallen in, the eyes were sunken and lightless; soon she would be dying, too. [28]

In my childhood—it had not been so long ago—I had thought her beautiful. She had been quick-witted and quick-moving and very generous with all the children and each of her visits had been an event. At one time one of my brothers and myself had thought of running away to live with her. Now she could no longer produce out of her handbag some unexpected and yet familiar delight. She made me feel pity and revulsion and fear. It was awful to realize that she no longer caused me to feel affection. The closer we came to the hospital the more querulous she became and at the same time, naturally, grew more dependent on me. Between pity and guilt and fear I began to feel that there was another me trapped in my skull like a jack-in-the-box who might escape my control at any moment and fill the air with screaming. [29]

She began to cry the moment we entered the room and she saw him lying there, all shriveled and still, like a little black monkey. The great, gleaming apparatus which fed him and would have compelled him to be still even if he had been able to move brought to mind, not beneficence, but torture; the tubes entering his arm made me think of pictures I had seen when a child, of Gulliver, tied down by the pygmies on that island. My aunt wept and wept, there was a whistling sound in my father's throat; nothing was said; he could not speak. I wanted to take his hand, to say something. But I do not know what I could have said, even if he could have heard me. He was not really in that room with us, he had at last really embarked on his journey; and though my aunt told me that he said he was going to meet Jesus, I did not hear anything except that whistling in his throat. The doctor came back and we left, into that unbearable train again, and home. In the morning came the telegram saying that he was dead. Then the house was suddenly full of relatives, friends, hysteria, and confusion and I quickly left my mother and the children to the care of those impressive women, who, in Negro communities at least, automatically appear at times of bereavement armed with lotions, proverbs, and patience, and an ability to cook. I went downtown. By the time I returned, later the same day, my mother had been carried to the hospital and the baby had been born. [30]

III

For my father's funeral I had nothing black to wear and this posed a nagging problem all day long. It was one of those problems, simple, or impossible of solution, to which the mind insanely clings in order to avoid the mind's real trouble. I spent most of that day at the downtown apartment of a girl I knew, celebrating my birthday with whiskey and wondering what to wear that night. When planning a birthday celebration one naturally does not expect that it will be up against competition from a funeral and this girl had anticipated taking me out that night, for a big dinner and a night club afterwards. Sometime during the course of that long day we decided that we would go out anyway, when my father's funeral service was over. I imagine I decided it, since, as the funeral hour approached, it became clearer and clearer to me that I would not know what to do with myself when it was over. The girl, stifling her very lively concern as to the possible effects of the whiskey on one of my father's chief mourners, concentrated on being conciliatory and practically helpful. She found a black shirt for me somewhere and ironed it and, dressed in the darkest pants and jacket I owned, and slightly drunk, I made my way to my father's funeral. [31]

The chapel was full, but not packed, and very quiet. There were, mainly, my father's relatives, and his children, and here and there I saw faces I had not seen since childhood, the faces of my father's one-time friends. They were very dark and solemn now, seeming somehow to suggest that they had known all along that something like this would happen. Chief among the mourners was my aunt, who had quarreled with my father all his life; by which I do not mean to suggest that her mourning was insincere or that she had not loved him. I suppose that she was one of the few people in the world who had, and their incessant quarreling proved precisely the strength of the tie that bound them. The only other person in the world, as far as I knew, whose relationship to my father rivaled my aunt's in depth was my mother, who was not there. [32]

It seemed to me, of course, that it was a very long funeral. But it was, if anything, a rather shorter funeral than most, nor, since there were no overwhelming, uncontrollable expressions of grief, could it be called—if I dare to use the word—successful. The minister who preached my father's funeral sermon was one of the few my father had still been seeing as he neared his end. He presented to us in his sermon a man whom none of us had ever seen—a man thoughtful, patient, and forbearing, a Christian inspiration to all who knew him, and a model for his children. And no doubt the children, in their disturbed and guilty state, were almost ready to believe this; he had been remote enough to be anything and, anyway, the shock of the incontrovertible, that it was really our father lying up there in that casket, prepared the mind for anything. His sister moaned and this grief-stricken moaning was taken as corroboration. The other faces held a dark, non-commital thoughtfulness. This was not the man they had known, but they had scarcely expected to be confronted with *him;* this was, in a sense deeper than questions of fact, the man they had not known, and the man they had not known may have been the real one. The real man, whoever he had been, had suffered and now he was dead: this was all that was sure and all that mattered now. Every man in the chapel hoped that when his hour came he, too, would be eulogized, which is to say forgiven, and that all of his lapses, greeds, errors, and strayings from the truth would be invested with coherence and looked upon with charity. This was perhaps the last thing human beings could give each other and it was what they demanded, after all, of the Lord. Only the Lord saw the midnight tears, only He was present when one of His children, moaning and wringing hands, paced up and down the room. When one slapped one's child in anger the recoil in the heart reverberated through heaven and became part of the pain of the universe. And when the children were hungry and sullen and distrustful and one watched them, daily, growing wilder, and further away, and running headlong into danger, it was the Lord who knew what the charged heart endured as the strap was laid to the backside; the Lord alone who knew what one *would* have said if one had had, like the Lord, the gift of the living word. It was the Lord who knew of the impossibility every parent in that room faced: how to prepare the child for the day when the child would be despised and how to *create* in the child—by what means?—a stronger antidote to this poison than one had found for oneself. The avenues, side streets, bars, billiard halls, hospitals, police stations, and even the playgrounds of

Harlem—not to mention the houses of correction, the jails, and the morgue—testified to the potency of the poison while remaining silent as to the efficacy of whatever antidote, irresistibly raising the question of whether or not such an antidote was desirable; perhaps poison should be fought with poison. With these several schisms in the mind and with more terrors in the heart than could be named, it was better not to judge the man who had gone down under an impossible burden. It was better to remember: *Thou knowest this man's fall; but thou knowest not his wrassling.* [33]

While the preacher talked and I watched the children—years of changing their diapers, scrubbing them, slapping them, taking them to school, and scolding them had had the perhaps inevitable result of making me love them, though I am not sure I knew this then—my mind was busily breaking out with a rash of disconnected impressions. Snatches of popular songs, indecent jokes, bits of books I had read, movie sequences, faces, voices, political issues—I thought I was going mad; all these impressions suspended, as it were, in the solution of the faint nausea produced in me by the heat and liquor. For a moment I had the impression that my alcoholic breath, inefficiently disguised with chewing gum, filled the entire chapel. Then someone began singing one of my father's favorite songs and, abruptly, I was with him, sitting on his knee, in the hot, enormous, crowded church which was the first church we attended. It was the Abyssinia Baptist Church on 138th Street. We had not gone there long. With this image, a host of others came. I had forgotten, in the rage of my growing up, how proud my father had been of me when I was little. Apparently, I had had a voice and my father had liked to show me off before the members of the church. I had forgotten what he had looked like when he was pleased but now I remembered that he had always been grinning with pleasure when my solos ended. I even remembered certain expressions on his face when he teased my mother—had he loved her? I would never know. And when had it all begun to change? For now it seemed that he had not always been cruel. I remembered being taken for a haircut and scraping my knee on the footrest of the barber's chair and I remembered my father's face as he soothed my crying and applied the stinging iodine. Then I remembered our fights, fights which had been the worst possible kind because my technique had been silence. [34]

I remembered the one time in all our life together when we had really spoken to each other. [35]

It was on a Sunday and it must have been shortly before I left home. We were walking, just the two of us, in our usual silence, to or from church. I was in high school and had been doing a lot of writing and I was, at about this time, the editor of the high school magazine. But I had also been a Young Minister and had been preaching from the pulpit. Lately, I had been taking fewer engagements and preached as rarely as possible. It was said in the church, quite truthfully, that I was "cooling off." [36]

My father asked me abruptly, "You'd rather write than preach, wouldn't you?" [37]

I was astonished at his question—because it was a real question. I answered, "Yes." [38]

That was all we said. It was awful to remember that that was all we had *ever* said. [39]

The casket now was opened and the mourners were being led up the aisle to look for the last time on the deceased. The assumption was that the family was too overcome with grief to be allowed to make this journey alone and I watched while my aunt was led to the casket and, muffled in black, and shaking, led back to her seat. I disapproved of forcing the children to look on their dead father, considering that the shock of his death, or, more truthfully, the shock of death as a reality, was already a little more than a child could bear, but my judgment in this matter had been overruled and there they were, bewildered and frightened and very small, being led, one by one, to the casket. But there is also something very gallant about children at such moments. It has something to do with their silence and gravity and with the fact that one cannot help him. Their legs, somehow, seem *exposed,* so that it is at once incredible and terribly clear that their legs are all they have to hold them up. [40]

I had not wanted to go to the casket myself and I certainly had not wished to be led there, but there was no way of avoiding either of these forms. One of the deacons led me up and I looked on my father's face. I cannot say that it looked like him at all. His blackness had been equivocated by powder and there was no suggestion in that casket of what his power had or could have been. He was simply an old man dead, and it was hard to believe that he had ever given anyone either joy or pain. Yet, his life filled that room. Further up the avenue his wife was holding his newborn child. Life and death so close together, and love and hatred, and right and wrong, said something to me which

I did not want to hear concerning man, concerning the life of man. [41]

After the funeral, while I was downtown desperately celebrating my birthday, a Negro soldier, in the lobby of the Hotel Braddock, got into a fight with a white policeman over a Negro girl. Negro girls, white policemen, in or out of uniform, and Negro males—in or out of uniform—were part of the furniture of the lobby of the Hotel Braddock and this was certainly not the first time such an incident had occurred. It was destined, however, to receive an unprecedented publicity, for the fight between the policeman and the soldier ended with the shooting of the soldier. Rumor, flowing immediately to the streets outside, stated that the soldier had been shot in the back, an instantaneous and revealing invention, and that the soldier had died protecting a Negro woman. The facts were somewhat different—for example, the soldier had not been shot in the back, and was not dead, and the girl seems to have been as dubious a symbol of womanhood as her white counterpart in Georgia usually is, but no one was interested in the facts. They preferred the invention because this invention expressed and corroborated their hates and fears so perfectly. It is just as well to remember that people are always doing this. Perhaps many of those legends, including Christianity, to which the world clings began their conquest of the world with just some such concerted surrender to distortion. The effect, in Harlem, of this particular legend was like the effect of a lit match in a tin of gasoline. The mob gathered before the doors of the Hotel Braddock simply began to swell and to spread in every direction, and Harlem exploded. [42]

The mob did not cross the ghetto lines. It would have been easy, for example, to have gone over Morningside Park on the west side or to have crossed the Grand Central railroad tracks at 125th Street on the east side, to wreak havoc in white neighborhoods. The mob seems to have been mainly interested in something more potent and real than the white face, that is, in white power, and the principal damage done during the riot of the summer of 1943 was to white business establishments in Harlem. It might have been a far bloodier story, of course, if, at the hour the riot began, these establishments had still been open. From the Hotel Braddock the mob fanned out, east and west along 125th Street, and for the entire length of Lenox, Seventh, and Eighth avenues. Along each of these avenues, and along each major side street —116th, 125th, 138th, and so on—bars, stores, pawnshops, restaurants, even little luncheonettes had been smashed open and entered and looted—looted, it might be added, with more haste than efficiency. The shelves really looked as though a bomb had struck them. Cans of beans and soup and dog food, along with toilet paper, corn flakes, sardines, and milk tumbled every which way, and abandoned cash registers and cases of beer leaned crazily out of the splintered windows and were strewn along the avenues. Sheets, blankets, and clothing of every description formed a kind of path, as though people had dropped them while running. I truly had not realized that Harlem *had* so many stores until I saw them all smashed open; the first time the word *wealth* ever entered my mind in relation to Harlem was when I saw it scattered in the streets. But one's first, incongruous impression of plenty was countered immediately by an impression of waste. None of this was doing anybody any good. It would have been better to have left the plate glass as it had been and the goods lying in the stores. [43]

It would have been better, but it would also have been intolerable, for Harlem had needed something to smash. To smash something is the ghetto's chronic need. Most of the time it is the members of the ghetto who smash each other, and themselves. But as long as the ghetto walls are standing there will always come a moment when these outlets do not work. That summer, for example, it was not enough to get into a fight on Lenox Avenue, or curse out one's cronies in the barber shops. If ever, indeed, the violence which fills Harlem's churches, pool halls, and bars erupts outward in a more direct fashion, Harlem and its citizens are likely to vanish in an apocalyptic flood. That this is not likely to happen is due to a great many reasons, most hidden and powerful among them the Negro's real relation to the white American. This relation prohibits, simply, anything as uncomplicated and satisfactory as pure hatred. In order really to hate white people, one has to blot so much out of the mind—and the heart—that this hatred itself becomes an exhausting and self-destructive pose. But this does not mean, on the other hand, that love comes easily: the white world is too powerful, too complacent, too ready with gratuitous humiliation, and, above all, too ignorant and too innocent for that. One is absolutely forced to make perpetual qualifications and one's own reactions are always canceling each other out. It is this, really, which has driven so many people mad, both white and black. One is always in the position of having to decide between amputation and gangrene. Amputation is swift but time may prove that the amputation was not necessary—or one may delay the amputation too long. Gangrene is slow, but it is impossible to be sure that one is reading one's symptoms right. The idea of going through life as a cripple is more than one can bear, and equally unbearable is the risk of swelling up slowly, in agony, with poison. And the trouble, finally, is that the risks are real even if the choices do not exist. [44]

"But as for me and my house," my father had said, "we will serve the Lord." I wondered, as we drove him to his resting place, what this line had meant for him. I had heard him preach it many times. I had preached it once myself, proudly giving it an interpretation different from my father's. Now the whole thing came back to me, as though my father and I were on our way to Sunday school and I were memorizing the golden text: *And if it seem evil unto you to serve the Lord, choose you this day whom you will serve; whether the gods which your fathers served that were on the other side of the flood, or the gods of the Amorites, in whose land ye dwell: but as for me and my house, we will serve the Lord.* I suspected in these familiar lines a meaning which had never been there for me before. All of my father's texts and songs, which I had decided were meaningless, were arranged before me at his death like empty bottles, waiting to hold the meaning which life would give them for me. This was his legacy: nothing is ever escaped. That bleakly memorable morning I hated the unbelievable streets and the Negroes and whites who had, equally, made them that way. But I knew that it was folly, as my father would have said, this bitterness was folly. It was necessary to hold on to the things that mattered. The dead man mattered, the new life mattered; blackness and whiteness did not matter; to believe that they did was to acquiesce in one's own destruction. Hatred, which could destroy so much, never failed to destroy the man who hated and this was an immutable law. [45]

It began to seem that one would have to hold in the mind forever two ideas which seemed to be in opposition. The first idea was acceptance, the acceptance, totally without rancor, of life as it is, and men as they are: in the light of this idea, it goes without saying that injustice is a commonplace. But this did not mean that one could be complacent, for the second idea was of equal power: that one must never, in one's own life, accept these injustices as commonplace but must fight them with all one's strength. This fight begins, however, in the heart and it now had been laid to my charge to keep my own heart free of hatred and despair. This intimation made my heart heavy and,

now that my father was irrecoverable, I wished that he had been beside me so that I could have searched his face for the answers which
only the future would give me now. [46]

PURPOSE AND STRUCTURE

1. The title of James Baldwin's essay—its diction and tone—prepares
the reader for the splintered and powerful first paragraph, and, indeed, for
the entire essay. "Notes" are free, personal, and fragmentary. "Native Son"
not only connotes organizations of native-born patriots, it also suggests
Richard Wright's powerful novel of the same title, a bitter attack on race
prejudice. What is the function of par. 1? Is this paragraph coherent?

2. Notice the transitional sentence at the beginning of par. 2: "The day
of my father's funeral had also been my nineteenth birthday." How does
this function as transition?

3. The announced themes of the first paragraph are concretely elaborated
in the three main sections of the essay. The wilderness between birth and
death, the wilderness of blackness and whiteness, is the subject of section I,
which ends,

> I could not get over two facts, both equally difficult for the imagina-
> tion to grasp, and one was that I could have been murdered. But the
> other was that I had been ready to commit murder. I saw nothing very
> clearly but I did see this: that my life, my *real* life, was in danger, and
> not from anything other people might do but from the hatred I carried
> in my own heart.

Every paragraph in section I touches upon or develops this theme of *hatred*.
Examine each one and show how. Notice that this theme is combined so
richly with other themes that Baldwin's conclusion to section II is surprising
and powerful.

4. Section II of the essay develops the identities in birth and death; section III combines and resolves the themes of the preceding sections. It
begins, "For my father's funeral I had nothing black to wear and this
posed a nagging problem all day long. It was one of those problems, simple,
or impossible of solution, to which the mind insanely clings in order to
avoid the mind's real trouble." Baldwin's thesis states the mind's real
trouble. What is the thesis?

5. The form of this essay, however, says more than can be stated in a
thesis. The free, personal, and fragmentary notes for which the title has
prepared the reader have moved in a pattern that is complex, concrete, and

structured. Personal experience has constantly been given a general significance. Polar opposites—birth-death, whiteness-blackness, love-hate, father-son—have collided, become identical, and stubbornly separated into new oppositions. Thus the last paragraph states the discoveries that have been made through the form of the essay. What are these discoveries?

6. Does the last sentence in par. 26 relate to the final paragraph of the essay?

DICTION AND TONE

1. See "Purpose and Structure": the tone of Baldwin's essay is in large part achieved through structure.

2. The diction of much of the following sentence in par. 2 is formal: "I had declined to believe in that apocalypse which had been central to my father's vision; very well, life seemed to be saying, here is something that will certainly pass for an apocalypse until the real thing comes along." The last few words are similar to the words of a popular song. Is this an accidental or planned allusion? Is the allusion effective or inappropriate?

3. In par. 10 Baldwin speaks of his father's voice as "vindictively polite." Is this possible? Is the phrase appropriate?

4. Why does Baldwin give the title of the movie and the name of the diner in par. 16?

5. The first two sentences of par. 30 refer to a monkey, torture, Gulliver, and pygmies. What tone results from these images? from the "whistling sound" of the next sentence?

APPLICATIONS TO WRITING

1. The diction and tone of "Notes of a Native Son" are sometimes personal and autobiographical, sometimes public and formal. But both the language and the attitudes expressed seem to grow directly out of experiences described in the essay. Write a composition showing how one of your ideas has grown out of concrete personal experiences.

2. In Baldwin's first paragraph the death of his father, the birth of a sister, and race riots are related to each other. Throughout his essay personal experiences acquire a general significance. Write a composition in

which you show a discovery about yourself to be a discovery about your family or nation.

3. Both Baldwin and Alex Haley seem able to communicate perceptions that go deeper than simple rationality. Yet their techniques differ radically. Compare *one* aspect of their selections: purpose, structure, diction, or tone.

Sight Into Insight

ANNIE DILLARD

When I was six or seven years old, growing up in Pittsburgh, I used to take a precious penny of my own and hide it for someone else to find. It was a curious compulsion; sadly, I've never been seized by it since. For some reason I always "hid" the penny along the same stretch of sidewalk up the street. I'd cradle it at the roots of a maple, say, or in a hole left by a chipped-off piece of sidewalk. Then I'd take a piece of chalk and, starting at either end of the block, draw huge arrows leading up to the penny from both directions. After I learned to write I labeled the arrows "SURPRISE AHEAD" or "MONEY THIS WAY." I was greatly excited, during all this arrow-drawing, at the thought of the first lucky passerby who would receive in this way, regardless of merit, a free gift from the universe. But I never lurked about. I'd go straight home and not give the matter another thought, until, some months later, I would be gripped by the impulse to hide another penny. [1]

There are lots of things to see, unwrapped gifts and free surprises. The world is fairly studded and strewn with pennies cast broadside from a generous hand. But—and this is the point—who gets excited by a mere penny? If you follow one arrow, if you crouch motionless on a bank to watch a tremulous ripple thrill on the water, and are rewarded by the sight of a muskrat kit paddling from its den, will you count that sight a chip of copper only, and go your rueful way? It is a very dire poverty indeed for a man to be so malnourished and fatigued that he won't stoop to pick up a penny. But if you cultivate a healthy poverty and simplicity, so that finding a penny will make your day, then, since the world is in fact planted in pennies, you have with your poverty bought a lifetime of days. What you see is what you get. [2]

Unfortunately, nature is very much a now-you-see-it, now-you-don't affair. A fish flashes, then dissolves in the water before my eyes like so much salt. Deer apparently ascend bodily into heaven; the brightest oriole fades into leaves. These disappearances stun me into stillness and concentration; they say of nature that it conceals with a grand nonchalance, and they say of vision that it is a deliberate gift, the revelation of a dancer who for my eyes only flings away her seven veils. [3]

For nature does reveal as well as conceal: now-you-don't-see-it, now-you-do. For a week this September migrating red-winged blackbirds were feeding heavily down by Tinker Creek at the back of the house. One day I went out to investigate the racket; I walked up to a tree, an Osage orange, and a hundred birds flew away. They simply materialized out of the tree. I saw a tree, then a whisk of color, then a tree again. I walked closer and another hundred blackbirds took flight. Not a branch, not a twig budged: the birds were apparently weightless as well as invisible. Or, it was as if the leaves of the Osage orange had been freed from a spell in the form of red-winged blackbirds; they flew from the tree, caught my eye in the sky, and vanished. When I looked again at the tree, the leaves had reassembled as if nothing had happened. Finally I walked directly to the trunk of the tree and a final hundred, the real diehards, appeared, spread, and vanished. How could so many hide in the tree without my seeing them? The Osage orange, unruffled, looked just as it had looked from the house, when three hundred red-winged blackbirds cried from its crown. I looked upstream where they flew, and they were gone. Searching, I couldn't spot one. I wandered upstream to force them to play their hand, but they'd crossed the creek and scattered. One show to a customer. These appearances catch at my throat: they are the free gifts, the bright coppers at the roots of trees. [4]

It's all a matter of keeping my eyes open. Nature is like one of those line drawings that are puzzles for children: Can you find hidden in the tree a duck, a house, a boy, a bucket, a giraffe, and a boot? Specialists can find the most incredibly hidden things. A book I read when I was young recommended an easy way to find caterpillars: you simply find some fresh caterpillar droppings, look up, and there's your caterpillar. More recently an author advised me to set my mind at ease about those piles of cut stems on the ground in grassy fields. Field mice make them; they cut the grass down by degrees to reach the seeds at the head. It seems that when the grass is tightly packed, as in a field of ripe grain, the blade won't topple at a single cut through the stem; instead, the cut stem simply drops vertically, held in the crush of grain. The mouse severs the bottom again and again, the stem keeps dropping an inch at a time, and finally the head is low enough for the mouse to reach the seeds. Meanwhile the mouse is positively littering the field with its little piles of cut stems into which, presumably, the author is constantly stumbling. [5]

If I can't see this minutiae, I still try to keep my eyes open. I'm always on the lookout for ant lion traps in sandy soil, monarch pupae near milkweed, skipper larvae in locust leaves. These things are utterly common, and I've not seen one. I bang on hollow trees near water, but so far no flying squirrels have appeared. In flat country I watch every sunset in hopes of seeing the green ray. The green ray is a seldom-seen streak of light that rises from the sun like a spurting fountain at the moment of sunset; it throbs into the sky for two seconds and disappears. One more reason to keep my eyes open. A photography professor at the University of Florida just happened to see a bird die in midflight; it jerked, died, dropped, and smashed on the ground. [6]

I squint at the wind because I read Stewart Edward White: "I have always maintained that if you looked closely enough you could *see* the wind—the dim, hardly-made-out, fine débris fleeing high in the air." White was an excellent observer, and devoted an entire chapter of *The Mountains* to the subject of seeing deer: "As soon as you can forget the naturally obvious and construct an artificial obvious, then you too will see deer." [7]

But the artificial obvious is hard to see. My eyes account for less than 1 percent of the weight of my head; I'm bony and dense; I see what I expect. I just don't know what the lover knows; I can't see the artificial obvious that those in the know construct. The herpetologist asks the native, "Are there snakes in that ravine?" "No, sir." And the herpetologist comes home with, yessir, three bags full. Are there butterflies on that mountain? Are the bluets in bloom? Are there arrowheads here, or fossil ferns in the shale? [8]

Peeping through my keyhole I see within the range of only about 30 percent of the light that comes from the sun; the rest is infrared and some little ultraviolet, perfectly apparent to many animals, but invisible to me. A nightmare network of ganglia, charged and firing without my knowledge, cuts and splices what I do see, editing it for my brain. Donald E. Carr points out that the sense impressions of one-celled animals are *not* edited for the brain: "This is philosophically interesting in a rather mournful way, since it means that only the simplest animals perceive the universe as it is." [9]

A fog that won't burn away drifts and flows across my field of vision. When you see fog move against a backdrop of deep pines, you don't see the fog itself, but streaks of clearness floating across the air in dark shreds. So I see only tatters of clearness through a pervading obscurity. I can't distinguish the fog from the overcast sky; I can't be sure if the light is direct or reflected. Everywhere darkness and the presence of the unseen appalls. We estimate now that only one atom dances alone in every cubic meter of intergalactic space. I blink and squint. What planet or power yanks Halley's Comet out of orbit? We haven't seen it yet; it's a question of distance, density, and the pallor of reflected light. We rock, cradled in the swaddling band of darkness. Even the simple darkness of night whispers suggestions to the mind. This summer, in August, I stayed at the creek too late. [10]

STRANGERS TO DARKNESS

Where Tinker Creek flows under the sycamore log bridge to the tear-shaped island, it is slow and shallow, fringed thinly in cattail marsh. At this spot an astonishing bloom of life supports vast breeding populations of insects, fish, reptiles, birds, and mammals. On windless summer evenings I stalk along the creek bank or straddle the sycamore log in absolute stillness, watching for muskrats. The night I stayed too late I was hunched on the log staring spellbound at spreading, reflected stains of lilac on the water. A cloud in the sky suddenly lighted as if turned on by a switch; its reflection just as suddenly materialized on the water upstream, flat and floating, so that I couldn't see the creek bottom, or life in the water under the cloud. Downstream, away from the cloud on the water, water turtles smooth as beans were gliding down with the current in a series of easy, weightless push-offs, as men bound on the moon. I didn't know whether to trace the progress of one turtle I was sure of, risking sticking my face in one of the bridge's spider webs made invisible by the gathering dark, or take a chance on seeing the carp, or scan the mudbank in hope of seeing a muskrat, or follow the last of the swallows who caught at my heart and trailed it after them like streamers as they appeared from directly below, under the log, flying upstream with their tails forked, so fast. [11]

But shadows spread and deepened and stayed. After thousands of years we're still strangers to darkness, fearful aliens in an enemy camp with our arms crossed over our chests. I stirred. A land turtle on the bank, startled, hissed the air from its lungs and withdrew to its shell. An uneasy pink here, an unfathomable blue there, gave great suggestion of lurking beings. Things were going on. I couldn't see whether that rustle I heard was a distant rattlesnake, slit-eyed, or a nearby sparrow kicking in the dry flood debris slung at the foot of a willow. Tremendous action roiled the water everywhere I looked, big action, inexplicable. A tremor welled up beside a gaping muskrat burrow in the bank and I caught my breath, but no muskrat appeared. The ripples continued to fan upstream with a steady, powerful thrust. Night was knitting an eyeless mask over my face, and I still sat transfixed. A distant airplane, a delta wing out of nightmare, made a gliding shadow on the creek's bottom that looked like a stingray cruising upstream. At once a black fin slit the pink cloud on the water, shearing it in two. The two halves merged together and seemed to dissolve before my eyes. Darkness pooled in the cleft of the creek and rose, as water collects in a well. Untamed, dreaming lights flickered over the sky. I saw hints of hulking underwater shadows, two pale splashes out of the water, and round ripples rolling close together from a blackened center. [12]

At last I stared upstream where only the deepest violet remained of the cloud, a cloud so high its underbelly still glowed, its feeble color reflected from a hidden sky lighted in turn by a sun halfway to China. And out of that violet, a sudden enormous black body arched over the water. Head and tail, if there was a head and tail, were both submerged in cloud. I saw only one ebony fling, a headlong dive to darkness; then the waters closed, and the lights went out. [13]

I walked home in a shivering daze, up hill and down. Later I lay open-mouthed in bed, my arms flung wide at my sides to steady the whirling darkness. At this latitude I'm spinning 836 miles an hour round the earth's axis; I feel my sweeping fall as a breakneck arch like the dive of dolphins, and the hollow rushing of wind raises the hairs on my neck and the side of my face. In orbit around the sun I'm moving 64,800 miles an hour. The solar system as a whole, like a merry-go-round unhinged, spins, bobs, and blinks at the speed of 43,200 miles an hour along a course set east of Hercules. Someone has piped, and we are dancing a tarantella until the sweat pours. I open my eyes and I see dark, muscled forms curl out of water, with flapping gills and flattened eyes. I close my eyes and I see stars, deep stars giving way to deeper stars, deeper stars bowing to deepest stars at the crown of an infinite cone. [14]

"Still," wrote Van Gogh in a letter, "a great deal of lights falls on everything." If we are blinded by darkness, we are also blinded by light. Sometimes here in Virginia at sunset low clouds on the southern or northern horizon are completely invisible in the lighted sky. I only know one is there because I can see its reflection in still water. The first time I discovered this mystery I looked from cloud to no-cloud in bewilderment, checking my bearings over and over, thinking maybe the ark of the covenant was just passing by south of Dead Man Mountain. Only much later did I learn the explanation: polarized light from the sky is very much weakened by reflection, but the light in clouds isn't polarized. So invisible clouds pass among visible clouds, till all slide over the mountains; so a greater light extinguishes a lesser as though it didn't exist. [15]

In the great meteor shower of August, the Perseid, I wail all day for the shooting stars I miss. They're out there showering down, committing hara-kiri in a flame of fatal attraction, and hissing perhaps at last into the ocean. But at dawn what looks like a blue dome clamps down over me like a lid on a pot. The stars and planets could smash and I'd never know. Only a piece of ashen moon occasionally climbs up or down the inside of the dome, and our local star without surcease explodes on our heads. We have really only that one light, one source for all power, and yet we must turn away from it by universal decree. Nobody here on the planet seems aware of this strange, powerful taboo, that we all walk about carefully averting our faces, this way and that, lest our eyes be blasted forever. [16]

Darkness appalls and light dazzles; the scrap of visible light that doesn't hurt my eyes hurts my brain. What I see sets me swaying. Size and distance and the sudden swelling of meanings confuse me, bowl me over. I straddle the sycamore log bridge over Tinker Creek in the summer. I look at the lighted creek bottom: snail tracks tunnel the mud in quavering curves. A crayfish jerks, but by the time I absorb what has happened, he's gone in a billowing smoke screen of silt. I look at the water: minnows and shiners. If I'm thinking minnows, a carp will fill my brain till I scream. I look at the water's surface: skaters, bubbles, and leaves sliding down. Suddenly, my own face, reflected, startles me witless. Those snails have been tracking my face! Finally, with a shuddering wrench of the will, I see clouds, cirrus clouds. I'm dizzy, I fall in. [17]

This looking business is risky. Once I stood on a humped rock on nearby Purgatory Mountain, watching through binoculars the great autumn hawk migration below, until I discovered that I was in danger of joining the hawks on a vertical migration of my own. I was used to binoculars, but not, apparently, to balancing on humped rocks while looking through them. I reeled. Everything advanced and receded by turns; the world was full of unexplained foreshortenings and depths. A distant huge object, a hawk the size of an elephant, turned out to be the browned bough of a nearby loblolly pine. I followed a sharp-shinned hawk against a featureless sky, rotating my head unawares as it flew, and when I lowered the glass a glimpse of my own looming shoulder sent me staggering. What prevents the men on Palomar from falling, voiceless and blinded, from their tiny, vaulted chairs? [18]

I reel in confusion; I don't understand what I see. With the naked eye I can see two million light-years to the Andromeda galaxy. Often I slop some creek water in a jar, and when I get home I dump it in a white china bowl. After the silt settles I return and see tracings of minute snails on the bottom, a planarian or two winding round the rim of water, roundworms shimmying frantically, and finally, when my eyes have adjusted to these dimensions, amoebae. At first the amoebae look like *muscae volitantes,* those curled moving spots you seem to see in your eyes when you stare at a distant wall. Then I see the amoebae as drops of water congealed, bluish, translucent, like chips of sky in the bowl. At length I choose one individual and give myself over to its idea of an evening. I see it dribble a grainy foot before it on its wet, unfathomable way. Do its unedited sense impressions include the fierce focus of my eyes? Shall I take it outside and show it Andromeda, and blow its little endoplasm? I stir the water with a finger, in case it's running out of oxygen. Maybe I should get a tropical aquarium with motorized bubblers and lights, and keep this one for a pet. Yes, it would tell its fissioned descendants, the universe is two feet by five, and if you listen closely you can hear the buzzing music of the spheres. [19]

Oh, it's mysterious, lamplit evenings here in the galaxy, one after the other. It's one of those nights when I wander from window to window, looking for a sign. But I can't see. Terror and a beauty insoluble are a riband of blue woven into the fringes of garments of things both great and small. No culture explains, no bivouac offers real haven or rest. But it could be that we are not seeing something. Galileo thought comets were an optical illusion. This is fertile ground: since we are certain that they're not, we can look at what our scientists have been saying with fresh hope. What if there are *really* gleaming, castellated cities hung upside-down over the desert sand? What limpid lakes and cool date palms have our caravans always passed untried? Until, one by one, by the blindest of leaps, we light on the road to these places, we must stumble in darkness and hunger. I turn from the window. I'm blind as a bat, sensing only from every direction the echo of my own thin cries. [20]

LEARNING TO SEE

I chanced on a wonderful book called *Space and Sight,* by Marius Von Senden. When Western surgeons discovered how to perform safe cataract operations, they ranged across Europe and America operating on dozens of men and women of all ages who had been blinded by cataracts since birth. Von Senden collected accounts of such cases; the histories are fascinating. Many doctors had tested their patients' sense perceptions and ideas of space both before and after the operations. The vast majority of patients, of both sexes and all ages, had, in Von Senden's opinion, no idea of space whatever. Form, distance, and size were so many meaningless syllables. A patient "had no idea of depth, confusing it with roundness." Before the operation a doctor would give a blind patient a cube and a sphere; the patient would tongue it or feel it with his hands, and name it correctly. After the operation the doctor would show the same objects to the patient without letting him touch them; now he had no clue whatsoever to what he was seeing. One patient called lemonade "square" because it pricked on his tongue as a square shape pricked on the touch of his hands. Of another postoperative patient the doctor writes, "I have found in her no notion of size, for example, not even within the narrow limits which she might have encompassed with the aid of touch. Thus when I asked her to show me how big her mother was, she did not stretch out her hands, but set her two index fingers a few inches apart." [21]

For the newly sighted, vision is pure sensation unencumbered by meaning. When a newly sighted girl saw photographs and paintings, she asked, " 'Why do they put those dark marks all over them?' 'Those aren't dark marks,' her mother explained, 'those are shadows. That is one of the ways the eye knows that things have shape. If it were not for shadows, many things would look flat.' 'Well, that's how things do look,' Joan answered. 'Everything looks flat with dark patches.' " [22]

In general the newly sighted see the world as a dazzle of "color-patches." They are pleased by the sensation of color, and learn quickly to name the colors, but the rest of seeing is tormentingly difficult. Soon after his operation, a patient "generally bumps into one of these colour-patches and observes them to be substantial, since they resist him as tactual objects do. In walking about it also strikes him—or can if he pays attention—that he is continually passing in between the colours he sees, that he can go past a visual object, that a part of it then stead-ily disappears from view; and that in spite of this, however he twists and turns—whether entering the room from the door, for example, or returning back to it—he always has a visual space in front of him. Thus he gradually comes to realize that there is also space behind him, which he does not see." [23]

The mental effort involved in these reasonings proves overwhelming for many patients. It oppresses them to realize, if they ever do at all, the tremendous size of the world, which they had previously conceived of as something touchingly manageable. It oppresses them to realize that they have been visible to people all along, perhaps unattractively so, without their knowledge or consent. A disheartening number of them refuse to use their new vision, continuing to go over objects with their tongues, and lapsing into apathy and despair. [24]

On the other hand, many newly sighted people speak well of the world, and teach us how dull our own vision is. To one patient, a human hand, unrecognized, is "something bright and then holes." Shown a bunch of grapes, a boy calls out, "It is dark, blue and shiny. . . . It isn't smooth, it has bumps and hollows." A little girl visits a garden. "She is greatly astonished, and can scarcely be persuaded to answer, stands speechless in front of the tree, which she only names on taking hold of it, and then as 'the tree with the lights in it.' " Another patient, a twenty-two-year-old girl, was dazzled by the world's brightness and kept her eyes shut for two weeks. When at the end of that time she opened her eyes again, she did not recognize any objects, but "the more she now directed her gaze upon everything about her, the more it could be seen how an expression of gratification and astonishment overspread her features; she repeatedly exclaimed: 'Oh God! How beautiful!' " [25]

I saw color-patches for weeks after I read this wonderful book. It was summer; the peaches were ripe in the valley orchards. When I woke in the morning, color-patches wrapped round my eyes, intricately, leaving not one unfilled spot. All day long I walked among shifting color-patches that parted before me like the Red Sea and closed again in silence, transfigured, wherever I looked back. Some patches swelled and loomed, while others vanished utterly, and dark marks flitted at random over the whole dazzling sweep. But I couldn't sustain the illusion of flatness. I've been around for too long. Form is condemned to an eternal danse macabre with meaning: I couldn't unpeach the peaches. Nor can I remember ever having seen without understanding; the color-patches of infancy are lost. My brain then must have been smooth as any balloon. I'm told I reached for the moon; many babies do. But the color-patches of infancy swelled as meaning filled them; they arrayed themselves in solemn ranks down distance which unrolled and stretched before me like a plain. The moon rocketed away. I live now in a world of shadows that shape and distance color, a world where space makes a kind of terrible sense. What Gnosticism is this, and what physics? The fluttering patch I saw in my nursery window—silver and green and shape-shifting blue—is gone; a row of Lombardy poplars takes its place, mute, across the distant lawn. That humming oblong creature pale as light that stole along the walls of my room at night, stretching exhilaratingly around the corners, is gone, too, gone the night I ate of the bittersweet fruit, put two and two together and puckered forever my brain. Martin Buber tells this tale: "Rabbi Mendel once boasted to his teacher Rabbi Elimelekh that evenings he saw the angel who rolls away the light before the darkness, and mornings the angel who rolls away the darkness before the light. 'Yes,' said Rabbi Elimelekh, 'in my youth I saw that too. Later on you don't see these things anymore.' " [26]

Why didn't someone hand these newly sighted people paints and brushes from the start, when they still didn't know what anything was?

Then maybe we all could see color-patches too, the world unraveled from reason, Eden before Adam gave names. The scales would drop from my eyes; I'd see trees like men walking; I'd run down the road against all orders, hallooing and leaping. [27]

SILVER FLASHES

Seeing is of course very much a matter of verbalization. Unless I call my attention to what passes before my eyes, I simply won't see it. If Tinker Mountain erupted, I'd be likely to notice. But if I want to notice the lesser cataclysms of valley life, I have to maintain in my head a running description of the present. It's not that I'm observant; it's just that I talk too much. Otherwise, especially in a strange place, I'll never know what's happening. Like a blind man at the ball game, I need a radio. [28]

When I see this way I analyze and pry. I hurl over logs and roll away stones; I study the bank a square foot at a time, probing and tilting my head. Some days when a mist covers the mountains, when the muskrats won't show and the microscope's mirror shatters, I want to climb up the blank blue dome as a man would storm the inside of a circus tent, wildly, dangling, and with a steel knife claw a rent in the top, peep, and, if I must, fall. [29]

But there is another kind of seeing that involves a letting go. When I see this way I sway transfixed and emptied. The difference between the two ways of seeing is the difference between walking with and without a camera. When I walk with a camera I walk from shot to shot, reading the light on a calibrated meter. When I walk without a camera, my own shutter opens, and the moment's light prints on my own silver gut. When I see this second way I am above all an unscrupulous observer. [30]

It was sunny one evening last summer at Tinker Creek; the sun was low in the sky, upstream. I was sitting on the sycamore log bridge with the sunset at my back, watching the shiners the size of minnows who were feeding over the muddy sand in skittery schools. Again and again, one fish, then another, turned for a split second across the current and flash! the sun shot out from its silver side. I couldn't watch for it. It was always just happening somewhere else, and it drew my vision just as it disappeared: flash! like a sudden dazzle of the thinnest blade, a sparkling over a dun and olive ground at chance intervals from every direction. Then I noticed white specks, some sort of pale petals, small, floating from under my feet on the creek's surface, very slow and steady. So I blurred my eyes and gazed toward the brim of my hat and saw a new world. I saw the pale white circles roll up, roll up, like the world's turning, mute and perfect, and I saw the linear flashes, gleaming silver, like stars being born at random down a rolling scroll of time. Something broke and something opened. I filled up like a new wineskin. I breathed an air like light; I saw a light like water. I was the lip of a fountain the creek filled forever; I was ether, the leaf in the zephyr; I was flesh-flake, feather, bone. [31]

When I see this way I see truly. As Thoreau says, I return to my senses. I am the man who watches the baseball game in silence in an empty stadium. I see the game purely; I'm abstracted and dazed. When it's all over and the white-suited players lope off the green field to their shadowed dugouts, I leap to my feet, I cheer and cheer. [32]

But I can't go out and try to see this way. I'll fail, I'll go mad. All I can do is try to gag the commentator, to hush the noise of useless interior babble that keeps me from seeing just as surely as a newspaper dangled before my eyes. The effort is really a discipline requiring a lifetime of dedicated struggle; it marks the literature of saints and monks of every order east and west, under every rule and no rule, discalced and shod. The world's spiritual geniuses seem to discover universally that the mind's muddy river, this ceaseless flow of trivia and trash, cannot be dammed, and that trying to dam it is a waste of effort that might lead to madness. Instead you must allow the muddy river to flow unheeded in the dim channels of consciousness; you raise your sights; you look along it, mildly, acknowledging its presence without interest and gazing beyond it into the realm of the real where subjects and objects act and rest purely, without utterance. "Launch into the deep," says Jacques Ellul, "and you shall see." [33]

The secret of seeing, then, is the pearl of great price. If I thought he could teach me to find it and keep it forever I would stagger barefoot across a hundred deserts after any lunatic at all. But although the pearl may be found, it may not be sought. The literature of illumination reveals this above all: although it comes to those who wait for it, it is always, even to the most practiced and adept, a gift and a total surprise. I return from one walk knowing where the killdeer nests in the field by the creek and the hour the laurel blooms. I return from the same walk a day later scarcely knowing my own name. Litanies hum in my ears; my tongue flaps in my mouth, *Alimonon,* alleluia! I cannot cause light; the most I can do is try to put myself in the path of its beam. It is possible, in deep space, to sail on solar wind. Light, be it particle or wave, has force: you rig a giant sail and go. The secret of seeing is to sail on solar wind. Hone and spread your spirit till you yourself are a sail, whetted, translucent, broadside to the merest puff. [34]

When her doctor took her bandages off and led her into the garden, the girl who was no longer blind saw "the tree with the lights in it." It was for this tree I searched through the peach orchards of summer, in the forests of fall and down winter and spring for years. Then one day I was walking along Tinker Creek thinking of nothing at all and I saw the tree with the lights in it. I saw the backyard cedar where the mourning doves roost charged and transfigured, each cell buzzing with flame. I stood on the grass with the lights in it, grass that was wholly fire, utterly focused and utterly dreamed. It was less like seeing than like being for the first time seen, knocked breathless by a powerful glance. The flood of fire abated, but I'm still spending the power. Gradually the lights went out in the cedar, the colors died, the cells unflamed and disappeared. I was still ringing. I had been my whole life a bell, and never knew it until at that moment I was lifted and struck. I have since only very rarely seen the tree with the lights in it. The vision comes and goes, mostly goes, but I live for it, for the moment when the mountains open and a new light roars in spate through the crack, and the mountains slam. [35]

PURPOSE AND STRUCTURE

1. What is the relationship between sight and insight (see Dillard's title)? Is seeing "of course very much a matter of verbalization" (par. 28)? What, then, is "the noise of useless interior babble that keeps me from seeing" (par. 33)? When Dillard saw the tree with the lights in it, "It was less like seeing than like being for the first time seen, knocked breathless by a powerful glance" (par. 35). Why? Compare with "Do its unedited sense impressions include the fierce focus of my eyes?" (par. 19).

2. There are four sections in Dillard's piece: pars. 1–10, 11–20, 21–27, 28–35. What is the purpose of each section? Is there a structural relation-

ship between them? How do the subtitles of the last three sections relate to their content?

3. Why begin with hidden pennies, "a free gift from the universe" (par. 1)? What are "the bright coppers at the roots of trees" (par. 4)?

4. Pars. 5–7 list the things that are invisible to Dillard that other observers see. Why introduce an essay on seeing with such a list?

5. What is the purpose of the last sentence in paragraph 10?

6. Why follow seeing the Andromeda galaxy with "Often I slop some creek water in a jar" (par. 19)?

7. The newly sighted see the world as a dazzle of " 'color-patches' " (par. 23). Why does Dillard (par. 26) also see color-patches for weeks after reading *Space and Sight*? Why does she lose this ability? Why do a disheartening number of the newly sighted refuse to use their new vision (par. 24)? Is Dillard inconsistent in her attitude toward color-patches?

DICTION AND TONE

1. Is Dillard searching for a particular tree: "It was for this tree I searched through the peach orchards of summer, in the forests of fall and down winter and spring for years" (par. 35)? Why does she find it in her own back yard? How can "mountains open" (par. 35)? Can a new light roar "in spate"? In what fashion can "mountains slam"? Discuss the diction and tone of par. 35.

2. What is the tone of "out of that violet, a sudden enormous black body arched over the water" (par. 13)? Comment on the diction of "I saw only one ebony fling" (par. 13).

3. Dillard's diction is sometimes curious: "I couldn't unpeach the peaches" (par. 26). Why?

4. What is the tone of " 'Everything looks flat with dark patches' " (par. 22)?

5. What is the tone of "I live now in a world of shadows that shape and distance color" (par. 26)?

6. Compare the two ways of seeing (pars. 29–30). What is an "unscrupulous observer" (par. 30)? Why does Dillard want to "climb up the blank blue dome" (par. 29)?

APPLICATIONS TO WRITING

1. Cultivate a "healthy poverty and simplicity" (par. 2): write of finding a penny; tell how you get what you see.

2. Par. 4 describes an action (approaching a tree) and three stages of a vision. Write your own paragraph.

3. Have you ever learned a new way of seeing? Describe the process. (Par. 26 may stimulate you.)

A Megalopolis Like New York
from *The Landscape of Our Lives*

ERIC SEVAREID

One way to go quietly insane is to think hard about the concept of eternity. Another way, for anyone living in a megalopolis like New York, is to think hard about "progress." [1]

The eerie sensation comes over one that true progress reached the end of its cable some years ago and is now recoiling upon us, an unstoppable juggernaut smashing masses of human beings back toward medieval conditions of life. [2]

The streets are littered with cigarette and cigar butts, paper wrappings, particles of food and dog droppings. How long before they become indistinguishable from the gutters of medieval towns when slop pails were emptied from the second-story windows? [3]

Thousands of New York women no longer attend evening services in their churches. They fear assault as they walk the few steps from bus or subway station to their apartment houses. The era of the medieval footpad has returned, and, as in the dark ages, the cry for help brings no assistance, for even grown men know they would be cut down before the police could arrive. [4]

A thousand years ago in Europe acres of houses and shops were demolished and their inhabitants forced elsewhere so that great cathedrals could be built. For decades the building process soaked up all available skilled labor; for decades the townspeople stepped around pits in the streets, clambered over ropes and piles of timber, breathed mortar dust and slept and woke to the crashing noise of construction. The cathedrals, when finished, stood half-empty six days a week, but most of them at least had beauty. Today the ugly office skyscrapers go up, shops and graceful homes are obliterated, their inhabitants forced away and year after year New Yorkers step around the pits, stumble through the wooden catwalks, breathe the fine mist of dust, absorb the hammering noise night and day and telephone in vain for carpenter or plumber. And the skyscrapers stand empty two days and seven nights a week. This is progress. [5]

At the rush hour men outrun old women for the available cab; the strong bodily crush back the weak for a place to stand in suffocating bus or subway car, no less destructive of human dignity than a cattle wagon in the time of Peter the Great. When the buses and subway cars began they represented progress. [6]

Great parking garages are built, immediately filled with cars; the traffic remains as before, and that is progress. The renowned New York constructionist, Robert Moses, builds hundreds of miles of access highways, and they are at once crammed bumper to bumper with automobiles as long as locomotives carrying an average of about two human beings apiece. Parkinson's general law applies here too, for vehicles will always increase in direct proportion to the increase in spaces to hold them. So skyscrapers and boxlike apartment houses will increase as the money to build them increases. So footpads will increase as the number of possible victims increases. But it's progress. [7]

I am not surprised that the English writer, Mervyn Jones, concludes after traveling throughout Russia and the United States that ordinary Americans and ordinary Russians are remarkably alike in at least two respects—in the sheer physical misery they are forced to endure in their cities and in the sheer ugliness of jumbled signs and billboards being spread across their once fair countryside. [8]

They are alike in a third respect. As Jones writes in *Horizon* magazine, both peoples complain remarkably little. Russians don't complain because they don't expect government authorities to listen. American dwellers in our megalopolises don't complain because they have long since abandoned hope. Their authorities may listen, but they know their authorities are helpless. A city like New York is ungovernable. [9]

The secret, terrible fact is that progress, in all measurable terms of human effort, grace and self-respect ended some years ago in the great ant-hill cities. The juggernaut of time and effort has turned around and is now destroying the recent progressive past. [10]

PURPOSE AND STRUCTURE

1. Sevareid does not tell us why thinking about "eternity" (par. 1) may cause us to go "quietly insane." But it may be because time seems to be going backwards. What has happened to "progress" in the great cities? Why is this a "secret" (par. 10)?

2. Why does Sevareid compare cathedrals and skyscrapers (par. 5)?

3. In the thesis of his talk, Sevareid refers to "true progress" (par. 2). Why does he wait until par. 10 to explain what he means by the phrase?

4. How do pars. 3–7 relate to Sevareid's thesis?

5. Pars. 8–9 are transitional to the climactic restatement of the thesis (par. 10). In what way do pars. 8–9 broaden the impact of par. 10?

DICTION AND TONE

1. If the "juggernaut of time and effort" (par. 10) has turned around "and is now destroying the recent progressive past," what does Sevareid mean by the word *progressive*? Is he referring to a political theory about "progress" or to a paradox about time? Or to both?

2. Pars. 5–7 end with the same word. Why?

3. Why is the sensation "eerie" (par. 2)?

4. One way to go "quietly insane" (par. 1) is to think hard about "progress." Why are city dwellers in Russia and the United States so quiet (par. 9)?

APPLICATIONS TO WRITING

1. Are "ant-hill cities" (par. 10) better adapted to ants than people? Answer the question by writing a fantasy or an argument.

2. Is *your* time going backwards? Are you losing rather than gaining? Are the pleasures of maturity overrated? Compare your past with your present "progress."

3. Is the "juggernaut of time" (which has destroyed our great cities) now destroying our countryside? Write of this new disaster.

Glossary

ABSTRACTION, LEVELS OF—distinguished in two ways: in the range between the general and the specific and in the range between the abstract and the concrete.

A general word refers to a class, genus, or group; a specific word refers to a member of that group. *Ship* is a general word, but *ketch, schooner, liner,* and *tugboat* are specific. It must be remembered, however, that the terms *general* and *specific* are relative, not absolute. *Ketch,* for example, is more specific than ship, for a ketch is a kind of ship. But *ketch,* on the other hand, is more general than *Tahiti ketch,* for a Tahiti ketch is a kind of ketch.

The distinction between the abstract and the concrete is also relative. Ideas and qualities that are usually embodied in physical things or dramatized by them, but that may be thought of separately (*redness, honor*), are called abstract; physical things such as *house, shoes,* and *horse* are concrete. Notice, however, that concrete words can not only range further into the specific (*bungalow, moccasin,* and *stallion*), but they can also range back toward the general (*domicile, clothing,* and *cattle*). In making these distinctions between the abstract and the concrete and between the general and the specific, there is no implication that good writing should be specific and concrete and that poor writing is general and abstract. Certainly most good writing is concrete and specific, but it is also general and abstract, constantly moving from the general to the specific and from the abstract, to the concrete. See Twain ("Memories of a Missouri Farm"); Forster; Boorstin; Anderson; Fairlie; Greer; Baldwin; Dillard.

ALLUSION—a reference to a person, place, or thing, whether real or imaginary: Woodrow Wilson or Zeus, Siam or Atlantis, kangaroo or Phoenix.

The allusion is an economical way to evoke an atmosphere, a historical era, or an emotion. See Wolfe; Jacobson; Russell; Trilling; Roszak; Broyard.

ANALOGY—in exposition, usually a comparison of some length in which the unknown is explained in terms of the known, the unfamiliar in terms of the familiar, the remote in terms of the immediate. See Sontag; Bettelheim; Huxley; E. B. White; Roszak.

In argument, an analogy consists of a series of likenesses between two or more dissimilar things, demonstrating that they are either similar or identical in other respects also. The use of analogy in argument is open to criticism, for two things alike in many respects are not necessarily alike in all (for example, lampblack and diamonds are both pure carbon; they differ significantly in their crystal structure). Although analogy never *proves* anything, its dramatic quality, its assistance in establishing tone, its vividness make it one of the most valuable techniques of the writer. See Bettelheim; Thomas; Mailer; Kopkind.

ANALYSIS—a method of exposition by logical division, applicable to anything that can be divided into component parts. For example, in "The Iks" Thomas has a double analysis: in the first half of the essay he analyzes the causes of the behavior of the Iks; in the second half, the causes of the behavior of communities of men. Martin analyzes a huge, inchoate list of types of professional wrestlers: "Crushers, Killers, Bruisers, and Butchers, Commies, Nazis, Japs, and A-rabs . . ." and eighteen more. But Boorstin simply divides his subject into four parts and then develops each part equally. In "Living Together," the editors of *Newsweek* attempt to establish some of the causes for the increase in cohabitation and for the decline of marriage. Like Boorstin, Roberts arbitrarily divides his subject into a number of reasonable parts and then richly illustrates each. In her discussion of Marilyn Monroe's personality, Trilling distinguishes among the possible causes of her suicide, and concludes that she is a victim of her own remarkable gifts. In the excerpt from his autobiography, Wright interweaves in his deceptively simple narrative a number of experiences and themes that are unified by their causal relationships: his omnivorous reading led to his discovery that words are indeed weapons; his increasing awareness of the vast distance between himself and the world in which he lived strengthened his fearsome determination to leave the South. Russell simplifies his long and complex career by dividing the forces governing his life into three overwhelming passions.

ARGUMENT AND PERSUASION—reciprocally related. Formal argument often consists of the following parts: the *proposition,* an assertion that leads to the *issue;* the *issue,* the aspect of the proposition that the writer is attempting to prove and the question on which the whole argument rests; the *evidence,* the facts and opinions that the author offers as testimony. He may order the evidence deductively by proceeding from certain premises to a *conclusion* or inductively by generalizing from a number of instances and drawing a *conclusion.* Informal arguments frequently make greater use of the methods of exposition than they do of formal logic. Argument is a mode of discourse; *the* argument, a line of reasoning. (See Deduction, Induction, Logic, and Analogy.)

The purpose of argument is to persuade. The attempt to distinguish between argument and persuasion is sometimes made by reference to means (argument makes appeals to reason; persuasion, to emotions); sometimes to ends (argument causes someone to change his mind; persuasion moves him to action). These distinctions, however, are more academic than functional, for in practice argument and persuasion are not discrete entities. Yet the proof in argument rests largely upon the objectivity of evidence; the proof in persuasion, upon a subtle and controlled use of language. The diction employed, as well as such literary devices as irony, satire, paradox, metaphor, and allusion, will establish the tone, which in turn may affect the reader's judgement of the objectivity of the evidence and the degree to which he is persuaded by it. Hoppe argues that today's university (Skarewe U) is a diploma mill. If we go back to the Good Old Medieval Campus (no credits, no grades, no requirements, no diplomas) we will end with well-educated students. Kauffmann argues that film is too easy a medium. The filmgoer sits in the dark in a near fetal position and falls into a "brothel lethargy." In "The Artist as Housewife" the formal components of Jong's argument are less arresting than the amusing digressions, the myriad, wry rhetorical questions, and the acerbic cumulative detail, all of which reflect the intensity of her effort to persuade. Mark Twain attacks the literary art of James Fenimore Cooper by presenting arguments that are so palpably exaggerated and so unfair that they are amusing—and, because they are so funny, they are persuasive. In the excerpt from *Man and Superman* the Devil supports his argument that man is "the most destructive of all destroyers" by alluding to a succession of his bestial acts. Although the argument in "Joan Baez: Where the Kissing Never Stops" can be divided into proposition, issue, evidence, and conclusion, Didion's power to persuade is largely dependent upon the tone of her discourse, which both disarms and delights the reader in its reliance upon irony, paradox, and subtle humor. Claiborne makes one argument for the Wasps: for three hundred years no Wasp nation has endured an absolute monarchy or dictatorship. The persuasive power of "A Modest Proposal" lies in its sustained irony: Swift simulates an amorality that is cumulatively revealed in an exaggerated rationality and a view of man that reduces him to an object to be used. Mailer's argument moves from the question of who finally would do the dishes to the ultimate responsibility of women to choose the fathers of their children. Leonard argues that "the natural condition of the human organism is joy" and that significant learning can take place only when accompanied by delight. Kopkind draws upon a variety of sources— from pop culture to psychology—to support his view that the acceptance of androgyny is crucial for the successful functioning of the next stages of social evolution. In his effort to persuade the reader of the limitations of conventional answers, Calandra employs a parable in which the student engages in an academic lark.

ASSUMPTION—that part of an argument that is unstated because it is either taken for granted by the reader and writer or undetected by them. When the reader consciously disagrees with an assumption, the writer has misjudged his audience by assuming what the reader refuses to concede. See Swift; Wolfe; Trilling; Roszak.

ATTITUDE—toward subject, see Tone. Toward audience, see Audience.

AUDIENCE—for the writer, his expected readers. When the audience is a general, unknown one and the subject matter is closely related to the writer's opinions, preferences, attitudes, and tastes, then the writer's relationship to his audience is in a very real sense his relatiosnhip to himself. The writer who distrusts the intelligence of his audience or who adapts his material to what he assumes are the tastes and interests of his readers compromises his integrity.

On the other hand, if the audience is generally known (a college class, for example), and the subject matter is factual information, then the beginning writer may well consider the education, interests, and tastes of his audience. Unless he keeps a definite audience in mind, the beginner is apt to shift levels of usage, use inappropriate diction, and lose the reader by appealing to none of his interests.

"It is now necessary to warn the writer that his concern for the reader must be pure; he must sympathize with the reader's plight (most readers are in trouble about half the time) but never seek to know his wants. The whole duty of a writer is to please and satisfy himself, and the true writer always plays to an audience of one. Let him start sniffing the air, or glancing at the Trend Machine, and he is as good as dead, although he may make a nice living." (Strunk and White, *The Elements of Style, Second Edition,* used with permission of Macmillan Publishing Co., Inc.)

CAUSE AND EFFECT—a seemingly simple method of development in which either the cause of a particular effect or the effects of a particular cause are investigated. However, because of the philosophical difficulties surrounding causality, the writer should be cautious in ascribing causes. For the explanation of most processes, it is probably safer to proceed in a sequential order, using transitional words to indicate the order of the process. See Baldwin; Huxley; Cox; Maynard; Kauffmann.

CLASSIFICATION—an arbitrary, systematic arrangement of categories (classes) so that the larger categories include the smaller. By definition, all members of a class have at least one characteristic in common. While Shulman's purpose is to amuse, his method is classification of logical fallacies. Cox's mode of classification reflects the basic human needs of those who turn East for fulfillment. Hertzberg and McClelland use a wide variety of methods to classify the types of paranoia. Packard arranges people shapers into four categories and then provides an example or illustration of each. McGlashan reviews a number of classic and contemporary theories of dream interpretation before focusing on the dream as a means of penetrating the mystery of the self.

COHERENCE—literally, a sticking together; therefore, the joining or linking of one point to another. It is the writer's obligation to make clear to the reader the relationship of sentence to sentence and paragraph to paragraph. Sometimes coherence is simply a matter of putting the parts in a sequence that is meaningful and relevant—logical sequence, chronological order, order of importance. Other times it is helpful to underscore the relationship. An elementary but highly useful method of underscoring relationships is the use of transitional words: *but, however, yet* inform the reader that what is to follow contrasts with what went before; *furthermore, moreover, in addition to* continue to expand what went before.

Another elementary way of achieving coherence is the enumeration of ideas—"first," "second," "third"—so as to remind the reader of the development. A more subtle transition can be gained by repetition at the beginning of a paragraph of a key word or idea from the end of the preceding paragraph. Such a transition reminds the reader of what has gone before and simultaneously prepares him for what is to come. See Haley; Russell; McGlashan; Cox; Fairlie.

COMPARISON AND CONTRAST—the presentation of a subject by the indication of similarities between two or more things (comparison) and by the demonstration of differences (contrast). The basic elements in a comparative process, then, are (1) the various entities compared, and (2) the points of likeness or difference between them. To be comparable, they should be members of the same class (see Classification). For example, nature lovers and nature haters, both members of the same class, are comparable. Democracy and communism are not comparable, because the former is a subdivision of a political system and the latter of an economic one. Although nearly all of Highet's essay develops a dramatic contrast between Diogenes and Alexander the Great, the essay ends with a surprising comparison between the two men. The range of effects that may be achieved in comparison and contrast is reflected in Roszak's graphic and moving description of the ways in which the symbols of flight have been debased to the level of a poor counterfeit; in Mencken's preposterous and paradoxical development of the distinctions between men and women; in Huxley's use of the familiar to explain the unfamiliar; in Ullman's mocking portrait of Hollywood's conspicuous consumption which is contrasted to the spartan life of a barren island in the Baltic; and in Eiseley's counterpointing of bird and machine to express his choice of all that is life supporting.

CONCRETENESS—see Abstraction, Levels of.

CONNOTATION—all that a word suggests or implies in addition to its literal meaning. However, this definition is arbitrary and, from the standpoint of the writer, artificial, because the meaning of a word includes *all* that it suggests and implies. For connotative language see Twain; Mencken; Didion; Jong; Greer; McFadden; Leonard; Broyard.

CONTRAST—see Comparison.

COORDINATION—elements of like importance in like grammatical construction. Less important elements should be placed in grammatically subordinate positions. See Parallelism and Subordination. See Boorstin; Allen; E. B. White.

DEDUCTIVE REASONING—in logic, deriving a conclusion about a particular example by recognizing that a predetermined generalization is applicable to it; by analogy, in rhetoric, that development that moves from the general to the specific. See Huxley; Swift; E. B. White.

DEFINITION—in logic, the placing of the word to be defined in a general class and then demonstrating how it differs from other members of the class; in rhetoric, the meaningful extension (usually enriched by the use of detail, concrete illustrations, anecdote, metaphor) of a logical definition in order to answer fully—though often implicitly—the question, "What is

. . . ?" Tom Wolfe defines the perfect crime by identifying the motives and goals of the criminals. E. B. White's evocative definition of democracy is developed by metaphor and analogy. Sontag defines the liberated woman in terms of her activities and responsibilities. Fairlie defines lust by comparing and contrasting it with love. Forster limits his subject by deliberately excluding peripheral questions and particularizing his general question by personal example. In Greer's extended definition of the female stereotype she excoriates its perpetrators by employing satire, hyperbole, and personification.

DENOTATION—the literal meaning of a word. See Connotation.

DESCRIPTION—that form of discourse whose primary purpose is to present factual information about an object or experience (objective description) or to report the impression or evaluation of an object or experience (subjective description). Most description combines the two purposes. *It was a frightening night* (an evaluation with which others might disagree). *The wind blew the shingles off the north side of the house and drove the rain under the door* (two facts about which there can be little disagreement). See Wells; Orwell; Twain ("Memories of a Missouri Farm"); Hersey; Dillard; Williams.

DICTION—style as determined by choice of words. Good diction is characterized by precision and appropriateness to subject matter, weak diction by the use of inappropriate, vague, or trite words. The relationship between the kinds of words a writer selects and his subject matter in large part determines tone. Broyard describes the sad plight of the last married couple in Connecticut, all of whose friends have divorced. Faulkner's impressions of Japan are paradoxical ("the overcast sinks slowly upward") and almost nonverbal ("the spashed symbols of the characters"), whereas Orwell's impressions of Marrakech have a cinematic immediacy. Du Plessix Gray believes that deceit and lying—used with compassion and civility—are necessary in the love relationship. Lee Strout White (E. B. White) bids farewell to the Model T Ford as an aging male kisses an old flame goodbye. Hersey's diction does not reflect his subject matter; his language is deliberately flat and reportorial. Baldwin's diction is a striking combination of formal public language and informal private language. Dillard shows that sight and insight are one: that it is "the noise of useless interior babble" that keeps us from seeing. Sevareid tells us that the modern city is becoming like a medieval town with its garbage in the streets and its footpads: "the juggernaut of time" is going backwards.

DISCOURSE, FORMS OF—traditionally, exposition, argument, description, and narration (see entries under each). These four kinds of traditional discourse are rarely found in a pure form. Argument and exposition may be interfused in the most complex fashion. Exposition often employs narration and description for purposes of illustration. It is important to remember, however, that in an effective piece of writing the use of more than one form of discourse is never accidental. It always serves the author's central purpose. For a combination of forms see selections under Identification.

EMPHASIS—the arrangement of the elements of a composition so that the important meanings occur in structurally important parts of the composition. Repetition, order of increasing importance, exclamation points, rhetorical questions, and figures of speech are all devices for achieving emphasis. See Shaw; Mencken ("The Libido for the Ugly"); Broyard; Highet.

EVIDENCE—that part of argument or persuasion that involves proof. It usually takes the form of facts, particulars deduced from general principles, or opinions of authorities. See Shaw; Didion; Claiborne; Leonard.

EXPOSITION—the form of discourse that explains or informs. Most papers required of college students are expository. The *methods* of exposition presented in this text are identification, definition, classification, illustration, comparison and contrast, and analysis (see separate entries in Glossary).

FIGURES OF SPEECH—a form of expression in which the meanings of words are extended beyond the literal. The common figures of speech are metaphor, simile, analogy. See Mailer; Huxley; Allen; McFadden; Faulkner.

GENERALIZATION—a general conception or principle derived from particulars. Often, simply a general statement. See Abstraction.

GRAMMAR—a systematic description of a language.

IDENTIFICATION—seeks to answer the question "Who am I?" or "Who are you?" or "What is that?" Maynard identifies the generation of which she is a member as one of "unfulfilled expectations." Alex Haley relies heavily on detail to give authenticity to his search for his ancestry. Steffens discovers what it means to become an educated person in the context of his experience as a student in the university. William Allen identifies the dreams of a young boy by evoking a mingled sense of hope and fear. Wells gives substance to his imaginary creatures, the Martians, by confronting us with bug-eyed monsters, whose menace is increased by their superiority to us. Twain ties memories to sensory experiences. Mencken identifies the "libido" for the ugly by the objects it creates. Dillard seeks to identify the fleeting moment, the present—catch it if you can.

ILLUSTRATION—at its simplest, a particular member of a class used to explain or dramatize the class. The individual member selected must be a fair representative of the distinctive qualities of the class. At its most complex, an illustration provides the particulars on which a generalization is based; the generalization—a type of person or thing, an idea or abstraction —may or may not be explicitly stated. McFadden illustrates the incidence of mental inertia and debasement of thought that characterizes those who resort to the cliché-ridden psychological patter of the fringe human potential movements. Anderson documents a revolution with illustrations of the changes made in each person's life. Thurber's amusing essay on his "university days" is pure illustration: he states no thesis or generalization. Excerpts from official reports illustrate Williams' sense that sharks are unpredictable. Bettelheim transforms what might have been a mere case history into an illustration of a predicament of contemporary man. The experience of his own life illustrates the irony of Mark Jacobson's thesis.

IMAGE—a word or statement that makes an appeal to the senses. Thus, there are visual images, auditory images, and so on. As the most direct experience of the world is through the senses, writing that makes use of sense impressions (images) can be unusually effective. See Orwell; Allen; McFadden; Dillard.

INDUCTIVE REASONING—in logic, the formulation of a generalization after the observation of an adequate number of particular instances; by analogy, in rhetoric, that development that moves from the particular to the general. See Forster; Huxley; Trilling; Maynard.

INTENTION—for the particular purpose or function of a single piece of writing, see Purpose. Intention determines the four forms of discourse. See Exposition, Argument, Description, Narration. These intentions may be explicitly or implicitly set forth by the writer.

IRONY—at its simplest, involves a discrepancy between literal and intended meaning; at its most complex, it involves an utterance more meaningful (and usually meaningful in a different way) to the listener than to the speaker (dramatic irony). For example, Oedipus' remarks about discovering the murderer of the king are understood by the audience in a way Oedipus himself cannot understand them. The inability to grasp the full implications of his own remark is frequently feigned by the satirist. See Swift; Hoppe; Twain ("Fenimore Cooper's Literary Offences"); Calandra; Greer.

ISSUE—the limitation of a general proposition to the precise point on which the argument rests. Defeating the issue defeats the argument. Typically the main proposition of an argument will raise at least one issue for discussion and controversy. See Mailer; Leonard; Callandra; Claiborne.

LIMITATION OF SUBJECT—restriction of the subject to one that can be adequately developed with reference to audience and purpose. See Forster; Steffens; Fairlie; Maynard.

METAPHOR—an implied comparison between two things that are seemingly different; a compressed analogy. Effectively used, metaphors increase clarity, interest, vividness, and concreteness. See Allen; Wolfe; Eiseley; Roszak; E. B. White; McFadden.

NARRATION—a form of discourse the purpose of which is to tell a story. If a story is significant in itself, the particulars appealing to the imagination, it is *narration*. If a story illustrates a point in exposition or argument, it may be called *illustrative narration*. If a story outlines a process step by step, the particulars appealing to the understanding, it is designated as *expository narration*. See Shulman; Wells.

ORGANIZATION, METHODS OF—vary with the form of discourse. Exposition uses in part, in whole, or in combination identification, definition, classification, illustration, comparison and contrast, and analysis. Argument and persuasion often use the method of organization of inductive or deductive reasoning, or analogy. Description is often organized either around a dominant impression or by means of a spatial arrangement. Narration, to give two examples, may be organized chronologically or in terms of point of view.

PARADOX—an assertion or sentiment seemingly self-contradictory, or opposed to common sense, which may yet be true. See Mencken ("The Feminine Mind"); Swift; Hoppe; Faulkner; du Plessix Gray.

PARAGRAPH—serves to discuss one topic or one aspect of a topic. The central thought is either implied or expressed in a topic sentence. Paragraphs have such a great variety of organization and function that it is almost impossible to generalize about them. See the various kinds of paragraph development referred to in the exercises.

Parallelism—elements of similar rhetorical importance in similar grammatical patterns. See Coordination. See Mencken ("The Feminine Mind"); Huxley; Shaw; Fairlie; Steffens; Trilling; Martin.

Parody—mimicking the language and style of another. See McFadden; Broyard.

Perspective—the vantage point chosen by the writer to achieve his purpose, his strategy. It is reflected in his close scrutiny of, or distance from, his subject; his objective representation or subjective interpretation of it. See Diction, Purpose, Tone. See Jong; Mailer; Cox; Hersey; Dillard; Shulman.

Persuasion—see Argument.

Point of View—in description, the vantage point from which the author looks at the described object—see Allen and Wells; in narration, the "central intelligence" through whom the author reports the events of the story—see Anderson; in exposition, the grammatical person (first person, third person, editorial we) through whom the author presents his explanation—see Baldwin; Hersey.

Proposition—see Argument.

Purpose—what the writer wants to accomplish with a particular piece of writing.

Rhetoric—the art of using language effectively.

Rhetorical Question—a question asked in order to induce thought and to provide emphasis rather than to evoke an answer. See Shaw; Forster.

Rhythm—in poetry and prose, patterned emphasis. Good prose is less regular in its rhythm than poetry. See Orwell; Russell; Faulkner.

Satire—the attempt to effect reform by exposing an object to laughter. Satire makes frequent recourse to irony, wit, ridicule, parody. It is usually classified under such categories as the following: social satire, personal satire, literary satire. See Swift; Hoppe; Steffens; Mencken ("The Libido for the Ugly"); Twain ("Fenimore Cooper's Literary Offences").

Style—"The essence of a sound style is that it cannot be reduced to rules —that it is a living and breathing thing, with something of the demoniacal in it—that it fits its proprietor tightly and yet ever so loosely, as his skin fits him. It is, in fact, quite as securely an integral part of him as that skin is. . . . In brief, a style is always the outward and visible symbol of a man, and it cannot be anything else." (H. L. Mencken, *On Style,* used with permission of Alfred A. Knopf, Inc.)

"Young writers often suppose that style is a garnish for the meat of prose, a sauce by which a dull dish is made palatable. Style has no such separate entity; it is nondetachable, unfilterable. The beginner should approach style warily, realizing that it is himself he is approaching, no other; and he should begin by turning resolutely away from all devices that are popularly believed to indicate style—all mannerisms, tricks, adornments. The approach to style is by way of plainness, simplicity, orderliness, sincerity." (Strunk and White, *The Elements of Style, Second Edition,* used with permission of Macmillan Publishing Co., Inc.)

SUBORDINATION—less important rhetorical elements in grammatically subordinate positions. See Parallelism, Coordination, and Emphasis.

SYLLOGISM—in formal logic, a deductive argument in three steps: a major premise, a minor premise, a conclusion. The major premise states a quality of a class (All men are mortal); the minor premise states that X is a member of the class (Socrates is a man); the conclusion states that the quality of a class is also a quality of a member of the class (Socrates is mortal). In rhetoric the full syllogism is rarely used; instead, one of the premises is usually omitted. "You can rely on him; he is independent," is an abbreviated syllogism. Major premise: Independent people are reliable; minor premise: He is independent; conclusion: He is reliable. Constructing the full syllogism frequently reveals flaws in reasoning, such as the above, which has an error in the major premise. See Huxley.

SYMBOL—a concrete image that suggests a meaning beyond itself. See Allen; Eiseley; Roszak; Callandra.

TOPIC SENTENCE—the thesis that the paragraph as a whole develops. Some paragraphs do not have topic sentences.

TRANSITION—the linking together of sentences, paragraphs, and larger parts of the composition to achieve coherence. See Coherence.

UNITY—the relevance of selected material to the central theme of an essay. See Coherence. See Didion; Haley; Sontag; Maynard; Greer; Shulman.

Biographical Notes

W I L L I A M   A L L E N (1940–   ), an assistant professor of English at Ohio State University, writes both articles and short stories for such publications as *Saturday Review* and *The New York Times*. *Starkweather* is his nonfiction book about a series of murders.

P O U L   A N D E R S O N (1926–   ) decided to become a writer after graduating with an honors degree in physics from the University of Minnesota. Although his work includes both historical and conventional fiction, he is best known for his science fiction, especially the "Flandry" stories and the "Hoka" tales. A prolific writer, Anderson has won many Hugo (1961, 1964, 1969, 1972, 1973) and Nebula (1971, 1972) awards.

J A M E S   B A L D W I N (1924–   ), born in Harlem, has lived much of his life in New York City. His first novel, *Go Tell It on the Mountain*, was published in 1954. A collection of essays, *Notes of a Native Son*, was published in 1955; his second novel, *Giovanni's Room*, in 1956. *Nobody Knows My Name* (1961), *The Fire Next Time* (1963), and *No Name in the Street* (1972) are his most recent books of essays. He has also written two plays, *Blues for Mr. Charlie* (1964) and *One Day, When I was Lost* (1973), and a novel, *Tell Me How Long the Train's Been Gone* (1968). In the spring of 1974 his first novel in six years, *If Beale Street Could Talk*, was published.

B R U N O   B E T T E L H E I M (1903–   ) was born in Austria and received his Ph.D. from the University of Vienna. He came to America in the late 1930's and is now a professor of educational psychology at the University of Chicago. He has published *Love Is Not Enough—The Treatment of*

535

Emotionally Disturbed Children (1950), *Truants from Life* (1955), *The Empty Fortress* (1967), and *The Children of the Dream* (1969).

DANIEL J. BOORSTIN (1914–   ), lawyer and distinguished internationally known historian, occupied the Chair of American History at the Sorbonne, Paris, and was elected a Fellow of Trinity College, Cambridge. He is currently the Librarian of Congress.

ANATOLE BROYARD (   ) grew up in Brooklyn and Greenwich Village. He has taught at the New School for Social Research and has published stories and articles in *Partisan Review, Discovery,* and *Commentary.* He reviews books for *The New York Times.*

ALEXANDER CALANDRA (1911–   ) is a professor of physics at Washington University, St. Louis. He is editor of the *Reporter,* a journal of the American Chemistry Society. The selection in this anthology appears in his book, *The Teaching of Elementary Science and Physics.*

ROBERT CLAIBORNE (1919–   ) has edited *Scientific American* and *Medical World News* and has contributed articles to *The Nation, Harper's,* and *Newsweek.*

HARVEY COX (1929–   ) is a writer, theologian, and member of the faculty of Harvard Divinity School. Among his books are *The Feast of Fools, The Seduction of the Spirit, The Secular City,* and *Turning East.*

JOAN DIDION (1935–   ), California-born writer, began her career when she won *Vogue's* Prix de Paris award in her senior year of college. She later became an associate editor of *Vogue* and has written columns for *Saturday Evening Post* and *Life.* Her novels, *Run River, Play It as It Lays,* and *The Book of Common Prayer,* and her collection of essays, *Slouching Towards Bethlehem,* have established her as an important American writer. She and her husband, writer John Gregory Dunne, have collaborated on several film plays.

ANNIE DILLARD (1945–   ) was awarded the Pulitzer Prize for her book *Pilgrim at Tinker Creek.* She has also published a book of poetry, *Tickets for a Prayer Wheel,* and a meditation on religious themes.

LOREN EISELY (1907–1977), famous anthropologist, historian of science, and university administrator, was the author of such popular works as *The Immense Journey, Firmament of Time, The Mind as Nature,* and *Francis Bacon and the Modern Dilemma.*

H ENRY F AIRLIE (1924–   ) is a contributing editor to *The New Republic* as well as a contributor to other journals. He is author of *The Spoiled Child of the Western World.* An expanded version of *Lust or Luxuria* will appear in a volume to be published in 1978 on the seven deadly sins in modern life.

W ILLIAM F AULKNER (1897–1962) lived most of his life in Mississippi and is best known for his novels portraying the dying aristocracy and the poor whites of his fictional Yoknapatawpha County, Mississippi. In 1950 he was awarded the Nobel Prize for literature. His novels include *The Sound and the Fury, Intruder in the Dust, Go Down Moses,* and *A Fable.*

E . M . F ORSTER (1879–1970) was a British novelist, educated at Kings College, Cambridge. He lived for a time in Italy, was a member of the Bloomsbury group of writers and artists in London, and spent the major part of his life at Cambridge. His works include *A Passage to India, Where Angels Fear to Tread,* and *A Room with a View.* His last novel, *Maurice,* and a collection of short stories, *The Life to Come,* were published posthumously.

F RANCINE DU P LESSIX G RAY (1931–   ) published her novel *Lovers and Tyrants* in 1976. She is also a versatile journalist whose work has been published in the *New Yorker,* the *New York Review of Books,* and *Vogue.* A study of Catholic radicalism, *Divine Disobedience,* won the National Catholic Book Award (1970).

G ERMAINE G REER (1939–   ) is an Australian-born writer and educator, best known as a standard-bearer of the women's liberation movement and as the author of the best-selling *The Female Eunuch* (1971). On leave of absence from the University of Warwick in England, Miss Greer is a freelance journalist and TV personality.

A LEX H ALEY (1921–   ) was born in Ithaca, New York, but moved to Henning, Tennessee, when only six weeks old. Retiring after having served twenty years in the Coast Guard, he became a professional writer. After ghostwriting *The Autobiography of Malcolm X,* he began his search for his own past, which culminated in the now famous book, *Roots.*

J OHN H ERSEY (1914–   ) is an American novelist, Pulitzer-Prize winner, and journalist. His works include the novels *A Bell for Adano* (1944), *The Wall* (1950), and *The Child Buyer* (1960), and his famous reports, *Hiroshima* (1946) and *The Algiers Motel Incident* (1968). His most recent books are *Letter to the Alumni* (1970) and *The Conspiracy* (1972).

HENDRIK HERTZBERG (1943–   ) is a staff writer for *The New Yorker* and the author of *One Million*.

GILBERT HIGHET (1906–1978) was an American classicist who was born in Glasgow, Scotland. His books include *The Classical Tradition, The Art of Teaching,* and *The Anatomy of Satire.*

ARTHUR HOPPE (1925–   ) writes a humorous column for the San Francisco *Chronicle* and other newspapers. His books include *Love Everybody Crusade, Dreamboat,* and *The Perfect Solution to Absolutely Everything.*

THOMAS HENRY HUXLEY (1825–1895), the foremost spokesman in England for Darwin's theory of evolution, devoted himself to the question of man's origin and place in nature, which he investigated in such works as *Science and Culture* (1881) and *Evolution and Ethics* (1893).

MARK JACOBSON (   )

ERICA JONG (1942–   ) has been awarded numerous prizes for her poetry. Her books include *Fruits and Vegetables* (1971) and *Half Lives* (1973). Her novel, *Fear of Flying* (1973), an exploration of modern marriage, reflects her interest in women's liberation. In 1978 she published *How to Save Your Own Life.*

STANLEY KAUFFMANN (1916–   ) is film critic for the *New Republic* magazine. He has been a member of the Washington Square Players, an editor for Bantam Books, Ballantine Books, and Alfred A. Knopf, drama critic for *The New York Times,* and professor at the City University of New York. His books include *The Hidden Hero, A World on Film,* and *Figures of Light.*

ANDREW KOPKIND (1935–   ) is author of *America: The Mixed Curse.* He has been a reporter for the *Washington Post,* a correspondent for *The New Statesman.*

GEORGE B. LEONARD (1923–   ) is a freelance journalist and writer. He was formerly senior editor for *Look Magazine.* Among his books are *Education and Ecstasy, The Transformation: A Guide to the Inevitable Changes in Humankind,* and *The Ultimate Athlete: Re-visioning Sports, Physical Education, and the Body.*

NORMAN MAILER (1929–   ) grew up in Brooklyn and was educated at Harvard. His novels include *The Naked and the Dead* (1948), *Barbary Shore* (1951), *The Deer Park* (1955), and *An American Dream* (1965). His journalism and commentary have appeared in *Esquire,* the *New York Post,* and *Life. Marilyn,* a study of the late Marilyn Monroe, was published in 1973.

WILLIAM C. MARTIN (1937–   ) is a professor of sociology at Rice University in Houston, Texas. He was born in San Antonio, Texas, and educated at Abilene Christian College, Harvard Divinity School, and Harvard University. He has written two books, *These Were God's People* and *Christians in Conflict.* His articles have appeared in *The Atlantic, Harper's, Esquire,* and *Texas Monthly.* His newest book, *The Electric Preacher,* will be published by Doubleday Anchor in 1979.

JOYCE MAYNARD (1953–   ) wrote *Looking Back: A Chronicle of Growing Up Old in the Sixties,* a book published when she was a sophomore at Yale University. She has been published in the *New York Times Magazine, Mademoiselle,* and other popular magazines.

DAVID C. K. McCLELLAND (1917–   ) is a psychologist. He is author of *Personality, Talent and Society, The Achieving Society,* and *The Roots of Consciousness.*

CYRA McFADDEN (1937–   ) has been an instructor in the English department at San Francisco State University and is author of *The Serial,* a best selling satire on the human potential movement and in particular on the use of psychological patter that substitutes for thought.

ALAN McGLASHAN (1898–   ) is a psychiatrist who in writing about his professional interests in *Savage and Beautiful Country* has been able to avoid professional jargon. He has written for the French magazine *Réalités* as well as for professional journals.

H. L. MENCKEN (1880–1956) is known as a caustic satirist of the culture of the 1920's, as editor of *Smart Set* and the *American Mercury,* and as author of six volumes of *Prejudices.* His scholarship is reflected in his exhaustive work, *The American Language.*

GEORGE ORWELL (1903–1950) was the pseudonym of Eric Blair, an English writer who at one time served with the Indian Imperial Police in Burma. He fought in the Spanish Civil War, an experience he recorded in *Homage to Catalonia*. His books include the satirical fantasy *Animal Farm* and the grim novel *1984*.

VANCE PACKARD (1914–   ) is a popularizer of the American sociological scene, as the titles of some of his books suggest: *The Hidden Persuaders, The Status Seekers, The Waste Makers, The Pyramid Climbers*, and *The Sexual Wilderness*.

PAUL ROBERTS (1917–1966), a specialist in structural linguistics, wrote texts for almost every level of instruction. His more popular works include *Understanding Grammar, Patterns of English, Understanding English*, and *English Sentences*.

THEODORE ROSZAK (1933–   ) is the author of *The Making of a Counter Culture* and co-author with his wife of *Masculine/Feminine*. His most recent books are *Where the Wasteland Ends*, from which this selection was taken, and *Pontifex: A Revolutionary Entertainment for the Mind's Eye*. He teaches at California State University at Hayward. He has been a recipient of a Guggenheim Fellowship and has published in *American Review, New Scientist*, and other journals.

BERTRAND RUSSELL (1872–1970), internationally famous British philosopher and mathematician, dedicated his long life to the unpopular side of many controversial causes. He won the Nobel Prize for literature in 1950. Among his many works are *Principia Mathematica, Unpopular Essays*, and *New Hopes for a Changing World*. "A Life Worth Living" is an excerpt from *The Autobiography of Bertrand Russell: 1872–1914*.

ERIC SEVAREID (1912–   ) is a famous newspaper correspondent, broadcaster, and TV commentator. His books include *Not So Wild a Dream, This Is Eric Sevareid*, and *The Landscape of Our Lives*.

GEORGE BERNARD SHAW (1856–1950), born in Dublin, began his career as an unsuccessful novelist. He gained his early reputation as a journalist-critic. In 1884 he was one of the founders of the Fabian Society. It is on his plays, however, that his reputation rests. Among his numerous plays are *Man and Superman* (1903); *Major Barbara* (1905); *Pygmalion* (1912), which was later produced on stage and film as *My Fair Lady;* and *Saint Joan* (1923). Shaw received the Nobel Prize for literature in 1925.

MAX SHULMAN (1919–) is a popular humorist. He is the author of *Barefoot Boy with Cheek, The Feather Merchants,* and *Rally Round the Flag, Boys* as well as of the TV series *Dobie Gillis.*

SUSAN SONTAG (1933–), who writes trenchantly about the modern cultural scene, was educated at the University of Chicago, Radcliffe College, Oxford University, and the Sorbonne. She teaches philosophy at the City College of New York and Columbia University, where she was writer in residence (1964–1965). She has written *The Benefactor, Death Kit,* and *Styles of Radical Will* and contributes numerous essays to *Partisan Review, The Nation,* and other periodicals. Her latest book, *On Photography,* won a National Book Award.

LINCOLN STEFFENS (1866–1936) was a newspaper man and editor of *McClure's Magazine* from 1902 to 1906, and associate editor of *American Magazine* and *Everybody's Magazine* from 1906 to 1911. He first attracted wide attention for his exposé of political and civic corruption in the United States (*The Shame of the Cities,* 1904). *The Autobiography of Lincoln Steffens* is recognized as a masterpiece of personal analysis and social criticism.

JONATHAN SWIFT (1667–1745) is generally acknowledged to be the greatest English prose satirist. With savage irony he probes beneath appearances and exposes harsh realities. His hatred of sham and oppression is reflected in *Gulliver's Travels* (1726), a tale delighting children and shocking and challenging adults by its bitter satire of human vices.

LEWIS THOMAS (1913–), president of the Memorial Sloan-Kettering Cancer Center, has spent his professional life in medical education, having served in important professorial and administrative posts at the University of Minnesota, the New York University-Bellevue Medical Center, and Yale Medical School. He is a member of the National Academy of Sciences. His *Lives of the Cell* won the National Book Award.

JAMES THURBER (1894–1961) recorded his incomparable wit and satire in short stories, essays, and line drawings. *The Thurber Carnival* and *The Thurber Album* represent his own selection of the best of his work; among his other books are *My Life and Hard Times, Let Your Mind Alone, My World and Welcome to It,* and *Thurber Country.*

DIANA TRILLING (1905–) is an essayist and critic. She has written for a variety of magazines and journals and has won a Guggenheim

Award. She is the author of *Claremont Essays* and *We Must March My Darlings: A Critical Decade* and editor of *The Portable D. H. Lawrence*.

MARK TWAIN (1835–1910) is the pen name of Samuel Clemens, American humorist and novelist. His best-loved novels, *The Adventures of Tom Sawyer* and *Huckleberry Finn*, grew out of his boyhood days in the Mississippi river town of Hannibal, Missouri. His experience for four years as a river pilot is recorded in *Life on the Mississippi*. Other favorites are *Innocents Abroad* and *A Connecticut Yankee in King Arthur's Court*.

LIV ULLMAN (1938–) was born in Norway. After a successful career making films with Swedish director Ingmar Bergman, she made movies in Hollywood. Her reputation is primarily based upon such films as *Persona, The Passion of Anna, Scenes from a Marriage,* and *Face to Face.* The selection included here is from her autobiography, *Changing.*

H. G. WELLS (1866–1946), novelist and social reformer, was an early writer of what later came to be called science fiction. *The Time Machine* and *The War of the Worlds* are his best-known works, but he also wrote traditional novels: *Tono-Bungay, Love and Mr Lewisham, Kipps,* and *Ann Veronica*. His later works include *The Outline of History* and *The Shape of Things to Come*.

E. B. WHITE (1899–), perhaps America's best personal essayist, was a contributor of a monthly department to *Harper's* magazine (1938–1943) and has been a contributing editor of *The New Yorker* magazine since 1926. His lightly satirical essays show great depth of feeling. They have been published under the titles *Quo Vadimus?, One Man's Meat, The Second Tree from the Corner,* and *The Points of My Compass.* Among his other books are *The Wild Flag, Stuart Little, Charlotte's Web, The Trumpet of the Swan,* and his revision, with additions, of William Strunk's *The Elements of Style.* Recently published are *The Letters of E. B. White* and a new collection of *The Essays of E. B. White*.

JOY WILLIAMS (1944–) is an essayist, novelist, and short-story writer whose work has appeared in such publications as *Antioch Review, Esquire,* and *Paris Review.* Her novel *State of Grace* won critical approval.

TOM WOLFE (1931–) has been called "supercontemporary," "parajournalistic," and the "poet laureate of pop." Probably the most famous of the "new journalists," he is the author of *The Kandy-Kolored Tangerine-Flake Streamline Baby, The Electric Kool-Aid Acid Test, The Pump House*

Gang, Radical Chic and Mau-Mauing the Flak Catchers. "The Perfect Crime" is a chapter from his most recent book, *Mauve Gloves & Madmen, Clutter & Vine.*

RICHARD WRIGHT (1908–1960) major American black writer, published stories, novels, an autobiography, and several books about America's racial problems. Among his best-known works are *Native Son, Black Boy,* and *White Man, Listen!*